WRITING A C COMPILER

Build a Real Programming Language from Scratch

by Nora Sandler

no starch press®

San Francisco

Printed in the United States of America

First printing

28 27 26 25 24   1 2 3 4 5

ISBN-13: 978-1-7185-0042-6 (print)
ISBN-13: 978-1-7185-0043-3 (ebook)

 Published by No Starch Press®, Inc.
245 8th Street, San Francisco, CA 94103
phone: +1.415.863.9900
www.nostarch.com; info@nostarch.com

Publisher: William Pollock
Managing Editor: Jill Franklin
Production Manager: Sabrina Plomitallo-González
Production Editor: Sydney Cromwell
Developmental Editors: Alex Freed and Eva Morrow
Cover Illustrator: James L. Barry
Interior Design: Octopod Studios
Technical Reviewer: Stephen Kell
Copyeditor: Rachel Head
Proofreader: Audrey Doyle
Indexer: Beth Nauman-Montana

Figure 13-1, courtesy of Codekaizen via Wikimedia Commons, has been reproduced under CC BY-SA 4.0, *https://creativecommons.org/licenses/by-sa/4.0*. The original image has been converted to grayscale, and fonts have been modified.

Library of Congress Control Number: 2023058768

For customer service inquiries, please contact info@nostarch.com. For information on distribution, bulk sales, corporate sales, or translations: sales@nostarch.com. For permission to translate this work: rights@nostarch.com. To report counterfeit copies or piracy: counterfeit@nostarch.com.

To Brian

About the Author

Nora Sandler is a software engineer based in Seattle. She holds a BS in computer science from the University of Chicago, where she researched the implementation of parallel programming languages. After several years as a penetration tester, she found her way back to compilers. Most recently, she worked on domain-specific languages at an endpoint security company. You can read her blog about pranks, compilers, and other computer science topics at *https://norasandler.com.*

About the Technical Reviewer

Stephen Kell is a researcher, educator, and consultant on the design and implementation of programming languages and systems. He has taught compilers and C programming in various settings over the past 12 years, served on an ISO study group on the evolution of the C language specification, and published numerous research papers on the specification, design, and implementation of C and its linking and debugging tools. These continue to be a focus of the research that he leads as an academic at King's College London.

BRIEF CONTENTS

CONTENTS IN DETAIL

PART II: TYPES BEYOND INT   241

11
LONG INTEGERS   243

12
UNSIGNED INTEGERS   273

14
POINTERS

15
ARRAYS AND POINTER ARITHMETIC

PART III: OPTIMIZATIONS   555

19
OPTIMIZING TACKY PROGRAMS   557

20
REGISTER ALLOCATION   613

ACKNOWLEDGMENTS

I was attending the Recurse Center in fall 2017 when I started on the series of blog posts that eventually turned into this book. I'm immensely grateful to the Recurse Center for giving me the time and space to follow my own curiosity, in a community of kind, brilliant people, without the pressure to produce anything. Without them, I would never have attempted this project.

I'm also grateful to everyone in the Recurse Center community whose advice, encouragement, and pair programming sessions shaped those initial blog posts. I'd particularly like to thank Julian Squires for pointing me toward Abdulaziz Ghuloum's "An Incremental Approach to Compiler Construction," the article that served as the starting point for this project. I'd also like to thank Raph Levien for teaching me about the precedence climbing method for expression parsing.

Thanks to Stephen Kell, this book's technical reviewer, whose thoughtful comments made the book clearer and more accurate. I'm particularly indebted to Stephen for undertaking the monumental task of reviewing the accompanying test suite and reference implementation. Alex Freed, who first reached out to me about writing a book, provided invaluable editorial guidance and encouragement, and Jill Franklin and Eva Morrow shepherded the book through the final stages of editing. James L. Barry provided the fabulous cover art. Thanks also to Sydney Cromwell for overseeing the production process, Rachel Head for copyediting, and the entire team at No Starch Press for their hard work making this book a reality.

Thanks to all the readers who emailed me and filed GitHub issues about earlier versions of this project, including the original blog posts and Early Access version. Their suggestions made the book better, and their enthusiasm for compilers reminded me why I was writing it.

Thank you to my friend Haney Maxwell for his thorough, insightful feedback on Chapter 13.

Last but never least, thanks to my partner, Brian, whose sound advice and ear for language I often relied on, who gamely agreed to "read this one paragraph and tell me whether it makes sense" whenever I asked, and who has always supported and believed in me.

INTRODUCTION

When we talk about how programming languages work, we tend to borrow metaphors from fantasy novels: compilers are magic, and the people who work on them are wizards. Dragons may be involved somehow. But in the day-to-day lives of most programmers, compilers behave less like magical artifacts and more like those universal translator earpieces from science fiction. They aren't flashy or dramatic; they don't demand a lot of attention. They just hum along in the background, translating a language you speak (or type) fluently into the alien language of machines.

For some reason, sci-fi characters rarely seem to wonder how their translators work. But once you've been coding for a while, it's hard not to feel curious about what your compiler is doing. A few years ago, this curiosity got the better of me, so I decided to learn more about compilers by writing one of my own. It was important to me to write a compiler for a real programming language, one that I'd used myself. And I wanted my compiler to generate assembly code that I could run without an emulator or virtual machine. But when I looked around, I found that most guides to compiler construction used toy languages that ran on idealized processors. Some of these guides were excellent, but they weren't quite what I was looking for.

I finally got unstuck when a friend pointed me toward a short paper titled "An Incremental Approach to Compiler Construction" by Abdulaziz Ghuloum (*http://scheme2006.cs.uchicago.edu/11-ghuloum.pdf*). It explained how to compile Scheme to x86 assembly, starting with the simplest possible programs and adding one new language construct at a time. I didn't particularly want to write a compiler for Scheme, so I adapted the paper to a language I was more interested in: C. As I kept working on the project, I switched from x86 to its modern counterpart, x64 assembly. I also built out support for a larger subset of C and added a few optimization passes. By this point, I had gone way beyond Ghuloum's original scheme (pun intended, sorry), but his basic strategy held up remarkably well: focusing on one small piece of the language at a time made it easy to stay on track and see that I was making progress. In this book, you'll tackle the same project. Along the way, you'll gain a deeper understanding of the code you write and the system it runs on.

Who This Book Is For

I wrote this book for programmers who are curious about how compilers work. Many books about compiler construction are written as textbooks for college or graduate-level classes, but this one is meant to be accessible to someone exploring the topic on their own. You won't need any prior knowledge of compilers, interpreters, or assembly code to complete this project. A basic understanding of computer architecture is helpful, but not essential; I'll discuss important concepts as they come up and occasionally point you to outside resources with more background information. That said, this is not a book for novice programmers. You should be comfortable writing substantive programs on your own, and you should be familiar with binary numbers, regular expressions, and basic data structures like graphs and trees. You'll need to know C well enough to read and understand small C programs, but you don't need to be an expert C programmer. We'll explore the ins and outs of the language as we go.

Although this book is geared toward newcomers to the subject, it will also be worthwhile for people who have some experience with compilers already. Maybe you implemented a toy language for a college class or personal project, and now you'd like to work on something more realistic. Or maybe you've worked on interpreters in the past, and you want to try your hand at compiling programs down to machine code. If you're in this category, this book will cover some material you already know, but it will provide plenty of new challenges too. At the very least, I promise you'll learn a few things about C.

Why Write a C Compiler?

I assume you're already sold on the idea of writing a compiler—you did pick up this book, after all. I want to talk a little bit about why we're writing a compiler for C in particular. The short answer is that C is a (relatively) simple language, but not a toy language. At its core, C is simple enough to implement even if you've never written a compiler before. But it's also a particularly clear example of how programming languages are shaped by the systems they run on and the people who use them. Some aspects of C vary based on what hardware you're targeting; others vary between operating systems; still others are left unspecified to give compiler writers more flexibility. Some bits of the language are historical artifacts that have stuck around to support legacy code, while others are more recent attempts to make C safer and more reliable.

These messy parts of C are worth tackling for a couple of reasons. First, you'll develop a solid mental model of how your compiler fits in with all the other pieces of your system. Second, you'll get a sense of the different perspectives that different groups of people bring to the language, from the specification authors trying to stamp out ambiguity and inconsistency, to compiler implementers looking for performance improvements, to ordinary programmers who just want their code to work.

I hope this project will make you think about *all* programming languages differently: not as fixed sets of rules enshrined in language standards, but as ongoing negotiations between the people who design, implement, and use them. Once you start looking at programming languages this way, they become richer, more interesting, and less frustrating to work with.

Compilation from 10,000 Feet

Before we go any further, let's take a high-level look at how source code turns into an executable and where the compiler fits into the process. We'll clear up some terminology and review a tiny bit of computer architecture while we're at it. A *compiler* is a program that translates code from one programming language to another. It's just one part (though often the most complex part) of the whole system that's responsible for getting your code up and running. We're going to build a compiler that translates C programs into *assembly code*, a textual representation of the instructions we want the processor to run.

Different processors understand different instructions; we'll focus on the x64 instruction set, also called x86-64 or AMD64. This is what most people's computers run. (The other instruction set you're likely to encounter is ARM. Most smartphones and tablets have ARM processors, and they're starting to show up in laptops too.)

The processor doesn't understand text, so it can't run our assembly code as is. We need to convert it into *object code*, or binary instructions that the processor can decode and execute. For example, the assembly instruction ret corresponds to the byte 0xc3. The *assembler* handles this conversion, taking in assembly programs and spitting out object files. Finally, the *linker* combines all the object files we need to include in our final program, resolves any references to variables or functions from other files, and adds some information about how to actually start up the program. The end result is an executable that we can run. This is a wildly oversimplified view of what happens, but it's good enough to get us started.

Aside from the compiler, assembler, and linker, compiling a C program requires yet another tool: the *preprocessor*, which runs right before the compiler. The preprocessor strips out comments, executes preprocessor directives like #include, and expands macros to produce preprocessed code that's ready to be compiled. The whole process looks something like Figure 1.

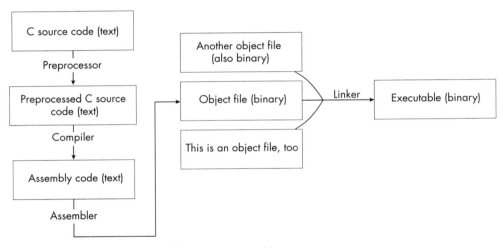

Figure 1: Transforming a source file into an executable

When you compile a program with a command like gcc or clang, you're actually invoking the *compiler driver*, a small wrapper that's responsible for calling the preprocessor, compiler, assembler, and linker in turn. You'll write your own compiler and compiler driver, but you won't write your own preprocessor, assembler, or linker. Instead, you'll use the versions of these tools already installed on your system.

What You'll Build

Over the course of this book, you'll build a compiler for a large subset of C. You can write your compiler in any programming language you like; I'll present key parts of the implementation in pseudocode. The book is organized into three parts. In Part I, The Basics, you'll implement the core features of C: expressions, variables, control-flow statements, and function calls.

Chapter 1: A Minimal Compiler In this chapter, you'll build a working compiler that can handle the simplest possible C programs, which just return integer constants. You'll learn about the different stages of compilation, how to represent a C program internally as an abstract syntax tree, and how to read simple assembly programs.

Chapter 2: Unary Operators Next, you'll start to expand your compiler by implementing two unary operators: negation and bitwise complement. This chapter introduces TACKY, a new intermediate representation that bridges the gap between the abstract syntax tree and assembly code. It also explains how to perform negation and bitwise complement in assembly, and how assembly programs store values in a region of memory called the stack.

Chapter 3: Binary Operators In this chapter, you'll implement the binary operators that perform basic arithmetic, like addition and subtraction. You'll use a technique called precedence climbing to parse arithmetic expressions with the correct associativity and precedence, and you'll learn how to do arithmetic in assembly.

Chapter 4: Logical and Relational Operators Here, you'll add support for the logical AND, OR, and NOT operators and relational operators like >, ==, and !=. This chapter introduces several new kinds of assembly instructions, including conditional instructions and jumps.

Chapter 5: Local Variables Next, you'll extend your compiler to support local variable declarations, uses, and assignments. You'll add a new compiler stage to perform semantic analysis in this chapter. This stage detects programming errors like using an undeclared variable.

Chapter 6: if Statements and Conditional Expressions In this chapter, you'll add support for if statements, your compiler's first control-flow structure, as well as conditional expressions of the form a ? b : c. Using TACKY as an intermediate representation will pay off here; you can implement both language constructs with existing TACKY instructions, so you won't need to touch later compiler stages.

Chapter 7: Compound Statements Here, you'll add support for compound statements, which group together statements and declarations and control the scope of identifiers. You'll take a close look at C's scoping rules and learn how to apply those rules during semantic analysis.

Chapter 8: Loops This chapter covers while, do, and for loops, as well as break and continue statements. You'll write a new semantic analysis pass to associate break and continue statements with their enclosing loops.

Chapter 9: Functions In this chapter, you'll implement function calls and declarations of functions other than main. You'll have two major tasks here: writing a type checker to detect semantic errors like calling functions with the wrong number of arguments, and generating assembly code. You'll learn all the ins and outs of the calling conventions for Unix-like systems, which dictate how function calls work in assembly. By meticulously following these conventions, you'll be able to compile code that calls external libraries.

Chapter 10: File Scope Variable Declarations and Storage-Class Specifiers Next, you'll add support for file scope variable declarations and the extern and static specifiers. This chapter discusses several properties of C identifiers, including linkage and storage duration. It walks through how to determine an identifier's linkage and storage duration in the semantic analysis stage and covers how those properties impact the assembly you ultimately generate. It also introduces a new region of memory, the data section, and describes how to define and operate on values stored there.

In Part II, Types Beyond int, you'll implement additional types. This is where we'll take the most in-depth look at the messy, confusing, and surprising bits of C.

Chapter 11: Long Integers In this chapter, you'll implement the long type and lay the groundwork to add more types in later chapters. You'll learn how to infer the type of every expression during type checking and how to operate on values of different sizes in assembly.

Chapter 12: Unsigned Integers Here, you'll implement the unsigned integer types. This chapter dives into the C standard's rules on integer type conversions and covers a few new assembly instructions that perform unsigned integer operations.

Chapter 13: Floating-Point Numbers Next, you'll add the floating-point double type. This chapter describes the binary representation of floating-point numbers and the perils of floating-point rounding error. It introduces a new set of assembly instructions for performing floating-point operations and explains the calling conventions for passing floating-point arguments and return values.

Chapter 14: Pointers In this chapter, you'll implement pointer types and the address and pointer dereference operators. You'll validate pointer operations in the type checker and add explicit memory access instructions to the TACKY intermediate representation.

Chapter 15: Arrays and Pointer Arithmetic This chapter picks up where Chapter 14 left off by adding support for array types and several related language features: the subscript operator, pointer arithmetic, and compound initializers. It digs into the relationship between arrays and pointers and lays out how the type checker should analyze these types.

Chapter 16: Characters and Strings This chapter covers the character types, character constants, and string literals. You'll learn about the different ways C programs use string literals, and you'll add new TACKY and assembly constructs to represent string constants. At the end of the chapter, you'll compile a couple of example programs that perform input/output (I/O) operations.

Chapter 17: Supporting Dynamic Memory Allocation   In this chapter, you'll implement the void type and sizeof operator, which will allow you to compile programs that call malloc and the other memory management functions. The biggest challenge here is handling void in the type checker. Because void is a type with no values, the type checker will treat it very differently from the other types you've implemented so far.

Chapter 18: Structures   Structures, along with the . and -> member access operators, are the last language features you'll add in this book. To implement them, you'll need all the skills you learned in earlier chapters. In the semantic analysis stage, you'll resolve structure tags according to C's scoping rules and analyze structure type declarations to determine how they're laid out in memory. When you generate TACKY, you'll translate member access operators into sequences of simple memory access instructions. And when you generate assembly, you'll follow the calling conventions for passing structures as arguments and return values.

In Part III, Optimizations, you won't add any new language features. Instead, you'll implement several classic compiler optimizations to generate more efficient assembly code. Part III is quite different from Parts I and II because these optimizations aren't specific to C; they work just as well for programs written in any language.

Chapter 19: Optimizing TACKY Programs   In this chapter, you'll add an optimization stage targeting TACKY programs. This stage will include four different optimizations: constant folding, unreachable code elimination, dead store elimination, and copy propagation. These four optimizations work together, making each one more effective than it would be by itself. This chapter introduces several tools for understanding a program's behavior, including control-flow graphs and data-flow analysis. You'll use these tools to discover ways to optimize programs without changing their behavior.

Chapter 20: Register Allocation   To cap off this project, you'll write a register allocator, which figures out how to store values in the assembly program in registers instead of memory. You'll use graph coloring to find a valid mapping from values to registers. Once the initial version of your register allocator is working, you'll use another technique, register coalescing, to make it even more effective and remove some unnecessary assembly instructions.

Next Steps   We'll wrap up with a few suggestions about how to keep learning and building out your compiler on your own.

Parts II and III both build on Part I, but they're independent of each other. You can complete either of them, both, or neither. The appendixes include some helpful information you can refer to along the way.

Appendix A: Debugging Assembly Code with GDB or LLDB   This appendix walks you through how to use GDB, the GNU debugger, and LLDB, the LLVM debugger, to debug assembly programs. When your compiler produces buggy assembly, these tools will help you figure out what's going on.

Appendix B: Assembly Generation and Code Emission Tables The tables in this appendix summarize how to convert each TACKY construct to assembly, and how to print each assembly construct during code emission. All of the chapters where we update these passes include similar tables showing what changed in that chapter; this appendix brings it all together.

Finally, a disclaimer: this book covers a lot of ground, but it doesn't cover everything. There are some really important parts of C that we won't implement: function pointers, variable-length argument lists, typedef, and type qualifiers like const, to name just a few. Instead of cramming in as many features as possible, we'll dive deep on the features we *do* implement so that you really understand how and why they work. That way, you'll learn all the skills and concepts you need to keep building on your own.

How to Use This Book

Each chapter is a detailed guide to implementing a particular feature. At the beginning of a chapter, I'll discuss the feature you're about to build and any important concepts you'll need to understand to get started. Then, we'll walk through how to update each stage of the compiler to support this new feature. I'll include pseudocode for any steps that are particularly tricky or important. Don't feel like you need to follow the pseudocode exactly; it's there to clarify what you want to accomplish, not to prescribe all the details of how you go about it.

Each chapter builds on the one before it, so you'll need to complete them in order, except that you can skip to Part III without completing Part II first.

The Test Suite

Every chapter includes a few checkpoints where you can stop and test your compiler with this book's test suite, which is available at *https://github.com/ nlsandler/writing-a-c-compiler-tests*. For each chapter, the test suite includes a set of invalid test programs that your compiler should reject with an error message and a set of valid test programs that it should compile successfully. Use the provided *test_compiler* script to run the tests.

Extra Credit Features

Some chapters mention additional language features that you can implement on your own; I call these "extra credit" features. An extra credit feature is related to the main feature covered in the chapter. You can implement it using techniques you've already learned, but you'll have to figure out the details for yourself. You might need to look at the assembly output for a few test programs to figure out how to handle them. You'll also need to consult outside references, like the C standard and the documentation for the x64 instruction set (you'll find links to these and other resources in "Additional Resources" on page xxxvi). The extra credit features are totally optional; try out the ones that seem interesting and skip the ones that don't.

Tests for these features are included in the test suite but aren't run by default. You can run them by passing the appropriate command line options to *test_compiler*.

Some Advice on Choosing an Implementation Language

While it's possible to write a compiler in any programming language, some languages are better suited to the task than others. We'll be creating a compiler *for* C, but I don't recommend writing it *in* C. Although C has its strengths as a programming language, this project doesn't play to any of them. You're better off choosing a language with easier memory management and a more extensive standard library.

You should also consider using a language with *pattern matching*. You can think of this as a kind of souped-up switch statement that lets you define different cases for values that have different structures and include different data. (Note that this is distinct from regular expression matching, which also gets called "pattern matching" occasionally.) Our very first snippet of pseudocode shows pattern matching in action:

```
greet(someone):
    match someone with
    | ImportantPerson(title, last_name) ->
        say("Good day to you, {title} {last_name}!")
    | Friend(first_name) -> say("Hello, {first_name}!")
    | Stranger -> say("Howdy, stranger!")
    | Animal(name, species) ->
        say("Hi, {name}! Who's a good {species}? It's you!")
```

This turns out to be extremely useful for analyzing and transforming programs, which generally contain several types of expressions, statements, and so on, like this:

```
do_something(expr):
    match expr with
    | Constant(int) -> do_something_for_int(int)
    | BinaryExpr(op, left, right) ->
        do_something(left)
        do_something(right)
    // handle more kinds of expressions
```

The pseudocode in this book uses pattern matching all over the place, so you'll have an easier time following along if you use a language that supports it.

For a long time, pattern matching was the province of functional languages like ML and Haskell. (It's no coincidence that these languages are very popular in programming language academia.) More recently, just about everyone else has noticed that pattern matching is great, and it's making its way into more mainstream languages. Rust and Swift both support pattern matching, Python added it in version 3.10, and Java has been gradually building out support for it since version 16. Before you start writing a compiler in your favorite language, do a little research to find out what sort of support it has for pattern matching. Depending on what you find, you might decide to use the latest and greatest version of the language, use a pattern matching library (C++, for example, has several), or use your second-favorite language instead. Or you might decide to ignore my advice; pattern matching is helpful, but you can get by without it.

System Requirements

To complete this project, you'll need a macOS or Linux system with an x64 processor (or a Mac with an Apple Silicon processor, which can emulate x64 without too much fuss). If you're on a Windows machine, you'll need to set up a Linux environment using Windows Subsystem for Linux (WSL). You can find setup instructions for WSL at *https://docs.microsoft.com/en-us/windows/wsl/install.*

This project has two dependencies. To run *test_compiler*, you'll need Python 3.8 or later. You may have a recent version of Python installed already; if not, you can download it from *https://www.python.org/downloads* or install it with your system's package manager. (See this book's web page at *https://norasandler.com/book/#setup* for more detailed installation instructions.) To check that you have a suitable version of Python installed, run:

```
$ python3 --version
```

You'll also need a real C compiler (or, strictly speaking, a real C compiler driver) to invoke the preprocessor, assembler, and linker. The test script depends on the compiler driver as well. If you're on Linux, use GCC as the compiler driver. If you're on macOS, use the version of Clang included in Xcode. (The test script uses the gcc command to invoke the compiler driver; Xcode's Clang gets installed under both the name clang and the alias gcc.) It's a good idea to install a debugger that can step through assembly code too, to help you debug the code that your compiler produces. I recommend debugging with GDB on Linux and LLDB on macOS.

Installing GCC and GDB on Linux

If you're running Linux, you should use GCC as the compiler driver and GDB as the debugger. To check whether they're already installed, run:

```
$ gcc -v
$ gdb -v
```

If either of these commands is missing, you can install them with your system's package manager. For example, to install both tools on Ubuntu, run:

```
$ sudo apt-get install gcc gdb
```

Installing the Command Line Developer Tools on macOS

The simplest option on macOS is to install the Xcode command line developer tools, which include the Clang compiler and LLDB debugger. To check whether they're already installed, run:

```
$ clang -v
```

If the tools aren't installed already, you'll be prompted to install them when you try to run this command.

The examples in this book were compiled with GCC, so if you compile them with Clang, the resulting assembly will sometimes look a little different. These differences won't impact your ability to complete the project.

Running on Apple Silicon

If your computer has an Apple Silicon processor (Apple's ARM chip), you'll need to use Rosetta 2 to run the programs you compile. The easiest solution is to run everything—including your compiler and the test script—as x64 binaries under Rosetta 2. To open an x64 shell, run:

```
$ arch -x86_64 zsh
```

You can run your compiler, Clang, the compiled programs, and *test_compiler* in this shell, and everything should work fine. Just make sure to build your compiler itself to run on x64 and not ARM.

If the arch command doesn't work, Rosetta 2 may not be installed yet. To install it, run:

```
$ softwareupdate --install-rosetta --agree-to-license
```

Validating Your Setup

The test script includes a --check-setup option that you can use to make sure your system is set up correctly. Run these commands to download the test suite and validate your setup:

```
$ git clone https://github.com/nlsandler/writing-a-c-compiler-tests.git
$ cd writing-a-c-compiler-tests
$ ./test_compiler --check-setup
All system requirements met!
```

If the test script doesn't report any issues, you're ready to get started!

Additional Resources

You can find errata, updates, links, and other resources on this book's web page at *https://norasandler.com/book/*. If you run into any problems with the project or the test script, check this page first. New versions of GCC, the Xcode command line tools, and the other tools this project depends on are released periodically; the book's web page includes any updates to the project that are needed to work with the latest versions of these tools.

If you get stuck and want to see a complete, working implementation of the project, refer to this book's reference implementation: NQCC2, the not-quite-C compiler, available at *https://github.com/nlsandler/nqcc2*. It's written in OCaml, but it has lots of comments to help you understand it if you're not an OCaml programmer.

Finally, here are a few external resources that you might find helpful. These will be especially useful if you decide to implement any of the extra credit features or otherwise build out your compiler beyond what's covered in this book:

- The **C standard** specifies how C programs are supposed to behave. We'll use C17 (ISO/IEC 9899:2018), which was the latest version of the standard at the time this book was being written. You can buy a copy from the International Standards Institute (ISO) at *https://www.iso.org/standard/74528.html*. Alternatively, if the idea of paying $200 for a PDF doesn't appeal to you, you can use a similar draft version of the standard, which is freely available at *https://www.open-std.org/JTC1/SC22/WG14/www/docs/n2310.pdf*. This is an early draft of C23—the next version of the standard after C17—with diff marks indicating what's changed. It's not the official ISO standard, so I wouldn't recommend using it to build a production C compiler, but it's close enough for this project.

- The **System V Application Binary Interface (ABI)** defines a set of conventions that executables follow on Unix-like operating systems. This will be important starting in Chapter 9, when we implement function calls. You can find the latest version of the System V ABI for x64 systems at *https://gitlab.com/x86-psABIs/x86-64-ABI*.

- The **Intel 64 Software Developer's Manual** (*https://www.intel.com/content/www/us/en/developer/articles/technical/intel-sdm.html*) is Intel's official documentation for the x64 instruction set. We care about Volume 2, the instruction set reference. There's also an unofficial version at *https://www.felixcloutier.com/x86/*, which is easier to browse.

- **Compiler Explorer** (*https://godbolt.org*) is an extremely nifty website where you can see how a variety of widely used compilers translate your code to assembly. It makes it easy to compare the output of different compilers and see the impact of various optimization levels and compiler flags.

NOTE *C23 is set to be published in 2024, superseding C17. For our purposes, the differences between C17 and C23 aren't significant. We won't implement the new language features introduced in C23, but we aren't implementing all of C17, either. The subset of C we* do *implement looks pretty much the same in both versions of the standard. If you're curious about what's different in C23, you can find a free, nearly final draft at* https://open-std.org/JTC1/SC22/WG14/www/docs/n3096.pdf *and an informal list of changes at* https://en.cppreference.com/w/c/23.

Let's Go!

We've covered all the preliminaries and we're ready to get started. In Chapter 1, we'll compile our first C program.

PART I

THE BASICS

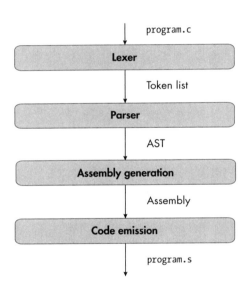

program.c

Lexer

Token list

Parser

AST

Assembly generation

Assembly

Code emission

program.s

1

A MINIMAL COMPILER

In this chapter, you'll write a minimal compiler that can handle only the simplest C programs. You'll learn how to read a simple assembly program, and you'll implement four basic compiler passes that you'll build on throughout the rest of the book. Let's start by looking at these compiler passes.

The Four Compiler Passes

The compiler you write in this chapter will process source code in four stages:

1. The *lexer* breaks up the source code into a list of *tokens*. Tokens are the smallest syntactic units of a program; they include delimiters, arithmetic symbols, keywords, and identifiers. If a program is like a book, tokens are like individual words.

2. The *parser* converts the list of tokens into an *abstract syntax tree (AST)*, which represents the program in a form we can easily traverse and analyze.

3. The *assembly generation* pass converts the AST into assembly. At this stage, we still represent the assembly instructions in a data structure that the compiler can understand, not as text.

4. The *code emission* pass writes the assembly code to a file so the assembler and linker can turn it into an executable.

This is a typical way of structuring a compiler, although the exact stages and intermediate representations vary. It's also overkill for this chapter—you could compile the programs you'll handle here in just one pass—but setting up this structure now makes it easier to expand your compiler in future chapters. As you implement more language features, you'll extend these compiler stages and add a few new ones. Each chapter starts with a current diagram of the compiler's architecture, including the stages you've already implemented and any you need to add. This chapter's diagram shows the four stages you're about to implement. In the diagrams for later chapters, new stages will be bolded.

Before you start coding, let's take a quick look at how to compile C to assembly with the C compiler already installed on your system, and how to read assembly programs.

Hello, Assembly!

The simplest C program looks like Listing 1-1.

```
int main(void) {
    return 2;
}
```

Listing 1-1: A simple program that returns the number 2

This program consists of a single function, main, containing a single return statement, which returns an integer (in this case, 2). Save this program as *return_2.c*, then use the gcc command to translate it into assembly:

```
$ gcc -S -O -fno-asynchronous-unwind-tables -fcf-protection=none return_2.c
```

If you're using macOS, this command may invoke Clang instead of GCC, but the command line options have the same effect. These options produce fairly readable assembly:

-S   Don't run the assembler or linker. This makes the compiler emit assembly instead of a binary file.

-O   Optimize the code. This eliminates some instructions we aren't concerned with right now.

-fno-asynchronous-unwind-tables Don't generate the unwind table, which is used for debugging. We don't need it.

-fcf-protection=none Disable control-flow protection, a security feature that adds extra instructions we aren't concerned with. Control-flow protection might already be disabled by default on your system, in which case this option won't do anything. Skip this option if you're using an old version of GCC or Clang that doesn't support it.

The result, stored in *return_2.s*, should look similar to Listing 1-2.

```
    .globl main
main:
    movl    $2, %eax
    ret
```

Listing 1-2: The program from Listing 1-1 translated into assembly

Your *.s* file might contain a few other lines, but you can safely ignore them for now. The four lines in Listing 1-2 are a complete assembly program. Assembly programs have several kinds of statements. The first line, .globl main, is an *assembler directive*, a statement that provides directions for the assembler. Assembler directives always start with a period. Here, main is a *symbol*, a name for a memory address. Symbols appear in assembly instructions as well as assembler directives; for example, the instruction jmp main jumps to whatever address the main symbol refers to.

The .globl main directive tells the assembler that main is a *global* symbol. By default, you can use a symbol only in the same assembly file (and therefore the same object file) where it's defined. But because main is global, other object files can refer to it too. The assembler records this fact in a section of the object file called the *symbol table*, which the linker uses when it links object files together. The symbol table contains information about all the symbols in an object file or executable.

On the second line, we use main as a *label* for the code that follows it. Labels consist of a string or number followed by a colon. A label marks the location that a symbol refers to. This particular label defines main as the address of the movl instruction on the following line. The assembler doesn't know this instruction's final memory address, but it knows what *section* of the object file it's in, as well as its offset from the start of that section. (An object file is made up of several sections that hold various kinds of data; there are separate sections for machine instructions, global variables, debug information, and so on. Different sections are loaded into different parts of the program's address space at runtime.) The address of main will be in the *text section*, which contains machine instructions. Because main refers to the very first machine instruction in this assembly file, its offset within the text section is 0. The assembler records this offset in the symbol table.

The movl instruction on the next line is a *machine instruction*, which appears in the final executable. The movl instruction in Listing 1-2 moves the value 2 into a *register*, which is a very small and fast storage slot that has its own name and sits right on the CPU. Here, we move 2 into the register named EAX, which can hold 32 bits. According to our platform's calling convention, return values are passed to the caller in EAX (or RAX, the 64-bit equivalent, depending on the return value's type). Since the caller also knows about this convention, it can retrieve the return value from EAX after the function returns. The l suffix in movl indicates that the operands to this instruction are *longwords*, or 32-bit integers (in x64 assembly, unlike most modern implementations of C, *long* means 32 bits). A movq instruction operates on *quadwords*, or 64-bit integers. I'll just write mov when I want to refer to this instruction without specifying its size.

Finally, we have another machine instruction, ret, which returns control to the caller. You might see retq here instead of ret, since this instruction implicitly operates on a 64-bit return address. I'm skipping a lot of details, including what calling conventions are, who decides on them, and how ret knows where the caller is. I'll revisit these when we add function calls in Chapter 9.

NOTE *All the assembly listings in this book use AT&T syntax. Elsewhere, you might see x64 assembly written in Intel syntax. They're two different notations for the same language; the biggest difference is that they put instruction operands in different orders.*

At this point, it's fair to ask who the caller is, since main is the only function in this program. You might also wonder why we need the .globl main directive, since there don't seem to be any other object files that could contain references to main. The answer is that the linker adds a bit of wrapper code called crt0 to handle setup before main runs and teardown after it exits. (The crt stands for *C Runtime*.) This wrapper code does the following:

1. Makes a function call to main. This is why main needs to be globally visible; if it isn't, crt0 can't call it.
2. Retrieves the return value from main.
3. Invokes the exit system call, passing it the return value from main. Then, exit handles whatever work needs to happen inside the operating system to terminate the process and turn the return value into an exit code.

The bottom line is that you don't need to worry about process startup or teardown; you can treat main like a normal function.

The linker also associates each entry in the symbol table with a memory address through a process called *symbol resolution*. It then performs *relocation*, updating every place that uses a symbol to use the corresponding address instead. (Actually, the linking process is a lot more complicated than this! If you'd like to learn more, see "Additional Resources" on page 21.)

To verify that the assembly in *return_2.s* works, assemble and link it, run it, and check the exit code with the $? shell operator:

```
$ gcc return_2.s -o return_2
$ ./return_2
$ echo $?
2
```

Note that you can pass an assembly file to the gcc command just like a regular source file. It assumes any input files with a *.s* extension contain assembly, so it assembles and links those files without trying to compile them first.

The Compiler Driver

As you learned in the Introduction, a compiler isn't very useful on its own. You also need a *compiler driver* that calls the preprocessor, compiler, assembler, and linker. So, you'll write a compiler driver before starting on the compiler itself. It should convert a source file to an executable in three steps:

1. Run this command to preprocess the source file:

   ```
   gcc -E -P INPUT_FILE -o PREPROCESSED_FILE
   ```

   This command preprocesses INPUT_FILE and then writes the result to PREPROCESSED_FILE. The -E option tells GCC to run only the preprocessor, not the later steps of the compilation process. By default, the preprocessor emits *linemarkers* indicating the original source file, and the starting line number within that source file, for each part of the preprocessed output. (A preprocessed file might include code from multiple source files because of #include directives.) The -P option tells the preprocessor not to emit linemarkers; our lexer and parser won't be able to process them. By convention, PREPROCESSED_FILE should have a *.i* file extension.

2. Compile the preprocessed source file and output an assembly file with a *.s* extension. You'll have to stub out this step, since you haven't written your compiler yet. Delete the preprocessed file when you're done with it.

3. Assemble and link the assembly file to produce an executable, using this command:

   ```
   gcc ASSEMBLY_FILE -o OUTPUT_FILE
   ```

   Delete the assembly file when you're done with it.

Your compiler driver must have a specific command line interface so this book's test script, *test_compiler*, can run it. It must be a command line program that accepts a path to a C source file as its only argument. If this command succeeds, it must produce an executable in the same directory as the input file, with the same name (minus the file extension). In other words, if you run *./YOUR_COMPILER /path/to/program.c*, it should produce an executable at */path/to/program* and terminate with an exit code of 0. If your compiler fails, the compiler driver should return a nonzero exit code and shouldn't write any assembly or executable files; that's how *test_compiler* verifies that your compiler catches errors in invalid programs. Finally, your compiler driver should support the following options, which *test_compiler* uses to test intermediate stages:

--lex   Directs it to run the lexer, but stop before parsing

--parse   Directs it to run the lexer and parser, but stop before assembly generation

--codegen   Directs it to perform lexing, parsing, and assembly generation, but stop before code emission

None of these options should produce any output files, and all should terminate with an exit code of 0 if they don't hit any errors. You might also want to add a -S option that directs your compiler to emit an assembly file, but not assemble or link it. You'll need this option to run the tests in Part III; it isn't required for Parts I and II, but it's useful for debugging.

Once you've written the compiler driver, you're ready to start working on the actual compiler. You need to implement the four compiler passes listed at the beginning of the chapter: the lexer, which produces a list of tokens; the parser, which turns those tokens into an abstract syntax tree; the assembly generation pass, which converts the abstract syntax tree into assembly; and the code emission pass, which writes that assembly to a file. Let's start with the lexer.

The Lexer

The lexer should read in a source file and produce a list of tokens. Before you can start writing the lexer, you need to know what tokens you might encounter. Here are all the tokens in Listing 1-1:

int   A keyword

main   An identifier, whose value is "main"

(An open parenthesis

void   A keyword

)   A close parenthesis

{   An open brace

return   A keyword

2   A constant, whose value is "2"

;   A semicolon

}   A close brace

I've used two lexer-specific terms here. An *identifier* is an ASCII letter or underscore followed by a mix of letters, underscores, and digits. Identifiers are case sensitive. An integer *constant* consists of one or more digits. (We'll add character and floating-point constants in Part II. We won't implement hexadecimal or octal integer constants in this book.)

Note that the identifier and constant in this list of tokens have values, but the other types of tokens don't. There are many possible identifiers (for example, `foo`, `variable1`, and `my_cool_function`), so each identifier token produced by the lexer must retain its specific name. Likewise, each constant token needs to hold an integer value. By contrast, there's only one possible return keyword, so a `return` keyword token doesn't need to store any extra information. Even though `main` is the only identifier right now, you should build the lexer to support arbitrary identifiers later on. Also note that there are no whitespace tokens. If we were compiling a language like Python, where whitespace is significant, we'd need to include whitespace tokens.

You can recognize each token type with a regular expression, or regex. Table 1-1 gives the corresponding regular expression for each token in Perl Compatible Regular Expressions (PCRE) syntax.

Table 1-1: Tokens and Their Regular Expressions

Token	Regular expression
Identifier	`[a-zA-Z_]\w*\b`
Constant	`[0-9]+\b`
int keyword	`int\b`
void keyword	`void\b`
return keyword	`return\b`
Open parenthesis	`\(`
Close parenthesis	`\)`
Open brace	`{`
Close brace	`}`
Semicolon	`;`

The process of tokenizing a program looks roughly like Listing 1-3.

```
while input isn't empty:
    if input starts with whitespace:
        trim whitespace from start of input
    else:
        find longest match at start of input for any regex in Table 1-1
        if no match is found, raise an error
        convert matching substring into a token
        remove matching substring from start of input
```

Listing 1-3: Converting a string to a sequence of tokens

Note that identifiers, keywords, and constants must end at word boundaries, indicated by `\b`. For example, the first three digits of `123;bar` match the regular expression for a constant, and you should convert them into the constant 123. This is because `;` isn't in the `\w` character class, so the boundary between 3 and `;` is a word boundary. However, the first three digits of `123bar` don't match the regular expression for a constant, because those digits are followed by more characters in the `\w` character class instead of a word boundary. If your lexer sees a string like `123bar`, it should raise an error, as the start of the string doesn't match the regular expression for any token.

Now you're ready to write your lexer. Here are a few tips to keep in mind:

Treat keywords like other identifiers.

The regex for identifiers also matches keywords. Don't try to simultaneously find the end of the next token and figure out whether it's a keyword. First, find the end of the token. Then, if it looks like an identifier, check whether it matches any keywords.

Don't split on whitespace.

It isn't a good idea to start by splitting the string on whitespace, since whitespace isn't the only boundary between tokens. For example, main(void) has four tokens and no whitespace.

You only need to support ASCII characters.

The test programs for this book contain only ASCII characters. The C standard provides a mechanism called *universal character names* to include non-ASCII characters in identifiers, but we won't implement them. Many C implementations let you use Unicode characters directly, but you don't need to support that either.

Once you've written your lexer, the next step is testing it.

TEST THE LEXER

You'll test your lexer against all the programs in *tests/chapter_1*. The programs in *tests/chapter_1/invalid_lex* contain invalid tokens, so they should cause the lexer to fail with an appropriate error message. The programs in *tests/chapter_1/invalid_parse* and *tests/chapter_1/valid* contain only valid tokens, so the lexer should process them successfully. Use the following command to test that your lexer fails on the programs in *tests/chapter_1/invalid_lex* and succeeds on everything else:

```
$ ./test_compiler /path/to/your_compiler --chapter 1 --stage lex
```

This command tests whether the lexer succeeds or fails, but it doesn't look at what tokens the lexer produces. Consider writing your own tests to validate that it produces the correct list of tokens for valid programs and emits an appropriate error message for invalid ones.

The Parser

Now that you have a list of tokens, you'll figure out how those tokens are grouped together into language constructs. In most programming languages, including C, this grouping is hierarchical: each language construct in the program is composed of several simpler constructs. Individual tokens represent the most basic constructs, like variables, constants, and arithmetic operators. Tree data structures are a natural way to express this hierarchical relationship. As I mentioned at the start of this chapter, the parser will accept the list of tokens produced by the lexer and generate a tree representation called an abstract syntax tree. After the parser has created the AST, the assembly generation stage will traverse it to figure out what assembly code to emit.

There are two approaches to writing a parser: you can write it by hand, or you can use a *parser generator* like Bison or ANTLR to produce your parsing code automatically. Using a parser generator is less work, but this book uses a handwritten parser. There are a few reasons for this. Most importantly, handwriting a parser provides you with a solid understanding of how your parser works. It's easy to use a parser generator without fully understanding the code it produces. Many parser generators also have a steep learning curve, and you're better off learning general techniques like recursive descent parsing *before* you spend time mastering specific tools.

Handwritten parsers also have some practical advantages over those produced by parser generators: they can be faster and easier to debug, they're more flexible, and they provide better support for error handling. In fact, both GCC and Clang use handwritten parsers, which shows that writing a parser by hand isn't just an academic exercise.

That said, if you'd rather use a parser generator, that's fine too. It all depends on what you're hoping to get out of this book. Note, however, that I won't talk about how to use those tools, so you'll have to figure that out on your own. If you go that route, make sure to research what parsing libraries are available in your implementation language of choice.

Whichever option you choose, you'll need to design the abstract syntax tree your parser should produce. Let's start by taking a look at an example of an AST.

An Example Abstract Syntax Tree

Consider the if statement in Listing 1-4.

```
if (a < b) {
    return 2 + 2;
}
```

Listing 1-4: A simple if *statement*

The root node of the corresponding AST represents the whole if statement. This node has two children:

1. The condition, a < b
2. The statement body, return 2 + 2;

Each of these constructs can be broken down further. For example, the condition is a binary operation with three children:

1. The left operand, variable a
2. The operator, <
3. The right operand, variable b

Figure 1-1 shows the whole AST for this code snippet, with an If AST node representing the root of the if statement, a Binary node representing the condition, and so on.

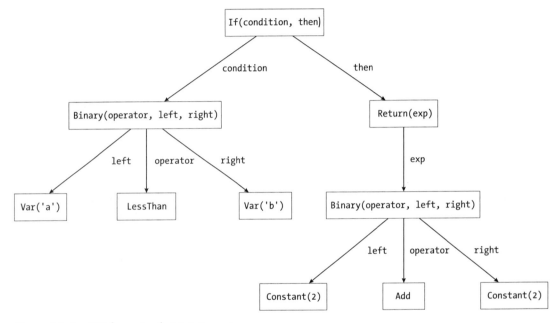

Figure 1-1: An AST for a simple if statement

The AST in Figure 1-1 contains the same information as Listing 1-4: it shows what actions the program will take, and in what order. But unlike Listing 1-4, this AST presents that information in a way your compiler can easily work with. In later stages, the compiler will traverse the tree, performing a different action at each type of node it encounters. Your compiler will use this general strategy to accomplish a bunch of different tasks, from resolving variable names to generating assembly.

Now let's look at the AST for the C program from Listing 1-1. Figure 1-2 shows this much simpler AST.

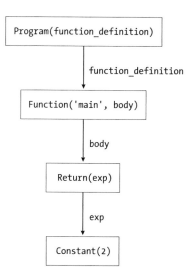

Figure 1-2: The AST for Listing 1-1

Next, you'll define the necessary data structures to construct ASTs like Figure 1-2 in code.

The AST Definition

This book gives AST descriptions in a language designed for specifying ASTs, the *Zephyr Abstract Syntax Description Language (ASDL)*. I'm using ASDL here as convenient, programming language–neutral notation. You won't use ASDL directly in your compiler; instead, you'll define equivalent data structures in your chosen implementation language. The next few paragraphs include a very brief overview of ASDL. You can find a link to the original paper, which describes the whole language, in "Additional Resources" on page 21.

Listing 1-5 has the ASDL definition for the tiny subset of C you'll implement in this chapter (programs like Listing 1-1).

```
program = Program(function_definition)
function_definition = Function(identifier name, statement body)
statement = Return(exp)
exp = Constant(int)
```

Listing 1-5: The abstract syntax tree definition for this chapter

Each line in Listing 1-5 describes how to build one type of AST node. Note that every AST node in Figure 1-2 has a corresponding definition in ASDL. The root of this AST is the `program` node. At the moment, this node can have exactly one child, of type `function_definition`. A function definition has two children: a function name, of type `identifier`, and a function body, of type `statement`. Right now, a function consists of a single statement and has no arguments. Later, you'll add support for function arguments and more complex function bodies. Note that name and body in this definition are *field names*, human-friendly labels that don't change the structure of the AST. Field names are optional in ASDL. When a field name is present, it comes immediately after the field type, like in identifier name.

In ASDL, identifier is a built-in type that represents function and variable names; they're basically strings, but we want to distinguish them from string literals like "Hello, World!" because they appear in different parts of an AST. Since identifier is a built-in type, it has no children. The other child of the function_definition node is statement. Right now, the only kind of statement is a return statement. This statement has one child: its return value, of type exp, short for *expression*. The only exp at the moment is a constant integer; int is another built-in ASDL type, so the AST is finished.

Of course, return statements aren't the only statements in C, and constants aren't the only expressions. In later chapters, we'll add new constructors to represent the other kinds of statements and expressions. For example, we'll add an If constructor to statement to represent if statements:

```
statement = Return(exp) | If(exp condition, statement then, statement? else)
```

The statement? type indicates an optional statement, since if statements don't always have an else clause. The | symbol separates constructors. Here, it tells us that a statement can be either a return statement, defined by the Return constructor, or an if statement, defined by the If constructor.

Now it's your turn to implement the AST definition in Listing 1-5 in whatever language you're using to write your compiler. The standard way to represent ASTs varies between programming languages. If you're implementing your compiler in a functional language like F#, ML, or Haskell, you can define the AST using algebraic data types. Enums in Rust are basically algebraic data types, so they can also represent ASTs. If you're using an object-oriented language like Java, you can define an abstract class for each type of node, then define classes that extend or inherit from those abstract classes for each constructor. For example, you might define an Exp abstract class and Constant and BinaryExp classes that extend it.

If you're still not sure how to write an AST definition, check out "Additional Resources" on page 21.

The Formal Grammar

An AST has all the information you'll need in later stages of the compiler. It does not, however, tell you exactly what tokens make up each language construct. For example, nothing in the AST description in Listing 1-5 says that a return statement must end with a semicolon or that a function body needs to be enclosed in braces. (This is why it's called an *abstract* syntax tree— by contrast, a *concrete* syntax tree includes every token from the original input.) Once you have an AST, those specific details are irrelevant, so it's convenient to leave them out. When you're parsing a sequence of tokens to construct your AST, though, those details matter a lot because they indicate where each language construct begins and ends.

So, in addition to an AST description, you need a set of rules defining how to build a language construct from a list of tokens. This ruleset is called a *formal grammar*, and it corresponds closely to the AST description. Listing 1-6 defines the formal grammar for C programs like Listing 1-1.

```
<program> ::= <function>
<function> ::= "int" <identifier> "(" "void" ")" "{" <statement> "}"
<statement> ::= "return" <exp> ";"
<exp> ::= <int>
<identifier> ::= ? An identifier token ?
<int> ::= ? A constant token ?
```

Listing 1-6: The formal grammar for this chapter

The grammar in Listing 1-6 is in *extended Backus-Naur form (EBNF)* notation. Each line of this grammar is a *production rule* that defines how a language construct can be formed from a sequence of other language constructs and tokens. Every symbol that appears on the left-hand side of a production rule (like `<function>`) is a *non-terminal symbol*. Individual tokens, like keywords, identifiers, and punctuation, are *terminal symbols*. All non-terminal symbols are wrapped in angle brackets, and specific tokens (like `;`) are wrapped in quotation marks. The `<identifier>` and `<int>` symbols represent individual identifier and constant tokens, respectively. Since these tokens aren't fixed strings like the other terminal symbols, we describe each of them using a *special sequence*: a plain English description of the symbol, wrapped in question marks.

Listing 1-6 looks a lot like the AST definition in Listing 1-5. In fact, it has the same structure; every AST node in Listing 1-5 corresponds to a non-terminal symbol in Listing 1-6. The only difference is that Listing 1-6 specifies exactly which tokens we'll find at each node of the tree, which helps us figure out when we need to start processing a new node at the next level down in the AST, and when we've finished processing a node and can go back up to its parent on the level above.

Just as later chapters will introduce multiple constructors for some AST nodes, they'll also introduce multiple production rules for the corresponding symbols. For example, here's how you'll add a production rule for `<statement>` to support if statements:

```
<statement> ::= "return" <exp> ";" | "if" "(" <exp> ")" <statement> [ "else" <statement> ]
```

Note that square brackets in EBNF indicate that something is optional, just like question marks in ASDL.

You'll refer to this formal grammar while writing the parser, but you won't explicitly define these grammar rules anywhere in your compiler.

Recursive Descent Parsing

Now that you have an AST definition and a formal grammar, let's talk about how to actually write the parser. We'll use a straightforward technique called *recursive descent parsing*, which uses a different function to parse each non-terminal symbol and return the corresponding AST node. For example, when the parser expects to encounter the <statement> symbol defined in Listing 1-6, it calls a function to parse that symbol and return the statement AST node from Listing 1-5. The main parsing function parses the <program> symbol, which corresponds to the entire program. With each function call to handle a new symbol, the parser descends to a lower level in the tree. That's where the *descent* in recursive descent comes from. (It's called *recursive* descent because the grammar rules are often recursive, in which case the functions to process them are too. For example, the operand of an expression could be another expression; we'll see an example of this in the next chapter.)

Let's walk through one of these parsing functions. The pseudocode in Listing 1-7 demonstrates how to parse a <statement> symbol.

```
parse_statement(tokens):
    expect("return", tokens)
    return_val = parse_exp(tokens)
    expect(";", tokens)
    return Return(return_val)

expect(expected, tokens):
    actual = take_token(tokens)
    if actual != expected:
        fail("Syntax error")
```

Listing 1-7: Parsing a statement

We call the parse_statement function when we expect the list of remaining tokens to start with a <statement>. According to Listing 1-6, a <statement> consists of three symbols: the return keyword, an <exp> symbol, and a ; token. First, we call a helper function, expect, to verify that the first token really is a return keyword. If it is, expect discards it so we can move on to the next token. If it isn't, we report a syntax error in the program. Next, we need to turn the <exp> symbol into an exp AST node. Since this is a different non-terminal symbol, it should be handled by a separate function, parse_exp, which I haven't defined here. We call parse_exp to get the AST node representing the return value; then we call expect again to verify that this expression is followed by the last token, a semicolon. Finally, we construct the Return AST node and return it.

Note that parse_statement removes all the tokens that made up the statement from the tokens list. After parse_statement returns, its caller keeps processing the remaining tokens in tokens. If there are any tokens left after parsing the entire program, that's a syntax error.

Right now, each symbol in the formal grammar has only one production rule. In later chapters, when some symbols have multiple production rules, the parser will need to figure out which production rule to use. It will do this by looking at the first few tokens in the list without removing them. Recursive descent parsers that look ahead a few tokens to figure out which production rule to use are called *predictive parsers*. The alternative to predictive parsing is *recursive descent with backtracking*, which involves trying each production rule in turn until you find one that works.

Now you can write your own recursive descent parser. Remember that you'll need to write one function to parse each non-terminal symbol in Listing 1-6. Here are a few tips to make it easier:

Write a pretty-printer.

A pretty-printer is a function that prints out your AST in a human-readable way. This will make debugging your parser a lot easier. A pretty-printed AST for the program in Listing 1-1 might look like this:

```
Program(
    Function(
        name="main",
        body=Return(
            Constant(2)
        )
    )
)
```

Give informative error messages.

This will also help you debug your parser, and it will make your compiler more user-friendly too. An error message like Expected ";" but found "return" is a lot more helpful than Fail.

TEST THE PARSER

Your parser should fail on the programs in *tests/chapter_1/invalid_parse* and succeed on the programs in *tests/chapter_1/valid*. To test the parser, run:

```
$ ./test_compiler /path/to/your_compiler --chapter 1 --stage parse
```

This command tests only whether the parser succeeds or fails, so you may want to write your own tests to confirm that it produces the correct AST for valid programs and emits an appropriate error for invalid ones.

Assembly Generation

The assembly generation stage should convert the AST into x64 assembly, traversing the AST in roughly the order the program executes to produce the appropriate assembly instructions for each node. First, define an appropriate data structure to represent the assembly program, just like you defined a data structure to represent the AST when you wrote the parser. You're adding yet another data structure, instead of writing assembly to a file right away, so that you can modify the assembly code after you've generated it. You won't need to rewrite any assembly in this chapter, but in later chapters you will.

I'll use ASDL again to describe the structure we'll use to represent assembly. Listing 1-8 has the definition.

```
program = Program(function_definition)
function_definition = Function(identifier name, instruction* instructions)
instruction = Mov(operand src, operand dst) | Ret
operand = Imm(int) | Register
```

Listing 1-8: The ASDL definition of an assembly program

This looks a lot like the AST definition from the last section! In fact, this *is* an AST definition, but for assembly programs, not C programs. Every node corresponds to a construct in assembly, like a single instruction, rather than a construct in C, like a statement. I'll refer to the data structure defined in Listing 1-8 as the *assembly AST* to distinguish it from the AST defined in Listing 1-5.

Let's walk through Listing 1-8. The program type represents a whole assembly program, which consists of a single function_definition. A function _definition has two fields: the function name and a list of instructions. The * in instruction* indicates that this field is a list. The instruction type has two constructors to represent the two instructions that can appear in our assembly programs: mov and ret. The mov instruction has two operands: it copies the first operand, the source, to the second operand, the destination. The ret instruction doesn't have any operands. The operand type defines the two possible operands to an instruction: a register and an *immediate value,* or constant. For now, you don't need to specify which register to operate on, because your generated code will use only EAX. You'll refer to other registers in later chapters. This stage has a similar structure to the parser: you need a function to handle each type of AST node, which calls other functions to handle that node's children. Table 1-2 describes the assembly you should generate for each AST node.

Table 1-2: Converting AST Nodes to Assembly

AST node	Assembly construct
Program(function_definition)	Program(function_definition)
Function(name, body)	Function(name, instructions)
Return(exp)	Mov(exp, Register) Ret
Constant(int)	Imm(int)

This translation is pretty straightforward, but there are a couple of things to note. The first is that a single statement results in multiple assembly instructions. The second is that this translation works only if an expression can be represented as a single assembly operand. This is true right now because the only expression is a constant integer, but it won't be once we add unary operators in the next chapter. At that point, your compiler will need to generate multiple instructions to calculate an expression and then figure out where that expression is stored in order to copy it into EAX.

TEST THE ASSEMBLY GENERATION STAGE

To test the assembly generation stage, run:

```
$ ./test_compiler /path/to/your_compiler --chapter 1 --stage codegen
```

This command tests that the assembly generation stage can handle every valid program without crashing. It also tests that your compiler rejects each invalid program, although you already confirmed that when you tested the lexer and parser.

Code Emission

Now that your compiler can generate assembly instructions, the last step is writing those instructions to a file. This file will look a lot like the assembly program in Listing 1-2, but a couple of details vary by platform. First, if you're on macOS, you should always add an underscore in front of the function name. For example, emit the label for the main function as _main. (Don't add this underscore on Linux.)

Second, if you're on Linux, you'll need to add this line to the end of the file:

```
.section .note.GNU-stack,"",@progbits
```

This line enables an important security hardening measure: it indicates that your code doesn't need an *executable stack*. A region of memory is *executable* if the processor is permitted to execute machine instructions stored there. The *stack*, which you'll learn more about in the next chapter, is a memory region that holds local variables and temporary values. It does not, under normal circumstances, hold machine instructions. Making the stack non-executable is a basic defense against certain security exploits, but this defense can't be enabled for every program, because a few programs that use certain nonstandard language extensions actually need an executable stack. Including this line in an assembly file signals that it does *not* require an executable stack, which allows this security measure to be enabled. None of the code we generate in this book will require an executable stack, so we'll always emit this line. (For more about executable stacks, see "Additional Resources" on page 21.)

The code emission stage should traverse the assembly AST and print each construct it encounters, much like the assembly generation stage traverses the AST from Listing 1-5. Because the assembly AST corresponds so closely to the final assembly program, the code emission stage will be very simple, even as you add more functionality to the compiler in later chapters.

Tables 1-3, 1-4, and 1-5 illustrate how to print each assembly construct.

Table 1-3: Formatting Top-Level Assembly Constructs

Assembly top-level construct	Output
Program(function_definition)	Print out the function definition. On Linux, add at end of file: .section .note.GNU-stack,"",@progbits
Function(name, instructions)	.globl *<name>* *<name>*: *<instructions>*

Table 1-4: Formatting Assembly Instructions

Assembly instruction	Output
Mov(src, dst)	movl *<src>*, *<dst>*
Ret	ret

Table 1-5: Formatting Assembly Operands

Assembly operand	Output
Register	%eax
Imm(int)	$*<int>*

Make sure to include line breaks between instructions. You should also emit readable, well-formatted assembly code because you'll spend a lot of time reading this assembly while you debug your compiler. You can make your assembly more readable by indenting every line except for labels, like in Listing 1-2. Consider including comments in your assembly programs too. A # symbol in assembly comments out the rest of the line, similar to // in C.

Once you've implemented the code emission stage, you'll be able to compile simple programs like Listing 1-1 into working executables.

TEST THE WHOLE COMPILER

To test your whole compiler, run:

```
$ ./test_compiler /path/to/your_compiler --chapter 1
```

This compiles each program in *tests/chapter_1/valid*, runs the resulting executable, and verifies that it produces the right exit code. It also validates that your compiler rejects each invalid test program, as it did for earlier stages.

Summary

In this chapter, you wrote a compiler that transforms a complete C program into an executable that runs on your computer. You learned how to interpret a program written in x64 assembly, a formal grammar in extended Backus-Naur form, and an AST definition in ASDL. The skills and concepts you learned in this chapter—and the four compiler stages you implemented—are the foundation for everything you'll do in the rest of the book.

In the next chapter, you'll add support for unary operators to your compiler. Along the way, you'll learn how assembly programs manage the stack, and you'll implement a new intermediate representation of the programs you compile to make them easier to analyze, transform, and optimize.

Additional Resources

To learn more about a few of the concepts introduced in this chapter, check out the following resources.

Linkers

- "Beginner's Guide to Linkers" by David Drysdale is a good starting point (*https://www.lurklurk.org/linkers/linkers.html*).

- Ian Lance Taylor's 20-part essay on linkers goes into a lot more depth. The first post is at *https://www.airs.com/blog/archives/38*, and there's a table of contents at *https://lwn.net/Articles/276782/*.

- "Position Independent Code (PIC) in Shared Libraries," a blog post by Eli Bendersky, provides an overview of how compilers, linkers, and assemblers work together to produce position-independent code, focusing on 32-bit machines (*https://eli.thegreenplace.net/2011/11/03/position -independent-code-pic-in-shared-libraries*).

- "Position Independent Code (PIC) in Shared Libraries on x64," also by Eli Bendersky, builds on the previous article, focusing on 64-bit systems (*https://eli.thegreenplace.net/2011/11/11/position-independent-code-pic-in-shared -libraries-on-x64*).

AST definitions

- "Abstract Syntax Tree Implementation Idioms" by Joel Jones provides a good overview of how to implement ASTs in various programming languages (*https://hillside.net/plop/plop2003/Papers/Jones-ImplementingASTs.pdf*).

- "The Zephyr Abstract Syntax Description Language" by Daniel Wang, Andrew Appel, Jeff Korn, and Christopher Serra is the original paper on ASDL. It includes examples of AST definitions in a few different languages (*https://www.cs.princeton.edu/~appel/papers/asdl97.pdf*).

Executable stacks

- "Executable Stack," a blog post by Ian Lance Taylor, discusses which programs need executable stacks and describes how Linux systems figure out whether a program's stack should be executable (*https://www.airs.com/blog/archives/518*).

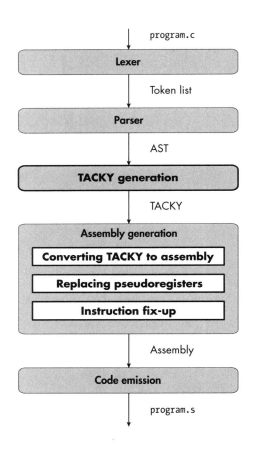

program.c

Lexer

Token list

Parser

AST

TACKY generation

TACKY

Assembly generation

Converting TACKY to assembly

Replacing pseudoregisters

Instruction fix-up

Assembly

Code emission

program.s

2

UNARY OPERATORS

C has several *unary operators*, which operate on a single value. In this chapter, you'll
extend your compiler to handle two unary
operators: negation and bitwise complement.
You'll transform complex, nested unary expressions into
simple operations that can be expressed in assembly.
Instead of performing this transformation in a single
compiler pass, you'll introduce a new intermediate representation between the AST produced by the parser
and the assembly AST produced by the assembly generation pass. You'll also break up assembly generation into
several smaller passes. The new passes are bolded in the
diagram at the start of this chapter.

To get started, let's look at a C program using the new unary operators and the corresponding assembly we'll generate.

Negation and Bitwise Complement in Assembly

In this chapter, you'll learn to compile programs like Listing 2-1.

```
int main(void) {
    return ~(-2);
}
```

Listing 2-1: A C program with negation and bitwise complement

This program contains a nested expression using both new unary operators. The first operator, *negation* (-), negates an integer—no surprise there. The *bitwise complement* (~) operator flips every bit in an integer, which has the effect of negating the integer and then subtracting one. (It has this effect because computers use a system called *two's complement* to represent signed integers. If you're not familiar with two's complement, see "Additional Resources" on page 45 for links to a few explanations of how it works.)

Your compiler will convert Listing 2-1 to the assembly code in Listing 2-2.

```
    .globl main
main:
    pushq    %rbp
    movq     %rsp, %rbp
    subq     $8, %rsp
❶ movl     $2, ❷ -4(%rbp)
❸ negl     -4(%rbp)
❹ movl     -4(%rbp), %r10d
❺ movl     %r10d, -8(%rbp)
❻ notl     -8(%rbp)
❼ movl     -8(%rbp), %eax
    movq     %rbp, %rsp
    popq     %rbp
    ret
```

Listing 2-2: The assembly code for Listing 2-1

The first three instructions after main form the *function prologue*, which sets up the current stack frame; I'll cover them in the next section, when I talk about the stack in detail. After the function prologue, we calculate the intermediate result, –2, and then the final result, 1, storing each of them at a unique memory address. This isn't very efficient, since we waste a lot of instructions copying values from one address to another. The optimizations we'll implement in Part III will clean up most of these unnecessary copies.

The first mov instruction ❶ stores 2 at an address in memory. The operand -4(%rbp) ❷ means "the value stored in the RBP register, minus four." The value in RBP is a memory address on the stack (more on this shortly), so -4(%rbp) refers to another memory address 4 bytes lower. Next, we negate the value at this address with the neg instruction ❸, so -4(%rbp) contains the value -2. (Just like mov, neg has an l suffix to indicate that it's operating on a 32-bit value.)

We then handle the outer bitwise complement expression. We start by copying the source value, stored in -4(%rbp), to the destination address at -8(%rbp). We can't do this in a single instruction, because mov can't have memory addresses as both its source and destination operands. At least one operand to mov needs to be a register or an immediate value. We get around this by copying -2 from memory into a scratch register, R10D ❹, and from there to the destination memory address ❺. Then, we take the bitwise complement of -2 with the not instruction ❻, so memory address -8(%rbp) now contains the value we want to return: ~(-2), which evaluates to 1. To return this value, we move it into EAX ❼. The final three instructions are the *function epilogue*, which tears down the stack frame and returns from the function.

NOTE *If you compile Listing 2-1 to assembly using GCC, Clang, or any other production C compiler, it won't look anything like Listing 2-2. That's because those compilers evaluate constant expressions at compile time, even when you've disabled optimizations! I'm guessing they behave this way because some constant expressions, like static variable initializers,* must *be evaluated at compile time, and evaluating all constant expressions at compile time is simpler than evaluating only some.*

The Stack

There are still two unanswered questions about Listing 2-2: what the function prologue and epilogue do, and why we refer to stack addresses relative to a value in the RBP register. To answer these questions, we need to talk about the segment of program memory called the *stack*. The RSP register, also called the *stack pointer*, always holds the address of the top of the stack. (RSP points to the last used stack slot, rather than the first free one.) As with any stack data structure, you can push values onto the stack and pop values off it; the push and pop assembly instructions do exactly that.

The stack grows toward lower memory addresses. When you push something onto the stack, you decrement RSP. That means the "top of the stack"—the address stored in RSP—is the *lowest* address on the stack. The stack diagrams in this book are oriented with lower memory addresses at the top, so the top of the stack is at the top of the diagram. Think of the memory addresses in these diagrams like line numbers in a code listing. The top of a code listing is line 1, and line numbers increase as you go down; similarly, the addresses in these diagrams increase as you go down the page or screen. Note that most stack diagrams in other books and articles use the opposite orientation: they put the top of the stack at the bottom of the diagram, so lower memory addresses appear lower on the page. I find that layout really confusing, but if you prefer it, just turn your book upside down.

An instruction like push $3 does two things:

1. Writes the value being pushed (in this example, 3) to the next empty spot on the stack. The push and pop instructions adjust the stack pointer in 8-byte increments, and the top value on the stack is currently at the address stored in RSP, so the next empty spot is RSP – 8.
2. Decrements RSP by 8 bytes. The new address in RSP is now the top of the stack, and the value at that address is 3.

Figure 2-1 illustrates the effect of a push instruction on the stack and RSP register.

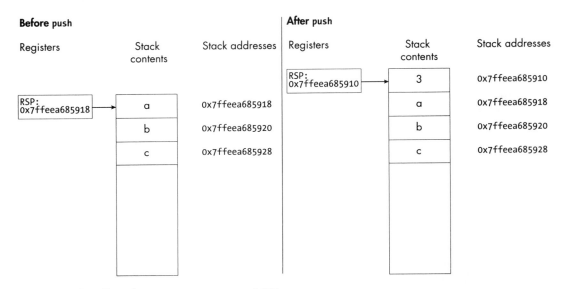

Figure 2-1: The effect of push $3 on memory and RSP

The pop instruction performs the opposite operation. For example, pop %rax copies the value at the top of the stack into the RAX register, then adds 8 bytes to RSP.

Since the push instruction decrements the stack pointer by 8 bytes, it has to push an 8-byte value. Likewise, the pop instruction always pops an 8-byte value off the stack. Values of type int—like the return value in Listing 2-1—are only 4 bytes. You can't push only 4 bytes onto the stack, but you can use movl to copy a 4-byte value into stack space you've already allocated. A couple of instructions do this in Listing 2-2, including movl $2, -4(%rbp). (On 32-bit systems, the reverse is true; you can push and pop 4-byte values but not 8-byte values. On both kinds of systems, it's also possible, though very unusual, to push and pop 2-byte values using the pushw and popw instructions; the w suffix, for *word*, indicates that the instruction takes a 2-byte operand. We won't use pushw, popw, or any other 2-byte instructions in this book.) Memory addresses on x64 systems are 8 bytes, so you can use push and pop to put them on and take them off the stack. This will come in handy in a moment.

The stack isn't just an undifferentiated chunk of memory; it's divided into sections called *stack frames*. Whenever a function is called, it allocates some memory at the top of the stack by decreasing the stack pointer. This memory is the function's stack frame, where it stores local variables and temporary values. Just before the function returns, it deallocates its stack frame, restoring the stack pointer to its previous value. By convention, the RBP register points to the base of the current stack frame; for this reason, it's sometimes called the *base pointer*. We refer to data in the current stack frame relative to the address stored in RBP. This means we don't need absolute addresses, which we can't know in advance. Since the stack grows toward lower memory addresses, every address in the current stack frame is lower than the address stored in RBP; this is why the addresses of local variables, like -4(%rbp), all have negative offsets from RBP. In later chapters, we'll also refer to data in the caller's stack frame, like function parameters, relative to RBP. (It's possible to refer to local variables and parameters relative to RSP instead, and not bother with RBP at all; most production compilers do this as an optimization.)

Now that you understand how the stack works, let's look at the function prologue and epilogue in more detail. The function prologue sets up the stack frame in three instructions:

1. pushq %rbp saves the current value of RBP, the address of the base of the caller's stack frame, onto the stack. We'll need this value when we restore the caller's stack frame later. This value will be at the bottom of the new stack frame established by the next instruction.

2. movq %rsp, %rbp makes the top of the stack the base of the new stack frame. At this point, the top and bottom of the current stack frame are the same. The current stack frame holds exactly one value, which both RSP and RBP point to: the base of the caller's stack frame, which we saved in the previous instruction.

3. subq $n, %rsp decrements the stack pointer by *n* bytes. The stack frame now has *n* bytes available to store local and temporary variables.

Figure 2-2 shows how each instruction in the function prologue affects the stack. In this figure, the subq instruction allocates 24 bytes, enough space for six 4-byte integers.

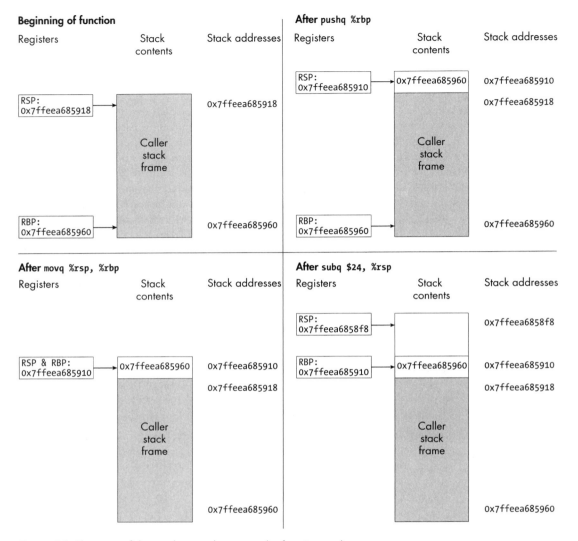

Figure 2-2: The state of the stack at each point in the function prologue

The function epilogue restores the caller's stack frame by setting RSP and RBP back to the same values they had before the function prologue. This requires two instructions:

1. `movq %rbp, %rsp` puts us back where we were after the second instruction of the function prologue: both RSP and RBP point to the bottom of the current stack frame, which holds the caller's value for RBP.

2. `popq %rbp` reverses the first instruction of the function prologue and restores the caller's values for the RSP and RBP registers. It restores RBP because the value at the top of the stack was the base address of the caller's stack frame that we saved at the start of the prologue. It restores RSP by removing the last value in this stack frame from the stack, leaving RSP pointing to the top of the caller's stack frame.

Figure 2-3 shows the effect of each instruction in the function epilogue.

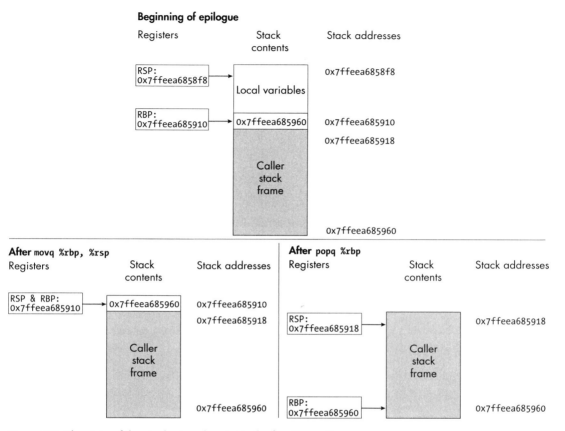

Figure 2-3: The state of the stack at each point in the function epilogue

Now that we know what output our compiler should produce, let's keep coding. We'll start by extending the lexer and parser.

The Lexer

In this chapter, you'll extend the lexer to recognize three new tokens:

~   A tilde, the bitwise complement operator

-     A hyphen, the negation operator

--   Two hyphens, the decrement operator

While you won't implement the decrement operator in this chapter, you still need to add a token for it. Otherwise, your compiler will accept programs it should reject, like the one in Listing 2-3.

```
int main(void) {
    return --2;
}
```

Listing 2-3: An invalid C program using the decrement operator

This shouldn't compile, because you can't decrement a constant. But if your compiler doesn't know that -- is a distinct token, it will think Listing 2-3 is equivalent to Listing 2-4, which is a perfectly valid program.

```
int main(void) {
    return -(-2);
}
```

Listing 2-4: A valid C program with two negation operators in a row

Your compiler should reject language features you haven't implemented; it shouldn't compile them incorrectly. That's why your lexer needs to know that -- is a single token, not just two negation operators in a row. (On the other hand, the lexer should lex ~~ as two bitwise complement operators in a row. Expressions like ~~2 are valid.)

You can process the new tokens the same way you handled punctuation like ; and (in Chapter 1. First, you need to define a regular expression for each new token. The regular expressions here are the strings ~, -, and --. Next, have your lexer check the input against these new regexes, as well as the regexes from the previous chapter, every time it tries to produce a token. When the start of the input stream matches more than one possible token, choose the longest one. For example, if your input stream starts with --, parse it as a decrement operator rather than two negation operators.

TEST THE LEXER

To test your lexer, run:

```
$ ./test_compiler /path/to/your_compiler --chapter 2 --stage lex
```

This command will validate that your compiler can successfully lex all the test cases for this chapter, including the valid test programs in *tests/chapter_2/valid* and the invalid test programs in *tests/chapter_2/invalid_parse*. It will also run the lexing test cases from Chapter 1, to make sure your lexer can still handle them.

The Parser

To parse the new operators in this chapter, we first need to extend the AST and formal grammar we defined in Chapter 1. Let's look at the AST first. Since unary operations are expressions, we represent them with a new constructor for the exp AST node. Listing 2-5 shows the updated AST definition, with new parts bolded.

```
program = Program(function_definition)
function_definition = Function(identifier name, statement body)
statement = Return(exp)
exp = Constant(int) | Unary(unary_operator, exp)
unary_operator = Complement | Negate
```

Listing 2-5: The abstract syntax tree with unary operations

The updated rule for exp indicates that an expression can be either a constant integer or a unary operation. A unary operation consists of one of the two unary operators, Complement or Negate, applied to an inner expression. Notice that the definition of exp is recursive: the Unary constructor for an exp node contains another exp node. This lets us construct arbitrarily deeply nested expressions, like -(~(-~-(-4))).

We also need to make the corresponding changes to the grammar, shown in Listing 2-6.

```
<program> ::= <function>
<function> ::= "int" <identifier> "(" "void" ")" "{" <statement> "}"
<statement> ::= "return" <exp> ";"
<exp> ::= <int> | <unop> <exp> | "(" <exp> ")"
<unop> ::= "-" | "~"
<identifier> ::= ? An identifier token ?
<int> ::= ? A constant token ?
```

Listing 2-6: The formal grammar with unary operations

Listing 2-6 includes a new production rule for unary expressions and a <unop> symbol to represent the two unary operators. These changes correspond to the additions to the AST in Listing 2-5. We've also added a third production rule for the exp symbol, which describes a parenthesized expression. It doesn't have a corresponding constructor in the AST because the rest of the compiler doesn't need to distinguish between an expression wrapped in parentheses and the same expression without parentheses. The expressions 1, (1), and ((((1)))) are all represented by the same AST node: Constant(1).

The decrement operator (--) doesn't show up anywhere in this grammar, so your parser should fail if it encounters a -- token.

To update the parsing stage, modify your compiler's AST data structure to match Listing 2-5. Then, update your recursive descent parsing code to reflect the changes in Listing 2-6. Parsing an expression gets a bit more complicated in this chapter because you need to figure out which of the three different production rules for the <exp> symbol to apply. The pseudo-code in Listing 2-7 demonstrates how to parse an expression.

```
parse_exp(tokens):
    next_token = peek(tokens)
❶ if next_token is an int:
        --snip--
❷ else if next_token is "~" or "-":
        operator = parse_unop(tokens)
        inner_exp = parse_exp(tokens)
      ❸ return Unary(operator, inner_exp)
❹ else if next_token == "(":
        take_token(tokens)
        inner_exp = parse_exp(tokens)
        expect(")", tokens)
      ❺ return inner_exp
❻ else:
        fail("Malformed expression")
```

Listing 2-7: Parsing an expression

First, we look at the next token in the input to figure out which production rule to apply. We call peek to look at this token without removing it from the input stream. Once we know which production rule to use, we'll want to process the whole input, including that first token, using that rule. So, we don't want to consume this token from the input just yet.

If the expression we're about to parse is valid, next_token should be an integer, a unary operator, or an open parenthesis. If it's an integer ❶, we parse it the same way as in the previous chapter. If it's a unary operator ❷, we apply the second production rule for <exp> from Listing 2-6 to construct a unary expression. This rule is <unop> <exp>, so we parse the unary operator and then the inner expression. The <unop> symbol is a single token, next_token, which we've already inspected. In Listing 2-7, we handle <unop> in a separate function (parse_unop, whose definition I've omitted). In practice, you probably don't need a separate function to parse one token. Either way, we end up with an AST node representing the appropriate unary operator. The next symbol in the production rule is <exp>, which we parse with a recursive call to parse_exp. (This is the recursive part of "recursive descent.") This call should return an exp AST node representing the operand of the unary expression. Now we have AST nodes for both the operator and the operand, so we return the AST node for the whole unary expression ❸.

If next_token is an open parenthesis ❹, we apply the third production rule for <exp>, which is "(" <exp> ")" . We remove the open parenthesis from the input stream, then call parse_exp recursively to handle the expression that follows. Next, we call expect to remove the closing parenthesis or throw a syntax error if it's missing. Since the AST doesn't need to indicate that there were parentheses, we return the inner expression as is ❺.

Finally, if next_token isn't an integer, a unary operator, or an open parenthesis ❻, the expression is malformed, so we throw a syntax error.

TACKY: A New Intermediate Representation

Converting the AST to assembly isn't as straightforward as it was in the last chapter. C expressions can have nested subexpressions, and assembly instructions can't. A single expression like -(~2) needs to be broken up into two assembly instructions: one to apply the inner bitwise complement operation and another to apply the outer negation operation.

We'll bridge the gap between C and assembly using a new intermediate representation (IR), *three-address code (TAC)*. In TAC, the operands of each instruction are constants or variables, not nested expressions. It's called three-address code because most instructions use at most three values: two source operands and a destination. (The instructions in this chapter use only one or two values; we'll introduce instructions that use three values when we implement binary operators in Chapter 3.) To rewrite nested expressions in TAC, we often need to introduce new temporary variables. For example, Listing 2-8 shows the three-address code for return 1 + 2 * 3;.

```
tmp0 = 2 * 3
tmp1 = 1 + tmp0
return tmp1
```

---

*Listing 2-8: The three-address code for return 1 + 2 * 3;*

There are two main reasons to use three-address code instead of converting an AST directly to assembly. First, it lets us handle major structural transformations—like removing nested expressions—separately from the details of assembly language, like figuring out which operands are valid for which instructions. This means we can write several smaller, simpler compiler passes, instead of having one huge, complicated assembly generation pass. Second, three-address code is well suited to several optimizations we'll implement in Part III. It has a simple, uniform structure, which makes it easy to answer questions like "Is the result of this expression ever used?" or "Will this variable always have the same value?" The answers to those questions determine what optimizations are safe to perform.

Most compilers use some form of three-address code internally, but the details vary. I've decided to name the intermediate representation in this book *TACKY*. (Naming your intermediate representations is, in my opinion, one of the best parts of compiler design.) I made up TACKY for this book, but it's similar to three-address code in other compilers.

Defining TACKY

We'll define TACKY in ASDL, like our other intermediate representations. The definition of TACKY in Listing 2-9 looks similar to the AST definition from Listing 2-5, but there are a few important differences.

```
program = Program(function_definition)
function_definition = Function(identifier, ❶ instruction* body)
instruction = Return(val) | Unary(unary_operator, val src, val dst)
val = Constant(int) | Var(identifier)
unary_operator = Complement | Negate
```

Listing 2-9: The TACKY intermediate representation

In TACKY, a function body consists of a list of instructions ❶ rather than a single statement. In this respect, it's similar to the assembly AST we defined in the previous chapter. For now, TACKY has two instructions: Return and Unary. Return returns a value; Unary performs some unary operation on src, the source value for the expression, and stores the result in dst, the destination. Both instructions operate on vals, which can be either constant integers (Constant) or temporary variables (Var). The TACKY we generate must meet one requirement that isn't explicit in Listing 2-9: the dst of a unary operation must be a temporary Var, not a Constant. Trying to assign a value to a constant wouldn't make sense.

Now that you've seen the ASDL definition of TACKY, you'll need to implement this definition in your own compiler, much like the definitions of the AST and assembly AST. Once you have your TACKY data structure, you're ready to write the IR generation stage, which converts the AST to TACKY.

Generating TACKY

Your TACKY generation pass should traverse an AST in the form defined in Listing 2-5 and return a TACKY AST in the form defined in Listing 2-9. The tricky part is turning an exp node into a list of instructions; once you have that figured out, handling the other AST nodes is easy. Table 2-1 lists a few examples of ASTs and the resulting TACKY.

Table 2-1: TACKY Representations of Unary Expressions

AST	TACKY
Return(Constant(3))	Return(Constant(3))
Return(Unary(Complement, Constant(2)))	Unary(Complement, Constant(2), Var("tmp.0")) Return(Var("tmp.0"))

Return(Unary(Negate,
      Unary(Complement,
         Unary(Negate, Constant(8))))))
	Unary(Negate, Constant(8), Var("tmp.0"))
	Unary(Complement, Var("tmp.0"), Var("tmp.1"))
	Unary(Negate, Var("tmp.1"), Var("tmp.2"))
	Return(Var("tmp.2"))

In these examples, we convert each unary operation into a Unary TACKY instruction, starting with the innermost expression and working our way out. We store the result of each Unary instruction in a temporary variable, which we then use in the outer expression or return statement. Listing 2-10 describes how to convert an exp AST node to TACKY.

```
emit_tacky(e, instructions):
    match e with
❶  | Constant(c) ->
        return ❷ Constant(c)
   | Unary(op, inner) ->
        src = emit_tacky(inner, instructions)
        dst_name = make_temporary()
        dst = Var(dst_name)
        tacky_op = convert_unop(op)
        instructions.append(Unary(tacky_op, src, dst))
        return dst
```

Listing 2-10: Converting an expression into a list of TACKY instructions

This pseudocode emits the instructions needed to calculate an expression by appending them to the instructions argument. It also returns a TACKY val that represents the result of the expression, which we'll use when translating the outer expression or statement.

The match statement in Listing 2-10 checks which type of expression we're translating, then runs the clause to handle that expression. If the expression is a constant, we return the equivalent TACKY Constant without generating any new instructions. Note that this code includes two different Constant constructs; the one we match on is a node in the original AST ❶, while the one we return is a node in the TACKY AST ❷. The same is true for the two Unary constructs that appear in the following clause.

If e is a unary expression, we construct TACKY values for the source and destination. First, we call emit_tacky recursively on the source expression to get the corresponding TACKY value. This also generates the TACKY instructions to calculate that value. Then, we create a new temporary variable for the destination. The make_temporary helper function generates a unique name for this variable. We use another helper function, convert_unop, to convert the unary operator to its TACKY equivalent. Once we have our source, destination, and unary operator, we construct the Unary TACKY instruction and append it to the instructions list. Finally, we return dst as the result of the whole expression.

Keep in mind that emit_tacky processes an expression, not a return statement. You need a separate function (which I won't provide pseudocode for) to convert a return statement to TACKY. This function should call emit_tacky to process the statement's return value, then emit a TACKY Return instruction.

Generating Names for Temporary Variables

It's clear that every temporary variable needs a distinct name. In later chapters, we'll also need to guarantee that these autogenerated names won't conflict with user-defined names for functions and global variables, or with autogenerated names from different functions. These identifiers must all be unique because we'll store all of them—autogenerated names and user-defined function and variable names—in the same table.

One simple solution is to maintain a global integer counter; to generate a unique name, increment the counter and use its new value as the name of the temporary variable. This name won't conflict with other temporary names because the counter produces a new value each time we increment it. It won't conflict with user-defined identifiers because integers aren't valid identifiers in C. In Table 2-1, I used a variation on this approach, concatenating a descriptive string, a period, and the value of the global counter to produce unique identifiers like tmp.0. These won't conflict with user-defined identifiers because C identifiers can't contain periods. With this naming scheme, you can encode useful information in autogenerated names, like the name of the function where they're used. (It's less useful if you name every variable tmp, like I've done here.)

Updating the Compiler Driver

To test out the TACKY generator, you need to add a new --tacky command line option to run your compiler through the TACKY generation stage, stopping before assembly generation. Like the existing --lex, --parse, and --codegen options, this new option shouldn't produce any output.

Assembly Generation

TACKY is closer to assembly, but it still doesn't specify exactly which assembly instructions we need. The next step is converting the program from TACKY into the assembly AST we defined in the last chapter. We'll do this in three small compiler passes. First, we'll produce an assembly AST, but still refer to temporary variables directly. Next, we'll replace those variables with concrete addresses on the stack. That step will result in some invalid instructions because many x64 assembly instructions can't use memory addresses for both operands. So, in the last compiler pass, we'll rewrite the assembly AST to fix any invalid instructions.

Converting TACKY to Assembly

We'll start by extending the assembly AST we defined in the last chapter. We need some new constructs to represent the neg and not instructions from Listing 2-2. We also need to decide how to represent the function prologue and epilogue in the assembly AST.

There are a few different ways to handle the prologue and epilogue. We could add the push, pop, and sub instructions to the assembly AST. We could add high-level instructions that correspond to the entire prologue and epilogue, instead of maintaining a one-to-one correspondence between assembly AST constructs and assembly instructions. Or we could leave out the function prologue and epilogue entirely and add them during code emission. I'll use a combination of the first and last options. This chapter's assembly AST, shown in Listing 2-11, includes a construct corresponding to the sub instruction (the third instruction in the function prologue). This construct specifies how many bytes we need to subtract from the stack pointer. The assembly AST doesn't include the other instructions from the prologue and epilogue; these instructions are always the same, so we can add them during code emission. That said, the other approaches to representing the function prologue and epilogue will also work, so choose whichever you like best.

We'll also introduce *pseudoregisters* to represent temporary variables. We use pseudoregisters as operands in assembly instructions, like real registers; the only difference is that we have an unlimited supply of them. Because they aren't real registers, they can't appear in the final assembly program; they'll need to be replaced by real registers or memory addresses in a later compiler pass. For now, we'll assign every pseudoregister to a distinct address in memory. In Part III, we'll write a *register allocator*, which assigns as many pseudoregisters as possible to hardware registers instead of memory addresses.

Listing 2-11 shows the updated assembly AST, with the new parts bolded.

```
program = Program(function_definition)
function_definition = Function(identifier name, instruction* instructions)
instruction = Mov(operand src, operand dst)
            | Unary(unary_operator, operand)
            | AllocateStack(int)
            | Ret
unary_operator = Neg | Not
operand = Imm(int) | Reg(reg) | Pseudo(identifier) | Stack(int)
reg = AX | R10
```

Listing 2-11: The assembly AST with unary operators

The instruction node has a couple of new constructors to represent our new assembly instructions. The Unary constructor represents a single not or neg instruction. It takes one operand that's used as both source and destination. The AllocateStack constructor represents the third instruction in the function prologue, subq $*n*, %rsp. Its one child, an integer, indicates the number of bytes we subtract from RSP.

We also have several new instruction operands. The Reg constructor represents a hardware register. It can specify either hardware register we've seen so far: EAX or R10D. The Pseudo operand lets us use an arbitrary identifier as a pseudoregister. We use this to refer to the temporary variables we produced while generating TACKY. Ultimately, we need to replace every pseudoregister with a location on the stack; we represent those with the Stack operand, which indicates the stack address at the given offset from RBP. For example, we'd represent the operand -4(%rbp) with the assembly AST node Stack(-4).

NOTE *Every hardware register has several aliases, depending on how many bytes of the register you need. EAX refers to the lower 32 bits of the 64-bit RAX register, and R10D refers to the lower 32 bits of the 64-bit R10 register. The names AL and R10B refer to the lower 8 bits of RAX and R10, respectively. Register names in the assembly AST are size agnostic, so AX in Listing 2-11 can refer to the register alias RAX, EAX, or AL, depending on context. (The name AX normally refers to the lower 16 bytes of RAX, but we won't use 16-byte register aliases in this book.)*

Now we can write a straightforward conversion from TACKY to assembly, shown in Tables 2-2 through 2-5. As Table 2-2 illustrates, we convert TACKY `Program` and `Function` nodes to the corresponding assembly constructs.

Table 2-2: Converting Top-Level TACKY Constructs to Assembly

TACKY top-level construct	Assembly top-level construct
Program(function_definition)	Program(function_definition)
Function(name, instructions)	Function(name, instructions)

We'll convert each TACKY instruction to a sequence of assembly instructions, as shown in Table 2-3. Since our new assembly instructions use the same operand for the source and destination, we copy the source value into the destination before issuing a unary neg or not instruction.

Table 2-3: Converting TACKY Instructions to Assembly

TACKY instruction	Assembly instructions
Return(val)	Mov(val, Reg(AX)) Ret
Unary(unary_operator, src, dst)	Mov(src, dst) Unary(unary_operator, dst)

Table 2-4 shows the corresponding assembly unary_operator for each TACKY unary_operator, and Table 2-5 shows the conversion from TACKY operands to assembly operands.

Table 2-4: Converting TACKY Arithmetic Operators to Assembly

TACKY operator	Assembly operator
Complement	Not
Negate	Neg

Table 2-5: Converting TACKY Operands to Assembly

TACKY operand	Assembly operand
Constant(int)	Imm(int)
Var(identifier)	Pseudo(identifier)

Note that we're not using the `AllocateStack` instruction yet; we'll add it in the very last pass before code emission, once we know how many bytes we need to allocate. We're also not using any `Stack` operands; we'll replace every `Pseudo` operand with a `Stack` operand in the next compiler pass. And we're not using the R10D register; we'll introduce it when we rewrite invalid instructions.

Replacing Pseudoregisters

Next, we write a compiler pass to replace each Pseudo operand with a Stack operand, leaving the rest of the assembly AST unchanged. In Listing 2-2, we used two stack locations: -4(%rbp) and -8(%rbp). This pass follows the same pattern: we replace the first temporary variable we see with Stack(-4), the next with Stack(-8), and so on. We subtract four for each new variable, since every temporary variable is a 4-byte integer. You'll need to maintain a map from identifiers to offsets as you go so you can replace each pseudoregister with the same address on the stack every time it appears. For example, if you process the instructions

```
Mov(Imm(2), Pseudo("a"))
Unary(Neg, Pseudo("a"))
```

you should replace Pseudo("a") with the same Stack operand in both instructions.

This compiler pass should also return the stack offset of the final temporary variable, because that tells us how many bytes to allocate on the stack in the next pass.

Fixing Up Instructions

Now we need to traverse the assembly AST one more time and make two small fixes. First, we'll insert the AllocateStack instruction at the very beginning of the instruction list in the function_definition. The integer argument to AllocateStack should be the stack offset of the last temporary variable we allocated in the previous compiler pass. That way, we'll allocate enough space on the stack to accommodate every address we use. For example, if we replace three temporary variables, replacing the last one with -12(%rbp), we'll insert AllocateStack(12) at the front of the instruction list.

The second fix is rewriting invalid Mov instructions. When we replaced pseudoregisters with stack addresses, we may have ended up with Mov instructions where both the source and destination are Stack operands. This happens when the unary expression in your program has at least one level of nesting. But mov, like many other instructions, can't have memory addresses as both the source and the destination. If you try to assemble a program with an instruction like movl -4(%rbp), -8(%rbp), the assembler will reject it. When you encounter an invalid mov instruction, rewrite it to first copy from the source address into R10D and then copy from R10D to the destination. For example, the instruction

```
movl    -4(%rbp), -8(%rbp)
```

becomes:

```
movl    -4(%rbp), %r10d
movl    %r10d, -8(%rbp)
```

I've chosen R10D as a scratch register because it doesn't serve any other special purpose. Some registers are required by particular instructions; for example, the idiv instruction, which performs division, requires the dividend to be stored in EAX. Other registers are used to pass arguments during function calls. Using any of these registers for scratch at this stage could cause conflicts. For example, you might copy a function argument into the correct register, but then accidentally overwrite it while using that register to transfer a different value between memory addresses. Because R10D doesn't have any special purpose, we don't have to worry about these conflicts.

TEST THE ASSEMBLY GENERATION STAGE

Once you've implemented all the passes in the assembly generation stage, use the --codegen option to test them out:

```
$ ./test_compiler /path/to/your_compiler --chapter 2 --stage codegen
```

You may also want to write your own unit tests for the individual assembly generation passes.

Code Emission

Finally, we'll extend the code emission stage to handle our new constructs and print out the function prologue and epilogue. Tables 2-6 through 2-9 show how to print out each assembly construct. New constructs and changes to the way we emit existing constructs are bolded.

Table 2-6 shows how to include the prologue when you emit an assembly Function.

Table 2-6: Formatting Top-Level Assembly Constructs

Assembly top-level construct	Output
Program(function_definition)	Print out the function definition. On Linux, add at end of file: .section .note.GNU-stack,"",@progbits

Function(name, instructions)	.globl *<name>*
	<name>:
	    pushq %rbp
	    movq %rsp, %rbp
	    <instructions>

Table 2-7 shows how to include the function epilogue just before the Ret instruction and how to emit the new Unary and AllocateStack instructions.

Table 2-7: Formatting Assembly Instructions

Assembly instruction	Output	
Mov(src, dst)	movl	\<src\>, \<dst\>
Ret	movq	%rbp, %rsp
	popq	%rbp
	ret	
Unary(unary_operator, operand)	\<unary_operator\>	\<operand\>
AllocateStack(int)	subq	$\<int\>, %rsp

As this table illustrates, you should emit AllocateStack as a subq instruction. Emit Unary as a negl or notl instruction, according to its unary_operator argument. Table 2-8 shows which unary_operator corresponds to each of these instructions.

Table 2-8: Instruction Names for Assembly Operators

Assembly operator	Instruction name
Neg	negl
Not	notl

Finally, Table 2-9 shows how to print out the new Reg and Stack operands.

Table 2-9: Formatting Assembly Operands

Assembly operand	Output
Reg(AX)	%eax
Reg(R10)	%r10d
Stack(int)	\<int\>(%rbp)
Imm(int)	$\<int\>

Because RBP and RSP contain memory addresses, which are 8 bytes, we always operate on them using quadword instructions, which have a q suffix. The movl instruction in Table 2-7 and the movq instruction in the prologue and epilogue are identical apart from the size of their operands.

Summary

In this chapter, you extended your compiler to implement negation and bitwise complement. You also implemented a new intermediate representation, wrote two new compiler passes that transform assembly code, and learned how stack frames are structured. Next, you'll implement binary operations like addition and subtraction. The changes to the backend in the next chapter are pretty simple; the tricky part is getting the parser to respect operator precedence and associativity.

Additional Resources

This chapter touched on *two's complement*, which is how all modern computers represent signed integers. Two's complement will show up throughout this book, so it's worth taking the time to understand it. Here are a couple of overviews of how it works:

- "Two's Complement" by Thomas Finley covers how and why two's complement representations work (*https://www.cs.cornell.edu/~tomf/notes/cps104/twoscomp.html*).

- Chapter 2 of *The Elements of Computing Systems* by Noam Nisan and Shimon Schocken (MIT Press, 2005) covers similar material from a more hardware-focused perspective. This is the companion book for the Nand to Tetris project. This chapter is freely available at *https://www.nand2tetris.org/course*; click the book icon under "Project 2: Boolean Arithmetic."

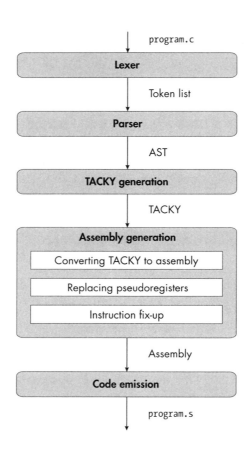

program.c

Lexer

Token list

Parser

AST

TACKY generation

TACKY

Assembly generation

Converting TACKY to assembly

Replacing pseudoregisters

Instruction fix-up

Assembly

Code emission

program.s

3

BINARY OPERATORS

In this chapter, you'll implement five new operators: addition, subtraction, multiplication, division, and the remainder operator. These are all *binary operators*, which take two operands. This chapter won't require any new compiler stages; you'll just extend each of the stages you've already written. In the parsing stage, you'll see why recursive descent parsing doesn't work well for binary expressions. Instead, you'll use a different technique, *precedence climbing*, which will be easier to build on in later chapters. Precedence climbing is the last major parsing technique you'll need. Once it's in place, you'll be able to add new syntax with relatively little effort for the rest of the book. In the assembly generation stage, you'll introduce several assembly instructions that perform binary operations. As usual, we'll start with the lexer.

The Lexer

The lexer needs to recognize four new tokens:

+   A plus sign, the operator for addition
*   An asterisk, the operator for multiplication
/   A forward slash, the division operator
%   A percent sign, the remainder operator

This list doesn't include the - token, because you added it in the last chapter. The lexing stage doesn't distinguish between negation and subtraction; it should produce the same token either way.

You should lex these tokens in the same way as the single-character tokens in the previous chapters.

TEST THE LEXER

To test your lexer, run:

```
$ ./test_compiler /path/to/your_compiler --chapter 3 --stage lex
```

Your compiler should successfully lex all the test cases in this chapter. As always, this command will also run the tests from the previous chapters.

The Parser

Now you're going to add another kind of expression to the AST: binary operations. Listing 3-1 shows the updated AST definition.

```
program = Program(function_definition)
function_definition = Function(identifier name, statement body)
statement = Return(exp)
exp = Constant(int)
    | Unary(unary_operator, exp)
    | Binary(binary_operator, exp, exp)
unary_operator = Complement | Negate
binary_operator = Add | Subtract | Multiply | Divide | Remainder
```

Listing 3-1: The abstract syntax tree with binary operations

Note that the parser, unlike the lexer, distinguishes between negation and subtraction. A - token is parsed as either Negate or Subtract, depending on where it appears in an expression.

Also note that the structure of the AST determines the order of evaluation of nested expressions. Let's look at a couple of examples to see how the AST's structure controls the order of operations. The AST in Figure 3-1 represents the expression 1 + (2 * 3), which evaluates to 7.

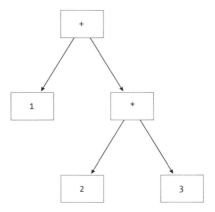

Figure 3-1: The AST for 1 + (2 * 3)

The + operation has two operands: 1 and (2 * 3). To evaluate this expression, you calculate 2 * 3 first, then add 1 to the result. The AST in Figure 3-2, on the other hand, represents the expression (1 + 2) * 3, which evaluates to 9.

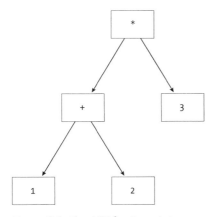

Figure 3-2: The AST for (1 + 2) * 3

In this case, you evaluate 1 + 2 first, then multiply by 3. As a general rule, before evaluating an AST node you need to evaluate both of its children. This pattern, where you process a node's children before the node itself, is called *postorder traversal*. Note that any tree data structure can be traversed in postorder, not just ASTs.

Your compiler traverses the AST to generate code, not to evaluate expressions, but the idea is the same. When you convert the AST for a binary expression to TACKY, you first generate instructions to calculate both operands, then generate instructions for the operation itself. (You also used postorder traversal to process unary operations in Chapter 2.)

It's crucial for your parser to group nested expressions correctly. If you try to parse 1 + (2 * 3) but end up with the AST from Figure 3-2, you'll ultimately compile the program incorrectly.

The examples we just looked at used parentheses to explicitly group nested expressions. Some expressions, like 1 + 2 * 3, don't parenthesize every nested expression. In those cases, we group expressions based on the *precedence* and *associativity* of the operators. Operators with higher precedence are evaluated first; since * has higher precedence than +, you'd parse 1 + 2 * 3 as 1 + (2 * 3). Associativity tells you how to handle operators at the same precedence level. If an operation is *left-associative*, you apply the operator on the left first, and if it's *right-associative*, you apply the operator on the right first. For example, since addition and subtraction are left-associative, 1 + 2 - 3 would be parsed as (1 + 2) - 3. All the new operators in this chapter are left-associative, and there are two precedence levels: *, /, and % have higher precedence, while + and - have lower precedence.

The Trouble with Recursive Descent Parsing

It's surprisingly tricky to write a recursive descent parser that correctly handles operator precedence and associativity. To see why, let's try adding a production rule for binary expressions to the formal grammar. This new rule is bolded in the definition of <exp> in Listing 3-2.

<exp> ::= <int> | <unop> <exp> | "(" <exp> ")" | **<exp> <binop> <exp>**

Listing 3-2: A simple grammar rule that doesn't work for recursive descent parsers

A binary expression consists of an expression, then a binary operator, then another expression, so <exp> <binop> <exp> is the obvious way to define it in the formal grammar. But there are a couple of reasons a recursive descent parser can't use this production rule.

First, Listing 3-2 is *ambiguous*: it allows you to parse certain inputs in more than one way. For example, according to this grammar, Figures 3-1 and 3-2 are equally valid parses of 1 + 2 * 3. We need to know the relative precedence of + and * to decide which parse to use, but the grammar doesn't capture that information.

Second, the new production rule is *left-recursive*: the leftmost symbol in this production rule for <exp> is, itself, <exp>. You can't apply a left-recursive rule in a recursive descent parser; if you try, you end up with unbounded recursion. Imagine trying to implement this production rule in parse_exp. The first symbol in this rule is <exp>, so parse_exp would have to process that symbol by calling itself recursively. But parse_exp wouldn't consume any tokens before the recursive call. It would call itself with exactly the same input, so it would never terminate.

We can solve these problems in a couple of ways. If we want a pure recursive descent parser, we can refactor the grammar to remove the ambiguity and left recursion. Since that approach has some drawbacks, we'll use precedence climbing, an alternative to recursive descent parsing. However, it's helpful to take a look at the pure recursive descent solution first.

The Adequate Solution: Refactoring the Grammar

If we refactor the grammar, we'll end up with one grammar rule for each precedence level, like in Listing 3-3.

```
<exp> ::= <term> { ("+" | "-") <term> }
<term> ::= <factor> { ("*" | "/" | "%") <factor> }
<factor> ::= <int> | <unop> <factor> | "(" <exp> ")"
```

Listing 3-3: A recursive descent–friendly grammar for binary operations

Using the grammar in Listing 3-3, there's only one way to parse 1 + 2 * 3, and there's no left recursion. The braces indicate repetition, so a single <exp>, for example, can contain any number of <term>s. It might be a <term>, or <term> + <term>, or <term> - <term> + <term>, and so on. The parser then groups that long string of terms into a left-associative tree to construct an exp AST node. (Note that we can't use a rule like <exp> ::= <term> "+" <exp> because it results in a right-associative tree. The grammar in Listing 3-3, on the other hand, doesn't specify the associativity, which allows the parser to build either a left-associative or a right-associative tree.)

This approach works, but it gets increasingly unwieldy as you add more precedence levels. We have three precedence levels now, if you count <factor>; we'll add four more when we introduce logical and relational operators in Chapter 4. If we went with this approach, we'd need to add a new symbol to the grammar—and a corresponding function to our parser—for each precedence level we add. That's a lot of boilerplate, since the functions to parse the expressions at different precedence levels would be almost identical.

The Better Solution: Precedence Climbing

Precedence climbing is a simpler way to parse binary expressions. It can handle production rules like <exp> <binop> <exp> while respecting the precedence of each binary operator. In precedence climbing, every operator has a numeric precedence level, and parse_exp takes a minimum precedence level as an argument. This lets you specify the appropriate precedence level for whatever subexpression you're parsing. For example, suppose you just saw a + token, and now you want to parse what comes next as the right-hand side of an addition expression: you'd specify that it should include only operations that have higher precedence than +. This solution makes it easy to add new operators; you have to assign each new operator a numeric precedence level, but you don't need to make any other changes to your parsing code.

Mixing Precedence Climbing with Recursive Descent

We can use precedence climbing to parse binary expressions and still use recursive descent to parse other language constructs. Remember that a recursive descent parser uses a different function to parse each symbol. That makes it easy to parse different symbols with different techniques: we use precedence climbing in the parse_exp function and recursive descent in the functions that parse all the other symbols. The parse_exp function will remove tokens from the input stream and return an AST node, just like the recursive descent–based parsing functions, but it will use a different strategy to get that result.

Since we already use recursive descent to parse unary and parenthesized expressions, let's represent those with a separate symbol from binary operations. Listing 3-4 shows the resulting grammar, with changes from Chapter 2 bolded.

```
<program> ::= <function>
<function> ::= "int" <identifier> "(" "void" ")" "{" <statement> "}"
<statement> ::= "return" <exp> ";"
<exp> ::= <factor> | <exp> <binop> <exp>
<factor> ::= <int> | <unop> <factor> | "(" <exp> ")"
<unop> ::= "-" | "~"
<binop> ::= "-" | "+" | "*" | "/" | "%"
<identifier> ::= ? An identifier token ?
<int> ::= ? A constant token ?
```

Listing 3-4: The final grammar to handle binary operations

The symbol we called <exp> in Listing 2-6 is now called <factor>; it represents a constant, a unary expression, or a parenthesized expression. (We'll keep the name *factor* from Listing 3-3 because this symbol can appear as a factor in a multiplication expression.) We parse a <factor> with the usual recursive descent approach. It has almost exactly the same definition that <exp> did in Chapter 2, except that we now allow binary expressions as well as factors inside parentheses. This means (1 + 2) is a factor, because "(" <exp> ")" is a production rule for <factor>. However, -1 + 2 is not, because <unop> <exp> is not a production rule for <factor>. An <exp> is either a binary operation, defined in the obvious way, or a factor. Because the rules for <exp> and <factor> refer to each other, the functions to parse those symbols are mutually recursive. Those functions both yield exp AST nodes; <factor> and <exp> are distinct symbols in the grammar, but not different types in the AST.

The pseudocode to parse factors is shown in Listing 3-5.

```
parse_factor(tokens):
    next_token = peek(tokens)
    if next_token is an int:
        --snip--
    else if next_token is "~" or "-":
        operator = parse_unop(tokens)
     ❶ inner_exp = parse_factor(tokens)
        return Unary(operator, inner_exp)
```

```
    else if next_token == "(":
        take_token(tokens)
    ❷ inner_exp = parse_exp(tokens)
        expect(")", tokens)
        return inner_exp
    else:
        fail("Malformed factor")
```

Listing 3-5: Parsing a factor

This looks a lot like the previous chapter's expression parsing code (shown in Listing 2-7). The only difference is that we call parse_factor where we expect a <factor> ❶ and parse_exp where we expect an <exp> ❷; before, we called parse_exp in both places.

Making Operators Left-Associative

Next, let's write the new version of parse_exp. We'll start with a simple version of the function that handles only the + and - operators, which are at the same precedence level. This simplified parse_exp needs to group expressions in a left-associative way, but it doesn't need to handle multiple precedence levels yet.

In this simple case, we'll encounter inputs like *factor1 + factor2 - factor3 + factor4*. These should always be parsed in a left-associative way to produce expressions like *((factor1 + factor2) - factor3) + factor4*. As a result, the right operand of every expression, including subexpressions, will be a single factor. For example, the right operand of *(factor1 + factor2)* is *factor2*, and the right operand of *((factor1 + factor2) - factor3)* is *factor3*.

Since the right operand of an expression is always a single factor, we can parse these expressions with the pseudocode in Listing 3-6.

```
parse_exp(tokens):
  ❶ left = parse_factor(tokens)
    next_token = peek(tokens)
  ❷ while next_token is "+" or "-":
        operator = parse_binop(tokens)
      ❸ right = parse_factor(tokens)
      ❹ left = Binary(operator, left, right)
        next_token = peek(tokens)
    return left
```

Listing 3-6: Parsing left-associative expressions without considering precedence level

We start by parsing a single factor ❶, which is either the whole expression or the left operand of a larger expression. Next, we check whether the following token is a binary operator ❷. If it is, we consume it from the input and convert it to a binary_operator AST node. Then, we construct a binary expression ❹ where the left operand is everything we've parsed so far and the right operand is the next factor, which we get by calling parse_factor ❸. We repeat this process until we see a token other than + or - after a factor; this means there are no binary expressions left to construct, so we're done.

Dealing with Precedence

Now let's extend Listing 3-6 to handle *, /, and %. These operators are also left-associative, but they're at a higher precedence level than + and -.

Once we add these operators, the right operand of every expression can be either a single factor or a subexpression involving only the new higher-precedence operators. For example, 1 + 2 * 3 + 4 would be parsed as (1 + (2 * 3)) + 4. The right operand of the whole expression is a single factor, 4. The right operand of the inner subexpression, 1 + (2 * 3), is a product, 2 * 3.

In other words, if the outermost expression is a + or - operation, its right operand contains only factors and *, /, and % operations. But if the outermost expression is itself a *, /, or % operation, its right operand must be single factor.

To generalize: when we parse an expression of the form e1 <op> e2, all the operators in e2 should have higher precedence than <op>. We can achieve this by tweaking the code from Listing 3-6, which gives us Listing 3-7.

```
parse_exp(tokens, min_prec):
    left = parse_factor(tokens)
    next_token = peek(tokens)
    while next_token is a binary operator and precedence(next_token) >= min_prec:
        operator = parse_binop(tokens)
        right = parse_exp(tokens, precedence(next_token) + 1)
        left = Binary(operator, left, right)
        next_token = peek(tokens)
    return left
```

Listing 3-7: Parsing left-associative expressions with precedence climbing

This pseudocode is our entire precedence climbing algorithm. The min_prec argument lets us state that all operators in the subexpression we're currently parsing need to exceed some precedence level. For example, we could include only operators that have higher precedence than +. We enforce this by comparing the precedence of the current operator to min_prec at each iteration of the while loop; we exclude the operator and anything that follows it from the current expression if its precedence is too low. Then, when we parse the right-hand side of an operation, we set the minimum precedence higher than the precedence of the current operator. This guarantees that higher-precedence operators will be evaluated first. Since operators at the same precedence level as the current operator won't be included in the right-hand expression, the resulting AST will be left-associative.

When you call parse_exp from any other function (including from parse _factor, to handle parenthesized expressions), start with a minimum precedence of zero so the result includes operators at every precedence level.

The code in Listing 3-7 requires us to assign every binary operator a precedence value. Table 3-1 shows the values I've assigned.

Table 3-1: Precedence Values of Binary Operators

Operator	Precedence
*	50
/	50
%	50
+	45
-	45

The exact precedence values don't matter, as long as higher-precedence operators have higher values. The numbers in Table 3-1 give us plenty of room to add lower-precedence operators later on.

Precedence Climbing in Action

Let's walk through an example where we parse the following expression:

```
1 * 2 - 3 * (4 + 5)
```

The following code snippets trace the execution of the precedence climbing code from Listing 3-7 as it parses this expression. We start by calling parse_exp on the whole expression with 0 as the minimum precedence argument:

```
parse_exp("1 * 2 - 3 * (4 + 5)", 0):
```

Next, inside parse_exp, we parse the first factor:

```
left = parse_factor("1 * 2 - 3 * (4 + 5)")
     = Constant(1)
next_token = "*"
```

This first call to parse_factor parses the token 1, returning Constant(1). Next, we peek at the token that follows, *. This token is a binary operator with a precedence greater than zero, so we enter the while loop.

The first iteration of the loop looks like this:

```
// loop iteration #1
operator = parse_binop("* 2 - 3 * (4 + 5)")
         = Multiply
right = parse_exp("2 - 3 * (4 + 5)", 51)
          left = parse_factor("2 - 3 * (4 + 5)")
               = Constant(2)
          next_token = "-"
          // precedence(next_token) < 51
      = Constant(2)
left = Binary(Multiply, Constant(1), Constant(2))
next_token = "-"
```

Inside the loop, parse_binop consumes next_token from the input and converts it to an AST node, Multiply, which leaves 2 - 3 * (4 + 5). Next, we call parse_exp recursively to get the right-hand side of this product. Since the precedence of * is 50, the second argument to parse_exp is 51. In the recursive call, we again get the next factor (2) and the token that follows it (-). The - token is a binary operator, but its precedence is only 45; it doesn't meet the minimum precedence of 51, so we don't enter the while loop. Instead, we return Constant(2).

Back in the outer call to parse_exp, we construct a Binary AST node for 1 * 2 from the values we've parsed so far. Then, we check the next token to see whether we have more subexpressions to process. The next token is -; we peeked at it, but didn't remove it from the input, inside the recursive call to parse_exp. Because - is a binary operator, and it exceeds our minimum precedence of zero, we jump back to the beginning of the while loop to parse the next subexpression:

```
// loop iteration #2
operator = parse_binop("- 3 * (4 + 5)")
         = Subtract
right = parse_exp("3 * (4 + 5)", 46)
              left = parse_factor("3 * (4 + 5)")
                   = Constant(3)
              next_token = "*"
              // loop iteration #1
              operator = parse_binop("* (4 + 5)")
                       = Multiply
              right = parse_exp("(4 + 5)", 51)
                       left = parse_factor("(4 + 5)")
                             parse_exp("4 + 5", 0)
                                --snip--
                             = Binary(Add, Constant(4), Constant(5))
                     = Binary(Add, Constant(4), Constant(5))
              left = Binary(
                        Multiply,
                        Constant(3),
                        Binary(Add, Constant(4), Constant(5))
                     )
         = Binary(
              Multiply,
              Constant(3),
              Binary(Add, Constant(4), Constant(5))
           )
left = Binary(
          Subtract,
          Binary(Multiply, Constant(1), Constant(2)),
          Binary(
             Multiply,
             Constant(3),
             Binary(Add, Constant(4), Constant(5))
          )
       )
```

The second time through the loop, we consume - from the input and make a recursive call to parse_exp. This time, because the precedence of - is 45, the second argument to parse_exp is 46.

Following our usual routine, we get the next factor (3) and the next token (*). Since the precedence of * exceeds the minimum precedence, we need to parse another subexpression. We consume *, leaving (4 + 5), then make yet another recursive call to parse_exp.

In this call to parse_exp, we start by calling parse_factor as usual. This call consumes the rest of our input and returns the AST node for 4 + 5. To handle that parenthesized expression, parse_factor needs to recursively call parse_exp with the minimum precedence reset to 0, but we won't step through that here. At this point, there are no tokens left in our expression. Let's assume this is a valid C program and the next token is a semicolon (;). Since the next token isn't a binary operator, we exit the loop and return the expression we got from parse_factor.

At the next level up, we construct the AST node for 3 * (4 + 5) from the subexpressions we've processed in this call. Once again, we peek at the next token, see that it isn't a binary operator, and return.

Finally, back in the original call to parse_exp, we construct the final expression from the left operand that we constructed in the first loop iteration (1 * 2), the current value of operator (-), and the right operand that was just returned from the recursive call (3 * (4 + 5)). For the last time, we check the next token, see that it isn't a binary operator, and return.

Now that you've seen how to parse binary expressions with precedence climbing, you're ready to extend your parser. Remember to use precedence climbing to parse binary expressions and recursive descent to parse all the other symbols in the grammar, including factors.

TEST THE PARSER

The parser should successfully parse every valid test case in *tests/chapter_3/ valid* and raise an error on every invalid test case in *tests/chapter_3/invalid _parse*. To test your parser against the test cases from this chapter and the ones before it, run:

```
$ ./test_compiler /path/to/your_compiler --chapter 3 --stage parse
```

Remember that the test suite checks only whether your compiler parses a program successfully or throws an error; it doesn't check that it produced the correct AST. Consider writing unit tests to validate the output of your parser; in this chapter, it's especially easy to write a parser that appears to succeed but generates the wrong AST.

TACKY Generation

Next, let's update the stage that converts the AST to TACKY. We'll start by adding binary operations to TACKY. Listing 3-8 defines the updated TACKY IR, with this chapter's additions bolded.

```
program = Program(function_definition)
function_definition = Function(identifier, instruction* body)
instruction = Return(val)
            | Unary(unary_operator, val src, val dst)
            | Binary(binary_operator, val src1, val src2, val dst)
val = Constant(int) | Var(identifier)
unary_operator = Complement | Negate
binary_operator = Add | Subtract | Multiply | Divide | Remainder
```

Listing 3-8: Adding binary operations to TACKY

We've added the Binary instruction to represent binary operations, and we've defined all the possible operators. Like unary operations, binary operations in TACKY operate on constants and variables, not nested sub-expressions. As Listing 3-9 illustrates, we can turn a binary expression into a sequence of TACKY instructions in basically the same way we handled unary expressions.

```
emit_tacky(e, instructions):
    match e with
    | --snip--
    | Binary(op, e1, e2) ->
        v1 = emit_tacky(e1, instructions)
        v2 = emit_tacky(e2, instructions)
        dst_name = make_temporary()
        dst = Var(dst_name)
        tacky_op = convert_binop(op)
        instructions.append(Binary(tacky_op, v1, v2, dst))
        return dst
```

Listing 3-9: Converting a binary expression to TACKY

We emit the TACKY instructions to evaluate each operand, then emit the Binary instruction that uses those source values. The only difference from how we handled unary expressions is that we're processing two operands instead of one.

Before we move on to assembly generation, I want to make a slightly tangential point. The TACKY we emit in Listing 3-9 evaluates a binary expression's first operand before the second, but it's just as correct to evaluate the second operand before the first. According to the C standard, subexpressions of the same operation are usually *unsequenced*; that is, they can be evaluated in any order. If two subexpressions would be unsequenced, but either or both of them is a function call, they're *indeterminately sequenced*, meaning that either one can execute first, but they can't interleave. In many cases, unsequenced and indeterminately sequenced evaluations can lead to unpredictable results. Consider the following program, which includes two indeterminately sequenced calls to printf:

```
#include <stdio.h>

int main(void) {
    return printf("Hello, ") + printf("World!");
}
```

You could compile this program with a C standard–compliant compiler, run it, and get either of these outputs:

```
Hello, World!
World!Hello,
```

There are a few exceptions where we must evaluate the first operand first: the logical && and || operators, which we'll cover in Chapter 4; the conditional ?: operator, which we'll cover in Chapter 6; and the comma operator, which we won't implement. For a more in-depth discussion of the order in which expressions are evaluated, see the "Order of Evaluation" page on cppreference.com, the C/C++ reference wiki (*https://en.cppreference.com/w/c/language/eval_order*). If you're curious about where all this is laid out in the C standard itself, see section 5.1.2.3 (which covers the general rules for evaluation order and defines the terms *unsequenced* and *indeterminately sequenced*) and section 6.5, paragraphs 1–3 (which address the evaluation order for expression operands in particular).

Unsequenced operations are one example of a broader pattern: there are a lot of circumstances where the C standard doesn't specify exactly how programs should behave. We'll see more examples of this throughout the book. By leaving some details about program behavior unspecified, the C standard puts a lot of power in the hands of compiler writers, allowing them to write sophisticated compiler optimizations. But there's an obvious trade-off: it's easy for programmers to write code that might not behave the way they expect.

TEST THE TACKY GENERATION STAGE

Test the TACKY generator with this command:

```
$ ./test_compiler /path/to/your_compiler --chapter 3 --stage tacky
```

This stage should be able to process every valid test case we've seen so far.

Assembly Generation

The next step is converting TACKY into assembly. We'll need several new assembly instructions to handle addition, subtraction, multiplication, division, and the remainder operation. Let's talk through how to use these instructions; then we'll make the necessary updates to each pass in the assembly generation stage.

Doing Arithmetic in Assembly

The instructions for addition, subtraction, and multiplication all take the form *op src, dst*, where:

op is an instruction.

src is an immediate value, register, or memory address.

dst is a register or memory address.

Each of these instructions applies *op* to *dst* and *src*, storing the result in *dst*. The instructions for addition, subtraction, and multiplication are add, sub, and imul, respectively. As usual, these instructions take an l suffix if their operands are 32 bits and a q suffix if their operands are 64 bits. Table 3-2 shows an example of each instruction.

Table 3-2: Assembly Instructions for Addition, Subtraction, and Multiplication

Instruction	Meaning
addl $2, %eax	eax = eax + 2
subl $2, %eax	eax = eax - 2
imull $2, %eax	eax = eax * 2

Note that *dst* is the *first* operand in the corresponding mathematical expression, so subl a, b computes b - a, not a - b.

These instructions are pretty easy to use and understand. If we lived in a perfect world, we could perform division in exactly the same way. But we don't, so we're stuck with the idiv instruction.

We use idiv to implement the division and remainder operations. Even though you need two numbers to perform division, it takes a single operand: the divisor. (In a / b, a is the dividend and b is the divisor.) This operand can't be an immediate value. In its 32-bit form, idiv gets the other value it needs, the dividend, from the EDX and EAX registers, which it treats as a single 64-bit value. It gets the most significant 32 bits from EDX and the least significant 32 bits from EAX. Unlike the other arithmetic instructions, idiv produces two results: the quotient and the remainder. It stores the quotient in EAX and the remainder in EDX. (The 64-bit version of idiv, written as idivq, uses RDX and RAX as the dividend instead of EDX and EAX.)

To calculate a / b with idiv, we need to take a—which will be either a 32-bit immediate value or a 32-bit value stored in memory—and turn it into a 64-bit value spanning both EDX and EAX. Whenever we need to convert a signed integer to a wider format, we use an operation called *sign extension*. This operation fills the upper 32 bits of the new 64-bit value with the sign bit of the original 32-bit value.

Sign extending a positive number just pads the upper 32 bits (4 bytes) with zeros. Sign extending the binary representation of 3, for example, turns

```
00000000000000000000000000000011
```

into:

```
0000000000000000000000000000000000000000000000000000000000000011
```

Both representations have the value 3; the second one just has more leading zeros. To sign extend a negative number, we fill the upper 4 bytes with ones. This transforms the binary representation of –3, for example, from

```
11111111111111111111111111111101
```

into:

```
1111111111111111111111111111111111111111111111111111111111111101
```

Thanks to the magic of two's complement, the value of both of these binary numbers is –3. (If you're not clear on how this works, check out Chapter 2's "Additional Resources" section on page 45.)

The cdq instruction does exactly what we want: it sign extends the value from EAX into EDX. If the number in EAX is positive, this instruction sets EDX to all zeros. If EAX is negative, it sets EDX to all ones. Putting it all together, as an example, the following assembly computes both 9 / 2 and 9 % 2:

```
movl    $2, -4(%rbp)
movl    $9, %eax
cdq
idivl   -4(%rbp)
```

This stores the result of 9 / 2, the quotient, in EAX. It stores the result of 9 % 2, the remainder, in EDX.

We've covered all the new instructions we'll need in this chapter: add, sub, imul, idiv, and cdq. Next, we'll add these instructions to the assembly AST and update the conversion from TACKY to assembly.

Converting Binary Operations to Assembly

Listing 3-10 defines the updated assembly AST, with this chapter's additions bolded.

```
program = Program(function_definition)
function_definition = Function(identifier name, instruction* instructions)
instruction = Mov(operand src, operand dst)
            | Unary(unary_operator, operand)
            | Binary(binary_operator, operand, operand)
            | Idiv(operand)
            | Cdq
            | AllocateStack(int)
            | Ret
unary_operator = Neg | Not
binary_operator = Add | Sub | Mult
operand = Imm(int) | Reg(reg) | Pseudo(identifier) | Stack(int)
reg = AX | DX | R10 | R11
```

Listing 3-10: The assembly AST with binary operators

Since the addition, subtraction, and multiplication instructions take the same form, we'll represent all of them using the Binary constructor for the instruction node. We'll also add constructors for the new idiv and cdq instructions. Finally, we'll add the EDX and R11 registers to the AST definition; we need EDX for division and R11 for the instruction fix-up pass.

Now we need to convert the new binary operations from TACKY to assembly. For addition, subtraction, and multiplication, we convert a single TACKY instruction into two assembly instructions. That is, we convert

```
Binary(op, src1, src2, dst)
```

to:

```
Mov(src1, dst)
Binary(op, src2, dst)
```

Division is a little more complicated; we move the first operand into EAX, sign extend it with cdq, issue the idiv instruction, and then move the result from EAX to the destination. So, we convert

```
Binary(Divide, src1, src2, dst)
```

to:

```
Mov(src1, Reg(AX))
Cdq
Idiv(src2)
Mov(Reg(AX), dst)
```

The remainder operation looks exactly the same, except that we ultimately want to retrieve the remainder from EDX instead of retrieving the quotient from EAX. We therefore convert

```
Binary(Remainder, src1, src2, dst)
```

to:

```
Mov(src1, Reg(AX))
Cdq
Idiv(src2)
Mov(Reg(DX), dst)
```

The idiv instruction can't operate on immediate values, so the assembly instructions for division and remainder won't be valid if src2 is a constant. That's okay; we'll fix this problem during the instruction fix-up pass. Tables 3-3 through 3-6 summarize the conversion from TACKY to assembly, with new and changed constructs bolded.

Table 3-3: Converting Top-Level TACKY Constructs to Assembly

TACKY top-level construct	Assembly top-level construct
Program(function_definition)	Program(function_definition)
Function(name, instructions)	Function(name, instructions)

Table 3-4: Converting TACKY Instructions to Assembly

TACKY instruction	Assembly instructions
Return(val)	Mov(val, Reg(AX)) Ret
Unary(unary_operator, src, dst)	Mov(src, dst) Unary(unary_operator, dst)
Binary(Divide, src1, src2, dst)	**Mov(src1, Reg(AX))** **Cdq** **Idiv(src2)** **Mov(Reg(AX), dst)**
Binary(Remainder, src1, src2, dst)	Mov(src1, Reg(AX)) Cdq Idiv(src2) Mov(Reg(DX), dst)
Binary(binary_operator, src1, src2, dst)	**Mov(src1, dst)** **Binary(binary_operator, src2, dst)**

Table 3-5: Converting TACKY Arithmetic Operators to Assembly

TACKY operator	Assembly operator
Complement	Not
Negate	Neg
Add	**Add**
Subtract	**Sub**
Multiply	**Mult**

Table 3-6: Converting TACKY Operands to Assembly

TACKY operand	Assembly operand
Constant(int)	Imm(int)
Var(identifier)	Pseudo(identifier)

Note that Table 3-4 includes three rows for the `Binary` TACKY instruction: one for division, one for the remainder operation, and one for everything else.

Replacing Pseudoregisters

Update this pass to replace pseudoregisters in the new `Binary` and `Idiv` instructions. You should treat them like the existing `Mov` and `Unary` instructions. When you see a pseudoregister in a `Mov`, `Unary`, `Binary`, or `Idiv` instruction, replace it with the corresponding stack address. If the pseudoregister hasn't been assigned to a stack address yet, assign it to the next available 4-byte address.

Fixing Up the idiv, add, sub, and imul Instructions

In the last compiler pass before emitting the final program, we rewrite any invalid instructions that we produced in earlier stages. We need to add a few more rewrite rules here. First, we need to fix `idiv` instructions that take constant operands. Whenever `idiv` needs to operate on a constant, we copy that constant into our scratch register first. For instance, we rewrite

```
idivl   $3
```

as:

```
movl    $3, %r10d
idivl   %r10d
```

The `add` and `sub` instructions, like `mov`, can't use memory addresses as both the source and destination operands. We rewrite them in the same way as `mov`, so that

```
addl    -4(%rbp), -8(%rbp)
```

becomes:

```
movl    -4(%rbp), %r10d
addl    %r10d, -8(%rbp)
```

The `imul` instruction can't use a memory address as its destination, regardless of its source operand. To fix an instruction's destination operand, we use the R11 register instead of R10. So, to fix `imul`, we load the destination into R11, multiply it by the source operand, and then store the result back to the destination address. In other words, the instruction

```
imull  $3, -4(%rbp)
```

becomes:

```
movl   -4(%rbp), %r11d
imull  $3, %r11d
movl   %r11d, -4(%rbp)
```

Using different registers to fix source and destination operands will become helpful in Part II, when we'll sometimes rewrite the source and destination of the same instruction. We'll need two registers so that the fix-up instructions for the different operands don't clobber each other.

Once you've updated the assembly generation, pseudoregister replacement, and instruction fix-up compiler passes, your compiler should be able to generate complete, correct assembly programs that perform basic arithmetic. All that's left is emitting those assembly programs in the right format.

TEST THE ASSEMBLY GENERATION STAGE

To test the assembly generation stage, run:

```
$ ./test_compiler /path/to/your_compiler --chapter 3 --stage codegen
```

Code Emission

The last step is extending the code emission stage to handle our new assembly instructions. Tables 3-7 through 3-10 show how to print out each construct, with new constructs bolded.

Table 3-7: Formatting Top-Level Assembly Constructs

Assembly top-level construct	Output
Program(function_definition)	Print out the function definition. On Linux, add at end of file: .section .note.GNU-stack,"",@progbits

Function(name, instructions)	.globl <name>
	 <name>:
	     pushq %rbp
	     movq %rsp, %rbp
	     <instructions>

Table 3-8: Formatting Assembly Instructions

Assembly instruction	Output		
Mov(src, dst)	movl	<src>, <dst>	
Ret	movq popq ret	%rbp, %rsp %rbp 	
Unary(unary_operator, operand)	<unary_operator>		<operand>
Binary(binary_operator, src, dst)	<binary_operator>		<src>, <dst>
Idiv(operand)	idivl	<operand>	
Cdq	cdq		
AllocateStack(int)	subq	$<int>, %rsp	

Table 3-9: Instruction Names for Assembly Operators

Assembly operator	Instruction name
Neg	negl
Not	notl
Add	addl
Sub	subl
Mult	imull

Table 3-10: Formatting Assembly Operands

Assembly operand	Output
Reg(AX)	%eax
Reg(DX)	%edx
Reg(R10)	%r10d
Reg(R11)	%r11d
Stack(int)	<int>(%rbp)
Imm(int)	$<int>

The new instructions operate on 32-bit values, so they get l suffixes (except cdq, which doesn't follow the usual naming conventions). Note that the subl instruction we use to subtract integers and the subq instruction we use to allocate space on the stack are 32-bit and 64-bit versions of the same instruction.

Extra Credit: Bitwise Operators

Now that you've learned how to compile binary operators, you can implement the bitwise binary operators on your own. These include bitwise AND (&), OR (|), XOR (^), left shift (<<), and right shift (>>). Your compiler can handle these much like the operators you just added. You'll need to look up the relative precedence of these operators, and you'll need to check the documentation for the x64 instruction set to see how to use the relevant assembly instructions.

Bitwise operations are optional; later test cases don't rely on them. If you do implement bitwise operations, use the --bitwise flag to include the test cases for this feature:

```
$ ./test_compiler /path/to/your_compiler --chapter 3 --bitwise
```

Include this flag when you run the test script in later chapters too, to include any test cases for those chapters that use bitwise operators.

Summary

In this chapter, you implemented several binary arithmetic operations in your compiler. You used a new technique, precedence climbing, to parse expressions that recursive descent parsers don't handle well. In the next chapter, you'll implement even more unary and binary operations: the logical operators !, &&, and ||, and relational operators like ==, <, and >. Some of these operators don't correspond closely to assembly instructions, so we'll break them down into lower-level instructions in TACKY. We'll also introduce conditional assembly instructions, which will be particularly important when we implement control-flow statements like if statements and loops later on.

Additional Resources

These blog posts helped me understand precedence climbing and how it relates to similar algorithms that solve the same problem; you might find them helpful too:

- "Parsing Expressions by Precedence Climbing" by Eli Bendersky is a solid overview of the precedence climbing algorithm (*https://eli.thegreenplace.net/2012/08/02/parsing-expressions-by-precedence-climbing*). The precedence climbing code in Listing 3-7 is loosely adapted from this blog post; it also inspired the presentation of the example in "Precedence Climbing in Action" on page 55.

- "Some Problems of Recursive Descent Parsers," also by Eli Bendersky, talks about how to handle binary expressions with a pure recursive descent parser (*https://eli.thegreenplace.net/2009/03/14/some-problems-of-recursive-descent-parsers*).

- Andy Chu has written two useful blog posts on precedence climbing. The first, "Pratt Parsing and Precedence Climbing Are the Same Algorithm," explores the fundamental similarities between precedence climbing and the Pratt Parsing algorithm (*https://www.oilshell.org/blog/2016/11/01.html*). The second, "Precedence Climbing Is Widely Used," discusses their differences (*https://www.oilshell.org/blog/2017/03/30.html*). These posts clarify some of the confusing terminology around different parsing algorithms.

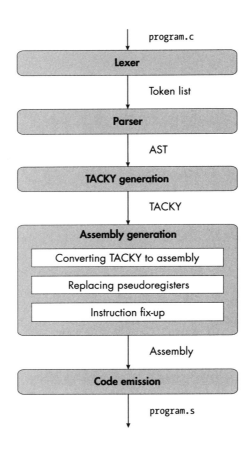

program.c

Lexer

Token list

Parser

AST

TACKY generation

TACKY

Assembly generation

Converting TACKY to assembly

Replacing pseudoregisters

Instruction fix-up

Assembly

Code emission

program.s

4

LOGICAL AND RELATIONAL OPERATORS

Now that you know how to compile binary operators, you're going to add a whole mess of them (plus one more unary operator). In this chapter, you'll add three logical operators: NOT (!), AND (&&), and OR (||). You'll also add the relational operators: <, >, ==, and so on. Each of these operators tests some condition, resulting in a value of 1 if that condition is true and 0 if it's false.

The && and || operators differ from the binary operators we've seen so far because they *short-circuit*: if you know the result after the first operand, you don't evaluate the second operand. To support short-circuiting logic, we'll add new instructions to TACKY that let us skip over blocks of code. We'll also introduce several new instructions in the assembly generation pass, including conditional assembly instructions that let us take specific actions only if some condition is met.

Let's start with a brief discussion of short-circuiting operators before moving on to the compiler passes.

Short-Circuiting Operators

The C standard guarantees that && and || short-circuit when you don't need the second operand. For example, consider the expression (1 - 1) && foo(). Because the first operand's value is 0, the whole expression will evaluate to 0 regardless of what foo returns, so we won't call foo at all. Likewise, if the first operand of || is nonzero, we don't evaluate the second operand.

This isn't just a performance optimization; the second operand might not change the result of the expression, but evaluating it can have visible side effects. For example, the foo function might perform I/O or update global variables. If your compiler doesn't implement && and || as short-circuiting operators, some compiled programs will behave incorrectly. (The standard defines this behavior in section 6.5.13, paragraph 4, for the && operator and in section 6.5.14, paragraph 4, for the || operator.)

Now that we've clarified how these operators work, you're ready to continue coding.

The Lexer

In this chapter, you'll add nine new tokens:

! An exclamation point, the logical NOT operator

&& Two ampersands, the logical AND operator

|| Two vertical bars, the logical OR operator

== Two equal signs, the "equal to" operator

!= An exclamation point followed by an equal sign, the "not equal to" operator

< The "less than" operator

> The "greater than" operator

<= The "less than or equal to" operator

>= The "greater than or equal to" operator

Your lexer should handle these the same way as the other operators you've added so far. Remember that the lexer should always choose the longest possible match for the next token. For example, if your input is <=something, the next token the lexer emits should be <=, not <.

The Parser

Next, we'll add the new operations to the AST definition. Listing 4-1 shows the updated definition, with these additions bolded.

```
program = Program(function_definition)
function_definition = Function(identifier name, statement body)
statement = Return(exp)
exp = Constant(int)
    | Unary(unary_operator, exp)
    | Binary(binary_operator, exp, exp)
unary_operator = Complement | Negate | Not
binary_operator = Add | Subtract | Multiply | Divide | Remainder | And | Or
                | Equal | NotEqual | LessThan | LessOrEqual
                | GreaterThan | GreaterOrEqual
```

Listing 4-1: The abstract syntax tree with comparison and logical operators

We also need to make the corresponding changes to the grammar, as shown in Listing 4-2.

```
<program> ::= <function>
<function> ::= "int" <identifier> "(" "void" ")" "{" <statement> "}"
<statement> ::= "return" <exp> ";"
<exp> ::= <factor> | <exp> <binop> <exp>
<factor> ::= <int> | <unop> <factor> | "(" <exp> ")"
<unop> ::= "-" | "~" | "!"
<binop> ::= "-" | "+" | "*" | "/" | "%" | "&&" | "||"
          | "==" | "!=" | "<" | "<=" | ">" | ">="
<identifier> ::= ? An identifier token ?
<int> ::= ? A constant token ?
```

Listing 4-2: The grammar with comparison and logical operators

In Listings 4-1 and 4-2, we've added some new operators, but we haven't made any other changes. Now we're ready to update the parsing code. First, update parse_factor to handle the new ! operator. It should parse ! the same way it parses the unary ~ and - operators.

Next, update parse_exp to handle the new binary operators. In Chapter 3, we associated every binary operator with a numeric precedence value. Now we'll give the new operators precedence values. These operators have lower precedence than the ones from Chapter 3, and they're all left-associative. Among the new operators, <, <=, >, and >= have the highest precedence, followed by the equality operators, == and !=. The && operator has lower precedence than the equality operators, and || has the lowest precedence of all. The precedence values I've chosen are listed in Table 4-1, with new operators bolded.

Table 4-1: Precedence Values of Old and New Binary Operators

Operator	Precedence
*	50
/	50
%	50
+	45
-	45
<	35
<=	35
>	35
>=	35
==	30
!=	30
&&	10
			5

These values are spaced far enough apart to leave room for the optional bitwise operators from Chapter 3. There's also room at the bottom of the scale for the = and ?: operators we'll add in the next two chapters. You don't need to use the exact values in this table as long as all operators have the correct precedence relative to each other.

You'll also need to extend the code that converts tokens into unary _operator and binary_operator AST nodes. For example, the function that converts a + token into an Add node should also convert a == token into an Equal node. (The pseudocode in the last two chapters called separate functions, parse_unop and parse_binop, to handle these conversions.)

Once you've updated your parser's table of precedence values, parse _binop, and parse_unop, you're done! The precedence climbing algorithm we implemented in the last chapter can handle the new operators without further changes.

TACKY Generation

Now that the lexer and parser are working properly, we can venture into less familiar territory: handling the new operators in TACKY. You can convert relational operators to TACKY in the same way as the binary operators you've already implemented. For example, given the expression e1 < e2, the resulting TACKY looks something like Listing 4-3.

```
<instructions for e1>
v1 = <result of e1>
<instructions for e2>
v2 = <result of e2>
Binary(LessThan, v1, v2, result)
```

Listing 4-3: Implementing the < operator in TACKY

You can't generate the && and || operators this way, though, because they short-circuit. The code in Listing 4-3 always evaluates both e1 and e2, but we need to generate code that sometimes skips e2. To support short-circuiting operators, we'll add an *unconditional jump* instruction, which lets us jump to a different point in the program. We'll also add two *conditional jump* instructions, which jump only when a particular condition is met.

Adding Jumps, Copies, and Comparisons to the TACKY IR

Listing 4-4 shows the latest TACKY IR, including the new jump instructions.

```
program = Program(function_definition)
function_definition = Function(identifier, instruction* body)
instruction = Return(val)
            | Unary(unary_operator, val src, val dst)
            | Binary(binary_operator, val src1, val src2, val dst)
            | Copy(val src, val dst)
            | Jump(identifier target)
            | JumpIfZero(val condition, identifier target)
            | JumpIfNotZero(val condition, identifier target)
            | Label(identifier)
val = Constant(int) | Var(identifier)
unary_operator = Complement | Negate | Not
```

```
binary_operator = Add | Subtract | Multiply | Divide | Remainder | Equal | NotEqual
                | LessThan | LessOrEqual | GreaterThan | GreaterOrEqual
```

Listing 4-4: Adding comparisons, jumps, and labels to TACKY

The Jump instruction works just like goto in C: it makes the program jump to the point labeled with some identifier, target. The Label instruction associates an identifier with a location in the program. The snippet of TACKY in Listing 4-5 shows how Jump and Label instructions work together.

```
  Unary(Negate, Constant(1), Var("tmp"))
  Jump("there")
❶ Unary(Negate, Constant(2), Var("tmp"))
  Label("there")
  Return(Var("tmp"))
```

Listing 4-5: A snippet of TACKY with a Jump instruction

This program stores -1 in tmp, then executes the Jump instruction, which jumps to the Label instruction. Next, it executes the Return instruction, which returns -1. The second Unary instruction ❶ won't execute at all, because we jumped over it.

The first conditional jump in the TACKY IR, JumpIfZero, jumps to the instruction indicated by target if the value of condition is 0. If condition is anything other than 0, we don't jump to target; instead, we execute the next instruction as usual. The second conditional jump, JumpIfNotZero, does the opposite: we jump to target only if condition isn't 0. We don't really need both of these instructions, since any behavior you can express with one can be expressed with the other plus a Not instruction. But adding both lets us generate simpler TACKY for the && and || operations, which will ultimately translate into simpler, shorter assembly.

The other new instruction is Copy. Since && and || ultimately return 1 or 0, we use this instruction to copy 1 or 0 into the temporary variable that holds the result of the expression.

Besides these five additional instructions, the latest TACKY IR includes the new relational and logical binary operators and the unary Not operator.

Converting Short-Circuiting Operators to TACKY

Let's use the new TACKY instructions to implement the && and || operators. The TACKY for the expression e1 && e2 should look like Listing 4-6.

```
<instructions for e1>
v1 = <result of e1>
JumpIfZero(v1, false_label)
<instructions for e2>
v2 = <result of e2>
JumpIfZero(v2, false_label)
result = 1
Jump(end)
Label(false_label)
```

```
result = 0
Label(end)
```

Listing 4-6: Implementing the && operator in TACKY

We start by evaluating e1. If it's 0, we short-circuit and set result to 0, without evaluating e2. We accomplish this with the JumpIfZero instruction; if v1 is 0, we jump straight to false_label, then set result to 0 with the Copy instruction. (I've written this out as result = 0 instead of Copy(0, result) to make it more readable. I'll take similar liberties with TACKY notation in later chapters.) If v1 isn't 0, we still need to evaluate e2. We handle the case where v2 is 0 exactly like the case where v1 is 0, by jumping to false_label with JumpIfZero. We reach the Copy instruction, result = 1, only if we didn't take either conditional jump. That means both e1 and e2 are nonzero, so we set result to 1. Then, we jump over result = 0 to the end label to avoid overwriting result.

I'll leave it to you to translate the || operation to TACKY on your own. The resulting TACKY will look similar to Listing 4-6, but it will use the JumpIfNotZero instruction instead of JumpIfZero. That leaves ! and all the relational operations; you can convert them to TACKY in the same way as the unary and binary operations you added in the previous chapters.

Generating Labels

Labels, like temporary variables, must be globally unique: an instruction like Jump("foo") is useless if the label foo shows up in multiple places. You can make sure they're unique by incorporating a global counter into labels, like you did with variable names in Chapter 2.

Unlike temporary variables, labels will appear in the final assembly program, so they must be identifiers that the assembler considers syntactically valid. They should contain only letters, digits, periods, and underscores. Choose descriptive labels to make your assembly programs easier to read and debug. For example, you could use the string and_falseN as false_label in Listing 4-6, where N is the current value of a global counter.

Although labels must not conflict with each other, it's okay for them to conflict with temporary variable names. It's also okay if the labels you generate here conflict with user-defined function names, even though both autogenerated labels and function names become labels in the final assembly program. We'll mangle our autogenerated labels during code emission so they don't conflict with user-defined identifiers.

TEST THE TACKY GENERATION STAGE

To test out TACKY generation, run:

```
$ ./test_compiler /path/to/your_compiler --chapter 4 --stage tacky
```

Comparisons and Jumps in Assembly

Before starting on the assembly generation pass, let's talk through the new assembly instructions we'll need. First, we'll discuss the `cmp` instruction, which compares two values, and the *conditional set* instructions, which set a byte to 1 or 0 based on the result of a comparison. We'll use these to implement relational operators like <. Next, we'll talk about conditional and unconditional jump instructions.

Comparisons and Status Flags

The "condition" that all conditional instructions depend on is the state of the RFLAGS register. Unlike EAX, RSP, and the other registers we've seen so far, we usually can't directly set RFLAGS. Instead, the CPU updates RFLAGS automatically every time it issues an instruction. As the name suggests, each bit in this register is a flag that reports some fact about the last instruction or the status of the CPU. Different instructions update different flags: the `add`, `sub`, and `cmp` instructions update all the flags we'll talk about in this section, and the `mov` instruction doesn't update any of them. We can ignore the effects of other instructions for now. Whenever I refer to the "last instruction" or "last result" while discussing RFLAGS, I mean the last instruction that affects the particular flag I'm talking about.

Right now, we care about three of these flags:

Zero flag (ZF)

ZF is set to 1 if the result of the last instruction was 0. It's set to 0 if the result of the last instruction was nonzero.

Sign flag (SF)

SF is set to 1 if the most significant bit of the last result was 1. It's set to 0 if the most significant bit of that result was 0. Remember that in two's complement, the most significant bit of a negative number is always 1, and the most significant bit of a positive number is always 0. Therefore, the sign flag tells us whether the result of the last instruction was positive or negative. (If the last result should be interpreted as an unsigned integer, it can't be negative, so the sign flag is meaningless.)

Overflow flag (OF)

OF is set to 1 if the last instruction resulted in a signed integer overflow, and 0 otherwise. An *integer overflow* occurs when the result of a signed integer operation can't be represented in the number of bits available. A positive result overflows when it's larger than the maximum value the type can hold. Suppose we're operating on 4-bit integers. The largest signed number we can represent is 7, or 0111 in binary. If we add one to it with the `add` instruction, the result is 1000. If we interpret this as an unsigned integer, its value is 8, but its value is −8 if we interpret it as a two's complement signed integer. The result of the computation should be positive, but since it overflowed, it appears negative. This computation sets the overflow flag to 1.

We also encounter integer overflow in the opposite situation: when the result should be negative, but it's below the smallest possible value. For example, in ordinary math, −8 − 1 = −9. But if we use the sub instruction to subtract one from the 4-bit two's complement representation of −8, which is 1000, we end up with 0111, or 7. The overflow flag is set to 1 in this case too.

An unsigned result can also be too large or small for its type to represent, but I won't refer to this as integer overflow in this book. Instead, I say the result *wrapped around*, which is more consistent with the terminology for unsigned operations in the C standard and in most discussions of x64 assembly. I draw this distinction because unsigned wraparound follows different rules from signed integer overflow in the C standard, and the CPU detects it differently. You'll learn how to handle unsigned wraparound in Part II. Like SF, OF is meaningless if the result is unsigned.

Tables 4-2 and 4-3 summarize the cases where each kind of integer overflow is possible. Table 4-2 describes the results of addition.

Table 4-2: Integer Overflow and Underflow from Addition

a + b	b > 0	b < 0
a > 0	Overflow from positive to negative	Neither
a < 0	Neither	Overflow from negative to positive

Table 4-3 describes the results of subtraction; it's just Table 4-2 with the columns swapped, since a - b and a + (- b) are equivalent.

Table 4-3: Integer Overflow and Underflow from Subtraction

a - b	b > 0	b < 0
a > 0	Neither	Overflow from positive to negative
a < 0	Overflow from negative to positive	Neither

The instruction cmp b, a computes a - b, exactly like the sub instruction, and has the same impact on RFLAGS, but it discards the result instead of storing it in a. This is more convenient when you want to subtract two numbers only in order to compare them and don't want to overwrite a.

Let's figure out the values of ZF and SF after the instruction cmp b, a:

- If a == b, then a - b is 0, so ZF is 1 and SF is 0.
- If a > b, then a - b is a positive number, so both SF and ZF are 0.
- If a < b, then a - b is a negative number, so SF is 1 and ZF is 0.

By issuing a cmp instruction and then checking ZF and SF, you can handle every comparison we're implementing in this chapter. But wait! That's not quite true, because a - b could overflow, which would flip SF. Let's consider how that impacts each case:

- If a == b, then a - b can't overflow because it's 0.
- If a > b, then a - b could overflow when a is positive and b is negative. The correct result in this case is positive, but if it overflows, the result will be negative. In that case, SF will be 1, and OF will be too.
- If a < b, then a - b could overflow when a is negative and b is positive. In this case, the correct result is negative, but the actual result will be positive. That means SF will be 0, but OF will be 1.

Table 4-4 gives the values of these flags in every case we've considered.

Table 4-4: Impact of cmp Instruction on Status Flags

	ZF	OF	SF
a == b	1	0	0
a > b, no overflow	0	0	0
a > b, overflow	0	1	1
a < b, no overflow	0	0	1
a < b, overflow	0	1	0

You can tell whether a or b is larger by checking whether SF and OF are the same. If they are, we know that a ≥ b. Either both are 0, because we got a positive (or 0) result with no overflow, or both are 1, because we got a large positive result that overflowed until it became negative. If SF and OF are different, we know that a < b. Either we got a negative result with no overflow, or we got a negative result that overflowed and became positive.

UNDEFINED BEHAVIOR ALERT!

If the add and sub instructions can overflow, why didn't we account for that in Chapter 3? We didn't need to because integer overflow in C is *undefined behavior*, where the standard doesn't tell you what should happen. Compilers are permitted to handle undefined behavior however they want—or not handle it at all.

When an expression in C overflows, for example, the result *usually* wraps around like the examples we saw earlier. However, it's equally acceptable for the program to generate a result at random, raise a signal, or erase your hard drive. That last option may sound unlikely, but production compilers really do handle undefined behavior in surprising (and arguably undesirable) ways. Take the following program:

```
#include <stdio.h>

int main(void) {
    for (int i = 2147483646; i > 0; i = i + 1)
        printf("The number is %d\n", i);
    return 0;
}
```

The largest value an int can hold is 2,147,483,647, so the expression i + 1 overflows the second time we execute it. When the add assembly instruction overflows, it produces a negative result, so we might expect this loop to execute twice, then stop because the condition i > 0 no longer holds. That's exactly what happens if you compile this program without optimizations, at least with the versions of Clang and GCC that I tried:

```
$ clang overflow.c
$ ./a.out
The number is 2147483646
The number is 2147483647
```

But if you enable optimizations, the behavior might change completely:

```
$ clang -O overflow.c
$ ./a.out
The number is 2147483646
The number is 2147483647
The number is -2147483648
The number is -2147483647
The number is -2147483646
The number is -2147483645
--snip--
```

What happened? The compiler tried to optimize the program by removing conditional checks that always succeed. The initial value of i is positive, and it's updated only in the expression i = i + 1, so the compiler concluded that the condition i > 0 is always true. That's correct, as long as i doesn't overflow. It's incorrect if i does overflow, of course, but that's undefined behavior, so the compiler didn't have to account for it. It therefore removed the condition entirely, resulting in a loop that never terminates.

I used Clang for this example because GCC produced completely different, even less intuitive behavior. You may well see different results if you compile this program on your own machine. Try it out with a few different optimization levels, and see what happens.

Note that setting the overflow flag in assembly doesn't necessarily indicate overflow in the source program. For example, when we implement an expression like a < 10 with cmp, that cmp instruction may set the overflow flag. But the result of a < 10 is either 0 or 1—both of which are in the range of int—so the

(continued)

expression itself does not overflow. This expression won't produce undefined behavior, regardless of how we implement it in assembly.

C has a bunch of different kinds of undefined behavior; integer overflow is just one example. It's a particularly ugly example, though, because it's difficult to avoid and can have dire consequences, including security vulnerabilities. To address this long-standing problem, the next version of the C standard, C23, adds a few standard library functions that perform checked integer operations. If you use the new ckd_add, ckd_sub, and ckd_mul functions instead of the +, -, and * operators, you'll get an informative return code instead of undefined behavior when the result is out of bounds. To learn more about these new library functions, see Jens Gustedt's blog post titled "Checked Integer Arithmetic in the Prospect of C23" (*https://gustedt.wordpress.com/2022/12/18/checked -integer-arithmetic-in-the-prospect-of-c23/*).

Undefined behavior is different from *unspecified behavior*. If some aspect of a program's behavior is unspecified, there are several possible ways it could behave, but it can't behave totally unpredictably. For example, in Chapter 3, we learned that the operands in a binary expression are unsequenced (or inde-terminately sequenced, if either is a function call), so their evaluation order is unspecified. This doesn't mean the expression's behavior is undefined. When we evaluate the expression printf("Hello, ") + printf("World!"), the program can print either "Hello, " or "World!" first, but it can't go off and do something else entirely. Unsequenced operations *can* produce undefined behavior under certain circumstances—say, if you perform two unsequenced updates to the same variable—but performing unsequenced or indeterminately sequenced operations is not an undefined behavior in and of itself.

Unspecified behavior is a normal part of any C program. It's a problem only if your program relies on a particular behavior that the standard doesn't specify, like in the Hello, World! example. Undefined behavior, on the other hand, is always a problem; if it occurs anywhere in your program, you can't count on any part of the program to work correctly.

To learn more about undefined behavior, and the trail of chaos and destruction it leaves in its wake, see "Additional Resources" on page 91.

Now that you understand how to set ZF, OF, and SF, let's take a look at a few instructions that depend on those flags.

Conditional Set Instructions

To implement a relational operator, we first set some flags using the cmp instruction, then set the result of the expression based on those flags. We perform that second step with a *conditional set* instruction. Each conditional set instruction takes a single register or memory address as an operand, which it sets to 0 or 1 based on the state of RFLAGS. The conditional set instructions are all identical, except that they test for different conditions. Table 4-5 lists the conditional set instructions we need in this chapter.

Table 4-5: Conditional Set Instructions

Instruction	Meaning	Flags
sete	Set byte if a == b	ZF set
setne	Set byte if a != b	ZF not set
setg	Set byte if a > b	ZF not set and SF == OF
setge	Set byte if a ≥ b	SF == OF
setl	Set byte if a < b	SF != OF
setle	Set byte if a ≤ b	ZF set or SF != OF

Unlike the other instructions we've seen so far, conditional set instructions take only 1-byte operands. For example, sete %eax is not a valid instruction, because EAX is a 4-byte register. The instruction sete %al, however, is valid; this sets the AL register, the least significant byte of EAX. To conditionally set the whole EAX register to 0 or 1, you need to zero out EAX before you set AL, because the conditional set instruction won't clear its upper bytes. For example, if EAX is

11111111111111111111111111111011

and you run

```
movl    $2, %edx
cmpl    $1, %edx
sete    %al
```

then the new value in EAX is

11111111111111111111111100000000

which is, of course, not 0. The sete instruction zeroed out the last byte of EAX, but not the rest of it.

If its operand is a memory address, a conditional set instruction will update the single byte at that address. Note that a memory address can be a 1-byte, 4-byte, or 8-byte operand, depending on context. In sete -4(%rbp), the operand -4(%rbp) indicates a single byte of memory at RBP − 4; in addl $1, -4(%rbp), it indicates the 4 bytes of memory starting at RBP − 4.

Jump Instructions

The jmp assembly instruction takes a label as an argument and performs an unconditional jump to that label. Jump assembly instructions manipulate another special-purpose register, RIP, which always holds the address of the next instruction to execute (IP stands for *instruction pointer*). To execute a sequence of instructions, the CPU carries out the *fetch-execute cycle*:

1. Fetch an instruction from the memory address in RIP and store it in a special-purpose *instruction register*. (This register doesn't have a name because you can't refer to it in assembly.)

2. Increment RIP to point to the next instruction. Instructions in x64 aren't all the same length, so the CPU has to check the length of the instruction it just fetched and increment RIP by that many bytes.

3. Run the instruction in the instruction register.

4. Repeat.

Normally, following these steps executes instructions in the order they appear in memory. But jmp puts a new value in RIP, which changes what instruction the CPU executes next. The assembler and linker convert the label in a jump instruction into a *relative offset* that tells you how much to increment or decrement RIP. Consider the snippet of assembly in Listing 4-7.

```
     addl    $1, %eax
     jmp     foo
     movl    $0, %eax
foo:
     ret
```

Listing 4-7: A snippet of assembly code with a jmp instruction

The machine instruction for movl $0, %eax is 5 bytes long. To jump over it and execute the ret instruction instead, jmp needs to increment RIP by an extra 5 bytes. The assembler and linker therefore convert jmp foo into the machine instruction for jmp 5. Then, when the CPU executes this instruction, it:

1. Fetches the instruction jmp 5 and stores it in the instruction register.

2. Increments RIP to point to the next instruction, movl $0, %eax.

3. Executes jmp 5. This adds 5 bytes to RIP so that it points to ret.

4. Fetches the instruction RIP points to, ret, and continues the fetch-execute cycle from there.

Note that labels aren't instructions: the CPU doesn't execute them, and they don't appear in the text section of the final executable (the section that contains machine instructions).

A *conditional jump* takes a label as an argument but jumps to that label only if the condition holds. Conditional jumps look a lot like conditional set instructions; they depend on the same conditions, using the same flags in RFLAGS. For example, the assembly in Listing 4-8 returns 3 if the EAX and EDX registers are equal, and 0 otherwise.

```
     cmpl    %eax, %edx
     je      return3
     movl    $0, %eax
     ret
```

```
return3:
    movl    $3, %eax
    ret
```

Listing 4-8: A snippet of assembly code with a conditional jump

If the values in EAX and EDX are equal, cmpl sets ZF to 1, so je jumps to return3. Then, the two instructions following return3 execute, so the function returns 3. If EAX and EDX aren't equal, je doesn't perform the jump, so the function returns 0. Similarly, jne jumps only if ZF is 0. There are also jump instructions that check other conditions, but we don't need them in this chapter.

Assembly Generation

Now that you understand the new assembly instructions you'll need, let's extend the assembly AST and update each assembly generation pass. Listing 4-9 defines the latest assembly AST, with additions bolded.

```
program = Program(function_definition)
function_definition = Function(identifier name, instruction* instructions)
instruction = Mov(operand src, operand dst)
            | Unary(unary_operator, operand)
            | Binary(binary_operator, operand, operand)
            | Cmp(operand, operand)
            | Idiv(operand)
            | Cdq
            | Jmp(identifier)
            | JmpCC(cond_code, identifier)
            | SetCC(cond_code, operand)
            | Label(identifier)
            | AllocateStack(int)
            | Ret
unary_operator = Neg | Not
binary_operator = Add | Sub | Mult
operand = Imm(int) | Reg(reg) | Pseudo(identifier) | Stack(int)
cond_code = E | NE | G | GE | L | LE
reg = AX | DX | R10 | R11
```

Listing 4-9: The assembly AST with comparisons and conditional instructions

Since all conditional jump instructions have the same form, we represent them with a single JmpCC instruction and distinguish between them using different condition codes. We do the same with conditional set instructions. We also treat labels like instructions at this stage, even though Label isn't really an instruction since labels aren't executed by the CPU.

To implement the TACKY `JumpIfZero` and `JumpIfNotZero` instructions, we use the new `JmpCC` assembly instruction. We convert

```
JumpIfZero(val, target)
```

to:

```
Cmp(Imm(0), val)
JmpCC(E, target)
```

We implement `JumpIfNotZero` the same way, but with `NE` instead of `E` as the condition code.

Similarly, we implement all the relational operators using conditional set instructions. For example, the TACKY instruction

```
Binary(GreaterThan, src1, src2, dst)
```

becomes:

```
Cmp(src2, src1)
Mov(Imm(0), dst)
SetCC(G, dst)
```

For all the other relational operators, replace `G` with the appropriate condition code. Remember to zero out the destination before the conditional set instruction, since it sets only the lowest byte. It's safe to perform a `mov` right after the `cmp` instruction because `mov` doesn't change RFLAGS. One potential wrinkle is that `SetCC` needs a 1-byte operand, but `dst` is 4 bytes; luckily, we can account for this in the code emission pass. If `dst` is a location in memory, `SetCC` sets the first byte at that location, which is the behavior we want. (Because x64 processors are *little-endian*, the first byte is the least significant, so setting that byte to 1 sets the whole 32-bit value to 1.) If `dst` is a register, we'll use the corresponding 1-byte register name when we emit `SetCC` during code emission. Registers in the assembly AST are size agnostic, so for now we represent `dst` the same way whether we're using it as a 4-byte or 1-byte operand.

Because `!x` is equivalent to `x == 0`, we also implement the unary `!` operator with a conditional set instruction. We convert the TACKY instruction

```
Unary(Not, src, dst)
```

into:

```
Cmp(Imm(0), src)
Mov(Imm(0), dst)
SetCC(E, dst)
```

The remaining TACKY instructions—`Jump`, `Label`, and `Copy`—are easy. A TACKY `Jump` becomes an assembly `Jmp`, `Label` becomes `Label`, and `Copy` becomes `Mov`. Tables 4-6 and 4-7 summarize how to convert each new

TACKY construct to assembly. Note that these tables include only new constructs, unlike the equivalent tables in Chapters 2 and 3.

Table 4-6 shows how to convert the new Copy, Label, and conditional and unconditional jump instructions to assembly, as well as Unary instructions with the new Not operator and Binary instructions with the new relational operators.

Table 4-6: Converting TACKY Instructions to Assembly

TACKY instruction	Assembly instructions
Unary(Not, src, dst)	Cmp(Imm(0), src) Mov(Imm(0), dst) SetCC(E, dst)
Binary(relational_operator, src1, src2, dst)	Cmp(src2, src1) Mov(Imm(0), dst) SetCC(relational_operator, dst)
Jump(target)	Jmp(target)
JumpIfZero(condition, target)	Cmp(Imm(0), condition) JmpCC(E, target)
JumpIfNotZero(condition, target)	Cmp(Imm(0), condition) JmpCC(NE, target)
Copy(src, dst)	Mov(src, dst)
Label(identifier)	Label(identifier)

Table 4-7 gives the corresponding condition code for each relational operator in TACKY.

Table 4-7: Converting TACKY Comparisons to Assembly

TACKY comparison	Assembly condition code
Equal	E
NotEqual	NE
LessThan	L
LessOrEqual	LE
GreaterThan	G
GreaterOrEqual	GE

From now on, the tables describing each chapter's conversion from TACKY to assembly will show only what's changed from the chapter before. Appendix B includes two sets of tables giving the complete conversion from TACKY to assembly: one shows the conversion at the end of Part I, and the other shows the conversion at the end of Part II.

Replacing Pseudoregisters

Update this pass to replace any pseudoregisters used by the new Cmp and SetCC instructions with stack addresses, just like you did for all the other instructions.

Fixing Up the cmp Instruction

The cmp instruction, much like mov, add, and sub, can't use memory addresses for both operands. We rewrite it in the usual way, turning

```
cmpl    -4(%rbp), -8(%rbp)
```

into:

```
movl    -4(%rbp), %r10d
cmpl    %r10d, -8(%rbp)
```

The second operand of a cmp instruction can't be a constant. This sort of makes sense if you remember that cmp follows the same form as sub; the second operand of a sub, add, or imul instruction can't be a constant either, since that operand holds the result. Even though cmp doesn't produce a result, the same rules apply. We rewrite

```
cmpl    %eax, $5
```

as:

```
movl    $5, %r11d
cmpl    %eax, %r11d
```

Following the convention from the previous chapter, we use R10 to fix a cmp instruction's first operand and R11 to fix its second operand.

TEST THE ASSEMBLY GENERATION STAGE

To test the assembly generation stage, run:

```
$ ./test_compiler /path/to/your_compiler --chapter 4 --stage codegen
```

Code Emission

We've generated a valid assembly program, and we're ready to emit it. Code emission is slightly more complicated in this chapter, for two reasons. First, we're dealing with both 1-byte and 4-byte registers. We'll print out a different name for a register depending on whether it appears in a conditional set instruction, which takes 1-byte operands, or any of the other instructions we've encountered so far, which take 4-byte operands.

The second issue is emitting labels. Some assembly labels are autogenerated by the compiler, while others—function names—are user-defined identifiers. Right now, the only function name is main, but eventually we'll compile programs with arbitrary function names. Because labels must be unique, autogenerated labels must not conflict with any function names that could appear in a program.

We'll avoid conflicts by adding a special *local label* prefix to our auto-generated labels. The local label prefix is .L on Linux and L on macOS. On Linux, these labels won't conflict with user-defined identifiers because identifiers in C can't contain periods. On macOS, they won't conflict because we prefix all user-defined names with underscores (so that main becomes _main, for example).

Local labels are handy for another reason: they won't confuse GDB or LLDB when you need to debug this code. The assembler puts most labels in the object file's symbol table, but it leaves out any that start with the local label prefix. If your autogenerated labels were in the symbol table, GDB and LLDB would mistake them for function names, which would cause problems when you tried to disassemble a function or view a stack trace.

Aside from those two issues, code emission is pretty straightforward. Tables 4-8 through 4-10 summarize the changes to this pass. From this point forward, the code emission tables will show only what's changed from the previous chapter, much like the tables describing the conversion from TACKY to assembly. See Appendix B for a complete overview of the code emission pass; it includes three sets of tables showing how this pass will look at the end of Part I, Part II, and Part III.

Table 4-8 shows how to print out this chapter's new assembly instructions. It uses the .L prefix for local labels; if you're on macOS, use an L prefix without a period instead.

Table 4-8: Formatting Assembly Instructions

Assembly instruction	Output
Cmp(operand, operand)	cmpl *<operand>*, *<operand>*
Jmp(label)	jmp .L*<label>*
JmpCC(cond_code, label)	j*<cond_code>* .L*<label>*
SetCC(cond_code, operand)	set*<cond_code>* *<operand>*
Label(label)	.L*<label>*:

The cmp instruction gets an l suffix to indicate that it operates on 4-byte values. Conditional set instructions don't take a suffix to indicate the operand size, because they support only 1-byte operands. Jumps and labels also don't use operand size suffixes, since they don't take operands. However, conditional jump and set instructions do need suffixes to indicate what condition they test. Table 4-9 gives the corresponding suffix for each condition code.

Table 4-9: Instruction Suffixes for
Condition Codes

Condition code	Instruction suffix
E	e
NE	ne
L	l
LE	le
G	g
GE	ge

Finally, Table 4-10 gives the 1-byte and 4-byte aliases for each register. The 4-byte aliases are the same as in the previous chapter; the new 1-byte aliases are bolded.

Table 4-10: Formatting Assembly Operands

Assembly operand		Output
Reg(AX)	4-byte	%eax
	1-byte	**%al**
Reg(DX)	4-byte	%edx
	1-byte	**%dl**
Reg(R10)	4-byte	%r10d
	1-byte	**%r10b**
Reg(R11)	4-byte	%r11d
	1-byte	**%r11b**

Emit the 1-byte names for registers when they appear in SetCC and the 4-byte names anywhere else.

TEST THE WHOLE COMPILER

To check that you're compiling every test program correctly, run:

```
$ ./test_compiler /path/to/your_compiler --chapter 4
```

Once all the tests pass, you're ready to move on to the next chapter.

Summary

Your compiler can now handle relational and logical operators. In this chapter, you added conditional jumps to TACKY to support short-circuiting operators, and you learned about several new assembly instructions. You also learned how the CPU keeps track of the current instruction and records the results of comparisons. The new TACKY and assembly instructions you introduced in this chapter will eventually help you implement complex control structures like `if` statements and loops. But first, you'll implement one of the most essential features of C: variables!

Additional Resources

For more in-depth discussions of undefined behavior, see these blog posts:

- "A Guide to Undefined Behavior in C and C++, Part 1" by John Regehr is a good overview of what undefined behavior means in the C standard and how it impacts compiler design (*https://blog.regehr.org/archives/213*).

- "With Undefined Behavior, Anything Is Possible" by Raph Levien explores some sources of undefined behavior in C and the history of how it got into the standard to begin with (*https://raphlinus.github.io/programming/rust/2018/08/17/undefined-behavior.html*).

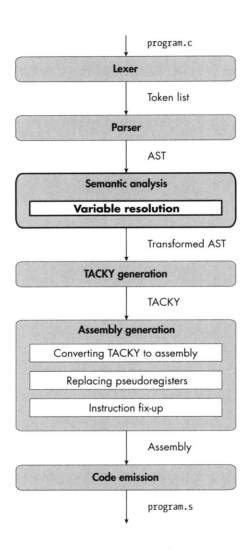

program.c

Lexer

Token list

Parser

AST

Semantic analysis

Variable resolution

Transformed AST

TACKY generation

TACKY

Assembly generation

Converting TACKY to assembly

Replacing pseudoregisters

Instruction fix-up

Assembly

Code emission

program.s

5

LOCAL VARIABLES

Up to this point, you've been able to compile only programs that return constant expressions. In this chapter, you'll implement local variables, which will let you compile far more interesting programs. Your compiler will need to support a more expressive grammar so it can parse C programs that declare, assign values to, and refer to variables. It will also need to contend with the ways that variables can be declared and used incorrectly. To catch these potential errors, you'll add a *semantic analysis* stage, which is bolded in the diagram at the beginning of this chapter. This stage validates that variables are not declared multiple times in the same scope or used before they're declared. It also assigns each variable a unique identifier that allows you to safely refer to it in TACKY.

Luckily, the TACKY and assembly IRs in your compiler already support variables, since they use temporary variables to store intermediate results. That means you won't have to change anything in your compiler after TACKY generation. Before jumping into the compiler passes, let's define the language features we need to support.

Variables, Declarations, and Assignment

For variables to be even remotely useful, we'll need to implement a few new language features. First of all, we need to support variable *declarations*. Every local variable in C must be declared before it can be used. A variable declaration consists of the variable's type, its name, and an optional expression, called an *initializer*, that specifies its initial value. Here's a declaration with an initializer:

```
int a = 2 * 3;
```

Here's a declaration without one:

```
int b;
```

Second, we must support using a variable's value in an expression, like b + 1. Just like an integer constant, a variable is a complete expression on its own but can also appear in more complex logical and arithmetic expressions.

Finally, we need to support variable *assignment*. In C, you update a variable using the assignment operator (=). Variable assignment in C is an expression, like addition, subtraction, and so forth. This means it evaluates to some result, which you can use in a return statement or as part of a larger expression. The result of an assignment expression is the updated value of the destination variable. For example, the expression 2 * (a = 5) evaluates to 10. First, you assign the value 5 to the variable a, then you multiply the new value of a by 2. Because assignment is an expression, you can perform multiple assignments at once in an expression like a = b = c. Unlike other binary operations we've seen so far, assignment is right-associative, so a = b = c is equivalent to a = (b = c). To evaluate this expression, you first perform the assignment b = c. Then, you assign the result of that expression, which is the new value of b, to a.

Variable assignment is the first expression we've encountered that has a *side effect*. That means it doesn't just reduce to a value; it also has some impact on the execution environment. In 2 * (a = 5), the subexpression a = 5 has a value (5), and it also has a side effect (updating a). Most of the time, we care only about the side effect of a variable assignment, not the resulting value.

An action counts as a side effect only if it's visible outside of the language construct in question. For example, updating a local variable is a side effect of an assignment expression because the variable's new value is visible outside of that expression. But it's *not* a side effect of the function that contains the assignment expression, because the effect isn't visible outside of that function. Updating a global variable, on the other hand, would be a side effect of the expression *and* the function.

Since we're implementing expressions with side effects, it also makes sense to add support for *expression statements*, which evaluate an expression but don't use the result. Statements that assign to variables, like

```
foo = 3 * 3;
```

are expression statements. This expression has the side effect of assigning the value 9 to foo. The result of the whole expression is also the value 9, but this result isn't used anywhere; only the side effect of updating foo affects the program.

You can also have expression statements with no side effect at all:

```
1 + a * 2;
```

You don't typically see expression statements without side effects, because they're completely useless, but they're perfectly valid.

Any expression can appear on the right side of the = operator, but only some expressions can appear on the left side. It makes sense to assign values to variables, array elements, and struct members:

```
x = 3;
array[2] = 100;
my_struct.member = x * 2;
```

But it doesn't make sense to assign values to constants or the results of logical or arithmetic expressions:

```
4 = 5;
foo && bar = 6;
a - 5 = b;
```

Expressions that can appear on the left side of an assignment are called *lvalues*. In this chapter, the only lvalues we'll handle are variables. You'll learn about more complex lvalues in Part II.

Local variables introduce new opportunities for undefined behavior, which you learned about in Chapter 4. For example, with a few exceptions, using the value of an uninitialized variable leads to undefined behavior. Consider the following function:

```
int foo(void) {
    int a;
    return a;
}
```

It's possible that this function will allocate stack space for a without initializing it, then return whatever value happens to already be in that uninitialized memory. In this case, although the return value of foo will be unpredictable, the rest of the program will behave reasonably. But because foo's behavior is undefined, it's also possible that it will do something completely different; calling foo could crash the program or even make other functions misbehave later on.

Let's look at a subtler example with two unsequenced variable assignments:

```
int main(void) {
    int a;
    (a = 4) + (a = 5);
    return a;
}
```

Remember that the operands of a binary operator like + are unsequenced; they can be evaluated in any order. It might look like this program has two possible behaviors: it could return either 4 or 5. But performing multiple unsequenced assignments to the same variable is undefined behavior, so there are no restrictions on how this program might behave. In practice, it probably *will* return 4 or 5, but that isn't guaranteed.

Similarly, the behavior is undefined if you use a variable's value and assign to it in unsequenced expressions, like so:

```
int main(void) {
    int a = 0;
    return (a = 1) + a;
}
```

These examples aren't an exhaustive overview of every possible undefined behavior involving local variables, but they illustrate how problems that appear to affect one small part of a program can make the entire program's behavior undefined.

Now that you understand the language features you're going to add in this chapter, let's extend the compiler.

The Lexer

You'll add one new token in this chapter:

=   An equal sign, the assignment operator

You don't need a new token to represent variable names. The lexer already recognizes identifiers, like the function name main, and variable names are just identifiers. We won't distinguish between function names and variable names until the parsing stage.

TEST THE LEXER

To test the lexer, run:

```
$ ./test_compiler /path/to/your_compiler --chapter 5 --stage lex
```

Your lexer should succeed on all of this chapter's test cases.

The Parser

As usual, we'll update the AST and grammar to support this chapter's new language constructs. We'll also update our precedence climbing code to correctly parse assignment expressions.

The Updated AST and Grammar

Let's start by extending our AST definition to support using, declaring, and assigning to variables. To support using variables in expressions, we'll add a Var constructor for the exp AST node. Since variable assignment is also an expression, we'll add an Assignment constructor for exp too. Listing 5-1 shows the updated definition of exp.

```
exp = Constant(int)
    | Var(identifier)
    | Unary(unary_operator, exp)
    | Binary(binary_operator, exp, exp)
    | Assignment(exp, exp)
```

Listing 5-1: The definition for the exp AST node, including Var and Assignment

A Var node holds the variable name. An Assignment consists of two parts: the lvalue being updated and the expression we're assigning to that lvalue.

When we parse the program, we'll allow any expression on the left-hand side of an assignment. In the semantic analysis stage, we'll make sure that expression is a valid lvalue. We validate lvalues during semantic analysis, rather than during parsing, because we'll need to support more complex lvalues in later chapters.

Next, we'll extend the statement AST node to support expression statements. We'll add a new Expression constructor, which takes a single exp node as an argument. We'll also add a Null constructor to represent *null statements*, which are expression statements without the expression:

```
statement = Return(exp) | Expression(exp) | Null
```

A null statement has no content; it's just a semicolon. It's a placeholder for when the grammar requires a statement, but you don't want that statement to do anything. Listing 5-2, which is taken from section 6.8.3, paragraph 5, of the C standard, illustrates why you might need a null statement.

```
char *s;
/* ... */
while (❶ *s++ != '\0')
    ❷ ;
```

Listing 5-2: An example of a null statement from the C standard

In this example, the while loop finds the end of a null-terminated string by iterating over each character until it reaches the null byte. The loop body doesn't need to do anything, because all the work happens in the controlling expression ❶, but omitting the loop body completely would be syntactically invalid. Instead, you can use a null statement ❷. Null statements don't really have anything to do with local variables, but we'll implement them here because they're technically a kind of expression statement. (They're also easy to implement.)

We'll need an AST node to represent variable declarations too:

```
declaration = Declaration(identifier name, exp? init)
```

A declaration consists of a name and an optional initializer. (The question mark in exp? means that field is optional.) We'll include type information for declarations in Part II, but we don't need it yet because int is the only possible type.

Declarations are a separate AST node, not another kind of statement, because declarations aren't statements! Conceptually, the difference is that statements are executed when the program runs, whereas declarations simply tell the compiler that some identifier exists and can be used later. This distinction will become obvious during TACKY generation: we'll handle declarations with initializers like normal variable assignments, but declarations without initializers will just disappear.

The more concrete difference, from the parser's perspective, is that there are parts of a program where a statement can appear but a declaration can't. For example, the body of an if statement is always another statement:

```
if (a == 2)
    return 4;
```

It can't be a declaration, because declarations aren't statements. So, this is invalid:

```
if (a == 2)
    int x = 0;
```

It might be surprising to hear that an if body is a single statement, since an if body often appears to be a list of statements and declarations, like this:

```
if (a == 2) {
    int x = 0;
    return x;
}
```

But a list of statements and declarations wrapped in braces is actually a single statement, called a *compound statement*. We'll implement compound statements in Chapter 7; for now, the key point is that we need to distinguish between statements and declarations in the AST.

Finally, we need to change how we define a function body so that we can parse functions that contain multiple declarations and statements, like Listing 5-3.

```
int main(void) {
    int a;
    a = 2;
    return a * 2;
}
```

Listing 5-3: A program with a declaration and multiple statements

Up until this point, we've defined a function body as a single statement:

```
function_definition = Function(identifier name, statement body)
```

Now, though, we need to define it as a list of statements and declarations, which are collectively called *block items*. We'll add a new AST node to represent block items:

```
block_item = S(statement) | D(declaration)
```

Then we can represent a function body as a list of block items:

```
function_definition = Function(identifier name, block_item* body)
```

The asterisk here indicates that body is a list. Putting it all together, Listing 5-4 shows the new AST definition, with this chapter's additions bolded.

```
program = Program(function_definition)
function_definition = Function(identifier name, block_item* body)
block_item = S(statement) | D(declaration)
declaration = Declaration(identifier name, exp? init)
statement = Return(exp) | Expression(exp) | Null
exp = Constant(int)
    | Var(identifier)
    | Unary(unary_operator, exp)
    | Binary(binary_operator, exp, exp)
    | Assignment(exp, exp)
unary_operator = Complement | Negate | Not
binary_operator = Add | Subtract | Multiply | Divide | Remainder | And | Or
                | Equal | NotEqual | LessThan | LessOrEqual
                | GreaterThan | GreaterOrEqual
```

Listing 5-4: The abstract syntax tree with variables, assignment expressions, and expression statements

Listing 5-5 shows the updated grammar.

```
<program> ::= <function>
<function> ::= "int" <identifier> "(" "void" ")" "{" { <block-item> } "}"
<block-item> ::= <statement> | <declaration>
<declaration> ::= "int" <identifier> [ "=" <exp> ] ";"
<statement> ::= "return" <exp> ";" | <exp> ";" | ";"
<exp> ::= <factor> | <exp> <binop> <exp>
<factor> ::= <int> | <identifier> | <unop> <factor> | "(" <exp> ")"
<unop> ::= "-" | "~" | "!"
<binop> ::= "-" | "+" | "*" | "/" | "%" | "&&" | "||"
         | "==" | "!=" | "<" | "<=" | ">" | ">=" | "="
<identifier> ::= ? An identifier token ?
<int> ::= ? A constant token ?
```

Listing 5-5: The grammar with variables, assignment expressions, and expression statements

Listing 5-5 introduces a couple of new bits of EBNF notation. Wrapping a sequence of symbols in braces indicates that it can be repeated zero or more times, so { <block-item> } indicates a list of <block-item> symbols. Note the difference between unquoted braces, which indicate repetition, and quoted braces, which indicate literal { and } tokens. In the rule for <function>, the expression "{" { <block-item> } "}" indicates a { token, then a list of <block-item> symbols, then a } token. The pseudocode in Listing 5-6 shows how to parse the list of block items in a function definition.

```
parse_function_definition(tokens):
    // parse everything up through the open brace as before...
    --snip--
    function_body = []
```

```
        while peek(tokens) != "}":
            next_block_item = parse_block_item(tokens)
            function_body.append(next_block_item)
        take_token(tokens)
        return Function(name, function_body)
```

Listing 5-6: Parsing a list of block items

You keep parsing block items until you see a close brace, which indicates the end of the function body. You can then remove that brace from the input stream and finish processing the function definition.

Just as braces indicate repetition in EBNF notation, wrapping a sequence of symbols in square brackets indicates that it's optional. We represent the optional initializer in declarations with the expression ["=" <exp>]. To handle this optional construct, your declaration parsing code should check whether the identifier in the grammar rule is followed by an = token, which means the initializer is present, or a ; token, which means the initializer is absent.

While parsing <block-item>, you need a way to tell whether the current block item is a statement or a declaration. To do this, peek at the first token; if it's the int keyword, it's a declaration, and otherwise it's a statement.

Listing 5-5 also includes a new production rule for the <factor> symbol, corresponding to the new Var constructor, and a new binary operator, =, to represent variable assignment. Even though we won't represent variable assignment with the Binary AST node, it looks just like any other binary operator in the grammar. This lets us parse variable assignments with the precedence climbing algorithm we've already implemented, although it will require a few tweaks.

An Improved Precedence Climbing Algorithm

There's just one problem with using our current precedence climbing code to parse assignment expressions: the = operator is right-associative, but our code can handle only left-associative operators. To remind ourselves why, let's look at the precedence climbing pseudocode again. We saw the full version of this algorithm in Listing 3-7; it's reproduced here as Listing 5-7.

```
parse_exp(tokens, min_prec):
    left = parse_factor(tokens)
    next_token = peek(tokens)
    while next_token is a binary operator and precedence(next_token) >= min_prec:
        operator = parse_binop(tokens)
        right = parse_exp(tokens, ❶ precedence(next_token) + 1)
        left = Binary(operator, left, right)
        next_token = peek(tokens)
    return left
```

Listing 5-7: Parsing left-associative operators with precedence climbing

When we make recursive calls to parse_exp, we set the minimum precedence higher than the precedence of the current operator ❶. So, if next_token is + and tokens is b + 4, a recursive call to parse_exp will return only b, because + won't meet the minimum precedence. That's how we get left-associative expressions like (left + b) + 4.

If next_token is right-associative, however, we shouldn't stop if we hit that same token in the recursive call to parse_exp; we should include it in the right-hand expression. To do that, we need to set the minimum precedence on the right-hand side *equal* to the precedence of the current token. In other words, when handling a right-associative token like =, the recursive call should be:

```
right = parse_exp(tokens, precedence(next_token))
```

Suppose you're parsing a = b = c. You'll parse the left-hand side into the factor a, then call parse_exp recursively to handle b = c. If the minimum precedence in this recursive call were precedence("=") + 1, it would parse only the next factor, b. But if the minimum precedence is precedence("="), it will parse the entire assignment, returning b = c as the right-hand side of the expression. The final result will be a = (b = c), which is exactly what we want.

The only other difference between parsing variable assignment and other binary expressions is that we need to construct an Assignment AST node instead of a Binary node. Listing 5-8 gives the updated pseudocode for precedence climbing with these adjustments.

```
parse_exp(tokens, min_prec):
    left = parse_factor(tokens)
    next_token = peek(tokens)
    while next_token is a binary operator and precedence(next_token) >= min_prec:
        if next_token is "=":
            take_token(tokens) // remove "=" from list of tokens
            right = parse_exp(tokens, precedence(next_token))
            left = Assignment(left, right)
        else:
            operator = parse_binop(tokens)
            right = parse_exp(tokens, precedence(next_token) + 1)
            left = Binary(operator, left, right)
        next_token = peek(tokens)
    return left
```

Listing 5-8: The extended precedence climbing algorithm

Finally, we need to add = to our precedence table. Table 5-1 lists the precedence values I'm using for all the binary operators, with the new operator bolded. It has lower precedence than any other operator we've implemented so far.

Table 5-1: Precedence Values of Binary Operators

Operator	Precedence
*	50
/	50
%	50
+	45
-	45
<	35
<=	35
>	35
>=	35
==	30
!=	30
&&	10
||	5
=	1

At this point, you know how to build a valid AST for every program you'll encounter in this chapter; you're ready to update the parser and test it out.

TEST THE PARSER

To test this chapter's changes to the parser, run:

```
$ ./test_compiler /path/to/your_compiler --chapter 5 --stage parse
```

The parser should successfully parse every test case in *tests/chapter_5/ valid* and *tests/chapter_5/invalid_semantics*. It should raise an error for every test case in *tests/chapter_5/invalid_parse*.

Semantic Analysis

Up to this point, the only errors we've had to worry about were syntax errors. If we could parse a program, we knew the remaining compiler passes would succeed. Now, a program can be syntactically correct but *semantically* invalid; in other words, it might just not make sense. For example, a program could assign a value to an expression that isn't assignable:

```
2 = a * 3; // ERROR: can't assign a value to a constant
```

Or it could declare the same variable twice in the same scope:

```
int a = 3;
int a; // ERROR: a has already been declared!
```

Or it could try to use a variable before it's been declared:

```
int main(void) {
    a = 4; // ERROR: a has not been declared yet!
    return a;
}
```

All of these examples use valid syntax, but you should get an error if you try to compile them. The semantic analysis stage detects this kind of error. This stage will eventually include several different passes that validate different aspects of the program. In this chapter, we'll add our first semantic analysis pass, *variable resolution.*

The variable resolution pass will track which variables are in scope throughout the program and *resolve* each reference to a variable by finding the corresponding declaration. It will report an error if a program declares the same variable more than once or uses a variable that hasn't been declared. It will also rename each local variable with a globally unique identifier. For example, it might convert the program

```
int main(void) {
    int a = 4;
    int b = a + 1;
    a = b - 5;
    return a + b;
}
```

into something like this:

```
int main(void) {
    int a0 = 4;
    int b1 = a0 + 1;
    a0 = b1 - 5;
    return a0 + b1;
}
```

(Of course, this pass actually transforms ASTs rather than source files, but I'm presenting these examples as C source code to make them more readable.)

This transformation may not seem too helpful—the variable names a and b were already unique—but it will be essential once we introduce multiple variable scopes, because different variables in different scopes can have the same name. For example, we might transform the program

```c
int main(void) {
    int a = 2;
    if (a < 5) {
        int a = 7;
        return a;
    }
    return a;
}
```

into:

```c
int main(void) {
    int a0 = 2;
    if (a0 < 5) {
        int a1 = 7;
        return a1;
    }
    return a0;
}
```

This makes it clear that a0 and a1 are two different variables, which will simplify later compiler stages.

Variable Resolution

Now we'll write the variable resolution pass. During this pass, we'll construct a map from the user-defined variable names to the unique names we'll use in later stages. We'll process block items in order, checking for errors and replacing variable names as we go. When we encounter a variable declaration, we'll add a new entry mapping that variable name to a unique name that we generate. Then, when we see an expression that uses a variable, we'll replace the variable name with the corresponding unique name from the map. The pseudocode in Listing 5-9 demonstrates how to resolve a variable declaration.

```
resolve_declaration(Declaration(name, init), variable_map):
❶ if name is in variable_map:
        fail("Duplicate variable declaration!")
    unique_name = make_temporary()
❷ variable_map.add(name, unique_name)
❸ if init is not null:
        init = resolve_exp(init, variable_map)
❹ return Declaration(unique_name, init)
```

Listing 5-9: Resolving a variable declaration

First, we check whether the variable being declared is already present in the variable map ❶. If it is, that means it was declared earlier in the function, so this is a duplicate declaration. In that case, we throw an error. Next, we associate the user-defined variable name with a unique autogenerated name in the variable map ❷.

After we update the variable map, we process the declaration initializer, if there is one ❸. The call to resolve_exp returns a new copy of the initializer with any variables renamed, throwing an error if the initializer uses an undeclared variable. Finally, we return a copy of the Declaration node ❹ that uses the new autogenerated name instead of the old user-defined one, along with the new initializer we got from resolve_exp.

The identifiers you generate in resolve_declaration must not conflict with the names of temporary TACKY variables. If you're using a global counter to generate unique identifiers, use the same counter across both the semantic analysis and TACKY generation stages.

These identifiers must not conflict with the names of functions or global variables, either. (In Chapter 10, you'll see that global variables keep their original names, like functions, instead of being renamed, like local variables.) You can rely on the usual trick of generating identifiers that wouldn't be syntactically valid in C. I recommend including a variable's original name in its autogenerated name to help with debugging; for example, you might rename a to a.0 and b to b.1.

NOTE *You might have noticed that the examples in the previous section used autogenerated identifiers that* are *syntactically valid in C, like a0 and b1, because those examples were presented as C source code. The naming scheme in those examples wouldn't work in practice, because the renamed variables could conflict with function names and with each other. For example, two local variables named a and a1 could both be renamed a12.*

USING VARIABLES IN THEIR OWN INITIALIZERS

Because Listing 5-9 updates the variable map before processing the initializer, it will happily process an initializer that uses the same variable it initializes. Take this example:

```
int foo = foo + 1;
```

When we process the initializer, foo + 1, the variable foo is already in the map, so the variable resolution pass won't complain. This is consistent with the C standard; a variable really is in scope in its own initializer. Still, this declaration isn't exactly legal. It will result in undefined behavior, because foo is uninitialized when it's used in foo + 1. (Remember that compilers don't need to detect undefined behavior, so it's okay not to report an error here.)

In other cases, using a variable in its own initializer makes sense. For example, in

unsigned int foo = sizeof foo;

we're still using foo before initializing it, but we consider only foo's size, not its value. Annex J of the C standard says we get undefined behavior when "an lvalue . . . is used in a context *that requires the value of the designated object,* but the object is uninitialized" (emphasis added). Since sizeof doesn't require foo's value, there's no undefined behavior in this declaration.

To resolve a return statement or expression statement, we just process the inner expression, as Listing 5-10 illustrates.

```
resolve_statement(statement, variable_map):
    match statement with
    | Return(e) -> return Return(resolve_exp(e, variable_map))
    | Expression(e) -> return Expression(resolve_exp(e, variable_map))
    | Null -> return Null
```

Listing 5-10: Resolving a statement

When we resolve an expression, we check that all the variable uses and assignments in that expression are valid. Listing 5-11 shows how to do that.

```
resolve_exp(e, variable_map):
    match e with
    | Assignment(left, right) ->
        if left is not a Var node:
            fail("Invalid lvalue!")
        return Assignment(❶ resolve_exp(left, variable_map), ❷ resolve_exp(right, variable_map))
    | Var(v) ->
        if v is in variable_map:
            return Var(❸ variable_map.get(v))
        else:
            fail("Undeclared variable!")
    | --snip--
```

Listing 5-11: Resolving an expression

When we encounter an Assignment expression, we check that the left side is a valid lvalue; for now, that means it must be a Var. We then recursively resolve the left ❶ and right ❷ subexpressions. When we encounter a Var, we replace the variable name with the unique identifier from the variable map ❸. If it's not in the variable map, that means it hasn't been declared yet, so we throw an error. Since we process both sides of an assignment recursively with resolve_exp, the Var case in resolve_exp handles variables on the left side of assignment expressions too.

To handle other kinds of expressions, we process any subexpressions recursively with resolve_exp. Ultimately, the variable resolution pass should return a complete AST that uses autogenerated instead of user-defined variable names.

THE TROUBLE WITH TYPEDEF

The way we've structured our compiler has one major limitation: we first parse the entire program, and then resolve variables. This approach works well for the subset of C we'll implement in this book, but to implement the whole language, you need to resolve identifiers *while* you parse the program. In particular, our approach can't handle typedef, which lets you declare names for arbitrary types:

```
typedef int foo;
```

The problem is that some statements can be parsed one way if an identifier like foo refers to a type and another way if it refers to a function or variable. Here's a simple illustration:

```
return (foo) * x;
```

If foo is the name of a type, this statement dereferences x, casts the result to type foo, and then returns it. But if foo is a variable, this statement instead multiplies foo by x and returns the result. To make matters worse, type names follow the same scoping rules as variable names. So, just as the same identifier might refer to two different variables at different points in a program, it might refer to a variable at one point and a type at a different point. To figure out whether a given identifier refers to a type or a variable, you need to resolve identifiers as you parse the program. Since the correct way to parse a C construct might depend on other parts of the program you've already parsed, we say that C has a *context-sensitive grammar*. (By contrast, a language has a *context-free grammar* if you can apply every production rule in isolation, without worrying about anything that came before it.)

Production C compilers generally deal with typedef by maintaining a symbol table (similar to our variable map) while they parse the program. Some of them feed the information from the symbol table back into the lexer, which then interprets type names as a different kind of token from other identifiers; this approach is called the *lexer hack*. Others use the same token type for all identifiers and do all the work of distinguishing between type names and other identifiers in the parser. If you want to implement typedef on your own, I recommend the latter approach.

Here's a quick sketch of how you could adapt our implementation to support typedef. First, you'll need to move all the variable resolution logic into the parser. You should pass around a variable map as you parse the program. Your parser should add declarations to the map and rename variables as it goes. It should also validate that variables are declared before they're used,

---

that there are no conflicting declarations, and so on. Once you're ready to add typedef, you can track type names in this map too, recording whether each entry in the map refers to a type or some other entity. You might want to convert type names to unique IDs during parsing, and then replace these names with the corresponding types in a separate pass. Alternatively, you could replace type names with the corresponding types right away as you parse the program. Either way, your parser will have enough information to distinguish types from other identifiers. The other semantic analysis passes that we'll add in later chapters should remain separate from the parser.

If you decide to implement typedef yourself, I recommend reading Eli Bendersky's blog post "The Context Sensitivity of C's Grammar, Revisited," which walks through some particularly ugly edge cases that you'll need to handle (*https://eli.thegreenplace.net/2011/05/02/the-context-sensitivity-of-cs-grammar-revisited*).

The --validate Option

To test out the new compiler pass, you'll need to add a --validate command line option to your compiler driver. This option should run your compiler through the semantic analysis stage, stopping before TACKY generation. In later chapters, after you've updated the semantic analysis stage to include multiple passes, this option should direct your compiler to run all of them.

Like the existing options to run the compiler up to a specific stage, this new option shouldn't produce any output files. As usual, it should return an exit code of 0 if compilation succeeds and a nonzero exit code if it fails.

TEST THE VARIABLE RESOLUTION PASS

To test out this pass, run:

```
$ ./test_compiler /path/to/your_compiler --chapter 5 --stage validate
```

This pass should reject every test case in *tests/chapter_5/invalid_semantics* and accept every test case in *tests/chapter_5/valid*. You may also want to write your own unit tests for this pass to verify that it updates variable names correctly.

TACKY Generation

We don't need to modify the TACKY IR at all in this chapter. We can already refer to variables with the TACKY Var constructor and assign values to them with the Copy instruction. The TACKY IR doesn't include variable declarations, because it doesn't need them. We got all the information we needed out of variable declarations during semantic analysis, and now we can discard them.

Although TACKY itself doesn't need to change, the TACKY generation pass does: we need to extend this pass to handle the latest additions to the AST. First, we'll deal with the two new kinds of expressions we added in this chapter. Next, we'll handle the other additions to the AST, including expression statements and declarations.

Variable and Assignment Expressions

We'll convert each Var in the AST to a Var in TACKY, keeping the same identifier. Because we autogenerated the identifier, we can guarantee that it won't conflict with any other identifiers in the TACKY program. To handle an Assignment AST node, we'll emit the instructions to evaluate the right-hand side, then emit a Copy instruction to copy the result to the left-hand side. Listing 5-12 shows how to handle both expressions.

```
emit_tacky(e, instructions):
    match e with
    | --snip--
    | Var(v) -> return Var(v)
    | Assignment(Var(v), rhs) ->
        result = emit_tacky(rhs, instructions)
        instructions.append(Copy(result, Var(v)))
        return Var(v)
```

Listing 5-12: Converting variable and assignment expressions to TACKY

This is an inefficient way to handle variable assignments; we'll often end up evaluating the right-hand side, storing the result in a temporary variable, and then copying it into variable v, instead of storing the result directly in v and avoiding the temporary variable entirely. The optimizations we implement in Part III will remove some of these superfluous copies.

Declarations, Statements, and Function Bodies

Now we'll handle declarations. As I mentioned earlier, we can discard variable declarations at this stage; in TACKY, you don't need to declare variables before using them. But we do need to emit TACKY to *initialize* variables. If a declaration includes an initializer, we'll handle it like a normal variable assignment. If a declaration doesn't have an initializer, we won't emit any TACKY at all.

We also need to handle expression statements and null statements. To convert an expression statement to TACKY, we'll just process the inner expression. This will return a new temporary variable that holds the result of the expression, but we won't use that variable again during TACKY generation. We won't emit any TACKY instructions for a null statement.

Finally, we'll deal with the fact that a function contains multiple block items instead of a single statement. We'll process the block items in the function body in order, emitting TACKY for each one. Suppose we're compiling the C function in Listing 5-13.

```
int main(void) {
    int b;
    int a = 10 + 1;
    b = a * 2;
    return b;
}
```

Listing 5-13: A C function with variable declarations and an assignment expression

Let's assume that we renamed a and b to a.1 and b.0 during variable resolution, and that we use the naming scheme tmp.n for all temporary variables, where *n* is the value of a global counter. Then, we'll generate the TACKY instructions shown in Listing 5-14 for the function body. (This listing, like Listing 4-6 in the previous chapter, uses the notation dst = src for Copy instructions, instead of Copy(src, dst). Similarly, it uses notation like dst = src1 + src2 for Binary instructions, instead of Binary(Add, src1, src2, dst).)

```
tmp.2 = 10 + 1
a.1 = tmp.2
tmp.3 = a.1 * 2
b.0 = tmp.3
Return(b.0)
```

Listing 5-14: Implementing Listing 5-13 in TACKY

We won't generate any TACKY for the declaration of b in Listing 5-13, because it doesn't include an initializer. We'll convert the declaration of a into the first two instructions of Listing 5-14, which calculate 10 + 1 and copy the result to a. We'll convert the expression statement b = a * 2; to the next two instructions, and we'll convert the return statement to the final Return instruction.

At this point, you know how to convert the whole AST to TACKY. But we're not quite done; we have one last edge case to consider.

Functions with No return Statement

Since our AST now supports more than one kind of statement, we might encounter functions without return statements, like Listing 5-15.

```
int main(void) {
    int a = 4;
    a = 0;
}
```

Listing 5-15: A main function with no return statement

What happens if you call this function? The C standard gives one answer for main and a different answer for any other function. (I'm ignoring functions with return type void, which don't return a value, because we haven't implemented them yet.) Section 5.1.2.2.3 says that "reaching the } that terminates the main function returns a value of 0," so the code in Listing 5-15 is equivalent to Listing 5-16.

```
int main(void) {
    int a = 4;
    a = 0;
    return 0;
}
```

Listing 5-16: A main function that returns 0

The situation is more complicated for other functions. According to section 6.9.1, paragraph 12, "Unless otherwise specified, if the } that terminates a function is reached, and the value of the function call is used by the caller, the behavior is undefined." This implicitly covers two possible cases. In the first case, shown in Listing 5-17, the caller tries to use the function's return value.

```
#include <stdio.h>

int foo(void) {
    printf("I'm living on the edge, baby!");
    // no return statement
}

int main(void) {
    return foo(); // try to use return value from foo
}
```

Listing 5-17: Trying to use a function's return value when it didn't return anything

This results in undefined behavior, which means all bets are off; the standard makes no guarantees about what will happen. In the second case, shown in Listing 5-18, we call the function but don't use its return value.

```
#include <stdio.h>

int foo(void) {
    printf("I'm living on the edge, baby!");
    // no return statement
}

int main(void) {
    foo();
    return 0;
}
```

Listing 5-18: Calling a function without using its return value

There's no undefined behavior in this program; it's guaranteed to print I'm living on the edge, baby! and then exit with a status code of 0. When we compile a function like foo, we don't know whether any of its callers use its return value, so we have to assume it's part of a program like Listing 5-18. In particular, we need to restore the caller's stack frame and return control to the caller at the end of foo. Because we aren't returning any particular value, we can set EAX to whatever we like, or not set it at all.

The easiest way to handle both cases is to add one extra TACKY instruction, Return(Constant(0)), to the end of every function body. This gives us the correct behavior for main and for programs like Listing 5-18. If a function already ends with a return statement, this extra instruction will never run, so it won't change the program's behavior. In Part III, you'll learn how to eliminate this extra Return instruction when it's not needed.

Once you've extended the TACKY generation stage, you're ready to test the whole compiler! Because we didn't change the TACKY IR, we don't need to change the assembly generation or code emission stages, either.

TEST THE WHOLE COMPILER

To test out your compiler, run:

```
$ ./test_compiler /path/to/your_compiler --chapter 5
```

Once these tests pass, you can either implement a couple of related extra credit features or go straight to the next chapter.

Extra Credit: Compound Assignment, Increment, and Decrement

Now that your compiler supports the simple assignment operator, =, you have the option of implementing several *compound assignment* operators: +=, -=, *=, /=, and %=. If you added the bitwise binary operators in Chapter 3, you should add the corresponding compound assignment operators here as well: &=, |=, ^=, <<=, and >>=.

You can also add the increment and decrement operators, ++ and --. Each of these operators can be used in two distinct ways: as a prefix operator in an expression like ++a, or as a postfix operator in an expression like a++. When you use ++ or -- as a prefix operator, it increments or decrements its operand and evaluates to its new value. A postfix ++ or -- operator also increments or decrements its operand, but it evaluates to the operand's original value. As with the other language constructs in this chapter, you can implement the compound assignment, increment, and decrement operators without changing any part of your compiler after TACKY generation.

To include test cases for the increment and decrement operators, use the --increment flag when you run the test suite. To include the test cases for compound assignment, use the --compound flag. The test script will run the test cases for bitwise compound assignment operators, like |=, only if you use both the --compound and --bitwise flags.

You can test all the extra credit features at once using the --extra-credit flag. The command

```
$ ./test_compiler /path/to/your_compiler --chapter 5 --extra-credit
```

is equivalent to:

```
$ ./test_compiler /path/to/your_compiler --chapter 5 --bitwise --compound --increment
```

When we introduce more extra credit features in later chapters, the --extra-credit flag will cover those too.

Summary

This chapter was a milestone in a few ways: you added a new kind of statement, and you implemented your first language construct that has a side effect. You also implemented a semantic analysis stage to catch new kinds of errors in the programs you compile. In later chapters, you'll keep expanding the semantic analysis stage to detect more errors and gather additional information that you'll need later in compilation. Next, you'll implement your first control-flow constructs: if statements and conditional expressions.

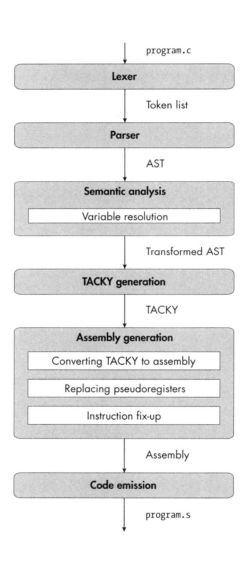

program.c

Lexer

Token list

Parser

AST

Semantic analysis

Variable resolution

Transformed AST

TACKY generation

TACKY

Assembly generation

Converting TACKY to assembly

Replacing pseudoregisters

Instruction fix-up

Assembly

Code emission

program.s

6

IF STATEMENTS AND CONDITIONAL EXPRESSIONS

In the last chapter, you learned how to compile programs that execute a list of statements. But most C programs have a more complicated execution path; they often need to decide what statements to execute at runtime based on the current state of the program. The order in which a program executes statements is its *control flow,* and the language constructs that let you change a program's control flow are called *control structures.*

In this chapter, you'll implement your first control structure: if statements. You'll also implement *conditional expressions.* Like if statements, conditional expressions let you control what code to run. For example, the conditional expression (a == 0) ? 3 : 4 evaluates to 3 if a is equal to 0 and 4 otherwise. We laid a lot of the groundwork for if statements and conditional expressions when we implemented the short-circuiting && and || operators in Chapter 4. We already have TACKY constructs that let us conditionally run or skip over code, so we don't need to change any stages after TACKY generation. Let's get started!

The Lexer

You'll add four tokens in this chapter:

if A keyword indicating the start of an if statement

else A keyword indicating the start of the else clause in an if statement

? A question mark, the delimiter between the first and second operands in a conditional expression

: A colon, the delimiter between the second and third operands in a conditional expression

Once your lexer supports these four tokens, you can test it out.

TEST THE LEXER

To test your lexer, run:

```
$ ./test_compiler /path/to/your_compiler --chapter 6 --stage lex
```

It should be able to process every test case in this chapter without errors.

The Parser

Now we'll update the parser to support if statements and conditional expressions. Because these are two distinct language constructs, we'll handle them one at a time, beginning with if statements.

Parsing if Statements

We'll start by extending the statement AST node to support if statements. Listing 6-1 gives the updated definition of this node.

```
statement = Return(exp)
          | Expression(exp)
          | If(exp condition, statement then, statement? else)
          | Null
```

Listing 6-1: The definition for the statement AST node, including if statements

The new If constructor takes three arguments. The condition expression, sometimes called the *controlling expression*, determines whether the body of the statement is executed. The then statement is the first clause of the if statement, which executes when the result of condition is nonzero. The second clause, the else statement, is optional. If it's present, it executes when the result of condition is 0.

As I mentioned in the previous chapter, each clause in an if statement is itself a single statement. Although it may look like multiple statements, the body of an if statement like the one in Listing 6-2 is really a single compound statement.

```
if (a == 3) {
    a = a + 1;
    int b = a * 4;
    return a && b;
}
```

Listing 6-2: An if statement whose body is a compound statement

We haven't implemented compound statements yet, so at this point we can't compile code like Listing 6-2. Listing 6-3 gives an example of an if statement that we can compile.

```
if (a == 3)
    return a;
else
    b = 8;
```

Listing 6-3: An if statement that doesn't contain any compound statements

We can also compile if statements nested inside other if statements, like Listing 6-4.

```
if (a)
    if (a > 10)
        return a;
    else
        return 10 - a;
```

Listing 6-4: An if statement nested inside another if statement

Note that the AST definition in Listing 6-1 doesn't have an else if construct, because an if statement can have at most one else clause. An else if clause is really just an else clause that contains another if statement. Take Listing 6-5 as an example.

```
if (a > 100)
    return 0;
else if (a > 50)
    return 1;
else
    return 2;
```

Listing 6-5: An if statement nested inside an else clause

Let's reformat this in a way that better reflects how it will be parsed:

```
if (a > 100)
    return 0;
else
    if (a > 50)
        return 1;
    else
        return 2;
```

The AST for Listing 6-5 will look like this:

```
If(
    condition=Binary(GreaterThan, Var("a"), Constant(100)),
    then=Return(Constant(0)),
    else=If(
        condition=Binary(GreaterThan, Var("a"), Constant(50)),
        then=Return(Constant(1)),
        else=Return(Constant(2))
    )
)
```

Listing 6-6 shows the changes to the grammar, which exactly mirror the changes to the AST.

```
<statement> ::= "return" <exp> ";"
              | <exp> ";"
              | "if" "(" <exp> ")" <statement> [ "else" <statement> ]
              | ";"
```

Listing 6-6: The grammar rules for statements, including if statements

We can handle this new production rule with straightforward recursive descent parsing. Interestingly, this rule is ambiguous, but that ambiguity won't pose any problems for our parser. Let's take another look at Listing 6-4:

```
if (a)
    if (a > 10)
        return a;
    else
        return 10 - a;
```

There are two ways to parse this listing that both follow our new grammar rule: we could group the else clause with either the first or the second if statement. In other words, we could parse this listing like this:

```
if (a) {
    if (a > 10)
        return a;
    else
        return 10 - a;
}
```

Or we could parse it like this:

```
if (a) {
    if (a > 10)
        return a;
}
else
    return 10 - a;
```

The C standard clarifies that the first of these alternatives is correct; an else clause should always be grouped with the closest if statement. However, the grammar by itself doesn't tell us which of these options to choose. This quirk of the grammar is called the *dangling else* ambiguity, and it can cause problems for parser generators that automatically convert formal grammars into parsing code.

Luckily, the dangling else ambiguity isn't an issue for handwritten recursive descent parsers like ours. Whenever we parse an if statement, we'll look for an else keyword right after the statement body; if we find one, we'll go ahead and parse the else clause. In cases like Listing 6-4, this means that we'll end up parsing the else clause as part of the inner if statement, which is the correct behavior.

Go ahead and implement this production rule now; then, we'll move on to conditional expressions.

Parsing Conditional Expressions

The conditional : ? operator is a *ternary* operator, which takes three operands. In Listing 6-7, we add this operator to the exp AST node.

```
exp = Constant(int)
    | Var(identifier)
    | Unary(unary_operator, exp)
    | Binary(binary_operator, exp, exp)
    | Assignment(exp, exp)
    | Conditional(exp condition, exp, exp)
```

Listing 6-7: The definition for the exp AST node, including conditional expressions

In Listing 6-8, we add it to the <exp> grammar rule.

```
<exp> ::= <factor> | <exp> <binop> <exp> | <exp> "?" <exp> ":" <exp>
```

Listing 6-8: The grammar rule for expressions, including conditional expressions

Now we need to figure out its precedence and associativity. It's not immediately obvious how precedence and associativity work for a ternary expression. The trick is to think of it as a binary expression where the operator in the middle is "?" <exp> ":". The "operator" is easy to parse because it's delimited by ? and : tokens; it just happens to include an entire subexpression. (You should think of it this way only during parsing, not during later stages. We can *parse* this like a binary expression, but we'll *evaluate* it completely differently!) This lets us define the conditional operator's precedence relative to other binary operators: it has higher precedence than assignment and lower precedence than everything else. For example, the expression

```
a = 1 ? 2 : 3
```

is parsed as

```
a = (1 ? 2 : 3)
```

but

```
a || b ? 2 : 3
```

is parsed as:

```
(a || b) ? 2 : 3
```

The same logic applies for the third operand. We parse

```
1 ? 2 : 3 || 4
```

as

```
1 ? 2 : (3 || 4)
```

but we parse

```
1 ? 2 : a = 5
```

as:

```
(1 ? 2 : a) = 5
```

The semantic analysis pass will reject this last expression, since 1 ? 2 : a isn't a valid lvalue. However, any expression can appear between the ? and : tokens, even an assignment expression. Those tokens act like parentheses, delimiting where an expression starts and ends. So, the conditional expression

```
x ? x = 1 : 2
```

is equivalent to:

```
x ? (x = 1) : 2
```

The same logic applies when you nest one conditional expression inside another, meaning

```
a ? b ? 1 : 2 : 3
```

is parsed as:

```
a ? (b ? 1 : 2) : 3
```

Next, let's look at associativity. The conditional operator is right-associative, so

```
a ? 1 : b ? 2 : 3
```

is parsed as:

```
a ? 1 : (b ? 2 : 3)
```

Since conditional expressions can be parsed like weird binary expressions, we can (almost) handle them with our existing precedence climbing code. First, we'll add ? to our precedence table; Table 6-1 lists all our precedence values.

Table 6-1: Precedence Values of Binary and Ternary Operators

Operator	Precedence
*	50
/	50
%	50
+	45
-	45
<	35
<=	35
>	35
>=	35
==	30
!=	30
&&	10
||	5
?	3
=	1

We look at only the first token of the ? <exp> : "operator" during precedence climbing, so ? goes in the table but : doesn't.

Next, we'll update our precedence climbing code again. In the previous chapter, we handled assignment as a special case so we could use the Assignment AST node for it. Now we'll treat conditional expressions as a special case too. Listing 6-9 shows the updated precedence climbing pseudocode. Changes from the previous version of this algorithm, in Listing 5-8, are bolded.

```
parse_exp(tokens, min_prec):
    left = parse_factor(tokens)
    next_token = peek(tokens)
    while next_token is a binary operator and precedence(next_token) >= min_prec:
        if next_token is "=":
            take_token(tokens) // remove "=" from list of tokens
            right = parse_exp(tokens, precedence(next_token))
            left = Assignment(left, right)
        else if next_token is "?":
            middle = parse_conditional_middle(tokens)
            right = parse_exp(tokens, precedence(next_token))
            left = Conditional(left, middle, right)
        else:
            operator = parse_binop(tokens)
            right = parse_exp(tokens, precedence(next_token) + 1)
            left = Binary(operator, left, right)
        next_token = peek(tokens)
    return left
```

Listing 6-9: Precedence climbing with support for conditional expressions

The parse_conditional_middle function, which I haven't included code for here, should just consume the ? token, then parse an expression (with the minimum precedence reset to 0), then consume the : token. Next, we parse the third operand the same way we parse the right-hand side of any other expression: by calling parse_exp recursively. Since the conditional operator is right-associative, like assignment, we set the minimum precedence on the recursive call to precedence(next_token), not precedence(next_token) + 1. Finally, we construct a Conditional AST node from our three operands.

Listing 6-10 gives the complete AST definition, with the changes to support if statements and conditional expressions bolded. These are the same changes we introduced earlier in this section; I've pulled them all together here for easier reference.

```
program = Program(function_definition)
function_definition = Function(identifier name, block_item* body)
block_item = S(statement) | D(declaration)
declaration = Declaration(identifier name, exp? init)
statement = Return(exp)
          | Expression(exp)
          | If(exp condition, statement then, statement? else)
          | Null
exp = Constant(int)
    | Var(identifier)
    | Unary(unary_operator, exp)
```

```
            | Binary(binary_operator, exp, exp)
            | Assignment(exp, exp)
            | Conditional(exp condition, exp, exp)
unary_operator = Complement | Negate | Not
binary_operator = Add | Subtract | Multiply | Divide | Remainder | And | Or
               | Equal | NotEqual | LessThan | LessOrEqual
               | GreaterThan | GreaterOrEqual
```

Listing 6-10: The abstract syntax tree with conditional expressions and if statements

Listing 6-11 shows the corresponding changes to the grammar.

```
<program> ::= <function>
<function> ::= "int" <identifier> "(" "void" ")" "{" { <block-item> } "}"
<block-item> ::= <statement> | <declaration>
<declaration> ::= "int" <identifier> [ "=" <exp> ] ";"
<statement> ::= "return" <exp> ";"
              | <exp> ";"
              | "if" "(" <exp> ")" <statement> [ "else" <statement> ]
              | ";"
<exp> ::= <factor> | <exp> <binop> <exp> | <exp> "?" <exp> ":" <exp>
<factor> ::= <int> | <identifier> | <unop> <factor> | "(" <exp> ")"
<unop> ::= "-" | "~" | "!"
<binop> ::= "-" | "+" | "*" | "/" | "%" | "&&" | "||"
          | "==" | "!=" | "<" | "<=" | ">" | ">=" | "="
<identifier> ::= ? An identifier token ?
<int> ::= ? A constant token ?
```

Listing 6-11: The grammar with conditional expressions and if statements

Once you've implemented these changes, you're ready to test your parser.

TEST THE PARSER

Your parser should succeed on every test case in *tests/chapter_6/valid* and *tests/chapter_6/invalid_semantics* and fail on the test cases in *tests/chapter_6/invalid_parse*. To test the parser, run:

```
$ ./test_compiler /path/to/your_compiler --chapter 6 --stage parse
```

You may want to write additional tests to verify that your parser handles conditional expressions correctly.

Variable Resolution

The changes to this pass are minor. You'll extend resolve_statement and resolve_exp to handle the new constructs we added in this chapter, traversing their substatements and subexpressions. That will update variable names in if statements and conditional expressions in exactly the same way as variables that appear in other constructs.

TACKY Generation

We can implement if statements and conditional expressions with our existing TACKY instructions. We'll use the same basic approach here as for the short-circuiting && and || operators in Chapter 4: first we'll evaluate the controlling expression, then we'll use conditional jumps to go to the appropriate clause of the statement or expression. Let's implement if statements first.

Converting if Statements to TACKY

A statement of the form if (*<condition>*) then *<statement>* should translate to the TACKY in Listing 6-12.

```
<instructions for condition>
c = <result of condition>
JumpIfZero(c, end)
<instructions for statement>
Label(end)
```

Listing 6-12: The TACKY for an if statement

That's it! First, we evaluate the controlling expression, *<condition>*. If the result is 0, we jump to the end of the whole if statement. Otherwise, we execute the instructions for *<statement>*. If the statement also has an else clause, the resulting TACKY is only a tiny bit more complicated. The statement if (*<condition>*) then *<statement1>* else *<statement2>* translates to the TACKY in Listing 6-13.

```
<instructions for condition>
c = <result of condition>
JumpIfZero(c, else_label)
<instructions for statement1>
Jump(end)
```

```
Label(else_label)
<instructions for statement2>
Label(end)
```

Listing 6-13: The TACKY for an if statement with an else clause

Just like in Listing 6-12, we evaluate the controlling expression, then perform a conditional jump if the result is 0. But instead of jumping to the end of the if statement, in this case we jump to else_label, then execute <*statement2*>. If the controlling expression evaluates to a nonzero value, we execute <*statement1*>, then jump to the end of the entire statement. We can handle conditional expressions in a similar way; we'll look at those next.

Converting Conditional Expressions to TACKY

For conditional expressions, like short-circuiting expressions, the C standard provides guarantees about which subexpressions are executed and when. To evaluate the expression <*condition*> ? <*clause1*> : <*clause2*>, you have to evaluate <*condition*> first, then evaluate either <*clause1*> or <*clause2*>, depending on the result of <*condition*>. You can't, for example, evaluate both clauses, then evaluate <*condition*> to decide which result to use, since that might produce unexpected side effects. The upshot is that we'll handle conditional expressions very similarly to if statements. The only difference is that an expression, unlike a statement, produces a result that we need to store in the right destination. The expression <*condition*> ? <*e1*> : <*e2*> will produce the TACKY in Listing 6-14.

```
<instructions for condition>
c = <result of condition>
JumpIfZero(c, e2_label)
<instructions to calculate e1>
v1 = <result of e1>
result = v1
Jump(end)
Label(e2_label)
<instructions to calculate e2>
v2 = <result of e2>
result = v2
Label(end)
```

Listing 6-14: The TACKY for a conditional expression

This looks almost exactly like the TACKY in Listing 6-13. The only difference is that we end each clause by copying the result into the temporary result variable.

As usual, all the labels and temporary variable names you generate while handling if statements and conditional expressions should be unique. Once your TACKY generation stage is working, you'll be able to compile this chapter's test cases.

Extra Credit: Labeled Statements and goto

Now that you have some practice adding new kinds of statements, you have the option to implement goto, the statement everyone loves to hate. You'll also need to add support for labeled statements so that goto has somewhere to go to. You can implement these two statements without changing anything after the TACKY generation stage; however, you'll need to detect a few new error cases, like using the same label for two labeled statements in the same function. I recommend writing a new semantic analysis pass to catch these errors, rather than trying to catch them in the variable resolution stage.

To test out this feature, run the test script with the --goto flag:

```
$ ./test_compiler /path/to/your_compiler --chapter 6 --goto
```

If you've implemented the extra credit features in the previous chapters as well, you can test all of them at once by using the --extra-credit flag instead.

Summary

You've just implemented your first control structures! All your work in the early chapters is starting to pay off. The basic TACKY instructions you added to support && and || let you easily implement the more complex features in this chapter. You also built on the parsing techniques you learned earlier, extending your precedence climbing code to handle ternary operators. But the sorts of if statements you can compile are still very limited; you can't declare variables or execute longer blocks of code in an if statement body. In the next chapter, you'll remove those limitations by adding support for compound statements. The most exciting changes will be in the semantic analysis stage, where you'll learn how to deal with nested scopes.

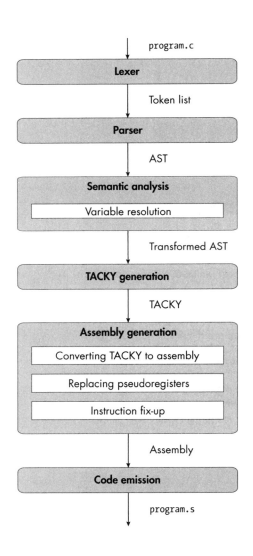

7

COMPOUND STATEMENTS

In this chapter, you'll implement compound statements. Compound statements serve two important purposes. As you saw in the two previous chapters, they group together other statements and declarations into a single unit that can appear in a larger construct, like an `if` statement. More interestingly, they also delineate the different *scopes* within a function. A variable's scope is the part of the program where that variable can be used; when you declare a variable inside a compound statement, its scope extends only to the end of that statement.

We'll spend a little time in this chapter extending the parser so we can group block items together, but our main task will be extending the variable resolution pass to keep track of each variable's scope. We'll barely change the TACKY generation stage, and we won't touch the lexer or the assembly generation stage at all. Before starting on the parser, I'll give a quick overview of how scoping works in C and define some terms that I'll use later in the chapter.

The Scoop on Scopes

A language construct that can contain declarations, and that determines the scope of those declarations, is called a *block*. Compound statements and function bodies are both blocks. So are loops, which we'll implement in Chapter 8. (Technically, if statements are too, but that doesn't matter for our implementation.) A local variable's scope begins at the point where that variable is declared. That means a variable's scope can begin in the middle of a block. Its scope extends until the end of the block in which it was declared. For example, in the program

```
int main(void) {
    int a ❶ = 5;
    return a;
❷ }
```

the variable a's scope begins right before its initializer ❶, and extends until the very end of the function ❷.

A compound statement can appear either on its own or inside another statement. In Listing 7-1, we use a compound statement as the body of an if statement.

```
int main(void) {
    if (1) {
        int a ❶ = 2;
        return a + 1;
  ❷ }
    return 0;
}
```

Listing 7-1: Using a compound statement as an if statement body

In this example, the variable a's scope runs from ❶ to the end of the compound statement ❷.

When you enter a new block, you can still use variables from the outer scope, as this code fragment illustrates:

```
int a = 2;
{
    int b = a + 2;
}
```

Although a is declared in the outer scope, we can refer to it when we initialize b in the inner scope. We therefore initialize b to 4. But let's see what happens in Listing 7-2, where we declare another variable named a inside the inner block.

```
❶ int a = 2;
  {
    ❷ int a = 3;
      int b = a + 2;
  }
```

Listing 7-2: Declaring two variables with the same name but different scopes

This time, when we initialize b, two different variables named a are in scope: the one declared in the outer scope ❶ and the one declared in the inner scope ❷. In cases like this, we always use the variable declared in the innermost scope. As a result, we initialize b to 5. Even though the outer a is still in scope, we can't access it; it's *hidden* (or *shadowed*) by the inner one.

Being hidden is different from being out of scope, because a hidden variable can become visible again later in the program. Listing 7-3, which is almost identical to Listing 7-2, illustrates this distinction.

```
❶ int a = 2;
  {
    ❷ int a = 3;
      int b = a + 2;
  }
❸ return a;
```

Listing 7-3: A hidden variable becoming visible again

As we saw in the previous example, the first declaration of a ❶ is hidden by the second declaration ❷. But the return statement ❸ comes after the end of the compound statement. At that point, the second a is no longer in scope, so the first one is visible again. We'll therefore use the first a in the return statement, returning 2.

What if we switched the order of the two statements in the inner block in Listing 7-2? Then we'd have:

```
int a = 2;
{
    int b = a + 2;
    int a = 3;
}
```

Now when we declare b, the inner a isn't in scope yet, so it doesn't hide the outer a. The expression a + 2 will refer to the first declaration of a, so we'll initialize b to 4.

You can have many layers of nested scopes, as Listing 7-4 demonstrates.

```
int main(void) {
  ❶ int x = 1;
    {
```

```
  ❷ int x = 2;
     if (x > 1) {
        ❸ x = 3;
        ❹ int x = 4;
     }
  ❺ return x;
  }
❻ return x;
}
```

Listing 7-4: Multiple nested scopes

In this listing, we declare three variables named x with three different scopes. We declare the first x at ❶ and the second at ❷. We assign the value 3 to the second x at ❸ and return it at ❺, so the whole program returns 3. The third variable named x, declared at ❹, is never used. We never reach the final return statement at ❻, but if we did, it would return 1, the value of the very first variable named x that was declared back at ❶.

We need to handle two error cases related to variable scope. (We covered both of these briefly in Chapter 5, but detecting them is a bit more complicated in programs with multiple scopes.) First, it's illegal to use a variable name if no variable with that name is in scope. Listing 7-5 illustrates this error.

```
int main(void) {
    {
        int x ❶ = 4;
  ❷ }
    return ❸ x;
    int x ❹ = 3;
❺ }
```

Listing 7-5: Using an undeclared variable

In this listing, we declare two different variables named x. The scope of the first declaration starts at ❶ and ends at ❷. The scope of the second declaration starts at ❹ and extends to the end of the function ❺. Neither of these declarations is in scope at ❸. It's an error to use the variable name x at that point, because that name doesn't refer to anything.

Second, you can't have multiple declarations of the same variable name with the same scope. We say that two variables have the same scope if their scopes end at exactly the same point; that is, if they're declared in the same block. For example, this code fragment is invalid:

```
int a = 3;
{
    int b = a;
    int b = 1;
}
```

The second declaration of b is illegal because it has the same scope as the first declaration.

Now that you understand the scoping rules you need to implement, let's start on the parser.

The Parser

A list of statements and declarations wrapped in braces can be either a function body or a compound statement. Let's define a block AST node to represent both constructs:

```
block = Block(block_item*)
```

Note that this AST node doesn't represent if statements and won't represent loops once we implement them in Chapter 8, even though they're technically also blocks.

Next, we'll extend the statement node to represent compound statements:

```
statement = Return(exp)
          | Expression(exp)
          | If(exp condition, statement then, statement? else)
          | Compound(block)
          | Null
```

And we'll change the function_definition node to use block too:

```
function_definition = Function(identifier name, block body)
```

Listing 7-6 gives the new AST definition with these changes bolded.

```
program = Program(function_definition)
function_definition = Function(identifier name, block body)
block_item = S(statement) | D(declaration)
block = Block(block_item*)
declaration = Declaration(identifier name, exp? init)
statement = Return(exp)
          | Expression(exp)
          | If(exp condition, statement then, statement? else)
          | Compound(block)
          | Null
exp = Constant(int)
    | Var(identifier)
    | Unary(unary_operator, exp)
    | Binary(binary_operator, exp, exp)
    | Assignment(exp, exp)
    | Conditional(exp condition, exp, exp)
unary_operator = Complement | Negate | Not
binary_operator = Add | Subtract | Multiply | Divide | Remainder | And | Or
                | Equal | NotEqual | LessThan | LessOrEqual
                | GreaterThan | GreaterOrEqual
```

Listing 7-6: The abstract syntax tree with compound statements

Listing 7-7 shows the corresponding changes to the grammar.

```
<program> ::= <function>
<function> ::= "int" <identifier> "(" "void" ")" <block>
<block> ::= "{" { <block-item> } "}"
<block-item> ::= <statement> | <declaration>
<declaration> ::= "int" <identifier> [ "=" <exp> ] ";"
<statement> ::= "return" <exp> ";"
             | <exp> ";"
             | "if" "(" <exp> ")" <statement> [ "else" <statement> ]
             | <block>
             | ";"
<exp> ::= <factor> | <exp> <binop> <exp> | <exp> "?" <exp> ":" <exp>
<factor> ::= <int> | <identifier> | <unop> <factor> | "(" <exp> ")"
<unop> ::= "-" | "~" | "!"
<binop> ::= "-" | "+" | "*" | "/" | "%" | "&&" | "||"
         | "==" | "!=" | "<" | "<=" | ">" | ">=" | "="
<identifier> ::= ? An identifier token ?
<int> ::= ? A constant token ?
```

Listing 7-7: The grammar with compound statements

Remember that the "{" and "}" in the definition of <block> are literal braces, and { and } indicate repetition. You can parse the updated grammar using the recursive descent techniques you're already familiar with. When you're parsing a <statement> symbol, a { token will tell you that you've hit a compound statement, just like the if keyword signals the beginning of an if statement and return signals the start of a return statement.

TEST THE PARSER

To test the parser, run:

```
$ ./test_compiler /path/to/your_compiler --chapter 7 --stage parse
```

Your parser should successfully parse every test program in *tests/chapter_7/ valid* and *tests/chapter_7/invalid_semantics*, and it should reject every test program in *tests/chapter_7/invalid_parse*.

Variable Resolution

Now we'll update the variable resolution pass to follow the scoping rules we talked about at the start of the chapter. Any local variables that share the same name in the original program will receive different names during this pass. In later passes, we won't have to think about scopes at all; because every variable will have a unique name, we can convert each variable in the AST to a TACKY variable, then a pseudoregister, and finally a memory address, exactly as we've done in earlier chapters, without worrying about which object each name refers to.

Resolving Variables in Multiple Scopes

As an example, let's take another look at the program from Listing 7-4:

```
int main(void) {
    int x = 1;
    {
        int x = 2;
        if (x > 1) {
            x = 3;
            int x = 4;
        }
        return x;
    }
    return x;
}
```

Listing 7-8 shows how this program looks after variable resolution.

```
int main(void) {
    int x0 = 1;
    {
        int x1 = 2;
        if (x1 > 1) {
            x1 = 3;
            int x2 = 4;
        }
        return x1;
    }
    return x0;
}
```

Listing 7-8: The program from Listing 7-4 after variable resolution

Now every variable has a different name. These new names make explicit which variable we're using at every point. For example, it's now clear that the variable declared at the start of the function (which we've renamed to x0) is used only once, at the very end.

Our basic approach to variable resolution is the same as in earlier chapters. We'll traverse the AST, maintaining a map from user-defined names to generated names as we go. But now our new scoping rules will dictate how we update this map. Table 7-1 shows how the variable map will look at each point in Listing 7-4.

Table 7-1: The Variable Map Throughout Listing 7-4

`int main(void) {`	(empty map)
`int x = 1;` `{`	x → x0

`int x = 2;`
       `if ( x > 1 ) {`
          `x = 3;`
	x → x1

`int x = 4;` `}`	x → x2
`return x;` `}`	x → x1
`return x;`	x → x0
`}`	

The state of the variable map changes in two cases. First, when a new variable is declared, we add it to the map, overwriting any existing variable with the same name. Second, when we exit a block, we revert to the same variable map we had before entering that block.

The first case is already familiar: whenever we encounter a variable declaration, we'll add a map entry. To handle the second case, we'll make a copy of the variable map whenever we enter a new block. As we process that block, we'll add new entries to that copy of the map, leaving the variable map for the outer scope unchanged.

Now that you have a basic idea of how this pass will work, let's walk through the pseudocode.

Updating the Variable Resolution Pseudocode

First, let's process declarations. In earlier chapters, the compiler would fail if it ever saw two declarations of the same variable name:

```
resolve_declaration(Declaration(name, init), variable_map):
    if name is in variable_map:
        fail("Duplicate variable declaration!")
    --snip--
```

But now things are a little more complicated. It's legal to reuse the same variable name in multiple declarations. However, it's illegal to declare the same variable name more than once *in the same block*. To enforce this rule, we'll track two facts about each entry in the variable map: its new auto-generated name and whether it was declared in the current block. Listing 7-9 gives the updated pseudocode to handle a declaration. Changes from the previous version of this pseudocode, in Listing 5-9, are bolded.

```
resolve_declaration(Declaration(name, init), variable_map):
    if name is in variable_map and variable_map.get(name).from_current_block:
        fail("Duplicate variable declaration!")
    unique_name = make_temporary()
    variable_map.add(name, MapEntry(new_name=unique_name, from_current_block=True))
```

```
if init is not null:
    init = resolve_exp(init, variable_map)
return Declaration(unique_name, init)
```

Listing 7-9: Resolving a variable declaration

Next, we need a function that can process block items in order (I'll call this resolve_block in later pseudocode listings). You've already written this code to process function bodies; now you just need to refactor it so you can reuse it to process compound statements too. Remember that changes you make while processing one block item (specifically, a declaration) must be visible when you process later block items.

We'll also update resolve_statement to handle compound statements. Listing 7-10 gives the updated pseudocode for resolve_statement, with changes from the previous version in Listing 5-10 bolded. The important detail here is that we'll pass a *copy* of the variable map when we traverse the compound statement, so any declarations we process inside the compound statement won't be visible outside of it.

```
resolve_statement(statement, variable_map):
    match statement with
    | Return(e) -> return Return(resolve_exp(e, variable_map))
    | Expression(e) -> return Expression(resolve_exp(e, variable_map))
    | Compound(block) ->
        new_variable_map = copy_variable_map(variable_map)
        return Compound(resolve_block(block, new_variable_map))
    | --snip--
```

Listing 7-10: Resolving compound statements

Finally, we'll implement copy_variable_map. This should create a copy of the variable map with the from_current_block flag set to False for every entry. That way, we won't throw an error when we process declarations in the inner scope that hide declarations from the outer scope.

Once you've made those changes, your variable resolution pass will be able to handle nested scopes!

TEST THE VARIABLE RESOLUTION PASS

The variable resolution pass should accept every test case in *tests/chapter_7/valid* and reject every test case in *tests/chapter_7/invalid_semantics*. To test it out, run:

```
$ ./test_compiler /path/to/your_compiler --chapter 7 --stage validate
```

You might also want to write your own tests to make sure variables are renamed consistently.

TACKY Generation

The last step is extending the TACKY generation stage to handle compound statements. It's pretty straightforward: to convert a compound statement to TACKY, just convert each block item inside it to TACKY. Basically, you should handle compound statements exactly like you're already handling function bodies. You don't need to touch later compiler stages at all; once you have TACKY generation working, you're done with the chapter!

TEST THE WHOLE COMPILER

To test out the whole compiler, run:

```
$ ./test_compiler /path/to/your_compiler --chapter 7
```

Summary

In this chapter, you implemented a new kind of statement by extending just a few stages in your compiler. You wrote a more sophisticated variable resolution pass that correctly resolves variables in multiple scopes, dramatically expanding the set of programs you can compile. Next, you'll implement loops, break statements, and continue statements. The work you did in this chapter will be especially important when you add support for for loops, since a single for loop contains two distinct scopes.

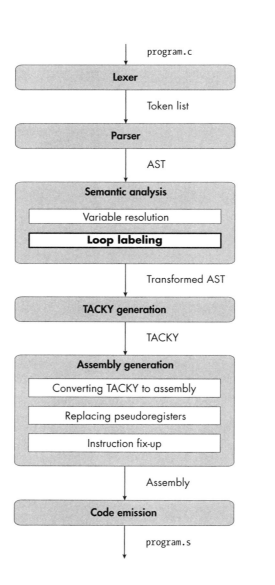

```
                              program.c
              ┌──────────────────────────────────┐
              │              Lexer                │
              └──────────────────────────────────┘
                              Token list
              ┌──────────────────────────────────┐
              │              Parser               │
              └──────────────────────────────────┘
                              AST
              ┌──────────────────────────────────┐
              │         Semantic analysis         │
              │  ┌────────────────────────────┐   │
              │  │    Variable resolution      │   │
              │  └────────────────────────────┘   │
              │  ┌────────────────────────────┐   │
              │  │      Loop labeling          │   │
              │  └────────────────────────────┘   │
              └──────────────────────────────────┘
                              Transformed AST
              ┌──────────────────────────────────┐
              │         TACKY generation          │
              └──────────────────────────────────┘
                              TACKY
              ┌──────────────────────────────────┐
              │        Assembly generation        │
              │  ┌────────────────────────────┐   │
              │  │  Converting TACKY to assembly│  │
              │  └────────────────────────────┘   │
              │  ┌────────────────────────────┐   │
              │  │   Replacing pseudoregisters │   │
              │  └────────────────────────────┘   │
              │  ┌────────────────────────────┐   │
              │  │     Instruction fix-up      │   │
              │  └────────────────────────────┘   │
              └──────────────────────────────────┘
                              Assembly
              ┌──────────────────────────────────┐
              │          Code emission            │
              └──────────────────────────────────┘
                              program.s
```

8

LOOPS

In this chapter, you'll add all things loop-related. That includes `for`, `while`, and `do` loops, plus `break` and `continue` statements to skip over parts of a loop. These are the last statements you'll implement in this book. Once you finish this chapter, if you've implemented all the extra credit features, your compiler will be able to handle *every* kind of C statement.

But you have work to do first! You'll update the lexer and parser to support all five new statements. Then, you'll add a new semantic analysis pass, which we'll call *loop labeling*. This new pass, which is bolded in the diagram at the start of the chapter, will annotate the AST to associate every `break` or `continue` statement with the loop that contains it. Finally, you'll translate every new statement into a sequence of TACKY instructions. You can implement all the new statements using the TACKY instructions you've already defined, so you won't change any stages after TACKY generation.

The new statements in this chapter introduce a few edge cases and errors we'll need to handle. We'll briefly discuss each of these statements before we start on the lexer.

Loops and How to Escape Them

Let's first look at the three kinds of loop statements, then consider the break and continue statements. Listing 8-1 shows an example of a while loop.

```
while (❶ a > 0)
    a = a / 2;
```

Listing 8-1: A while loop

First, we evaluate the statement's *controlling expression* ❶. If it's 0 (that is, false), the loop ends and we move on to the next statement. If it's nonzero, we execute the while loop body, then go back to the controlling expression, rinse, and repeat.

A do loop, like the one in Listing 8-2, is almost exactly the same.

```
do
    a = a + 1;
while (a < 100);
```

Listing 8-2: A do loop

The only difference is that we execute the loop body first, *then* check the controlling expression. That means the loop body will be executed at least once. Like an if statement body, a loop body is a single statement, which can be a compound statement that contains declarations. Any variables you declare in the loop body will not be in scope in the controlling expression. For example, Listing 8-3 is invalid.

```
do {
    int a = a + 1;
} while (a < 100);
```

Listing 8-3: A do loop where the controlling expression uses an out-of-scope variable

Things start to get more complicated with for loops. These come in two different flavors. In the first, shown in Listing 8-4, the loop header consists of three expressions.

```
int a;
for (❶ a = 0; ❷ a < 5; ❸ a = a + 1)
    b = b * 2;
```

Listing 8-4: A for loop where the initial clause is an expression

The initial expression ❶ is evaluated once before the first loop iteration. Then, on each iteration, we:

1. Evaluate the controlling expression ❷. If it's false, the loop terminates. Otherwise, we . . .
2. Execute the statement body.
3. Evaluate the final expression ❸.

You can omit any or all of the expressions in the loop header. If you omit the initial expression or the final expression, nothing happens when that clause would normally be evaluated. If you omit the controlling expression, the loop behaves as though its controlling expression is always true (that is, nonzero). That means it will never terminate, unless it contains a break, goto, or return statement that transfers control out of the loop body.

Listing 8-5 shows the second kind of for loop, in which the initial clause is a declaration rather than an expression.

```
for (int a = 0; a < 5; a = a + 1)
    b = b * 2;
```

Listing 8-5: A for loop with a declaration in the initial clause

The for loop header introduces a new scope, so you can write code like Listing 8-6.

```
int a = 5;
for (int a = 0; a < 5; a = a + 1)
    b = b + a;
```

Listing 8-6: Declaring two variables with the same name before a for loop and in the loop header

In this listing, the variable a declared in the header hides the variable a declared on the previous line. And since a compound statement always introduces a new scope, including when it appears as a loop body, Listing 8-7 is also valid.

```
❶ int a = 5;
for (❷ int a = 0; a < 5; a = a + 1) {
    ❸ int a = 1;
        b = b + a;
}
```

Listing 8-7: Declaring three variables with the same name before a for loop, in the loop header, and in the loop body

In Listing 8-7, there are three distinct variables named a: one declared before the start of the loop ❶, one declared in the loop header ❷, and one declared in the loop body ❸.

Although the expressions in a for loop header are optional, the loop body is required. (It's required for do and while loops too.) A loop body can, however, be a null statement, like in Listing 8-8.

```
while ((a = a + 1) < 10)
    ;
```

Listing 8-8: Using a null statement as a loop body

The lone ; here is a null statement. Even though this statement doesn't do anything, we need to include it so the parser can figure out where the loop ends. As we saw when we implemented them in Chapter 5, null statements aren't a loop-specific construct; you can use them anywhere you can use any other kind of statement. In practice, though, they mostly appear in loop bodies because they're rarely useful anywhere else.

Now let's talk about break and continue statements. Both can appear only inside loops. (Actually, that's not entirely true; a break statement can also appear inside a switch statement, which you can implement as an extra credit feature in this chapter.) A break statement, like the one in Listing 8-9, jumps to the point just after the end of the loop.

```
while (1) {
    a = a - 1;
    if (a < 0)
        break;
}
return a;
```

Listing 8-9: A break statement

When we hit this break statement, we'll jump to the return statement after the while loop.

A break statement terminates only the innermost loop. For example, consider the code snippet in Listing 8-10.

```
while (b > 0) {
    do {
        a = a - 1;
        if (a < 0)
            break;
    } while (1);
    b = b * a;
}
return b;
```

Listing 8-10: Using a break statement to break out of the inner of two nested loops

When we reach the break statement in this listing, we'll break out of the inner loop, but not the outer loop, so we'll jump to b = b * a;. Throughout this chapter, I'll call the innermost loop that contains a break or continue statement its *enclosing loop*. (Calling this the "smallest enclosing loop" would be more in line with the terminology in the C standard, but that's a bit of a mouthful.)

A continue statement jumps to the point just after the last statement in the body of the enclosing loop. Consider the example in Listing 8-11.

```
while (a > 0) {
    a = a * b;
    if (b > 0)
        continue;
    b = b + 1;
    return b;
❶ }
```

Listing 8-11: A continue statement

When we reach the continue statement, we skip over all the statements that follow it and jump to the end of the loop body ❶. From there, the while loop executes as usual, which means it jumps back to the controlling expression. A continue statement in a for loop, like the one in Listing 8-12, works the same way.

```
for (int i = 0; i < 5; ❶ i = i + 1) {
    a = a * i;
    if (b > 0)
        continue;
    b = b + 1;
❷ }
```

Listing 8-12: A continue statement inside a for loop

In this listing, we still jump from the continue statement to the end of the loop body ❷. Then, we jump to the final expression ❶, as usual.

If a break or continue statement appears outside of a loop, like in Listing 8-13, compilation should fail.

```
int main(void) {
    break;
}
```

Listing 8-13: An invalid break statement

It's perfectly fine, however, for one of these statements to appear nested deep inside a loop, like the break statement in Listing 8-14.

```
while (1) {
    if (a > 4) {
        b = b * 2;
        return a + b;
    } else {
        int c = a ? b : 5;
        {
            int d = c;
            break;
        }
```

```
    }
    return 0;
}
return 1;
```

Listing 8-14: A break statement appearing a few layers deep inside a loop

This break statement jumps to return 1; because that's the point right after the end of the loop.

It's legal to have multiple break and continue statements in one loop, like in Listing 8-15.

```
for (int i = 0; i < 10; i = i + 1) {
    if (i % 2 == 0)
        continue;
    if (x > y)
        continue;
    break;
}
```

Listing 8-15: Multiple break and continue statements inside a loop

Now that we've covered the key things you need to know about the statements we'll add in this chapter, we can get started on implementing them. The first step, as usual, is updating the lexer.

The Lexer

You'll add five keywords in this chapter:

do

while

for

break

continue

You won't need any other new tokens.

TEST THE LEXER

To test out your lexer, run:

```
$ ./test_compiler /path/to/your_compiler --chapter 8 --stage lex
```

Lexing should succeed for every test case in this chapter.

The Parser

Next, we'll update the AST. We'll add five new statements:

```
statement = Return(exp)
          | Expression(exp)
          | If(exp condition, statement then, statement? else)
          | Compound(block)
          | Break
          | Continue
          | While(exp condition, statement body)
          | DoWhile(statement body, exp condition)
          | For(for_init init, exp? condition, exp? post, statement body)
          | Null
```

The break and continue statements are as simple as it gets. The while and do statements are also relatively simple; both have a body and a controlling expression. The for statement is the most complex: it includes an initial clause, an optional controlling expression, an optional final expression, and a body. The initial clause can be a declaration, an expression, or nothing, so we need a new AST node to describe it:

```
for_init = InitDecl(declaration) | InitExp(exp?)
```

Putting it all together gives us the latest AST definition, shown in Listing 8-16.

```
program = Program(function_definition)
function_definition = Function(identifier name, block body)
block_item = S(statement) | D(declaration)
block = Block(block_item*)
declaration = Declaration(identifier name, exp? init)
for_init = InitDecl(declaration) | InitExp(exp?)
statement = Return(exp)
          | Expression(exp)
          | If(exp condition, statement then, statement? else)
          | Compound(block)
          | Break
          | Continue
          | While(exp condition, statement body)
          | DoWhile(statement body, exp condition)
          | For(for_init init, exp? condition, exp? post, statement body)
          | Null
exp = Constant(int)
    | Var(identifier)
    | Unary(unary_operator, exp)
    | Binary(binary_operator, exp, exp)
    | Assignment(exp, exp)
    | Conditional(exp condition, exp, exp)
unary_operator = Complement | Negate | Not
```

```
binary_operator = Add | Subtract | Multiply | Divide | Remainder | And | Or
                | Equal | NotEqual | LessThan | LessOrEqual
                | GreaterThan | GreaterOrEqual
```

Listing 8-16: The abstract syntax tree with loops and break and continue statements

Updating the AST in this chapter involves one complication. The loop labeling pass will annotate every break, continue, and loop statement in the program with a label (we'll use these labels to associate each break and continue statement with its enclosing loop). That means you'll need some way to attach these labels to the new statements in the AST. There are a few different options. One is to include a label argument for each new constructor, like this:

```
statement = --snip--
          | Break(identifier label)
          | Continue(identifier label)
          | While(exp condition, statement body, identifier label)
          | DoWhile(statement body, exp condition, identifier label)
          | For(for_init init, exp? condition, exp? post, statement body, identifier label)
```

If you go with this option, you may need to use dummy labels during parsing, then replace them with real labels in the loop labeling pass. Another option is to define two AST data structures: one without annotations to use before loop labeling and one with annotations to use afterward. The right approach depends on what language you're writing your compiler in (and on your personal taste).

After updating the AST, we'll make the corresponding changes to the grammar, as shown in Listing 8-17.

```
<program> ::= <function>
<function> ::= "int" <identifier> "(" "void" ")" <block>
<block> ::= "{" { <block-item> } "}"
<block-item> ::= <statement> | <declaration>
<declaration> ::= "int" <identifier> [ "=" <exp> ] ";"
<for-init> ::= <declaration> | [ <exp> ] ";"
<statement> ::= "return" <exp> ";"
              | <exp> ";"
              | "if" "(" <exp> ")" <statement> [ "else" <statement> ]
              | <block>
              | "break" ";"
              | "continue" ";"
              | "while" "(" <exp> ")" <statement>
              | "do" <statement> "while" "(" <exp> ")" ";"
              | "for" "(" <for-init> [ <exp> ] ";" [ <exp> ] ")" <statement>
              | ";"
<exp> ::= <factor> | <exp> <binop> <exp> | <exp> "?" <exp> ":" <exp>
<factor> ::= <int> | <identifier> | <unop> <factor> | "(" <exp> ")"
<unop> ::= "-" | "~" | "!"
<binop> ::= "-" | "+" | "*" | "/" | "%" | "&&" | "||"
          | "==" | "!=" | "<" | "<=" | ">" | ">=" | "="
```

```
<identifier> ::= ? An identifier token ?
<int> ::= ? A constant token ?
```

Listing 8-17: The grammar with loops and break and continue statements

I recommend writing a helper function to parse optional expressions. You can use this helper function to parse the two optional expressions in a for loop header, plus expression statements and null statements. The helper function should let you specify which token marks the end of the optional expression; most of the optional expressions in the grammar are followed by a semicolon, but the third clause in a for loop header is followed by a closing parenthesis.

TEST THE PARSER

To test your parser, run:

```
$ ./test_compiler /path/to/your_compiler --chapter 8 --stage parse
```

Your parser should successfully parse every test program in *tests/chapter_8/ valid* and *tests/chapter_8/invalid_semantics*, and it should raise an error for every test program in *tests/chapter_8/invalid_parse*.

Semantic Analysis

The semantic analysis stage of your compiler currently performs one task: it resolves variable names. In this chapter, it will take on a completely new task: loop labeling. The loop labeling pass associates each break and continue statement with its enclosing loop. More concretely, this pass assigns every loop statement a unique ID and annotates each break and continue statement with the ID of its enclosing loop. If it finds a break or continue statement outside of a loop, it will throw an error. During TACKY generation, we'll use these annotations to convert each break and continue statement into a jump to the correct spot relative to its enclosing loop.

We'll resolve variable names and label loops in two separate passes, traversing the whole program each time. Let's start by extending the variable resolution pass to handle this chapter's new statements; then we'll implement the loop labeling pass.

Extending Variable Resolution

You'll need to extend resolve_statement to traverse the five new statements you added in this chapter. You'll treat while and do loops just like if statements, processing every substatement and subexpression recursively.

Resolving break and continue statements is even simpler; since they don't have any substatements or subexpressions, you don't have to do anything.

Resolving a for loop is a tiny bit more complicated because the loop header introduces a new variable scope. Listing 8-18 demonstrates how to handle for loops in resolve_statement.

```
resolve_statement(statement, variable_map):
    match statement with
    | --snip--
    | For(init, condition, post, body) ->
        new_variable_map = copy_variable_map(variable_map)
        init = resolve_for_init(init, new_variable_map)
        condition = resolve_optional_exp(condition, new_variable_map)
        post = resolve_optional_exp(post, new_variable_map)
        body = resolve_statement(body, new_variable_map)
        return For(init, condition, post, body)
```

Listing 8-18: Resolving a for loop

We start by making a new copy of the variable map, just like we do at the beginning of a compound statement. Copying the map ensures that a variable declared in the loop header won't be visible outside of the loop and that it won't trigger a compiler error if it hides a variable from the outer scope.

Next, we process the initial clause with resolve_for_init, which we'll look at in a moment. We then traverse the for loop's controlling expression, final expression, and body, all using the new variable map. I won't provide pseudocode for resolve_optional_exp, which handles the optional controlling expression and final expression; it just calls resolve_exp if the expression is present and does nothing if it's absent.

Listing 8-19 shows the pseudocode for resolve_for_init.

```
resolve_for_init(init, variable_map):
    match init with
    | InitExp(e) -> return InitExp(resolve_optional_exp(e, variable_map))
    | InitDecl(d) -> return InitDecl(resolve_declaration(d, variable_map))
```

Listing 8-19: Resolving the initial clause of a for loop

We resolve an expression or declaration in the initial clause exactly the same way we would resolve it if it appeared elsewhere in the program. If the clause is a declaration, calling resolve_declaration will add the newly declared variable to the variable map so it's visible throughout the rest of the loop.

Loop Labeling

After resolving variables, we'll traverse the program again, labeling each loop, break, and continue statement with an ID. Whenever we encounter a loop statement, we'll generate a unique ID for it. Then, when we traverse the loop body, we'll attach that same ID to any break and continue statements we encounter. Let's look at a few examples. In the next three listings, the markers ❶ and ❷ represent IDs attached to the AST. Although the loop labeling pass annotates the AST rather than source files, these listings are presented as source code for the sake of readability.

Listing 8-20 illustrates how we'll annotate a code fragment that contains two loops in succession.

```
❶ while (1) {
       a = a - 1;
       if (a < 0)
         ❶ break;
   }

❷ for (int b = 0; b < 100; b = b + 1) {
       if (b % 2 == 0)
         ❷ continue;
       a = a * b;
   }
   return a;
```

Listing 8-20: Annotating break and continue statements and their enclosing loops

Each of the two loops in this listing gets its own ID. We annotate the while loop with ID ❶ and the for loop with ID ❷. Each break or continue statement is annotated with the ID of its enclosing loop, so we annotate the break statement with ID ❶ and the continue statement with ID ❷.

If several break or continue statements are in the same enclosing loop, they're all annotated with the same ID, as Listing 8-21 demonstrates.

```
❶ for (int i = 0; i < 10; i = i + 1) {
       if (i % 2 == 0)
         ❶ continue;
       if (x > y)
         ❶ continue;
     ❶ break;
   }
```

Listing 8-21: Annotating multiple break and continue statements in the same loop

Since the for loop labeled ❶ is the enclosing loop of the two continue statements and the break statement, we annotate all three of those statements with ID ❶.

If a break or continue statement appears inside nested loops, we annotate it with the ID of its enclosing loop, which is the innermost loop. Listing 8-22 illustrates how to annotate nested loops.

```
❶ while (a > 0) {
     ❷ for (int i = 0; i < 10; i = i + 1) {
           if (i % 2 == 0)
             ❷ continue;
           a = a / 2;
       }
```

```
    if (a == b)
      ❶ break;
}
```

Listing 8-22: Annotating nested loops

The outer while loop and inner for loop are labeled ❶ and ❷, respectively. Since the continue statement appears in the inner loop, we annotate it with ID ❷. The break statement is in the outer loop, so we annotate it with ID ❶.

Implementing Loop Labeling

To implement this compiler pass, we pass the current loop ID along as an argument when we traverse the AST, much like we pass the variable map as an argument to resolve_statement, resolve_exp, and so on during the variable resolution pass. When we're outside of a loop, the current ID is null, or None, or whatever your implementation language uses to indicate an absent value. When we hit a loop statement, we generate a new ID and annotate the statement with it. We then pass it along as the current ID when we traverse the loop body. When we hit a break or continue statement, we annotate it with the ID that was passed to us. The pseudocode in Listing 8-23 illustrates how to annotate statements with loop IDs.

```
label_statement(statement, current_label):
    match statement with
    | Break ->
        if current_label is null:
            fail("break statement outside of loop")
        return ❶ annotate(Break, current_label)
    | Continue ->
        if current_label is null:
            fail("continue statement outside of loop")
        return ❷ annotate(Continue, current_label)
    | While(condition, body) ->
        new_label = ❸ make_label()
        labeled_body = label_statement(body, new_label)
        labeled_statement = While(condition, labeled_body)
        return ❹ annotate(labeled_statement, new_label)
    | --snip--
```

Listing 8-23: The loop annotation algorithm

The make_label helper function ❸ generates unique loop IDs; you can use the same helper function here that you use to generate unique labels in TACKY. The annotate helper function takes a statement AST node and a label and returns a copy of that AST node annotated with that label. Here, we use it to annotate the Break ❶, Continue ❷, and While ❹ statements. I haven't provided the definition of annotate because it will depend on how exactly you represent loop annotations in your AST. I've also omitted the pseudocode to handle DoWhile, For, and all the statements we added in earlier chapters. You can process DoWhile and For essentially the same way as While. To process any other kind of statement, call `label_statement` recursively for every substatement, passing along the same value of `current_label`.

Once you've updated the loop labeling pass, you're ready to test out the whole semantic analysis stage.

TACKY Generation

Next, we'll convert each new statement to TACKY. We won't change the TACKY IR in this chapter, because we can implement these statements with our existing TACKY instructions.

break and continue Statements

A break statement unconditionally jumps to some other point in the program, so we implement it with a single `Jump` instruction. The same is true for continue statements. The only question is where to jump to. The loop annotations we added in the last section help us answer that question.

Whenever we convert a loop statement to TACKY, we'll emit a `Label` right after the instructions for the loop body. Any continue statement in that loop can be implemented as a jump to that label, which I'll call the *continue label*. We'll emit another `Label` as the final instruction for the whole loop; I'll call this the *break label*.

We'll derive these labels from the IDs we added during the loop annotation pass. For example, if a loop is labeled `loop0`, its break and continue labels might be `break_loop0` and `continue_loop0`. Using this example naming scheme, we'd convert a `Break` AST node annotated with ID `loop0` to the following TACKY instruction:

```
Jump("break_loop0")
```

We'd convert a Continue node with the same annotation to:

```
Jump("continue_loop0")
```

You don't need to use this particular naming scheme (although your naming scheme must guarantee that these labels won't conflict with any other labels in the TACKY program). The important point is that you can derive the same label when you convert a break or continue statement to TACKY as when you convert its enclosing loop to TACKY, because that statement and its enclosing loop are annotated with the same ID.

do Loops

We can execute the statement do <*body*> while (<*condition*>); in three steps. First, we execute the loop body. Then, we evaluate the condition and compare the result to zero. Finally, if the result was not zero, we jump back to the beginning of the loop. Listing 8-24 demonstrates how to implement these steps in TACKY.

```
Label(start)
<instructions for body>
<instructions for condition>
v = <result of condition>
JumpIfNotZero(v, start)
```

Listing 8-24: The TACKY instructions for a do loop

We also need break and continue labels. The continue label goes between the body and the condition, and the break label goes at the very end, after JumpIfNotZero. Adding both of these labels gives us the complete TACKY for a do loop, as shown in Listing 8-25.

```
Label(start)
<instructions for body>
Label(continue_label)
<instructions for condition>
v = <result of condition>
JumpIfNotZero(v, start)
Label(break_label)
```

Listing 8-25: The TACKY instructions for a do loop, with break and continue labels

Now any continue statements in the loop body will jump to the continue label, and any break statements will jump to the break label. These labels are necessary only if a break or continue statement shows up somewhere in the loop body—otherwise, they won't be used—but to keep things simple, we'll always emit them. That way, we don't need to figure out whether a loop contains break or continue statements.

while Loops

We'll handle while loops similarly to do loops, but in this case we'll execute
the condition before the loop body, then use JumpIfZero to exit the loop
if the condition is false. We can convert the statement while (*<condition>*)
<body> to the TACKY in Listing 8-26.

```
Label(start)
<instructions for condition>
v = <result of condition>
JumpIfZero(v, end)
<instructions for body>
❶ Jump(start)
Label(end)
```

Listing 8-26: The TACKY instructions for a while loop

Now let's figure out where to put the break and continue labels. This
time, we don't need extra Label instructions; we can reuse the Label instructions that are already present in Listing 8-26. We'll put the break label
in the Label instruction at the end of this listing. It will be the target for
both the JumpIfZero instruction and any break statements in the loop body.

Likewise, we'll put the continue label in the Label instruction at the
start of this listing. This has the same effect as putting the continue label
just after the end of the loop body ❶, because the instruction after the loop
body is an unconditional jump that immediately takes us back to the start
of the loop. Having continue statements jump directly to the start of the
loop lets them bypass that Jump instruction, which makes them a little bit
more efficient.

Listing 8-27 shows where to use the break and continue labels when we
convert while loops to TACKY.

```
Label(continue_label)
<instructions for condition>
v = <result of condition>
JumpIfZero(v, break_label)
<instructions for body>
Jump(continue_label)
Label(break_label)
```

Listing 8-27: The TACKY instructions for a while loop, with break and continue labels

This TACKY is identical to Listing 8-26, except that it uses continue_label
and break_label instead of start and end.

for Loops

Our final task is to convert for loops to TACKY. We'll convert the statement
for (*<init>* ; *<condition>* ; *<post>*) *<body>* into the TACKY in Listing 8-28,
which includes the break and continue labels.

```
<instructions for init>
Label(start)
<instructions for condition>
v = <result of condition>
JumpIfZero(v, break_label)
<instructions for body>
Label(continue_label)
<instructions for post>
Jump(start)
Label(break_label)
```

Listing 8-28: The TACKY instructions for a for loop

First, we execute <init>. Then, we execute the controlling expression, <condition>, and check whether the result is zero. If it is, we jump to Label(break_label) at the very end, without executing the loop body or the final expression. Otherwise, we execute the loop body followed by the final expression, <post>, then jump back to Label(start) and start another loop iteration. We won't execute <init> again, since Label(start) comes after <init>. Note that the continue label appears at the end of the loop body, just before <post>, and the break label appears at the very end of the loop, where it does double duty as the target of the JumpIfZero instruction and any break statements.

Next, let's break down how to handle each of the three clauses in the loop header. The first clause can be an expression, a declaration, or nothing. If it's a declaration or expression, we'll handle it the same way as a declaration or expression outside of a for loop. If it's absent, we won't emit any instructions.

The second clause is the controlling expression. If this expression is present, we'll convert it to TACKY exactly like the controlling expressions in while and do loops. If it's absent, the C standard says that this expression is "replaced by a nonzero constant" (section 6.8.5.3, paragraph 2). We could just use a nonzero constant in the conditional jump:

```
JumpIfZero(Const(1), break_label)
```

But this instruction doesn't do anything; Const(1) will never equal zero, so we'll never jump. Instead, we'll leave out the JumpIfZero instruction entirely, since that's a more efficient way to produce the same behavior.

Finally, we need to handle the third clause, <post>. If it's present, we'll convert it to TACKY; if it's absent, we won't emit any instructions.

TEST THE WHOLE COMPILER

Now you're ready to test out your whole compiler. To compile and execute this chapter's test cases, run:

```
$ ./test_compiler /path/to/your_compiler --chapter 8
```

Extra Credit: switch Statements

You have the option of implementing switch, case, and default statements in this chapter. To support these statements, you'll need to make significant changes to the semantic analysis stage. First, you'll need to change the loop annotation pass, because break statements can break out of switch statements as well as loops. You can't, however, use a continue statement inside a switch statement, so this pass will need to treat continue statements differently from break statements.

You'll need additional analysis, probably in a separate compiler pass, to collect the cases that appear inside each switch statement. To generate the TACKY for a switch statement, you'll need a list of all the cases in that statement. However, that information isn't immediately available in the AST. The cases in a switch statement may be nested several layers deep, or the switch statement body may not include any cases at all. You'll need to attach that information to the AST in a more usable form.

Use the --switch flag to enable the tests for switch statements:

```
$ ./test_compiler /path/to/your_compiler --chapter 8 --switch
```

Or enable every extra credit test with the --extra-credit flag, as usual.

Summary

In this chapter, you implemented your last set of control-flow statements. You added support for three different loop statements, plus break and continue statements. You implemented a new semantic analysis pass to associate break and continue statements with their enclosing loops, and you saw how to convert each of these complex structures into a list of TACKY instructions.

Although we're done with control-flow *statements*, you'll add support for one more control-flow *expression* in the next chapter: function calls. You'll learn about the calling conventions that dictate how function calls work in assembly and write a simple type checker. Best of all, you'll end the chapter by compiling "Hello, World!"

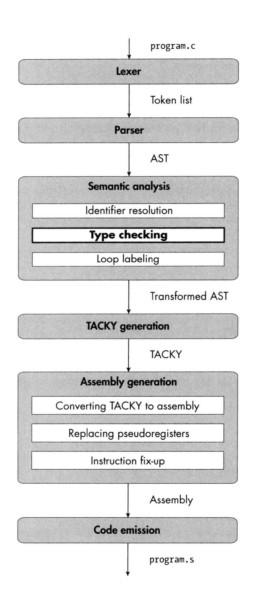

program.c

Lexer

Token list

Parser

AST

Semantic analysis

Identifier resolution

Type checking

Loop labeling

Transformed AST

TACKY generation

TACKY

Assembly generation

Converting TACKY to assembly

Replacing pseudoregisters

Instruction fix-up

Assembly

Code emission

program.s

9

FUNCTIONS

Functions—chunks of code that can be defined in one place and invoked somewhere else—are a fundamental concept in every mainstream programming language. They're so fundamental, in fact, that there are dedicated processor instructions just for making function calls. In this chapter, you'll implement function calls and definitions according to the standard *calling convention* for Unix-like systems, which defines exactly how function calls should work at the assembly level. Calling conventions make it possible for binaries that were compiled separately (and might even have been written in different source languages) to interoperate. By following your system's calling convention, you'll be able to compile programs that call functions in external libraries, including the standard library. The programs you compile will finally be able to perform I/O operations! Programs built by other compilers will also be able to use libraries built by your compiler.

We'll spend most of this chapter on semantic analysis and assembly code generation. In the semantic analysis stage, we'll add a new *type checking* pass, which is bolded in the diagram at the start of this chapter. This pass is pretty bare-bones for now, but we'll build on it as we add new types throughout Part II. In the assembly generation stage, we'll dig into our system's calling convention, which tells us how to set up stack frames, pass arguments and return values, and transfer control from one function to another.

To get started, let's define exactly what features we're about to implement.

Declaring, Defining, and Calling Functions

In this chapter, you'll implement function calls, function declarations, and function definitions. A function *declaration* tells you a function's name and type. The declaration brings the function name into scope so it can be called later. A function *definition* is a declaration that includes a function body. (All function definitions are declarations, but not all declarations are definitions.) Your compiler already has some support for function definitions, since it can compile main. Now you'll generalize it to compile other functions.

Declarations and Definitions

A function declaration, like the one in Listing 9-1, must include the function's return type, its name, and a type and name for each parameter.

```
int foo(int param1, int param2, int param3);
```

Listing 9-1: A function declaration

For now, a function's return type and parameter types all have to be int. As we've already seen, if a function has no parameters, its parameter list is just the void keyword:

```
int foo(void);
```

A function definition looks just like the function declaration from Listing 9-1, plus a body. Listing 9-2 shows an example of a function definition.

```
int foo(int param1, int param2, int param3) {
    return param1 + param2 + param3;
}
```

Listing 9-2: A function definition

You can declare the same function as many times as you like, but all the declarations must be compatible: the return type, parameter types, and number of parameters must be the same. The parameter names can vary between declarations, because only the parameter names in the function definition are used. Listing 9-3, for example, is perfectly valid.

```
int foo(int x, int y, int z);

int main(void) {
    return foo(1, 2, 3);
}

int foo(int param1, int param2, int param3);

int foo(int a, int b, int c) {
    return a + b + c;
}
```

Listing 9-3: Declaring a function multiple times with different parameter names

While it's legal to declare a function multiple times, you cannot define a function more than once; if you did, when the function was called, there would be no way to tell which definition to execute.

You can declare functions in two places: at the top level and inside the body of other functions. Listing 9-4 includes both kinds of declarations.

```
int foo(int a, int b);

int main(void) {
    int foo(int a, int b);
    return foo(1, 2);
}
```

Listing 9-4: Nested and top-level function declarations

You can't define a function in the body of another function, however. The C standard supports function definitions only at the top level, so it doesn't allow programs like Listing 9-5.

```
int main(void) {
    int foo(int a, int b) { return a + b; };
    return foo(1, 2);
}
```

Listing 9-5: A nested function definition (not supported)

Some compilers support nested function definitions as a language extension and will compile Listing 9-5 just fine. We won't implement this language extension; we're sticking with features that are in the C standard.

SOME THINGS WE'RE NOT IMPLEMENTING

C provides a handful of slightly different ways to declare functions. To simplify things, we won't support all of them; we'll only handle declarations in the form given in Listing 9-1. For instance, we won't support old-style function definitions, which look like this:

```
int foo(param1, param2, param3)
int param1, param2, param3;
{
    return param1 + param2 + param3;
}
```

In C17, the reference version of the C standard used in this book, old-style function definitions are an obsolescent feature. The C standard designates a feature *obsolescent* if it might be removed in the future and shouldn't be used in new code. The next version of the standard, C23, does, in fact, remove this feature from the language.

We'll also reject function declarations without parameter lists, like this one:

```
int foo();
```

According to the C17 standard, a function declaration without a parameter list or function body provides no information about that function's parameters. In other words, this declaration indicates that some function foo is in scope and returns an integer, but it doesn't tell us how many parameters it has.

Empty parameter lists are also obsolescent in C17. In C23, they're permitted, but their meaning has changed: instead of declaring a function without specifying its parameters, an empty parameter list declares a function with *no* parameters. In other words, the declarations int foo(); and int foo(void); are equivalent in C23.

In function declarations that aren't definitions, the C standard lets you specify just the parameters' types and omit their names, but we'll require a name for every parameter. Omitting the identifiers from a parameter list is not an obsolescent feature; we just aren't bothering with it.

We're also omitting a few more significant features, including functions with variable numbers of arguments and function specifiers like inline or _Noreturn. Finally, we won't implement *function pointers*, which are variables that hold the addresses of functions. If you want to implement function pointers on your own, I recommend waiting until we add arrays in Chapter 15. C's type system handles expressions of array type and function type in surprisingly similar ways: in most contexts, expressions of array type are implicitly converted to pointers, and expressions of function type are implicitly converted to function pointers.

Function Calls

A function call consists of a function name followed by a sequence of comma-separated arguments, wrapped in parentheses:

```
foo(1, 2, 3);
```

While the identifiers in a function declaration are called function *parameters*, the expressions passed into a function call are called function *arguments*. For example, in Listing 9-6, a, b, and c are parameters of foo, while a + b and 2 * c are arguments to bar.

```
int foo(int a, int b, int c) {
    return bar(a + b, 2 * c);
}
```

Listing 9-6: Function parameters and arguments

As Listing 9-7 illustrates, a function must be declared, but not necessarily defined, before it can be called.

```
int foo(int arg1, int arg2, int arg3);

int main(void) {
    return foo(1, 2, 3);
}
```

Listing 9-7: Declaring and then calling a function

The definition of foo may appear later in the same file, or it may appear in a separate library. It's up to the linker, not your compiler, to find the definition of every function your program calls. If it can't find the definition, linking will fail.

It's illegal to call a function before it's declared, so Listing 9-8 is invalid.

```
int main(void) {
    return foo(1, 2, 3);
}

int foo(int arg1, int arg2, int arg3);
```

Listing 9-8: Calling a function before it's declared

In practice, many compilers warn about programs that call undeclared functions, but don't reject them. Our implementation is stricter and rejects programs like Listing 9-8 during semantic analysis.

It's also illegal to call a function with the wrong number of arguments, or to call a variable as a function. (Function pointers would be an exception to this second point if we were implementing them.)

Identifier Linkage

Function and variable names are both identifiers. They exist in the same namespace and follow the same scoping rules. Function names, like variable names, can be shadowed by other declarations in inner scopes. Consider Listing 9-9, where the variable name foo shadows the function name foo.

```
int foo(int a, int b);

int main(void) {
    int foo = 3;
    return foo;
}
```

Listing 9-9: A variable name shadowing a function name

This program compiles without error and returns 3. Function names can also shadow variable names, as Listing 9-10 demonstrates.

```
int main(void) {
    int a = 3;
    if (a > 0) {
        int a(void);
        return a();
    }
    return 0;
}
```

Listing 9-10: A function name shadowing a variable name

Here, the function name a shadows the variable name a; this program compiles without error too, as long as the function a is defined somewhere else.

In other ways, however, function declarations are resolved very differently from the local variable declarations we've seen so far. Every local variable declaration refers to a different variable, even if some of those variables have the same name (we make this explicit when we give a unique name to each variable in the variable resolution pass). But multiple function declarations with the same name all refer to the same function. Consider Listing 9-11, which includes three function declarations that use the name incr.

```
int two(void) {
    int incr(int i);
    return incr(1);
}

int incr(int i);
```

```
int main(void) {
    return two() + incr(3);
}

int incr(int i) {
    return i + 1;
}
```

Listing 9-11: Multiple function declarations that refer to a single definition

Each of these declarations ultimately refers to the same function definition. This listing doesn't contain declarations of three different functions
called incr; it contains three declarations of the same function.

In the C standard, a declaration's *linkage* determines how it relates to
other declarations of the same identifier. There are a few different kinds of
linkage. According to section 6.2.2, paragraph 2, of the C standard, "each
declaration of a particular identifier with *external linkage* denotes the same
object or function." In Listing 9-11, every declaration of incr has external
linkage, so these declarations all refer to the same function definition.
Declarations with external linkage can refer to the same object or function
even if they appear in different translation units. (A *translation unit* is just a
preprocessed source file.)

Consider a program made up of two different files. In one file, shown
in Listing 9-12, we define a function.

```
int library_fun(int a, int b) {
    return a + b;
}
```

Listing 9-12: Defining a library function in one file

In the other file, which is shown in Listing 9-13, we declare and use that
function.

```
int library_fun(int a, int b);

int main(void) {
    return library_fun(1, 2);
}
```

Listing 9-13: Declaring and calling the library function in a different file

Even though library_fun is declared in two different files, the linker
will recognize that both of these declarations refer to the same thing: the
definition of library_fun in Listing 9-12. It will then update every use of
library_fun in the binary code for Listing 9-13 to point to the definition in
Listing 9-12.

In this chapter, all function identifiers have external linkage. Local
variables, on the other hand, have no linkage. Section 6.2.2, paragraph 2,
of the C standard says that "each declaration of an identifier with *no linkage*

denotes a unique entity." A local variable can't refer to the same object as another local variable, and it can't refer to the same thing as an identifier with external linkage, like a function name.

NOTE *It may look like an identifier's linkage depends only on whether it's a function or a variable, but in the next chapter you'll see that this isn't the case. We'll implement global variable declarations with external linkage, and we'll implement function and variable declarations with a third kind of linkage,* internal linkage. *Declarations with internal linkage can be linked to other declarations in the same translation unit, but not in other translation units.*

Since all declarations of a given function name must refer to the same function definition, they must be compatible even if they appear in different scopes. Listing 9-14 contains two incompatible function declarations.

```
int main(void) {
    int f(int x);
    int ret = f(1);
    if (ret) {
        int f(int a, int b);
        return f(0, 1);
    }
    return 0;
}
```

Listing 9-14: Conflicting function declarations

The two declarations of f should refer to the same function, since they both have external linkage. But no function definition could satisfy both declarations, since the numbers of parameters differ. Because the two declarations conflict, this code won't compile.

IDENTIFIER LINKAGE AT LINK TIME

Linkage is easier to understand if you know how the linker handles each kind of identifier. Identifiers with external linkage become global symbols in the final assembly program. We've already encountered global symbols, which we declare with the .globl directive:

```
    .globl main
main:
```

Because main is global, the linker can resolve references to it that appear in other object files. It's normal to define a global symbol in one object file

---

and use it in other object files, but if a global symbol is defined in two different object files, linking will fail.

An identifier with internal linkage appears in the assembly program as a *local symbol*. A local symbol is declared the same way as a global symbol, but without the .globl directive:

```
local:
```

The linker will resolve any references to local symbols in the same object file, but it won't resolve references to them in other object files. If two object files both contain local symbols named foo, for instance, the linker will assume they refer to two different objects.

If an identifier has no linkage, the linker isn't aware of it, because it doesn't correspond to a symbol in the assembly program. It just corresponds to a stack address at some offset from RBP.

Now that we've covered some background information on functions, we can get to work on the compiler. But we won't start with the lexer right away. First, we need to update the compiler driver.

Compiling Libraries

In previous chapters, we could compile only stand-alone executables. Every source file we compiled defined a main function, which was the program's entry point. Now that we can handle other functions, we should also be able to compile libraries, which don't have an entry point. When your compiler translates source code into assembly, it doesn't care whether it's processing a library or an executable. Your compiler driver, however, does care, because the linker expects a complete program to include main. If you try to compile a source file with no main function using your current compiler driver, you'll get a linker error, which might look something like this:

```
/usr/bin/ld: .../x86_64-linux-gnu/Scrt1.o: in function `_start':
(.text+0x24): undefined reference to `main'
collect2: error: ld returned 1 exit status
```

This error means the linker is trying and failing to link your code against crt0, the wrapper code that invokes main.

The gcc command accepts a -c command line flag that tells it not to invoke the linker; when this flag is present, it generates an object file instead of an executable. To work with the test suite, your compiler driver should recognize the -c flag as well. When it's passed this flag, the compiler driver should first convert the source program to assembly as usual, then run the following command to convert the assembly program into an object file:

```
gcc -c ASSEMBLY_FILE -o OUTPUT_FILE
```

The output filename should be the original filename with a *.o* suffix. In other words, `./YOUR_COMPILER -c /path/to/program.c` should produce an object file at */path/to/program.o*.

NOTE   *If you wanted to compile and distribute a real library, you wouldn't just produce an object file; you'd create a shared library (a .so file on Linux or a .dylib file on macOS). If you like, you can add another option to your compiler driver to produce shared libraries; your driver can convert an assembly program into a shared library instead of an object file by invoking GCC or Clang with the appropriate flags. But there's a major limitation on your compiler's ability to produce shared libraries, particularly on Linux; we'll talk more about this in Chapter 10.*

At this point, you might also want to extend your compiler driver to accept multiple input source files. The test suite doesn't require this feature, but you'll need it if you want to compile multifile programs. To handle multiple source files, your compiler driver should convert each one to assembly separately, then use the gcc command to assemble them and link them together.

The Lexer

You'll add one token in this chapter:

, A comma

Lists of function parameters or arguments are comma-separated.

TEST THE LEXER

To test out your lexer, run:

```
$ ./test_compiler /path/to/your_compiler --chapter 9 --stage lex
```

Your lexer should successfully process all of this chapter's test programs.

The Parser

We need to extend the AST in a couple of spots to support function calls, declarations, and definitions. Let's start with function calls, which are a kind of expression:

```
exp = Constant(int)
    | Var(identifier)
    | Unary(unary_operator, exp)
    | Binary(binary_operator, exp, exp)
    | Assignment(exp, exp)
    | Conditional(exp condition, exp, exp)
    | FunctionCall(identifier, exp* args)
```

The AST node for a function call includes the function name and a list of arguments. Each argument is an expression.

Next, we'll refactor the declaration node so that it can represent either function or variable declarations:

```
declaration = FunDecl(function_declaration) | VarDecl(variable_declaration)
variable_declaration = (identifier name, exp? init)
```

We've renamed the function_definition node to function_declaration. (We'll walk through the other changes to this node in a moment.) The variable_declaration node includes the same information that declaration did in earlier chapters: a variable name and an optional initializer. But it looks a little different from the other AST nodes we've seen so far; it doesn't include a named constructor like FunDecl or VarDecl. When a node in ASDL has multiple constructors—like the declaration node and most of the other AST nodes do—each constructor needs a distinct name so we can tell them apart. But since the variable_declaration node has only one constructor, we aren't required to name that constructor. In ASDL jargon, a node definition with exactly one unnamed constructor is a *product type*. The other nodes we've used up until now are *sum types*, because they all have named constructors. Product types are just a syntactic convenience so that we aren't forced to use clunky, redundant constructor names.

Now let's update function_declaration. Here's the existing function _definition node:

```
function_definition = Function(identifier name, block body)
```

We need to make a few changes here. First, as I already noted, we'll rename it to the more accurate function_declaration. We'll also add function parameters, and we'll make the function body optional so this node can represent both function declarations and function definitions. Lastly, for consistency with variable_declaration, we'll remove the Function constructor name to turn this into a product type. Our revised AST node for representing function declarations and definitions is:

```
function_declaration = (identifier name, identifier* params, block? body)
```

Finally, we need to change the top-level definition of a program. Now, instead of a single main function, a program is a list of function definitions and declarations:

```
program = Program(function_declaration*)
```

Listing 9-15 shows the complete updated AST.

```
program = Program(function_declaration*)
declaration = FunDecl(function_declaration) | VarDecl(variable_declaration)
variable_declaration = (identifier name, exp? init)
function_declaration = (identifier name, identifier* params, block? body)
block_item = S(statement) | D(declaration)
block = Block(block_item*)
for_init = InitDecl(variable_declaration) | InitExp(exp?)
statement = Return(exp)
          | Expression(exp)
          | If(exp condition, statement then, statement? else)
          | Compound(block)
          | Break
          | Continue
          | While(exp condition, statement body)
          | DoWhile(statement body, exp condition)
          | For(for_init init, exp? condition, exp? post, statement body)
          | Null
exp = Constant(int)
    | Var(identifier)
    | Unary(unary_operator, exp)
    | Binary(binary_operator, exp, exp)
    | Assignment(exp, exp)
    | Conditional(exp condition, exp, exp)
    | FunctionCall(identifier, exp* args)
unary_operator = Complement | Negate | Not
binary_operator = Add | Subtract | Multiply | Divide | Remainder | And | Or
                | Equal | NotEqual | LessThan | LessOrEqual
                | GreaterThan | GreaterOrEqual
```

Listing 9-15: The abstract syntax tree with function calls, declarations, and definitions

A declaration can appear as a block item, but only a variable_declaration can appear in a for loop header. Note that this AST can represent nested function definitions, like the one in Listing 9-5, even though we don't support them. We'll check for nested function definitions during the semantic analysis stage and throw an error if we encounter any.

Listing 9-16 shows the updated grammar.

```
<program> ::= { <function-declaration> }
<declaration> ::= <variable-declaration> | <function-declaration>
<variable-declaration> ::= "int" <identifier> [ "=" <exp> ] ";"
<function-declaration> ::= "int" <identifier> "(" <param-list> ")" ( <block> | ";")
<param-list> ::= "void" | "int" <identifier> { "," "int" <identifier> }
<block> ::= "{" { <block-item> } "}"
<block-item> ::= <statement> | <declaration>
```

```
<for-init> ::= <variable-declaration> | [ <exp> ] ";"
<statement> ::= "return" <exp> ";"
              | <exp> ";"
              | "if" "(" <exp> ")" <statement> [ "else" <statement> ]
              | <block>
              | "break" ";"
              | "continue" ";"
              | "while" "(" <exp> ")" <statement>
              | "do" <statement> "while" "(" <exp> ")" ";"
              | "for" "(" <for-init> [ <exp> ] ";" [ <exp> ] ")" <statement>
              | ";"
<exp> ::= <factor> | <exp> <binop> <exp> | <exp> "?" <exp> ":" <exp>
<factor> ::= <int> | <identifier> | <unop> <factor> | "(" <exp> ")"
           | <identifier> "(" [ <argument-list> ] ")"
<argument-list> ::= <exp> { "," <exp> }
<unop> ::= "-" | "~" | "!"
<binop> ::= "-" | "+" | "*" | "/" | "%" | "&&" | "||"
          | "==" | "!=" | "<" | "<=" | ">" | ">=" | "="
<identifier> ::= ? An identifier token ?
<int> ::= ? A constant token ?
```

Listing 9-16: The grammar with function calls, declarations, and definitions

The <param-list> and <argument-list> symbols in Listing 9-16 don't have equivalent nodes in the AST. I've factored them out of the production rules for function declarations and function calls, respectively, to make those rules a bit more readable. A <param-list> consists of just the void keyword if a function has no parameters; otherwise, it consists of a comma-separated list of parameters, each with a type and name. An <argument-list> consists of a comma-separated list of expressions. Note that <param-list> is required in a function declaration, but <argument-list> is optional in a function call. Parsing a comma-separated list of arguments or parameters is similar to parsing a list of block items; just consume the , tokens between list elements, and stop when you see a) token.

Function calls have higher precedence than any binary or ternary operator, so you should handle them when parsing the <factor> symbol. If a <factor> starts with an identifier, look ahead one token to figure out whether the expression is a variable or a function call. If the next token is (, you can assume it's a function call. Similarly, you'll need to check for a (token to distinguish between function and variable declarations.

TEST THE PARSER

To test your parser, run:

```
$ ./test_compiler /path/to/your_compiler --chapter 9 --stage parse
```

Your parser should raise an error for every test program in *tests/chapter_9/ invalid_parse* and successfully parse all other test cases.

Semantic Analysis

During the variable resolution pass, we give every local variable a new, unique name. However, we shouldn't rename entities with external linkage. Two declarations of local variables named var refer to distinct memory addresses, so we assign them distinct names. But two declarations of a function named fun refer to the same code, so those declarations should keep the same name throughout compilation. Furthermore, an object with external linkage must retain the name from the original source code because the linker will rely on that name during symbol resolution. The linker won't be able to link an object file that calls fun to the object file that defines fun unless the name fun was preserved when each of those object files was compiled.

We'll therefore need to update the variable resolution pass to rename identifiers with no linkage but leave identifiers with external linkage unchanged. (Since this pass will handle functions as well as variables, I'll call it *identifier resolution* instead of variable resolution from now on.) We'll check for all the usual error conditions, like duplicate declarations and undeclared identifiers; we'll also validate that there are no nested function definitions. The logic to catch duplicate declarations will change slightly, since it's legal to declare a name with external linkage more than once in the same scope. For instance, Listing 9-17 is perfectly valid.

```
int main(void) {
    int foo(void);
    int foo(void);
    return foo();
}
```

Listing 9-17: Multiple function declarations in the same scope

Because both declarations of foo have external linkage, they refer to the same function, so they don't conflict. Duplicate declarations of an identifier conflict only when they refer to different entities; when you use that identifier later in the same scope, there's no way to tell which entity it should refer to.

We also have a few other error cases to check for. We must validate that every declaration of a function has the same number of parameters and that no function is defined more than once. Also, we must validate that variables aren't used as functions and that functions are called with the right number of arguments. These errors aren't that similar to the error cases we already check for, because they're not really about what identifiers are in scope. They're *type errors*, which occur when different declarations of an object have conflicting types or when an object is used in a way its type doesn't support.

We'll define a separate type checking pass to catch these errors. This pass will also build up a symbol table to store the type of every identifier in the program, along with a few other properties of identifiers that we need to track. We'll refer back to the symbol table in later compiler stages. (This is different from the symbol table in an object file, which the linker uses during symbol resolution. The symbol table we build in the type checker is internal to the compiler.)

At the end of this chapter, the semantic analysis stage will consist of three passes: identifier resolution, type checking, and loop labeling. The loop labeling pass can happen at any point relative to the other two passes.

Extending Identifier Resolution

Let's update the identifier resolution pass to handle function calls, function declarations, and function definitions. We'll need to track one new piece of information for each entry in the identifier map: whether it has external linkage. As you build up your identifier map, don't assume that functions always have external linkage and variables never do. That assumption holds right now, but it won't in the next chapter.

We'll also update a couple of names in our pseudocode: we'll change variable_map to identifier_map, and we'll rename the from_current_block field in the identifier map to from_current_scope, since function declarations can appear outside of blocks, at the top level.

Function Calls

A function name, like a variable name, needs to be present in the identifier map before you can use it. Listing 9-18 demonstrates how resolve_exp should handle function calls.

```
resolve_exp(e, identifier_map):
    match e with
    | --snip--
    | FunctionCall(fun_name, args) ->
        if fun_name is in identifier_map:
            new_fun_name = identifier_map.get(fun_name).new_name
            new_args = []
            for arg in args:
                new_args.append(resolve_exp(arg, identifier_map))
            return FunctionCall(new_fun_name, new_args)
        else:
            fail("Undeclared function!")
```

Listing 9-18: Resolving function calls

First, we look up the function name in the identifier map to confirm that it's in scope at this point in the program. Then, we replace this name with the new name from the identifier map. In a valid program, this new name will be the same as the original name, since we don't rename identifiers with external linkage. But we also need to consider invalid programs. Maybe fun_name is actually the name of a local variable instead of a function; in that case, trying to call it like a function is a type error. Resolving fun _name here will allow us to catch this type error during type checking. We'll also wait until the type checking pass to make sure this function call has the right number of arguments.

After we replace the function's name, we recursively call `resolve_exp` on each function argument, just like we recursively resolve each subexpression in unary, binary, and ternary expressions.

Function Declarations

Now let's consider function declarations. We can handle a function declaration in almost exactly the same way whether it appears in a block or at the top level. First, we add the function name to the current scope. Then, we process its parameters, adding them to a new inner scope. Finally, if there's a function body, we process that too. Listing 9-19 illustrates how to resolve function declarations.

```
resolve_function_declaration(decl, identifier_map):
    if decl.name is in identifier_map:
        prev_entry = identifier_map.get(decl.name)
  ❶    if prev_entry.from_current_scope and (not prev_entry.has_linkage):
            fail("Duplicate declaration")

  ❷ identifier_map.add(decl.name, MapEntry(
        new_name=decl.name, from_current_scope=True, has_linkage=True
    ))

  ❸ inner_map = copy_identifier_map(identifier_map)
    new_params = []
    for param in decl.params:
        new_params.append(resolve_param(param, inner_map))

    new_body = null
    if decl.body is not null:
        new_body = resolve_block(decl.body, inner_map)
    return (decl.name, new_params, new_body)
```

Listing 9-19: Resolving function declarations

Before we update the identifier map, we need to make sure that we're not illegally redeclaring an identifier ❶. If the identifier isn't already in scope, there's no conflict. If the identifier was declared in an outer scope, that's also fine; the new declaration shadows the existing one. So far, this is exactly the same as how we handle variable declarations. However, we also need to consider linkage. Multiple declarations of an identifier with external linkage can appear in the same scope. We already know the new declaration has external linkage because it's a function declaration, so it's legal as long as the old declaration has external linkage too. But if the old declaration has no linkage (because it declares a local variable), we'll throw an error. The `has_linkage` attribute in the identifier map tells us whether an identifier has external linkage. (In the next chapter, it will track whether the identifier has any linkage at all, either internal or external.)

If there's no conflicting declaration, we add this name to `identifier_map` ❷. We don't generate new names for functions; the `new_name` attribute for this map entry should just be the original name. Because this declaration has external linkage, the has_linkage attribute should be True.

Next, we resolve the parameter names. The list of function parameters in a declaration starts a new scope, so we make a copy of the identifier map to keep track of them ❸. Parameter names can shadow names from the outer scope, but two parameters in the same function declaration can't share a name. So, this is legal:

```
int a;
int foo(int a);
```

But this is not:

```
int foo(int a, int a);
```

I've left out the pseudocode for resolve_param, but it should be the same as your existing code to resolve variable declarations: it should make sure the parameter name isn't already declared in the current scope, generate a unique name for it, add it to the identifier map, and return the new name. You may want to write one helper function to resolve both parameters and local variable declarations, since the logic is the same in both cases.

We resolve the function's parameters for two reasons. First, we need to validate that there are no duplicate parameter names. Second, we need to make sure the parameters are in scope when we process the function body. When we process a function declaration with no body, the second point doesn't matter; we could get away with checking for duplicate parameters without renaming them or updating the inner scope. However, I think it's easiest to process function declarations in a uniform way whether they have a body or not.

The last step in Listing 9-19 is processing the function body, if there is one. We handle this with resolve_block, as usual; we just need to make sure to pass in inner_map so the function parameters will be in scope. The function name itself is also in scope because we added it to the outer map before making a copy; we'll therefore be able to handle functions that call themselves recursively.

The function parameters and function body are in the same scope, so you should pass in inner_map, and not a copy of it, when you process the function body. This, for example, is illegal:

```
int foo(int a) {
    int a = 3;
    return a;
}
```

The variable declaration int a = 3; is an illegal duplicate declaration because it's in the same scope as parameter a.

At this point, we can return the updated function_declaration node. While the function name itself hasn't changed, the list of parameters and any variables declared in the function body have been renamed in this new node.

Local Declarations

You can process local variable declarations exactly the same way as in previous chapters; just be sure to record in the identifier map that these declarations do not have linkage. To process a local function declaration, first check if it has a body. If it does, throw an error; otherwise, call `resolve_function_declaration`, which we defined in Listing 9-19.

Top-Level Processing

Finally, we need to put all this together to process a list of function declarations. Just process them in order, building up the identifier map as you go. Each function name you add will remain in scope as you process later function declarations. The parameter names and local variables in a function won't be visible in later functions, because they were added to an inner scope.

TEST THE IDENTIFIER RESOLUTION PASS

At this point, you'll want to test that the identifier resolution pass handles every valid program without error and catches undeclared identifiers and duplicate declarations. This pass should successfully process every test case in *tests/chapter_9/valid* and *tests/chapter_9/invalid_types* and reject every test case in *tests/chapter_9/invalid_declarations*. Run these tests with:

```
$ ./test_compiler /path/to/your_compiler --chapter 9 --stage validate
```

The test script will report some test failures, because your compiler won't detect errors for the test cases in *tests/chapter_9/invalid_types*. Those tests will pass once you implement the type checking pass in the next section.

Writing the Type Checker

Our remaining validation is all type checking. Every identifier, whether it's a function or a variable, has a type. Variables can have types like int, long, and double, but at this point in our project the type of every variable is int. A function's type depends on its return type and the types of its parameters. For example, a function can have a type like "function that takes three int parameters and returns an int." Right now, we support only functions that take int parameters and return int results, so only the number of parameters varies.

The type checking pass validates that all declarations and uses of an identifier have compatible types. For example, if you declare that x is a variable, you can't call it like a function:

```
int x = 3;
return x();
```

You can't declare a function in multiple places with different types:

```
int foo(int a, int b);
int foo(int a);
```

You can't call a function with the wrong number of parameters:

```
int foo(int a, int b);

int main(void) {
    return foo(1);
}
```

And you can't define the same function more than once:

```
int foo(void) {
    return 1;
}

int foo(void) {
    return 2;
}
```

This last error isn't a type error per se, but it's easiest to check here.

To type check the program, we'll record the type of every identifier in the symbol table. We'll also record whether each function we encounter is defined or just declared; that is, whether it has a body. The symbol table will be our central source of information about every identifier in the program. In this chapter, we'll primarily use the symbol table to catch type errors. We'll add more information to this table, and find more uses for it, in future chapters.

To build a symbol table, we need a way to represent types in the compiler, just like we need a way to represent ASTs. Right now, your type definition should look something like this:

```
type = Int | FunType(int param_count)
```

Every variable has type int, and the only information we need about a function's type is how many parameters it has. We'll add more types in Part II.

We'll build the symbol table by traversing the program in the usual fashion. When we encounter a function or variable declaration, we'll record its type in the symbol table. The type checker doesn't transform the AST like the identifier resolution pass does, so the individual type checking methods won't return transformed AST nodes; they'll just add symbol table entries and report errors. (The type checker *will* transform the AST in Part II.)

Listing 9-20 shows how to type check a variable declaration.

```
typecheck_variable_declaration(decl, symbols):
    symbols.add(decl.name, Int)
    if decl.init is not null:
        typecheck_exp(decl.init, symbols)
```

Listing 9-20: Type checking variable declarations

Every variable has a unique name by this point, so we know that this declaration won't conflict with any existing entry in the symbol table. We just add it to the symbol table and then type check its initializer, if it has one. Functions are a little trickier. Because you can declare a function more than once, it might already have an entry in the symbol table. So, before adding a function to the symbol table, you need to validate it against what's already there. Listing 9-21 gives the pseudocode to type check a function declaration.

```
typecheck_function_declaration(decl, symbols):
    fun_type = FunType(length(decl.params))
    has_body = decl.body is not null
    already_defined = False

    if decl.name is in symbols:
        old_decl = symbols.get(decl.name)
    ❶ if old_decl.type != fun_type:
            fail("Incompatible function declarations")
        already_defined = old_decl.defined
    ❷ if already_defined and has_body:
            fail("Function is defined more than once")

  ❸ symbols.add(decl.name, fun_type, defined=(already_defined or has_body))

  ❹ if has_body:
        for param in decl.params:
            symbols.add(param, Int)
        typecheck_block(decl.body)
```

Listing 9-21: Type checking function declarations

We first check that the function hasn't already been declared with a different type ❶. Then, we make sure we're not redefining a function that was already defined ❷. The defined attribute in a function's symbol table entry tracks whether we've already type checked a definition of that function. (The symbol table entries for variables don't need this attribute.)

After validation, we add the function to the symbol table ❸. This will overwrite the existing symbol table entry, if there is one. That's okay, because the type won't change. We just need to take the old entry into account when setting the defined attribute. If the function was already defined, or if the current declaration has a body, we'll set defined to True. Finally, if the current declaration has a body ❹, we'll add each of the function's parameters to the symbol table, then type check the function body.

Keep in mind that the symbol table includes every declaration we've type checked so far, even if it's not in scope. Consider this example:

```
int main(void) {
❶   int foo(int a);
    return foo(1);
}

❷ int foo(int a, int b);
```

The nested function declaration ❶ is not in scope when the function is declared again ❷. Nonetheless, declaration ❶ will be in the symbol table when we type check declaration ❷. So, we'll detect that these two declarations conflict and throw an error.

We'll validate uses of identifiers as well as declarations. An identifier can be used as a variable in a Var AST node or as a function name in a FunctionCall AST node. In both cases, you should validate that the identifier has the expected type. Listing 9-22 demonstrates how to type check both kinds of expressions.

```
typecheck_exp(e, symbols):
    match e with
    | FunctionCall(f, args) ->
        f_type = symbols.get(f).type
❶       if f_type == Int:
            fail("Variable used as function name")
❷       if f_type.param_count != length(args):
            fail("Function called with the wrong number of arguments")
❸       for arg in args:
            typecheck_exp(arg, symbols)
    | Var(v) ->
❹       if symbols.get(v).type != Int:
            fail("Function name used as variable")
    | --snip--
```

Listing 9-22: Type checking expressions

When an identifier is called as a function, you need to validate that it was declared as a function, not an int ❶. You also need to validate that it's called with the correct number of arguments ❷, then recursively type check each of its arguments ❸. When an identifier is used as a variable, you need to validate that it was declared as a variable and not a function ❹.

Remember that your symbol table will need to be accessible in later compiler passes. I recommend making the symbol table a global variable (or a singleton, depending on your implementation language) so that it's easy to access from anywhere in the compiler. In our type checking pseudocode, the symbol table is an explicit argument to the typecheck_* functions instead of a global variable, for the sake of clarity. But in a real implementation, I've found that using a global variable is less cumbersome.

TACKY Generation

Now that we're sure the input program is valid, let's convert it to TACKY. We'll need to make a few changes to the TACKY IR. First, we need a new TACKY instruction to represent function calls. Second, we need to include parameters in TACKY function definitions. Finally, we'll define a whole TACKY program as a list of functions instead of a single function. Listing 9-23 shows the updated definition of the TACKY IR.

```
program = Program(function_definition*)
function_definition = Function(identifier, identifier* params, instruction* body)
instruction = Return(val)
            | Unary(unary_operator, val src, val dst)
            | Binary(binary_operator, val src1, val src2, val dst)
            | Copy(val src, val dst)
            | Jump(identifier target)
            | JumpIfZero(val condition, identifier target)
            | JumpIfNotZero(val condition, identifier target)
            | Label(identifier)
            | FunCall(identifier fun_name, val* args, val dst)
val = Constant(int) | Var(identifier)
unary_operator = Complement | Negate | Not
binary_operator = Add | Subtract | Multiply | Divide | Remainder | Equal | NotEqual
                | LessThan | LessOrEqual | GreaterThan | GreaterOrEqual
```

Listing 9-23: Adding function calls to TACKY

These changes correspond closely to the changes to the AST in Listing 9-15. The TACKY IR requires fewer changes than the AST, however, because we don't represent function declarations in TACKY. Like variable declarations without initializers, function declarations without bodies are discarded during IR generation. Only function definitions are converted to TACKY.

The new FunCall instruction requires a function name, a list of arguments, and a destination for the return value. Just like the operands of other TACKY instructions, function arguments must be constants or variables, not expressions.

To convert an entire program to TACKY, process the top-level function declarations one at a time, converting each function definition to a TACKY function_definition and discarding any declaration without a body. To convert a function call to TACKY, generate the instructions to evaluate each argument and construct a list of the resulting TACKY values. The TACKY for the function call fun(e1, e2, ...) will look like Listing 9-24.

```
<instructions for e1>
v1 = <result of e1>
<instructions for e2>
v2 = <result of e2>
--snip--
result = FunCall(fun, [v1, v2, ...])
```

Listing 9-24: Converting a function call to TACKY

This is the same approach we use to handle other expressions with nested subexpressions, like unary and binary operations. Now we're just generalizing it to an arbitrary number of nested expressions, since a function can have an arbitrary number of arguments.

Remember to add a Return(0) instruction to the end of every function body, to make sure it returns to the caller even if some execution paths are missing a return statement. Next, we'll tackle the trickiest part of this chapter: implementing function calls in assembly.

TEST THE TACKY GENERATION STAGE

To make sure that TACKY generation succeeds for all valid programs, run:

```
$ ./test_compiler /path/to/your_compiler --chapter 9 --stage tacky
```

Assembly Generation

We're going to make two big changes to the TACKY-to-assembly conversion pass in this chapter: putting function parameters on the stack so they can be accessed in the function body and converting the new FunCall instruction to assembly. We'll also make a couple of smaller changes to the pseudoregister replacement and instruction fix-up passes. But before we make these changes, we need to understand the calling convention we're going to use.

Understanding Calling Conventions

A *calling convention* is a contract between the caller and callee about how a function will be called. It answers questions like:

- How are arguments passed to the callee? Are they passed in registers or on the stack?
- How is a function's return value passed back to the caller?
- Is the callee or caller responsible for removing arguments from the stack at the end of a function?
- Which registers is the callee allowed to overwrite, and which does it need to preserve?

A shared calling convention allows the caller and callee to work together. The caller knows where to put arguments, and the callee knows where to look for them. The callee knows where to store a return value, and the caller knows where to find it after the callee returns. The callee and caller both know which registers they need to save to ensure that the callee won't clobber any values the caller will use after the function call. This ensures that both functions can access the information they need.

A calling convention is part of a larger specification, called the *application binary interface (ABI)*, that makes it possible to link object files that were built by different compilers. As long as the object files all share the same ABI, they'll be able to interoperate. In addition to calling conventions, the ABI specifies how different C types are represented in memory, which will be important in Part II. Most of the other details that make up the ABI—like executable file formats—are handled by the assembler, linker, and operating system, so we don't need to worry about them.

If your compiler adheres to the calling conventions on your platform, you can compile programs that depend on the standard library and any other libraries you might want to use. You'll be able to compile programs that make system calls and perform I/O operations. You still can't compile the standard library itself—it relies on all sorts of language features that we haven't implemented—but since it's already compiled and lives on your system, you can link to it.

Every Unix-like system uses the standard calling convention defined in the *System V ABI*. (This ABI takes its name from Unix System V, an early commercial version of Unix.) Since we're targeting macOS and Linux, we'll use the System V calling convention. There are different versions of the System V ABI for different processor architectures; we'll use the version for x64 processors. Windows has its own ABI, which we won't worry about. If you're doing this project on Windows Subsystem for Linux, you'll still be able to use the System V calling convention. Next, we'll look at how this calling convention works.

Calling Functions with the System V ABI

In the previous section, I listed a few questions that a calling convention must answer. Let's see how the System V calling convention answers these questions, and the other requirements it imposes:

Argument passing

The first six integer arguments to a function are passed in the EDI, ESI, EDX, ECX, R8D, and R9D registers, in that order (64-bit integers are passed using these registers' 64-bit names instead: RDI, RSI, RDX, RCX, R8, and R9). Any remaining arguments are pushed onto the stack *in reverse order*. For example, to implement the function call foo(a, b, c, d, e, f, g, h), you first copy variable a into EDI, then copy b into ESI, and so on, up to f. Then, you push h, the last argument, onto the stack. Finally, you push g onto the stack.

Return values

As we know, a function's return value is passed in EAX (or RAX if you're returning a 64-bit integer). The return value must be in EAX when the ret instruction is executed.

Argument cleanup

After the callee returns, the caller removes any arguments from the stack. The callee does not clean up arguments.

Caller-saved and callee-saved registers

If a register is *caller-saved*, the callee is allowed to overwrite it. The caller must therefore save the register's value to the stack before issuing the call instruction if it will need it later. It can then pop that value off the stack after the function returns. (If the value in a register won't be used after the function call, the caller doesn't need to save it.) If a register is *callee-saved*, it must have the same contents when a function returns as it did at the start of the function. If the callee needs to use the register, it typically pushes the register's value onto the stack during the function prologue, then pops it back off the stack during the function epilogue. Registers RAX, R10, R11, and all the parameter passing registers are caller-saved; the remaining registers are callee-saved.

Stack alignment

The System V ABI requires the stack to be 16-byte aligned. In other words, the address stored in RSP, the stack pointer, must be divisible by 16 when we issue a call instruction. The ABI imposes this requirement because some instructions require 16-byte-aligned operands. It's easier to maintain the correct alignment of these operands if the stack is 16-byte aligned to begin with.

You can find the full System V x64 ABI at *https://gitlab.com/x86-psABIs/x86-64-ABI*. However, looking at an example might be more useful than reading the spec. Consider Listing 9-25.

```
int fun(int a, int b, int c, int d, int e, int f, int g, int h) {
    return a + h;
}

int caller(int arg) {
    return arg + fun(1, 2, 3, 4, 5, 6, 7, 8);
}
```

Listing 9-25: A C program that includes a function call

Listing 9-26 gives the assembly code for fun. It's more optimized than what your compiler will produce, in order to illustrate the System V calling convention more clearly.

```
        .globl fun
fun:
    pushq   %rbp
    movq    %rsp, %rbp
    # copy first argument into EAX
    movl    %edi, %eax
    # add last argument to EAX
    addl    24(%rbp), %eax
    # epilogue
    movq    %rbp, %rsp
    popq    %rbp
    ret
```

Listing 9-26: The assembly code for fun in Listing 9-25

Listing 9-27 gives the assembly code to call fun from caller.

```
    # save RDI before function call
    pushq   %rdi
    # fix stack alignment
    subq    $8, %rsp
    # pass first six arguments in registers
    movl    $1, %edi
    movl    $2, %esi
    movl    $3, %edx
    movl    $4, %ecx
    movl    $5, %r8d
    movl    $6, %r9d
    # pass last two arguments on the stack
    pushq   $8
    pushq   $7
    # transfer control to fun
    call    fun
    # restore the stack and RDI
    addq    $24, %rsp
    popq    %rdi
```

Listing 9-27: The assembly code to call fun in Listing 9-25

Let's walk through this function call and see how the program state changes at each step. In the following diagrams, the left column shows the contents of the stack and general-purpose registers, and the right column shows the contents of RIP, which always holds the address of the next instruction to execute. (Note that the instruction addresses in these diagrams aren't realistic. These addresses suggest that every instruction is 1 byte long, but instruction length varies, and it's usually more than a single byte!)

Figure 9-1 shows the initial state of the program before the call to fun.

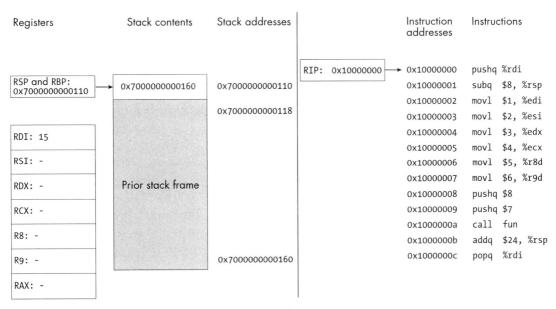

Figure 9-1: The initial state of the program in Listing 9-25

In Figure 9-1, RSP and RBP point to the same address. There are no local variables in caller, so we don't need to allocate any stack space. The registers in this diagram all hold 64-bit values, but we'll usually use 32-bit register names, like EDI, ESI, and EDX, because all our function arguments and return values are 32-bit integers. However, we'll use 64-bit register names when saving to and restoring from the stack, because push and pop require 64-bit operands.

The one argument to caller, arg, is passed in RDI. Let's say the value of arg is 15. To call fun, we need to pass all eight arguments according to the System V calling convention. The first six arguments will be passed in registers, and the last two will be passed on the stack. But copying the first argument into RDI will clobber arg, which we'll need again after the function call. So, the very first step, before passing any arguments, is to save arg onto the stack:

```
# save RDI before function call
pushq    %rdi
```

Next, we adjust RSP so it will be 16-byte aligned when we issue the call instruction. We need to work backward from the number of arguments and saved registers we put on the stack. Before the start of the function call, we can assume that the stack pointer is a multiple of 16. (To guarantee this, we'll allocate stack space in multiples of 16 bytes in the function prologue.) We'll then push some registers and function arguments onto the stack; each of these will be 8 bytes. If the total number of registers and arguments pushed onto the stack is even, the stack will be 16-byte aligned after we've added all of them. If the number of registers and arguments on the stack is odd, we need to subtract 8 bytes from the stack pointer to get the right alignment.

In this example, we push one register, RDI. We'll also need to push two arguments onto the stack, g and h. In total, we'll push three values, totaling 24 bytes, onto the stack before issuing the call instruction. Therefore, we need to adjust the stack by another 8 bytes after saving RDI:

```
# fix stack alignment
subq    $8, %rsp
```

Now we're ready to set up the arguments to fun. We start with the first six arguments, which will be passed in registers. Because the arguments are all 32-bit integers, we'll use 32-bit register names here:

```
# pass first six arguments in registers
movl    $1, %edi
movl    $2, %esi
movl    $3, %edx
movl    $4, %ecx
movl    $5, %r8d
movl    $6, %r9d
```

Next, we push the remaining two arguments onto the stack, in reverse order:

```
# pass last two arguments on the stack
pushq   $8
pushq   $7
```

Each of these instructions will push a 64-bit constant onto the stack, because the push instruction can push only 64-bit values. Figure 9-2 shows the state of the program after we save RDI, adjust the stack, and set up the function arguments.

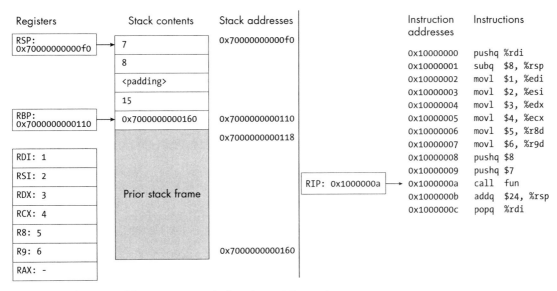

Registers	Stack contents	Stack addresses		Instruction addresses	Instructions

RSP: 0x70000000000f0

7	0x70000000000f0
8	
\<padding\>	
15	

RBP: 0x7000000000110

| 0x7000000000160 | 0x7000000000110 |
| | 0x7000000000118 |

RDI: 1

RSI: 2

RDX: 3

RCX: 4

R8: 5

R9: 6

RAX: -

Prior stack frame

0x7000000000160

RIP: 0x1000000a

0x10000000 pushq %rdi
0x10000001 subq $8, %rsp
0x10000002 movl $1, %edi
0x10000003 movl $2, %esi
0x10000004 movl $3, %edx
0x10000005 movl $4, %ecx
0x10000006 movl $5, %r8d
0x10000007 movl $6, %r9d
0x10000008 pushq $8
0x10000009 pushq $7
0x1000000a call   fun
0x1000000b addq $24, %rsp
0x1000000c popq   %rdi

Figure 9-2: The state of the program just before the call instruction

You can tell that the stack is indeed 16-byte aligned because the stack pointer is divisible by 16 (or 0x10 in hexadecimal). Once our arguments are set up, we call fun with the call assembly instruction:

```
# transfer control to fun
call    fun
```

The call instruction does two things. First, it pushes the address of the instruction that immediately follows it, the return address, onto the stack. Then, it transfers control to the instruction labeled fun by copying that instruction's address into RIP. Figure 9-3 shows the state of the program just after the call instruction.

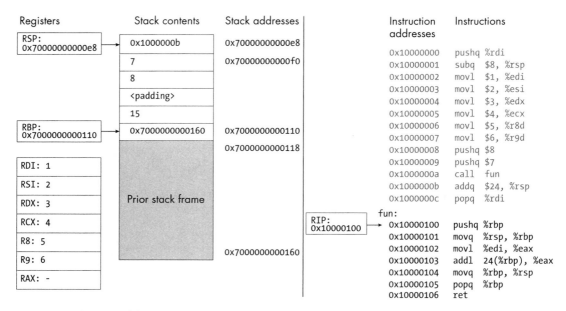

Figure 9-3: The state of the program just after the call instruction

The function prologue, which we're already familiar with, sets up the stack frame for fun, which puts the program in the state shown in Figure 9-4.

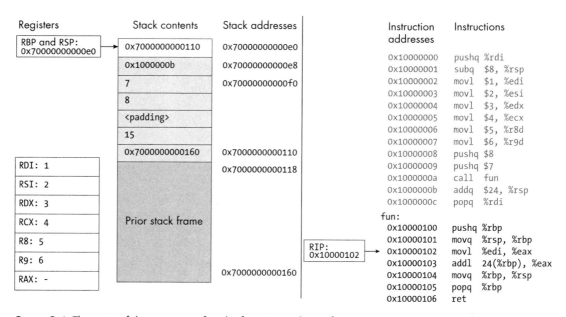

Figure 9-4: The state of the program after the function prologue for fun

In this diagram, the portion of the stack with a white background is fun's stack frame. The portion with a light gray background is caller's stack frame. In fun, we need to calculate a + h. This requires us to access one parameter that was passed in a register (a) and one that was passed on the stack (h). The next instruction in fun copies the value of a into EAX:

```
# copy first argument into EAX
movl    %edi, %eax
```

Next, we want to add h, which was passed on the stack, to the value in EAX. Stack arguments, just like local variables, can be addressed relative to RBP. We know that RBP points to the stack slot that contains the base address of the caller's stack frame. The stack slot just below that, at 8(%rbp), contains the return address in the caller. The value below that, at 16(%rbp), will be the first stack argument, g. (Remember that we pushed stack arguments in reverse order. That means g, the first stack argument, was pushed onto the stack last and is now closest to the current stack frame.) The next argument, h, will be 8 bytes below that, at 24(%rbp), and we can access it accordingly:

```
# add last argument to EAX
addl    24(%rbp), %eax
```

We pushed a 64-bit constant, 8, onto the stack, but addl needs a 32-bit operand. It will therefore interpret the 4 bytes starting at 24(%rbp) as a 32-bit integer, effectively dropping the upper 32 bits. Since those bits are just leading zeros, the resulting value will still be 8. That is, even though each argument pushed onto the stack must be 64 bits, we can still interpret them as 32-bit integers in the callee.

VARIADIC FUNCTIONS

Pushing the last argument onto the stack first makes it easier to support *variadic functions*, or functions with a varying number of arguments. The most obvious example is printf, where the number of arguments depends on the format string you pass in. Because we push arguments onto the stack from right to left, the seventh argument (the first stack argument) will always be at 16(%rbp), no matter how many arguments we pass. This means a variadic function can easily iterate over its arguments without knowing the total number of arguments in advance: it can just increase the offset from RBP to get the next argument. If we pushed arguments in order, the more arguments we passed, the larger the offset would be from RBP to the first argument on the stack. A variadic function would need to figure out the total number of arguments it had received (by, for example, inspecting the format string in the first argument to printf) and recalculate the address of each argument from there.

At this point, we have the correct return value in EAX. We're ready for the function epilogue:

```
# epilogue
movq    %rbp, %rsp
popq    %rbp
```

Note that the movq instruction is unnecessary in this particular program. Usually, this instruction deallocates the current stack frame, putting the old value of RBP back at the top of the stack. But we didn't allocate any stack space for fun, so RSP and RBP already have the same value.

The epilogue puts the stack back the way it was before the prologue. Figure 9-5 shows how things will look at this point.

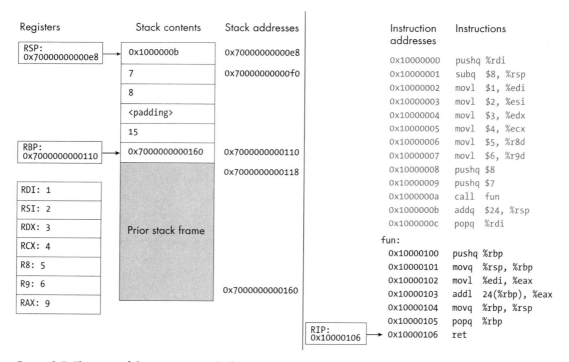

Figure 9-5: The state of the program just before returning to the caller

We return to the caller with the ret instruction, which pops the return address off the stack and transfers control to that address. Figure 9-6 shows the state of the program after we return to the caller.

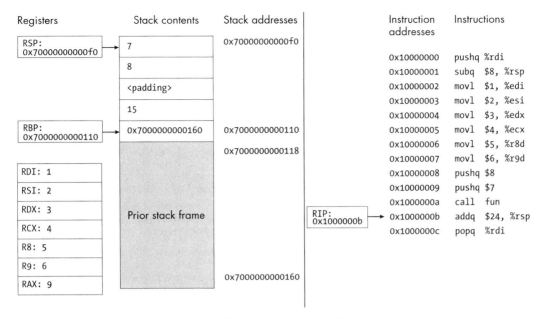

Figure 9-6: The state of the program just after returning to the caller

At this point, the stack is in exactly the same state as it was just before the call instruction. The last step is to clean up the padding and stack arguments and restore arg to RDI:

```
# restore the stack and RDI
addq    $24, %rsp
popq    %rdi
```

Now the stack is back the way it was before the function call, and RDI has been restored to its original state. The RAX register contains the return value, which we can use later in the function body. Because the other registers were uninitialized before the call to fun, we don't need to clean them up now. Figure 9-7 shows the state of the program once we've finished cleaning up after the function call.

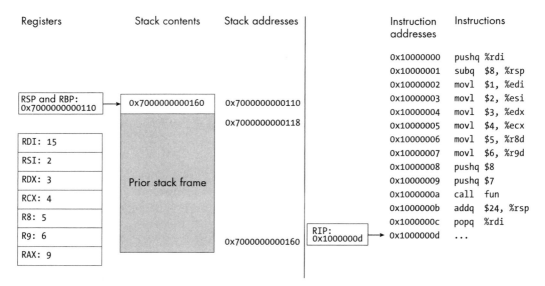

Figure 9-7: The state of the program after the function call has been completed

At this point, you should have a clear understanding of how to call functions and access function parameters in assembly. We're ready to update the assembly generation stage.

Converting Function Calls and Definitions to Assembly

We're going to extend our assembly AST now, for the first time since Chapter 4. Listing 9-28 defines the new AST, with changes bolded.

```
program = Program(function_definition*)
function_definition = Function(identifier name, instruction* instructions)
instruction = Mov(operand src, operand dst)
            | Unary(unary_operator, operand)
            | Binary(binary_operator, operand, operand)
            | Cmp(operand, operand)
            | Idiv(operand)
            | Cdq
            | Jmp(identifier)
            | JmpCC(cond_code, identifier)
            | SetCC(cond_code, operand)
            | Label(identifier)
            | AllocateStack(int)
            | DeallocateStack(int)
            | Push(operand)
            | Call(identifier)
            | Ret

unary_operator = Neg | Not
binary_operator = Add | Sub | Mult
operand = Imm(int) | Reg(reg) | Pseudo(identifier) | Stack(int)
```

```
cond_code = E | NE | G | GE | L | LE
reg = AX | CX | DX | DI | SI | R8 | R9 | R10 | R11
```

Listing 9-28: The assembly AST with support for function calls

First, we change the top-level definition of Program to support multiple function definitions. We also introduce three new instructions. To adjust the stack alignment before a function call, we can use the AllocateStack instruction we already have, which will eventually be emitted as a subq instruction. To remove arguments and padding after a function call, we add a corresponding DeallocateStack instruction, which will be emitted as addq. We also need the Push instruction to push arguments onto the stack. We've already used push in the function prologue, but in such a limited way that we could add it mechanically during code emission. Now that we're going to be using it more extensively, we need to add it to the assembly AST. And, of course, we need the Call instruction to actually call functions. Lastly, we need a few new registers for argument passing: CX, DI, SI, R8, and R9. Arguments are also passed in the DX register, which is already in our AST. Like in previous chapters, the AST doesn't distinguish between the different aliases for each register: DI, for example, will be emitted as %rdi, %edi, or %dil, depending on whether we want to use the whole register, its lower 4 bytes, or its lowest byte.

With these additions to the assembly AST in place, we can update the TACKY-to-assembly conversion. Remember that we made three changes to the TACKY IR: we defined a program as a list of functions instead of a single function, added parameters to each function definition, and added a FunCall instruction. Accounting for the first change is straightforward: we convert a list of functions in TACKY to a list of functions in assembly. Next, we'll make function parameters accessible in assembly. Then, we'll see how to convert the new FunCall instruction to assembly.

Accessing Function Parameters in Assembly

At the start of a function, each parameter is stored in the register or stack location dictated by our calling convention. We could access function parameters in assembly code by referring directly to those locations. The assembly code for fun in Listing 9-26 took this approach; when we needed to add parameters a and h, we referred to their calling convention–defined locations, %edi and 24(%rbp). This works, but it has a few disadvantages. It requires us to push parameter passing registers onto the stack just before function calls and pop them off again afterward, like we had to push and pop RDI before and after the call to fun in Listing 9-27. It also leads to conflicts with other instructions that use parameter passing registers. For example, idiv writes to the EDX register, potentially clobbering the function parameter stored there. Finally, it makes the pseudoregister allocation phase more complex, because parameters must be handled differently from local variables.

We'll take a different approach that bypasses these problems: at the start of each function body, we'll copy each parameter from its calling convention–defined register or memory address into a slot in the current function's stack frame. Let's look at a simple example. Listing 9-29 defines a function with one parameter.

```
int simple(int param) {
    return param;
}
```

Listing 9-29: A function with a single parameter

When we generate the assembly for this function, we'll include an extra Mov instruction at the start of the function body:

```
Mov(Reg(DI), Pseudo("param"))
```

This instruction copies the function's first parameter into the param pseudoregister. Keep in mind that any uses of Var("param") in TACKY will be translated to uses of Pseudo("param") in assembly.

The generated assembly for the whole function will look like this:

```
Mov(Reg(DI), Pseudo("param"))
Mov(Pseudo("param"), Reg(AX))
Ret
```

(Really, param would be renamed during identifier resolution, and we would emit an extra Return(0) instruction during TACKY generation, but neither of these details matter for this example.)

We'll replace pseudoregisters with stack locations in the usual fashion. Since param is our only pseudoregister, we'll assign it to Stack(-4). We'll ultimately emit the assembly program shown in Listing 9-30.

```
        .globl simple
simple:
    pushq   %rbp
    movq    %rsp, %rbp
    subq    $16, %rsp
    movl    %edi, -4(%rbp)
    movl    -4(%rbp), %eax
    movq    %rbp, %rsp
    popq    %rbp
    ret
```

Listing 9-30: The assembly program for Listing 9-29

Copying parameters onto the stack keeps code generation simple. We won't need to save caller-saved registers before function calls or restore them afterward, because we use these registers only in very transient ways. When we pass function parameters in registers, we save them to the stack immediately, instead of leaving them in those registers long term. Aside from function parameters, the only values we store in caller-saved registers are return values, the results of `idiv` instructions, and values that are temporarily copied into R10D or R11D during the instruction rewriting stage. Just like parameters, these values are either used or copied to the stack right away. The upshot is that the values in caller-saved registers will never need to persist across function calls; that's why we don't need to save or restore them. (Meanwhile, the callee doesn't need to save or restore most callee-saved registers because we don't use them at all. The sole exceptions are the RBP and RSP registers, which we save and restore in the function prologue and epilogue.)

Along the same lines, we don't have to worry about the `idiv` instruction clobbering the parameter in EDX. We don't need any extra logic to handle function parameters during pseudoregister allocation, either: we can assign them to stack locations just like local variables.

On the other hand, copying parameters to the stack is inefficient. First of all, we're generating extra `mov` instructions. Second, we're forcing the program to access memory, which is usually slower than registers, every time it reads or writes a parameter. Luckily, we'll be able to get rid of most of these extra instructions and memory accesses when we implement register allocation in Part III.

When you generate these parameter-copying instructions, start by moving the first parameter from `Reg(DI)` into a pseudoregister, the second from `Reg(SI)`, and so on, up to the sixth parameter (or until you run out of parameters, if the function has fewer than six). Then, copy the seventh parameter from `Stack(16)`, the eighth from `Stack(24)`, and so on until you've handled every parameter. As we saw earlier, the top of the caller's stack frame, `8(%rbp)`, is the return address, and the seventh parameter—the first parameter passed on the stack—is always just below it, at `16(%rbp)`. From there, the offset increases by 8 bytes for each additional parameter, because the caller pushes them onto the stack as 8-byte values (even though the callee interprets them as 4-byte values).

Implementing FunCall

Earlier, we stepped through the assembly code for a function call. Now let's look at how to generate this assembly code. Listing 9-31 gives the pseudocode to convert a `FunCall` TACKY instruction to assembly.

```
convert_function_call(FunCall(fun_name, args, dst)):
    arg_registers = [ DI, SI, DX, CX, R8, R9 ]

    // adjust stack alignment
    register_args, stack_args = first 6 args, remaining args
    if length(stack_args) is odd:
        stack_padding = 8
    else:
        stack_padding = 0

    if stack_padding != 0:
        emit(AllocateStack(stack_padding))
```

```
// pass args in registers
reg_index = 0
for tacky_arg in register_args:
    r = arg_registers[reg_index]
    assembly_arg = convert_val(tacky_arg)
    emit(Mov(assembly_arg, Reg(r)))
    reg_index += 1

// pass args on stack
for tacky_arg in reverse(stack_args):
    assembly_arg = convert_val(tacky_arg)
    if assembly_arg is a Reg or Imm operand:
      ❶ emit(Push(assembly_arg))
    else:
      ❷ emit(Mov(assembly_arg, Reg(AX)))
        emit(Push(Reg(AX)))

// emit call instruction
emit(Call(fun_name))

// adjust stack pointer
bytes_to_remove = 8 * length(stack_args) + stack_padding
if bytes_to_remove != 0:
    emit(DeallocateStack(bytes_to_remove))

// retrieve return value
assembly_dst = convert_val(dst)
emit(Mov(Reg(AX), assembly_dst))
```

Listing 9-31: Emitting assembly for a function call

The first step is to make sure the stack is properly aligned. We must do this before passing arguments on the stack; if we add extra padding between the arguments and the callee's stack frame, the callee won't be able to find them. When we walked through the function call in Listing 9-27, we saw that if we pushed an even number of arguments and caller-saved registers to the stack, it would still be 16-byte aligned afterward—no padding required. If we pushed an odd number, we'd need to subtract another 8 bytes from the stack pointer to maintain the correct alignment. Now, thanks to the parameter-copying trick from the previous section, we need to consider only arguments that are pushed onto the stack, not caller-saved registers. So, we just check how many arguments we'll push onto the stack, then emit an AllocateStack instruction if that number is odd.

Next, we pass the function arguments. As we process each argument, we convert it from a TACKY value to an assembly operand with the convert_val helper function. (I've omitted the pseudocode for convert_val, since you already know how to perform this conversion.) The first six arguments are copied into the appropriate registers. A function may, of course, have fewer than six arguments; in that case, we copy every argument into a register.

If the function has more than six arguments, the remainder must be passed on the stack. We push the last argument, then the second-to-last, and so on, up through the seventh argument. Keep in mind that our arguments are 4-byte integers, but we need to push 8 bytes onto the stack for each of them (because the ABI requires it, and because pushq takes only 8-byte operands). However, the callee will use only the lower 4 bytes of each argument. If an argument is a Reg or Imm operand, we pass it with a single Push instruction ❶. If it's in memory, we first copy the argument into AX, then push that ❷. Using an immediate value in an instruction like pushq $7 pushes the 8-byte representation of that value. Pushing a Reg operand pushes the entire 8-byte register, whose lower 4 bytes we can access with the corresponding 4-byte alias. (The code emission pass will use 4-byte register aliases like %eax in most instructions, including movl, and 8-byte aliases like %rax in pushq instructions.)

If we used a 4-byte memory operand directly in an instruction like pushq -4(%rbp), we'd push the 4 bytes of our operand followed by 4 bytes of whatever happened to follow it in memory. This would usually be fine, if a bit kludgy. But if the 4 bytes that followed our operand weren't readable memory, trying to access those bytes would trigger a segmentation fault and crash the program. This issue won't come up when we push an operand from the stack; the bytes right after it will hold either some other temporary value from the current function or the saved base address of the caller's stack frame. But it could come up when we push static variables, which we'll implement in Chapter 10. A static variable might appear at the very end of a valid memory region; in this case, the memory addresses just past that variable could be invalid. (You can read more about this edge case in Randall Hyde's *The Art of 64-Bit Assembly, Volume 1* [No Starch Press, 2021]; see section 5.5.3.3, "Passing Parameters on the Stack.") Copying the operand from memory into a register before we push it avoids this problem. Note that AX is the only register we can use to help push memory operands onto the stack, because we have to preserve the callee-saved registers, we've already put arguments in the parameter passing registers, and we've reserved R10 and R11 for the instruction fix-up phase.

Once every argument is in place, we issue the call instruction to transfer control to the callee. After the call returns, we no longer need the arguments that were passed on the stack, and we certainly don't need the padding. We add the total size of those arguments and the padding to the stack pointer with the DeallocateStack instruction. After deallocating this space, the stack pointer will be back where it was before we started preparing for the function call.

Finally, we retrieve the function's return value. This value will be in EAX, and we copy it to its destination with a mov instruction.

Tables 9-1 and 9-2 summarize this chapter's changes to the conversion from TACKY to assembly. New constructs and changes to existing constructs are bolded.

Table 9-1: Converting Top-Level TACKY Constructs to Assembly

TACKY top-level construct	Assembly top-level construct
Program(**function_definitions**)	Program(**function_definitions**)

Function(name, **params**, instructions)	Function(name,
	    [Mov(Reg(DI), param1),
	      Mov(Reg(SI), param2),
	      <copy next four parameters from registers>,
	      Mov(Stack(16), param7),
	      Mov(Stack(24), param8),
	      <copy remaining parameters from stack>] +
	    instructions)

Table 9-2: Converting TACKY Instructions to Assembly

TACKY instruction	Assembly instructions
FunCall(fun_name, args, dst)	*<fix stack alignment>* *<set up arguments>* Call(fun_name) *<deallocate arguments/padding>* Mov(Reg(AX), dst)

The assembly for a function call is too complex to fully specify in a table, so the conversion for FunCall in Table 9-2 is more of a rough outline.

Replacing Pseudoregisters

Next, we'll update the pseudoregister replacement pass. Most of the logic here won't change: we'll replace pseudoregisters in each function definition exactly the same way as in past chapters. As we saw earlier, pseudoregisters that represent function parameters don't require any special handling. They'll get assigned locations on the stack, just like local variables.

However, we do need to make a couple of updates. First, we'll extend this pass to replace pseudoregisters in the new Push instruction. (We don't directly push pseudoregisters now, but we will in Part II.) Second, we'll change how we track the stack space needed by each function. Previously, this whole pass returned a single number because the program contained a single function. Now we need to return a stack size for each function we process. You could record each function's stack size in the symbol table, or annotate each function with its stack size in the assembly AST.

Note that parameters count toward a function's stack size, whether they were passed on the stack or in registers, since we copy them into the function's stack frame.

Allocating Stack Space During Instruction Fix-Up

We need to make one small adjustment to the instruction fix-up pass: we'll change how we add AllocateStack to each function definition. First, we'll look up the stack space needed by each function wherever we recorded it during pseudoregister replacement. Next, we'll round that stack size up to the next multiple of 16. Rounding up the size of the stack frame makes it easier to maintain the correct stack alignment during function calls.

Code Emission

Now we need to make sure the code emission stage can handle all our new instructions and operands. Most of this is pretty straightforward, but there are a few platform-specific details to consider. As we've already seen, function names are prefixed with an underscore on macOS, but not on Linux. This applies in call instructions too, so on macOS you'll emit

```
call _foo
```

and on Linux you'll emit:

```
call foo
```

On Linux, you'll also call functions in external libraries differently from functions defined in the same file. If foo isn't defined in the current translation unit, you'll emit:

```
call foo@PLT
```

PLT stands for *procedure linkage table*, a section in ELF executables. (*ELF*, short *for Executable and Linkable Format*, is the standard file format for object files and executables on Linux and most other Unix-like systems; macOS uses a different file format called *Mach-O*.) Programs use the PLT to call functions in shared libraries. We've already learned that the linker combines object files and resolves symbols to concrete locations in memory in order to produce an executable. On modern systems, these locations are typically encoded as offsets from the current instruction rather than absolute memory addresses. When we define and use a symbol in the same executable, the linker can figure out the symbol's relative offset from the instruction that uses it and resolve the reference.

Shared libraries are a different story. When a program uses a shared library, the linker doesn't copy the whole library into the executable. Instead, the library is loaded into memory separately at runtime. The linker doesn't know exactly where this library will live in memory, so it can't resolve the names of shared library functions. Another piece of software, called the *dynamic linker*, must resolve these names at runtime. The dynamic linker can resolve symbols in a few different ways, but the most common approach is *lazy binding*. Using lazy binding, we don't figure out a function's address until the program tries to call that function. That's where the PLT comes in. The operand foo@PLT doesn't refer to the function foo. It refers to a tiny bit of code in the PLT that determines the address of foo if we don't already know it, and then calls foo. The linker is responsible for generating this code, which is called a *PLT entry*.

If foo isn't defined in the current translation unit, it might be defined in a shared library or in another object file that the linker will include in the final executable. In the latter case, we don't need the PLT: the linker will be able to figure out the address of foo (or, more precisely, its offset from the call instruction that refers to it). The code emission pass can't tell these two cases apart, so it should include the @PLT suffix either way; there's no harm in including this suffix when we don't need it.

NOTE   *For a more in-depth explanation of how the PLT works and why we need it, see the two blog posts on position-independent code listed in Chapter 1's "Additional Resources" on page 21.*

On Linux, to check whether a function was defined in the current translation unit—and therefore whether it requires the @PLT modifier—you'll need to look it up in the symbol table. On macOS, which handles lazy binding slightly differently, you don't need the @PLT modifier at all.

Tables 9-3 through 9-5 show the changes to the code emission pass for this chapter, with new constructs and updates to existing constructs bolded.

Table 9-3: Formatting Top-Level Assembly Constructs

Assembly top-level construct	Output
Program(**function_definitions**)	**Print out each function definition.** On Linux, add at end of file: .section .note.GNU-stack,"",@progbits

Table 9-4: Formatting Assembly Instructions

Assembly instruction	Output	
DeallocateStack(int)	addq	$*<int>*, %rsp
Push(operand)	pushq	*<operand>*
Call(label)	call or call	*<label>* *<label>*@PLT

Table 9-5: Formatting Assembly Operands

Assembly operand		Output
Reg(AX)	**8-byte**	**%rax**
	4-byte	%eax
	1-byte	%al
Reg(DX)	**8-byte**	**%rdx**
	4-byte	%edx
	1-byte	%dl
Reg(CX)	**8-byte**	**%rcx**
	4-byte	**%ecx**
	1-byte	**%cl**
Reg(DI)	**8-byte**	%rdi
	4-byte	%edi
	1-byte	%dil
Reg(SI)	**8-byte**	**%rsi**
	4-byte	**%esi**
	1-byte	**%sil**
Reg(R8)	**8-byte**	%r8
	4-byte	%r8d
	1-byte	%r8b
Reg(R9)	**8-byte**	**%r9**
	4-byte	**%r9d**
	1-byte	**%r9b**
Reg(R10)	**8-byte**	%r10
	4-byte	%r10d
	1-byte	%r10b
Reg(R11)	**8-byte**	**%r11**
	4-byte	%r11d
	1-byte	%r11b

We now have 8-byte, 4-byte, and 1-byte names for every register. We'll use 8-byte register names in push instructions, 1-byte names in conditional set instructions, and 4-byte names everywhere else.

Calling Library Functions

Once you've updated the backend of your compiler, you'll be able to compile programs that call standard library functions. You won't be able to use #include directives, because any standard library header file will use language features your compiler doesn't support. Instead, you'll need to explicitly declare any library functions you want to use.

There aren't many library functions we can call at this point. Because the only type we've implemented is int, we can't call functions that use any non-int type as either a return type or a parameter type. But we can call putchar, which takes an int argument and prints the corresponding ASCII character to stdout. This is enough for us to compile Listing 9-32, which is a slightly unorthodox implementation of "Hello, World!"

```
int putchar(int c);

int main(void) {
    putchar(72);
    putchar(101);
    putchar(108);
    putchar(108);
    putchar(111);
    putchar(44);
    putchar(32);
    putchar(87);
    putchar(111);
    putchar(114);
    putchar(108);
    putchar(100);
    putchar(33);
    putchar(10);
}
```

Listing 9-32: Hello, World!

Try compiling Listing 9-32 with your compiler and running it. If you've implemented everything correctly, it will write to stdout:

```
$ ./hello_world
Hello, World!
```

This is a big milestone! Take a moment to bask in your sense of accomplishment before running the remaining test cases.

TEST THE WHOLE COMPILER

To test out the whole compiler, run:

```
$ ./test_compiler /path/to/your_compiler --chapter 9
```

There are a couple of new kinds of tests in this chapter. Some of the test programs use putchar to write to stdout. The test script will validate anything written to stdout as well as the return code. Other test programs for this chapter contain multiple source files. The *tests/chapter_9/valid/libraries* directory contains several pairs of libraries and clients. Each library, *<LIB>.c*, contains one or more function definitions. The corresponding client program, *<LIB>_client.c*, calls those library functions. For each client and library, the test script runs two separate tests. First, it compiles the client with your compiler and the library with the production compiler installed on your system (GCC or Clang). Then, it compiles the client with the system's compiler and the library with your compiler. In both cases, it then links the client and library together, runs the resulting executable, and checks that it produces the expected behavior. This validates that your compiler adheres to the System V calling convention on both the caller and callee sides.

I recommend debugging any test failures in several stages. First, get the test cases without function arguments to pass. Then, to make sure you're accessing function parameters correctly, work on the test cases for library functions in *tests/chapter_9/valid/libraries* that don't call any functions themselves. Since the clients are compiled by the system compiler, you can test out the function definitions separately from the corresponding function calls. Once those tests pass, work on the tests of function calls with fewer than six arguments. Finally, debug any failing tests of function calls with more than six arguments.

Summary

Function calls are the most powerful, and most complicated, feature we've seen so far. To implement them, you expanded the semantic analysis stage to understand different kinds of identifiers and learned the ins and outs of the System V calling convention. All that work paid off: you can finally compile programs that interact with the outside world!

You've also laid the groundwork for other language features. You'll expand on the idea of identifier linkage and build on the latest changes to the identifier resolution pass when you implement file scope variables and storage-class specifiers in the next chapter (the last chapter of Part I!). And you'll continue to extend the type checker as you add more types throughout Part II.

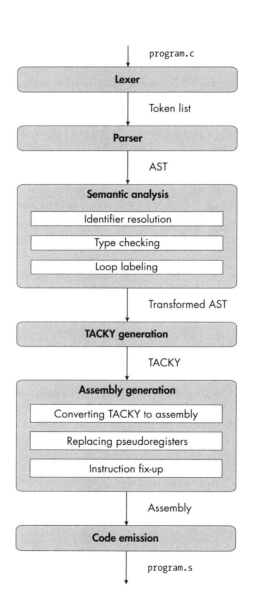

program.c

Lexer

Token list

Parser

AST

Semantic analysis

Identifier resolution

Type checking

Loop labeling

Transformed AST

TACKY generation

TACKY

Assembly generation

Converting TACKY to assembly

Replacing pseudoregisters

Instruction fix-up

Assembly

Code emission

program.s

10

FILE SCOPE VARIABLE DECLARATIONS AND STORAGE-CLASS SPECIFIERS

We'll wrap up Part I by implementing a few important features related to function and variable declarations. We'll add support for variable declarations at *file scope*—that is, at the top level of a source file—and introduce the static and extern keywords. These keywords are *storage-class specifiers* that control a declaration's linkage and the *storage duration* of the declared object (how long that object exists in memory).

We'll spend most of this chapter on the semantic analysis stage, determining the linkage and storage duration of every declaration. We'll also need a few new assembly directives to define and initialize different kinds of variables, but the changes to the compiler backend will be relatively simple. Let's start by reviewing what the C standard has to say about declarations and storage-class specifiers. I recommend reading the following section even if you already know C pretty well. This part of the language looks very different to a compiler developer than it does to a C programmer, largely because your compiler needs to support behavior that no sensible C programmer would use.

All About Declarations

Every declaration in a source file has several properties we need to track, each of which we'll examine in this section. These include the declaration's scope, its linkage, and whether it's a definition as well as a declaration. (Its type is also important, but we won't have anything new to say about that in this chapter.) We also need to track the storage duration of every variable in the program.

The rules for determining these properties are baroque. They depend on whether an identifier refers to a function or variable, whether it's declared at file scope or at *block scope* (inside a function body), and which storage-class specifier is applied to it. The static specifier has two distinct meanings, which apply in different contexts. The extern specifier has multiple, seemingly unrelated effects; these also depend on context. (The other storage-class specifiers—auto, register, _Thread_local, and typedef—serve a hodgepodge of different purposes that I won't get into here. We won't be implementing those.) Basically, this part of the C standard is a mess, but we'll do our best to wade through it.

The terminology around declarations in C can be inconsistent, so I'll spell out how I'm using a few terms before we get started:

- A *file* or *source file* is a preprocessed source file, referred to in the C standard (and the previous chapter) as a "translation unit."

- A *static variable* is a variable with static storage duration (discussed in "Storage Duration" on page 212), not just a variable declared with the static storage-class specifier. All variables with the static specifier are static variables, but not all static variables are declared with that specifier.

- An *automatic variable* is a variable with automatic storage duration (also discussed in "Storage Duration"), as opposed to static storage duration. All the variables we encountered in earlier chapters were automatic variables.

- An *external variable* is any variable with internal or external linkage, not just a variable declared with the extern storage-class specifier. As we'll see, all external variables are also static variables, but not all static variables are external.

Scope

Functions and variables follow the same scoping rules. Variables can be declared at either file scope or block scope, just like functions. File scope variables, like functions and block scope variables, must be declared before they can be used and may be shadowed by later block scope identifiers.

Since you already know the rules for determining an identifier's scope, there's not much more to say here.

Linkage

Up to this point, function declarations have always had external linkage: every declaration of a particular function name referred to the same function definition. The local variable declarations we've seen so far had no linkage: different declarations of the same variable name always referred to different objects. By default, variable declarations at file scope have external linkage, just like function declarations. Whenever there are multiple file scope declarations of the same identifier, the compiler needs to either reconcile them, so they can all refer to the same thing, or throw an error.

Using the static specifier, we can also declare functions and variables with *internal linkage*. Internal linkage works like external linkage, except that declarations with internal linkage never refer to entities in other files. To illustrate the difference, let's consider a program made up of two source files. Listing 10-1 shows the first file.

```
❶ int foo(void) {
      return 1;
  }

❷ int bar(void) {
      return 2;
  }
```

Listing 10-1: A source file defining two functions with external linkage

Listing 10-2 shows the second file.

```
❸ int foo(void);
❹ static int bar(void);

  int main(void) {
      return foo() + bar();
  }

❺ static int bar(void) {
      return 4;
  }
```

Listing 10-2: A source file declaring one function with internal linkage (bar) and two functions with external linkage (foo and main)

In Listing 10-1, we define two functions with external linkage: foo ❶ and bar ❷. Listing 10-2 also includes declarations of identifiers foo ❸ and bar ❹❺. First, let's figure out what foo means in Listing 10-2. Because the declaration at ❸ does not include the static specifier, it has external linkage. Therefore, declarations ❶ and ❸ refer to the same function, which is defined at ❶.

Next, let's consider bar. Because the declaration at ❹ includes the static specifier, it has internal linkage. That means it doesn't refer to the definition at ❷. Instead, it declares a brand-new function. The definition of this function appears later, at ❺. Since declarations ❹ and ❺ both have internal linkage and appear in the same file, they refer to the same function. Therefore, main will use the definition of bar at ❺ to compute 1 + 4 and return 5.

Note that identifiers with internal linkage don't shadow identifiers with external linkage, or vice versa. The declaration of bar in Listing 10-2 doesn't shadow the definition at ❷ in Listing 10-1; rather, that definition was never visible in Listing 10-2 to begin with, because no declaration in Listing 10-2 refers to it. If an identifier is declared with both internal and external linkage in the same file, the behavior is undefined, and most compilers will throw an error.

Section 6.2.2 of the C standard lays out the rules for determining identifier linkage, which I'll summarize here. A declaration's linkage depends on two things: what storage-class specifier it includes, if any, and whether it's declared at block or file scope. Function declarations with no storage-class specifier are always handled as though they include an extern specifier, which we'll discuss momentarily. If variable declarations with no storage-class specifier appear at block scope, they have no linkage. If they appear at file scope, they have external linkage.

At file scope, the static specifier indicates that a function or variable has internal linkage. At block scope, the static specifier controls storage duration, not linkage. Variables declared with this specifier at block scope have no linkage, just like variables declared with no specifier. It's illegal to declare static functions at block scope, because functions don't have storage duration.

The extern specifier is more complicated. If an identifier is declared with extern at a point where a prior declaration of that identifier is visible, and the prior declaration has internal or external linkage, the new declaration will have the same linkage as the previous one. If no prior declaration is visible, or the prior declaration had no linkage, an extern declaration will have external linkage.

In Listing 10-3, we use extern to declare an identifier that's already visible.

```
static int a;
extern int a;
```

Listing 10-3: Declaring an identifier with extern when a prior declaration is visible

The first declaration of a has internal linkage because of the static keyword. Because the second declaration is declared with the extern keyword at a point where the first declaration is visible, it will have internal linkage too.

In Listing 10-4, on the other hand, we use extern at a point where no prior declaration is visible.

```
int main(void) {
    extern int a;
    return a;
}

int a = 5;
```

Listing 10-4: Using extern *to declare a variable with external linkage at block scope*

The declaration of a inside `main` and the definition of a later in the file both have external linkage, so they refer to the same object. Therefore, `main` will return 5.

You can use `extern` to bring a variable with external linkage back into scope if it's shadowed by a local variable. Listing 10-5 shows how this works.

```
int a = 4;
int main(void) {
    int a = 3;
    {
      ❶ extern int a;
        return a;
    }
}
```

Listing 10-5: Using extern *to bring a shadowed variable with external linkage back into scope*

When we declare a with the `extern` specifier in `main` ❶, no prior declaration with internal or external linkage is visible. (The initial file scope declaration of a has external linkage, but it's hidden by the second declaration at block scope. The block scope declaration is visible, but it has no linkage.) Therefore, this extern declaration has external linkage. Since the earlier file scope declaration of a also has external linkage, both declarations refer to the same variable. We then use this variable in the return statement on the next line. As a result, `main` returns 4.

Earlier, I mentioned that function declarations without a storage-class specifier are always handled as though they include the extern specifier. Consider how this rule impacts the linkage of the function definition in Listing 10-6.

```
static int my_fun(void);
int my_fun(void) {
    return 0;
}
```

Listing 10-6: A function declaration with the static *specifier, followed by a definition of that function with no storage-class specifier*

As we saw in Listing 10-3, a declaration with the extern specifier takes on the same linkage as the previous declaration of that identifier, if one is visible. Since we treat the definition of `my_fun` as if it had the extern specifier, it will take on the same linkage as the declaration on the previous line; that is, internal linkage. This rule implies that including extern on function declarations is always redundant (with the exception of inline functions, which we won't implement).

Next, we'll consider a concept that's new to this chapter: storage duration.

Storage Duration

Storage duration is a property of variables; functions don't have storage duration. Section 6.2.4, paragraphs 1–2, of the C standard provides the following description: "An object has a *storage duration* that determines its lifetime. . . . The *lifetime* of an object is the portion of program execution during which storage is guaranteed to be reserved for it. An object exists, has a constant address, and retains its last-stored value throughout its lifetime." In other words, during an object's lifetime, you can work with it in the usual fashion: you can write to it, read from it, and get back the last value you wrote. The object won't be deallocated or reinitialized during that time.

In this chapter, we'll consider two kinds of storage duration: automatic and static. All the variables we saw in earlier chapters had *automatic storage duration*. The lifetime of a variable with automatic storage duration starts when you enter the block where it's declared and ends when you exit that block. This means you can't, for example, use an automatic variable to track how many times a function has been called. To understand why, take a look at Listing 10-7, which tries to do exactly that.

```
#include <stdio.h>

int recursive_call(int count_was_initialized) {
    int count;
    if(!count_was_initialized) {
        count = 0;
        count_was_initialized = 1;
    }
    count = count + 1;
    printf("This function has been called %d times\n", count);
    if (count < 20) {
        recursive_call(count_was_initialized);
    }
    return 0;
}
```

Listing 10-7: An incorrect attempt to share an automatic variable's value among multiple function calls

The recursive_call function in Listing 10-7 tries to initialize a local variable, count, the first time it's called, then increment it on every subsequent invocation. This won't work, because count has automatic storage duration; every invocation of recursive_call will allocate a new, uninitialized copy of count, which is then deallocated when that invocation returns.

If a variable has *static storage duration*, on the other hand, its lifetime lasts for the entire duration of the program. Variables with static storage duration are initialized once, before the program starts, and their lifetime ends when the program exits.

The rules for determining storage duration are simple: all variables declared at file scope have static storage duration, as do all variables declared at block scope with the `static` or `extern` keyword. All variables declared at block scope without a storage-class specifier have automatic storage duration. The standard also defines *allocated storage duration*, which we'll discuss when we add support for `malloc` in Part II, and *thread storage duration*, which we won't implement in this book.

We can use a static counter to fix Listing 10-7. Listing 10-8 shows the correct implementation of `recursive_call`.

```
#include <stdio.h>

int recursive_call(void) {
❶ static int count = 0;
    count = count + 1;
    printf("This function has been called %d times\n", count);
    if (count < 20) {
        recursive_call();
    }
    return 0;
}
```

Listing 10-8: Correctly sharing a static variable's value among multiple function calls

Now, because `count` is declared with the `static` keyword ❶, it has static storage duration. We'll allocate `count` and initialize it to `0` just once, before the program starts. Then, we'll increment that same `count` variable on each invocation of `recursive_call`.

We don't initialize `count` again when we reach its declaration inside `recursive_call`. The declaration marks the point in the program where the variable is brought into scope, not the point during execution when it's initialized. It's important to understand that a static variable's scope and its lifetime are unrelated. In Chapter 7, I described a variable's scope as the part of the program where it can be used. Now we need to refine that definition and specify that it's the part of the program's *source code* where the variable can be used. A variable's lifetime, on the other hand, is the part of *program execution* when the variable has an address and a value. For automatic variables, scope and lifetime are so closely linked that this distinction is almost irrelevant: the variable's lifetime begins when you start executing the block where it's in scope and ends when you finish executing that block. But a static variable's lifetime is independent of its scope. In Listing 10-8, for example, the lifetime of `count` lasts for the whole duration of the program, but its scope extends only from the point where it's declared in `recursive _call` until the end of the function.

Because static variables are initialized before startup, their initializers must be constant. Listing 10-9 shows two file scope declarations, one of which has an invalid initializer.

```
int first_var = 3;
int second_var = first_var + 1;
```

Listing 10-9: File scope variable declarations with valid and invalid initializers

Both first_var and second_var have static storage duration because they're declared at file scope. The initializer for first_var is valid because it's a constant. However, the initializer for second_var is invalid because you can't compute expressions like first_var + 1 before the program starts.

NOTE   *The C standard permits static variables to be initialized with constant expressions, like 1 + 1, because those can be computed at compile time. To make our lives a little easier, our compiler will support only constant values in initializers, not constant expressions.*

Definitions vs. Declarations

In the previous chapter, we had to distinguish between function definitions and function declarations. In this chapter, we'll extend that distinction to variables. If a variable is defined, our assembly program will need to allocate storage for it and possibly initialize it. If it's declared but not defined, we won't allocate storage for it; we'll rely on the linker to find the definition in another object file. Like a function, a variable can be declared many times but defined only once.

It's easy to recognize function definitions, because they have bodies. Figuring out what counts as a variable definition is a little trickier. Let's walk through the rules so you know which variable declarations are also definitions and which ones aren't. We'll also discuss how (and when) to initialize variables that are defined without explicit initializers.

First, every variable declaration with an initializer is a definition. This is unsurprising, since you can't initialize a variable if you haven't allocated storage for it. Second, every variable declaration without linkage is a definition. A variable declaration that didn't have linkage and wasn't a definition would be completely useless: a variable with no linkage can't be declared more than once, so you'd have no way to define the variable elsewhere in the program.

How we initialize a variable without linkage depends on its storage duration. Recall that local variables in previous chapters were allocated space on the stack, but not necessarily initialized. Local static variables, as we'll see in a moment, are allocated space in a different memory segment, and they're always initialized. If no explicit initializer is provided, they're initialized to zero.

If a variable declaration has the extern specifier and no initializer, it's not a definition. Note that extern variable declarations at block scope can't have initializers. Therefore, they are never definitions. (This is analogous to the fact that you can declare functions at block scope, but not define them.) We can use the extern specifier to declare variables that are defined elsewhere in the same file, like in Listing 10-10.

```
extern int three;

int main(void) {
    return three;
}

int three = 3;
```

Listing 10-10: Declaring an external variable at the start of a file and defining it at the end

The declaration at the beginning of the listing brings three into scope, and the definition at the end of the listing determines its initial value, 3. The extern specifier also lets us declare variables that are defined in other files, like in Listing 10-11.

```
extern int external_var;

int main(void) {
    return 1 + external_var;
}
```

Listing 10-11: Declaring a variable without defining it

Because external_var isn't defined in this file, the compiler won't allocate or initialize it. The linker will either find its definition in another file or throw an error.

A variable declaration with internal or external linkage, no extern specifier, and no initializer is a *tentative definition*. Listing 10-12 shows an example.

```
int x;

int main(void) {
    return x;
}
```

Listing 10-12: A tentative definition

The only definition of x in this file is the tentative definition on the first line. If a variable is tentatively defined, we'll initialize it to zero. Therefore, the first line of Listing 10-12 is treated exactly like the following nontentative definition:

```
int x = 0;
```

If a file contains both a tentative definition and an explicitly initialized definition of the same variable, like in Listing 10-13, the explicit definition takes precedence.

```
int x;

int main(void) {
    return x;
}

int x = 3;
```

Listing 10-13: A tentative definition followed by an explicit definition

This listing starts with a tentative definition of x and ends with a non-tentative definition. The non-tentative definition takes precedence, so x is initialized to 3. The first line is treated like a declaration, exactly as it would be if it included the extern specifier.

Although it's illegal to define a variable more than once, having multiple tentative definitions of a variable is perfectly fine. Consider the file scope declarations in Listing 10-14.

```
int a;
int a;
extern int a;
int a;
```

Listing 10-14: Three tentative definitions and a declaration

Here, we have three tentative definitions of a and one declaration of a that isn't a definition due to its extern specifier. Because there are no non-tentative definitions of a, it will be initialized to zero. Listing 10-14 therefore will be compiled as though it contained the following line:

```
int a = 0;
```

Tables 10-1 and 10-2 summarize how an identifier's linkage, storage duration, and status as a definition are determined. The leftmost columns, Scope and Specifier, refer to a declaration's syntax; we'll know a declaration's scope and storage-class specifier after parsing. The remaining columns are properties that we'll need to determine during the semantic analysis stage based on the declaration's syntax.

Table 10-1 covers variable declarations.

Table 10-1: Properties of Variable Declarations

Scope	Specifier	Linkage	Storage duration	Definition? With initializer	Definition? Without initializer
File scope	None	External	Static	Yes	Tentative
	static	Internal	Static	Yes	Tentative
	extern	Matches prior visible declaration; external by default	Static	Yes	No

Scope	Specifier	Linkage	Storage duration	Definition?	
				With initializer	Without initializer
Block scope	None	None	Automatic	Yes	Yes (defined but uninitialized)
	static	None	Static	Yes	Yes (initialized to zero)
	extern	Matches prior visible declaration; external by default	Static	Invalid	No

Table 10-2 covers function declarations.

Table 10-2: Properties of Function Declarations

Scope	Specifier	Linkage	Definition?	
			With body	Without body
File scope	None or extern	Matches prior visible declaration; external by default	Yes	No
	static	Internal	Yes	No
Block scope	None or extern	Matches prior visible declaration; external by default	Invalid	No
	static	Invalid	Invalid	Invalid

Note that the parameters in a function definition have automatic storage duration and no linkage, much like block scope variables with no storage-class specifier.

At this point, you understand the most important properties of declarations. You know how to determine a declaration's linkage, its storage duration, and whether it defines an entity as well as declaring it. You also understand how these properties affect what you can do with an identifier. Next, let's talk about what can go wrong.

Error Cases

We'll need to detect a whole slew of error cases in this chapter. Some of these error cases will be familiar from earlier chapters, although the details will change to account for our new language constructs. Other error cases we'll handle are brand-new.

Conflicting Declarations

There are a bunch of ways that declarations can conflict. Our compiler already detects some of them. For example, it detects the error when two declarations of an identifier appear in the same local scope and at least one of them has no linkage. This is an error because you can't resolve later uses of that identifier to a single entity.

As I mentioned earlier, it's also an error to declare the same identifier with both internal and external linkage. This is an issue even if the two declarations are in completely different parts of the source file. For example, Listing 10-15 includes conflicting declarations.

```
int main(void) {
    extern int foo;
    return foo;
}

static int foo = 3;
```

Listing 10-15: Variable declarations with conflicting linkage

At the point where foo is declared in main, no other declaration is visible. (When a variable becomes visible depends on where it's declared in the source code of the program, not when it's initialized during program execution.) Based on the rules we discussed earlier, this means that foo has external linkage. Later in the listing, however, foo is declared at file scope with internal linkage. You can't define the same object with both internal and external linkage, so this is illegal.

UNDEFINED BEHAVIOR ALERT!

Declaring an identifier with both internal and external linkage results in undefined behavior. Compilers aren't technically required to throw an error when declarations have conflicting linkage, but they almost always do. Interestingly, the following program features an edge case where GCC throws an error but Clang doesn't:

```
static int foo = 0;

int main(void) {
    int foo = 1;
    {
        extern int foo;
        return foo;
    }
}
```

I couldn't figure out why GCC was rejecting this program, until I found a nice explanation by Joseph Myers in the GCC bug tracker (*https://gcc.gnu.org/bugzilla/show_bug.cgi?id=90472#c3*). The defining feature of this edge case is the block scope extern declaration of a variable that's already in scope, but shadowed. The first declaration of foo has internal linkage. The extern declaration in main should have external linkage, because it occurs when the first declaration isn't visible. That would result in a conflict with the first declaration.

GCC reports this conflict and fails. However, Clang gives the extern declaration internal linkage and carries on without complaint, as though the first declaration were visible. We'll handle this edge case the way Clang does and not throw an error.

Finally, two declarations of the same entity conflict if they have different types. Declaring an external variable and a function with the same name is illegal. Again, this is the case even in programs like Listing 10-16, where the conflicting declarations are in completely different parts of the program.

```
int foo = 3;

int main(void) {
    int foo(void);
    return foo();
}
```

Listing 10-16: Declarations with conflicting types

Because both declarations of foo have external linkage, they should refer to the same entity, but that's impossible since one is a function declaration and one is a variable declaration. This program is therefore invalid.

Multiple Definitions

We've already seen that it's illegal to define a function multiple times in the same program. Having multiple definitions of an external variable is illegal too. If an external variable is defined multiple times in the same file, your compiler should produce an error. If a function or variable is defined in more than one file, your compiler can't catch the error, but the linker will.

UNDEFINED BEHAVIOR ALERT!

A tentative definition is tentative only within the file where it's declared. It still conflicts with definitions of the same variable in other files. Let's look at a program that includes two source files. Here's the first file:

```
int var = 4;
```

(continued)

And here's the second:

```
int var;
int main(void) {
    return var;
}
```

This program's behavior is undefined because var is defined more than once. The first file explicitly defines and initializes var. The second file includes one tentative definition of var, which should be treated like a definition because var isn't defined elsewhere in the file.

We normally get an error at link time if a variable is defined in two different files. But, given the right compiler options, both Clang and GCC will compile this program without errors or warnings. They can avoid errors at link time thanks to *common symbols*, which are essentially tentative definitions at the binary level. A common symbol tells the linker to allocate space for and initialize a symbol, unless that symbol is defined in another object file.

Our implementation doesn't use common symbols, so it can't compile this program.

No Definitions

This kind of error applies to both functions and variables. If you use an identifier that's declared but never defined, you'll get an error at link time, when the linker tries to find the definition and fails. Because this is a link-time error, your compiler doesn't need to detect it.

Invalid Initializers

As we've already seen, the initializer for a static variable must be a constant. An extern declaration at block scope can't have any initializer, not even a constant one.

Restrictions on Storage-Class Specifiers

You can't apply the extern or static specifier to function parameters or variables declared in for loop headers. You also can't apply static to function declarations at block scope. (You can apply extern to them, but it doesn't do anything.)

Linkage and Storage Duration in Assembly

As we extend each stage of the compiler—especially the semantic analysis stage—it will be helpful to understand how the concepts we covered in the previous section translate into assembly. I'll discuss linkage first, then storage duration. Linkage is pretty straightforward: if an identifier has external linkage, we'll emit a `.globl` directive for the corresponding assembly label. If an identifier doesn't have external linkage, we won't emit a `.globl` directive. The `.globl` directive applies the same way to both function and variable names.

Now let's talk storage duration. The variables we dealt with in earlier chapters, which had automatic storage duration, all lived on the stack. Static variables live in a different part of memory, the *data section*. (Some static variables live in the closely related BSS section, which I'll discuss in a moment.) Like the stack, the data section is a region in memory that the program can read from and write to.

However, while the stack is divided into frames, which are managed by a well-established calling convention, the data section is one big chunk of memory that exists regardless of what function you're in. This makes the data section the ideal place to store variables with static storage duration: objects in the data section won't be deallocated or overwritten when we call and return from functions. We don't have dedicated registers like RSP or RBP that point to particular spots in the data section, and we don't need them; as you'll see in a moment, we can refer to variables in this section by name instead.

By default, the assembler writes to the text section, which is the region of memory that holds machine instructions. The `.data` directive tells the assembler to start writing to the data section instead. Listing 10-17 initializes a variable in the data section.

```
        .data
        .align 4
var:
        .long 3
```

Listing 10-17: Initializing a variable in the data section

The first line of Listing 10-17 indicates that we're writing to the data section. The `.align` directive on the next line determines the alignment of the next value we write; a 4-byte alignment means that this value's address in bytes must be divisible by 4. The meaning of the `.align` directive varies by platform. On Linux, `.align` n produces an n-byte alignment. On macOS, `.align` n produces a 2^n-byte alignment. That means `.align 4` results in the next value being 4-byte aligned on Linux and 16-byte aligned on macOS.

The third line is a label; you can label locations in the data section just like locations in the text section. Finally, the last line writes the 32-bit integer 3 to the current section; this is the data section because of the earlier `.data` directive. Since *long* means 32 bits in x64 assembly, the `.long` directive always writes a 32-bit integer. (Recall that the l suffix on instructions with 32-bit operands, like `movl`, stands for *long*.)

Like any other label, the var label is internal to this object file by default. We could include the .globl directive to make it visible in other object files too:

```
.globl var
```

I mentioned earlier that some static variables are stored in the *BSS section*. (For obscure historical reasons, BSS stands for *Block Started by Symbol*.) This section works almost exactly like the data section, except that it holds only variables that are initialized to zero. This is a trick to save space on disk; an executable or object file needs to record only the size of the BSS section, not its contents, because its contents are all zeros.

Listing 10-18 initializes a variable in the BSS section.

```
        .bss
        .align 4
var:
        .zero 4
```

Listing 10-18: Initializing a variable in the BSS section

This code differs from Listing 10-17 in two ways. First, we use the .bss directive to write to the BSS section instead of the data section. Second, we use the .zero *n* directive to write *n* bytes of zeros. For example, .zero 4 initializes a 4-byte integer to zero. We use the .align directive, declare a label, and include or omit the .globl directive in exactly the same way whether we're dealing with the data or BSS section.

If a variable is declared, but not defined, in the file you're compiling, you won't write anything to the data or BSS section.

Finally, let's see how to refer to labels from the data section in assembly instructions. This line writes the immediate value 4 to the memory address labeled var:

```
movl    $4, var(%rip)
```

Operands like var(%rip) use *RIP-relative addressing*, which refers to memory addresses relative to the instruction pointer. We obviously can't refer to symbols in the data section relative to RBP and RSP, the way we refer to stack variables. We also can't replace them with absolute addresses at link time, because we're compiling position-independent code, which can be loaded into any spot in program memory. Instead, we use the RIP register, which holds the address of the current instruction in the program's text section, to calculate the address of a variable like var in the program's data section.

The details of RIP-relative addressing are involved, so I won't go into them here. Instead, I'll once again recommend Eli Bendersky's excellent blog posts on position-independent code, which I provided links to in Chapter 1's "Additional Resources" on page 21.

Now that you understand how storage duration, linkage, and variable initialization work in both C and assembly, you're ready to extend your compiler.

The Lexer

You'll add two new keywords in this chapter:

```
static
extern
```

The Parser

In this chapter, we're going to make two changes to the AST: we'll add variable declarations as a top-level construct, and we'll add optional storage-class specifiers to both function and variable declarations. Listing 10-19 shows the updated AST definition.

```
program = Program(declaration*)
declaration = FunDecl(function_declaration) | VarDecl(variable_declaration)
variable_declaration = (identifier name, exp? init, storage_class?)
function_declaration = (identifier name, identifier* params,
                        block? body, storage_class?)
storage_class = Static | Extern
block_item = S(statement) | D(declaration)
block = Block(block_item*)
for_init = InitDecl(variable_declaration) | InitExp(exp?)
statement = Return(exp)
          | Expression(exp)
          | If(exp condition, statement then, statement? else)
          | Compound(block)
          | Break
          | Continue
          | While(exp condition, statement body)
          | DoWhile(statement body, exp condition)
          | For(for_init init, exp? condition, exp? post, statement body)
          | Null
exp = Constant(int)
    | Var(identifier)
    | Unary(unary_operator, exp)
    | Binary(binary_operator, exp, exp)
    | Assignment(exp, exp)
    | Conditional(exp condition, exp, exp)
    | FunctionCall(identifier, exp* args)
unary_operator = Complement | Negate | Not
binary_operator = Add | Subtract | Multiply | Divide | Remainder | And | Or
                | Equal | NotEqual | LessThan | LessOrEqual
                | GreaterThan | GreaterOrEqual
```

Listing 10-19: The abstract syntax tree with file scope variables and storage-class specifiers

We've already defined a declaration AST node that includes both function and variable declarations. Now that we support file scope variable declarations, we'll use declaration nodes at the top level.

Listing 10-20 shows the corresponding changes to the grammar.

```
<program> ::= { <declaration> }
<declaration> ::= <variable-declaration> | <function-declaration>
<variable-declaration> ::= { <specifier> }+ <identifier> [ "=" <exp> ] ";"
<function-declaration> ::= { <specifier> }+ <identifier> "(" <param-list> ")" ( <block> | ";")
<param-list> ::= "void" | "int" <identifier> { "," "int" <identifier> }
<specifier> ::= "int" | "static" | "extern"
<block> ::= "{" { <block-item> } "}"
```

```
<block-item> ::= <statement> | <declaration>
<for-init> ::= <variable-declaration> | [ <exp> ] ";"
<statement> ::= "return" <exp> ";"
              | <exp> ";"
              | "if" "(" <exp> ")" <statement> [ "else" <statement> ]
              | <block>
              | "break" ";"
              | "continue" ";"
              | "while" "(" <exp> ")" <statement>
              | "do" <statement> "while" "(" <exp> ")" ";"
              | "for" "(" <for-init> [ <exp> ] ";" [ <exp> ] ")" <statement>
              | ";"
<exp> ::= <factor> | <exp> <binop> <exp> | <exp> "?" <exp> ":" <exp>
<factor> ::= <int> | <identifier> | <unop> <factor> | "(" <exp> ")"
           | <identifier> "(" [ <argument-list> ] ")"
<argument-list> ::= <exp> { "," <exp> }
<unop> ::= "-" | "~" | "!"
<binop> ::= "-" | "+" | "*" | "/" | "%" | "&&" | "||"
          | "==" | "!=" | "<" | "<=" | ">" | ">=" | "="
<identifier> ::= ? An identifier token ?
<int> ::= ? A constant token ?
```

Listing 10-20: The grammar with file scope variables and storage-class specifiers

We define a <program> as a list of <declaration> symbols, just like we did in Listing 10-19. We also introduce a new <specifier> symbol, which represents both type and storage-class specifiers, and we require every declaration to start with a list of specifiers. We've added a new bit of EBNF notation here: wrapping something in braces followed by a + symbol indicates that it must be repeated at least once. Therefore, { <specifier> }+ represents a non-empty list of specifiers. Note that the <param-list> rule hasn't changed; we still expect each parameter to be declared with a single int keyword, not a list of specifiers. If the parser encounters a static or extern parameter, it should throw an error.

Parsing Type and Storage-Class Specifiers

We lump type and storage-class specifiers into a single symbol because they can appear in any order in a declaration. In other words, the declaration

```
static int a = 3;
```

is equivalent to:

```
int static a = 3;
```

Things will get even more complicated when we add more type specifiers in Part II. A declaration might include multiple type specifiers (like long and unsigned), which can appear in any order relative to storage-class specifiers and each other.

To construct the AST, the parser needs to consume the list of specifiers at the start of a declaration, then convert them into exactly one type and at most one storage-class specifier. The pseudocode in Listing 10-21 outlines how to process the specifier list.

```
parse_type_and_storage_class(specifier_list):
    types = []
    storage_classes = []
❶ for specifier in specifier_list:
        if specifier is "int":
            types.append(specifier)
        else:
            storage_classes.append(specifier)

    if length(types) != 1:
        fail("Invalid type specifier")
    if length(storage_classes) > 1:
        fail("Invalid storage class")

❷ type = Int

    if length(storage_classes) == 1:
      ❸ storage_class = parse_storage_class(storage_classes[0])
    else:
        storage_class = null

    return (type, storage_class)
```

Listing 10-21: Determining a declaration's type and storage class

We start by partitioning our list into type specifiers and storage-class specifiers ❶. Then, we validate each list. The list of type specifiers must have exactly one value. The list of storage-class specifiers could be empty, or it could contain exactly one value. Finally, we return our results. At the moment, Int is the only possible type ❷. If the storage-class specifier list isn't empty, we'll convert its one element to the corresponding storage_class AST node ❸. (I've omitted the pseudocode for parse_storage_class, since there's not much to it.) If the storage-class specifier list is empty, the declaration doesn't have a storage class.

Listing 10-21 is a bit more complicated than we need right now, but it will be easy to extend as we add more type specifiers in later chapters.

Distinguishing Between Function and Variable Declarations

Our one remaining challenge is that we can't distinguish between <function -declaration> and <variable-declaration> symbols without parsing the whole list of type and storage-class specifiers. Once we support more complex declarations in later chapters, these two symbols will have even more parsing logic in common. This means that it isn't practical to write separate functions to parse these two grammar symbols; instead, you should write a single function to parse both and return a `declaration` AST node. The one spot where you can have one kind of declaration but not the other is the initial clause of a `for` loop. To handle this case, just parse the whole declaration, then fail if it turns out to be a function declaration.

Now you have everything you need to extend the parser.

TEST THE PARSER

To test your parser, run:

```
$ ./test_compiler /path/to/your_compiler --chapter 10 --stage parse
```

Your compiler should raise an error for every test program in *tests/chapter_10/invalid_parse* and successfully parse all the programs in *tests/chapter_10/invalid_declarations*, *tests/chapter_10/invalid_types*, and *tests/chapter_10/valid*.

There are several error cases in *tests/chapter_10/invalid_types* that would be just as easy to catch in the parser. These include storage-class specifiers on variable declarations in for loop headers, `static` specifiers on block scope function declarations, and block scope `extern` variables with initializers. You can have the parser catch these errors instead of catching them in the semantic analysis stage if you like. Just be aware that if you do this, the tests for those error cases will fail when you run the command to test the parser.

Semantic Analysis

Next, we need to extend the identifier resolution and type checking passes. In the identifier resolution pass, we'll handle top-level variable declarations and check for duplicate declarations in the same scope. In the type checking pass, we'll add storage class and linkage information to the symbol table because we'll need that information when we generate assembly. We'll also deal with our remaining error cases in the type checker.

Identifier Resolution: Resolving External Variables

Like functions, external variables aren't renamed during the identifier resolution pass. Our identifier map will track whether each identifier has linkage (either internal or external) or not. We don't need to distinguish between internal and external linkage until the type checking pass.

We'll need separate code to process block scope and file scope variable declarations, since different rules for determining linkage apply at these different scopes. Listing 10-22 demonstrates how to resolve variable declarations at file scope.

```
resolve_file_scope_variable_declaration(decl, identifier_map):
    identifier_map.add(decl.name, MapEntry(new_name=decl.name,
                                           from_current_scope=True,
                                           has_linkage=True))
    return decl
```

Listing 10-22: Resolving file scope variable declarations

As you'll see shortly, this is much simpler than the code to handle block scope variable declarations. We don't need to generate a unique name, since external variables retain their original names throughout this stage. We don't need to worry about previous declarations of this variable; any previous declarations must also have internal or external linkage, so they'll refer to the same object and have the same entry in the identifier map. (File scope declarations can conflict in other ways, but we'll deal with those conflicts in the type checker.) We can handle declarations uniformly whether they're static or not. Since we don't need to distinguish internal from external linkage, we'll keep using the Boolean has_linkage attribute from the previous chapter. This attribute is always True for file scope identifiers. We also don't need to recursively process the initializer, because it should be a constant and therefore shouldn't contain any variables we need to rename. If the initializer isn't a constant, we'll catch that during type checking.

Now let's consider variables at block scope. If a variable is declared with the extern keyword, we record that it has linkage in the identifier map and retain its original name. Otherwise, we handle it just like we've handled local variables in the past. If an identifier is declared both with and without linkage in the same scope, we can't maintain a consistent identifier map, so we throw an error. Listing 10-23 shows how to do this in pseudocode.

```
resolve_local_variable_declaration(decl, identifier_map):
    if decl.name is in identifier_map:
        prev_entry = identifier_map.get(decl.name)
      ❶ if prev_entry.from_current_scope:
            if not (prev_entry.has_linkage and decl.storage_class == Extern):
                fail("Conflicting local declarations")

    if decl.storage_class == Extern:
      ❷ identifier_map.add(decl.name, MapEntry(new_name=decl.name,
                                               from_current_scope=True,
                                               has_linkage=True))
        return decl
    else:
        unique_name = make_temporary()
      ❸ identifier_map.add(decl.name, MapEntry(new_name=unique_name,
                                               from_current_scope=True,
                                               has_linkage=False))
        --snip--
```

Listing 10-23: Resolving block scope variable declarations

First, we check for conflicting declarations ❶. If this identifier has already been declared in the current scope, we check the previous declaration's linkage. If it has linkage and the current declaration does too (as indicated by the extern keyword), they both refer to the same object. In that case, the declarations are consistent, at least for the purposes of identifier resolution. If either or both of the identifiers have no linkage, they refer to two different objects, so we throw an error.

Assuming there's no conflict, we update the identifier map. If this declaration has linkage, it retains its current name ❷; otherwise, we rename it ❸. Note that variables without linkage are handled identically here whether they're static or not. Also note that we don't need to recursively process the initializers of extern variables, because they shouldn't have initializers at all. (I've snipped out the code to resolve the initializers of variables without linkage, because it's unchanged from earlier chapters.)

You don't need to change how this pass processes function declarations, with one small exception: you should throw an error if a block scope function declaration includes the static specifier. It's easy to do this during identifier resolution, in the same spot where you validate that block scope function declarations don't have bodies. However, throwing this error in the type checker, or even the parser, works just as well.

Type Checking: Tracking Static Functions and Variables

Next, we'll update the symbol table and handle the remaining error cases. We'll add several new pieces of information to the symbol table. First, we'll record each variable's storage duration. Second, we'll record the initial values of variables with static storage duration. Finally, we'll record whether functions and variables with static storage duration are globally visible. Each of these pieces of information will impact the assembly we generate later.

Most of the logic we're adding to the type checker isn't type checking per se, since an identifier's storage class and linkage are separate from its type. But the type checker is a natural place for this logic because we'll track each identifier's type, linkage, and storage class together in the symbol table.

Identifier Attributes in the Symbol Table

We need to track different information in the symbol table for each kind of identifier: functions, variables with static storage duration, and variables with automatic storage duration. Listing 10-24 gives one way to represent all this information.

```
identifier_attrs = FunAttr(bool defined, bool global)
                 | StaticAttr(initial_value init, bool global)
                 | LocalAttr

initial_value = Tentative | Initial(int) | NoInitializer
```

Listing 10-24: The symbol table attributes for different kinds of identifiers

StaticAttr represents the attributes we need to track for variables with static storage duration. The initial_value type lets us distinguish between variable definitions with an initializer, tentative definitions with no initializer, and extern variable declarations. FunAttr represents functions, and LocalAttr represents function parameters and variables with automatic storage duration. Each symbol table entry should include both a type (as defined in the previous chapter) and identifier_attrs.

Now that we can represent the information we need in the symbol table, let's look at the three kinds of declarations we need to type check: function declarations, file scope variable declarations, and block scope variable declarations.

Function Declarations

Most of the logic here will stay the same. We'll check that the current declaration is the same type as any prior declarations and that the function isn't defined more than once. The only difference is that we'll also record whether the function is globally visible. The pseudocode in Listing 10-25 captures how we'll type check function declarations, with changes from Listing 9-21 bolded and some unchanged code omitted. (I've also made some changes to the code to accommodate changes to our symbol table representation, even though the logic is essentially the same. These are not bolded.)

```
typecheck_function_declaration(decl, symbols):
    fun_type = FunType(length(decl.params))
    has_body = decl.body is not null
    already_defined = False
❶ global = decl.storage_class != Static

❷ if decl.name is in symbols:
        old_decl = symbols.get(decl.name)
        if old_decl.type != fun_type:
            fail("Incompatible function declarations")
        already_defined = old_decl.attrs.defined
        if already_defined and has_body:
            fail("Function is defined more than once")

        if old_decl.attrs.global and decl.storage_class == Static:
            fail("Static function declaration follows non-static")
    ❸ global = old_decl.attrs.global

    attrs = FunAttr(defined=(already_defined or has_body), global=global)
    symbols.add(decl.name, fun_type, attrs=attrs)
    --snip--
```

Listing 10-25: Type checking function declarations

First, we look at the function's storage class ❶. If it's static, the function won't be globally visible, because its linkage is internal. If it's extern (or absent entirely, which amounts to the same thing), we tentatively say the function is globally visible, because its linkage is external. However, this can change depending on what other declarations are in scope.

Next, we look at those other declarations, if there are any ❷. We check for type mismatches and duplicate definitions, just like in the previous chapter. Then, we consider linkage. If the current declaration includes an explicit or implied extern keyword, we'll retain the previous declaration's linkage (and thus its global attribute). If both the current and past declarations have internal linkage, there's no conflict. Either way, the linkage from the previous declaration remains unchanged ❸. But if the function was previously declared with external linkage and is now declared with the static keyword, the declarations conflict, so we throw an error.

I've snipped out the rest of this function because it's the same as in the previous chapter.

File Scope Variable Declarations

When we encounter a variable declaration at file scope, we need to determine the variable's initial value and whether it's globally visible. These properties depend on both the current declaration and any previous declarations of the same variable. Listing 10-26 shows how to type check a file scope variable declaration.

```
typecheck_file_scope_variable_declaration(decl, symbols):
    if decl.init is constant integer i: ❶
        initial_value = Initial(i)
    else if decl.init is null: ❷
        if decl.storage_class == Extern:
            initial_value = NoInitializer
        else:
            initial_value = Tentative
    else: ❸
        fail("Non-constant initializer!")

    global = (decl.storage_class != Static) ❹

    if decl.name is in symbols: ❺
        old_decl = symbols.get(decl.name)
        if old_decl.type != Int:
            fail("Function redeclared as variable")
        if decl.storage_class == Extern:
            global = old_decl.attrs.global
        else if old_decl.attrs.global != global:
            fail("Conflicting variable linkage")

        if old_decl.attrs.init is a constant:
            if initial_value is a constant:
                fail("Conflicting file scope variable definitions") ❻
            else:
                initial_value = old_decl.attrs.init
        else if initial_value is not a constant and old_decl.attrs.init == Tentative:
            initial_value = Tentative
```

```
        attrs = StaticAttr(init=initial_value, global=global)
        symbols.add(decl.name, Int, attrs=attrs) ❼
```

Listing 10-26: Type checking file scope variable declarations

First, we determine the variable's initial value. This depends on the declaration's initializer and its storage-class specifier. If the initializer is a constant, we'll use it ❶. If it's absent ❷, we'll record that this variable is either
tentatively defined or not defined at all, depending on whether this is an
extern declaration. If the initializer is any expression other than a constant,
we'll throw an error ❸.

Next, we determine whether the variable is globally visible ❹. We tentatively say it's visible unless the storage-class specifier is static.

Then, if we recorded prior declarations of this identifier in the symbol
table, we factor those in too ❺. We validate that the prior declaration has
type Int, not a function type, and then we try to reconcile the global attribute with the previous declaration. If this is an extern declaration, we just
adopt the prior declaration's global attribute. Otherwise, we throw an error
if the new and old global attributes disagree.

Accounting for the previous declaration's initializer is more complicated. If either this declaration or the prior one has an explicit initializer,
we'll use that. Otherwise, if either the new declaration or the prior one
was a tentative definition, we'll use a Tentative initializer. If we haven't seen
any explicit or tentative definitions so far, we'll stick with NoInitializer. If
the new and old declarations both have explicit initializers, we'll throw
an error ❻.

Finally, we add (or update) this variable's entry in the symbol table ❼.

Block Scope Variable Declarations

We'll use the pseudocode in Listing 10-27 to type check variable declarations at block scope.

```
typecheck_local_variable_declaration(decl, symbols):
    if decl.storage_class == Extern:
        if decl.init is not null: ❶
            fail("Initializer on local extern variable declaration")
        if decl.name is in symbols:
            old_decl = symbols.get(decl.name)
            if old_decl.type != Int: ❷
                fail("Function redeclared as variable")
        else:
            symbols.add(decl.name, Int, attrs=StaticAttr(init=NoInitializer, global=True)) ❸

    else if decl.storage_class == Static:
        if decl.init is constant integer i: ❹
            initial_value = Initial(i)
        else if decl.init is null: ❺
            initial_value = Initial(0)
```

```
    else:
        fail("Non-constant initializer on local static variable")
    symbols.add(decl.name, Int, attrs=StaticAttr(init=initial_value, global=False)) ❻

else:
    symbols.add(decl.name, Int, attrs=LocalAttr) ❼
    if decl.init is not null:
        typecheck_exp(decl.init, symbols)
```

Listing 10-27: Type checking block scope variable declarations

To handle an extern variable, we first make sure it doesn't have an initializer ❶ and it wasn't previously declared as a function ❷. Then, if this variable wasn't declared earlier, we record in the symbol table that it's globally visible and not initialized ❸. If it was already declared, we do nothing: a local extern declaration will never change the initial value or linkage we've already recorded.

A static local variable has no linkage, so we don't need to consider earlier declarations. We just check the variable's initializer: if it's a constant, we use it ❹; if it's absent, we initialize the variable to zero ❺; and if it's not a constant, we throw an error. Then, we add the variable to the symbol table, recording that it is not globally visible ❻.

We'll include the LocalAttr attribute in the symbol table entries for automatic variables ❼. Aside from this detail, we type check these variables the same way we did in the previous chapter.

When you process a declaration in a for loop header, validate that it doesn't include a storage-class specifier before you call the code in Listing 10-27. (Alternatively, you can handle this error case during the identifier resolution pass, or even during parsing.)

That's it for the type checking pass! It took a lot of work to implement the C standard's byzantine rules around definitions, declarations, linkage, and storage duration. Luckily, now that the symbol table has all the information we need, the rest of the chapter should be pretty easy.

TEST THE SEMANTIC ANALYSIS STAGE

To test the semantic analysis stage, run:

```
$ ./test_compiler /path/to/your_compiler --chapter 10 --stage validate
```

The identifier resolution pass should reject the programs in *tests/chapter_10/ invalid_declarations* and the type checker should reject the programs in *tests/ chapter_10/invalid_types*, although some error cases could reasonably be caught in either pass. Both passes should handle the test cases in *tests/chapter_10/ valid* without error.

TACKY Generation

We need to make two additions to the TACKY IR. First, we'll add a new global field to function definitions, which corresponds to the .globl directive in the final assembly output:

```
Function(identifier, bool global, identifier* params, instruction* body)
```

Second, we'll add a top-level construct to represent static variables:

```
StaticVariable(identifier, bool global, int init)
```

We'll use this construct to represent both external and local static variables. We'll ultimately translate each StaticVariable construct into a set of assembly directives to initialize an object in the data or BSS section. Listing 10-28 presents the whole TACKY IR, with changes from the previous chapter bolded.

```
program = Program(top_level*)
top_level = Function(identifier, bool global, identifier* params, instruction* body)
          | StaticVariable(identifier, bool global, int init)
instruction = Return(val)
            | Unary(unary_operator, val src, val dst)
            | Binary(binary_operator, val src1, val src2, val dst)
            | Copy(val src, val dst)
            | Jump(identifier target)
            | JumpIfZero(val condition, identifier target)
            | JumpIfNotZero(val condition, identifier target)
            | Label(identifier)
            | FunCall(identifier fun_name, val* args, val dst)
val = Constant(int) | Var(identifier)
unary_operator = Complement | Negate | Not
binary_operator = Add | Subtract | Multiply | Divide | Remainder | Equal | NotEqual
                | LessThan | LessOrEqual | GreaterThan | GreaterOrEqual
```

Listing 10-28: Adding static variables and the global attribute to TACKY

We've renamed the function_definition node to top_level, since it doesn't just represent functions anymore. Note that when we translate a program into TACKY, we move local static variable definitions to the top level; they become StaticVariable constructs, not instructions in a function body.

When we traverse the AST and convert it to TACKY, we'll set the new global attribute on each top-level Function. We can look up this attribute in the symbol table. We won't generate any TACKY for file scope variable declarations or for local variable declarations with static or extern specifiers. Instead, *after* we've traversed the AST, we'll perform an additional step where we examine every entry in the symbol table and generate StaticVariable constructs for some of these entries. Our final TACKY program will include both function definitions converted from the original AST and variable definitions generated from the symbol table.

Listing 10-29 demonstrates how to convert symbol table entries into TACKY variable definitions.

```
convert_symbols_to_tacky(symbols):
    tacky_defs = []
    for (name, entry) in symbols:
        match entry.attrs with
        | StaticAttr(init, global) ->
            match init with
            | Initial(i) -> tacky_defs.append(StaticVariable(name, global, i))
            | Tentative -> tacky_defs.append(StaticVariable(name, global, 0))
            | NoInitializer -> continue
        | _ -> continue
    return tacky_defs
```

Listing 10-29: Converting symbol table entries to TACKY

We look at each symbol table entry to determine whether it should be converted into a StaticVariable. If it doesn't have a StaticAttr attribute, we skip over it because it's not a static variable. If its initial value is NoInitializer, we skip over it because it's not defined in this translation unit. Any symbol we don't skip over is converted into a TACKY StaticVariable and added to the TACKY program. Static variables with tentative definitions get initialized to zero.

Right now, it doesn't matter whether we process the AST or the symbol table first. Starting in Chapter 16, it will be important that we process the AST first and the symbol table second. In that chapter, we'll add new static objects to the symbol table as we convert the AST to TACKY; then, when we traverse the symbol table, we'll convert those new entries to TACKY constructs.

TEST THE TACKY GENERATION STAGE

To test TACKY generation, run:

```
$ ./test_compiler /path/to/your_compiler --chapter 10 --stage tacky
```

Assembly Generation

We'll make a few small changes to the assembly AST in this chapter. These changes are bolded in Listing 10-30.

```
program = Program(top_level*)
top_level = Function(identifier name, bool global, instruction* instructions)
          | StaticVariable(identifier name, bool global, int init)
```

```
instruction = Mov(operand src, operand dst)
            | Unary(unary_operator, operand)
            | Binary(binary_operator, operand, operand)
            | Cmp(operand, operand)
            | Idiv(operand)
            | Cdq
            | Jmp(identifier)
            | JmpCC(cond_code, identifier)
            | SetCC(cond_code, operand)
            | Label(identifier)
            | AllocateStack(int)
            | DeallocateStack(int)
            | Push(operand)
            | Call(identifier)
            | Ret

unary_operator = Neg | Not
binary_operator = Add | Sub | Mult
operand = Imm(int) | Reg(reg) | Pseudo(identifier) | Stack(int) | Data(identifier)
cond_code = E | NE | G | GE | L | LE
reg = AX | CX | DX | DI | SI | R8 | R9 | R10 | R11
```

Listing 10-30: The assembly AST with static variables

Just like in TACKY, we rename function_definition to top_level and add a top-level StaticVariable that indicates each static variable's name, its initial value, and whether it's globally visible. We also add a global attribute to function definitions. Finally, we add a new assembly operand, Data, for RIP-relative accesses to the data and BSS sections. We'll replace pseudoregisters with Data operands as needed during the pseudoregister replacement pass.

Generating Assembly for Variable Definitions

Converting our new TACKY constructs to assembly is simple, since we're just passing a few fields from TACKY to the equivalent assembly constructs. Table 10-3 summarizes the latest updates to this conversion, with new constructs and changes to existing constructs bolded. Appendix B includes the complete TACKY-to-assembly conversion pass for this chapter, which is also the final version of this pass for Part I.

Table 10-3: Converting Top-Level TACKY Constructs to Assembly

TACKY top-level construct	Assembly top-level construct
Program(top_level_defs)	**Program(top_level_defs)**
Function(name, **global**, params, instructions)	Function(name, **global**, [Mov(Reg(DI), param1), Mov(Reg(SI), param2), *<copy next four parameters from registers>*, Mov(Stack(16), param7), Mov(Stack(24), param8), *<copy remaining parameters from stack>*] + instructions)
StaticVariable(name, global, init)	**StaticVariable(name, global, init)**

The way we convert all the other TACKY constructs to assembly won't change. In particular, we'll convert every TACKY `Var` operand to an assembly `Pseudo` operand, regardless of whether it has static or automatic storage duration. This means the name `Pseudo` doesn't quite fit anymore; the term *pseudoregister* usually refers to operands that could theoretically live in registers, which static variables cannot. We won't bother to rename this operand, but you should bear in mind that we're using the term *pseudoregister* in a slightly unusual way.

Replacing Pseudoregisters According to Their Storage Duration

Next, we'll adjust how we replace pseudoregisters with concrete locations. In previous chapters, every pseudoregister was assigned a spot on the stack. This time, not every variable belongs on the stack; some of them are stored in the data or BSS section. We'll check the symbol table to tell which are which. Recall that we build a map from pseudoregisters to concrete addresses throughout the pseudoregister replacement pass. When we encounter a pseudoregister that isn't in this map, we look it up in the symbol table. If we find that it has static storage duration, we'll map it to a `Data` operand by the same name. Otherwise, we'll assign it a new slot on the stack, as usual. (If it's not in the symbol table, that means it's a TACKY temporary, so it has automatic storage duration.) For example, if foo is a static variable, the assembly instruction

```
Mov(Imm(0), Pseudo("foo"))
```

should be rewritten as:

```
Mov(Imm(0), Data("foo"))
```

Because static variables don't live on the stack, they don't count toward the total stack size we need to track for each function.

Fixing Up Instructions

You've already written several rewrite rules that apply if one or both operands are memory addresses. Keep in mind that `Data` operands are memory addresses too! For example, if you encounter the instruction

```
Mov(Data("x"), Stack(-4))
```

you should apply the usual rewrite rule for a `Mov` instruction where the source and destination are both in memory. The rewritten assembly will be:

```
Mov(Data("x"), Reg(R10))
Mov(Reg(R10), Stack(-4))
```

Otherwise, this pass won't change.

Code Emission

To wrap up this chapter, you'll extend the code emission pass to handle the changes in Listing 10-30. You should include or omit the .globl directive for functions based on the global attribute in the assembly AST. You should also include a .text directive at the start of each function definition. This directive tells the assembler to write to the text section; you need to include it now that you also write to the data and BSS sections.

Emit Data operands using RIP-relative addressing. For example, Data("foo") will be foo(%rip) on Linux or _foo(%rip) on macOS. Emit each StaticVariable as a list of assembly directives. On Linux, if you have a StaticVariable(name, global, init), where global is true and init is nonzero, you should emit the assembly in Listing 10-31.

```
    .globl <name>
    .data
    .align 4
<name>:
    .long <init>
```

Listing 10-31: The assembly for a global, nonzero static variable

If global is true and init is zero, you should emit the assembly in Listing 10-32.

```
    .globl <name>
    .bss
    .align 4
<name>:
    .zero 4
```

Listing 10-32: The assembly for a global static variable, initialized to zero

If global is false, emit Listing 10-31 or 10-32 without the .globl directive.

On macOS, you'll emit nearly the same assembly for a StaticVariable, with a couple of minor differences. First, symbols should start with an underscore, as usual. Second, you should use the .balign directive instead of .align. I noted earlier that the .align directive's behavior is platform-specific, so .align 4 will produce 16-byte-aligned values on macOS. The `.balign` directive works just like `.align`, except that its behavior is consistent across platforms: `.balign` *n* always aligns a value to *n* bytes instead of 2^n bytes. (On Linux, `.balign` and `.align` are interchangeable, so it's fine to use either one.)

Tables 10-4 and 10-5 summarize the latest updates to the code emission pass, with new constructs and changes to existing constructs bolded. Appendix B includes the complete code emission pass for this chapter (which is also the complete code emission pass for Part I).

Table 10-4: Formatting Top-Level Assembly Constructs

Assembly top-level construct		Output
Program(**top_levels**)		**Print out each top-level construct.** On Linux, add at end of file: `.section .note.GNU-stack,"",@progbits`

Function(name, **global**, instructions)		*<global-directive>*
		`.text`
		<name>:
		    `pushq` `%rbp`
		    `movq` `%rsp, %rbp`
		    <instructions>

StaticVariable(name, global, init)	**Initialized to zero**	*<global-directive>*
		`.bss`
		<alignment-directive>
		<name>:
		    `.zero 4`

	Initialized to nonzero value	*<global-directive>* `.data` *<alignment-directive>* *<name>*: `.long` *<init>*
Global directive		**If** `global` **is true:** `.globl` *<identifier>* **Otherwise, omit this directive.**
Alignment directive	**Linux only**	`.align 4`
	macOS or Linux	`.balign 4`

Table 10-5: Formatting Assembly Operands

Assembly operand	Output
Data(identifier)	*<identifier>*`(%rip)`

Once you've updated the code emission pass, you're ready to test your compiler.

Summary

You've just completed Part I of the book! Your compiler can handle identifiers with all kinds of linkage and with both static and automatic storage duration. You've also learned how to write assembly programs that define and use values in the data and BSS sections of an object file.

You've now implemented all the basic mechanics of C, from local and file scope variables to control-flow statements to function calls. You've also taken the first steps toward a type system by distinguishing between function types and int. In Part II, you'll implement more types, including signed and unsigned integers of various sizes, floating-point numbers, pointers, arrays, and structures. Or, if you want, you can skip straight to Part III, where you'll implement several classic compiler optimizations. The work you've done so far is a solid foundation for whichever part you decide to work on next.

PART II

TYPES BEYOND INT

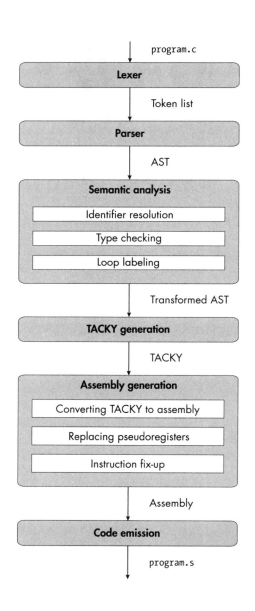

program.c

Lexer

Token list

Parser

AST

Semantic analysis

Identifier resolution

Type checking

Loop labeling

Transformed AST

TACKY generation

TACKY

Assembly generation

Converting TACKY to assembly

Replacing pseudoregisters

Instruction fix-up

Assembly

Code emission

program.s

11

LONG INTEGERS

In this chapter, you'll add a new type: `long`. This is a signed integer type, just like `int`; the only difference between the two types is the range of values they hold. You'll also add an explicit cast operation, which converts a value to a different type.

Because `long` is so similar to the `int` type we already support, we won't need to add many new assembly or TACKY instructions or implement complicated type casting logic. Instead, we'll focus on laying the groundwork we'll need for the rest of Part II. We'll track the types of constants and variables, attach type information to the AST, identify implicit casts and make them explicit, and determine the operand sizes for assembly instructions. We'll need to make at least a small change to every stage of the compiler except for loop labeling. Before we get started, let's see what operations on `long`s look like in assembly.

Long Integers in Assembly

The C standard doesn't specify the sizes of integer types, but the System V x64 ABI says that an int is 4 bytes and a long is 8. To wildly oversimplify things, C expressions with long operands are ultimately translated into assembly instructions on quadwords (8-byte operands). For example, the following assembly instructions operate on quadwords to calculate 2 + 2 and produce a quadword result:

```
movq    $2, %rax
addq    $2, %rax
```

This looks almost identical to the equivalent code using longwords, which are 4 bytes:

```
movl    $2, %eax
addl    $2, %eax
```

The only differences are the suffix on the mov and add instructions and whether we use the whole RAX register or just EAX, its lower 4 bytes.

NOTE *The terms* word, longword, *and* quadword *date back to the era of 16-bit processors, when an int was 2 bytes and a* long *was 4 bytes. To make matters worse, 4-byte values are often called* doublewords *instead of longwords. I use the term* longword *to mirror AT&T assembly syntax, but Intel's documentation uses* doubleword.

Most quadword instructions accept only 8-byte operands and produce 8-byte results, just as most longword instructions accept only 4-byte operands and produce 4-byte results. Expressions in C, on the other hand, often use several operand types at once or assign a value of one type to an object of a different type. During compilation, we'll decompose these expressions into simple instructions that either take operands of a single type and produce results of the same type or explicitly perform type conversions. Luckily, the C standard tells us exactly where these type conversions occur.

Type Conversions

Section 6.3.1.3, paragraph 1, of the C standard defines how to convert between integer types: "If the value can be represented by the new type, it is unchanged." In other words, if some expression evaluates to, say, 3, and then you cast it to a different integer type, the result of that cast expression should still be 3.

Because long is larger than int, we can safely cast any int to a long without changing its value. We're using a two's complement representation of signed integers, so we'll cast from int to long using sign extension, which you learned about in Chapter 3. Specifically, we'll use the movsx (or "move with sign extension") assembly instruction. This instruction moves a 4-byte source into an 8-byte destination, sign extending the value into the destination's upper 4 bytes.

Converting a long to an int is trickier because it may be too large or too small to represent as an int. Paragraph 3 of section 6.3.1.3 goes on to tell us that when "the new type is signed and the value cannot be represented in it[,] either the result is implementation-defined or an implementation-defined signal is raised." In other words, it's up to us to decide what to do. Our implementation will handle this conversion in the same way as GCC, as specified in its documentation: "For conversion to a type of width N, the value is reduced modulo 2^N to be within range of the type; no signal is raised" (*https://gcc.gnu.org/onlinedocs/gcc/Integers-implementation.html*).

Reducing a value modulo 2^{32} means adding or subtracting a multiple of 2^{32} to bring it into the range of int. Here's a quick example. The largest value you can represent as an int is $2^{31} - 1$, or 2,147,483,647. Suppose you need to convert the next largest integer value (2^{31}, or 2,147,483,648) from a long to an int. Subtracting 2^{32} from this value gives you -2^{31}, or −2,147,483,648, which is the smallest value that int can represent.

In practice, we'll convert a long to an int by dropping its upper 4 bytes. If a long can be represented as an int, dropping those bytes won't change its value. For example, here's the 8-byte binary representation of −3:

```
11111111 11111111 11111111 11111111 11111111 11111111 11111111 11111101
```

And here's the 4-byte representation of the same value:

```
                            11111111 11111111 11111111 11111101
```

If a long can't be represented as an int, dropping its upper 4 bytes has the effect of reducing its value modulo 2^{32}. To return to our earlier example, the long 2,147,483,648 has the following binary representation:

```
00000000 00000000 00000000 00000000 10000000 00000000 00000000 00000000
```

After we convert it to an int, the result, with the value −2,147,483,648, has the following binary representation:

```
                            10000000 00000000 00000000 00000000
```

To drop a long's upper bytes, we just copy its lower bytes with a movl instruction. For example, the following instruction truncates a value stored in RCX:

```
movl    %ecx, %eax
```

When we store a value in a register's lower 4 bytes, the register's upper 4 bytes will be zeroed out.

Static Long Variables

Variables with static storage duration are defined in assembly in basically the same way regardless of their type, but there are a few small differences between static quadwords and longwords. Consider the following file scope variable declaration:

```
static long var = 100;
```

We'll convert this declaration to the assembly in Listing 11-1.

```
        .data
        .align 8
var:
        .quad 100
```

Listing 11-1: Initializing an 8-byte value in the data section

This differs from the assembly we generate for a static int in two ways: the alignment is 8 instead of 4, and we use the .quad directive to initialize an 8-byte value instead of using .long to initialize 4 bytes.

The System V x64 ABI specifies that long and int are 8-byte and 4-byte aligned, respectively. The C standard leaves their alignment, like their size, unspecified.

Now that we have some idea of what assembly we want to generate, let's get to work on the compiler!

The Lexer

You'll add the following two tokens in this chapter:

long   A keyword.

Long integer constants   These differ from our current integer constants because they have an l or L suffix. A long constant token matches the regex [0-9]+[lL]\b.

The Parser

We'll add long constants, cast expressions, and type information to the AST in this chapter. Listing 11-2 shows the updated AST definition.

```
program = Program(declaration*)
declaration = FunDecl(function_declaration) | VarDecl(variable_declaration)
variable_declaration = (identifier name, exp? init,
                    ❶ type var_type, storage_class?)
function_declaration = (identifier name, identifier* params, block? body,
                    ❷ type fun_type, storage_class?)
❸ type = Int | Long | FunType(type* params, type ret)
storage_class = Static | Extern
block_item = S(statement) | D(declaration)
block = Block(block_item*)
for_init = InitDecl(variable_declaration) | InitExp(exp?)
statement = Return(exp)
          | Expression(exp)
          | If(exp condition, statement then, statement? else)
          | Compound(block)
          | Break
          | Continue
          | While(exp condition, statement body)
          | DoWhile(statement body, exp condition)
          | For(for_init init, exp? condition, exp? post, statement body)
          | Null
```

```
       exp = Constant(const)
           | Var(identifier)
     ❹ |  Cast(type target_type, exp)
           | Unary(unary_operator, exp)
           | Binary(binary_operator, exp, exp)
           | Assignment(exp, exp)
           | Conditional(exp condition, exp, exp)
           | FunctionCall(identifier, exp* args)
   unary_operator = Complement | Negate | Not
   binary_operator = Add | Subtract | Multiply | Divide | Remainder | And | Or
                   | Equal | NotEqual | LessThan | LessOrEqual
                   | GreaterThan | GreaterOrEqual
 ❺ const = ConstInt(int) | ConstLong(int)
```

Listing 11-2: The abstract syntax tree with long constants, type information, and cast expressions

The type AST node can represent int, long, and function types ❸. Rather than defining a brand-new data structure here, we can extend the type structure we started using in symbol table entries in Chapter 9. From now on, we'll use that data structure in both the symbol table and the AST.

In Chapter 9, we defined type like this:

```
type = Int | FunType(int param_count)
```

In Listing 11-2, we modify this definition by adding Long and tracking additional information about function types, including the return type and the list of parameter types. We didn't need that information before, because the type of every parameter and the return type had to be int. Note that our new, recursive definition of type can represent some invalid types, like functions that return functions, but the parser will never produce those invalid types.

Once we've updated how we represent type, we attach type information to variable ❶ and function declarations ❷. We don't add type information to params in function declarations because the function's type already includes the types of its parameters. We also extend the exp AST node to represent cast expressions ❹ and define a new const AST node with distinct constructors for long and int constants ❺. We'll need to distinguish between different types of constants during type checking.

If your implementation language has signed 64-bit and 32-bit integer types and supports conversions between those types with the same semantics as conversions between long and int in our implementation of C, I recommend using those types to represent ConstLong and ConstInt in the AST. (Most languages provide fixed-width integer types with these semantics, either by default or through a library.) This will make it easier to cast static initializers to the correct type at compile time; it will also simplify constant folding, an optimization we'll implement in Part III. If your implementation language doesn't have integer types with the right semantics, you should at least make sure the ConstLong node uses an integer type that can represent all long values.

After updating the AST, we'll make the corresponding changes to the grammar, shown in Listing 11-3.

```
<program> ::= { <declaration> }
<declaration> ::= <variable-declaration> | <function-declaration>
<variable-declaration> ::= { <specifier> }+ <identifier> [ "=" <exp> ] ";"
<function-declaration> ::= { <specifier> }+ <identifier> "(" <param-list> ")" ( <block> | ";")
<param-list> ::= "void"
              | { <type-specifier> }+ <identifier> { "," { <type-specifier> }+ <identifier> }
<type-specifier> ::= "int" | "long"
<specifier> ::= <type-specifier> | "static" | "extern"
<block> ::= "{" { <block-item> } "}"
<block-item> ::= <statement> | <declaration>
<for-init> ::= <variable-declaration> | [ <exp> ] ";"
<statement> ::= "return" <exp> ";"
              | <exp> ";"
              | "if" "(" <exp> ")" <statement> [ "else" <statement> ]
              | <block>
              | "break" ";"
              | "continue" ";"
              | "while" "(" <exp> ")" <statement>
              | "do" <statement> "while" "(" <exp> ")" ";"
              | "for" "(" <for-init> [ <exp> ] ";" [ <exp> ] ")" <statement>
              | ";"
<exp> ::= <factor> | <exp> <binop> <exp> | <exp> "?" <exp> ":" <exp>
<factor> ::= <const> | <identifier>
           | "(" { <type-specifier> }+ ")" <factor>
           | <unop> <factor> | "(" <exp> ")"
           | <identifier> "(" [ <argument-list> ] ")"
<argument-list> ::= <exp> { "," <exp> }
<unop> ::= "-" | "~" | "!"
<binop> ::= "-" | "+" | "*" | "/" | "%" | "&&" | "||"
          | "==" | "!=" | "<" | "<=" | ">" | ">=" | "="
<const> ::= <int> | <long>
<identifier> ::= ? An identifier token ?
<int> ::= ? An int token ?
<long> ::= ? An int or long token ?
```

Listing 11-3: The grammar with long constants, the long type specifier, and cast expressions

We need to handle two slightly tricky details here. First, whenever we parse a list of type specifiers, we need to convert them into a single type AST node. A long integer can be declared with the long specifier or with both long and int, in either order. Listing 11-4 illustrates how to turn a list of type specifiers into a type.

```
parse_type(specifier_list):
    if specifier_list == ["int"]:
        return Int
    if (specifier_list == ["int", "long"]
        or specifier_list == ["long", "int"]
        or specifier_list == ["long"]):
        return Long
    fail("Invalid type specifier")
```

Listing 11-4: Determining a type from a list of type specifiers

This works for types with no storage class, which we'll find in parameter lists or cast expressions. For function and variable declarations, we'll build on the specifier parsing code from Listing 10-21. Listing 11-5 reproduces that code, with changes bolded.

```
parse_type_and_storage_class(specifier_list):
    types = []
    storage_classes = []
    for specifier in specifier_list:
        if specifier is "int" or "long":
            types.append(specifier)
        else:
            storage_classes.append(specifier)

    type = parse_type(types)

    if length(storage_classes) > 1:
        fail("Invalid storage class")
    if length(storage_classes) == 1:
        storage_class = parse_storage_class(storage_classes[0])
    else:
        storage_class = null

    return (type, storage_class)
```

Listing 11-5: Determining type and storage class from a list of specifiers

We still separate type specifiers from storage class specifiers and determine storage class just like we did in Listing 10-21, but we've made a few small changes here. First, we recognize long as a type specifier. Second, we no longer expect the list of type specifiers to have exactly one element (this change isn't bolded because we just deleted some existing code). Third, rather than always setting type to Int, we use the new parse_type function to determine the type.

The second tricky detail is parsing constant tokens. Listing 11-6 shows how to convert these into const AST nodes.

```
parse_constant(token):
    v = integer value of token
    if v > 2^63 - 1:
        fail("Constant is too large to represent as an int or long")

    if token is an int token and v <= 2^31 - 1:
        return ConstInt(v)

    return ConstLong(v)
```

Listing 11-6: Converting a constant token to an AST node

We parse an integer constant token (without an l or L suffix) into a ConstInt node unless its value is outside the range of the int type. Similarly, we parse a long constant token (with an l or L suffix) into a ConstLong node unless its value is outside the range of long. If an integer constant token is outside the range of int but in the range of long, we parse it to a ConstLong node. If an integer or long constant token is too large for long to represent, we throw an error.

An int is 32 bits, so it can hold any value between -2^{31} and $2^{31} - 1$, inclusive. By the same logic, a long can hold any value between -2^{63} and $2^{63} - 1$. Your parser should check each constant token against the maximum value of the corresponding type. It doesn't need to check against the minimum value, because these tokens can't represent negative numbers; the negative sign is a separate token.

TEST THE PARSER

To test your parser, run:

```
$ ./test_compiler /path/to/your_compiler --chapter 11 --stage parse
```

It should fail on all the test cases in the *tests/chapter_11/invalid_parse* directory, which contains test programs with missing and invalid type specifiers. None of the test cases include constants that are too large to fit into a long, since they may still be valid in a C implementation that supports larger integer types. Your parser should be able to handle every test case in *tests/chapter_11/invalid_types* and *tests/chapter_11/valid*.

Semantic Analysis

Next, we'll extend the compiler passes that perform semantic analysis. We'll make one tiny mechanical change to identifier resolution: we'll extend resolve_exp to traverse cast expressions the same way it traverses other kinds of expressions. I won't always explicitly mention this sort of modification in later chapters; from now on, whenever we add a new expression that contains subexpressions, go ahead and extend the identifier resolution pass to traverse it. Once we've made this change, we can turn to the more interesting problem of extending the type checker.

Just as every object in a C program has a type, the result of every expression has a type too. For example, performing any binary arithmetic operation on two int operands results in an int, performing the same operation on two long operands results in a long, and calling a function with a particular return type produces a result of that type.

During the type checking pass, we'll annotate every expression in the AST with the type of its result. We'll use this type information to determine the types of the temporary variables we generate in TACKY to hold intermediate results. That, in turn, will tell us the appropriate operand sizes for assembly instructions and the amount of stack space we need to allocate for each temporary variable.

While we're annotating expressions with type information, we'll also identify any implicit type conversions in the program and make them explicit by inserting Cast expressions in the AST. Then, we can easily generate the correct type casting instructions during TACKY generation.

Adding Type Information to the AST

Before we update the type checker, we need a way to attach type information to exp AST nodes. The obvious solution, shown in Listing 11-7, is to mechanically add a type field to every exp constructor.

```
exp = Constant(const, type)
    | Var(identifier, type)
    | Cast(type target_type, exp, type)
    | Unary(unary_operator, exp, type)
    | Binary(binary_operator, exp, exp, type)
    | Assignment(exp, exp, type)
    | Conditional(exp condition, exp, exp, type)
    | FunctionCall(identifier, exp* args, type)
```

Listing 11-7: Adding type information to exp nodes

This is easy enough if you're using an object-oriented implementation language and you have a common base class for every exp. You can just add a type field to the base class, as shown in Listing 11-8.

```
class BaseExp {
    --snip--
    type expType;
}
```

Listing 11-8: Adding a type to the base class for exp nodes

If, on the other hand, you've implemented your AST using algebraic data types, this approach is deeply annoying. Not only will you have to update every single exp constructor, but you'll also have to pattern match on every constructor whenever you want to get an expression's type. A slightly less tedious approach, shown in Listing 11-9, is to define mutually recursive exp and typed_exp AST nodes.

```
typed_exp = TypedExp(type, exp)
exp = Constant(const)
    | Var(identifier)
    | Cast(type target_type, typed_exp)
    | Unary(unary_operator, typed_exp)
    | Binary(binary_operator, typed_exp, typed_exp)
    | Assignment(typed_exp, typed_exp)
    | Conditional(typed_exp condition, typed_exp, typed_exp)
    | FunctionCall(identifier, typed_exp* args)
```

Listing 11-9: Another way to add type information to exp nodes

Whichever option you choose, you'll need to either define two separate AST data structures—one with type information and one without—or initialize every exp with a null or dummy type when you build the AST in the parser. There's no one right answer here; it depends on your implementation language and personal taste. Rather than imposing a specific approach, the pseudocode in the rest of the book will use two functions to handle type information in the AST: set_type(e, t) returns a copy of e annotated with type t, and get_type(e) returns the type annotation from e.

THE AST TYPING PROBLEM

The challenge of defining an AST that you can easily annotate with type information, without resorting to hacks or producing a lot of boilerplate, is sometimes called the *AST typing problem*. It's a problem because nobody has a great solution to it (the options I've presented here, for example, have obvious drawbacks). The AST typing problem generally comes up when you're writing a compiler in functional languages like ML or Haskell. Compiler authors have proposed a wide range of solutions in these languages, some of them quite elaborate. If you'd like to learn about a few different approaches, "The AST Typing Problem" by Edward Yang is a good overview (*http://blog.ezyang.com/2013/05/the-ast-typing-problem/*).

Type Checking Expressions

Once we've extended our AST definition, we'll rewrite typecheck_exp, which we defined in Chapter 9, to return a new annotated copy of each exp AST node it processes.

Listing 11-10 shows how to type check a variable.

```
typecheck_exp(e, symbols):
    match e with
    | Var(v) ->
        v_type = symbols.get(v).type
        if v_type is a function type:
            fail("Function name used as variable")
        return set_type(e, v_type)
```

Listing 11-10: Type checking a variable

First, we look up the variable's type in the symbol table. Then, we validate that we're not using a function name as a variable, just like we did in earlier chapters. Finally, we annotate the expression with the variable's type and return it.

Listing 11-11 shows how to type check a constant. This is easy, since different types of constants have different constructors in the AST.

```
| Constant(c) ->
    match c with
    | ConstInt(i) -> return set_type(e, Int)
    | ConstLong(l) -> return set_type(e, Long)
```

Listing 11-11: Type checking a constant

For the remaining expressions, we'll need to traverse any subexpressions and annotate them too. The result of a cast expression has whatever type we cast it to. We type check these in Listing 11-12.

```
| Cast(t, inner) ->
    typed_inner = typecheck_exp(inner, symbols)
    cast_exp = Cast(t, typed_inner)
    return set_type(cast_exp, t)
```

Listing 11-12: Type checking a cast expression

The results of expressions that evaluate to 1 or 0 to indicate true or false, including comparisons and logical operations like !, have type int. The results of arithmetic and bitwise expressions have the same type as their operands. This is straightforward for unary expressions, which we type check in Listing 11-13.

```
| Unary(op, inner) ->
    typed_inner = typecheck_exp(inner, symbols)
    unary_exp = Unary(op, typed_inner)
    match op with
    | Not -> return set_type(unary_exp, Int)
    | _   -> return set_type(unary_exp, get_type(typed_inner))
```

Listing 11-13: Type checking a unary expression

Binary expressions are more complicated because the two operands may have different types. This doesn't matter for logical && and || operations, which can evaluate the truth value of each operand in turn. It does matter for comparisons and arithmetic operations, which need to use both operands at once. The C standard defines a set of rules, called the *usual arithmetic conversions*, for implicitly converting both operands of an arithmetic expression to the same type, called its *common type* or *common real type*.

Given the types of two operands, Listing 11-14 shows how to find their common real type. For now this is simple, since there are only two possible types.

```
get_common_type(type1, type2):
    if type1 == type2:
        return type1
    else:
        return Long
```

Listing 11-14: Finding the common real type

If the two types are already the same, no conversion is necessary. If they're different, we convert the smaller type (which must be Int) to the larger type (which must be Long), so the common type is Long. Once we add more types, finding the common type won't be quite this straightforward.

Once we know the common type that both operands will be converted to, we can use the convert_to helper function, shown in Listing 11-15, to make those type conversions explicit.

```
convert_to(e, t):
    if get_type(e) == t:
        return e
    cast_exp = Cast(t, e)
    return set_type(cast_exp, t)
```

Listing 11-15: Making an implicit type conversion explicit

If an expression already has the correct result type, convert_to returns it unchanged. Otherwise, it wraps the expression in a Cast AST node, then annotates the result with the correct type.

With both of these helper functions in place, we can type check binary expressions. Listing 11-16 shows the relevant clause of typecheck_exp.

```
| Binary(op, e1, e2) ->
  ❶ typed_e1 = typecheck_exp(e1, symbols)
    typed_e2 = typecheck_exp(e2, symbols)
    if op is And or Or:
        binary_exp = Binary(op, typed_e1, typed_e2)
        return set_type(binary_exp, Int)
  ❷ t1 = get_type(typed_e1)
    t2 = get_type(typed_e2)
    common_type = get_common_type(t1, t2)
    converted_e1 = convert_to(typed_e1, common_type)
    converted_e2 = convert_to(typed_e2, common_type)
    binary_exp = Binary(op, converted_e1, converted_e2)
  ❸ if op is Add, Subtract, Multiply, Divide, or Remainder:
        return set_type(binary_exp, common_type)
    else:
        return set_type(binary_exp, Int)
```

Listing 11-16: Type checking a binary expression

We start by type checking both operands ❶. If the operator is And or Or, we don't perform any type conversions. Otherwise, we perform the usual arithmetic conversions ❷. We first get the common type, then convert both operands to that type. (In practice, at least one operand will have the correct type already, so convert_to will return it unchanged.) Next, we construct our new Binary AST node using these converted operands. Finally, we annotate the new AST node with the correct result type ❸. If this is an arithmetic operation, the result will have the same type as its operands, which is the common type we found earlier. Otherwise, it's a comparison that results in an integer representation of true or false, so the result type is Int.

In assignment expressions, we convert the value being assigned to the type of the object it's assigned to. Listing 11-17 gives the pseudocode for this case.

```
| Assignment(left, right) ->
    typed_left = typecheck_exp(left, symbols)
    typed_right = typecheck_exp(right, symbols)
    left_type = get_type(typed_left)
    converted_right = convert_to(typed_right, left_type)
    assign_exp = Assignment(typed_left, converted_right)
    return set_type(assign_exp, left_type)
```

Listing 11-17: Type checking an assignment expression

Remember that the result of an assignment expression is the value of the left-hand side after assignment; unsurprisingly, the result has the type of the left-hand side as well.

Conditional expressions work a lot like binary arithmetic expressions: we find the common type of both branches, convert both branches to that common type, and annotate the result with that type. We'll type check the controlling condition, but we don't need to convert it to anything. I won't give you the pseudocode for this case.

Last but not least, Listing 11-18 shows how to type check function calls.

```
| FunctionCall(f, args) ->
    f_type = symbols.get(f).type
    match f_type with
    | FunType(param_types, ret_type) ->
        if length(param_types) != length(args):
            fail("Function called with the wrong number of arguments")
        converted_args = []
      ❶ for (arg, param_type) in zip(args, param_types):
            typed_arg = typecheck_exp(arg, symbols)
            converted_args.append(convert_to(typed_arg, param_type))
        call_exp = FunctionCall(f, converted_args)
      ❷ return set_type(call_exp, ret_type)
    | _ -> fail("Variable used as function name")
```

Listing 11-18: Type checking a function call

We start by looking up the function type in the symbol table. Just like in previous chapters, we need to make sure that the identifier we're trying to call is actually a function and that we're passing it the right number of arguments. Then, we iterate over the function's arguments and parameters together ❶. We type check each argument, then convert it to the corresponding parameter type. Finally, we annotate the whole expression with the function's return type ❷.

Type Checking return Statements

When a function returns a value, it's implicitly converted to the function's return type. The type checker needs to make this implicit conversion explicit. To type check a return statement, we look up the enclosing function's return type and convert the return value to that type. This requires us to keep track of the name, or at least the return type, of whatever function we're currently type checking. I'll omit the pseudocode to type check return statements, since it's straightforward.

Type Checking Declarations and Updating the Symbol Table

Next, we'll update how we type check function and variable declarations and what information we store in the symbol table. First, we'll need to record the correct type for each entry in the symbol table; we can't just assume that every variable, parameter, and return value is an int. Second, whenever we check for conflicting declarations, we'll need to validate that the current and previous declarations have the same type. It's not enough to check whether a variable was previously declared as a function or a function was previously declared with a different number of parameters; the types must be identical. For example, if a variable is declared as an int and then redeclared as a long, the type checker should throw an error. Third, when we type check an automatic variable, we'll need to convert its initializer to the type of the variable, much like we convert the right-hand side of an assignment expression to the type of the left-hand side.

Finally, we'll change how we represent static initializers in the symbol table. A static initializer, like a constant expression, can now be either an int or a long. Listing 11-19 gives the updated definition for static initializers.

```
initial_value = Tentative | Initial(static_init) | NoInitializer
static_init = IntInit(int) | LongInit(int)
```

Listing 11-19: Static initializers in the symbol table

This definition of static_init may seem redundant, since it's basically identical to the const AST node defined in Listing 11-2, but they'll diverge in later chapters. As with the ConstInt and ConstLong AST nodes, you should carefully choose what integer types in your implementation language you use to represent both initializers. It's particularly important to make sure that LongInit can accommodate any signed 64-bit integer.

You may need to perform type conversions when converting expressions to static initializers. For example, suppose a program contains the following declaration:

```
static int i = 100L;
```

The constant 100L will be parsed as a ConstLong in our AST. Since it's being assigned to a static int, we'll need to cast it from a long to an int at compile time and store it as an IntInit(100) in the symbol table. This sort of conversion is especially tricky when a variable with type int is initialized with a long constant that's too large to be represented in 32 bits, as in this declaration:

```
static int i = 2147483650L;
```

According to the implementation-defined behavior we specified earlier, we need to subtract 2^{32} from this value until it's small enough to fit in an int. That results in $-2,147,483,646$, so the initial value we record in the symbol table should be IntInit(-2147483646). Ideally, you can use signed integer types that already have the right semantics for type conversions so you won't have to mess with the binary representations of these constants yourself.

Here are a couple of tips to help you handle static initializers:

Make your constant type conversion code reusable.

The type checker isn't the only place where you'll convert constants to a different type. In Part III, you'll implement constant folding in TACKY. The constant folding pass will evaluate constant expressions, including type conversions. You may want to structure your type conversion code as a separate module that you can reuse for constant folding later.

Don't call typecheck_exp on static initializers.

Convert each static initializer directly to a static_init, without calling typecheck_exp first. This will simplify things in later chapters, when typecheck_exp will transform expressions in more complex ways.

TEST THE TYPE CHECKER

To test the type checking pass, run:

```
$ ./test_compiler /path/to/your_compiler --chapter 11 --stage validate
```

Your compiler should fail on the test cases in *tests/chapter_11/invalid _types*. It should succeed on every test case in *tests/chapter_11/valid*.

TACKY Generation

We'll make a few changes to the TACKY AST in this chapter. First, we'll add a type to each top-level StaticVariable and represent each static variable's initial value with our newly defined static_init construct:

```
StaticVariable(identifier, bool global, type t, static_init init)
```

We'll also reuse the const construct from the AST in Listing 11-2 to represent constants:

```
val = Constant(const) | Var(identifier)
```

Finally, we'll introduce a couple of new instructions to convert values between types:

```
SignExtend(val src, val dst)
Truncate(val src, val dst)
```

The SignExtend and Truncate instructions convert from int to long and long to int, respectively. Listing 11-20 gives the complete updated TACKY IR. This listing uses type, static_init, and const without defining them, since we've defined these three constructs already.

```
program = Program(top_level*)
top_level = Function(identifier, bool global, identifier* params, instruction* body)
          | StaticVariable(identifier, bool global, type t, static_init init)
instruction = Return(val)
            | SignExtend(val src, val dst)
            | Truncate(val src, val dst)
            | Unary(unary_operator, val src, val dst)
            | Binary(binary_operator, val src1, val src2, val dst)
            | Copy(val src, val dst)
            | Jump(identifier target)
            | JumpIfZero(val condition, identifier target)
            | JumpIfNotZero(val condition, identifier target)
            | Label(identifier)
            | FunCall(identifier fun_name, val* args, val dst)
val = Constant(const) | Var(identifier)
unary_operator = Complement | Negate | Not
binary_operator = Add | Subtract | Multiply | Divide | Remainder | Equal | NotEqual
                | LessThan | LessOrEqual | GreaterThan | GreaterOrEqual
```

Listing 11-20: Adding support for long integers to TACKY

We'll handle the changes to StaticVariable by looking up type and initializer information in the symbol table during TACKY generation. If a static variable has a tentative definition in the symbol table, we'll initialize it to IntInit(0) or LongInit(0), depending on its type.

Handling constants is even easier; the logic is essentially unchanged from earlier chapters. We'll convert a Constant AST node directly to a TACKY Constant, since they both use the same definition of const.

Recall that when we convert a logical && or || expression to TACKY, we explicitly assign 1 or 0 to the variable that holds the result of the expression. Since these logical expressions both have type int, we represent their results as ConstInt(1) and ConstInt(0).

Listing 11-21 shows how to convert cast expressions to TACKY. We'll use the type information we added in the previous pass to determine what type we're casting from.

```
emit_tacky(e, instructions, symbols):
    match e with
    | --snip--
```

```
| Cast(t, inner) ->
    result = emit_tacky(inner, instructions, symbols)
    if t == get_type(inner):
      ❶ return result
    dst_name = make_temporary()
    symbols.add(dst_name, t, attrs=LocalAttr)
    dst = Var(dst_name)
    if t == Long:
      ❷ instructions.append(SignExtend(result, dst))
    else:
      ❸ instructions.append(Truncate(result, dst))
    return dst
```

Listing 11-21: Converting a cast expression to TACKY

If the inner expression already has the type we want to cast it to, the cast has no effect; we emit TACKY to evaluate the inner expression but don't do anything else ❶. Otherwise, we emit either a SignExtend instruction to cast an int to a long ❷ or a Truncate instruction to cast a long to an int ❸.

Tracking the Types of Temporary Variables

When we create the temporary variable dst in Listing 11-21, we add it to the symbol table with the appropriate type. We need to do this for every temporary variable we create so that we can look up their types during assembly generation. The assembly generation stage will use this type information in two ways: to determine the operand size of each assembly instruction and to figure out how much stack space to allocate for each variable.

Every temporary variable we add holds the result of an expression, so we can determine its type by checking the expression's type annotation. Let's take another look at Listing 3-9, which demonstrated how to convert a binary arithmetic expression to TACKY. Listing 11-22 demonstrates the same conversion, with changes from Listing 3-9 bolded.

```
emit_tacky(e, instructions, symbols):
    match e with
    | --snip--
    | Binary(op, e1, e2) ->
        v1 = emit_tacky(e1, instructions, symbols)
        v2 = emit_tacky(e2, instructions, symbols)
        dst_name = make_temporary()
        symbols.add(dst_name, get_type(e), attrs=LocalAttr)
        dst = Var(dst_name)
        tacky_op = convert_binop(op)
        instructions.append(Binary(tacky_op, v1, v2, dst))
        return dst
    | --snip--
```

Listing 11-22: Tracking temporary variable types when converting a binary expression to TACKY

The main change here is adding dst to the symbol table. Since dst holds the result of expression e, we look up e's type annotation to figure out dst's type. Like every temporary variable, dst is a local, automatic variable, so we'll give it the LocalAttr attribute in the symbol table.

Let's refactor this into a helper function, shown in Listing 11-23.

```
make_tacky_variable(var_type, symbols):
    var_name = make_temporary()
    symbols.add(var_name, var_type, attrs=LocalAttr)
    return Var(var_name)
```

Listing 11-23: A helper function for generating TACKY variables

From now on, we'll use make_tacky_variable whenever we generate a new temporary variable in TACKY.

Generating Extra Return Instructions

In Chapter 5, I mentioned that we add an extra Return instruction to the end of each TACKY function, in case not every execution path in the original C function reaches a return statement. This extra instruction can always return ConstInt(0), even when the function's return type isn't int. When we return from main, this is the correct return type. When we return from any other function that's missing an explicit return statement, the return value is undefined. We still need to return control to the caller, but we aren't obligated to return any particular value, so it doesn't matter if we get the type wrong.

TEST THE TACKY GENERATION STAGE

To test TACKY generation, run:

```
$ ./test_compiler /path/to/your_compiler --chapter 11 --stage tacky
```

Assembly Generation

We'll make several changes to the assembly AST in this chapter. Listing 11-24 gives the complete definition, with changes bolded.

```
program = Program(top_level*)
assembly_type = Longword | Quadword
top_level = Function(identifier name, bool global, instruction* instructions)
          | StaticVariable(identifier name, bool global, int alignment, static_init init)
instruction = Mov(assembly_type, operand src, operand dst)
            | Movsx(operand src, operand dst)
            | Unary(unary_operator, assembly_type, operand)
```

```
            | Binary(binary_operator, assembly_type, operand, operand)
            | Cmp(assembly_type, operand, operand)
            | Idiv(assembly_type, operand)
            | Cdq(assembly_type)
            | Jmp(identifier)
            | JmpCC(cond_code, identifier)
            | SetCC(cond_code, operand)
            | Label(identifier)
            | Push(operand)
            | Call(identifier)
            | Ret
unary_operator = Neg | Not
binary_operator = Add | Sub | Mult
operand = Imm(int) | Reg(reg) | Pseudo(identifier) | Stack(int) | Data(identifier)
cond_code = E | NE | G | GE | L | LE
reg = AX | CX | DX | DI | SI | R8 | R9 | R10 | R11 | SP
```

Listing 11-24: The assembly AST with support for quadword operands and 8-byte static variables

The biggest change is tagging most instructions with the type of their operands. That allows us to choose the correct suffix for each instruction during assembly emission. We'll also add a type to Cdq, since the 32-bit version of Cdq extends EAX into EDX and the 64-bit version extends RAX into RDX. There are just three instructions that take an operand but don't need a type: SetCC, which takes only byte-size operands; Push, which always pushes quadwords; and the new Movsx instruction, which we'll cover in a moment.

Instead of reusing the source-level type we defined earlier, we'll define a new assembly_type construct. This will simplify working with assembly types as we introduce more C types in later chapters. For example, we'll add unsigned integers in Chapter 12, but assembly doesn't distinguish between signed and unsigned integers.

During assembly generation, we'll figure out each instruction's type based on the type of its operands. For example, we'll convert the TACKY instruction

```
Binary(Add, Constant(ConstInt(3)), Var("src"), Var("dst"))
```

to these assembly instructions:

```
Mov(Longword, Imm(3), Pseudo("dst"))
Binary(Add, Longword, Pseudo("src"), Pseudo("dst"))
```

Since the first operand is a ConstInt, we know that the resulting mov and add instructions should use longword operands. We can assume that the second operand and the destination have the same type as the first operand, since we inserted the appropriate type conversion instructions during TACKY generation. If an operand is a variable instead of a constant, we'll look up its type in the symbol table.

We'll also figure out how to pass stack arguments based on their type. Listing 11-25 reproduces the relevant part of convert_function_call, which we defined back in Listing 9-31, with this change bolded.

```
convert_function_call(FunCall(fun_name, args, dst)):
    --snip--
    // pass args on stack
    for tacky_arg in reverse(stack_args):
        assembly_arg = convert_val(tacky_arg)
        if assembly_arg is a Reg or Imm operand or has type Quadword:
            emit(Push(assembly_arg))
        else:
            emit(Mov(Longword, assembly_arg, Reg(AX)))
            emit(Push(Reg(AX)))
    --snip--
```

Listing 11-25: Passing quadwords on the stack in convert_function_call

In Chapter 9, we learned that we could run into trouble if we used an 8-byte pushq instruction to push a 4-byte operand from memory onto the stack. To work around this issue, we emit two instructions to push a 4-byte Pseudo onto the stack: we copy it into EAX, then push RAX. An 8-byte Pseudo doesn't require this workaround; we pass it on the stack with a single Push instruction, the same way we pass an immediate value.

To handle conversions from int to long, we'll use the sign extension instruction, movsx. At the moment, this instruction doesn't need type information, since its source must be an int and its destination must be a long. We'll convert

```
SignExtend(src, dst)
```

to:

```
Movsx(src, dst)
```

To truncate a value, we just move its lowest 4 bytes into the destination using a 4-byte movl instruction. We'll convert

```
Truncate(src, dst)
```

to:

```
Mov(Longword, src, dst)
```

We've also tweaked the StaticVariable construct:

```
StaticVariable(identifier name, bool global, int alignment, static_init init)
```

We hold onto the static_init construct from TACKY, so we know whether to initialize 4 or 8 bytes for each static variable. We add an alignment field too, since we'll need to specify each static variable's alignment in assembly.

Finally, we've removed the DeallocateStack and AllocateStack instructions from the assembly AST. These instructions were just placeholders for quadword addition and subtraction, which we can now represent with ordinary addq and subq instructions. Since DeallocateStack and AllocateStack represented adding to and subtracting from RSP, we've also added the RSP register to the assembly AST so we can use it in normal instructions. In earlier chapters, we maintained the stack alignment before function calls with the instruction:

AllocateStack(bytes)

Now we'll use this instruction instead:

Binary(Sub, Quadword, Imm(bytes), Reg(SP))

Similarly, instead of

DeallocateStack(bytes)

---

we'll use

Binary(Add, Quadword, Imm(bytes), Reg(SP))

---

to restore the stack pointer after function calls.

Tables 11-1 through 11-4 summarize this chapter's updates to the conversion from TACKY to assembly. New constructs and changes to the conversions for existing constructs are bolded.

Table 11-1: Converting Top-Level TACKY Constructs to Assembly

TACKY top-level construct	Assembly top-level construct
Function(name, global, params, instructions)	Function(name, global, [Mov(*<param1 type>*, Reg(DI), param1), Mov(*<param2 type>*, Reg(SI), param2), *<copy next four parameters from registers>*, Mov(*<param7 type>*, Stack(16), param7), Mov(*<param8 type>*, Stack(24), param8), *<copy remaining parameters from stack>*] + instructions)
StaticVariable(name, global, **t**, init)	StaticVariable(name, global, *<alignment of t>*, init)

Table 11-2: Converting TACKY Instructions to Assembly

TACKY instruction	Assembly instructions
Return(val)	Mov(**<val type>**, val, Reg(AX)) Ret
Unary(Not, src, dst)	Cmp(**<src type>**, Imm(0), src) Mov(**<dst type>**, Imm(0), dst) SetCC(E, dst)
Unary(unary_operator, src, dst)	Mov(**<src type>**, src, dst) Unary(unary_operator, **<src type>**, dst)
Binary(Divide, src1, src2, dst)	Mov(**<src1 type>**, src1, Reg(AX)) Cdq(**<src1 type>**) Idiv(**<src1 type>**, src2) Mov(**<src1 type>**, Reg(AX), dst)
Binary(Remainder, src1, src2, dst)	Mov(**<src1 type>**, src1, Reg(AX)) Cdq(**<src1 type>**) Idiv(**<src1 type>**, src2) Mov(**<src1 type>**, Reg(DX), dst)
Binary(arithmetic_operator, src1, src2, dst)	Mov(**<src1 type>**, src1, dst) Binary(arithmetic_operator, **<src1 type>**, src2, dst)
Binary(relational_operator, src1, src2, dst)	Cmp(**<src1 type>**, src2, src1) Mov(**<dst type>**, Imm(0), dst) SetCC(relational_operator, dst)
JumpIfZero(condition, target)	Cmp(**<condition type>**, Imm(0), condition) JmpCC(E, target)
JumpIfNotZero(condition, target)	Cmp(**<condition type>**, Imm(0), condition) JmpCC(NE, target)
Copy(src, dst)	Mov(**<src type>**, src, dst)
FunCall(fun_name, args, dst)	*<fix stack alignment>* *<set up arguments>* Call(fun_name) *<deallocate arguments/padding>* Mov(**<dst type>**, Reg(AX), dst)
SignExtend(src, dst)	**Movsx(src, dst)**
Truncate(src, dst)	**Mov(Longword, src, dst)**

Table 11-3: Converting TACKY Operands to Assembly

TACKY operand	Assembly operand
Constant(**ConstInt(int)**)	Imm(int)
Constant(**ConstLong(int)**)	**Imm(int)**

Table 11-4: Converting Types to Assembly

Source type	Assembly type	Alignment
Int	Longword	4
Long	Quadword	8

In Table 11-3, we convert both types of TACKY constants to `Imm` operands. In assembly, there's no distinction between 4-byte and 8-byte immediate values. The assembler infers how large an immediate value should be based on the operand size of the instruction where it appears.

Table 11-4 gives the conversion from source-level to assembly types, as well as each type's alignment. Note that this conversion fits into the whole compiler pass a bit differently than the conversions in Tables 11-1 through 11-3, because when we traverse a TACKY program, we won't encounter type AST nodes that we can convert directly to `assembly_type` nodes in the assembly program. As we've seen, we typically need to infer a TACKY instruction's operand type before we can convert it to an assembly type. The one TACKY construct with an explicit type is `StaticVariable`, but we don't need to convert this type to an assembly type; we only need to calculate its alignment. We'll use the conversion shown in Table 11-4 again in the next step of this compiler pass, where we'll construct a new symbol table to track assembly types.

Tracking Assembly Types in the Backend Symbol Table

After converting the TACKY program to assembly, we'll convert the symbol table to a form that's better suited to the remaining compiler passes. This new symbol table will store variables' assembly types, rather than their source types. It will also store a handful of other properties that we'll need to look up in the pseudoregister replacement, instruction fix-up, and code emission passes. I'll call this new symbol table the *backend symbol table*. I'll call the existing one either the *frontend symbol table* or just the *symbol table*.

The backend symbol table maps each identifier to an `asm_symtab_entry` construct, defined in Listing 11-26.

```
asm_symtab_entry = ObjEntry(assembly_type, bool is_static)
                 | FunEntry(bool defined)
```

Listing 11-26: The definition of an entry in the backend symbol table

We'll use `ObjEntry` to represent variables (and, in later chapters, constants). We'll track each object's assembly type and whether it has static storage duration. `FunEntry` represents functions. We don't need to track the types of functions—which is just as well, since `assembly_type` can't represent function types—but we do track whether they're defined in the current translation unit. If you're tracking each function's stack frame size in the symbol table, add an extra `stack_frame_size` field to the `FunEntry` constructor. I recommend making the backend symbol table a global variable or singleton, just like the existing frontend symbol table.

At the very end of the TACKY-to-assembly conversion pass, you should iterate over the frontend symbol table and convert each entry to an entry in the backend symbol table. This process is simple enough that I won't provide the pseudocode for it. You'll also need to update any spots in the pseudoregister replacement, instruction fix-up, and code emission passes that refer to the frontend symbol table and have them use the backend symbol table instead.

Replacing Longword and Quadword Pseudoregisters

The pseudoregister replacement pass requires a couple of changes. First, we'll extend it to replace pseudoregisters in the new movsx instruction. Second, whenever we assign a stack address to a pseudoregister, we'll look up the pseudoregister's type in the backend symbol table to determine how much space to allocate. If it's a Quadword, we'll allocate 8 bytes; if it's a Longword, we'll allocate 4 bytes, as before. Finally, we'll make sure that the address of each Quadword pseudoregister is 8-byte aligned on the stack. Consider the following fragment of assembly:

```
Mov(Longword, Imm(0), Pseudo("foo"))
Mov(Quadword, Imm(1), Pseudo("bar"))
```

Suppose we look up the type of foo in the backend symbol table and see that it's 4 bytes. We'll assign it to -4(%rbp), as usual. Next, we'll look up bar and see that it's 8 bytes. We could assign it to -12(%rbp), which is 8 bytes below foo. But then bar would be misaligned, since its address wouldn't be a multiple of 8 bytes. (Remember that the address in RBP is always 16-byte aligned.) To maintain the correct alignment, we'll round down to the next multiple of 8 and store bar at -16(%rbp) instead. Alignment requirements are part of the System V ABI; if you ignore them, your code may not interact correctly with code in other translation units.

Fixing Up Instructions

We'll make several updates to the instruction fix-up pass in this chapter. First, we need to specify operand sizes for all the instructions in our existing rewrite rules. These should always have the same operand size as the original instruction being rewritten.

Next, we'll rewrite the movsx instruction. It can't use a memory address as a destination or an immediate value as a source. If both operands to movsx are invalid, we'll need to use both R10 and R11 to fix them. For example, we'll rewrite

```
Movsx(Imm(10), Stack(-16))
```

to:

```
Mov(Longword, Imm(10), Reg(R10))
Movsx(Reg(R10), Reg(R11))
Mov(Quadword, Reg(R11), Stack(-16))
```

It's important to use the right operand size for each mov instruction in this rewrite rule. Since the source operand of movsx is 4 bytes, we specify a longword operand size when moving that operand into a register. Since the result of movsx is 8 bytes, we specify a quadword operand size when we move the result to its final memory location.

The quadword versions of our three binary arithmetic instructions (addq, imulq, and subq) can't handle immediate values that don't fit into an int, and neither can cmpq or pushq. If the source of any of these instructions is a constant outside the range of int, we'll need to copy it into R10 before we can use it.

The movq instruction can move these very large immediate values into registers, but not directly into memory, so

```
Mov(Quadword, Imm(4294967295), Stack(-16))
```

should be rewritten as:

```
Mov(Quadword, Imm(4294967295), Reg(R10))
Mov(Quadword, Reg(R10), Stack(-16))
```

NOTE *The assembler permits an immediate value in addq, imulq, subq, cmpq, or pushq only if it can be represented as a* signed *32-bit integer. That's because these instructions all sign extend their immediate operands from 32 to 64 bits. If an immediate value can be represented in 32 bits only as an* unsigned *integer—which implies that its upper bit is set—sign extending it will change its value. For more details, see this Stack Overflow question:* https://stackoverflow.com/questions/64289590/integer-overflow-in-gas.

We'll also fix how we allocate stack space at the start of each function. Instead of adding AllocateStack(bytes) to each function to allocate space on the stack, we'll add the following instruction, which does the same thing:

```
Binary(Sub, Quadword, Imm(bytes), Reg(SP))
```

We'll add one last rewrite rule to placate the assembler, although it isn't strictly necessary. Remember that we convert the Truncate TACKY instruction to a 4-byte movl, which means we can generate movl instructions that move 8-byte immediate values to 4-byte destinations:

```
Mov(Longword, Imm(4294967299), Reg(R10))
```

Since movl can't use 8-byte immediate values, the assembler automatically truncates these values to 32 bits. When it processes the instruction movl $4294967299, %r10d, for example, it will convert the immediate value 4294967299 to 3. The GNU assembler issues a warning when it performs this conversion, although the LLVM assembler doesn't. To avoid these warnings, we'll truncate 8-byte immediate values in movl instructions ourselves. That means we'll rewrite the previous instruction as:

```
Mov(Longword, Imm(3), Reg(R10))
```

Assembler warnings aside, your assembly programs will still work even if you don't include this rewrite rule.

Code Emission

Our final task is to extend the code emission stage. We'll add the appropriate suffix to every instruction, emit the correct alignment and initial value for static variables, and handle the new Movsx instruction. Whenever an instruction uses a register, we'll emit the appropriate register name for that instruction's operand size.

Instructions with 4-byte operands have an l suffix, for longword, and instructions with 8-byte operands have a q suffix, for quadword, with one exception: the 8-byte version of cdq has a completely different mnemonic, cqo. The Movsx instruction takes suffixes for both its source and destination operand sizes. For example, movslq sign extends a longword to a quadword. For now, we'll always emit this instruction with an lq suffix; we'll need more suffixes as we add more assembly types in later chapters. (You may also see this instruction written as movsx when it's possible for the assembler to infer the size of both operands. For example, the assembler will accept the instruction movsx %r10d, %r11, since it can infer the source and destination sizes from the register names.)

Tables 11-5 through 11-10 summarize this chapter's updates to the code emission pass. New constructs and changes to existing constructs are bolded.

Table 11-5: Formatting Top-Level Assembly Constructs

Assembly top-level construct		Output
StaticVariable(name, global, **alignment**, init)	Initialized to zero	*<global-directive>* .bss *<alignment-directive>* *<name>*: **<init>**
	Initialized to nonzero value	*<global-directive>* .data *<alignment-directive>* *<name>*: **<init>**
Alignment directive	Linux only	.align **<alignment>**
	macOS or Linux	.balign **<alignment>**

Table 11-6: Formatting Static Initializers

Static initializer	Output
IntInit(0)	.zero 4
IntInit(i)	.long *<i>*
LongInit(0)	.zero 8
LongInit(i)	.quad *<i>*

Table 11-7: Formatting Assembly Instructions

Assembly instruction	Output
Mov(t, src, dst)	mov*<t>* *<src>*, *<dst>*
Movsx(src, dst)	movslq *<src>*, *<dst>*
Unary(unary_operator, t, operand)	*<unary_operator><t>* *<operand>*
Binary(binary_operator, t, src, dst)	*<binary_operator><t>* *<src>*, *<dst>*
Idiv(t, operand)	idiv*<t>* *<operand>*
Cdq(Longword)	cdq
Cdq(Quadword)	**cqo**
Cmp(t, operand, operand)	cmp*<t>* *<operand>*, *<operand>*

Table 11-8: Instruction Names for Assembly Operators

Assembly operator	Instruction name
Neg	**neg**
Not	**not**
Add	**add**
Sub	**sub**
Mult	**imul**

Table 11-9: Instruction Suffixes for Assembly Types

Assembly type	Instruction suffix
Longword	l
Quadword	q

Table 11-10: Formatting Assembly Operands

Assembly operand	Output
Reg(SP)	%rsp

Table 11-6 shows how to print out the static_init constructs representing static variable initializers. Table 11-8 shows the mapping from unary and binary operators to instruction names without suffixes; the suffix now depends on the instruction's type (as shown in Table 11-9). Aside from the suffix, these instruction names are the same as in earlier chapters.

Once you've updated the code emission stage, you're ready to test out your compiler.

TEST THE WHOLE COMPILER

To test the whole compiler, run:

```
$ ./test_compiler /path/to/your_compiler --chapter 11
```

The test programs in *tests/chapter_11/valid/long_expressions* validate that the expressions we implemented in earlier chapters, like addition, subtraction, and comparisons, work correctly with long operands. The programs in *tests/chapter_11/valid/explicit_casts* test explicit casts between int and long, and the programs in *tests/chapter_11/valid/implicit_casts* test that we perform the correct implicit type conversions to evaluate expressions involving both types. Finally, the test cases in *tests/chapter_11/valid/libraries* validate that compiled code dealing with long integers conforms to the System V ABI.

Summary

Your compiler has a type system now! In this chapter, you annotated the AST with type information, used the symbol table to track type information through multiple compiler stages, and added support for multiple operand sizes during assembly generation. Long integers aren't the flashiest language feature, so it might feel like you've done a lot of work and don't have much to show for it. But the infrastructure you created in this chapter is the basis for everything you'll do in the rest of Part II. In the next chapter, you'll build on that work by implementing unsigned integers.

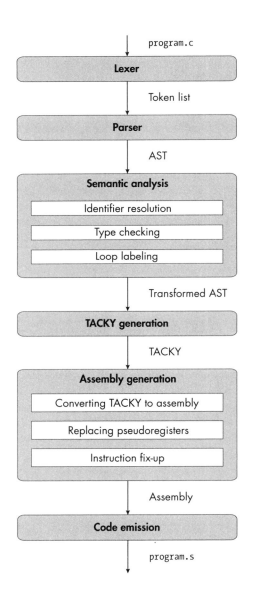

12

UNSIGNED INTEGERS

In this chapter, you'll implement the unsigned counterparts to our two signed integer types: unsigned int and unsigned long. You'll extend the usual arithmetic conversions to handle unsigned integers and implement casts between signed and unsigned types. On the backend, you'll use a few new assembly instructions to do unsigned integer arithmetic.

In Chapter 11, we focused on inferring and tracking type information in general; now we'll be able to build on that work to add new types with relatively little effort. Before we modify the compiler, let's start with a quick overview of conversions between signed and unsigned types.

Type Conversions, Again

Every integer type conversion has two aspects we need to consider: how the integer's value changes and how its binary representation changes. We saw this in the conversions between int and long in the previous chapter. Sign extension changes a signed integer's representation from 32 to 64 bits without changing its value. Truncating a long to an int also changes its representation, and it changes its value too if the original value can't fit in the new type.

With that distinction in mind, I'll break our type conversions down into four cases. In each case, I'll describe how the integer's representation will change. Then, I'll explain how that corresponds with the rules in the C standard about how its value should change.

Converting Between Signed and Unsigned Types of the Same Size

The first case is when we convert between signed and unsigned types of the same size: that is, between int and unsigned int or between long and unsigned long. These conversions don't change the binary representation of the integer. The only thing that changes is whether we use two's complement to interpret its value. Let's consider the effect of that change in interpretation.

If a signed integer is positive, its upper bit will be 0, so interpreting it as an unsigned integer won't change its value. The reverse is also true: if an unsigned integer is smaller than the maximum value the signed type can represent, its upper bit must be 0. Therefore, if we reinterpret it using two's complement, its value won't change. As you learned in the previous chapter, when we convert an integer to a new type, the standard requires us to preserve its value if we can. We're satisfying that requirement here.

That leaves integers whose upper bit is 1. When we reinterpret a signed negative integer as unsigned, we change the upper bit's value from negative to positive. If the upper bit is 1, this has the effect of adding 2^N to the value, where N is the number of bits in the type. This is exactly the behavior the standard requires; section 6.3.1.3, paragraph 2, states that if the value can't be represented by the new type and the new type is unsigned, "the value is converted by repeatedly adding or subtracting one more than the maximum value that can be represented in the new type until the value is in the range of the new type."

Conversely, converting an unsigned type with a leading 1 to the corresponding signed type will subtract 2^N from its value. This matches the implementation-defined behavior we chose in the last chapter for conversions to signed integers, following GCC: "The value is reduced modulo $2^{\wedge}N$ to be within range of the type."

Converting unsigned int to a Larger Type

The second case is when we convert unsigned int to a larger type, either long or unsigned long. To handle this case, we'll *zero extend* the integer by filling the upper bits of the new representation with zeros. This conversion always preserves the original value, since we're just adding leading zeros to a positive number.

Converting signed int to a Larger Type

The third case is when we convert a signed int to a long or unsigned long. We already convert int to long using sign extension. We'll convert int to unsigned long the same way. If an int is positive, sign extension will just add leading zeros, which preserves its value whether you interpret the result as signed or unsigned. If the value is negative, sign extending and then interpreting the result as an unsigned long will add 2^{64} to its value, as the standard requires.

Converting from Larger to Smaller Types

In the final case, we convert a larger type (long or unsigned long) to a smaller one (int or unsigned int). We always handle this case by truncating the value. This has the effect of adding or subtracting 2^{32} until the value is in the range of the new type—or, equivalently, reducing the value modulo 2^{32}—which is the behavior we want. I won't walk you through why truncating the integer produces the correct value in every case; you can work through some examples on your own, or just take my word for it.

Now that you know what to expect from type conversions, let's get to work on the compiler.

The Lexer

You'll add four new tokens in this chapter:

signed   A keyword used to specify a signed integer type.

unsigned   A keyword used to specify an unsigned integer type.

Unsigned integer constants   Integer constants with a u or U suffix. An unsigned constant token matches the regex [0-9]+[uU]\b.

Unsigned long integer constants   Integer constants with a case-insensitive ul or lu suffix. An unsigned long constant token matches the regex [0-9]+([lL][uU]|[uU][lL])\b.

Update your lexer to support these tokens, then test it out.

TEST THE LEXER

To test your lexer, run:

```
$ ./test_compiler /path/to/your_compiler --chapter 12 --stage lex
```

The lexer should fail on the test cases in *tests/chapter_12/invalid_lex*, which include invalid constant tokens. It should successfully process the test cases in all the other subdirectories of *tests/chapter_12*.

The Parser

Next, we'll update the AST to support the two new unsigned types and their corresponding constants. These updates are bolded in Listing 12-1.

```
program = Program(declaration*)
declaration = FunDecl(function_declaration) | VarDecl(variable_declaration)
variable_declaration = (identifier name, exp? init,
                        type var_type, storage_class?)
function_declaration = (identifier name, identifier* params, block? body,
                        type fun_type, storage_class?)
type = Int | Long | UInt | ULong | FunType(type* params, type ret)
storage_class = Static | Extern
block_item = S(statement) | D(declaration)
block = Block(block_item*)
for_init = InitDecl(variable_declaration) | InitExp(exp?)
statement = Return(exp)
          | Expression(exp)
          | If(exp condition, statement then, statement? else)
          | Compound(block)
          | Break
          | Continue
          | While(exp condition, statement body)
          | DoWhile(statement body, exp condition)
          | For(for_init init, exp? condition, exp? post, statement body)
          | Null
exp = Constant(const)
    | Var(identifier)
    | Cast(type target_type, exp)
    | Unary(unary_operator, exp)
    | Binary(binary_operator, exp, exp)
    | Assignment(exp, exp)
    | Conditional(exp condition, exp, exp)
    | FunctionCall(identifier, exp* args)
unary_operator = Complement | Negate | Not
binary_operator = Add | Subtract | Multiply | Divide | Remainder | And | Or
                | Equal | NotEqual | LessThan | LessOrEqual
                | GreaterThan | GreaterOrEqual
const = ConstInt(int) | ConstLong(int) | ConstUInt(int) | ConstULong(int)
```

Listing 12-1: The abstract syntax tree with unsigned types and unsigned constants

Just like when you added ConstLong in the previous chapter, you need to make sure ConstUInt can represent the full range of unsigned int and ConstULong can represent the full range of unsigned long. If your implementation language has unsigned 32-bit and 64-bit integer types, use them here.

Listing 12-2 shows the updated grammar, with the changes bolded.

```
<program> ::= { <declaration> }
<declaration> ::= <variable-declaration> | <function-declaration>
<variable-declaration> ::= { <specifier> }+ <identifier> [ "=" <exp> ] ";"
<function-declaration> ::= { <specifier> }+ <identifier> "(" <param-list> ")" ( <block> | ";")
<param-list> ::= "void"
              | { <type-specifier> }+ <identifier> { "," { <type-specifier> }+ <identifier> }
```

```
<type-specifier> ::= "int" | "long" | "unsigned" | "signed"
<specifier> ::= <type-specifier> | "static" | "extern"
<block> ::= "{" { <block-item> } "}"
<block-item> ::= <statement> | <declaration>
<for-init> ::= <variable-declaration> | [ <exp> ] ";"
<statement> ::= "return" <exp> ";"
              | <exp> ";"
              | "if" "(" <exp> ")" <statement> [ "else" <statement> ]
              | <block>
              | "break" ";"
              | "continue" ";"
              | "while" "(" <exp> ")" <statement>
              | "do" <statement> "while" "(" <exp> ")" ";"
              | "for" "(" <for-init> [ <exp> ] ";" [ <exp> ] ")" <statement>
              | ";"
<exp> ::= <factor> | <exp> <binop> <exp> | <exp> "?" <exp> ":" <exp>
<factor> ::= <const> | <identifier>
           | "(" { <type-specifier> }+ ")" <factor>
           | <unop> <factor> | "(" <exp> ")"
           | <identifier> "(" [ <argument-list> ] ")"
<argument-list> ::= <exp> { "," <exp> }
<unop> ::= "-" | "~" | "!"
<binop> ::= "-" | "+" | "*" | "/" | "%" | "&&" | "||"
          | "==" | "!=" | "<" | "<=" | ">" | ">=" | "="
<const> ::= <int> | <long> | <uint> | <ulong>
<identifier> ::= ? An identifier token ?
<int> ::= ? An int token ?
<long> ::= ? An int or long token ?
<uint> ::= ? An unsigned int token ?
<ulong> ::= ? An unsigned int or unsigned long token ?
```

Listing 12-2: The grammar with the signed and unsigned type specifiers and unsigned constants

Parsing type specifiers is more complicated than in the previous chapter because there are so many different ways to refer to the same type. For example, these are all valid ways to specify the long type:

```
long

long int

signed long

signed long int
```

The order of type specifiers doesn't matter, so long signed, long int signed, and so on all specify the same type. The pseudocode in Listing 12-3 provides one way to impose order on this chaos.

```
parse_type(specifier_list):
    if (specifier_list is empty
        or specifier_list contains the same specifier twice
        or specifier_list contains both "signed" and "unsigned"):
        fail("Invalid type specifier")
    if specifier_list contains "unsigned" and "long":
        return ULong
```

```
if specifier_list contains "unsigned":
    return UInt
if specifier_list contains "long":
    return Long
return Int
```

Listing 12-3: Determining a type from a list of type specifiers

We start by checking for error cases. You need at least one specifier to indicate a type, and you can't include the same specifier twice. You can't specify a type as int long int, for example. (The long long type specifier would complicate this validation check, but we're not implementing it.) You also can't include the signed and unsigned specifiers in the same type specification, since they contradict each other.

Once we know our input specifies a valid type, we check for the unsigned and long specifiers. If both are present, the type is unsigned long. Otherwise, if unsigned is present, the type is unsigned int; if long is present, the type is long; if neither is present, the type is int. Basically, int is the default type, and the unsigned and long specifiers can indicate a type other than the default. Section 6.7.2, paragraph 2, of the C standard enumerates all the ways you can specify each type.

We also need to deal with constant tokens. In the previous chapter, Listing 11-6 demonstrated how to parse signed constant tokens. I won't include the corresponding pseudocode for unsigned constant tokens here, but the logic is the same. We parse an unsigned integer constant token as ConstUInt if it's within the range of values an unsigned int can hold; that is, between 0 and $2^{32} - 1$, inclusive. Otherwise, we parse it as a ConstULong.

An unsigned long constant token will always be parsed to a ConstULong. If either kind of unsigned constant token isn't in the range for unsigned long (between 0 and $2^{64} - 1$), we'll throw an error. If you're curious, section 6.4.4.1 of the C standard has the full rules for determining the types of integer constants.

TEST THE PARSER

To test your parser, run:

```
$ ./test_compiler /path/to/your_compiler --chapter 12 --stage parse
```

It should fail on all the test cases in *tests/chapter_12/invalid_parse* and succeed on all the test cases in *tests/chapter_12/invalid_types* and *tests/chapter_12/valid*.

The Type Checker

We don't need to change the loop labeling or identifier resolution passes in this chapter. We just need to handle unsigned integers in the type checker.

First, we'll update our implementation of the usual arithmetic conversions, which implicitly convert the operands in a binary expression to a common type. Let's walk through the usual arithmetic conversion rules for integer types, which are defined in section 6.3.1.8, paragraph 1, of the C standard. The first rule is pretty self-explanatory:

> If both operands have the same type, then no further conversion is needed.

The second one is a little harder to follow:

> Otherwise, if both operands have signed integer types or both have unsigned integer types, the operand with the type of the lesser integer conversion rank is converted to the type of the operand with greater rank.

This just means "if both integers have the same signedness, convert the smaller type to the bigger one." We already do this when we implicitly convert values from int to long. Section 6.3.1.1, paragraph 1, specifies the *integer conversion rank* of every integer type, which provides a relative order on their sizes without nailing down those sizes exactly. Of the types we have so far, long and unsigned long have the highest rank, then int and unsigned int. The signed and unsigned versions of the same type always have the same rank. Because of their relative conversion ranks, long is guaranteed to be at least as large as int but not necessarily larger. (In fact, the two types are the same size on most 32-bit systems.) Regardless of their exact sizes, the common type of long and int is long, and the common type of unsigned long and unsigned int is unsigned long. No big surprises here.

The third rule talks about cases with one signed operand and one unsigned operand:

> Otherwise, if the operand that has unsigned integer type has rank greater or equal to the rank of the type of the other operand, then the operand with signed integer type is converted to the type of the operand with unsigned integer type.

So, if the two types are the same size, or if the unsigned type is bigger, we go with the unsigned type. For example, the common type of int and unsigned int is unsigned int, and the common type of int and unsigned long is unsigned long. That leaves the case where the signed type is bigger, which is covered by the fourth rule:

> Otherwise, if the type of the operand with signed integer type can represent all of the values of the type of the operand with unsigned integer type, then the operand with unsigned integer type is converted to the type of the operand with signed integer type.

Under the System V x64 ABI, a long can represent every value of type unsigned int, so the common type of unsigned int and long is long. This isn't true in implementations where `long` and `int` are the same size. In these implementations, `long` has a higher rank than `int` but can't represent every value of type `unsigned int`. The fifth and final rule covers these implementations. Even though this rule doesn't apply to us, I'll include it for the sake of completeness:

> Otherwise, both operands are converted to the unsigned integer type corresponding to the type of the operand with signed integer type.

So, on systems where `long` and `int` are the same size, the common type of `long` and `unsigned int` is `unsigned long`.

This all boils down to three rules for finding the common type, which Listing 12-4 describes in pseudocode.

```
get_common_type(type1, type2):
❶ if type1 == type2:
      return type1
❷ if size(type1) == size(type2):
      if type1 is signed:
          return type2
      else:
          return type1
❸ if size(type1) > size(type2):
      return type1
  else:
      return type2
```

Listing 12-4: Finding the common type of two integers

First, if the types are the same, pick either one ❶. Otherwise, if they're the same size, choose the unsigned one ❷. If they're not the same size, choose the bigger one ❸. Apart from the usual arithmetic conversions, we'll make one tiny update to the logic for type checking expressions: we'll annotate unsigned constants with the correct type, in the same way that we already annotate signed constants.

Next, let's look at how we record the initial values of static variables in the symbol table. We'll add two new kinds of static initializers, just like we added two new kinds of constants:

```
static_init = IntInit(int) | LongInit(int) | UIntInit(int) | ULongInit(int)
```

We need to convert each initializer to the type of the variable it's initializing, according to the type conversion rules presented at the beginning of this chapter. Consider the following declaration:

```
static unsigned int u = 4294967299L;
```

The value 4,294,967,299 is outside the range of `unsigned int`. When adding `u` to the symbol table, we'll convert this value to an `unsigned int` by subtracting 2^{32} from it. (In practice, you can probably just use the equivalent integer type conversion in your implementation language.) The resulting initializer will be UIntInit(3).

Along the same lines, this declaration initializes an int with a value outside of its range:

```
static int i = 4294967246u;
```

Once we reduce this value modulo 2^{32}, the resulting initializer will be IntInit(-50).

It isn't strictly necessary to have different static initializers for signed and unsigned variables. Instead, you could use IntInit to represent both int and unsigned int initializers and use LongInit to represent both long and unsigned long initializers. Ultimately, the assembler will write out the same bytes for an initializer whether you represent it as a signed or unsigned value: the directives .long -50 and .long 4294967246 mean exactly the same thing. Having separate UIntInit and ULongInit initializers just makes our type conversions easier to keep track of.

TEST THE TYPE CHECKER

To test the type checking pass, run:

```
$ ./test_compiler /path/to/your_compiler --chapter 12 --stage validate
```

Your type checker should fail on the test cases in *tests/chapter_12/invalid_types*. These tests include declarations with conflicting types. The type checker should succeed on every test case in *tests/chapter_12/valid*.

TACKY Generation

We'll make one addition to TACKY in this chapter: a ZeroExtend instruction. Listing 12-5 defines the whole TACKY IR.

```
program = Program(top_level*)
top_level = Function(identifier, bool global, identifier* params, instruction* body)
          | StaticVariable(identifier, bool global, type t, static_init init)
instruction = Return(val)
          | SignExtend(val src, val dst)
          | Truncate(val src, val dst)
          | ZeroExtend(val src, val dst)
          | Unary(unary_operator, val src, val dst)
          | Binary(binary_operator, val src1, val src2, val dst)
          | Copy(val src, val dst)
          | Jump(identifier target)
          | JumpIfZero(val condition, identifier target)
```

```
                | JumpIfNotZero(val condition, identifier target)
                | Label(identifier)
                | FunCall(identifier fun_name, val* args, val dst)
val = Constant(const) | Var(identifier)
unary_operator = Complement | Negate | Not
binary_operator = Add | Subtract | Multiply | Divide | Remainder | Equal | NotEqual
                | LessThan | LessOrEqual | GreaterThan | GreaterOrEqual
```

Listing 12-5: Adding the ZeroExtend instruction to TACKY

Now we have to generate the right TACKY for cast expressions that convert to and from unsigned types. At the beginning of this chapter, we discussed how converting an integer to a new type affected its binary representation in four different cases. Listing 12-6 demonstrates what TACKY instructions to emit in each of those cases.

```
emit_tacky(e, instructions, symbols):
    match e with
    | --snip--
    | Cast(t, inner) ->
        result = emit_tacky(inner, instructions, symbols)
        inner_type = get_type(inner)
        if t == inner_type:
            return result
        dst = make_tacky_variable(t, symbols)
    ❶ if size(t) == size(inner_type):
            instructions.append(Copy(result, dst))
    ❷ else if size(t) < size(inner_type):
            instructions.append(Truncate(result, dst))
    ❸ else if inner_type is signed:
            instructions.append(SignExtend(result, dst))
    ❹ else:
            instructions.append(ZeroExtend(result, dst))
        return dst
```

Listing 12-6: Converting a cast expression to TACKY

As in the previous chapter, the cast expression does nothing if the inner expression already has the correct type. Otherwise, we check if the original type and the target type are the same size ❶. If they are, we don't need to extend, truncate, or otherwise change the inner value, because its representation in assembly won't change. We just copy it into a temporary variable with the correct type. The Copy instruction here may seem redundant, but we need it to help us track type information during assembly generation. We'll generate different assembly for certain TACKY instructions depending on whether their operands are signed or unsigned. If we don't store the result of each expression in a variable of the correct type, we'll generate incorrect assembly.

Next, we check whether the target type is smaller than the original type ❷. In that case, we'll issue a Truncate instruction. If that check also fails, this cast expression converts a smaller type to a larger one. We issue a SignExtend instruction if the original type is signed ❸ and a ZeroExtend instruction if it's unsigned ❹.

Once your compiler generates the correct TACKY for unsigned constants and cast expressions, you can test it out.

TEST THE TACKY GENERATION STAGE

To test TACKY generation, run:

```
$ ./test_compiler /path/to/your_compiler --chapter 12 --stage tacky
```

Unsigned Integer Operations in Assembly

In most cases, we can use exactly the same assembly instructions to operate on signed and unsigned values. However, there are two cases where we handle unsigned values differently: comparisons and division. We'll need to translate the new ZeroExtend instruction to assembly too. Before we update the assembly generation stage, let's look at how unsigned comparisons, unsigned division, and zero extension work in assembly.

Unsigned Comparisons

In Chapter 4, you learned how to compare two integers: issue a cmp instruction to set the RFLAGS register, then issue a conditional instruction whose behavior depends on the state of that register. We'll use the same approach to compare unsigned integers, but we need different condition codes that rely on different flags.

Several instructions that perform arithmetic, including add, sub, and cmp, don't distinguish between signed and unsigned values. Listing 12-7 demonstrates how a single operation can implement both signed and unsigned addition.

```
   1000
+ 0010
------
   1010
```

Listing 12-7: Adding binary integers

If we interpret the operands and the result as unsigned 4-bit integers, Listing 12-7 calculates $8 + 2 = 10$. If we interpret them as signed 4-bit integers, it calculates $-8 + 2 = -6$. As long as we interpret both operands and the result consistently, we get the right answer either way. You can think of the results of add, sub, and most other arithmetic assembly instructions as sequences of bits with two possible values, one signed and one unsigned.

After the processor executes one of these instructions, some flags in RFLAGS tell us about the signed value of the result, others tell us about its unsigned value, and still others apply to both values. (Some flags have nothing to do with the results of these instructions, but we don't care about them.) We discussed three flags in Chapter 4: ZF, the zero flag; SF, the sign flag; and OF, the overflow flag. ZF applies whether we interpret the result as signed or unsigned, since zero is represented the same way in either case. The SF and OF flags, however, give us meaningful information only about the result's signed value.

SF, for example, indicates that the result is negative. In Chapter 4, we used this flag to conclude that a - b was negative. In that case, assuming there was no overflow, we knew that a was less than b. That won't work for unsigned values, which are positive by definition. Consider Listing 12-8, which uses unsigned 4-bit integers to calculate 15 − 3.

```
  1111
- 0011
------
  1100
```

Listing 12-8: Subtracting binary integers

Since 15 is greater than 3, the result of this operation is a positive number, 12. The fact that the result has a leading 1 doesn't tell us anything about which operand is larger. Similarly, OF tells us that the signed value of some instruction's result wrapped around from positive to negative, or vice versa, which doesn't tell us anything useful about its unsigned value.

To compare unsigned integers, we'll use CF, the *carry flag*. This flag indicates that the unsigned value of a result wrapped around because the correct value was less than zero or greater than the maximum value the type could hold. For example, suppose we want to compute 15 + 1 with unsigned 4-bit integers. The 4-bit unsigned representation of 15 is 1111; when we increment it, it wraps around to 0000. This computation will set the carry flag to 1. The carry flag will also be set if we try to calculate 0 − 1 and the result wraps around in the other direction to 1111, or 15. If a < b, the result of a - b will always wrap around and set the carry flag. If a > b, the result will always be representable as an unsigned integer, so it won't have to wrap around. Let's walk through how cmp b, a will impact CF and ZF when we interpret a and b as unsigned integers:

- If a == b, then a - b will be 0, so ZF will be 1 and CF will be 0.
- If a > b, then a - b will be a positive number. It will be greater than 0 but less than or equal to a, so it won't wrap around. ZF and CF will both be 0.
- If a < b, then a - b will be negative, so it will have to wrap around. ZF will be 0 and CF will be 1.

Note that ZF and CF are mutually exclusive; one operation will never set both of them. All the condition codes we need in this chapter depend on one or both of these flags. Table 12-1 lists these condition codes.

Table 12-1: Condition Codes for Unsigned Comparisons

Condition code	Meaning	Flags
E	a == b	ZF set
NE	a != b	ZF not set
A	a > b	CF not set and ZF not set
AE	a >= b	CF not set
B	a < b	CF set
BE	a <= b	CF set or ZF set

We use the existing E and NE condition codes to test for equality and inequality, but we'll use new codes to determine which of two operands is larger. The A and B in the new codes are mnemonics for "above" and "below." The new condition codes can appear in conditional jump and set instructions, just like the old ones. Listing 12-9 demonstrates how to set EAX to 1 if the unsigned value in EDX is greater than 10.

```
cmpl    $10, %edx
movl    $0, %eax
seta    %al
```

Listing 12-9: Performing an unsigned comparison in assembly

This follows exactly the same pattern as signed comparisons: we issue the cmp instruction, then zero out the destination, and finally issue a set instruction with a suffix for the appropriate condition code.

UNSIGNED WRAPAROUND VS. SIGNED OVERFLOW

You learned in Chapter 4 that when the result of an operation on signed integers overflows, the behavior is undefined. This isn't true for unsigned integers. Section 6.2.5, paragraph 9, of the C standard specifies how to deal with an unsigned integer operation when the result doesn't fit in the result type: "A computation involving unsigned operands can never overflow, because a result that cannot be represented by the resulting unsigned integer type is reduced modulo the number that is one greater than the largest value that can be represented by the resulting type."

It's no coincidence that this is exactly the same behavior that the standard requires when we convert a value to an unsigned type. It's also the same

(continued)

---

implementation-defined behavior we chose for conversions to signed types. In all three cases, we get this behavior by truncating the result to the appropriate width.

The assembly instructions we're using to perform arithmetic already handle unsigned wraparound correctly, so we don't need to do anything special to account for it here. We will need to account for it, however, when we implement constant folding in Part III.

Unsigned Division

For most arithmetic operations, the same instruction can operate correctly on both signed and unsigned integers. But for division, this doesn't work. Suppose we want to calculate 1000 / 0010. If we interpret these values as signed 4-bit integers, this is –8 / 2 and the result is –4, represented as 1100. If they're unsigned 4-bit integers, this is 8 / 2 and the result is 4, or 0100. There's no way a single instruction can produce the correct result in both cases.

So, we'll need a new instruction, div, to perform unsigned division. This instruction works just like idiv. It takes one operand, which is its divisor. Its dividend is the value stored in EDX and EAX, or RDX and RAX if we're working with quadwords. It stores the quotient in EAX or RAX, and it stores the remainder in EDX or RDX.

Since the dividend is unsigned, we zero extend it from EAX into EDX (or from RAX into RDX) instead of sign extending it. We accomplish this by zeroing out RDX instead of emitting a cdq instruction.

Zero Extension

The last operation we need to implement is zero extension. We can zero extend a longword to a quadword by moving it into a register; this zeroes out the register's upper 4 bytes. Then, if we need to store the value in memory, we can move the whole 8-byte value to its final destination. The following code zero extends the value at -4(%rbp) and then saves the result to -16(%rbp):

```
movl    -4(%rbp), %eax
movq    %rax, -16(%rbp)
```

We use the 4-byte movl instruction to copy the value into the register and the 8-byte movq instruction to copy it back out. If the final destination of the zero extension operation is a register instead of a location in memory, we need only the first 4-byte movl instruction.

There's also a separate movz instruction, which zero extends source values that are smaller than 4 bytes. We don't need this instruction yet, but we'll use it when we implement character types in Chapter 16.

Assembly Generation

Now that you know how to work with unsigned integers in assembly, you're ready to extend the assembly generation stage. Listing 12-10 defines the latest assembly AST, with this chapter's additions bolded.

```
program = Program(top_level*)
assembly_type = Longword | Quadword
top_level = Function(identifier name, bool global, instruction* instructions)
          | StaticVariable(identifier name, bool global, int alignment, static_init init)
instruction = Mov(assembly_type, operand src, operand dst)
            | Movsx(operand src, operand dst)
            | MovZeroExtend(operand src, operand dst)
            | Unary(unary_operator, assembly_type, operand)
            | Binary(binary_operator, assembly_type, operand, operand)
            | Cmp(assembly_type, operand, operand)
            | Idiv(assembly_type, operand)
            | Div(assembly_type, operand)
            | Cdq(assembly_type)
            | Jmp(identifier)
            | JmpCC(cond_code, identifier)
            | SetCC(cond_code, operand)
            | Label(identifier)
            | Push(operand)
            | Call(identifier)
            | Ret

unary_operator = Neg | Not
binary_operator = Add | Sub | Mult
operand = Imm(int) | Reg(reg) | Pseudo(identifier) | Stack(int) | Data(identifier)
cond_code = E | NE | G | GE | L | LE | A | AE | B | BE
reg = AX | CX | DX | DI | SI | R8 | R9 | R10 | R11 | SP
```

Listing 12-10: The assembly AST with unsigned operations

We've added the new condition codes and unsigned div instruction we discussed in the previous section. We've also added a MovZeroExtend instruction to handle zero extension. For now, this instruction is only a placeholder. During the instruction fix-up pass, we'll replace it with either one or two mov instructions, depending on whether its destination is in memory or a register. (At the moment, the destination will always be in memory, so we'll always need two mov instructions; this will change once we implement register allocation in Part III.) When we add character types, MovZeroExtend will also represent the real movz instruction to zero extend 1-byte values.

Let's recap the changes we'll need to make to the assembly generation pass. First, when we convert source-level types to assembly types, we lose the distinction between signed and unsigned integers. Both long and unsigned long values in TACKY become quadwords in assembly, and int and unsigned int values become longwords.

When we convert a comparison instruction from TACKY to assembly, we start by looking up the type of either operand (both operands are guaranteed to have the same type). We then choose the appropriate condition code, depending on whether that type is signed. For example, to handle

```
Binary(LessThan, Var("src1"), Var("src2"), Var("dst"))
```

we start by looking up the type of either src1 or src2 in the symbol table. Let's say the type is UInt. In this case, we'll generate the following assembly instructions:

```
Cmp(Longword, Pseudo("src2"), Pseudo("src1"))
Mov(Longword, Imm(0), Pseudo("dst"))
SetCC(B, Pseudo("dst"))
```

These are exactly the same instructions we'd generate for a signed comparison, except that we use the B condition code instead of L.

To handle a TACKY Divide or Remainder operation, we copy the first operand into EAX, as before. Then, if the operands are signed, we sign extend EAX into EDX and issue an idiv instruction. If they're unsigned, we zero out EDX and issue a div instruction. (Naturally, we'll use RAX and RDX instead of EAX and EDX if the operands are quadwords.) For example, we'll translate

```
Binary(Remainder, ConstULong(100), Var("x"), Var("dst"))
```

into:

```
Mov(Quadword, Imm(100), Reg(AX))
Mov(Quadword, Imm(0), Reg(DX))
Div(Quadword, Pseudo("x"))
Mov(Quadword, Reg(DX), Pseudo("dst"))
```

Finally, we'll convert each ZeroExtend TACKY instruction into a MovZero Extend assembly instruction.

Tables 12-2 through 12-5 summarize the latest updates to the conversion from TACKY to assembly. New constructs and changes to the way we convert existing constructs are bolded.

Table 12-2: Converting TACKY Instructions to Assembly

TACKY instruction		Assembly instructions
Binary(Divide, src1, src2, dst)	Signed	Mov(*<src1 type>*, src1, Reg(AX)) Cdq(*<src1 type>*) Idiv(*<src1 type>*, src2) Mov(*<src1 type>*, Reg(AX), dst)
	Unsigned	**Mov(*<src1 type>*, src1, Reg(AX))** **Mov(*<src1 type>*, Imm(0), Reg(DX))** **Div(*<src1 type>*, src2)** **Mov(*<src1 type>*, Reg(AX), dst)**

TACKY instruction		Assembly instructions
Binary(Remainder, src1, src2, dst)	Signed	Mov(<src1 type>, src1, Reg(AX)) Cdq(<src1 type>) Idiv(<src1 type>, src2) Mov(<src1 type>, Reg(DX), dst)
	Unsigned	Mov(<src1 type>, src1, Reg(AX)) Mov(<src1 type>, Imm(0), Reg(DX)) Div(<src1 type>, src2) Mov(<src1 type>, Reg(DX), dst)
ZeroExtend(src, dst)		MovZeroExtend(src, dst)

Table 12-3: Converting TACKY Comparisons to Assembly

TACKY comparison		Assembly condition code
LessThan	Signed	L
	Unsigned	B
LessOrEqual	Signed	LE
	Unsigned	BE
GreaterThan	Signed	G
	Unsigned	A
GreaterOrEqual	Signed	GE
	Unsigned	AE

Table 12-4: Converting TACKY Operands to Assembly

TACKY operand	Assembly operand
Constant(ConstUInt(int))	Imm(int)
Constant(ConstULong(int))	Imm(int)

Table 12-5: Converting Types to Assembly

Source type	Assembly type	Alignment
UInt	Longword	4
ULong	Quadword	8

Next, we'll update the pseudoregister replacement and instruction fix-up passes.

Replacing Pseudoregisters

We'll extend this pass to handle the new Div and MovZeroExtend instructions. Otherwise, there's nothing to change here. This pass looks at each operand's assembly type rather than its source-level type, so it doesn't distinguish between signed and unsigned operands.

Fixing Up the Div and MovZeroExtend Instructions

Next, we'll rewrite both `Div` and `MovZeroExtend`. Like `Idiv`, the new `Div` instruction can't use a constant operand. We'll rewrite it the same way as `Idiv`, copying its operand into R10 if we need to.

We'll replace `MovZeroExtend` with one or two `mov` instructions. If its destination is a register, we'll issue a single `movl` instruction. For example, we'll rewrite

```
MovZeroExtend(Stack(-16), Reg(AX))
```

as:

```
Mov(Longword, Stack(-16), Reg(AX))
```

If its destination is in memory, we'll use a `movl` instruction to zero extend into R11, then move it from there to the destination. So, we'll rewrite

```
MovZeroExtend(Imm(100), Stack(-16))
```

as:

```
Mov(Longword, Imm(100), Reg(R11))
Mov(Quadword, Reg(R11), Stack(-16))
```

We won't make any other changes to this pass.

TEST THE ASSEMBLY GENERATION STAGE

To test the assembly generation stage, run:

```
$ ./test_compiler /path/to/your_compiler --chapter 12 --stage codegen
```

Code Emission

We'll make a few changes to the code emission stage in this chapter. First, we'll add the `div` instruction and the new condition codes. We'll also add our two new static initializers, `UIntInit` and `ULongInit`, which we'll emit exactly like their signed counterparts, `IntInit` and `LongInit`. Tables 12-6 through 12-8 demonstrate how to emit these new constructs.

Table 12-6: Formatting Static Initializers

Static initializer	Output
UIntInit(0)	.zero 4
UIntInit(i)	.long <i>
ULongInit(0)	.zero 8
ULongInit(i)	.quad <i>

Table 12-7: Formatting Assembly Instructions

Assembly instruction	Output
Div(t, operand)	div<t> <operand>

Table 12-8: Instruction Suffixes for Condition Codes

Condition code	Instruction suffix
A	a
AE	ae
B	b
BE	be

I haven't bolded the new constructs and changes in these tables like I normally do, because all of these assembly constructs are new.

TEST THE WHOLE COMPILER

To test out the whole compiler, run:

```
$ ./test_compiler /path/to/your_compiler --chapter 12
```

The programs in *tests/chapter_12/valid/type_specifiers* test that your compiler correctly determines a function or variable's type based on a list of type specifiers. The programs in *tests/chapter_12/valid/unsigned_expressions* test that you've correctly implemented arithmetic operations on unsigned values, including unsigned comparisons and division. The programs in *tests/chapter_12/valid/explicit_casts* test that you've implemented explicit conversions to and from unsigned types correctly, and the programs in *tests/chapter_12/valid/implicit_casts* test that you add implicit type conversions in the right places. The programs in *tests/chapter_12/valid/libraries* test that compiled code dealing with unsigned integers conforms to the System V ABI.

Summary

In this chapter, you built on the foundations you laid in Chapter 11 to implement two unsigned integer types. You waded through the C standard's rules for type conversions and explored how those conversions impact both an integer's representation and its value. In the type checker, you learned how signed and unsigned integers are converted to a common type. During assembly generation, you implemented zero extension and unsigned division and comparisons.

In Chapter 13, you'll add a floating-point type, double. Floating-point numbers are processed very differently from integers in hardware; they even get their own set of registers! As you'll see, those hardware differences impact everything from type conversions to function calling conventions.

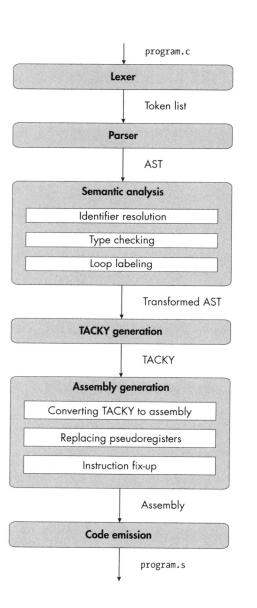

13

FLOATING-POINT NUMBERS

Your compiler now supports four different integer types, but it still doesn't support non-integral values. It also doesn't support values outside the range of `long` and `unsigned long`. In this chapter, you'll address these shortcomings by implementing the `double` type. This type uses a *floating-point* binary representation, which is totally different from the signed and unsigned integer representations we've seen so far. The C standard also defines two other floating-point types, `float` and `long double`, but we won't implement those in this book.

We'll have two major tasks in this chapter. The first task is figuring out exactly what behavior we're trying to implement. We can't just check the C standard, because many aspects of floating-point behavior are implementation-defined. Instead, we'll consult yet another standard,

IEEE 754, to fill in most of the details that the C standard doesn't specify. Our second major task is generating assembly code; we'll need a whole new set of specialized assembly instructions and registers to operate on floating-point numbers.

We'll start with a quick look at the IEEE 754 standard, which defines the binary format of `double` and some other aspects of floating-point behavior. Then, we'll consider all the ways that rounding error can creep into floating-point operations and decide how our implementation will handle them. We won't cover every aspect of floating-point arithmetic, but you can find links to the standard itself and more comprehensive explanations of IEEE 754, rounding error, and other aspects of floating-point behavior in "Additional Resources" on page 343.

IEEE 754, What Is It Good For?

The IEEE 754 standard specifies several floating-point formats and how to work with them. It defines a set of floating-point operations, including basic arithmetic operations, conversions, and comparisons. It also defines several rounding modes, which control how the results of these operations are rounded, and various floating-point exceptions, like overflow and division by zero. The standard can be used as a specification for any system that implements floating-point arithmetic, whether that system is a processor or a high-level programming language. In processors, the required operations are typically implemented as machine instructions. In most programming languages, including C, some IEEE 754 operations are implemented as primitive operators like + and -, while others are implemented as standard library functions.

Virtually all modern programming languages represent floating-point numbers in IEEE 754 format (because they run on hardware using that format), but they have varying degrees of support for other aspects of the standard. For example, not all programming languages let you detect floating-point exceptions or use nondefault rounding modes.

In theory, you could implement C without using IEEE 754 at all; the C standard doesn't dictate how to represent `double` and other floating-point types. However, the standard is designed to be compatible with IEEE 754. Annex F, an optional section of the C standard, specifies how to fully support IEEE 754 and explicitly binds C types, operations, and macros to their IEEE 754 equivalents. (Note that the standard refers to "IEC 60559," which is just another name for IEEE 754.)

While the C standard doesn't specify how to represent floating-point types, the System V x64 ABI does. Implementations that follow this ABI, including ours, must represent these types in IEEE 754 format. However, the ABI doesn't deal with the other aspects of IEEE 754.

Most C implementations provide command line options to control exactly how strictly they conform to IEEE 754. Our compiler won't provide these options; instead, it will roughly match the default behavior of Clang and GCC. This means we'll implement mathematical floating-point operations according to IEEE 754, and we'll correctly handle most special values, but we'll ignore floating-point exceptions and nondefault rounding modes.

In the next couple of sections, I'll discuss the parts of IEEE 754 that you'll need to know about as you work on your compiler. I won't discuss operations that are implemented in the underlying hardware (like addition and subtraction) or in the C standard library (like square root and remainder). You don't need to know the details of how those are specified, since they're handled for you. But you *do* need to know a bit about the binary format of IEEE 754 numbers, so we'll start with that.

The IEEE 754 Double-Precision Format

The System V x64 ABI tells us to represent double using the IEEE 754 *double-precision* format, which is 64 bits wide. Figure 13-1 illustrates this format. (This figure is reproduced with slight modifications from *https:// en.wikipedia.org/wiki/Double-precision_floating-point_format.*)

Figure 13-1: The IEEE 754 double-precision floating-point format

The double-precision floating-point format has three fields: the sign bit, the exponent field, and the fraction field. These fields encode three values: the sign s, the exponent e, and the significand f, respectively. (Sometimes f is called the *mantissa* instead of the significand.) A number in this format has the value $(-1)^s \times f \times 2^e$, except for a few special cases that we'll discuss shortly.

The significand f is a *binary fraction*, which is analogous to a decimal number. In decimal numbers, the digits to the left of the decimal point (the *integer part*) represent nonnegative powers of 10, and the digits to the right (the *fractional part*) represent negative powers of 10: 1/10, 1/100, and so on. Similarly, each bit in the integer part of a binary fraction represents a nonnegative power of 2, like 1, 2, 4, or 8, and each bit in the fractional part represents a negative power of 2, like 1/2, 1/4, or 1/8.

The integer part of f is always 1; the 52 bits of the fraction field encode only the fractional part. This means that the value of f is always greater than or equal to 1 and less than 2. For example, the fraction field

1000000000000000000000000000000000000000000000000000

indicates that the fractional part of f is 0.1, so the overall value of f is the binary fraction 1.1, which is 1.5 in decimal notation. The implied leading 1 lets the 52-bit fraction field represent binary fractions up to 53 bits long.

The value of e is between –1,022 and 1,023. The exponent field uses a *biased* encoding: we interpret the 11 bits in this field as an unsigned integer and then subtract 1,023 to get the value of e. For example, suppose this field has the following bits:

00000000010

Interpreted as an ordinary unsigned integer, these bits represent the number 2. The value of the exponent e is therefore 2 – 1,023, or –1,021. Setting the exponent field to all 1s or all 0s indicates one of the special values we'll discuss in a moment.

Since f is always positive, the whole floating-point number will be negative if the sign bit is 1 and positive if it's 0. Essentially, floating point lets us express numbers in scientific notation, but with powers of 2 instead of powers of 10.

The IEEE 754 standard also defines a few special values that are interpreted differently than ordinary floating-point numbers:

Zero and negative zero

If a floating-point number is all zeros, its value is 0.0. If it's all zeros except for its sign bit, its value is -0.0. This value compares equal to 0.0 but follows the usual rules for determining the sign of arithmetic results. For example, -1.0 * 0.0 and 1.0 * -0.0 both evaluate to -0.0.

Subnormal numbers

As we just saw, most floating-point numbers have a significand between 1 and 2. We say that these numbers are *normalized*. The smallest magnitude a normalized double can represent is $1 \times 2^{-1,022}$, since the minimum exponent is –1,022. In a *subnormal* number, the significand is smaller than 1, which lets us represent values that are even closer to zero. An all-zero exponent field indicates that a number is subnormal, so its exponent is –1,022 and the integer part of its significand is 0 instead of 1. Subnormal numbers are much slower to work with in hardware than normalized numbers, so some C implementations let users disable them and round any subnormal results to zero.

Infinity

At the opposite end of the spectrum, the largest magnitude a normalized double can represent is the largest possible value of the significand (just shy of 2) multiplied by $2^{1,023}$. Anything larger gets rounded to infinity. The result of dividing a nonzero number by zero is also infinity. The IEEE standard defines both positive and negative infinity; for example, the expression -1.0 / 0.0 evaluates to negative infinity. A number whose exponent is all 1s and whose fraction field is all 0s represents infinity. The sign bit indicates whether it's negative or positive infinity.

NaN

NaN is short for *not-a-number*. A few operations, including 0.0 / 0.0, produce NaN. The IEEE 754 standard defines both *signaling NaNs*, which raise an exception if you try to use them, and *quiet NaNs*, which don't. A number whose exponent is all 1s and whose fraction field is nonzero represents NaN.

We'll support all of these values except for NaN. Quiet NaNs are an extra credit feature because handling them correctly in comparisons requires a bit of extra work. We can support negative zero, subnormal numbers, and infinity with no extra work on our part; the processor will deal with them for us.

Aside from the double-precision format, IEEE 754 defines a few other floating-point formats that we won't use, including *single precision*, which corresponds to float, and *double extended precision*, which usually corresponds to long double. These formats include the same three fields as double precision, use the same formula to determine a floating-point number's value, and have the same special values; they just have different widths.

Rounding Behavior

You can't represent every real number exactly as a double. There are infinitely many real numbers, and a double has only 64 bits. We're not particularly interested in *all* the real numbers; we care only about the numbers that show up in C programs. Unfortunately, a double can't represent most of those exactly either, so we'll need to round them. Let's start by examining how IEEE 754 tells us to round real numbers to double. Then, we'll look at the three cases where we can encounter rounding error: when converting constants from decimal to binary floating point, performing type conversions, and performing arithmetic operations.

Rounding Modes

IEEE 754 defines several different rounding modes, including rounding to nearest, rounding toward zero, rounding toward positive infinity, and rounding toward negative infinity. Modern processors support all four of these rounding modes and provide instructions to let programs change the current rounding mode. We'll support only the default IEEE rounding mode, *round-to-nearest, ties-to-even* rounding. As the name suggests, in this mode the real value of a result is always rounded to the nearest representable double. "Ties-to-even" means that if a result is exactly between two representable values, it's rounded to the one whose least significant bit is 0. We'll use this rounding mode when converting constants to floating point, when converting from integer types to double, and in arithmetic operations.

Rounding Constants

C programmers generally write `double` constants in decimal. At compile time, we'll convert constants from this decimal representation to a double-precision floating-point representation. This conversion is inexact, since most decimal constants can't be represented exactly in binary floating point. For example, you can't represent the decimal number 0.1 in binary floating point, because each bit in a binary fraction represents a power of 2, but you can't add up powers of 2 and get 0.1. If the source code of a C program includes the constant `0.1`, the compiler will round this constant to the value in Listing 13-1, which is the nearest value we can represent as a `double`.

```
0.1000000000000000055511151231257827021181583404541015625
```

Listing 13-1: The closest double to 0.1, in decimal notation

Unlike 0.1, this value can be represented exactly as a 53-bit binary fraction multiplied by a power of 2, as shown in Listing 13-2.

```
1.1001100110011001100110011001100110011001100110011001101 * 2^-4
```

Listing 13-2: The closest double to 0.1, represented as a binary fraction

Representing 0.1 as a `double` is analogous to trying to write 1/3 in decimal notation; since you can't break it down into powers of 10, you can't write it out exactly using any number of decimal places. Instead, you have to round 1/3 to the nearest value you can represent in the space available. For example, a calculator that can display up to four digits would display 1/3 as `.3333`.

NOTE *IEEE 754 defines several decimal floating-point formats, which can represent decimal constants without this sort of rounding error. These formats encode numbers as decimal significands multiplied by powers of 10. C23 includes new decimal floating-point types that correspond to these formats.*

Rounding Type Conversions

We may also need to round when we convert an integer to a `double`. This issue arises because of the spacing between values that `double` can represent. The gap between representable values grows larger as the magnitude of the values themselves increases. At a certain point, the gap becomes larger than 1, which means you can't represent all integers in that range. To illustrate this problem, let's imagine a decimal format with three digits of precision. This format can represent any integer smaller than 1,000; for example, we can write 992 and 993 as 9.92×10^2 and 9.93×10^2. But it can't represent every integer larger than 1,000. We can represent 1,000 exactly as 1.00×10^3, but the next representable value is 1.01×10^3, or 1,010; there's a gap of 10. The gap increases to 100 once we hit 10,000, and continues to grow at larger magnitudes. We'll encounter precisely the same issue when converting from long or unsigned long to double. A double has 53 bits of precision, since the significand is a 53-bit binary fraction. A long or unsigned long, however, has 64 bits of precision. Suppose we need to convert 9223372036854775803 from a long to a double. The binary representation of this long is:

111111111111111111111111111111111111111111111111111111111111011

That's 63 bits, so it won't fit in the significand of a double! We'll need to round it to the nearest double, which is 9223372036854775808.0, or 1×2^{63}.

Rounding Arithmetic Operations

Finally, we may need to round the results of basic floating-point operations like addition, subtraction, and multiplication. Once again, this is due to the gaps between representable values. For example, let's try computing $993 + 45$ in the three-digit decimal format from the previous section. The correct result, 1,038, can't be represented in only three digits; we'll need to round it to 1.04×10^3. Division can also produce values that aren't representable at any precision, just like the result of 1 / 3 isn't representable in any number of decimal digits. Thankfully, we can basically ignore this category of rounding error; the assembly instructions for floating-point arithmetic will round correctly without any extra effort on our part.

Now that you understand the basics of the IEEE 754 format and the rounding behavior you need to implement, you're ready to get to work on the compiler. We'll start with a change to the compiler driver.

Linking Shared Libraries

This chapter's test suite uses functions from <math.h>, the standard math library. We'll add a new command line option to the compiler driver that lets us link in shared libraries like <math.h>. This option takes the form -l<lib>, where <lib> is the name of a library. You should pass this option through to the gcc command to assemble and link the program, placing it after the names of any input assembly files in that command. For example, if your compiler is invoked with the command

---

./YOUR_COMPILER /path/to/program.c -lm

---

it should assemble and link the program with the command:

---

gcc /path/to/program.s -o /path/to/program -lm

If you're on macOS, you don't need to add this new option, because the standard math library is linked in by default. You may want to add it anyway, though, since being able to link in shared libraries is generally useful.

The Lexer

You'll introduce two new tokens in this chapter:

double   A keyword

Floating-point constants   Constants that use scientific notation or contain a decimal point

You'll also change how the lexer recognizes the end of a constant token; this will affect both the new floating-point constants and the integer constants you already support.

Let's start by walking through the format of floating-point constants. Then, we'll see how to recognize the end of a constant. Finally, we'll define the new regular expressions for each constant token.

Recognizing Floating-Point Constant Tokens

Numerals with decimal points, like 1.5 and .72, are valid tokens that represent floating-point numbers. We'll call a sequence of digits that includes a decimal point a *fractional constant*. A fractional constant may include a decimal point with no digits after it. For example, 1. is a valid fractional constant with the same value as 1.0.

A floating-point constant can also be written in scientific notation. A token that uses scientific notation consists of:

- A significand, which may be an integer or fractional constant
- An uppercase or lowercase E
- An exponent, which is an integer with an optional leading + or - sign

100E10, .05e-2, and 5.E+3 are all valid floating-point constants. These constants are all in decimal, and their exponents are powers of 10. For example, 5.E+3 is 5×10^3, or 5,000. The C standard also defines hexadecimal floating-point constants, but we won't implement them. There's no constant for infinity. The <math.h> header defines an INFINITY macro, which is supposed to translate to the constant for positive infinity, but our compiler can't include this header, since it uses float, struct, and other language features we don't support. Therefore, we won't support this macro (or any other macros defined in <math.h>, for that matter).

It's a bit tricky to write a regex that will match every floating-point constant, so let's break it down into steps. The regex in Listing 13-3 matches a fractional constant.

```
[0-9]*\.[0-9]+|[0-9]+\.
```

Listing 13-3: The regex for a fractional constant

The first part of this regex, [0-9]*\.[0-9]+, matches any constant with digits after the decimal point, like .03 or 3.14. The part after the | matches constants like 3. with nothing after the decimal point. Listing 13-4 defines a similar regex to match the significand of a constant in scientific notation.

```
[0-9]*\.[0-9]+|[0-9]+\.?
```

Listing 13-4: The regex for the significand of a constant in scientific notation

The only difference from Listing 13-3 is that the trailing decimal point in the second clause is optional, so it matches both integers and fractional constants with trailing decimal points.

We'll use the regex in Listing 13-5 to match the exponent part of a floating-point constant.

```
[Ee][+-]?[0-9]+
```

Listing 13-5: The regex for the exponent of a constant in scientific notation

This regex includes the case-insensitive E that marks the start of the exponent, an optional sign, and the integer value of the exponent. To match any floating-point constant, we'll assemble one giant regex of the form `<Listing 13-4> <Listing 13-5> | <Listing 13-3>`, which gives us Listing 13-6.

```
([0-9]*\.[0-9]+|[0-9]+\.?)[Ee][+-]?[0-9]+|[0-9]*\.[0-9]+|[0-9]+\.
```

Listing 13-6: The regex to match every part of a floating-point constant

In other words, a floating-point constant is either a significand followed by an exponent, or a fractional constant. Listing 13-6 isn't quite complete, though: we need one more component to match the boundary between the end of this token and the start of the next one.

Matching the End of a Constant

Until now, we've required constants to end at word boundaries. Given the string 123foo, for example, we wouldn't accept the substring 123 as a constant. Now we'll add another requirement: a constant token can't be immediately followed by a period. This means, for example, that the lexer will recognize the start of the string 123L; as a long integer constant token, 123L, but it will reject the string 123L.bar; as malformed. Along the same lines, the lexer will accept the string 1.0+x but reject 1.0.+x, and it will accept 1.} but reject 1..}. Note that the last character in a floating-point constant like 1. can be a period, but the first character *after* the constant cannot.

NOTE *If you're curious about where in the C standard this requirement comes from, see the definition of preprocessing numbers in section 6.4.8, the list of translation phases in section 5.1.1.2, and the discussion of tokens and preprocessing tokens in section 6.4, paragraph 3. These sections describe a multiphase process for dividing a source file into preprocessing tokens and then converting them into tokens. We don't follow this process, but we define each token in a way that produces the same results for the subset of C that we support.*

To enforce this new requirement, we'll end the regular expression for each constant token with the [^\w.] character class instead of the special word boundary character \b. The [^\w.] character class matches any single character except for a word character (a letter, digit, or underscore) or a period. This single non-word, non-period character marks the end of the constant but isn't part of the constant itself, so we'll define a capture group within each regex to match the actual constant.

For example, our old regular expression for a signed integer constant was [0-9]+\b. Our new regular expression is ([0-9]+)[\w.]. This regex matches the entire string 100;, including the ; at the end. The capture group ([0-9]+) matches just the constant 100, not the final ; character. Whenever your lexer recognizes a constant, it should consume only the constant itself from the input, not the character that immediately follows it.

In Listing 13-7, we finally define the whole regular expression to recognize a floating-point constant.

```
((([0-9]*\.[0-9]+|[0-9]+\.?)[Ee][+-]?[0-9]+|[0-9]*\.[0-9]+|[0-9]+\.)[^\w.]
```

Listing 13-7: The complete regex to recognize a floating-point constant

This is just the regular expression we defined in Listing 13-6, wrapped in parentheses to form a capture group and followed by the [^\w.] character class.

Table 13-1 defines the new regular expressions for all of our constant tokens.

Table 13-1: Regular Expressions for Constant Tokens

Token	Regular expression
Signed integer constant	([0-9]+)[^\w.]
Unsigned integer constant	([0-9]+[uU])[^\w.]
Signed long integer constant	([0-9]+[lL])[^\w.]
Unsigned long integer constant	([0-9]+([lL][uU]|[uU][lL]))[^\w.]
Floating-point constant	((([0-9]*\.[0-9]+|[0-9]+\.?)[Ee][+-]?[0-9]+|[0-9]*\.[0-9]+|[0-9]+\.)[^\w.]

Go ahead and add the new floating-point constant token and update how you recognize the constant tokens from earlier chapters. Don't forget to add the double keyword too!

The Parser

The changes to the parser are pretty limited. Listing 13-8 gives the updated AST, which includes the double type and floating-point constants.

```
program = Program(declaration*)
declaration = FunDecl(function_declaration) | VarDecl(variable_declaration)
variable_declaration = (identifier name, exp? init,
                        type var_type, storage_class?)
function_declaration = (identifier name, identifier* params, block? body,
                        type fun_type, storage_class?)
type = Int | Long | UInt | ULong | Double | FunType(type* params, type ret)
storage_class = Static | Extern
block_item = S(statement) | D(declaration)
block = Block(block_item*)
for_init = InitDecl(variable_declaration) | InitExp(exp?)
statement = Return(exp)
          | Expression(exp)
          | If(exp condition, statement then, statement? else)
          | Compound(block)
          | Break
          | Continue
          | While(exp condition, statement body)
          | DoWhile(statement body, exp condition)
          | For(for_init init, exp? condition, exp? post, statement body)
          | Null
exp = Constant(const)
    | Var(identifier)
    | Cast(type target_type, exp)
    | Unary(unary_operator, exp)
    | Binary(binary_operator, exp, exp)
    | Assignment(exp, exp)
    | Conditional(exp condition, exp, exp)
    | FunctionCall(identifier, exp* args)
unary_operator = Complement | Negate | Not
binary_operator = Add | Subtract | Multiply | Divide | Remainder | And | Or
                | Equal | NotEqual | LessThan | LessOrEqual
                | GreaterThan | GreaterOrEqual
```

```
const = ConstInt(int) | ConstLong(int)
      | ConstUInt(int) | ConstULong(int)
      | ConstDouble(double)
```

Listing 13-8: The abstract syntax tree with the double *type and floating-point constants*

Your AST should represent double constants using the double-precision floating-point format, since that's how they'll be represented at runtime. You'll need to look up which type in your implementation language uses this format. If you use a representation with less precision than double, you might not be able to represent the closest double to every constant in the source code, so you'll end up with incorrectly rounded constants in the compiled program.

Surprisingly, storing constants with *more* precision than double can also cause problems. Storing a floating-point number in a higher-precision format and then rounding to a lower-precision format can produce a different result than rounding exactly once. This phenomenon is called *double rounding error*. (The word *double* here refers to rounding twice, not to the double type.) We'll explore double rounding error in more depth during assembly generation.

After updating the AST, we'll make the corresponding changes to the grammar. Listing 13-9 shows the complete grammar with these changes bolded.

```
<program> ::= { <declaration> }
<declaration> ::= <variable-declaration> | <function-declaration>
<variable-declaration> ::= { <specifier> }+ <identifier> [ "=" <exp> ] ";"
<function-declaration> ::= { <specifier> }+ <identifier> "(" <param-list> ")" ( <block> | ";")
<param-list> ::= "void"
              | { <type-specifier> }+ <identifier> { "," { <type-specifier> }+ <identifier> }
<type-specifier> ::= "int" | "long" | "unsigned" | "signed" | "double"
<specifier> ::= <type-specifier> | "static" | "extern"
<block> ::= "{" { <block-item> } "}"
<block-item> ::= <statement> | <declaration>
<for-init> ::= <variable-declaration> | [ <exp> ] ";"
<statement> ::= "return" <exp> ";"
              | <exp> ";"
              | "if" "(" <exp> ")" <statement> [ "else" <statement> ]
              | <block>
              | "break" ";"
              | "continue" ";"
              | "while" "(" <exp> ")" <statement>
              | "do" <statement> "while" "(" <exp> ")" ";"
              | "for" "(" <for-init> [ <exp> ] ";" [ <exp> ] ")" <statement>
              | ";"
<exp> ::= <factor> | <exp> <binop> <exp> | <exp> "?" <exp> ":" <exp>
<factor> ::= <const> | <identifier>
           | "(" { <type-specifier> }+ ")" <factor>
           | <unop> <factor> | "(" <exp> ")"
           | <identifier> "(" [ <argument-list> ] ")"
<argument-list> ::= <exp> { "," <exp> }
<unop> ::= "-" | "~" | "!"
```

```
<binop> ::= "-" | "+" | "*" | "/" | "%" | "&&" | "||"
          | "==" | "!=" | "<" | "<=" | ">" | ">=" | "="
<const> ::= <int> | <long> | <uint> | <ulong> | <double>
<identifier> ::= ? An identifier token ?
<int> ::= ? An int token ?
<long> ::= ? An int or long token ?
<uint> ::= ? An unsigned int token ?
<ulong> ::= ? An unsigned int or unsigned long token ?
<double> ::= ? A floating-point constant token ?
```

Listing 13-9: The grammar with the double *type specifier and floating-point constants*

In the last two chapters, we had to deal with the many different ways to specify integer types. Luckily, there's only one way to specify the double type: with the double keyword. Listing 13-10 demonstrates how to handle double when we process a list of type specifiers.

```
parse_type(specifier_list):
    if specifier_list == ["double"]:
        return Double
    if specifier_list contains "double":
        fail("Can't combine 'double' with other type specifiers")
    --snip--
```

Listing 13-10: Determining a type from a list of type specifiers

Either double should be the only specifier in the list, or it shouldn't appear at all; it can't be combined with long, unsigned, or any other type specifier we've introduced so far. (It can, however, appear alongside storage-class specifiers like static and extern.)

Next, we'll convert floating-point constant tokens to constants in the AST. We saw earlier that most decimal constants can't be represented exactly in binary floating point, so we'll need to round them. According to the C standard, the rounding direction here is implementation-defined and doesn't necessarily need to match the runtime rounding mode. We'll use round-to-nearest mode here, like we do everywhere else. Your implementation language's built-in string-to-floating point conversion utilities should handle this correctly.

When we parse integer constants, we need to ensure that they're within the range the type can hold. Floating-point constants, however, can't go out of range. Since double supports positive and negative infinity, its range includes all real numbers. So, our parser shouldn't run into any errors when parsing double constants.

TEST THE PARSER

To test your parser, run:

```
$ ./test_compiler /path/to/your_compiler --chapter 13 --stage parse
```

The Type Checker

We'll make a handful of changes to account for double in the type checker. First, we'll make sure to annotate double constants with the correct type. Then, we'll update how we find the common real type of two values. The rule here is simple: if either value is a double, the common real type is double. Listing 13-11 shows how to update the get_common_type helper function to handle double.

```
get_common_type(type1, type2):
    if type1 == type2:
        return type1
    if type1 == Double or type2 == Double:
        return Double
    --snip--
```

Listing 13-11: Finding the common real type of two values

We also need to detect a couple of new type errors. The bitwise complement operator, ~, and the remainder operator, %, accept only integer operands. We'll validate that both of these operators are used correctly in typecheck_exp. Listing 13-12 demonstrates how to type check the ~ operator.

```
typecheck_exp(e, symbols):
    match e with
    | --snip--
    | Unary(Complement, inner) ->
        typed_inner = typecheck_exp(inner, symbols)
    ❶ if get_type(typed_inner) == Double:
            fail("Can't take the bitwise complement of a double")
        unary_exp = Unary(Complement, typed_inner)
        return set_type(unary_exp, get_type(typed_inner))
```

Listing 13-12: Type checking a bitwise complement expression

First, we type check the operand. Then, we validate that the operand is an integer ❶. Finally, we annotate the expression with the type of its result. Only the validation step differs from earlier chapters. We can handle the % operator in a similar way.

To wrap up the changes to the type checker, we'll deal with static variables of type double. We'll add a new kind of initializer for these variables:

```
static_init = IntInit(int) | LongInit(int) | UIntInit(int) | ULongInit(int)
             | DoubleInit(double)
```

As usual, we'll convert each initializer to the type of the variable it initializes, using the same rules that we'd apply at runtime. The C standard requires us to truncate toward zero when we convert from double to an integer type. For example, we would convert 2.8 to 2. If the truncated value is out of range of the resulting integer type, the result is undefined, so you can handle it however you like. The cleanest option here is to just throw an error.

When we convert an integer to a double, we'll preserve its value if it can be represented exactly. Otherwise, we'll round to the nearest representable value. You should be able to use your implementation language's built-in type conversion utilities to cast from double to integer types and vice versa.

TACKY Generation

In TACKY, we'll add a few new instructions to handle conversions between double and integer types. Listing 13-13 gives the updated TACKY IR.

```
program = Program(top_level*)
top_level = Function(identifier, bool global, identifier* params, instruction* body)
          | StaticVariable(identifier, bool global, type t, static_init init)
instruction = Return(val)
            | SignExtend(val src, val dst)
            | Truncate(val src, val dst)
            | ZeroExtend(val src, val dst)
            | DoubleToInt(val src, val dst)
            | DoubleToUInt(val src, val dst)
            | IntToDouble(val src, val dst)
            | UIntToDouble(val src, val dst)
            | Unary(unary_operator, val src, val dst)
            | Binary(binary_operator, val src1, val src2, val dst)
            | Copy(val src, val dst)
            | Jump(identifier target)
            | JumpIfZero(val condition, identifier target)
            | JumpIfNotZero(val condition, identifier target)
            | Label(identifier)
            | FunCall(identifier fun_name, val* args, val dst)
val = Constant(const) | Var(identifier)
unary_operator = Complement | Negate | Not
binary_operator = Add | Subtract | Multiply | Divide | Remainder | Equal | NotEqual
                | LessThan | LessOrEqual | GreaterThan | GreaterOrEqual
```

Listing 13-13: Adding conversions between double and the integer types to TACKY

Listing 13-13 introduces four new instructions to convert between double and the signed and unsigned integer types: DoubleToInt, DoubleToUInt,

IntToDouble, and UIntToDouble. We don't have different instructions for integer operands of different sizes; for example, DoubleToInt can cast to either int or long.

To update the TACKY generation pass, just emit the appropriate cast instruction when you encounter a cast to or from double.

TEST THE TACKY GENERATION STAGE

To test TACKY generation, run:

```
$ ./test_compiler /path/to/your_compiler --chapter 13 --stage tacky
```

Floating-Point Operations in Assembly

Before we get to work on the assembly generation pass, we need to understand how to work with floating-point numbers in assembly. Because floating-point numbers use a completely different binary representation from signed and unsigned integers, we can't operate on them with our existing arithmetic instructions. Instead, we'll use a set of specialized instructions called the *Streaming SIMD Extension (SSE)* instructions. This instruction set includes operations on both floating-point values and integers. It gets its name because it includes *single-instruction, multiple data (SIMD)* instructions, which perform the same operation on a vector of several values simultaneously (or two vectors of values, in the case of binary operations). For example, a SIMD addition instruction whose operands were the two-element vectors [1.0, 2.0] and [4.0, 6.0] would add their corresponding elements together to produce the vector [5.0, 8.0].

The term *SSE* is a bit misleading because only some SSE instructions perform SIMD operations on vectors. Others operate on single values. When we talk about SSE instructions, we refer to vectors as *packed* operands and single values as *scalar* operands. SSE instructions that use these different types of operands are called packed and scalar instructions, respectively. Our implementation will primarily use scalar instructions, although we will need one packed instruction.

The SSE instructions were first introduced as an extension to the x86 instruction set; they weren't available on every x86 processor. Over time, new groups of SSE instructions were added, creatively named SSE2, SSE3, and SSE4. The SSE and SSE2 instructions were eventually incorporated into the core x64 instruction set, so they're available on every x64 processor. The first generation of floating-point SSE instructions support only single-precision operands, which correspond to the float type in C. SSE2 added support for double-precision operands. Since we're working with double-precision operands, we'll use only SSE2 instructions in this chapter.

The x64 and x86 instruction sets include an older set of floating-point instructions that were first introduced with the Intel 8087 floating-point unit (FPU), a separate processor that handled floating-point math. These are called x87 or FPU instructions (sometimes simply referred to as floating-point instructions). Be aware that some resources on floating-point assembly—particularly older ones—discuss only x87 instructions and don't mention SSE.

Just like the general-purpose instructions we're already familiar with, SSE instructions take suffixes that describe their operands. Instructions that operate on scalar double-precision values use the sd suffix. Instructions that take packed double-precision values use the pd suffix. Scalar and packed single-precision instructions use the ss and ps suffixes, respectively. The next few sections introduce the SSE instructions we'll need in this chapter.

Working with SSE Instructions

There are two major differences between SSE instructions and the assembly instructions you learned about in earlier chapters. The first difference is that SSE instructions use a separate set of registers, called the *XMM registers*. There are 16 XMM registers: XMM0, XMM1, and so on, up to XMM15. Each XMM register is 128 bits wide, but we'll use only their lower 64 bits. From now on, I'll refer to all the non-XMM registers we know and love—like RAX, RSP, and so on—as *general-purpose registers*. SSE instructions can't use general-purpose registers, and non-SSE instructions can't use XMM registers. Both SSE and non-SSE instructions can refer to values in memory.

The second difference is that SSE instructions can't use immediate operands. If we need to use a constant in an SSE instruction, we'll define that constant in read-only memory. Then, the constant can be accessed with RIP-relative addressing, just like a static variable. Listing 13-14, which computes 1.0 + 1.0 in assembly, illustrates how to use XMM registers and floating-point constants.

```
    .section .rodata
    .align 8
.L_one:
    .double 1.0
    .text
one_plus_one:
    movsd   .L_one(%rip), %xmm0
    addsd   .L_one(%rip), %xmm0
    --snip--
```

Listing 13-14: Computing 1.0 + 1.0 in assembly

At the start of the listing, we define the constant 1.0. We can define and initialize this constant in almost exactly the same way as a static variable. The key difference is that we don't store this value in the data or BSS section; instead, we use the .section .rodata directive to put it in the *read-only data section*. As the name suggests, the program can read data from this section at runtime, but it can't write to it.

The `.section` directive can be used to write to any section. We use it here because we don't have a dedicated directive to write to the read-only data section the way we have dedicated `.text`, `.bss`, and `.data` directives. In the object file format used on macOS, there are several read-only data sections; we'll use the `.literal8` directive to write to the section that holds 8-byte constants.

We use a new directive, `.double`, to initialize the memory address labeled `.L_one` to the floating-point value `1.0`. The `.L` prefix on `.L_one` makes it a local label. As you learned back in Chapter 4, local labels are omitted from the symbol table in the object file. Compilers typically use local labels for floating-point constants.

Now that we've defined the data we need, let's look at the start of the assembly function `one_plus_one`. The first instruction, `movsd .L_one(%rip), %xmm0`, copies the constant `1.0` from memory into the XMM0 register. The `movsd` instruction, like `mov`, copies data from one location to another. We'll use `movsd` to copy values between XMM registers or between an XMM register and memory.

Finally, we use the `addsd` instruction to perform floating-point addition. This instruction adds the constant at `.L_one` to the value in XMM0 and stores the result in XMM0. The source of `addsd` can be an XMM register or a memory address, and the destination must be an XMM register.

Now that you have a high-level understanding of how to use SSE instructions, let's dig into some specifics. First, we'll explore how the System V calling convention handles floating-point function arguments and return values. Then, we'll cover how individual floating-point operations, like arithmetic, comparisons, and type conversions, are implemented in assembly. At that point, you'll finally be ready to add floating-point support to the backend of your compiler.

Using Floating-Point Values in the System V Calling Convention

In Chapter 9, you learned that a function's first six arguments are passed in general-purpose registers and its return value is passed in the EAX register (or RAX, depending on its size). The System V calling convention handles floating-point values a bit differently: they're passed and returned in XMM registers instead of general-purpose registers.

A function's first eight floating-point arguments are passed in registers XMM0 through XMM7. Any remaining floating-point arguments are pushed onto the stack in reverse order, just like integer arguments are. Floating-point return values are passed in XMM0 instead of RAX. Consider the function in Listing 13-15, which takes two `double` arguments, adds them together, and returns the result.

```
double add_double(double a, double b) {
    return a + b;
}
```

Listing 13-15: Adding two double arguments

We could compile this function to the assembly in Listing 13-16.

```
    .text
    .globl add_double
add_double:
    addsd    %xmm1, %xmm0
    ret
```

Listing 13-16: add_double in assembly

According to the System V calling convention, arguments a and b will be passed in registers XMM0 and XMM1, respectively. The instruction addsd %xmm1, %xmm0 will therefore add b to a, storing the result in XMM0. Since double values are returned in XMM0, the function's return value is already in the right place after that addsd instruction. At that point, the function can return immediately. This code is more optimized than what your compiler will produce—it doesn't include the function prologue and epilogue, for example—but it illustrates how to pass and return floating-point values in assembly.

When a function contains a mix of double and integer arguments, it can be tricky to push the right arguments onto the stack in the right order. First, we need to assign parameters to registers, working from the start of the parameter list. Then, we push any remaining unassigned parameters of any type onto the stack, starting from the back of the parameter list. Let's work through a few examples, starting with Listing 13-17.

```
long pass_parameters_1(int i1, double d1, int i2, unsigned long i3,
                       double d2, double d3, long i4, int i5);
```

Listing 13-17: A function declaration with integer and double parameters

This example is simple because we can pass every parameter in a register. Figure 13-2 illustrates the state of each register just before invoking pass_parameters_1 with a call instruction.

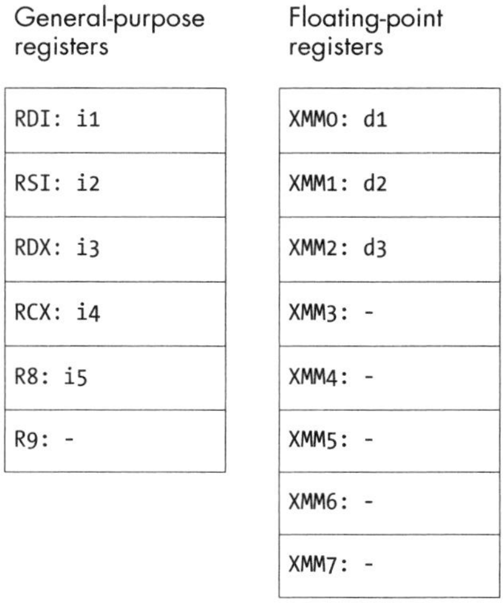

General-purpose registers

| RDI: i1 |
| RSI: i2 |
| RDX: i3 |
| RCX: i4 |
| R8: i5 |
| R9: - |

Floating-point registers

| XMM0: d1 |
| XMM1: d2 |
| XMM2: d3 |
| XMM3: - |
| XMM4: - |
| XMM5: - |
| XMM6: - |
| XMM7: - |

Figure 13-2: Passing parameters from Listing 13-17

Listing 13-18 shows a slightly more complicated example, where some integer parameters are passed on the stack.

```
double pass_parameters_2(double d1, long i1, long i2, double d2, int i3,
                         long i4, long i5, double d3, long i6, long i7,
                         int i8, double d4);
```

Listing 13-18: A function declaration with even more parameters

We'll pass every double argument to this function in a register, but the last two integer arguments, i7 and i8, will be passed on the stack. Figure 13-3 illustrates where each parameter will wind up.

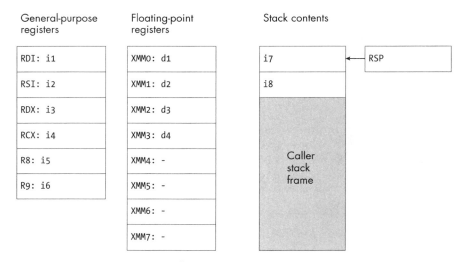

Figure 13-3: Passing parameters from Listing 13-18

After we've assigned parameters to all the available registers, only i7 and i8 are left. Because we push stack arguments in reverse order, we push i8 first, then i7, which puts i7 at the top of the stack.

Finally, let's consider the function declared in Listing 13-19. When we call this function, we'll need to pass both double and integer parameters on the stack.

```
int pass_parameters_3(double d1, double d2, int i1, double d3, double d4,
                      double d5, double d6, unsigned int i2, long i3,
                      double d7, double d8, unsigned long i4, double d9,
                      int i5, double d10, int i6, int i7, double d11,
                      int i8, int i9);
```

Listing 13-19: A function declaration with way too many parameters

We'll pass the first six integer parameters, i1 through i6, and the first eight double parameters, d1 through d8, in registers. Listing 13-20 reproduces Listing 13-19, with parameters that will be passed on the stack bolded.

```
int pass_parameters_3(double d1, double d2, int i1, double d3, double d4,
                      double d5, double d6, unsigned int i2, long i3,
                      double d7, double d8, unsigned long i4, double d9,
                      int i5, double d10, int i6, int i7, double d11,
                      int i8, int i9);
```

Listing 13-20: The declaration of pass_parameters_3, with parameters passed on the stack bolded

Going in reverse order, we'll push i9, then i8, d11, i7, d10, and d9. Figure 13-4 illustrates where we'll put each parameter.

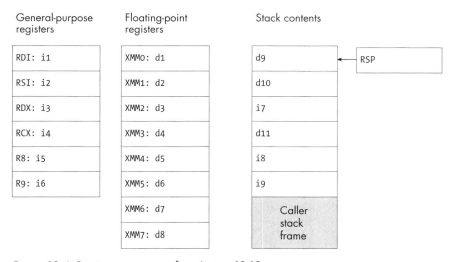

Figure 13-4: Passing parameters from Listing 13-19

Now that we understand how our calling convention handles floating-point values, let's look at basic arithmetic and comparisons.

Doing Arithmetic with SSE Instructions

We need to support five arithmetic operations on floating-point numbers: addition, subtraction, multiplication, division, and negation. We've already seen an example of addition with the addsd instruction. There are equivalent SSE instructions for the other binary operations: subsd for subtraction, mulsd for multiplication, and divsd for division. All four of these SSE instructions follow the same pattern as the integer add, sub, and imul instructions: take a source and destination operand, use them in a binary operation, and store the result in the destination. These four floating-point instructions all require an XMM register or memory address as a source and an XMM register as a destination. Floating-point division follows the same pattern as the other arithmetic instructions; it doesn't require special handling like integer division does.

There's no floating-point negation instruction. To negate a floating-point value, we'll XOR it with -0.0, which has its sign bit set but is otherwise all zeros. This has the effect of flipping the value's sign bit, which negates it. This operation correctly negates normal numbers, subnormal numbers, positive and negative zero, and positive and negative infinity.

The only complication is that there's no `xorsd` instruction to XOR two `doubles`. Instead, we'll use the `xorpd` instruction, which XORs two packed vectors of two `doubles` each. Each operand to `xorpd` is 16 bytes wide; the lower 8 bytes hold the first element of the vector and the upper 8 bytes hold the second. We'll use the lower 8 bytes of each operand and ignore the upper bytes. Like `addsd` and the other arithmetic floating-point instructions, `xorpd` takes an XMM register or memory address as a source operand and an XMM register as a destination. Unlike those other instructions, `xorpd` only accepts memory addresses that are 16-byte aligned; using a misaligned source operand causes a runtime exception.

Suppose we want to negate the `double` at `-8(%rbp)`, then store the result in `-16(%rbp)`. First, we define the constant `-0.0`:

```
    .section .rodata
    .align 16
.L_negative.zero:
    .double -0.0
```

We use the `.align 16` directive to ensure that this constant is 16-byte aligned. Next, we XOR it with our source value:

```
    movsd    -8(%rbp), %xmm0
    xorpd    .L_negative.zero(%rip), %xmm0
    movsd    %xmm0, -16(%rbp)
```

The first `movsd` instruction moves the source value into the lower 8 bytes of XMM0, zeroing out the upper 8 bytes. The `xorpd` instruction XORs the lower 8 bytes of XMM0 with the 8-byte value at `.L_negative.zero`, which is `-0.0`. It simultaneously XORs the upper 8 bytes of XMM0 with 8 bytes of whatever happens to immediately follow `-0.0` in memory. After this instruction, the lower bytes of XMM0 hold our negated value, and the upper 8 bytes hold junk. The final `movsd` instruction copies the lower bytes of XMM0 to their final destination at `-16(%rbp)`.

We'll also use `xorpd` to zero out registers. Because the result of XORing any number with itself is 0, an instruction like `xorpd %xmm0, %xmm0` is the easiest way to zero out a floating-point register.

NOTE *The XOR trick works for general-purpose registers too; for example, `xorq %rax, %rax` will zero out RAX. In fact, most compilers zero out both floating-point and general-purpose registers this way because it's slightly faster than using a `mov` instruction. Since we're prioritizing clarity and simplicity over performance, we use `mov` instead of `xor` to zero out general-purpose registers. But for XMM registers, zeroing with `xor` is the simpler option.*

Comparing Floating-Point Numbers

We'll compare floating-point values using the comisd instruction, which works similarly to cmp. Executing comisd b, a sets ZF to 1 if the values are equal and 0 otherwise. It sets CF to 1 if a is less than b and 0 otherwise. These are the same flags that characterize the result of an unsigned comparison. Unlike cmp, the comisd instruction always sets SF and OF to 0. We'll therefore use the same condition codes for floating-point comparisons that we use for unsigned comparisons: A, AE, B, and BE.

The comisd instruction handles subnormal numbers, infinity, and negative zero correctly without any special effort on our part. It treats 0.0 and -0.0 as equal, like the IEEE 754 standard requires. Handling NaN, which is an extra credit feature in this chapter, *does* require special effort. When either operand is NaN, comisd reports an *unordered* result, which we can't detect with the condition codes we've learned about so far. For more details, see "Extra Credit: NaN" on page 342.

Converting Between Floating-Point and Integer Types

In Listing 13-13, we defined TACKY instructions for four different type conversions: IntToDouble, DoubleToInt, UIntToDouble, and DoubleToUInt. The SSE instruction set includes conversions to and from signed integer types, so implementing IntToDouble and DoubleToInt is easy. It doesn't include conversions to and from unsigned integer types, so implementing UIntToDouble and DoubleToUInt takes a little ingenuity. There's more than one way to implement these trickier conversions; we'll implement them roughly the same way that GCC does.

Let's walk through these four conversions one at a time.

Converting a double to a Signed Integer

The cvttsd2si instruction converts a double to a signed integer. It truncates its source operand toward zero, which is what the C standard requires for conversions from double to integer types. This instruction takes a suffix that indicates the size of the result: cvttsd2sil converts the source value to a 32-bit integer, and cvttsd2siq converts it to a 64-bit integer.

Since double can represent a much wider range of values than either int or long, the source of cvttsd2si might be outside the range of the destination type. In that case, the instruction results in the special *indefinite integer* value, which is the minimum integer the destination type supports. It also sets a status flag indicating that the operation was invalid. Converting a double to an integer type is undefined behavior when it's outside the range of that type, so we're free to handle this case however we want. We'll just use the indefinite integer as the result of the conversion and ignore the status flag.

A more user-friendly compiler might check the status flag and raise a runtime error when a conversion is out of range, instead of silently returning a bogus result. It might do the same for the conversions from double to the unsigned integer types, which we'll consider next. Our approach makes it easy for C programmers to shoot themselves in the foot, but at least we're in good company: by default, GCC and Clang handle out-of-range conversions the same way we do.

Converting a double to an Unsigned Integer

It's not always possible to convert a double to an unsigned integer with the cvttsd2si instruction. We'll run into trouble when the double is in the range of an unsigned integer type but outside the range of the corresponding signed type. Consider the following C cast expression:

```
(unsigned int) 4294967290.0
```

This should evaluate to 4294967290, which is a perfectly valid unsigned int. But if we try to convert 4294967290.0 with the cvttsd2sil instruction, it will produce the indefinite integer instead of the right answer, because that value is outside the range of signed int. There's no SSE instruction to convert a double to an unsigned integer, either. We'll need to be a bit clever to work around these limitations.

NOTE   *A newer instruction set extension called AVX does include conversions from double to unsigned integer types, but not all x64 processors support this extension.*

To convert a double to an unsigned int, we'll first convert it to a signed long and then truncate the result. For example, to convert a double in XMM0 to an unsigned int and then store it on the stack, we can use the assembly in Listing 13-21.

```
cvttsd2siq  %xmm0, %rax
movl        %eax, -4(%rbp)
```

Listing 13-21: Converting a double to an unsigned int in assembly

Any value in the range of unsigned int is also in the range of signed long, so cvttsd2siq will handle it correctly. If the value is outside the range of unsigned int, the behavior is undefined, so we don't care what the result will be.

Converting from double to unsigned long is trickier. First, we'll check whether the double we want to convert is in the range of signed long. If it is, we can convert it with the cvttsd2siq instruction. If it's not, we'll subtract the value of LONG_MAX + 1 from our double to get a result in the range of signed long. We'll convert that result to an integer with the cvttsd2siq instruction, then add LONG_MAX + 1 again after the conversion. Listing 13-22 demonstrates how we might convert a double stored in XMM0 to an unsigned long in RAX.

```
    .section .rodata
    .align 8
.L_upper_bound:
 ❶  .double 9223372036854775808.0
    .text
```

```
        --snip--
❷ comisd   .L_upper_bound(%rip), %xmm0
  jae      .L_out_of_range
❸ cvttsd2siq      %xmm0, %rax
  jmp      .L_end
.L_out_of_range:
  movsd    %xmm0, %xmm1
❹ subsd    .L_upper_bound(%rip), %xmm1
  cvttsd2siq      %xmm1, %rax
  movq     $9223372036854775808, %rdx
  addq     %rdx, %rax
.L_end:
```

Listing 13-22: Converting a double *to an* unsigned long *in assembly*

We define a constant double with a value of LONG_MAX + 1, or 2^{63} ❶. To perform the conversion, we first check whether the value in XMM0 is below this constant ❷. If it is, we can convert it to an integer with a cvttsd2siq instruction ❸, then jump over the instructions for the other case.

If XMM0 is greater than the .L_upper_bound constant, it's too large for cvttsd2siq to convert. To handle this case, we jump to the .L_out_of_range label. We first copy the source value into XMM1 to avoid overwriting the original value, then subtract .L_upper_bound from it ❹. If the original value was within the range of unsigned long, the new value will be within the range of long. Therefore, we can convert XMM1 to a signed long with the cvttsd2siq instruction. (If the original value wasn't within the range of unsigned long, the behavior is undefined according to the C standard and cvttsd2siq will result in the indefinite integer.) At this point, the value in RAX is exactly 2^{63} (or 9,223,372,036,854,775,808) less than the correct answer, so we add 9223372036854775808 to get the final result.

Listing 13-22 includes a decimal value, .L_upper_bound, which the assembler will convert to a double-precision floating-point number. It also includes floating-point subtraction. We know that both of these operations can potentially introduce rounding error. Could this rounding error lead to an incorrect result?

Luckily for us, it won't. We can prove that Listing 13-22 won't require any rounding at all. First of all, 9223372036854775808.0 can be represented exactly as a double, where the significand is 1 and the exponent is 63. (That's why we use this constant instead of LONG_MAX, which double cannot represent exactly.) A double can also represent the exact result of subsd .L_upper_bound(%rip), %xmm0 in every case we care about. Specifically, we care about the cases where the source value is greater than or equal to 9223372036854775808.0, which is 2^{63}, but not greater than ULONG_MAX, which is $2^{64} - 1$. That means we can write this value as $1.x \times 2^{63}$, for some sequence of bits x. Because a double has 53 bits of precision, x can't be more than 52 bits long. When we subtract 1×2^{63} from the source value, the result will be exactly $x \times 2^{62}$, which requires at most 52 bits of precision to represent exactly. (This is a special case of the *Sterbenz lemma*, in case you want to look it up.)

Therefore, this subtraction will give us an exact result, and adding 9223372036854775808 to that result after converting it to an integer will give us an exact final answer.

Converting a Signed Integer to a double

The cvtsi2sd instruction converts a signed integer to a double. You write it with an l or q suffix, depending on whether the source operand is a 32-bit or 64-bit integer. If the result can't be represented exactly as a double, it will be rounded according to the CPU's current rounding mode, which we can assume is round-to-nearest.

Converting an Unsigned Integer to a double

The cvtsi2sd instruction interprets its source operand as a two's complement value, meaning any value with its upper bit set gets converted to a negative double. Unfortunately, there's no unsigned equivalent to cvtsi2sd that we can use instead. We're back in a similar situation to the previous section on unsigned integers, so we'll rely on similar techniques.

To convert an unsigned int to a double, we can zero extend it to a long and then convert it to a double with cvtsi2sdq. Listing 13-23 illustrates how we can use this approach to convert the unsigned integer 4294967290 to a double.

```
movl   $4294967290, %eax
cvtsi2sdq  %rax, %xmm0
```

Listing 13-23: Converting an unsigned int to a double in assembly

Recall that a movl instruction moves a value into a register's lower 32 bits and zeroes out its upper 32 bits. The first instruction in this listing effectively moves and zero extends 4294967290 into the RAX register. This zero-extended number has the same value whether we interpret it as signed or unsigned, so the cvtsi2sdq instruction will convert it correctly, storing the floating-point value 4294967290.0 in XMM0.

That leaves the conversion from unsigned long to double. To handle this case, we'll first check whether the value is in the range that signed long can represent. If it is, we can use cvtsi2sdq directly. Otherwise, we'll halve the source value to bring it into the range of signed long, convert it with cvtsi2sdq, and then double the result of the conversion. A naive attempt to perform this conversion in assembly might look like Listing 13-24.

```
❶ cmpq    $0, -8(%rbp)
   jl     .L_out_of_range
❷ cvtsi2sdq   -8(%rbp), %xmm0
   jmp    .L_end
.L_out_of_range:
   movq   -8(%rbp), %rax
❸ shrq    %rax
   cvtsi2sdq   %rax, %xmm0
```

```
        addsd   %xmm0, %xmm0
.L_end:
```

Listing 13-24: Incorrectly converting an unsigned long to a double in assembly

We first check whether the source value, at -8(%rbp), is out of bounds by performing a signed comparison to zero ❶. If the signed value is greater than or equal to zero, we can use cvtsi2sdq directly ❷ and then jump over the instructions for the out-of-range case.

Otherwise, we jump to the .L_out_of_range label. We copy the source value into RAX, then halve it by shifting it 1 bit to the right with the unary shrq instruction ❸. (The mnemonic shr is short for *shift right*.) Next, we use cvtsi2sdq to convert the halved value to the nearest representable double. Finally, we add the result to itself, producing the double representation of the original value (or at least the closest value that double can represent exactly).

But there's a problem with this code: the result won't always be correctly rounded. When we halve an integer with shrq, we round down; halving 9, for example, gives us 4 as the result. If this rounded-down integer happens to be at the exact midpoint between two consecutive values that double can represent, cvtsi2sdq might round down again, even though the original integer was closer to the double above it than the one below it. We've hit a double rounding error!

Let's work through a concrete example. (To make this example more readable, I'll bold the digits that differ between large numbers that are near each other.) We'll convert 922337203685477**6833** to a double according to Listing 13-24. The closest double values to our source operand are 9223372036854775**808.0**, which is 1,025 less than the source value, and 9223372036854777**856.0**, which is 1,023 more than it. We should convert the source value to the higher double, since it's closer.

Halving the source value with shrq gives us 4611686018427388**416**. This integer is exactly at the midpoint between two adjacent double values: 4611686018427387**904.0** and 4611686018427388**928.0**.

Written out as a binary fraction, the lower value is

```
1.0000000000000000000000000000000000000000000000000000 * 2^62
```

and the higher one is:

```
1.0000000000000000000000000000000000000000000000000001 * 2^62
```

This notation shows us the significands of both values, written out with the full available precision. Since we round ties to even, we pick the value with a 0 in the least significant bit of the significand. In this particular example, that means rounding down, so cvtsi2sd produces the lower double, 4611686018427387**904.0**. We then add that to itself, which gives us a final answer of 9223372036854775**808.0**. Instead of getting the double just above our initial value, which was the correctly rounded result, we got the double just below it. Figure 13-5 illustrates how double rounding here leads to an incorrect result. (To reduce the size of the figure, we only show the first and last few digits of each number.)

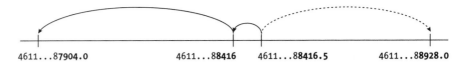

4611...87904.0   4611...88416   4611...88416.5   4611...88928.0

Figure 13-5: A double rounding error when converting from an unsigned long to a double

The dotted arrow shows the correct rounding of 9223372036854776**833** / 2 to the nearest double. The two solid lines demonstrate the actual result of double rounding.

To avoid this error, we need to make sure that when we halve the initial value, we don't round the result to a midpoint between two values that double can represent. We'll do this with a technique called *rounding to odd*. When we halve the source value, we won't truncate it toward zero. Instead, we'll round to the nearest odd number. Using this rounding rule, we'll round 9 / 2 up to 5 instead of down to 4. Similarly, we'll round 7 / 2 down to 3, and we'll round 9223372036854776**833** / 2 up to 4611686018427388**417**. If the result of dividing by 2 is already an integer, we don't need to round; for example, 16 / 2 will still be 8. (Only the result of shrq needs to be rounded to odd; cvtsi2sdq will still round to nearest.)

Rounding to odd works in this situation because the midpoints we want to avoid are always even integers. The gaps between binary floating-point numbers are always powers of 2, and they get bigger at larger magnitudes. Remember that we halve an integer for this conversion only if it's too big to fit in a long. The halved value will therefore be between (LONG_MAX + 1) / 2 and ULONG_MAX / 2. In that range, the gap between representable double values is 1,024, so every midpoint is a multiple of 512, which is even.

Figure 13-6 illustrates a few different cases of rounding to odd in action.

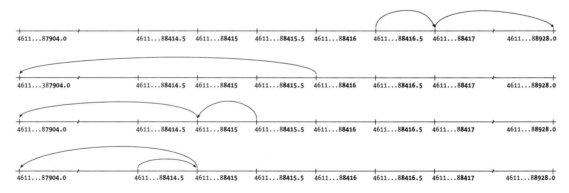

Figure 13-6: Using rounding to odd to avoid a double rounding error

In the first case, rounding to odd prevents us from rounding to a midpoint and then down to an incorrect result. In the remaining cases, it doesn't change the final result; whether we round these cases to odd or toward zero on the first rounding, we'll get the same answer as if we'd rounded only once using round-to-nearest, ties-to-even mode. Sometimes rounding to odd is necessary to get the right answer, and sometimes it has no impact, but it never gives us the wrong answer.

Now that we understand why rounding to odd works, let's figure out how to implement it in assembly. Listing 13-25 demonstrates how to halve the value stored in RAX and round the result to odd.

```
movq    %rax, %rdx
shrq    %rdx
andq    $1, %rax
orq     %rax, %rdx
```

Listing 13-25: Rounding to odd after halving an integer with shrq

This listing includes two new instructions: and and or. If you did the extra credit section in Chapter 3, you're already familiar with them. These instructions perform bitwise AND and OR operations, respectively; they're used exactly like our other instructions that perform binary operations on integers, including add and sub.

Let's figure out why this code works. First, we copy the value we want to halve into RDX and halve it with shrq. Next, we take the bitwise AND of 1 and the original value in RAX; this produces 1 if the original value was odd and 0 if it was even.

Now we need to decide what to do about the halved value in RDX. At this point, one of three things is true:

1. The original value was even, so RDX contains the exact result of halving that value. Therefore, we don't need to round it.

2. The original value was odd, and the result of shrq is also odd. For example, if the original value was 3, halving it with shrq will produce 1. In this case, the result is already rounded to odd and doesn't need to change.

3. The original value was odd, and the result of shrq is even. For example, if the original value was 5, halving it with shrq will produce 2. In this case, the result is not rounded to odd, and we need to increment it.

In each of these three cases, the final instruction, orq %rax, %rdx, has the desired effect. In the first case, it does nothing because RAX is 0, thanks to the prior and instruction. In the second case, it does nothing because the least significant bit of RDX is already 1. In the third case, it flips the least significant bit of RDX from 0 to 1 and makes the value odd.

Putting it all together, Listing 13-26 shows the complete assembly to convert an unsigned long to a correctly rounded double.

```
cmpq     $0, -8(%rbp)
jl       .L_out_of_range
cvtsi2sdq    -8(%rbp), %xmm0
jmp      .L_end
```

```
.L_out_of_range:
    movq    -8(%rbp), %rax
    movq    %rax, %rdx
    shrq    %rdx
    andq    $1, %rax
    orq     %rax, %rdx
    cvtsi2sdq    %rdx, %xmm0
    addsd   %xmm0, %xmm0
.L_end:
```

Listing 13-26: Correctly converting an unsigned long to a double in assembly

This code is identical to the original conversion in Listing 13-24, except for the bolded changes: we round the result of shrq to odd and use the rounded value in RDX as the source of the cvtsi2sdq instruction.

We've now discussed how to implement every floating-point operation we need; we're ready to update the assembly generation pass!

Assembly Generation

As usual, our first task is to update the assembly AST. We'll add a new Double assembly type:

```
assembly_type = Longword | Quadword | Double
```

We'll also add a new top-level construct to represent floating-point constants:

```
StaticConstant(identifier name, int alignment, static_init init)
```

This construct is almost identical to StaticVariable. The one difference is that we can omit the global attribute, since we'll never define global constants. For now, we'll define only floating-point constants; in later chapters, we'll use this construct to define constants of other types as well.

Next, we'll add two new instructions, Cvtsi2sd and Cvttsd2si:

```
instruction = --snip--
            | Cvttsd2si(assembly_type dst_type, operand src, operand dst)
            | Cvtsi2sd(assembly_type src_type, operand src, operand dst)
```

Each of these takes an assembly_type parameter to specify whether it operates on Longword or Quadword integers.

We'll reuse the existing Cmp and Binary instructions to represent floating-point comparisons with comisd and arithmetic with addsd, subsd, and so on. We'll add a new DivDouble binary operator to represent floating-point division. (Recall that the assembly AST doesn't include a binary operator for integer division because div and idiv don't follow the same pattern as the other arithmetic instructions.) We'll also add the Xor binary operator we need to negate floating-point values, as well as the bitwise And and Or operators we need to convert an unsigned long to a double:

```
binary_operator = --snip-- | DivDouble | And | Or | Xor
```

We need the unary Shr operator for that type conversion too:

```
unary_operator = --snip-- | Shr
```

Finally, we'll add the XMM registers. We'll need XMM0 through XMM7 for parameter passing, plus a couple more scratch registers for instruction rewrites. You can use any registers apart from XMM0 through XMM7 for scratch; I'll use XMM14 and XMM15. You can either add all 16 registers to the AST or just add the ones we need right now:

```
reg = --snip-- | XMM0 | XMM1 | XMM2 | XMM3 | XMM4 | XMM5 | XMM6 | XMM7 | XMM14 | XMM15
```

Listing 13-27 gives the entire assembly AST, with changes bolded.

```
program = Program(top_level*)
assembly_type = Longword | Quadword | Double
top_level = Function(identifier name, bool global, instruction* instructions)
          | StaticVariable(identifier name, bool global, int alignment, static_init init)
          | StaticConstant(identifier name, int alignment, static_init init)
instruction = Mov(assembly_type, operand src, operand dst)
            | Movsx(operand src, operand dst)
            | MovZeroExtend(operand src, operand dst)
            | Cvttsd2si(assembly_type dst_type, operand src, operand dst)
            | Cvtsi2sd(assembly_type src_type, operand src, operand dst)
            | Unary(unary_operator, assembly_type, operand)
            | Binary(binary_operator, assembly_type, operand, operand)
            | Cmp(assembly_type, operand, operand)
            | Idiv(assembly_type, operand)
            | Div(assembly_type, operand)
            | Cdq(assembly_type)
            | Jmp(identifier)
            | JmpCC(cond_code, identifier)
            | SetCC(cond_code, operand)
            | Label(identifier)
            | Push(operand)
            | Call(identifier)
            | Ret
unary_operator = Neg | Not | Shr
binary_operator = Add | Sub | Mult | DivDouble | And | Or | Xor
operand = Imm(int) | Reg(reg) | Pseudo(identifier) | Stack(int) | Data(identifier)
cond_code = E | NE | G | GE | L | LE | A | AE | B | BE
reg = AX | CX | DX | DI | SI | R8 | R9 | R10 | R11 | SP
    | XMM0 | XMM1 | XMM2 | XMM3 | XMM4 | XMM5 | XMM6 | XMM7 | XMM14 | XMM15
```

Listing 13-27: The assembly AST with floating-point constants, instructions, and registers

We already understand how to perform floating-point operations in assembly, but there are a few implementation details we still need to discuss. We'll deal with constants first.

Floating-Point Constants

In previous chapters, we converted integer constants in TACKY to `Imm` operands in assembly. This approach won't work for floating-point constants. Instead, when we encounter a `double` constant in TACKY, we'll generate a new top-level `StaticConstant` construct with a unique identifier. To use that constant in an instruction, we refer to it with a `Data` operand, just like a static variable. For example, suppose we need to convert the following TACKY instruction to assembly:

```
Copy(Constant(ConstDouble(1.0)), Var("x"))
```

First, we'll generate a unique label, `const_label`, that won't conflict with any of the names in the symbol table or any of the internal labels we use as jump targets. Then, we'll define a new top-level constant like this:

```
StaticConstant(const_label, 8, DoubleInit(1.0))
```

This top-level constant must be 8-byte aligned to conform to the System V ABI. After defining this constant, we'll emit the following assembly instruction:

```
Mov(Double, Data(const_label), Pseudo("x"))
```

Keep track of every `StaticConstant` you define throughout the entire assembly generation pass. Then, at the end of this pass, add these constants to your list of top-level constructs.

Aside from constant handling, this example demonstrates a few things about assembly generation that won't change. First, we'll still convert the TACKY `Copy` instruction to a `Mov` instruction in assembly, whether we're copying an integer or a `double`. Second, TACKY variables are still converted to `Pseudo` operands, regardless of their type.

There are a couple of optional tweaks you can make here to bring your top-level constants more in line with what a production compiler would generate:

Avoiding duplicate constants

Don't generate multiple equivalent `StaticConstant` constructs. Instead, whenever you see a `double` constant in TACKY, check whether you've already generated a `StaticConstant` with the same value and alignment. If you have, refer to that constant in your assembly code instead of generating a new one. Just keep in mind that `0.0` and `-0.0` are distinct constants that require separate `StaticConstant` constructs, even though they compare equal in most languages.

Using local labels for top-level constants

Compilers typically use local labels starting with `L` (on macOS) or `.L` (on Linux) for floating-point constants, so they don't show up as symbols in the final executable. (Recall that we already use local labels for jump targets.) If you want to follow this naming convention, don't add the local label prefix just yet; wait until the code emission pass. For now, add top-level constants to the backend symbol table and use a new attribute to distinguish them from variables. Listing 13-28 shows how to update the original backend symbol table entry from Listing 11-26 to include this attribute.

```
asm_symtab_entry = ObjEntry(assembly_type, bool is_static, bool is_constant)
                 | FunEntry(bool defined)
```

Listing 13-28: Definition of an entry in the backend symbol table, including the is_constant attribute

During code emission, we'll use this new attribute to figure out which operands should get a local label prefix. The is_static attribute should also be true for constants, since we store them in the read-only data section and access them with RIP-relative addressing. We're waiting until code emission to add local labels instead of generating them right off the bat because it will be easier to extend this approach when we add more kinds of top-level constants in Chapter 16.

Feel free to make both of these tweaks, skip both of them, or make one but not the other.

Unary Instructions, Binary Instructions, and Conditional Jumps

We'll convert floating-point addition, subtraction, and multiplication instructions from TACKY to assembly just like their integer equivalents. Floating-point division will follow the same pattern as these other instructions, even though integer division doesn't. Consider the following TACKY instruction:

```
Binary(Divide, Var("src1"), Var("src2"), Var("dst"))
```

If the type of its operands is double, we'll generate the following assembly:

```
Mov(Double, Pseudo("src1"), Pseudo("dst"))
Binary(DivDouble, Double, Pseudo("src2"), Pseudo("dst"))
```

We'll also translate floating-point negation differently from its integer counterpart. To negate a double, we'll XOR it with -0.0. For example, to translate the TACKY instruction

```
Unary(Negate, Var("src"), Var("dst"))
```

we'll start by defining a new 16-byte-aligned constant:

```
StaticConstant(const, 16, DoubleInit(-0.0))
```

Then we'll generate the following assembly instructions:

```
Mov(Double, Pseudo("src"), Pseudo("dst"))
Binary(Xor, Double, Data(const), Pseudo("dst"))
```

We need to align -0.0 to 16 bytes so that we can use it in the xorpd instruction. This is the only time we align a double to 16 bytes instead of 8. We don't need to worry about the alignment of dst; xorpd's destination must be a register, and we'll take care of that requirement during instruction fix-up.

Next, let's talk about how to handle our relational binary operators: Equal, LessThan, and so on. Because comisd sets the CF and ZF flags, we'll handle floating-point comparisons just like unsigned integer comparisons. Here's an example:

```
Binary(LessThan, Var("x"), Var("y"), Var("dst"))
```

If x and y are floating-point values, we'll produce the following assembly:

```
Cmp(Double, Pseudo("y"), Pseudo("x"))
Mov(Longword, Imm(0), Pseudo("dst"))
SetCC(B, Pseudo("dst"))
```

We'll take a similar approach to the three TACKY instructions that compare a value to zero: JumpIfZero, JumpIfNotZero, and the unary Not operation. We'll convert

```
JumpIfZero(Var("x"), "label")
```

to the following assembly:

```
Binary(Xor, Double, Reg(XMM0), Reg(XMM0))
Cmp(Double, Pseudo("x"), Reg(XMM0))
JmpCC(E, "label")
```

Note that we need to zero out an XMM register with xorpd in order to perform the comparison. You don't need to use XMM0 here, but you shouldn't use the scratch registers you've chosen for the rewrite pass. It's easier to avoid conflicting uses of registers if you strictly separate which registers you introduce in each backend pass.

Type Conversions

Since we've already covered the assembly for each of our type conversions, I won't present it again here, but I will flag a couple of details we haven't discussed yet. First, you'll need to choose which hard registers to use in these conversions. All four conversions between double and the unsigned integer types use XMM registers, general-purpose registers, or both. For example, Listing 13-26 uses RAX and RDX to halve an integer and then round to odd. You don't need to stick with the same registers we used when we walked through these conversions earlier; just avoid the callee-saved registers (RBX, R12, R13, R14, and R15) and the registers you use in the rewrite pass (R10 and R11, plus your two scratch XMM registers; mine are XMM14 and XMM15).

Second, when you process a conversion from unsigned int to double, be sure to generate a MovZeroExtend instruction to explicitly zero extend the source value, rather than a Mov instruction. This will become important when we implement register allocation in Part III. We'll use a technique called *register coalescing* to delete redundant mov instructions as we allocate registers; using MovZeroExtend instead of Mov here signals that you're using this instruction to zero out bytes and not just to move values around, so it shouldn't be deleted.

Concretely, if x is an unsigned int, you'll translate the TACKY instruction

```
UIntToDouble(Var("x"), Var("y"))
```

into this assembly:

```
MovZeroExtend(Pseudo("x"), Reg(AX))
Cvtsi2sd(Quadword, Reg(AX), Pseudo("y"))
```

You can use a register other than RAX here, as long as it meets the requirements we just discussed.

Function Calls

The tricky part of handling floating-point values in function calls is figuring out where each argument is passed. We'll use this information in two places. First, we'll need it to pass arguments correctly when we translate the TACKY FunCall instruction. Second, we'll use it to set up parameters at the beginning of each function body. We'll write a helper function, classify_parameters, to handle the bookkeeping we need in both of these places. Given a list of TACKY values, this helper function will convert each one to an assembly operand and determine its assembly type. It will also partition the list in three: one list of operands passed in general-purpose registers, one list of operands passed in XMM registers, and one list of operands passed on the stack. Listing 13-29 gives the pseudocode for classify_parameters.

```
classify_parameters(values):
    int_reg_args = []
    double_reg_args = []
    stack_args = []

    for v in values:
        operand = convert_val(v)
        t = assembly_type_of(v)
      ❶ typed_operand = (t, operand)
        if t == Double:
          ❷ if length(double_reg_args) < 8:
```

```
        ❸ double_reg_args.append(operand)
          else:
              stack_args.append(typed_operand)
      else:
          if length(int_reg_args) < 6:
              ❹ int_reg_args.append(typed_operand)
          else:
              stack_args.append(typed_operand)

  return (int_reg_args, double_reg_args, stack_args)
```

Listing 13-29: Classifying function arguments or parameters

To process each parameter, we first convert it from a TACKY value to an assembly operand and convert its type to the corresponding assembly type. (I won't give you the pseudocode for assembly_type_of, which just finds the type of a TACKY value and converts it to assembly.) We package these up into a pair, typed_operand ❶. The elements of int_reg_args and stack_args will all be pairs in this form. The elements of double_reg_args will be plain assembly operands; since they're all doubles, it would be redundant to specify each one's type explicitly.

Next, we figure out which list to add the operand to. We'll see if we can pass it in an available register for its type. For example, if its type is Double, we check whether double_reg_args already contains eight values ❷. If it does, registers XMM0 through XMM7 are already taken. If it doesn't, there's at least one XMM register still available.

If we can pass the operand in an XMM register, we'll add operand to double_arg_regs ❸. If we can pass it in a general-purpose register, we'll add typed_operand to int_arg_regs ❹. If there are no registers of the correct type available, we'll add typed_operand to stack_args. Once we've processed every value, we return all three lists.

As we build up these three lists, we preserve the order in which the values appear. In particular, we add values to stack_args in the same order they appear in the original list of values, not in reverse. That means the first value in stack_args will be pushed last and will appear at the top of the stack. From the callee's perspective, the first value will be stored at 16(%rbp), the second value at 24(%rbp), and so on.

Recall that at the start of a function body, we copy any parameters from their initial locations into pseudoregisters. Listing 13-30 demonstrates how to use classify_parameters to perform this setup.

```
set_up_parameters(parameters):

    // classify them
    int_reg_params, double_reg_params, stack_params = classify_parameters(parameters)

    // copy parameters from general-purpose registers
    int_regs = [ DI, SI, DX, CX, R8, R9 ]
    reg_index = 0
    for (param_type, param) in int_reg_params:
        r = int_regs[reg_index]
```

```
    emit(Mov(param_type, Reg(r), param))
    reg_index += 1

// copy parameters from XMM registers
double_regs = [ XMM0, XMM1, XMM2, XMM3, XMM4, XMM5, XMM6, XMM7 ]
reg_index = 0
for param in double_reg_params:
    r = double_regs[reg_index]
    emit(Mov(Double, Reg(r), param))
    reg_index += 1

// copy parameters from the stack
offset = 16
for (param_type, param) in stack_params:
    emit(Mov(param_type, Stack(offset), param))
    offset += 8
```

Listing 13-30: Setting up parameters in function bodies

In this listing, set_up_parameters takes a list of a TACKY Vars representing a function's parameter list. We process this list with classify_parameters, then handle the three resulting lists of assembly operands. To process parameters passed in general-purpose registers, we copy the value in EDI (or RDI, depending on the type) to the pseudoregister for the first parameter, copy the value in ESI to the second parameter, and so on. We handle parameters passed in XMM registers the same way. Finally, we handle parameters passed on the stack: we copy the value at Stack(16) to the first pseudoregister in stack_params, then increase the stack offset by 8 for each subsequent parameter until we've processed the whole list.

We'll also use classify_parameters to implement the TACKY FunCall instruction. Let's revisit the pseudocode to convert FunCall to assembly, which we first introduced in Listing 9-31 and updated in Listing 11-25. Listing 13-31 presents this pseudocode again, with the new logic to process floating-point arguments and return values bolded. (I haven't bolded minor changes like renaming arg_registers to int_registers.)

```
convert_function_call(FunCall(fun_name, args, dst)):
    int_registers = [ DI, SI, DX, CX, R8, R9 ]
    double_registers = [ XMM0, XMM1, XMM2, XMM3, XMM4, XMM5, XMM6, XMM7 ]

    // classify arguments
    int_args, double_args, stack_args = classify_parameters(args)

    // adjust stack alignment
    if length(stack_args) is odd:
        stack_padding = 8
    else:
        stack_padding = 0

    if stack_padding != 0:
        emit(Binary(Sub, Quadword, Imm(stack_padding), Reg(SP)))
```

```
// pass args in registers
reg_index = 0
for (assembly_type, assembly_arg) in int_args:
    r = int_registers[reg_index]
    emit(Mov(assembly_type, assembly_arg, Reg(r)))
    reg_index += 1

reg_index = 0
for assembly_arg in double_args:
    r = double_registers[reg_index]
    emit(Mov(Double, assembly_arg, Reg(r)))
    reg_index += 1

// pass args on stack
for (assembly_type, assembly_arg) in reverse(stack_args):
    if (assembly_arg is a Reg or Imm operand
        or assembly_type == Quadword
        or assembly_type == Double):
        emit(Push(assembly_arg))
    else:
        emit(Mov(assembly_type, assembly_arg, Reg(AX)))
        emit(Push(Reg(AX)))

// emit call instruction
emit(Call(fun_name))

// adjust stack pointer
bytes_to_remove = 8 * length(stack_args) + stack_padding
if bytes_to_remove != 0:
    emit(Binary(Add, Quadword, Imm(bytes_to_remove), Reg(SP)))

// retrieve return value
assembly_dst = convert_val(dst)
return_type = assembly_type_of(dst)
if return_type == Double:
    emit(Mov(Double, Reg(XMM0), assembly_dst))
else:
    emit(Mov(return_type, Reg(AX), assembly_dst))
```

Listing 13-31: Supporting double in function calls

Let's walk through the changes in this listing. To start, we need to catego-
rize our arguments with classify_parameters. The arguments in int_args are
passed in general-purpose registers the same way as before (possibly with a
few tweaks, not bolded here, to account for the fact that we're iterating over
typed assembly operands rather than TACKY values). We add a new step to
copy each argument in double_args into the corresponding XMM register.

Next, we update how we pass arguments on the stack. We make two tiny
changes from Listing 11-25, where we last looked at this step. First, Pseudo
operands of Double type, like operands of Quadword type, are pushed directly
onto the stack without copying them into a register first, since they're the
correct operand size for the Push instruction. Second, in cases where we
move an operand into the AX register before we push it onto the stack, we no
longer hardcode Longword as the type of the Mov instruction; instead, we use

the operand type we determined in classify_parameters. This future-proofs our code against later chapters, where we'll add more assembly types.

Finally, we update how we retrieve the function's return value. If the return value is a double, we'll copy it from XMM0 to the destination. Otherwise, we'll copy it from EAX (or RAX), as usual. We don't need to change how we adjust the stack alignment before a function call, issue the call instruction itself, or clean up arguments afterward.

Return Instructions

Last but not least, we'll change how we translate the TACKY Return instruction. For example, given the TACKY instruction

```
Return(Var("x"))
```

we'll look up the type of x in the backend symbol table. If it's an integer, we can handle it as before. If it's a double, we'll copy it into XMM0 and then return:

```
Mov(Double, Pseudo("x"), Reg(XMM0))
Ret
```

And with that, we've covered every update to the assembly generation pass.

The Complete Conversion from TACKY to Assembly

Tables 13-2 through 13-7 summarize this chapter's changes to the conversion from TACKY to assembly. As usual, new constructs and changes to the conversions for existing constructs are bolded. The *⟨R⟩* and *⟨X⟩* placeholders in Table 13-3 indicate arbitrary general-purpose and XMM registers, respectively.

Table 13-2: Converting Top-Level TACKY Constructs to Assembly

TACKY top-level construct	Assembly top-level construct
Program(top_level_defs)	Program(top_level_defs + *⟨all StaticConstant constructs for floating-point constants⟩*)
Function(name, global, params, instructions)	Function(name, global, [Mov(*⟨first int param type⟩*, Reg(DI), *⟨first int param⟩*), Mov(*⟨second int param type⟩*, Reg(SI), *⟨second int param⟩*), *⟨copy next four integer parameters from registers⟩*, **Mov(Double, Reg(XMM0), ⟨first double param⟩),** **Mov(Double, Reg(XMM1), ⟨second double param⟩),** **⟨copy next six double parameters from registers⟩,** Mov(*⟨first stack param type⟩*, Stack(16), *⟨first stack param⟩*), Mov(*⟨second stack param type⟩*, Stack(24), *⟨second stack param⟩*), *⟨copy remaining parameters from stack⟩*] + instructions)

Table 13-3: Converting TACKY Instructions to Assembly

TACKY instruction		Assembly instructions
Return(val)	Integer	Mov(<*val type*>, val, Reg(AX)) Ret
	double	Mov(Double, val, Reg(XMM0)) Ret
Unary(Not, src, dst)	Integer	Cmp(<*src type*>, Imm(0), src) Mov(<*dst type*>, Imm(0), dst) SetCC(E, dst)
	double	Binary(Xor, Double, Reg(<*X*>), Reg(<*X*>)) Cmp(Double, src, Reg(<*X*>)) Mov(<*dst type*>, Imm(0), dst) SetCC(E, dst)
Unary(Negate, src, dst) (double **negation**)		Mov(Double, src, dst) Binary(Xor, Double, Data(<*negative-zero*>), dst) **And add a top-level constant:** StaticConstant(<*negative-zero*>, 16, DoubleInit(-0.0))
Binary(Divide, src1, src2, dst) **(integer division)**	Signed	Mov(<*src1 type*>, src1, Reg(AX)) Cdq(<*src1 type*>) Idiv(<*src1 type*>, src2) Mov(<*src1 type*>, Reg(AX), dst)
	Unsigned	Mov(<*src1 type*>, src1, Reg(AX)) Mov(<*src1 type*>, Imm(0), Reg(DX)) Div(<*src1 type*>, src2) Mov(<*src1 type*>, Reg(AX), dst)
JumpIfZero(condition, target)	Integer	Cmp(<*condition type*>, Imm(0), condition) JmpCC(E, target)
	double	Binary(Xor, Double, Reg(<*X*>), Reg(<*X*>)) Cmp(Double, condition, Reg(<*X*>)) JmpCC(E, target)
JumpIfNotZero(condition, target)	Integer	Cmp(<*condition type*>, Imm(0), condition) JmpCC(NE, target)
	double	Binary(Xor, Double, Reg(<*X*>), Reg(<*X*>)) Cmp(Double, condition, Reg(<*X*>)) JmpCC(NE, target)
FunCall(fun_name, args, dst)		*<fix stack alignment>* *<move arguments to general-purpose registers>* *<move arguments to XMM registers>* *<push arguments onto the stack>* Call(fun_name) *<deallocate arguments/padding>* Mov(<*dst type*>, *<dst register>*, dst)
IntToDouble(src, dst)		Cvtsi2sd(<*src type*>, src, dst)
DoubleToInt(src, dst)		Cvttsd2si(<*dst type*>, src, dst)

TACKY instruction		Assembly instructions
UIntToDouble(src, dst)	unsigned int	MovZeroExtend(src, Reg(\<R\>)) Cvtsi2sd(Quadword, Reg(\<R\>), dst)
	unsigned long	Cmp(Quadword, Imm(0), src) JmpCC(L, \<label1\>) Cvtsi2sd(Quadword, src, dst) Jmp(\<label2\>) Label(\<label1\>) Mov(Quadword, src, Reg(\<R1\>)) Mov(Quadword, Reg(\<R1\>), Reg(\<R2\>)) Unary(Shr, Quadword, Reg(\<R2\>)) Binary(And, Quadword, Imm(1), Reg(\<R1\>)) Binary(Or, Quadword, Reg(\<R1\>), Reg(\<R2\>)) Cvtsi2sd(Quadword, Reg(\<R2\>), dst) Binary(Add, Double, dst, dst) Label(\<label2\>)
DoubleToUInt(src, dst)	unsigned int	Cvttsd2si(Quadword, src, Reg(\<R\>)) Mov(Longword, Reg(\<R\>), dst)

	unsigned long	Cmp(Double, Data(\<upper-bound\>), src)
		JmpCC(AE, \<label1\>)
		Cvttsd2si(Quadword, src, dst)
		Jmp(\<label2\>)
		Label(\<label1\>)
		Mov(Double, src, Reg(\<X\>))
		Binary(Sub, Double, Data(\<upper-bound\>),
		        Reg(\<X\>))
		Cvttsd2si(Quadword, Reg(\<X\>), dst)
		Mov(Quadword, Imm(9223372036854775808), Reg(\<R\>))
		Binary(Add, Quadword, Reg(\<R\>), dst)
		Label(\<label2\>)
		And add a top-level constant:
		StaticConstant(\<upper-bound\>, 8,
		           DoubleInit(9223372036854775808.0))

Table 13-4: Converting TACKY Arithmetic Operators to Assembly

TACKY operator	Assembly operator
Divide (double division)	DivDouble

Table 13-5: Converting TACKY Comparisons to Assembly

TACKY comparison		Assembly condition code
LessThan	Signed	L
	Unsigned **or double**	B
LessOrEqual	Signed	LE
	Unsigned **or double**	BE

(continued)

Table 13-5: Converting TACKY Comparisons to Assembly *(continued)*

TACKY comparison		Assembly condition code
GreaterThan	Signed	G
	Unsigned **or double**	A
GreaterOrEqual	Signed	GE
	Unsigned **or double**	AE

Table 13-6: Converting TACKY Operands to Assembly

TACKY operand	Assembly operand
Constant(ConstDouble(double))	Data(*<ident>*) **And add top-level constant:** StaticConstant(*<ident>*, 8, DoubleInit(double))

Table 13-7: Converting Types to Assembly

Source type	Assembly type	Alignment
Double	Double	8

As the row for the top-level Program construct in Table 13-2 indicates, you'll need to add every StaticConstant you define in this pass to the list of top-level definitions. From this point on, updating the rest of the backend is relatively smooth sailing.

Pseudoregister Replacement

You should allocate 8 bytes on the stack for each double pseudoregister and make sure it's 8-byte aligned. If the backend symbol table indicates that a double has static storage duration, you should replace any references to it with Data operands, like you do for other static variables. In short, this pass can treat Double and Quadword pseudoregisters identically, since they have the same size and alignment.

As usual, you should also extend this pass to handle the new assembly instructions in this chapter.

Instruction Fix-Up

Next, we'll rewrite invalid SSE instructions. We'll also need to rewrite the new bitwise instructions that operate on integers. Let's handle the SSE instructions first. You should dedicate one XMM register to fixing instructions' source operands and one to fixing destinations. I'll use XMM14 for the former and XMM15 for the latter.

The destination of `cvttsd2si` must be a register. For example, we'll rewrite

```
Cvttsd2si(Quadword, Stack(-8), Stack(-16))
```

as:

```
Cvttsd2si(Quadword, Stack(-8), Reg(R11))
Mov(Quadword, Reg(R11), Stack(-16))
```

The `cvtsi2sd` instruction has two constraints: the source can't be a constant, and the destination must be a register. We'll therefore rewrite

```
Cvtsi2sd(Longword, Imm(10), Stack(-8))
```

as:

```
Mov(Longword, Imm(10), Reg(R10))
Cvtsi2sd(Longword, Reg(R10), Reg(XMM15))
Mov(Double, Reg(XMM15), Stack(-8))
```

The `comisd` instruction has different constraints from `cmp`. Its second operand, in the "destination" position, must be a register. So, we'll rewrite

```
Cmp(Double, Stack(-8), Stack(-16))
```

as:

```
Mov(Double, Stack(-16), Reg(XMM15))
Cmp(Double, Stack(-8), Reg(XMM15))
```

The destination of an `addsd`, `subsd`, `mulsd`, `divsd`, or `xorpd` instruction must be a register as well, so we'll rewrite all of these instructions accordingly. The `xorpd` instruction also requires either a register or a 16-byte-aligned memory address as its source operand, but we don't need a rewrite rule for this since all the `xorpd` instructions we generate already satisfy this requirement.

We'll use the same rewrite rule for `movsd` that we introduced for the general-purpose `mov` instruction in Chapter 2, because it's subject to the same constraint: its operands can't both be in memory. (The one difference, of course, is that we'll use an XMM register instead of R10 as the scratch register.)

That leaves the new bitwise instructions. We won't need to rewrite `shr`. The `and` and `or` instructions are subject to the same constraints as integer `add` and `sub`: the operands can't both be memory addresses, and they can't take immediate source operands outside the range of `int`.

There's one other constraint that we'll ignore for now: the `push` instruction can't push an XMM register. We'll wait until the next chapter to add the rewrite rule for invalid `push` instructions because it will use a new kind of assembly operand that we haven't added yet. We won't actually need this rewrite rule until we implement register allocation in Part III; until then, we'll push only immediate values and memory operands (and the RBP register in the function prologue).

TEST THE ASSEMBLY GENERATION STAGE

Your compiler should now generate complete, valid assembly programs for each of this chapter's test cases. To test it out, run:

```
$ ./test_compiler /path/to/your_compiler --chapter 13 --stage codegen
```

Code Emission

As always, the last step is printing out the newest additions to the assembly AST. The most fiddly bit of this pass is emitting floating-point constants and static variables. Let's walk through how to format floating-point numbers in assembly, how to label floating-point constants, and how to store floating-point constants and variables in the correct section.

Formatting Floating-Point Numbers

There are a few different ways to format floating-point numbers in assembly. One option is to print these numbers as *hexadecimal floating-point* constants, where the significand is a hexadecimal number and the exponent is a power of 2. This notation can represent a double exactly, without any rounding. The significand of a hexadecimal floating-point constant has an 0x prefix, and the exponent has a p or P prefix. For example, 20.0 in hexadecimal floating point is 0x2.8p+3. The hexadecimal number 0x2.8 is 2.5 in decimal, and $2.5 \times 2^3 = 20$. We can use this notation in a .double directive, like so:

```
.L_twenty:
    .double 0x2.8p+3
```

When you emit a double in this notation, you'll need up to 14 hexadecimal digits to represent it exactly. Unfortunately, not every assembler understands this format. The LLVM assembler, which is the default assembler on macOS, does; GAS, the GNU assembler, doesn't.

If your assembler doesn't support hexadecimal floating-point constants, you can emit a quadword with the same binary representation as the required double. Printing out 20.0 with this approach results in:

```
.L_twenty:
    .quad 4626322717216342016
```

This isn't the most readable assembly, but it works perfectly well as long as your implementation language provides a way for you to get at the binary representation of a floating-point number. Your last option is to use decimal floating-point constants, which we used in earlier assembly examples:

```
.L_twenty:
    .double 20.0
```

Decimal can be less compact than hexadecimal floating point. For example, consider 0x1.999999999999ap-4, the closest double to the decimal number 0.1. The exact decimal representation of this value is:

```
1.000000000000000055511151231257827021181583404541015625e-1
```

You don't need to emit this entire value; 17 digits is always enough to guarantee a *round-trip conversion* back to the original double. In other words, you can print out a 17-digit decimal approximation of 0x1.999999999999ap-4, like this:

```
1.0000000000000001e-1
```

This isn't exactly the right value, but it's close enough that when the assembler converts it back to a double you'll get the original value of 0x1.999999999999ap-4.

Labeling Floating-Point Constants

If you're using local labels for top-level constants, you should include the local label prefix (L on macOS, .L on Linux) any time you emit these constants' identifiers. You'll need to check the backend symbol table to distinguish between Data operands that represent static variables and those that represent constants. If an object's is_constant attribute is true, it takes a local label prefix; otherwise, it's a variable, so it doesn't.

If you're not using local labels, you'll need to emit all Data operands uniformly. On macOS, that means prefixing the labels for both constants and static variables with an underscore.

Storing Constants in the Read-Only Data Section

The name of the section that holds constants is platform-specific. On Linux, you should specify this section with the .section .rodata directive. On macOS, 8-byte-aligned and 16-byte-aligned constants are stored in different sections. If a constant is 8-byte aligned, use the .literal8 directive to store it in the correct section. For our one 16-byte-aligned constant (-0.0, which we use to implement negation), use the .literal16 directive.

The macOS linker expects 16-byte-aligned constants to be 16 bytes long, but -0.0 is only 8 bytes. Emit a .quad 0 directive right after the directive for -0.0 to bring the total size of the section holding this constant up to 16 bytes and satisfy the linker's requirements.

Initializing Static Variables to 0.0 or −0.0

We won't store static variables of type double in the BSS section or initialize them with the .zero directive, even if they're initialized to zero. This side-steps any potential confusion about whether a double is really initialized to 0.0 or -0.0. (These two values usually compare equal, but we can't store -0.0 in the BSS section or initialize it with the .zero directive because its binary representation isn't all zeros.)

Putting It All Together

Aside from floating-point constants and static variables, the code emission stage needs to handle the new XMM registers, the new instructions, and the sd suffix on the floating-point versions of existing instructions. These changes are extensive, but they don't require much discussion. Tables 13-8 through 13-13 summarize this chapter's updates to the code emission pass. New constructs and changes to the way we emit existing constructs are bolded.

Table 13-8: Formatting Top-Level Assembly Constructs

Assembly top-level construct		Output

StaticVariable(name, global, alignment, init)	Integer initialized to zero	`<global-directive>`
		`.bss`
		`<alignment-directive>`
		`<name>:`
		`    <init>`

	Integer with nonzero initializer, **or any double**	`<global-directive>`
		`.data`
		`<alignment-directive>`
		`<name>:`
		`    <init>`

StaticConstant(name, alignment, init)	**Linux**	`.section .rodata`
		`<alignment-directive>`
		`<name>:`
		`    <init>`

	macOS (8-byte-aligned constants)	`.literal8`
		`.balign 8`
		`<name>:`
		`    <init>`

	macOS (16-byte-aligned constants)	`.literal16`
		`.balign 16`
		`<name>:`
		`    <init>`
		`    .quad 0`

Table 13-9: Formatting Static Initializers

Static initializer	Output

DoubleInit(d)	`.double <d>`
	or
	`.quad <d-interpreted-as-long>`

Table 13-10: Formatting Assembly Instructions

Assembly instruction	Output
Cvtsi2sd(t, src, dst)	cvtsi2sd<t> <src>, <dst>
Cvttsd2si(t, src, dst)	cvttsd2si<t> <src>, <dst>
Binary(Xor, Double, src, dst)	xorpd <src>, <dst>
Binary(Mult, Double, src, dst)	mulsd <src>, <dst>
Cmp(Double, operand, operand)	comisd <operand>, <operand>

Table 13-11: Instruction Names for Assembly Operators

Assembly operator	Instruction name
Shr	shr
DivDouble	div
And	and
Or	or

Table 13-12: Instruction Suffixes for Assembly Types

Assembly type	Instruction suffix
Double	sd

Table 13-13: Formatting Assembly Operands

Assembly operand	Output
Reg(XMM0)	%xmm0
Reg(XMM1)	%xmm1
Reg(XMM2)	%xmm2
Reg(XMM3)	%xmm3
Reg(XMM4)	%xmm4
Reg(XMM5)	%xmm5
Reg(XMM6)	%xmm6
Reg(XMM7)	%xmm7
Reg(XMM14)	%xmm14
Reg(XMM15)	%xmm15

Note that Table 13-8 doesn't include local label prefixes on constants, although you have the option to include them, as we've discussed. Also note that the xorpd, comisd, and mulsd instructions in Table 13-10 require special handling. As a packed instruction, xorpd doesn't use the standard sd suffix, and the `comisd` and `mulsd` instructions have different names than their integer counterparts.

Once you've worked through all these changes, you're ready to test the whole compiler.

Extra Credit: NaN

You can add support for quiet NaNs as an extra credit feature. Arithmetic operations should just work, without any extra effort on your part, because the SSE instructions will propagate NaNs appropriately. You don't need to handle type conversions, either, since conversions from NaN to integers are undefined. The only operations you need to worry about are comparisons.

When you compare any value to NaN, the result is unordered. If x is NaN, then x > y, x < y, and x == y are all false. NaN even compares unequal to itself. The `comisd` instruction indicates an unordered result by setting three flags to 1: ZF, CF, and PF, the *parity flag*. Just as there are condition codes that rely on ZF, CF, and the other status flags we've already encountered, the P condition code relies on the parity flag. For example, the `jp` instruction will jump only if PF is 1. You'll need to use this condition code to properly account for NaN in floating-point comparisons.

Use the `--nan` flag to include test cases with NaN when you run the test suite:

```
$ ./test_compiler /path/to/your_compiler --chapter 13 --nan
```

Or use the `--extra-credit` flag to enable all extra credit tests, as usual.

Summary

Your compiler now supports floating-point numbers! In this chapter, you learned how to define floating-point constants in assembly, how to use SSE instructions, and how to pass floating-point arguments according to the System V calling convention. You also dealt with rounding error throughout the compiler, from the parser all the way through code emission. Above all, you've seen how difficult floating-point arithmetic is to get right. Many programmers know, in a general way, that floating-point arithmetic can be imprecise; writing a compiler forces you to understand exactly how it can go awry. In the next chapter, you'll add a very different type: pointers. You'll deal with tricky parsing issues, expand the type checker, and add a few extremely useful constructs to the TACKY and assembly ASTs.

Additional Resources

These are the resources I relied on while writing this chapter, roughly organized by the section where they're most relevant. I've also included a couple of online floating-point visualization tools that I found particularly helpful.

IEEE 754

- The IEEE 754 standard is available for purchase on the IEEE website for $100 (*https://ieeexplore.ieee.org/document/8766229*). But you can probably get any answers you need from the following resources, which are free:

  - The "Double-Precision Floating-Point Format" article on Wikipedia gives a thorough description of the binary encoding of IEEE 754 double-precision values (*https://en.wikipedia.org/wiki/Double-precision _floating-point_format*).

  - "What Every Computer Scientist Should Know About Floating-Point Arithmetic" by David Goldberg is one of the best-known introductions to floating-point math, if not the most readable (*https://docs .oracle.com/cd/E19957-01/806-3568/ncg_goldberg.html*). I found the discussion of the IEEE 754 format in the section "The IEEE Standard" especially useful. The article also covers some important topics that I've glossed over completely, like exceptions and error handling.

  - The Floating-Point Guide, a website created by Michael Borgwardt, covers the basics of working with IEEE 754 floating-point numbers in an approachable way (*https://floating-point-gui.de*). Start here if the other two articles are too dense.

- To learn more about support for the IEEE 754 standard in GCC and Clang, see the following resources:

  - "Semantics of Floating Point Math in GCC" on the GCC wiki summarizes the state of floating-point support in GCC, describes the default floating-point behavior, and discusses some of the challenges of fully conforming to IEEE 754 (*https://gcc.gnu.org/wiki/FloatingPointMath*).

  - The section "Controlling Floating-Point Behavior" in the Clang Compiler User's Manual discusses IEEE 754 compliance in Clang (*https://clang.llvm.org/docs/UsersManual.html#controlling-floating-point-behavior*).

Reference for "Rounding Behavior" on page 299

- "The Spacing of Binary Floating-Point Numbers," a blog post by Rick Regan, discusses the gaps between consecutive floating-point numbers (*https://www.exploringbinary.com/the-spacing-of-binary-floating-point-numbers/*). I found that focusing on the gaps in the number line was the key to understanding floating-point rounding error. After I read this blog post, other discussions of this topic suddenly made a lot more sense.

References for "Floating-Point Operations in Assembly" on page 310

- For details about the System V calling convention, see the System V x64 ABI (*https://gitlab.com/x86-psABIs/x86-64-ABI*).

- For details about individual SSE instructions, including how they deal with overflow and rounding, see the Intel 64 Software Developer's Manual (*https://www.intel.com/content/www/us/en/developer/articles/technical/intel-sdm.html*).

- "Sometimes Floating Point Math Is Perfect," a blog post by Bruce Dawson, gives an overview of cases where floating-point calculations *don't* produce rounding error (*https://randomascii.wordpress.com/2017/06/19/sometimes-floating-point-math-is-perfect/*). It helped me think through why our assembly to convert from double to unsigned long won't have rounding error.

- Pascal Cuoq has written an excellent answer to a Stack Overflow question about the assembly-level conversion from unsigned long to double (*https://stackoverflow.com/a/26799227*). This is the best explanation of this conversion I've been able to find.

- "GCC Avoids Double Rounding Errors with Round-to-Odd," another post by Rick Regan, provides more background information on double rounding error (*https://www.exploringbinary.com/gcc-avoids-double-rounding-errors-with-round-to-odd/*).

References for "Code Emission" on page 338

I drew on two of Rick Regan's blog posts on Exploring Binary to handle floating-point constants during code emission:

- "Hexadecimal Floating-Point Constants" talks about representing floating-point numbers in hexadecimal to avoid rounding error (*https://www.exploringbinary.com/hexadecimal-floating-point-constants/*).
- "Number of Digits Required for Round-Trip Conversions" explains why 17 decimal digits is enough to represent a floating-point constant (*https://www.exploringbinary.com/number-of-digits-required-for-round-trip-conversions/*).

Floating-point visualization tools

These tools let you experiment with the IEEE 754 representations of decimal numbers:

- The Decimal to Floating-Point Converter, created by Rick Regan, lets you convert a decimal number to the nearest representable `double` and display it in a wide range of formats, including raw binary, hexadecimal floating point, and binary scientific notation (*https://www.exploringbinary.com/floating-point-converter/*).
- Float Exposed, created by Bartosz Ciechanowski, lets you view and edit the sign, exponent, and significand fields within a `double` as well as its raw binary representation (*https://float.exposed*).

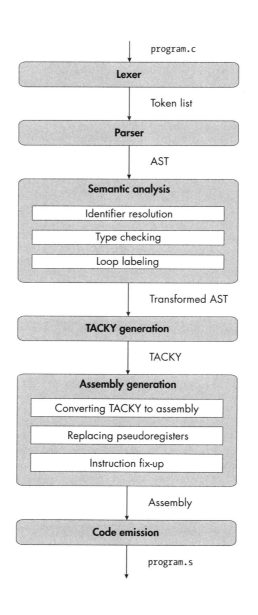

14

POINTERS

So far, you've implemented only *arithmetic types*. These types have a lot in common; they all support the same basic mathematical operations, and you can always implicitly convert from one type to another. In the rest of Part II, we'll add several non-arithmetic types, like pointers, arrays, and structures. These types are quite different both from the arithmetic types and from each other. They don't support ordinary arithmetic. Instead, each type supports its own distinct set of operations.

In this chapter, you'll implement *pointer types*, which represent memory addresses. You'll also add two new operators for working with pointers: the address operator, &, and the dereference operator, *. You'll learn how to parse complex type specifiers and how to detect several new kinds of type errors. During TACKY and assembly generation, you'll add a few new constructs to read from and write to locations in memory. You'll continue to build on these changes as you add more non-arithmetic types in later chapters.

First, let's discuss a few key concepts that I'll refer to throughout this chapter: objects, values, and lvalue conversion.

Objects and Values

Objects and values have come up in earlier chapters, but I never precisely defined either term or explained how they differ from each other. You can think of a *value* as a sequence of bits with a type. For example, the bits

---

11111111111111111111111111111111

---

with the type int have the value -1. So far, we've encountered only integer and floating-point values.

An *object* is a location in memory that contains a value. Variables are the only objects we've seen so far. From the programmer's perspective, every object has a memory address, which is fixed throughout its lifetime, and a value, which you can update using an assignment expression. (In practice, some objects may be stored in registers rather than memory, and you can't update every object's value, but we can ignore those exceptions for now.)

In Chapter 5, I described an lvalue as an expression that can appear on the left side of an assignment expression. Now we can use the more precise definition from section 6.3.2.1, paragraph 1, of the C standard: "An lvalue is an expression . . . that potentially designates an object." (Note that an lvalue is *not* a value, in spite of its name; it's an expression.) Evaluating a non-lvalue expression produces a value. Evaluating an lvalue, on the other hand, "determin[es] the identity of the designated object," according to section 5.1.2.3, paragraph 2, of the standard. If an expression designates an object, you can assign to it. Otherwise, you can't.

When you use an object in an expression like x + 1, you're actually using its current value. But when you assign to an object, you don't care about its current value, which you're just going to overwrite; you care about its location, which you're trying to write to. In other words, if x is a variable of type int, you sometimes treat it like a value of type int and sometimes like a container where you can store a value of type int. The C standard refers to the first case, where you use an object's value in an expression, as *lvalue conversion*. This is a "conversion" in the sense that you're converting an lvalue, which designates an object, into an ordinary value. If an lvalue appears as the left operand of an assignment expression or as the operand of the & operator, it doesn't undergo lvalue conversion. If it appears anywhere else in an expression, it does. For example, x is an lvalue in the expressions x = 3 and y = &x, but it's not an lvalue in the expressions foo(x), x == y, and a = x. In later chapters, we'll encounter other expressions that aren't lvalue converted.

This terminology lets us talk about pointers without getting hopelessly confused. Now we can discuss precisely what operations pointers support.

Operations on Pointers

In this section I'll introduce the address operator, &, which gets a pointer to an object, and the dereference operator, *, which you use to access an object through a pointer. I'll also discuss casting and comparing pointers, plus one special case involving the & operator. I won't talk about pointer addition or subtraction yet; we'll implement those in the next chapter.

Address and Dereference Operations

To see how the & and * operations work, let's walk through the program in Listing 14-1. We'll pay special attention to which expressions in this program designate objects and which ones result in values.

```
int main(void) {
    int x = 0;
    int *ptr = &x;
    *ptr = 4;
    return *ptr;
}
```

*Listing 14-1: A simple program using & and * operations*

We start by declaring a variable, x. Since x is an object, it has an address, although that address won't be the same every time you run the program. Let's say that, during one run of Listing 14-1, x winds up at memory address 0x7ffeee67b938. It also has a value, 0. Since the type of x is int, we'll interpret its value as an int too.

Next, we declare the variable ptr, which is also an object. The type of ptr is int *, or "pointer to int," which represents the address of an object with type int. Like x, ptr has an address; let's say it's 0x7ffeee67b940. It also has a value: the result of the expression &x. The & operator takes the address of its operand, which implies that its operand must designate an object with an address. In other words, the operand must be an lvalue. The result of the & operator, however, is not an object; it's a value of pointer type.

In the expression &x, the operand is the lvalue x. Evaluating &x results in the value 0x7ffeee67b938, which is the address of x. We assign this value to the variable ptr, just like we can assign any value to a variable with a compatible type. To help us keep things straight, Figure 14-1 shows the contents of the stack at this point in the program.

Figure 14-1: The addresses and initial
values of the objects declared in
Listing 14-1

As this figure shows, 0x7ffeee67b938 is both the address of x and the
value of ptr. I said earlier that a value is a sequence of bits with a type; the
type of the value 0x7ffeee67b938 is int * because it's the address of an object
of type int.

On the next line of Listing 14-1, we have the assignment expression
*ptr = 4, which consists of several subexpressions. On the right, we have the
constant 4; on the left, we have the variable ptr, itself part of the dereference
expression *ptr. The constant isn't particularly interesting, but the other
two subexpressions are. The innermost of these expressions, ptr, designates
an object of type int *. We don't assign to it or take its address; we just read
its value. Therefore, we implicitly lvalue convert it, which results in a *value*
of type int *, 0x7ffeee67b938. We use this value in a dereference expression,
*ptr. A dereference expression is an lvalue, so its result is an object. In this
case, it's the object at address 0x7ffeee67b938, since that's the value being
dereferenced. Because we're assigning to the object *ptr, rather than using
its value, it doesn't undergo lvalue conversion. Figure 14-2 shows the contents of the stack after this statement.

Stack contents   Stack addresses

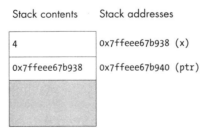

Figure 14-2: The contents of the
stack after assignment through a
dereferenced pointer

We dereference ptr one more time in the final return statement. Once
again, the result of *ptr is the object at address 0x7ffeee67b938. This time,
however, we aren't assigning to this object or applying the & operator to it.
Therefore, we perform lvalue conversion, which results in the object's current value, 4.

Now that you understand how * and & operate on objects and values, let's talk about conversions to and from pointer types.

Null Pointers and Type Conversions

An integer constant expression whose value is 0, called a *null pointer constant*, can be converted implicitly to any pointer type. The result of this conversion is a *null pointer*:

```
int *null = 0;
```

Because a null pointer is not a valid memory address, the result of dereferencing it is undefined. In practice, dereferencing a null pointer will likely crash your program. The C standard permits constant expressions like (long) 0 and 10 - 10 as null pointer constants, but we'll support only constant literals like 0 and 0ul. (This is the same limitation we placed on static initializers in Chapter 10.)

With the exception of null pointer constants, it's illegal to implicitly convert integers to pointers or vice versa. Consider this code snippet:

```
int x = 0;
int *ptr = x;
```

Because x has type int, it's illegal to assign it to ptr, which has type int *. For the same reason, it's illegal to assign a nonzero constant to a pointer:

```
int *ptr1 = 3;
int *ptr2 = 0x7ffeee67b938;
```

These declarations of ptr1 and ptr2 are both illegal because 3 and 0x7ffeee67b938 are integers, not pointers. Note that the type of an expression has nothing to do with whether its value is a valid memory address. Even if 0x7ffeee67b938 happens to be a valid address, the constant expression 0x7ffeee67b938 is still a long rather than a pointer.

It's also illegal to implicitly convert from one pointer type to another (with the exception of conversions to and from void *, which I'll introduce in Chapter 17). For example, you can't implicitly convert a double * to a long *:

```
double *d = 0;
long *l = d;
```

GCC warns about the implicit conversions in the previous three code snippets, but it still compiles them. We'll take a stricter approach and treat these implicit conversions as errors.

On the other hand, *explicit* casts between pointer types, and between pointer and integer types, are legal. Listing 14-2 shows an example of an explicit cast from double * to unsigned long *.

```
   double negative_zero = -0.0;
   double *d = &negative_zero;
❶ unsigned long *l = (unsigned long *) d;
```

Listing 14-2: An explicit pointer type conversion

After the explicit cast and assignment ❶, d and l contain the same memory address, interpreted as two different pointer types.

One important caveat is that dereferencing l after this cast would result in undefined behavior. With a few exceptions, if we declare an object with some type (called its *effective type*) and then access it using an expression of a different type, the result is undefined. In other words, casting from one pointer type to another is always legal, but using the result of that cast expression may not be. In Listing 14-2, the effective type of negative_zero is double, so we can't access it with the expression *l, which has type unsigned long. The complete set of rules about which types of expressions you can use to access an object—unofficially called the *strict aliasing rules*—are spelled out in section 6.5, paragraphs 6–7, of the C standard. Luckily, since we don't need to detect undefined behavior or handle it gracefully, we can ignore these rules; our implementation will happily compile programs that violate them.

Finally, you can explicitly cast between pointer types and integer types. When you cast a null pointer constant to a pointer type, the result is a null pointer. When you cast any other integer to a pointer type, or any pointer to an integer type, the result is implementation-defined. On an x64 system, memory addresses are unsigned 64-bit integers, like 0x7ffeee67b938. Therefore, if you convert an unsigned long to a pointer (or vice versa), its value won't change. Casting any other integer type to or from a pointer type has the same effect as casting to or from unsigned long. For example, if you cast a signed int or a long with value -1 to a pointer type, it will result in the largest representable memory address, 0xffffffffffffffff. This address is unlikely to hold a valid object, so dereferencing it will probably result in undefined behavior.

Casting a pointer type to a double or a double to a pointer type is illegal.

Pointer Comparisons

You can compare pointers of the same type with the == and != operators. Two non-null pointers compare equal if they point to the same object (or just past the end of the same array, once we implement arrays). They compare unequal otherwise. A pointer to a valid object always compares unequal to a null pointer, and two null pointers always compare equal to each other. You can also use a pointer in any construct that compares an expression to zero, including logical !, &&, and || expressions; the condition in a conditional expression; and the controlling condition in an if statement or loop. In each of these cases, a null pointer counts as zero, and any non-null pointer is nonzero.

You can also compare pointers using the other relational operators, like >, but we won't support that yet. This sort of pointer comparison is most useful when you're working with pointers to array elements, so we'll implement it when we add arrays in the next chapter.

& Operations on Dereferenced Pointers

We saw earlier that the operand of the & operator must be an lvalue. Since a dereferenced pointer is an lvalue, you can take its address with this operator, like we do in Listing 14-3.

```
int *ptr = &var;
int *ptr2 = &*ptr;
```

Listing 14-3: Taking the address of a dereferenced pointer

The expression &*ptr is valid, but it's not very useful. The inner expression designates the object stored at some address, and the outer expression takes the address of that object. You just end up with the value of ptr, which is the address you dereferenced to begin with.

In fact, the C standard treats &*<exp> as a special case: section 6.5.3.2, paragraph 3, states that "neither [the * operator] nor the & operator is evaluated and the result is as if both were omitted, except that the constraints on the operators still apply and the result is not an lvalue." In other words, the result of &*<exp> is always the value of <exp>. Usually, like in Listing 14-3, it doesn't matter whether we evaluate the * and & operators; we end up with <exp> either way. The one exception is when <exp> is not a valid memory address, like in Listing 14-4.

```
int *null_ptr = 0;
int *ptr2 = &*null_ptr;
```

Listing 14-4: Taking the address of a dereferenced null pointer

Dereferencing null_ptr would usually cause a runtime error. However, since the & and * expressions in Listing 14-4 aren't evaluated, this code is equivalent to:

```
int *null_ptr = 0;
int *ptr2 = null_ptr;
```

Therefore, Listing 14-4 runs without error; it initializes both null_ptr and ptr2 as null pointers.

Now that we're experts on pointer semantics, let's start on the lexer!

The Lexer

In this chapter, you'll add a single token:

&   An ampersand, the address operator

You already added the * token to support multiplication. If you implemented the bitwise operators for extra credit in Chapter 3, you've already added the & token too, so you won't need to modify the lexer at all.

The Parser

Next, we'll add pointer types and the two new pointer operators to the AST. A pointer type is constructed recursively from the type of the object it points to; int *, double *, and unsigned long * are all valid types. You can also declare pointers to pointers, so int **, long ***, and so on are valid types as well. Therefore, the AST defines pointer types recursively:

```
type = Int | Long | UInt | ULong | Double
     | FunType(type* params, type ret)
     | Pointer(type referenced)
```

In C, types that are built up from simpler types are called *derived types*. Pointer types and function types are both derived types. The array and structure types we'll implement in later chapters are derived types too. The type that a pointer points to is its *referenced type*. For example, the referenced type of int * is int.

We'll extend the exp AST node to represent the dereference and address operators:

```
exp = --snip--
    | Dereference(exp)
    | AddrOf(exp)
```

Syntactically, these are both unary operators, so you can extend unary _operator instead of exp if you want. But I think it's easier to make them distinct expressions because we'll handle these quite differently from the other unary operators during type checking and TACKY generation. Listing 14-5 shows the updated AST, with this chapter's additions bolded.

```
program = Program(declaration*)
declaration = FunDecl(function_declaration) | VarDecl(variable_declaration)
variable_declaration = (identifier name, exp? init,
                        type var_type, storage_class?)
```

```
function_declaration = (identifier name, identifier* params, block? body,
                        type fun_type, storage_class?)
type = Int | Long | UInt | ULong | Double
     | FunType(type* params, type ret)
     | Pointer(type referenced)
storage_class = Static | Extern
block_item = S(statement) | D(declaration)
block = Block(block_item*)
for_init = InitDecl(variable_declaration) | InitExp(exp?)
statement = Return(exp)
          | Expression(exp)
          | If(exp condition, statement then, statement? else)
          | Compound(block)
          | Break
          | Continue
          | While(exp condition, statement body)
          | DoWhile(statement body, exp condition)
          | For(for_init init, exp? condition, exp? post, statement body)
          | Null
exp = Constant(const)
    | Var(identifier)
    | Cast(type target_type, exp)
    | Unary(unary_operator, exp)
    | Binary(binary_operator, exp, exp)
    | Assignment(exp, exp)
    | Conditional(exp condition, exp, exp)
    | FunctionCall(identifier, exp* args)
    | Dereference(exp)
    | AddrOf(exp)
unary_operator = Complement | Negate | Not
binary_operator = Add | Subtract | Multiply | Divide | Remainder | And | Or
                | Equal | NotEqual | LessThan | LessOrEqual
                | GreaterThan | GreaterOrEqual
const = ConstInt(int) | ConstLong(int)
      | ConstUInt(int) | ConstULong(int)
      | ConstDouble(double)
```

Listing 14-5: The abstract syntax tree with pointer types and the dereference and address operators

Next, we'll update the grammar and figure out how to parse it. We can parse the * and & operators like any other unary operator, so we add them to the <unop> grammar rule:

```
<unop> ::= "-" | "~" | "!" | "*" | "&"
```

Parsing pointer types in declarations and cast expressions is more challenging. We need an approach that we can extend to handle derived types in general, not just pointers; otherwise, we'll have to completely rewrite it to deal with arrays in the next chapter. We'll start by updating the parser to support derived types in declarations. Then, we'll handle derived types in cast expressions.

Parsing Declarations

A function or variable declaration consists of three parts: a list of specifiers, a declarator, and an optional initializer or function body. You already know what initializers and function bodies look like, so I won't talk about them here. The specifiers are also familiar from earlier chapters: they include storage class specifiers like static, which determine the identifier's storage class and linkage, and type specifiers like int, which determine what I'll call its *basic type*. The basic type is either the type of the identifier or the starting point for deriving its type. (This particular term doesn't appear in the C standard, but it sometimes shows up in other discussions of C declarations.) The *declarator* is everything else: it indicates the identifier being declared and the sequence of derivations we'll apply to the basic type. For example, var, *var, foo(int a), and foo[3] are all declarators.

The simplest declarator is an identifier:

```
int var;
```

Here, the basic type is int and the declarator is var, so it declares a variable named var with type int. This declaration doesn't include any type derivations.

To derive a new type, we nest a declarator like var inside another declarator:

```
int *(var);
```

Here, we have a pointer declarator, *(var), which contains the nested declarator var. A pointer declarator takes some type *t* and derives the type "pointer to *t*," so this declaration declares var with the type "pointer to int." Note that C's syntax allows us to wrap any declarator in parentheses. I've wrapped var in parentheses to make the nesting here explicit, but the declaration has the same meaning if we omit them:

```
int *var;
```

We use multiple layers of nested declarators to specify multiple type derivations; these are applied from the outside in to determine the final type. The innermost declarator is always a plain identifier. Here's an example with three nested declarators:

```
int *(*(var));
```

The full declarator is *(*(var)), which contains *(var), which contains var. As in the previous example, the parentheses in this declarator have no effect; I've just included them for clarity.

Let's walk through the type derivations here. Working from the outside in, we start with the basic type, int. Next, we see a pointer declarator, so we derive the type "pointer to int." Then, we see another pointer declarator, so we derive "pointer to pointer to int." Finally, we encounter the identifier, which completes the declaration but doesn't add any type information. We end up with a variable var whose type is "pointer to pointer to int."

The other two kinds of declarators are *function declarators*, which we already support, and *array declarators*, which we'll add in the next chapter. A function declarator takes a type *t* and derives the type "function returning *t*." Let's break down a function declaration:

```
int foo(void);
```

The full declarator here is foo(void), which contains the nested declarator foo. Parenthesizing each declarator gives us the following equivalent declaration:

```
int ((foo)(void));
```

We start with the basic type int. The outer declarator tells us to derive the type "function returning int," and the inner declarator indicates that we're declaring the identifier foo. Of course, a function declarator also declares the function's parameters. Each parameter, much like a declaration, includes a basic type and a declarator:

```
int foo(int a, int *b);
```

As we already know, a parameter list of the form (void) is a special case: it declares that the function has no parameters.

Finally, an array declarator starts with type *t* and derives the type "array of *n* elements of type *t*." For example, the following code includes the declarator arr[3], which has a nested declarator arr:

```
int arr[3];
```

This declares that arr is an array of three elements of type int.

More complicated declarations can include a mix of nested pointer, array, and function declarators. The function and array declarators, which we indicate with postfix expressions, have higher precedence than the pointer declarator, so

```
int *arr[3];
```

is equivalent to:

```
int *(arr[3]);
```

To interpret this declaration, we start with int, apply the outer pointer declarator to derive "pointer to int," apply the inner array declarator to derive "array of three pointers to int," and end with the innermost declarator, arr. To declare a pointer to an array instead, we override this precedence with parentheses:

```
int (*arr)[3];
```

Along the same lines, this declaration declares a pointer to a function with a single parameter:

```
int (*fptr)(int a);
```

Function pointers are legal in C, but we won't implement them in this book. You can also nest declarators to specify types that are straight-up illegal. For example, int foo(void)(void); declares a function that returns a function that returns an int. This declaration is syntactically well formed but semantically invalid; a function can't return another function.

Now that you understand the basic syntax of declarators, we're ready to write grammar rules for them. For the full description of declarators, see section 6.7.6 of the C standard. I also recommend "Reading C Type Declarations" by Steve Friedl, which describes their syntax in a more comprehensible way than the standard does (*http://unixwiz.net/techtips/reading -cdecl.html*).

Since declarators have several precedence levels, we need several grammar rules to define their syntax. At the highest precedence level, a <simple-declarator> is a single identifier or parenthesized declarator:

```
<simple-declarator> ::= <identifier> | "(" <declarator> ")"
```

At the next precedence level, we have what the C grammar calls *direct declarators*, including function and array declarators. We support only function declarators in this chapter:

```
<direct-declarator> ::= <simple-declarator> [ <param-list> ]
<param-list> ::= "(" "void" ")" | "(" <param> { "," <param> } ")"
<param> ::= { <type-specifier> }+ <declarator>
```

In the definition of <direct-declarator>, a direct declarator may be either a simple declarator or a function declarator, indicated by the presence of a parameter list. Notice that we've changed <param-list> a bit from previous chapters, refactoring this symbol to include the parentheses around the parameter list and moving the definition of a single parameter into a separate <param> symbol. Most importantly, the definition of <param> now includes a declarator instead of a plain identifier. This lets us parse parameters with pointer types (and eventually with array types as well). Finally, we'll define a top-level <declarator> that includes pointer declarators:

```
<declarator> ::= "*" <declarator> | <direct-declarator>
```

Unfortunately, this grammar doesn't really correspond with our AST definition. One minor problem is that it allows us to specify types we don't support, including function pointers, functions that return functions, and functions that take other functions as arguments. A more serious problem is that in our grammar, type derivations are applied from the outside in, but in the AST definition, they're applied from the inside out. Let's revisit a declaration we looked at earlier:

```
int (*arr)[3];
```

We want to parse this declaration and construct the type "pointer to array of three elements of type int." What happens if we try to construct this type using recursive descent parsing? First, we'll encounter the basic type, int. Then, we'll see an open parenthesis, which indicates the start of a direct declarator. Inside that direct declarator, we'll find a pointer declarator—and then we'll be stuck. We should derive a pointer type, but a pointer to what? The basic type we've seen so far is int, but "pointer to int" is incorrect. Because type derivations are applied from the outside in, we ought to derive the array type first. But we can't, because the parser has to consume the inner, parenthesized declarator before it can reach the [3] that specifies the array type.

We get stuck here because the order in which we can recognize grammar symbols doesn't match the order in which we apply type derivations. When we parse a declaration, we can't derive its type as we go. Instead, we'll first parse each declarator to a one-off representation that more closely mirrors the grammar, like the one in Listing 14-6.

```
declarator = Ident(identifier)
           | PointerDeclarator(declarator)
           | FunDeclarator(param_info* params, declarator)

param_info = Param(type, declarator)
```

Listing 14-6: Representing the syntax of a declarator

We can produce a declarator construct with standard recursive descent parsing, following the grammar rules we just introduced.

The next step is to traverse that declarator and derive all the information we'll use to construct an AST node: the declaration's type, its identifier, and the identifiers of any parameters. At every layer, we'll apply the appropriate type derivation, then recursively handle the inner declarator. Listing 14-7 presents the pseudocode for this step.

```
process_declarator(declarator, base_type):
    match declarator with
    | Ident(name) -> return (name, base_type, []) ❶
    | PointerDeclarator(d) -> ❷
        derived_type = Pointer(base_type)
        return process_declarator(d, derived_type)
```

```
    | FunDeclarator(params, d) -> ❸
        match d with
        | Ident(name) -> ❹
            param_names = []
            param_types = []
            for Param(p_base_type, p_declarator) in params: ❺
                param_name, param_t, _ = process_declarator(p_declarator, p_base_type)
                if param_t is a function type:
                    fail("Function pointers in parameters aren't supported")
                param_names.append(param_name)
                param_types.append(param_t)

            derived_type = FunType(param_types, base_type)
            return (name, derived_type, param_names)
        | _ -> fail("Can't apply additional type derivations to a function type")
```

Listing 14-7: Deriving type and identifier information from a declarator

The process_declarator function takes two arguments. The first is the declarator itself. The second, base_type, is the type we've derived so far. Initially, this will be the basic type indicated by the list of specifiers at the start of the declaration. For example, if we were processing the declaration double **fun(int x), we'd start with a base_type of double. The result of process_declarator will be a tuple of three values: the declaration's identifier, its derived type, and the names of any parameters. If the declaration declares a variable, or if it declares a function with no parameters, the list of parameter names will be empty. Using these three values, we'll be able to construct a declaration AST node.

Let's walk through how to extract these values from a declarator construct. In the simplest case, the declarator is an identifier ❶. We don't need to apply any type derivations or introduce any parameters, so we return the identifier, the unchanged base_type, and an empty list of parameter names. For example, while processing the declaration int x;, we'd immediately reach this case and return ("x", Int, []).

In the second case, we handle pointer declarators ❷. In this case, we derive a pointer type from base_type. We then call process_declarator recursively on the type we just derived and the inner declarator that still needs to be processed.

In the last case, we handle function declarators ❸. This case is a little different because the inner declarator must be a plain identifier. If it's another function declarator, we'll end up with a function that returns a function, which isn't legal. If it's a pointer declarator, we'll end up with a function pointer, which we aren't implementing. Therefore, we validate that the inner declarator is a plain identifier instead of parsing it recursively ❹.

Assuming the inner declarator is valid, the next step is figuring out the function type and parameter names. We'll iterate over the parameters in the declarator, recursively calling process_declarator to get the type and name of each one ❺. While we're at it, we'll validate that none of these function parameters are functions themselves. (The C standard actually lets you declare parameters with function type, but it requires the compiler to implicitly adjust them to function pointer type. Since we don't support function pointers, we'll reject them.) Once we've handled every parameter, we construct the whole function type and return all the relevant information about this declaration.

Listing 14-8 shows how to put all the pieces together to parse an entire declaration.

```
parse_declaration(tokens):
    specifiers = parse_specifier_list(tokens)
    base_type, storage_class = parse_type_and_storage_class(specifiers)
    declarator = parse_declarator(tokens)
    name, decl_type, params = process_declarator(declarator, base_type)
    if decl_type is a function type:
        <construct function_declaration>
    else:
        <construct variable_declaration>
```

Listing 14-8: Parsing an entire declaration

We first determine the declaration's base type in the usual way: we consume a list of specifiers from tokens, then convert those specifiers to a type and storage class. Next, we parse the declarator, and then we call process _declarator to determine its complete type and name. Finally, we examine the resulting type to determine whether it's a function or variable declaration and parse the rest of the declaration accordingly.

Parsing Type Names

Pointer types can also appear in cast expressions:

```
int *result_of_cast = (int *) exp;
```

But you can't use a declarator in a cast expression, because a declarator must contain an identifier. C syntax solves this problem with *abstract declarators*, which are declarators without identifiers. We'll add abstract pointer declarators now and abstract array declarators in the next chapter. (We won't need abstract function declarators, because they're used only to specify function pointers.)

An abstract declarator might be a sequence of one or more * tokens, indicating a sequence of pointer type derivations:

```
(int ***) exp;
```

Abstract declarators can be parenthesized, like their non-abstract counterparts:

```
(int (*)) exp;
```

And an outer abstract declarator can contain an inner parenthesized one:

```
(int *(*)) exp;
```

The parentheses are pointless at the moment. They'll be more useful when we add arrays in the next chapter. For example, the expression

```
(int *[3]) exp;
```

casts exp to an array of three pointers to int because the abstract array declarator [3] is parsed with higher precedence. This cast expression is illegal because you can't cast expressions to array type. On the other hand, this expression is fine:

```
(int (*)[3]) exp;
```

This casts exp to a pointer to an array of three int elements; the parenthesized pointer declarator has higher precedence, so the array declarator is applied to int first.

We define abstract declarators using two grammar rules:

```
<abstract-declarator> ::= "*" [ <abstract-declarator> ]
                        | <direct-abstract-declarator>
<direct-abstract-declarator> ::= "(" <abstract-declarator> ")"
```

An `<abstract-declarator>`, like a regular `<declarator>`, consists of either a pointer declarator or a direct declarator. The key difference between the two is that in an abstract pointer declarator, the inner declarator is optional. In other words, * by itself is a valid abstract declarator but not a valid regular declarator.

A `<direct-abstract-declarator>` is an `<abstract-declarator>` wrapped in parentheses. In the next chapter, this symbol will cover abstract array declarators too. We'll parse abstract declarators to a one-off abstract_declarator structure, like we did with normal declarators. Listing 14-9 defines this structure.

```
abstract_declarator = AbstractPointer(abstract_declarator)
                    | AbstractBase
```

Listing 14-9: Representing the syntax of an abstract declarator

AbstractBase represents the base case, where a * token isn't followed by an inner declarator. For example, we'd parse the abstract declarator *(*) to AbstractPointer(AbstractPointer(AbstractBase)). At the moment, abstract _declarator just tells us how many layers of pointer indirection we found (two, in this example). This is a fairly elaborate way to convey a single number, but it lays the groundwork for array declarators in the next chapter.

The type name in a cast expression is a sequence of type specifiers followed by an optional abstract declarator, all wrapped in parentheses:

```
<factor> ::= --snip--
           | "(" { <type-specifier> }+ [ <abstract-declarator> ] ")" <factor>
           | --snip--
```

To handle cast expressions, you'll need a process_abstract_declarator function, similar to process_declarator from Listing 14-7, to convert a basic type and an abstract_declarator into a derived type. This function will be simpler than process_declarator; it won't deal with function declarators and it will return only a type, not an identifier or a list of parameters.

Putting It All Together

We've covered every change we'll make to the parser. Listing 14-10 shows the full grammar, with this chapter's changes bolded.

```
<program> ::= { <declaration> }
<declaration> ::= <variable-declaration> | <function-declaration>
<variable-declaration> ::= { <specifier> }+ <declarator> [ "=" <exp> ] ";"
<function-declaration> ::= { <specifier> }+ <declarator> ( <block> | ";")
<declarator> ::= "*" <declarator> | <direct-declarator>
<direct-declarator> ::= <simple-declarator> [ <param-list> ]
<param-list> ::= "(" "void" ")" | "(" <param> { "," <param> } ")"
<param> ::= { <type-specifier> }+ <declarator>
<simple-declarator> ::= <identifier> | "(" <declarator> ")"
<type-specifier> ::= "int" | "long" | "unsigned" | "signed" | "double"
<specifier> ::= <type-specifier> | "static" | "extern"
<block> ::= "{" { <block-item> } "}"
<block-item> ::= <statement> | <declaration>
<for-init> ::= <variable-declaration> | [ <exp> ] ";"
<statement> ::= "return" <exp> ";"
            | <exp> ";"
            | "if" "(" <exp> ")" <statement> [ "else" <statement> ]
            | <block>
            | "break" ";"
            | "continue" ";"
            | "while" "(" <exp> ")" <statement>
            | "do" <statement> "while" "(" <exp> ")" ";"
            | "for" "(" <for-init> [ <exp> ] ";" [ <exp> ] ")" <statement>
            | ";"
<exp> ::= <factor> | <exp> <binop> <exp> | <exp> "?" <exp> ":" <exp>
<factor> ::= <const> | <identifier>
            | "(" { <type-specifier> }+ [ <abstract-declarator> ] ")" <factor>
            | <unop> <factor> | "(" <exp> ")"
            | <identifier> "(" [ <argument-list> ] ")"
<argument-list> ::= <exp> { "," <exp> }
<abstract-declarator> ::= "*" [ <abstract-declarator> ]
            | <direct-abstract-declarator>
<direct-abstract-declarator> ::= "(" <abstract-declarator> ")"
<unop> ::= "-" | "~" | "!" | "*" | "&"
<binop> ::= "-" | "+" | "*" | "/" | "%" | "&&" | "||"
            | "==" | "!=" | "<" | "<=" | ">" | ">=" | "="
<const> ::= <int> | <long> | <uint> | <ulong> | <double>
<identifier> ::= ? An identifier token ?
<int> ::= ? An int token ?
<long> ::= ? An int or long token ?
<uint> ::= ? An unsigned int token ?
<ulong> ::= ? An unsigned int or unsigned long token ?
<double> ::= ? A floating-point constant token ?
```

Listing 14-10: The grammar with pointer types and the dereference and address operators

We've made three major changes to the grammar. First, we're using the <declarator> symbol instead of simple identifiers in function, variable, and parameter declarations. Second, we use the corresponding symbol to specify pointer types in cast expressions. Third, we've added the new unary & and * operators.

TEST THE PARSER

To test your parser, run:

```
$ ./test_compiler /path/to/your_compiler --chapter 14 --stage parse
```

The tests in *tests/chapter_14/invalid_parse* validate that your compiler rejects malformed declarators and abstract declarators. They don't test whether your compiler rejects function pointers. If you want to be really ambitious and implement function pointers on your own, you can still use these tests.

Semantic Analysis

On to semantic analysis! We'll extend the type checker to validate expressions that involve pointers and infer the types of these expressions. The identifier resolution pass will change a little bit too; we'll move one piece of validation from this pass into the type checker.

We need to detect three kinds of type errors:

1. Applying an operator to a type it doesn't support. For example, you can't multiply or divide pointers, and you can't dereference arithmetic values.

2. Operating on values of two incompatible types. This includes errors like trying to compare a pointer to a double. We run into this kind of error because C generally doesn't allow implicit conversions to and from pointer types, the way it does for arithmetic types.

3. Not using an lvalue where one is required. We already require the left side of an assignment expression to be an lvalue. Now we'll require the operand of an AddrOf expression to be an lvalue too. We'll also expand our definition of lvalue to include dereferenced pointers as well as variables.

This third kind of error is the one we currently handle during identifier resolution. Remove this validation from the identifier resolution pass now; you'll add it to the type checker in a moment. (While you're at it, make sure the identifier resolution pass traverses the new Dereference and `AddrOf` expressions.) Next, we'll update the logic to type check expressions.

Type Checking Pointer Expressions

We need to tweak how we type check almost every expression we support. Let's start with the new `Dereference` and `AddrOf` expressions. Then, we'll update the type checking logic for our existing constructs.

Dereference and AddrOf Expressions

A `Dereference` expression must take an operand of pointer type. It produces a result with its operand's referenced type (the type it points to). Listing 14-11 demonstrates how to type check a `Dereference` expression and annotate it with the correct result type.

```
typecheck_exp(e, symbols):
    match e with
    | --snip--
    | Dereference(inner) ->
        typed_inner = typecheck_exp(inner, symbols)
        match get_type(typed_inner) with
        | Pointer(referenced_t) ->
            deref_exp = Dereference(typed_inner)
            return set_type(deref_exp, referenced_t)
        | _ -> fail("Cannot dereference non-pointer")
```

Listing 14-11: Type checking a `Dereference` expression

We start by type checking the expression's operand, as usual. Then, we look up the operand's type. If it's a pointer to some type, `referenced_t`, we set `referenced_t` as the result type of the whole expression. Otherwise, we throw an error.

To type check an `AddrOf` expression, we first check that its operand is an lvalue (that is, a `Var` or `Dereference` expression). Then, we record its result type, which is a pointer to the type of its operand. Listing 14-12 demonstrates how to type check `AddrOf`.

```
    | AddrOf(inner) ->
        if inner is an lvalue:
            typed_inner = typecheck_exp(inner, symbols)
            referenced_t = get_type(typed_inner)
            addr_exp = AddrOf(typed_inner)
            return set_type(addr_exp, Pointer(referenced_t))
        else:
            fail("Can't take the address of a non-lvalue!")
```

Listing 14-12: Type checking an `AddrOf` expression

Next, we'll type check pointer comparisons with `Equal` and `NotEqual`. (We'll deal with other pointer comparisons using `GreaterThan`, `LessThan`, and the other relational operators in Chapter 15.) We'll also handle conditional expressions, which follow similar typing rules.

Comparisons and Conditional Expressions

As you learned in earlier chapters, both operands in a comparison must have the same type, or at least be implicitly converted to the same type. However, we can't perform implicit conversions to or from pointer types. Therefore, if either operand to an Equal or NotEqual operation is a pointer, we require the types of both operands to be the same. At the moment, null pointer constants are the one exception to this rule; they're the only expressions that we can implicitly convert to a pointer type. (Once we implement void, we'll also permit implicit conversions between void * and other pointer types.)

For example, this code snippet compares a pointer to a null pointer constant:

```
double *d = get_pointer();
return d == 0;
```

When we type check d == 0 in this example, we implicitly cast 0 to a null pointer with type double *. Listing 14-13 defines a helper function to identify null pointer constants.

```
is_null_pointer_constant(e):
    match e with
    | Constant(c) ->
        match c with
        | ConstInt(0) -> return True
        | ConstUInt(0) -> return True
        | ConstLong(0) -> return True
        | ConstULong(0) -> return True
        | _ -> return False
    | _ -> return False
```

Listing 14-13: Checking whether an expression is a null pointer constant

This function captures our three requirements for an expression to count as a null pointer constant: it must be a constant literal, it must be an integer, and its value must be 0. (Remember that we're defining null pointer constants more narrowly than the C standard does; the standard permits more complex constant expressions as well as constant literals.)

Listing 14-14 defines another helper function to determine whether two expressions, at least one of which results in a pointer, have compatible types.

```
get_common_pointer_type(e1, e2):
    e1_t = get_type(e1)
    e2_t = get_type(e2)
    if e1_t == e2_t:
        return e1_t
```

```
    else if is_null_pointer_constant(e1):
        return e2_t
    else if is_null_pointer_constant(e2):
        return e1_t
    else:
        fail("Expressions have incompatible types")
```

Listing 14-14: Getting the common type of two expressions, where at least one has pointer type

When an expression that operates on pointers expects both its operands to have the same type, get_common_pointer_type will determine what that type should be. If its arguments have different types and neither of them is a null pointer constant, they're incompatible, so we throw an error.

Now that we've defined get_common_pointer_type, we're finally ready to type check Equal and NotEqual expressions. Listing 14-15 demonstrates how to type check an Equal expression; we'll handle NotEqual the same way.

```
typecheck_exp(e, symbols):
    match e with
    | --snip--
    | Binary(Equal, e1, e2) ->
        typed_e1 = typecheck_exp(e1, symbols)
        typed_e2 = typecheck_exp(e2, symbols)
        t1 = get_type(typed_e1)
        t2 = get_type(typed_e2)
        if t1 or t2 is a pointer type:
          ❶ common_type = get_common_pointer_type(typed_e1, typed_e2)
        else:
          ❷ common_type = get_common_type(t1, t2)
        converted_e1 = convert_to(typed_e1, common_type)
        converted_e2 = convert_to(typed_e2, common_type)
        equality_exp = Binary(Equal, converted_e1, converted_e2)
        return set_type(equality_exp, Int)
```

Listing 14-15: Type checking an Equal expression

This follows the usual pattern for type checking comparisons: we type check both operands, find their common type, convert them both to that type, and then set the type of the result to Int. The key change from earlier chapters is how we find the common type. If either operand is a pointer, we use the helper function that we just defined ❶. Otherwise, we'll stick with get_common_type ❷.

When we convert two operands to a common pointer type, we'll see one of three possible outcomes:

1. Both operands already have the same type, so neither convert_to call has any effect.

2. One operand is a null pointer constant, which we implicitly convert to the other operand's type.

3. The operands have incompatible types, so get_common_pointer_type throws an error.

We'll use similar logic to type check conditional expressions. The second and third operands in the expression *<cond>* ? *<clause1>* : *<clause2>* are subject to the same type constraints as the operands in an Equal or NotEqual expression. If either one is a pointer, we'll validate both operands and find their common type using get_common_pointer_type, then convert them to that type. The *<cond>* expression can be either a pointer or an arithmetic value, since we can compare it to zero either way.

Assignment and Conversion as if by Assignment

Next, we'll handle assignment expressions. We first validate that the left-hand side of an assignment expression is an lvalue. Then, we convert the value on the right side of the expression to the type of the object on the left, or fail if the conversion is illegal. What the C standard calls type conversion "as if by assignment" turns up in a few places, not just in assignment expressions, so we'll write yet another helper function to handle it. Listing 14-16 defines this helper function.

```
convert_by_assignment(e, target_type):
    if get_type(e) == target_type:
        return e
    if get_type(e) is arithmetic and target_type is arithmetic:
        return convert_to(e, target_type)
    if is_null_pointer_constant(e) and target_type is a pointer type:
        return convert_to(e, target_type)
    else:
        fail("Cannot convert type for assignment")
```

Listing 14-16: Converting an expression to a target type as if by assignment

The rules here are unsurprising: we can assign a value to an object of the same type, we can implicitly convert any arithmetic type to any other arithmetic type, and we can implicitly convert a null pointer constant to any pointer type. Otherwise, we'll raise an error.

We'll use this helper function to convert the right side of assignment expressions and in a few other spots too. To type check a function call, we'll use convert_by_assignment to convert each argument to the type of the corresponding parameter. We'll also use it to convert variable initializers to the correct type and to detect initializers with invalid types, like the following:

```
int *d = 2.0;
```

Finally, we'll use convert_by_assignment to convert the value in a return statement to the function's return type and detect functions that return the wrong type, like Listing 14-17.

```
int *bad_pointer(void) {
    return 2.0;
}
```

Listing 14-17: A function that returns a value with an incompatible type

Later, when we implement void, we'll extend both `get_common_pointer_type` and `convert_by_assignment` to accept implicit conversions to and from void *.

Other Expressions

We still need to deal with cast expressions, unary operators, and binary operators besides `Equal` and `NotEqual`. Let's start with casts. As you learned earlier, it's illegal to cast a pointer to a `double` or a `double` to a pointer. If your type checker encounters this kind of cast, it should throw an error. Otherwise, it can handle casts to and from pointer types exactly like any other cast expression.

Next, we'll handle unary operators. Applying the `Negate` or `Complement` operator to a pointer is illegal, since negating or taking the bitwise complement of a memory address won't produce a meaningful result. Applying the `Not` operator to a pointer is fine, since it makes sense to compare a memory address to zero.

Binary operators deal with pointers in several different ways. First, we have the Boolean `And` and `Or` operators. The type checking logic for these operators won't change. Like `Not`, they both accept pointers. Since they don't convert their operands to a common type, they can operate on any combination of pointer and arithmetic operands.

The arithmetic `Multiply`, `Divide`, and `Remainder` operators, on the other hand, don't accept pointers. Applying any of these to an operand of pointer type should produce an error. Pointer addition and subtraction are legal, as are pointer comparisons with `GreaterThan`, `LessThan`, `GreaterOrEqual`, and `LessOrEqual`, but we won't implement them until the next chapter. They won't come up in this chapter's tests. For now, your compiler can either assume it will never see these expressions or explicitly reject them.

Tracking Static Pointer Initializers in the Symbol Table

Now let's talk about static initializers. Static variables of pointer type, like non-static variables, can be initialized to null pointers:

```
static int *ptr = 0;
```

We therefore need a way to represent a null pointer as a `static_init` in the symbol table. Rather than defining a dedicated construct for null pointers, we'll use the `ULongInit(0)` initializer, since pointers are unsigned 64-bit integers.

It's also legal to initialize static variables of pointer type with the address of other static variables:

```
static int a;
static int *a_ptr = &a;
```

However, our implementation won't support this sort of static initializer; we've already decided that constant literals are the only static initializers we'll accept.

TACKY Generation

We'll introduce three new TACKY instructions that operate on pointers in this chapter. The first, GetAddress, corresponds to the AddrOf operator in the AST:

```
GetAddress(val src, val dst)
```

This instruction copies the address of src—which must be a variable, not a constant—into dst. We'll also add two instructions to dereference pointers:

```
Load(val src_ptr, val dst)
Store(val src, val dst_ptr)
```

The Load instruction takes a memory address, src_ptr, as its source operand. It retrieves the current value at that memory address and copies it to dst. The Store instruction takes a memory address, dst_ptr, as its destination operand and writes the value of src to that address. Listing 14-18 defines the complete TACKY IR, with the three new instructions bolded.

```
program = Program(top_level*)
top_level = Function(identifier, bool global, identifier* params, instruction* body)
          | StaticVariable(identifier, bool global, type t, static_init init)
instruction = Return(val)
            | SignExtend(val src, val dst)
            | Truncate(val src, val dst)
            | ZeroExtend(val src, val dst)
```

```
            | DoubleToInt(val src, val dst)
            | DoubleToUInt(val src, val dst)
            | IntToDouble(val src, val dst)
            | UIntToDouble(val src, val dst)
            | Unary(unary_operator, val src, val dst)
            | Binary(binary_operator, val src1, val src2, val dst)
            | Copy(val src, val dst)
            | GetAddress(val src, val dst)
            | Load(val src_ptr, val dst)
            | Store(val src, val dst_ptr)
            | Jump(identifier target)
            | JumpIfZero(val condition, identifier target)
            | JumpIfNotZero(val condition, identifier target)
            | Label(identifier)
            | FunCall(identifier fun_name, val* args, val dst)
val = Constant(const) | Var(identifier)
unary_operator = Complement | Negate | Not
binary_operator = Add | Subtract | Multiply | Divide | Remainder | Equal | NotEqual
                | LessThan | LessOrEqual | GreaterThan | GreaterOrEqual
```

Listing 14-18: Adding pointer operations to TACKY

It's tricky to convert Dereference and AddrOf to TACKY, because these conversions depend on context. A Dereference expression can be used in one of three ways: you can lvalue convert it, assign to it, or take its address. We'll produce different TACKY instructions in each of these three cases. Similarly, we'll process AddrOf one way if its operand is a variable and a different way if its operand is a dereferenced pointer. First, let's see what instructions we should generate in each case. Then, I'll present a strategy for TACKY conversion that minimizes the number of special cases we need to handle.

Pointer Operations in TACKY

To dereference a pointer and then lvalue convert the result, we'll use the Load instruction. In this case, we can translate the expression *<exp> to Listing 14-19.

```
<instructions for exp>
ptr = <result of exp>
result = Load(ptr)
```

Listing 14-19: The TACKY implementation of a pointer dereference that undergoes lvalue conversion

We'll use Store when we want to assign to a dereferenced pointer instead of lvalue converting it. We'll translate an assignment expression of the form *<left> = <right> to Listing 14-20.

```
<instructions for left>
ptr = <result of left>
<instructions for right>
```

```
result = <result of right>
Store(result, ptr)
```

Listing 14-20: The TACKY implementation of a pointer dereference on the left-hand side of an assignment expression

We first calculate ptr, which is the address of some object, and result, which is the value we want to assign to that object. Then, we use Store to perform the assignment. Note that the single Store instruction here implements both the deference and assignment operations from the original expression.

Finally, let's consider the AddrOf expression. If its operand is a variable, we'll get a pointer to it with GetAddress. Therefore, we'll translate &var to:

```
result = GetAddress(var)
```

But if the operand is a dereferenced pointer, neither the outer AddrOf nor the inner Dereference expression is evaluated. When we see an expression of the form &*<exp>, we'll translate only the inner <exp> to TACKY.

A Strategy for TACKY Conversion

To manage all these different cases, we'll use two different functions to convert expressions to TACKY. The first is our existing emit_tacky function. This function will no longer return a TACKY operand. Instead, it will return a new construct, exp_result, which represents an expression result that hasn't been lvalue converted. The second function, emit_tacky_and_convert, will call emit_tacky, lvalue convert the result (if it's an lvalue rather than a constant), and return it as a TACKY operand. In most contexts, we'll process expressions with emit_tacky_and_convert. But to process expressions that shouldn't be lvalue converted—like the left-hand side of assignment expressions—we'll call emit_tacky directly.

First, let's define exp_result:

```
exp_result = PlainOperand(val) | DereferencedPointer(val)
```

A DereferencedPointer represents the object designated by a dereferenced pointer, as the name suggests. It takes a single argument: a TACKY operand of pointer type. A PlainOperand represents an ordinary constant or variable. Its argument is a TACKY operand of any type. The exp_result construct isn't a TACKY operand itself, so it doesn't appear in TACKY instructions. It just helps us process AddrOf and assignment expressions, which operate on objects instead of values. For each of these expressions, we'll generate different instructions depending on whether its operand is a dereferenced pointer or a normal variable. In later chapters, we'll add more operators that dereference pointers, like array subscripting and the -> operator to access structure members. At that point, the DereferencedPointer constructor will be especially useful because it will let us represent the results of all of these different operators in a uniform way.

Now let's update emit_tacky. We'll make a couple of changes throughout this function. First, wherever we currently call emit_tacky recursively on a subexpression—except on the left-hand side of an assignment expression—we'll instead call emit_tacky_and_convert. This function will convert the subexpression to TACKY and then lvalue convert the result. Second, wherever we currently return a TACKY operand, we'll wrap that operand in a PlainOperand constructor. Listing 14-21 shows how to handle unary expressions, with this chapter's changes bolded.

```
emit_tacky(e, instructions, symbols):
    match e with
    | --snip--
    | Unary(op, inner) ->
        src = emit_tacky_and_convert(inner, instructions, symbols)
        dst = make_tacky_variable(get_type(e), symbols)
        tacky_op = convert_unop(op)
        instructions.append(Unary(tacky_op, src, dst))
        return PlainOperand(dst)
```

Listing 14-21: Translating a unary expression to TACKY

We'll make the same changes for every kind of expression that emit_tacky currently handles.

Next, let's deal with Dereference expressions. Listing 14-22 demonstrates how to handle these in emit_tacky.

```
    | Dereference(inner) ->
        result = emit_tacky_and_convert(inner, instructions, symbols)
        return DereferencedPointer(result)
```

Listing 14-22: Translating a Dereference expression to TACKY

To process this expression, we first process and lvalue convert its operand. This produces a TACKY operand of pointer type, result. Then, we return a DereferencedPointer to represent the object result points to.

After emit_tacky returns an exp_result, we either assign to it, get its address, or lvalue convert it. Listing 14-23 illustrates how to handle assignment.

```
    | Assignment(left, right) ->
    ❶ lval = emit_tacky(left, instructions, symbols)
    ❷ rval = emit_tacky_and_convert(right, instructions, symbols)
        match lval with
        | PlainOperand(obj) ->
        ❸ instructions.append(Copy(rval, obj))
            return lval
        | DereferencedPointer(ptr) ->
        ❹ instructions.append(Store(rval, ptr))
            return PlainOperand(rval)
```

Listing 14-23: Translating an assignment expression to TACKY

We don't lvalue convert the left side of the assignment expression ❶, but we do lvalue convert the right side ❷. If the left side is a PlainOperand, we issue a Copy instruction, like in earlier chapters ❸. If it's a DereferencedPointer, we issue a Store instruction to write to the location that the inner pointer indicates ❹. Note that even when we assign through a pointer, we return a PlainOperand as the result. That's because the result of an assignment expression is the value stored in the object on the left-hand side, not the object itself.

We use a similar pattern to process AddrOf. Listing 14-24 gives the pseudocode.

```
| AddrOf(inner) ->
  ❶ v = emit_tacky(inner, instructions, symbols)
    match v with
    | PlainOperand(obj) ->
        dst = make_tacky_variable(get_type(e), symbols)
      ❷ instructions.append(GetAddress(obj, dst))
        return PlainOperand(dst)
    | DereferencedPointer(ptr) ->
      ❸ return PlainOperand(ptr)
```

Listing 14-24: Translating an AddrOf expression to TACKY

We process the expression's operand without lvalue converting it ❶, then pattern match on the result to decide how to proceed. If it's a normal value, we emit a GetAddress instruction ❷. If it's a dereferenced pointer, we drop the dereference and return the pointer ❸.

Finally, in Listing 14-25, we define emit_tacky_and_convert, which performs lvalue conversions.

```
emit_tacky_and_convert(e, instructions, symbols):
    result = emit_tacky(e, instructions, symbols)
    match result with
    | PlainOperand(val) -> return val
    | DereferencedPointer(ptr) ->
        dst = make_tacky_variable(get_type(e), symbols)
        instructions.append(Load(ptr, dst))
        return dst
```

Listing 14-25: Translating an expression to TACKY and performing lvalue conversion

To lvalue convert a dereferenced pointer, we'll retrieve its value with a Load instruction. Other operands can be returned as is, without emitting any extra instructions. A *full expression*, which isn't part of another expression, always undergoes lvalue conversion. That means you should use emit_tacky_and _convert, not emit_tacky, to process a full expression and get its result. For example, you'll use emit_tacky_and_convert to process the controlling expressions in loops and if statements.

The results of some full expressions—specifically, expression statements and the first and third clauses in for loop headers—are not used.

As an optimization, you can process these expressions with emit_tacky, which saves you an unnecessary Load instruction.

To wrap up this section, we'll implement casts to and from pointer types. For the purposes of casting, we treat pointer types exactly like unsigned long. For example, we cast from int to any pointer type with a SignExtend instruction and from a pointer type to int with Truncate. The TACKY implementations of other expressions, like logical operations and comparisons, won't change.

Assembly Generation

In the previous section, we added Load and Store instructions that allow us to read from and write to memory. This means that TACKY has finally caught up with assembly, which we've been using to read from and write to memory since Chapter 2. The operand -4(%rbp), for example, identifies a location in memory, which we can read or write with a mov instruction.

There's nothing special about RBP, though; we can access memory through an address stored in any register. Here's how to read the value from an address stored in the RAX register and copy it into RCX:

```
movq    (%rax), %rcx
```

Note that (%rax) is equivalent to 0(%rax).

The assembly AST will change slightly to handle operands like (%rax). First, we'll add the RBP register to the AST:

```
reg = AX | CX | DX | DI | SI | R8 | R9 | R10 | R11 | SP | BP | --snip--
```

Then, we'll replace the Stack operand, which lets us access memory at some offset from the address in RBP, with a more generic Memory operand, which can use a base address stored in any register:

```
operand = Imm(int) | Reg(reg) | Pseudo(identifier) | Memory(reg, int) | Data(identifier)
```

This makes converting a Load or Store instruction to assembly very simple. We'll translate

---

```
Load(ptr, dst)
```

---

to:

```
Mov(Quadword, ptr, Reg(AX))
Mov(<dst type>, Memory(AX, 0), dst)
```

In the first instruction, we move the memory address ptr to a register. In the second instruction, we move the value stored at that address, which we access with a Memory operand, to the destination. In this example, we copy ptr into RAX, but any general-purpose register will do (aside from R10, R11, or a callee-saved register).

Along the same lines, we'll translate

```
Store(src, ptr)
```

---

to:

```
Mov(Quadword, ptr, Reg(AX))
Mov(<src type>, src, Memory(AX, 0))
```

Note that when we copy a pointer into a register, we use the Quadword operand type, since pointers are 8 bytes. But when we copy a value to or from the memory location that a pointer indicates, the value's type determines the type of the mov instruction.

We'll implement GetAddress using a new assembly instruction: lea, which is short for *load effective address*. The instruction lea src, dst copies the *address* of its source (which must be a memory operand) to its destination. For example, lea (%rbp), %rax is equivalent to mov %rbp, %rax. You can also use lea to get RIP-relative addresses, so

---

```
lea     x(%rip), %rax
```

---

stores the address of the symbol x in the RAX register.

With this new instruction, converting GetAddress to assembly is straightforward. We'll translate

---

```
GetAddress(src, dst)
```

---

to:

```
Lea(src, dst)
```

As I mentioned earlier, src here must be a memory operand, not a constant or register, for obvious reasons. At the moment, we're guaranteed to satisfy this constraint; we map every pseudoregister to a memory address, and the type checker catches any attempts to take the address of a constant. But in Part III, when we implement register allocation, we'll store some variables in registers instead of in memory. At that point, it will take some extra work to make sure that lea never tries to load the address of a register.

Listing 14-26 defines the whole assembly AST, including the new Memory operand, BP register, and Lea instruction.

```
program = Program(top_level*)
assembly_type = Longword | Quadword | Double
top_level = Function(identifier name, bool global, instruction* instructions)
          | StaticVariable(identifier name, bool global, int alignment, static_init init)
          | StaticConstant(identifier name, int alignment, static_init init)
instruction = Mov(assembly_type, operand src, operand dst)
            | Movsx(operand src, operand dst)
            | MovZeroExtend(operand src, operand dst)
            | Lea(operand src, operand dst)
            | Cvttsd2si(assembly_type dst_type, operand src, operand dst)
            | Cvtsi2sd(assembly_type src_type, operand src, operand dst)
            | Unary(unary_operator, assembly_type, operand)
            | Binary(binary_operator, assembly_type, operand, operand)
            | Cmp(assembly_type, operand, operand)
            | Idiv(assembly_type, operand)
            | Div(assembly_type, operand)
            | Cdq(assembly_type)
            | Jmp(identifier)
            | JmpCC(cond_code, identifier)
            | SetCC(cond_code, operand)
            | Label(identifier)
            | Push(operand)
            | Call(identifier)
            | Ret

unary_operator = Neg | Not | Shr
binary_operator = Add | Sub | Mult | DivDouble | And | Or | Xor
operand = Imm(int) | Reg(reg) | Pseudo(identifier) | Memory(reg, int) | Data(identifier)
cond_code = E | NE | G | GE | L | LE | A | AE | B | BE
reg = AX | CX | DX | DI | SI | R8 | R9 | R10 | R11 | SP | BP
    | XMM0 | XMM1 | XMM2 | XMM3 | XMM4 | XMM5 | XMM6 | XMM7 | XMM14 | XMM15
```

Listing 14-26: The assembly AST with the Memory operand, BP register, and Lea instruction

When we translate other TACKY instructions to assembly, we'll treat pointer types exactly like unsigned long. We'll convert pointer types to the Quadword assembly type, compare pointers with the cmp instruction, pass return values of pointer type in the RAX register, and pass parameters of pointer type in the same general-purpose registers as integer parameters.

We'll also make one entirely mechanical change: everywhere we previously used an operand of the form Stack(<i>), we'll use Memory(BP, <i>) instead. Tables 14-1 through 14-3 summarize this chapter's updates to the conversion from TACKY to assembly; as usual, new constructs and changes to the conversions for existing constructs are bolded.

Table 14-1: Converting Top-Level TACKY Constructs to Assembly

TACKY top-level construct	Assembly top-level construct

Function(name, global, params, instructions)	Function(name, global,
	    [Mov(*<first int param type>*, Reg(DI),
	        <first int param>),
	      Mov(*<second int param type>*, Reg(SI),
	        <second int param>),
	      <copy next four integer parameters from registers>,
	      Mov(Double, Reg(XMM0), *<first double param>*),
	      Mov(Double, Reg(XMM1), *<second double param>*),
	      <copy next six double parameters from registers>,
	      Mov(*<first stack param type>*, **Memory(BP, 16)**,
	        <first stack param>),
	      Mov(*<second stack param type>*, **Memory(BP, 24)**,
	        <second stack param>),
	      <copy remaining parameters from stack>] +
	    instructions)

Table 14-2: Converting TACKY Instructions to Assembly

TACKY instruction	Assembly instructions
Load(ptr, dst)	Mov(Quadword, ptr, Reg(*<R>*)) Mov(*<dst type>*, Memory(*<R>*, 0), dst)
Store(src, ptr)	Mov(Quadword, ptr, Reg(*<R>*)) Mov(*<src type>*, src, Memory(*<R>*, 0))
GetAddress(src, dst)	Lea(src, dst)

Table 14-3: Converting Types to Assembly

Source type	Assembly type	Alignment
Pointer(referenced_t)	Quadword	8

Next, we'll update the pseudoregister replacement and instruction fix-up passes.

Replacing Pseudoregisters with Memory Operands

We'll use the new Memory operand instead of the old Stack operand throughout this pass. We'll also extend this pass to replace pseudoregisters in the lea instruction. We won't make any other changes. When we converted TACKY pointer variables to pseudoregisters, we assigned them the Quadword assembly type; now we'll allocate stack space for them like any other Quadword.

Fixing Up the lea and push Instructions

The destination of the lea instruction must be a register; we'll rewrite it in the usual fashion. We'll also add a new rewrite rule for push instructions.

As I mentioned in the previous chapter, it's illegal to push an XMM register, so we'll rewrite an instruction like

```
pushq    %xmm0
```

as:

```
subq     $8, %rsp
movsd    %xmm0, (%rsp)
```

A push instruction decrements the stack pointer by 8 bytes, then moves its operand to the top of the stack. When we can't use push, we'll perform the same operation in two instructions: sub followed by mov. The (%rsp) operand designates the memory location at the top of the stack.

Because we don't generate any push instructions that operate on XMM registers, this rewrite rule isn't strictly necessary yet. It will become necessary once we implement register allocation in Part III; then, values that we currently store in memory might be assigned to XMM registers instead.

TEST THE ASSEMBLY GENERATION STAGE

To test that your compiler can generate assembly programs without throwing an error, run:

```
$ ./test_compiler /path/to/your_compiler --chapter 14 --stage codegen
```

Code Emission

Our final task will be to update the code emission stage to handle the new Lea instruction, Memory operand, and BP register. Tables 14-4 and 14-5 summarize how to print out these new constructs. (I haven't bolded new constructs and changes in these tables, because all three of these constructs are entirely new.)

Table 14-4: Formatting Assembly Instructions

Assembly instruction	Output
Lea(src, dst)	leaq <src>, <dst>

Table 14-5: Formatting Assembly Operands

Assembly operand	Output
Reg(BP)	%rbp
Memory(reg, int)	<int>(<reg>)

We'll always use the 8-byte aliases for the base register in a Memory operand and the destination register in an Lea instruction, because memory addresses are 8-byte integers.

When the offset in a Memory operand is zero, you can either print it or omit it; (%rax) and 0(%rax) are equally valid.

TEST THE WHOLE COMPILER

To test out the whole compiler, run:

```
$ ./test_compiler /path/to/your_compiler --chapter 14
```

Summary

In this chapter, you added support for pointers to your compiler. You learned how to parse complex declarators into derived types and how to type check operations on pointers. During TACKY generation, you established a uniform way to process pointer dereference expressions, regardless of how they're used. On the backend, you took the existing Stack operand that accessed memory relative to the address in RBP and tweaked it to work with addresses stored in any register.

In the next chapter, you'll implement arrays, your first non-scalar type. You'll also implement array subscripting and pointer arithmetic and explore the ways in which they're equivalent. Because pointers and arrays are so closely related, the concepts, techniques, and instructions introduced in this chapter will be crucial in the next chapter too.

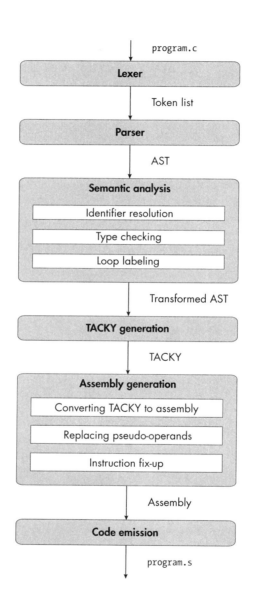

program.c

Lexer

Token list

Parser

AST

Semantic analysis

Identifier resolution

Type checking

Loop labeling

Transformed AST

TACKY generation

TACKY

Assembly generation

Converting TACKY to assembly

Replacing pseudo-operands

Instruction fix-up

Assembly

Code emission

program.s

15

ARRAYS AND POINTER ARITHMETIC

In this chapter, you'll implement array types. You'll also add the main language features that programmers use to work with arrays: compound initializers, subscript operators, and pointer arithmetic. Arrays and pointers are distinct but closely related types. Many expressions of array type are implicitly converted to pointers, and many pointer operations, like subscripting, are meant to operate on pointers to array elements. So, to support arrays, you'll build on the support for pointers that you added in the previous chapter.

The type checker plays an especially critical role here. It will handle the implicit conversions from arrays to pointers and annotate the AST with the type information you'll rely on to perform pointer arithmetic. Once the type checker has done all the hard work, it will be relatively easy to break down subscript operators and compound initializers into simple pointer operations during TACKY generation. You won't add any new assembly instructions in this chapter, but you'll introduce new operands to represent objects in memory and elements within those objects.

As usual, we'll start with an overview of the language constructs we're going to add. We'll pay special attention to the relationship between pointers and arrays and how this relationship plays out in pointer arithmetic and subscript expressions. This is a particularly confusing aspect of C, and it's key to everything we'll do in this chapter.

Arrays and Pointer Arithmetic

Let's define a few terms up front. In the last chapter, we divided every object type we knew about into two categories: arithmetic types and non-arithmetic types. Now we'll introduce another distinction. A *scalar type* represents a single value. The pointer and arithmetic types we've already implemented are all scalar types. An *aggregate type* represents a collection of values. Arrays are aggregate types; so are structures, which we'll implement in Chapter 18. All the values in an array have the same type, which is the array's *element type*.

Array Declarations and Initializers

When we declare an array, we specify its element type and how many elements it contains. For example, we could declare an array of three int objects:

```
int int_array[3];
```

Or we could declare an array of five pointers to double:

```
double *(ptr_array[5]);
```

(Remember that we interpret a declaration by starting with the basic type—double, in this case—and then applying type derivations from the outside in.)

Both of these examples use scalar element types, but we can use aggregate element types too. The following example declares an array of three elements, where each element is itself an array of two long objects:

```
long nested_array[3][2];
```

Arrays of arrays like this one are called *multidimensional arrays*. Note that we still apply type derivations from the outside in to determine this array's type. We start with the base type long, apply the derivation specified by [2] to get the type "array of two long objects," and then apply the derivation specified by [3] to get the type "array of three arrays of two long objects."

You can initialize an array with a *compound initializer*, which specifies an initial value for each element:

```
int int_array[3] = {1, foo(), a * 4};
```

And you can initialize a multidimensional array with nested compound initializers:

```
long nested_array[3][2] = {{a, a + 1}, {31, -4}, {foo(), 6}};
```

Here, the three nested compound initializers initialize the three elements of the outer array. Each of those three elements is, itself, an array of two long objects. The nested initializer for each of these elements specifies two arithmetic values (which can be implicitly converted to long).

You can also leave an array uninitialized. If it has automatic storage duration, its initial value will be undefined. If it has static storage duration, it will be initialized to all zeros. In other words, we treat uninitialized arrays exactly like uninitialized scalar objects.

Memory Layout of Arrays

At this point, it's helpful to talk a bit about the memory layout of flat and multidimensional arrays. If you declare an array of *n* objects, those *n* objects will be laid out sequentially in memory. Consider the array in Listing 15-1, which has a scalar element type.

```
int six_ints[6] = {1, 2, 3, 4, 5, 6};
```

Listing 15-1: An array of scalar values

Figure 15-1 shows what six_ints might look like in memory right after it's initialized (the memory addresses in this figure are just for illustration; they wouldn't be valid on a real system).

Memory contents	1	2	3	4	5	6
Memory address	0x10	0x14	0x18	0x1c	0x20	0x24

Figure 15-1: The layout of six_ints in memory

Compare this declaration to Listing 15-2, which declares a multidimensional array with the same number and type of scalar elements as six_ints.

```
int three_arrays[3][2] = {{1, 2}, {3, 4}, {5, 6}};
```

Listing 15-2: An array of nested arrays

The memory that holds three_arrays will also look like Figure 15-1. In memory, there's no indication of where one element ends and another begins, so the two arrays are indistinguishable. Although the nested structure of three_arrays doesn't impact its layout in memory, it does impact how you access individual array elements, as we'll see shortly.

Array-to-Pointer Decay

Once we've defined and initialized an array, what can we do with it? Not a lot, as it turns out. In fact, there are only two valid operations on objects of array type. First, we can get an array's size with the sizeof operator, which we'll implement in Chapter 17. Second, we can get its address with the & operator:

```
int my_array[3] = {1, 2, 3};
int (*my_pointer)[3] = &my_array;
```

That's it! There are no other valid operations on arrays. That probably sounds ridiculous, since C programs read and write array elements all the time. What's going on here? The C standard (section 6.3.2.1, paragraph 3) provides the solution to this puzzle: "Except when it is the operand of the sizeof operator, or the unary & operator . . . an expression that has type 'array of *type*' is converted to an expression with type 'pointer to *type*' that points to the initial element of the array object and is not an lvalue."

This implicit conversion from arrays to pointers is called *array-to-pointer decay*. (I'll sometimes say that an array decays to a pointer, and sometimes that it's implicitly converted to a pointer. They both mean the same thing.) While we can't do much with arrays, we can perform all sorts of useful operations on pointers. We've already implemented some of these operations, and we'll add a few more in this chapter.

The code snippet in Listing 15-3 shows an example of array decay.

```
int my_array[3] = {1, 2, 3};
int *my_pointer = ❶ my_array;
return ❷ *my_pointer;
```

Listing 15-3: Implicitly converting an array to a pointer

Let's say my_array starts at address 0x10. When my_array appears on the right side of the assignment expression in this listing, it will be implicitly converted to a pointer whose type is int * and whose value is 0x10 ❶. We can then assign this pointer's value to my_pointer. When we dereference my_pointer, the result is the int object stored in the first 4 bytes of my_array ❷. Therefore, we'll return this object's current value, 1. Note that the address 0x10 can be interpreted in a couple of different ways, depending on its type. As an int *, it points to the array's initial element, which we can read or write through a pointer dereference operation. The expression &my_array has the same value, 0x10, but it points to the whole array and its type is int (*)[3].

It's especially important to keep track of a pointer's type when working with multidimensional arrays. Consider Listing 15-4, which tries to assign to two array elements.

```
int nested_array[2][2] = {{1, 2}, {3, 4}};
**nested_array = 10;
*nested_array = 0;
```

Listing 15-4: Legal and illegal assignments to array elements

The first assignment expression, which assigns to **nested_array, is valid. First, we implicitly convert the variable nested_array to a pointer to the array's initial element. That element has type int[2], so the type of the pointer is int(*)[2]. The first dereference operation on this pointer results in an array object with type int[2]. We implicitly convert *this* array to a pointer with type int *. The second pointer dereference therefore produces an int object, which we can assign to. The assignment expression overwrites that object's current value, 1, with a new value, 10. The int(*)[2] and int * pointers in this expression both point to the start of nested_array; only their types differ.

The next assignment expression, which assigns to *nested_array, is illegal. It starts out as before: we implicitly convert nested_array to a pointer of type int(*)[2], dereference it, and implicitly convert the result to a pointer of type int *. We then try to assign directly to this pointer, but the C standard states that the result of this implicit conversion "is not an lvalue," so we can't assign to it. It's not clear what this assignment would do even if it were permitted; it would be like assigning to the result of an & operation.

Now we know how to access an array's initial element in any dimension. We can even read and write to the initial scalar object in an array. However, we usually want to access an array's other elements too. For that, we'll need pointer arithmetic.

Pointer Arithmetic to Access Array Elements

Once we have a pointer to an array's initial element, we'll use pointer addition to produce pointers to its other elements. Let's work through the example in Listing 15-5.

```
int array[3] = {1, 2, 3};
int *ptr = array + 1;
```

Listing 15-5: Accessing later array elements with pointer arithmetic

We'll use 0x10 again as the array's starting address. In the expression array + 1, the variable array decays to a pointer to the initial array element, as usual. When we add 1 to this pointer, the result is a pointer to the next int element in the array. Since each int is 4 bytes, we need to multiply 1 by a scale of 4 to calculate how many bytes to add to array's address. The resulting pointer's value is 0x14. If we dereferenced this pointer, we would get the int object at address 0x14, whose current value is 2. Array elements are zero indexed, so we say the initial element of array is at index 0 and the next element is at index 1.

More generally, when we add an integer *n* to a pointer, the result is a pointer to another array element at the position *n* elements further along in the array. Similarly, we can move backward in an array by subtracting an integer (or adding a negative integer). If the result would be outside the bounds of the array in either direction, the behavior is undefined.

NOTE *If x is an n-element array, x + n points one past the end of x. This pointer is a special case. It's not considered out of bounds, and you can use it in pointer arithmetic. For example, you can compare it to other pointers to elements in the same array. (When you're looping through array elements, this is a useful way to test whether you've reached the end.) But dereferencing it is undefined behavior, because it doesn't point to an element of the array.*

When we perform pointer arithmetic, the nested structure of the array we point into matters, because it dictates what counts as a single element. Let's look at Listing 15-6 to see how this plays out for the two arrays we defined in Listings 15-1 and 15-2, which had identical contents in memory.

```
int six_ints[6] = {1, 2, 3, 4, 5, 6};
int three_arrays[3][2] = {{1, 2}, {3, 4}, {5, 6}};
❶ int *int_ptr = six_ints + 1;
❷ int (*array_ptr)[2] = three_arrays + 1;
```

Listing 15-6: Pointer arithmetic with flat and nested arrays

The result of the expression six_ints + 1 is a pointer to the element at index 1 in six_ints ❶. This element is an int with the value 2. Similarly, when we compute three_arrays + 1, we get a pointer to the array element at index 1 in three_arrays ❷. In this case, however, this element is itself an array of two int objects, whose current values are 3 and 4. Although six_ints and three_arrays may have identical contents in memory, performing the same operation on both of them produces very different results.

So how can we access the scalar objects in three_arrays? For example, how could we read the last int in this array, whose value is 6? First, we'll get a pointer to the last element in three_arrays:

```
int (*outer_ptr)[2] = three_arrays + 2;
```

This points to the entire two-element array {5, 6}. We'll dereference it to get a pointer to a single scalar element in this array instead:

```
int *inner_ptr = *outer_ptr;
```

This dereference expression results in an array of type int[2], which decays to a pointer with type int *. Now inner_ptr points to the first int in this nested array, whose value is 5. We'll increment it to point to the next int, whose value is 6:

```
inner_ptr = inner_ptr + 1;
```

At that point, we can access its value with a normal pointer dereference:

```
int result = *inner_ptr;
```

We can consolidate these statements into the single expression in Listing 15-7.

```
int result = *( *(three_arrays + 2) + 1);
```

Listing 15-7: Accessing the last int in three_arrays

Through repeated pointer addition, dereferencing, and implicit conversions from arrays to pointers, we can access any element in a multidimensional array. This is, obviously, a huge pain. The subscript operator, [ ], provides more convenient syntax to accomplish the same thing. The expression a[i] is equivalent to *(a + i), so we can rewrite Listing 15-7 as Listing 15-8.

```
int result = three_arrays[2][1];
```

Listing 15-8: A more convenient way to access the last int in three_arrays

The last point I want to emphasize is that subscripting and pointer arithmetic apply to all pointers, not just pointers that decayed from arrays. If a pointed-to object isn't in an array, we'll treat it like the sole element in a one-element array. For example, Listing 15-9 is perfectly valid.

```
int a = 5;
int *ptr = &a;
return ptr[0] == 5;
```

Listing 15-9: Subscripting a pointer to a scalar object

When we add 0 to ptr and dereference the result, we get back the object a. Therefore, the expression ptr[0] == 5 evaluates to 1 (that is, true).

Even More Pointer Arithmetic

We'll support two other operations on pointers. The first is subtraction; Listing 15-10 gives an example.

```
int arr[3] = {1, 2, 3};
int *ptr = arr + 2;
return ptr - arr;
```

Listing 15-10: Subtracting two pointers

When we subtract pointers to two elements in the same array, the result is the difference between their indices. In this example, unsurprisingly, we return 2.

We can also compare pointers to array elements, like in Listing 15-11.

```
int arr[3] = {1, 2, 3};
int *ptr = arr + 2;
return ptr > arr;
```

Listing 15-11: Comparing pointers

The pointer to the element with the higher array index compares greater than the one with the lower index. In this example, ptr points to the element at index 2 and arr decays to a pointer to the element at index 0, so the comparison ptr > arr evaluates to 1. If two pointers don't point into the same array, the result of subtracting or comparing them is undefined.

Array Types in Function Declarations

It's illegal for a function to return an array, like in the following declaration:

```
int foo(void)[3];
```

A function can't take arrays as parameters, either. Weirdly enough, the C standard lets you *declare* a function with array parameters, but it requires the compiler to adjust your function signature to take pointers instead. For example, the declaration

```
int foo(int array_of_three_elements[3]);
```

will be turned into:

```
int foo(int *array_of_three_elements);
```

We'll adjust parameters with array types to have the corresponding pointer types in the type checker.

> **"IT'S FOR HISTORICAL REASONS"**
>
> It doesn't make sense that you can declare function parameters of array type, only to have the compiler treat them like pointers. When I learned about this behavior, it struck me as confusing and useless. Whenever I run into a feature of C that doesn't make sense, I assume it's for historical reasons. In this case, that turns out to be true! Dennis Ritchie talks about this in his paper "The Development of the C Language" (ACM, 1993). In a parameter declaration like int a[], he notes, the array declarator [] is "a living fossil. . . . The notation survived in part for the sake of compatibility, in part under the rationalization that it would allow programmers to communicate to their readers an intent to pass [a function] a pointer generated from an array, rather than a reference to

a single integer. Unfortunately, it serves as much to confuse the learner as to alert the reader."

The paper goes into more detail about how C's pointer and array semantics have changed over time; you can read it at *https://www.bell-labs.com/usr/ dmr/www/chist.html*.

Things We Aren't Implementing

The features we won't support are significant enough that I'll mention them explicitly. We won't implement variable-length arrays, whose length is determined at runtime, like this one:

```
int variable_length_array[x];
```

We'll permit only constants as the dimensions in array declarations. We also won't permit declarations of incomplete array types:

```
int array[];
```

C requires you to specify an array's dimensions when you define it, but not when you declare it. However, we'll require array dimensions in declarations as well as definitions.

We won't implement *compound literals*, which let you construct array objects (and other aggregate objects) outside of initializers:

```
int *p = (int []){2, 4};
```

Finally, we won't fully support C's semantics for initializing aggregate objects. Compound initializers are a bit of a free-for-all; you can omit braces, wrap scalar values in braces, or initialize some elements but not others. This makes it tricky to figure out which expression is supposed to initialize which element. We'll take a much stricter approach. First of all, we'll require braces around the initializers for each nested array. In other words, we'll accept the declaration

```
int arr[2][2] = {{1, 2}, {3, 4}};
```

but we'll reject the following equivalent declaration, even though the C standard permits it:

```
int arr[2][2] = {1, 2, 3, 4};
```

We'll also reject braces around scalar initializers, like in the following example:

```
int i = { 3 };
```

And we won't support designators, which let you initialize elements out of order:

```
int arr[3] = { 0, [2] = 1 };
```

However, we *will* allow compound initializers that don't initialize every array element, like the following:

```
int arr[3] = {1, 2};
```

In this case, we'll pad out any remaining elements with zeros; that's the behavior the C standard requires. Now that we've clarified exactly what we will and won't build, we can move on to the lexer.

The Lexer

You'll add two tokens in this chapter:

[An open square bracket

] A close square bracket

After adding these tokens, you can test out your lexer.

TEST THE LEXER

To test the lexer, run:

```
$ ./test_compiler /path/to/your_compiler --chapter 15 --stage lex
```

Lexing should succeed for every test case in this chapter.

The Parser

Next, we'll add array types, subscript expressions, and compound initializers to the AST. An array's type indicates the number of elements in the array and the type of those elements:

```
type = --snip-- | Array(type element, int size)
```

We can nest `Array` constructors to specify a multidimensional array. For example, we'll represent the type of the declaration

```
int x[3][4];
```

as `Array(Array(Int, 4), 3)`. Since we won't support variable-length arrays, every array type must have a constant size.

A subscript expression contains two subexpressions, a pointer and an index:

```
exp = --snip--
    | Subscript(exp, exp)
```

Surprisingly, the order in which these two subexpressions appear doesn't matter; the expressions `x[1]` and `1[x]` are equivalent.

Finally, we'll add an `initializer` construct to support both scalar and compound variable initializers:

```
initializer = SingleInit(exp) | CompoundInit(initializer*)
```

We'll use `CompoundInit` to initialize arrays and `SingleInit` to initialize scalar objects, including individual array elements. We'll use a nested `CompoundInit` construct for each row in a multidimensional array. Listing 15-12 shows how to represent the initializer `{{1, 2}, {3, 4}, {5, 6}}`.

```
CompoundInit([
    CompoundInit([SingleInit(Constant(ConstInt(1))),
                  SingleInit(Constant(ConstInt(2)))]),
    CompoundInit([SingleInit(Constant(ConstInt(3))),
                  SingleInit(Constant(ConstInt(4)))]),
    CompoundInit([SingleInit(Constant(ConstInt(5))),
                  SingleInit(Constant(ConstInt(6)))])
])
```

Listing 15-12: Representing the initializer for three_arrays, from Listing 15-2, as an AST node

The type checker will annotate initializers with their types, just like it does for exp nodes. However you support type annotations on exp nodes, you should do the same thing for initializer.

Listing 15-13 gives the complete AST definition, with this chapter's additions bolded.

```
program = Program(declaration*)
declaration = FunDecl(function_declaration) | VarDecl(variable_declaration)
variable_declaration = (identifier name, initializer? init,
                        type var_type, storage_class?)
function_declaration = (identifier name, identifier* params, block? body,
                        type fun_type, storage_class?)
initializer = SingleInit(exp) | CompoundInit(initializer*)
```

```
type = Int | Long | UInt | ULong | Double
     | FunType(type* params, type ret)
     | Pointer(type referenced)
     | Array(type element, int size)
storage_class = Static | Extern
block_item = S(statement) | D(declaration)
block = Block(block_item*)
for_init = InitDecl(variable_declaration) | InitExp(exp?)
statement = Return(exp)
          | Expression(exp)
          | If(exp condition, statement then, statement? else)
          | Compound(block)
          | Break
          | Continue
          | While(exp condition, statement body)
          | DoWhile(statement body, exp condition)
          | For(for_init init, exp? condition, exp? post, statement body)
          | Null
exp = Constant(const)
    | Var(identifier)
    | Cast(type target_type, exp)
    | Unary(unary_operator, exp)
    | Binary(binary_operator, exp, exp)
    | Assignment(exp, exp)
    | Conditional(exp condition, exp, exp)
    | FunctionCall(identifier, exp* args)
    | Dereference(exp)
    | AddrOf(exp)
    | Subscript(exp, exp)
unary_operator = Complement | Negate | Not
binary_operator = Add | Subtract | Multiply | Divide | Remainder | And | Or
                | Equal | NotEqual | LessThan | LessOrEqual
                | GreaterThan | GreaterOrEqual
const = ConstInt(int) | ConstLong(int)
      | ConstUInt(int) | ConstULong(int)
      | ConstDouble(double)
```

Listing 15-13: The abstract syntax tree with array types, compound initializers, and subscript expressions

Let's walk through how to parse each of these additions to the AST.

Parsing Array Declarators

You learned how to parse pointer and function declarators in the previous chapter; now we'll extend that code to handle array declarators too. Listing 15-14 shows how to extend the declarator construct that we defined in Listing 14-6.

```
declarator = Ident(identifier)
           | PointerDeclarator(declarator)
           | ArrayDeclarator(declarator, int size)
           | FunDeclarator(param_info* params, declarator)
```

Listing 15-14: Representing array declarators

Next, we'll add array declarators to the grammar. Since they have higher precedence than pointer declarators, they belong in the <direct-declarator> grammar rule:

```
<direct-declarator> ::= <simple-declarator> [ <declarator-suffix> ]
<declarator-suffix> ::= <param-list> | { "[" <const> "]" }+
```

A direct declarator is a simple declarator with an optional suffix: either a parenthesized list of function parameters or a sequence of constant array dimensions of the form [*const*]. Each ArrayDeclarator specifies just one array dimension, so we'll parse a <declarator-suffix> with multiple dimensions to a sequence of multiple nested ArrayDeclarator nodes. For example, we'd parse the declarator array[1][2] to:

```
ArrayDeclarator(ArrayDeclarator(Ident("array"), 1), 2)
```

The grammar rule for <declarator-suffix> permits floating-point constants as array dimensions, but the C standard requires array dimensions to be integers. When you parse a <declarator-suffix>, you should reject floating-pointing constants and accept constants of any integer type. The C standard also requires array dimensions to be greater than zero, but Clang and GCC support zero-length arrays as a language extension. It's up to you whether to accept zero-length arrays or reject them; the test suite doesn't cover this case.

Finally, we'll update process_declarator, which converts a declarator construct into an AST node. Listing 15-15 illustrates how to handle array declarators in process_declarator.

```
process_declarator(declarator, base_type):
    match declarator with
    | --snip--
    | ArrayDeclarator(inner, size) ->
        derived_type = Array(base_type, size)
        return process_declarator(inner, derived_type)
```

Listing 15-15: Applying array type derivations

This listing follows the same pattern we introduced to derive pointer types in Chapter 14.

Parsing Abstract Array Declarators

Next, let's deal with abstract declarators, which specify types without declaring identifiers. We'll parse abstract array declarators according to the grammar rule in Listing 15-16.

```
<direct-abstract-declarator> ::= "(" <abstract-declarator> ")" { "[" <const> "]" }
                               | { "[" <const> "]" }+
```

Listing 15-16: The grammar rule for abstract array declarators

A direct abstract declarator is either a parenthesized declarator, optionally followed by a sequence of array dimensions, or just a sequence of array dimensions. (Remember that {} in EBNF syntax indicates zero or more repetitions, while {}+ indicates one or more repetitions.) We'll take the same steps here that we took to support normal declarators. Listing 15-17 shows how to extend the `abstract_declarator` construct.

```
abstract_declarator = AbstractPointer(abstract_declarator)
                    | AbstractArray(abstract_declarator, int size)
                    | AbstractBase
```

Listing 15-17: Representing abstract array declarators

After updating `abstract_declarator`, we'll change our parsing code to handle the grammar rule in Listing 15-16. (This code should accept integer constants as array dimensions and reject floating-point constants, just like the code to parse ordinary declarators.) Finally, we'll update `process_abstract_declarator`.

Parsing Compound Initializers

Now let's define the grammar rule for initializers:

```
<initializer> ::= <exp> | "{" <initializer> { "," <initializer> } ["," ] "}"
```

This rule is straightforward: an initializer is either an expression or a brace-enclosed list of one or more nested initializers. Note that there can be a trailing comma after the last element in an initializer list: { 1, 2, 3 } and { 1, 2, 3, } are both valid compound initializers.

Parsing Subscript Expressions

The last new language feature we need to parse is the subscript operator. Subscripting is a *postfix* operator, which follows the expression it modifies. Postfix operators have higher precedence than prefix operators like &, -, or ~. We'll break up the `<factor>` grammar rule to reflect this difference in precedence. At the highest precedence level, we'll have constants, variables, parenthesized expressions, and function calls:

```
<primary-exp> ::= <const> | <identifier> | "(" <exp> ")"
                | <identifier> "(" [ <argument-list> ] ")"
```

Then, we'll define a postfix expression as a primary expression, optionally followed by a sequence of subscript operators:

```
<postfix-exp> ::= <primary-exp> { "[" <exp> "]" }
```

Each subscript operator is an expression enclosed in square brackets. Finally, we'll define unary expressions, which include both prefix and cast operators:

```
<unary-exp> ::= <unop> <unary-exp>
             | "(" { <type-specifier> }+ [ <abstract-declarator> ] ")" <unary-exp>
             | <postfix-exp>
```

Listing 15-18 shows the complete grammar, with this chapter's changes bolded.

```
<program> ::= { <declaration> }
<declaration> ::= <variable-declaration> | <function-declaration>
<variable-declaration> ::= { <specifier> }+ <declarator> [ "=" <initializer> ] ";"
<function-declaration> ::= { <specifier> }+ <declarator> ( <block> | ";")
<declarator> ::= "*" <declarator> | <direct-declarator>
<direct-declarator> ::= <simple-declarator> [ <declarator-suffix> ]
<declarator-suffix> ::= <param-list> | { "[" <const> "]" }+
<param-list> ::= "(" "void" ")" | "(" <param> { "," <param> } ")"
<param> ::= { <type-specifier> }+ <declarator>
<simple-declarator> ::= <identifier> | "(" <declarator> ")"
<type-specifier> ::= "int" | "long" | "unsigned" | "signed" | "double"
<specifier> ::= <type-specifier> | "static" | "extern"
<block> ::= "{" { <block-item> } "}"
<block-item> ::= <statement> | <declaration>
<initializer> ::= <exp> | "{" <initializer> { "," <initializer> } [ "," ] "}"
<for-init> ::= <variable-declaration> | [ <exp> ] ";"
<statement> ::= "return" <exp> ";"
              | <exp> ";"
              | "if" "(" <exp> ")" <statement> [ "else" <statement> ]
              | <block>
              | "break" ";"
              | "continue" ";"
              | "while" "(" <exp> ")" <statement>
              | "do" <statement> "while" "(" <exp> ")" ";"
              | "for" "(" <for-init> [ <exp> ] ";" [ <exp> ] ")" <statement>
              | ";"
<exp> ::= <unary-exp> | <exp> <binop> <exp> | <exp> "?" <exp> ":" <exp>
<unary-exp> ::= <unop> <unary-exp>
             | "(" { <type-specifier> }+ [ <abstract-declarator> ] ")" <unary-exp>
             | <postfix-exp>
<postfix-exp> ::= <primary-exp> { "[" <exp> "]" }
<primary-exp> ::= <const> | <identifier> | "(" <exp> ")"
               | <identifier> "(" [ <argument-list> ] ")"
<argument-list> ::= <exp> { "," <exp> }
<abstract-declarator> ::= "*" [ <abstract-declarator> ]
                        | <direct-abstract-declarator>
<direct-abstract-declarator> ::= "(" <abstract-declarator> ")" { "[" <const> "]" }
                               | { "[" <const> "]" }+
<unop> ::= "-" | "~" | "!" | "*" | "&"
<binop> ::= "-" | "+" | "*" | "/" | "%" | "&&" | "||"
          | "==" | "!=" | "<" | "<=" | ">" | ">=" | "="
<const> ::= <int> | <long> | <uint> | <ulong> | <double>
```

```
<identifier> ::= ? An identifier token ?
<int> ::= ? An int token ?
<long> ::= ? An int or long token ?
<uint> ::= ? An unsigned int token ?
<ulong> ::= ? An unsigned int or unsigned long token ?
<double> ::= ? A floating-point constant token ?
```

Listing 15-18: The grammar with array types, compound initializers, and subscript expressions

Once you've updated your parser to account for all of the changes in Listing 15-18, you're ready to test it out.

TEST THE PARSER

To test your parser, run:

```
$ ./test_compiler /path/to/your_compiler --chapter 15 --stage parse
```

The parser should fail on every test case in *tests/chapter_15/invalid_parse*, which includes programs with malformed declarators, initializers, and subscript expressions. It should handle every test case in *tests/chapter_15/invalid_types* and *tests/chapter_15/valid* without error.

The Type Checker

The type checker will do most of the heavy lifting in this chapter. It will add type information to subscript and pointer arithmetic expressions; validate the dimensions of compound initializers; and detect type errors, like casting an expression to an array type. It will also handle implicit conversions from array to pointer types. Just as we insert Cast expressions into the AST to make implicit type conversions explicit, we'll insert AddrOf expressions to make conversions from arrays to pointers explicit.

Converting Arrays to Pointers

We'll convert any array type expression to a pointer, unless it's already the operand of an AddrOf expression. This might sound familiar from the previous chapter, where we lvalue converted the result of every expression, except when we took its address or assigned to it. In Chapter 14, we introduced a new emit_tacky_and_convert helper function to manage lvalue conversions; now we'll use a similar design pattern in a different compiler pass. We'll define a new typecheck_and_convert function, shown in Listing 15-19.

```
typecheck_and_convert(e, symbols):
    typed_e = typecheck_exp(e, symbols)
```

```
match get_type(typed_e) with
| Array(elem_t, size) ->
    addr_exp = AddrOf(typed_e)
    return set_type(addr_exp, Pointer(elem_t))
| _ -> return typed_e
```

Listing 15-19: Implicitly converting an array to a pointer

If an expression has array type, we insert an AddrOf operation to get its address. We then record its result type, which is a pointer to the array's element type. This is a different result type than we'd get from an explicit & operator, which always produces a pointer to the type of its operand. Take the following declaration:

```
int arr[3];
```

The expression &arr has type int (*)[3]. The expression arr, on the other hand, has type int *. In the type checked AST, we're using AddrOf to represent two ways of taking an object's address, which yield different result types: through an implicit conversion or an explicit & operator.

Once we've introduced typecheck_and_convert, we'll use it in place of typecheck_exp to check both subexpressions and full expressions. The one exception is type checking the operand of AddrOf. This operand should not be converted from an array to a pointer, so we'll continue to process it by calling typecheck_exp directly.

Validating Lvalues

We'll change a couple of details about how we validate lvalues. First, we should recognize Subscript expressions as lvalues, in addition to Var and Dereference.

Second, we need to reject assignment expressions that try to assign to arrays. Once an array decays to a pointer, it's no longer an lvalue and can't be assigned to. To catch these invalid assignment expressions, we'll process the left operand with typecheck_and_convert before we check whether it's an lvalue. Listing 15-20 shows the latest logic to type check assignment expressions.

```
typecheck_exp(e, symbols):
    match e with
    | --snip--
    | Assignment(left, right) ->
        typed_left = typecheck_and_convert(left, symbols)
        if typed_left is not an lvalue:
            fail("Tried to assign to non-lvalue")
        typed_right = typecheck_and_convert(right, symbols)
        --snip--
```

Listing 15-20: Type checking assignment expressions

If the left operand is an array, typecheck_and_convert will wrap it in an AddrOf operation. Then, since AddrOf isn't an lvalue, the type checker will throw an error.

Type Checking Pointer Arithmetic

Next, we'll extend addition, subtraction, and the relational operators to work with pointers. Adding any integer type to a pointer is valid. Listing 15-21 demonstrates how to type check addition.

```
| Binary(Add, e1, e2) ->
    typed_e1 = typecheck_and_convert(e1, symbols)
    typed_e2 = typecheck_and_convert(e2, symbols)
    t1 = get_type(typed_e1)
    t2 = get_type(typed_e2)
    if t1 and t2 are arithmetic:
        --snip--
    else if t1 is a pointer type and t2 is an integer type:
      ❶ converted_e2 = convert_to(typed_e2, Long)
        add_exp = Binary(Add, typed_e1, converted_e2)
      ❷ return set_type(add_exp, t1)
  ❸ else if t2 is a pointer type and t1 is an integer type:
        --snip--
    else:
        fail("Invalid operands for addition")
```

Listing 15-21: Type checking pointer addition

To type check addition involving a pointer and an integer, we first convert the integer operand to a long ❶. This will simplify later compiler passes, when pointer indices will need to be 8 bytes wide so that we can add them to 8-byte memory addresses. This conversion doesn't come from the C standard; we're just adding it for our own convenience. But it also doesn't violate the standard; converting a valid array index to long won't change its value, so the result of the whole expression is the same either way. (If an integer is too big to represent as a long, we can safely assume that it's not a valid array index, since no hardware supports arrays with anywhere close to 2^{63} elements.)

The result of pointer addition has the same type as the pointer operand ❷. We use the same logic whether the first or second operand is the pointer, so I've omitted the pseudocode for the latter case ❸. Finally, in any case other than adding a pointer to an integer or adding two arithmetic operands, we throw an error.

Subtracting an integer from a pointer works the same way: we convert the integer operand to a long and annotate the result with the same type as the pointer operand. The only difference is that operand order matters. You can subtract an integer from a pointer, but you can't subtract a pointer from an integer.

When we subtract one pointer from another, both operands must have the same type, and the result has an implementation-defined signed integer type. We'll use long as the result type here, which is the norm on 64-bit systems. This type is supposed to be aliased as ptrdiff_t in the <stddef.h> header, to help users write more portable code. Since we don't support typedef and therefore can't compile <stddef.h>, we'll ignore this requirement.

Listing 15-22 demonstrates how to type check both cases of pointer subtraction.

```
| Binary(Subtract, e1, e2) ->
    typed_e1 = typecheck_and_convert(e1, symbols)
    typed_e2 = typecheck_and_convert(e2, symbols)
    t1 = get_type(typed_e1)
    t2 = get_type(typed_e2)
    if t1 and t2 are arithmetic:
        --snip--
❶ else if t1 is a pointer type and t2 is an integer type:
        converted_e2 = convert_to(typed_e2, Long)
        sub_exp = Binary(Subtract, typed_e1, converted_e2)
        return set_type(sub_exp, t1)
❷ else if t1 is a pointer type and t1 == t2:
        sub_exp = Binary(Subtract, typed_e1, typed_e2)
        return set_type(sub_exp, Long)
    else:
        fail("Invalid operands for subtraction")
```

Listing 15-22: Type checking pointer subtraction

If an expression subtracts an integer from a pointer, we handle it just like pointer addition ❶. If it subtracts two pointers of the same type, we record long as the result type ❷. In any other case—if an expression subtracts two pointers of different types, subtracts a double from a pointer, or subtracts a pointer from an arithmetic value—we'll throw an error.

Finally, let's deal with the <, <=, >, and >= operators. Each of these accepts two pointer operands of the same type and returns an int. These are pretty simple to type check, so I won't provide pseudocode for this case.

Note that none of these operators accept null pointer constants; they compare pointers to elements in the same array, but a null pointer, by definition, doesn't point to an array element. By the same logic, you can't subtract a pointer from a null pointer constant. If x is a pointer, the expressions x == 0 and x != 0 are legal, but 0 - x, 0 < x, and x >= 0 are not. (Clang and GCC are more permissive than the standard here; as a language extension, they both let you use null pointer constants with any relational operator. With this extension, any non-null pointer will compare greater than the null pointer constant.)

Type Checking Subscript Expressions

One operand of a subscript expression must be a pointer, and the other must be an integer. The pointer's referenced type is the result type. Remember that these two operands can appear in either order; we can't assume that the pointer will be the first operand. Listing 15-23 shows how to type check subscript expressions.

```
| Subscript(e1, e2) ->
    typed_e1 = typecheck_and_convert(e1, symbols)
    typed_e2 = typecheck_and_convert(e2, symbols)
    t1 = get_type(typed_e1)
    t2 = get_type(typed_e2)
❶ if t1 is a pointer type and t2 is an integer type:
      ptr_type = t1
    ❷ typed_e2 = convert_to(typed_e2, Long)
   else if t1 is an integer type and t2 is a pointer type:
      ptr_type = t2
      typed_e1 = convert_to(typed_e1, Long)
   else:
      fail("Subscript must have integer and pointer operands")
   subscript_exp = Subscript(typed_e1, typed_e2)
❸ return set_type(subscript_exp, ptr_type.referenced)
```

Listing 15-23: Type checking a subscript expression

First, we validate that one operand is a pointer and the other is an integer ❶. We then convert the integer operand to a long ❷. Finally, we annotate the whole expression with the pointer's referenced type ❸.

Type Checking Cast Expressions

This one is easy: you can't cast an expression to an array type. For example, the expression

```
(int[3]) foo;
```

is invalid and should produce a type error.

Type Checking Function Declarations

When we process a function declaration, we consider both its return type and its parameter types. If a function returns an array type, we throw an error. If any of its parameters has an array type, we adjust it to a pointer type instead. Listing 15-24 describes how to validate and implicitly adjust a function type.

```
typecheck_function_declaration(decl, symbols):
    if decl.fun_type.ret is an array type:
        fail("A function cannot return an array!")
    adjusted_params = []
    for t in decl.fun_type.params:
        match t with
        | Array(elem_t, size) ->
            adjusted_type = Pointer(elem_t)
            adjusted_params.append(adjusted_type)
        | _ -> adjusted_params.append(t)
    decl.fun_type.params = adjusted_params
    --snip--
```

Listing 15-24: Adjusting array types in function declarations

You should add this logic to the very beginning of `typecheck_function_declaration`, in order to adjust a function's parameter types before you check whether it conflicts with prior definitions of the same identifier. You should also ensure that both the symbol table and the AST node itself use the adjusted parameter types.

Type Checking Compound Initializers

We need to annotate each initializer with its type and emit an error if an initializer is incompatible with the type of the object it's supposed to initialize. To type check a compound initializer, we first validate that the object it initializes is an array. Then, we recursively type check each nested initializer, validating that it's compatible with the array's element type. Listing 15-25 illustrates this approach.

```
typecheck_init(target_type, init, symbols):
    match target_type, init with
    | _, SingleInit(e) -> ❶
        typechecked_exp = typecheck_and_convert(e, symbols)
        cast_exp = convert_by_assignment(typechecked_exp, target_type)
        return set_type(SingleInit(cast_exp), target_type)
    | Array(elem_t, size), CompoundInit(init_list) -> ❷
        if length(init_list) > size:
            fail("wrong number of values in initializer") ❸
        typechecked_list = []
        for init_elem in init_list:
            typechecked_elem = typecheck_init(elem_t, init_elem, symbols) ❹
            typechecked_list.append(typechecked_elem)
        while length(typechecked_list) < size:
            typechecked_list.append(zero_initializer(elem_t)) ❺
        return set_type(CompoundInit(typechecked_list), target_type) ❻
    | _ -> fail("can't initialize a scalar object with a compound initializer") ❼
```

Listing 15-25: Type checking initializers

In the base case, an initializer is a single expression ❶. We'll type check this expression, then call `convert_by_assignment`, which we defined in Chapter 14, to convert it to the target type. If it's not compatible with the target type, `convert_by_assignment` will throw an error (this includes cases where the target type is an array type).

In the recursive case, we'll initialize an array using a compound initializer ❷. Each item in the list will initialize one element in the array. First, we'll check that the list doesn't contain too many elements ❸. Then, we'll type check each list item recursively, using the array's element type as the target type ❹. If the initializer list contains too few elements, we'll pad it with zeros ❺. We'll use the `zero_initializer` helper function, which I haven't provided pseudocode for, to produce zero-valued initializers that we can add to the initializer list. Given a scalar type, `zero_initializer` should return a `SingleInit` of that type with the value 0. Given an array type, it should return a `CompoundInit` whose scalar elements (which may be nested several layers deep) have the value 0. For example, calling zero_initializer on the type UInt should return

```
SingleInit(Constant(ConstUInt(0)))
```

and calling it on the type Array(Array(Int, 2), 2) should return:

```
CompoundInit([
    CompoundInit([SingleInit(Constant(ConstInt(0))),
                  SingleInit(Constant(ConstInt(0)))]),
    CompoundInit([SingleInit(Constant(ConstInt(0))),
                  SingleInit(Constant(ConstInt(0)))])
])
```

Once we've finished building the type checked list of initializers, we'll package it into a CompoundInit, which we'll annotate with the target type ❻. If the initializer isn't a single expression and the target type isn't an array type, we're trying to initialize a scalar object with a compound initializer, so we'll throw an error ❼.

Initializing Static Arrays

As with other static variables, we'll store the initial values of static arrays in the symbol table. We'll need to update the data structures we use to represent these initial values. We'll represent the initializer for every object as a list of scalar values:

```
initial_value = Tentative | Initial(static_init* init_list) | NoInitializer
```

For scalar objects, init_list will have only one element. The declaration

```
static int a = 3;
```

will have this initializer:

```
Initial([IntInit(3)])
```

For multidimensional arrays, we'll flatten out any nested structures. Therefore, the declaration

```
static int nested[3][2] = {{1, 2}, {3, 4}, {5, 6}};
```

will have this initializer:

```
Initial([IntInit(1),
         IntInit(2),
         IntInit(3),
         IntInit(4),
         IntInit(5),
         IntInit(6)])
```

Next, we'll add a static_init constructor to represent zeroed-out objects of any size:

```
static_init = IntInit(int) | LongInit(int) | UIntInit(int) | ULongInit(int)
            | DoubleInit(double) | ZeroInit(int bytes)
```

The bytes argument to ZeroInit specifies how many bytes to initialize to zero. If a static array is only partially initialized, we'll use ZeroInit to pad out any uninitialized elements. For example, the declaration

```
static int nested[3][2] = {{100}, {200, 300}};
```

will have this initializer:

```
Initial([IntInit(100),
        ZeroInit(4),
        IntInit(200),
        IntInit(300),
        ZeroInit(8)])
```

The second element of this initializer list, ZeroInit(4), initializes the int at nested[0][1]; the last element, ZeroInit(8), initializes both elements of the nested array nested[2].

Once you've updated the initial_value and static_init data structures, write a function to convert a compound initializer to a static_init list. You'll need to validate that initializers for static arrays have the correct size and structure, just like initializers for non-static arrays; you should reject initializers with too many elements, scalar initializers for arrays, and compound initializers for scalar objects. I won't provide pseudocode for this transformation, since it's similar to the way we type check non-static initializers in Listing 15-25.

Initializing Scalar Variables with ZeroInit

You can also use ZeroInit to initialize scalar variables to zero. For instance, given the declaration

```
static long x = 0;
```

you could use this initializer:

```
Initial([ZeroInit(8)])
```

Using ZeroInit here is optional, but it makes code emission simpler because you can easily tell which initializers belong in .data and which belong in .bss. Just be careful about using ZeroInit to initialize doubles; use it only if you're sure the double's initial value is 0.0 and not -0.0.

TACKY Generation

To accommodate pointer arithmetic and compound initializers, we'll make a few changes to the TACKY IR. First, since we changed how we represent initializers in the symbol table, we'll make the corresponding change in TACKY:

```
top_level = Function(identifier, bool global, identifier* params, instruction* body)
          | StaticVariable(identifier, bool global, type t, static_init* init_list)
```

We'll also introduce a new instruction to support pointer arithmetic:

```
AddPtr(val ptr, val index, int scale, val dst)
```

We'll use this instruction to add or subtract an integer from a pointer, but not to subtract one pointer from another. The scale operand is the size, in bytes, of each element in the array that ptr points into. For example, if ptr is an int *, the scale operand will be 4, since an int is 4 bytes. If ptr is an int (*)[3], a pointer to an array of three int objects, then scale will be 12. The index operand tells us how many elements forward or back to move from the base pointer. At runtime, the program will multiply index by scale to determine how many bytes to add to the base pointer. It would be possible to implement pointer arithmetic using the existing TACKY instructions for multiplication and addition. However, introducing a specialized AddPtr instruction here will help us take advantage of the x64 architecture's built-in support for pointer arithmetic.

We'll introduce one more instruction to support compound initializers:

```
CopyToOffset(val src, identifier dst, int offset)
```

In this instruction, src is a scalar value, dst is the name of some variable of aggregate type, and offset specifies the number of bytes between the start of dst and the position we should copy src to. It's important to note that dst designates an array, *not* a pointer to an array element. In other words, CopyToOffset doesn't use the value of dst; it uses dst to identify an object with a fixed location in memory. Because this instruction operates directly on arrays, rather than pointers, it's useful for array initialization but not for subscripting. In Chapter 18, we'll use it to initialize and update structures too.

Listing 15-26 shows the updated TACKY IR, with this chapter's changes bolded.

```
program = Program(top_level*)
top_level = Function(identifier, bool global, identifier* params, instruction* body)
          | StaticVariable(identifier, bool global, type t, static_init* init_list)
instruction = Return(val)
            | SignExtend(val src, val dst)
            | Truncate(val src, val dst)
            | ZeroExtend(val src, val dst)
            | DoubleToInt(val src, val dst)
            | DoubleToUInt(val src, val dst)
            | IntToDouble(val src, val dst)
            | UIntToDouble(val src, val dst)
            | Unary(unary_operator, val src, val dst)
            | Binary(binary_operator, val src1, val src2, val dst)
            | Copy(val src, val dst)
            | GetAddress(val src, val dst)
            | Load(val src_ptr, val dst)
            | Store(val src, val dst_ptr)
            | AddPtr(val ptr, val index, int scale, val dst)
            | CopyToOffset(val src, identifier dst, int offset)
            | Jump(identifier target)
            | JumpIfZero(val condition, identifier target)
            | JumpIfNotZero(val condition, identifier target)
            | Label(identifier)
            | FunCall(identifier fun_name, val* args, val dst)
val = Constant(const) | Var(identifier)
unary_operator = Complement | Negate | Not
binary_operator = Add | Subtract | Multiply | Divide | Remainder | Equal | NotEqual
                | LessThan | LessOrEqual | GreaterThan | GreaterOrEqual
```

Listing 15-26: Adding support for arrays to the TACKY IR

With these additions, we can implement every new operator and construct in this chapter. Let's handle each of them in turn.

Pointer Arithmetic

We'll implement the pointer arithmetic expression *<ptr>* + *<int>* with an AddPtr instruction, as Listing 15-27 demonstrates.

```
<instructions for ptr>
p = <result of ptr>
<instructions for int>
i = <result of int>
result = AddPtr(p, i, <size of referenced type of ptr>)
```

Listing 15-27: Adding an integer to a pointer in TACKY

There are a couple of things to note about this listing. First, the pointer is always the first operand to the AddPtr instruction and the integer is always the second, regardless of which was the first operand in the original expression. Second, you need to calculate the size of the pointer's referenced type at compile time, since the scale operand is a constant rather than a TACKY value.

The TACKY to subtract an integer from a pointer is almost identical; we just negate the index before we include it in AddPtr. We'll convert *<ptr>* - *<int>* to the TACKY in Listing 15-28.

```
<instructions for ptr>
p = <result of ptr>
<instructions for int>
i = <result of int>
j = Unary(Negate, i)
result = AddPtr(p, j, <size of referenced type of ptr>)
```

Listing 15-28: Subtracting an integer from a pointer in TACKY

Subtracting one pointer from another works a bit differently. First, we calculate the difference in bytes, using an ordinary Subtract instruction. Then, we divide this result by the number of bytes in one array element, to calculate the difference between the two pointers in terms of array indices. In other words, we'll convert *<ptr1>* - *<ptr2>* to the TACKY in Listing 15-29.

```
<instructions for ptr1>
p1 = <result of ptr1>
<instructions for ptr2>
p2 = <result of ptr2>
diff = Binary(Subtract, p1, p2)
result = Binary(Divide, diff, <size of referenced type of ptr1>)
```

Listing 15-29: Subtracting two pointers in TACKY

We'll calculate the size of the referenced type at compile time. You can use the type of either operand here, since the type checker already validated that they both have the same type.

We'll compare pointers exactly like arithmetic values, using the LessThan, LessOrEqual, GreaterThan, and GreaterOrEqual operators.

Subscripting

According to the C standard, the subscript expression *<ptr>*[*<int>*] is equivalent to *(*<ptr>* + *<int>*). So, to implement a subscript expression, we'll generate the TACKY for pointer addition from Listing 15-27 but return a DereferencedPointer(result) to the caller instead of a PlainOperand(result). Generating the right TACKY here is simple, but understanding why it works, especially for multidimensional arrays, is a little trickier. To explore this further, let's work through the example in Listing 15-30.

```
int arr[3][4];
--snip--
return arr[i][j];
```

Listing 15-30: Returning the result of a subscript operator

Listing 15-31 shows the TACKY implementation of the return statement in this example.

```
❶ tmp0 = GetAddress(arr)
  tmp1 = AddPtr(tmp0, i, 16)
  tmp2 = AddPtr(tmp1, j, 4)
❷ tmp3 = Load(tmp2)
  Return(tmp3)
```

Listing 15-31: Implementing Listing 15-30 in TACKY

First, we issue a GetAddress instruction to get a pointer to the first element in arr. Then, we issue two AddPtr instructions to calculate a pointer to the array element at arr[i][j]. Finally, we use a Load instruction to read that array element's current value into a temporary variable, which we return. Listing 15-31 is efficient, without any superfluous instructions. We saw earlier that array subscripting requires us to repeatedly get the addresses of array elements, perform pointer arithmetic, and dereference the result. But in this listing, we get an array's address only once, at the beginning ❶, and we use a Load instruction to dereference a pointer only once, at the end ❷. How does our strategy for TACKY generation produce this result?

Listing 15-32 gives the AST for the return statement in Listing 15-30. Let's figure out how each subexpression in this AST is converted to TACKY.

```
❶ Return(
    ❷ Subscript(
        ❸ AddrOf(
            ❹ Subscript(
                ❺ AddrOf(Var("arr")),
                  Var("i")
              )
          ),
          Var("j")
      )
  )
```

Listing 15-32: The AST for Listing 15-30

The AST includes the two AddrOf expressions we inserted during type checking. The inner one ❺ gets the address of arr, and the outer one ❸ gets the address of arr[i]. Of course, arr, i, and j would have been renamed during identifier resolution, but we'll ignore that detail in this example (and in the later examples in this chapter).

As always, we convert this AST to TACKY in postorder, processing each expression's operands before we process the expression itself. The first non-leaf AST node we process is the inner AddrOf expression, which takes the address of arr ❺. We convert it to a GetAddress instruction:

```
tmp0 = GetAddress(arr)
```

Next, to implement the inner Subscript expression ❹, we emit an AddPtr instruction:

```
tmp1 = AddPtr(tmp0, i, 16)
```

The scale here is 16 because tmp0 points to a four-int array. The second part of a subscript operation is dereferencing the result, so we'll return DereferencedPointer(tmp1) to the caller.

In the caller, we process the outer AddrOf expression ❸. When we take the address of a dereferenced pointer, the operations cancel out. Therefore, we return PlainOperand(tmp1) as the result of this expression, without emitting any further instructions.

Now we process the outer Subscript expression ❷. Once again, we emit an AddPtr instruction:

```
tmp2 = AddPtr(tmp1, j, 4)
```

We then return DereferencedPointer(tmp2) to the caller. Because this Subscript expression appears in a Return statement ❶, not an AddrOf or assignment expression, we lvalue convert this result. That means we emit a Load instruction:

```
tmp3 = Load(tmp2)
```

Now tmp3 contains the lvalue-converted result of the whole expression, so we return it:

```
Return(tmp3)
```

As this example illustrates, when we index into a multidimensional array the dereference operations and implicit address loads cancel each other out, without producing any extra instructions. Therefore, any subscript and dereference operators work out to pure pointer arithmetic in TACKY, without any Load or Store instructions, until we reach a scalar array element.

Compound Initializers

To process a compound initializer, we evaluate each scalar expression in the initializer and copy it to the appropriate location in memory with a CopyToOffset instruction. For example, we'll convert the initializer

```
long arr[3] = {11, 21, 31};
```

to the following sequence of instructions:

```
CopyToOffset(1l, "arr", 0)
CopyToOffset(2l, "arr", 8)
CopyToOffset(3l, "arr", 16)
```

Since a long is 8 bytes, the offset increases by eight with each element. Even when we process a nested initializer, we only need to copy the scalar values at the leaves to the correct memory locations. For example, we'll convert

```
long nested[2][3] = { {1l, 2l, 3l}, {4l, 5l, 6l} };
```

to:

```
CopyToOffset(1l, "nested", 0)
CopyToOffset(2l, "nested", 8)
CopyToOffset(3l, "nested", 16)
CopyToOffset(4l, "nested", 24)
CopyToOffset(5l, "nested", 32)
CopyToOffset(6l, "nested", 40)
```

This conversion is pretty straightforward, so I'll omit the pseudocode for it. I will note, however, that you should use the type information the type checker added to each compound initializer to calculate the offset of each element.

Tentative Array Definitions

Recall that when we convert symbol table entries to StaticVariable constructs, we initialize tentatively defined variables to zero. That goes for tentatively defined arrays too. You should use the new initializer we added in the previous section, ZeroInit(*n*), to initialize an *n*-byte array to zero.

You can also use ZeroInit to initialize tentatively defined scalar variables. For consistency, you should only use ZeroInit here if you're using it to initialize explicitly defined scalar variables to zero in the type checker.

TEST THE TACKY GENERATION STAGE

To test out TACKY generation, run:

```
$ ./test_compiler /path/to/your_compiler --chapter 15 --stage tacky
```

Assembly Generation

We won't introduce any new assembly instructions in this chapter. We will, however, introduce a new memory addressing mode, sometimes called *indexed addressing.* Right now, we can specify a memory operand with a base address in a register and a constant offset, like 4(%rax). Using indexed addressing, we can store the base address in one register and an index in another. We can also specify a scale, which must be one of the constants 1, 2, 4, or 8. Here's an example of indexed addressing in action:

```
movl    $5, (%rax, %rbx, 4)
```

To find the destination address of this movl instruction, the CPU will calculate RAX + RBX × 4. Then, it will store the 4-byte constant 5 at this address. This addressing mode is convenient for array accesses. If RAX holds the address of an array of int objects and RBX holds an index *i* into that array, the operand (%rax, %rbx, 4) specifies the element at index *i*.

USING INDEXED ADDRESSING FOR
GENERAL-PURPOSE ARITHMETIC

Although indexed addressing was designed for pointer arithmetic, it's an efficient way to add and multiply ordinary integers too. For example, the instruction

```
lea     (%rax, %rbx, 2), %rax
```

produces the same result as these instructions:

```
imulq   $2, %rbx
addq    %rbx, %rax
```

Our compiler uses indexed addressing only for pointer operations, but other compilers frequently use it for general-purpose integer arithmetic as well.

We'll add a new operand to support indexed addressing:

```
Indexed(reg base, reg index, int scale)
```

We'll also make a few other changes to the assembly AST to help with bookkeeping in later backend passes. For starters, we'll add another operand to represent aggregate objects that haven't been assigned a fixed address yet:

```
PseudoMem(identifier, int)
```

The PseudoMem operand serves a similar purpose to the existing Pseudo operand; it lets us represent variables in assembly before we've allocated registers or memory locations for them. The difference is that PseudoMem represents aggregate objects, which we'll always store in memory (even once we implement register allocation in Part III). Pseudo, on the other hand, represents scalar objects that could potentially be stored in registers. The PseudoMem operand also lets us specify a byte offset into the object in question. Note that the identifier in this operand designates an aggregate object, not a pointer to an aggregate object.

Next, we'll add a new assembly type to represent arrays. In assembly, we'll treat an array like an undifferentiated chunk of memory. We no longer need to track how many objects will be stored in that chunk of memory or what those objects' types will be. We do, however, care about its alignment and how much space it takes up, so we can allocate stack space for it. Therefore, we'll convert array types to a new ByteArray type:

```
assembly_type = Longword | Quadword | Double | ByteArray(int size, int alignment)
```

Finally, we'll adjust how we represent static variables. As in earlier compiler passes, we'll initialize a static variable with a list of static_init values, instead of just one:

```
StaticVariable(identifier name, bool global, int alignment, static_init* init_list)
```

Listing 15-33 highlights all the changes to the assembly AST in this chapter.

```
program = Program(top_level*)
assembly_type = Longword | Quadword | Double | ByteArray(int size, int alignment)
top_level = Function(identifier name, bool global, instruction* instructions)
          | StaticVariable(identifier name, bool global, int alignment, static_init* init_list)
          | StaticConstant(identifier name, int alignment, static_init init)
instruction = Mov(assembly_type, operand src, operand dst)
            | Movsx(operand src, operand dst)
            | MovZeroExtend(operand src, operand dst)
            | Lea(operand src, operand dst)
            | Cvttsd2si(assembly_type dst_type, operand src, operand dst)
            | Cvtsi2sd(assembly_type src_type, operand src, operand dst)
            | Unary(unary_operator, assembly_type, operand)
            | Binary(binary_operator, assembly_type, operand, operand)
            | Cmp(assembly_type, operand, operand)
            | Idiv(assembly_type, operand)
            | Div(assembly_type, operand)
            | Cdq(assembly_type)
            | Jmp(identifier)
            | JmpCC(cond_code, identifier)
            | SetCC(cond_code, operand)
            | Label(identifier)
            | Push(operand)
            | Call(identifier)
            | Ret
unary_operator = Neg | Not | Shr
binary_operator = Add | Sub | Mult | DivDouble | And | Or | Xor
operand = Imm(int) | Reg(reg) | Pseudo(identifier) | Memory(reg, int) | Data(identifier)
        | PseudoMem(identifier, int) | Indexed(reg base, reg index, int scale)
```

```
cond_code = E | NE | G | GE | L | LE | A | AE | B | BE
reg = AX | CX | DX | DI | SI | R8 | R9 | R10 | R11 | SP | BP
    | XMM0 | XMM1 | XMM2 | XMM3 | XMM4 | XMM5 | XMM6 | XMM7 | XMM14 | XMM15
```

Listing 15-33: The assembly AST with support for aggregate objects and indexed addressing

Once we've updated the assembly AST, we'll update the conversion from TACKY to assembly.

Converting TACKY to Assembly

First, we'll deal with TACKY variables of array type. To distinguish these from scalar values, we'll convert them to PseudoMem operands, instead of Pseudo operands. For example, if arr is an array, we'll convert

```
GetAddress(Var("arr"), Var("dst"))
```

to:

```
Lea(PseudoMem("arr", 0), Pseudo("dst"))
```

Whenever we convert an aggregate TACKY Var to assembly, we'll use an offset of zero, in order to designate the whole object.

Next, let's deal with the new CopyToOffset and AddPtr instructions. We'll use a PseudoMem operand with the appropriate offset to represent the destination of a CopyToOffset instruction. Therefore, we'll convert

```
CopyToOffset(src, dst, offset)
```

to:

```
Mov(<src type>, src, PseudoMem(dst, offset))
```

We'll implement AddPtr with an Lea instruction using the new Indexed operand. The details will vary depending on the scale and index. First, let's consider the case where the scale is 1, 2, 4, or 8. We'll convert

```
AddPtr(ptr, index, scale, dst)
```

to Listing 15-34.

```
Mov(Quadword, ptr, Reg(AX))
Mov(Quadword, index, Reg(DX))
Lea(Indexed(AX, DX, scale), dst)
```

Listing 15-34: Implementing AddPtr in assembly

First, we copy ptr and index into registers; I've used RAX and RDX here, but anything other than the callee-saved registers or our scratch registers will do. Then, we emit an Lea instruction to compute ptr + index * scale and store the result in dst.

The scale of `AddPtr` may not be one of the four values that `Indexed` supports, especially if we're indexing into a multidimensional array instead of an array of scalar objects. In that case, we'll use a separate instruction to multiply the scale by the index, as Listing 15-35 illustrates.

```
Mov(Quadword, ptr, Reg(AX))
Mov(Quadword, index, Reg(DX))
Binary(Mult, Quadword, Imm(scale), Reg(DX))
Lea(Indexed(AX, DX, 1), dst)
```

Listing 15-35: Implementing `AddPtr` in assembly with a nonstandard scale

If the index operand is a constant, we can save an instruction by computing index * scale at compile time. Then, we'll generate just the two instructions in Listing 15-36.

```
Mov(Quadword, ptr, Reg(AX))
Lea(Memory(AX, index * scale), dst)
```

Listing 15-36: Implementing `AddPtr` with a constant index

Next, we'll deal with pointer comparisons. We'll implement these exactly like unsigned integer comparisons, using the unsigned condition codes: A, AE, B, and BE.

Finally, let's talk about the alignment requirements for arrays. There are a couple of cases where we need to calculate an array's alignment: when we convert a `StaticVariable` of array type from TACKY to assembly (a `StaticVariable` in assembly includes an `alignment` field), and when we convert a frontend symbol table entry of array type to the corresponding entry in the backend symbol table. The assembly type of each array in the backend symbol table will be a `ByteArray` with the appropriate size and alignment. The size will be the size of the array's element type in bytes, multiplied by the number of elements. The rules for calculating alignment are a bit less obvious.

If an array is smaller than 16 bytes, it has the same alignment as its scalar elements. For example, an array with type `int[2]` and an array with type `int[2][1]` both have an alignment of 4. If an array-type variable is 16 bytes or larger, its alignment is always 16, no matter what type its elements are. This requirement makes it possible to use SSE instructions to operate on multiple array elements at once. We don't use SSE instructions this way, but we need to maintain ABI compatibility with other object files that might.

Note that this alignment requirement applies only to variables, not to nested arrays. For example, if we declare the variable

```
int nested[3][5];
```

then `nested` needs to start at a 16-byte-aligned address because its total size is 60 bytes. But its first and second elements start at 20 and 40 bytes, respectively, from the start of `nested`, so they aren't 16-byte aligned, even though each of these elements is also larger than 16 bytes.

Tables 15-1 through 15-5 summarize this chapter's updates to this compiler pass; as usual, new constructs and changes to the conversions for existing constructs are bolded.

Table 15-1: Converting Top-Level TACKY Constructs to Assembly

TACKY top-level construct	Assembly top-level construct
StaticVariable(name, global, t, **init_list**)	StaticVariable(name, global, *<alignment of t>*, init_list)

Table 15-2: Converting TACKY Instructions to Assembly

TACKY instruction		Assembly instructions
AddPtr(ptr, index, scale, dst)	**Constant index**	Mov(Quadword, ptr, Reg(*<R>*)) Lea(Memory(*<R>*, index * scale), dst)
	Variable index and scale of 1, 2, 4, or 8	Mov(Quadword, ptr, Reg(*<R1>*)) Mov(Quadword, index, Reg(*<R2>*)) Lea(Indexed(*<R1>*, *<R2>*, scale), dst)
	Variable index and other scale	Mov(Quadword, ptr, Reg(*<R1>*)) Mov(Quadword, index, Reg(*<R2>*)) Binary(Mult, Quadword, Imm(scale), Reg(*<R2>*)) Lea(Indexed(*<R1>*, *<R2>*, 1), dst)
CopyToOffset(src, dst, offset)		Mov(*<src type>*, src, PseudoMem(dst, offset))

Table 15-3: Converting TACKY Comparisons to Assembly

TACKY comparison		Assembly condition code
LessThan	Signed	L
	Unsigned, **pointer**, or double	B
LessOrEqual	Signed	LE
	Unsigned, **pointer**, or double	BE
GreaterThan	Signed	G
	Unsigned, **pointer**, or double	A
GreaterOrEqual	Signed	GE
	Unsigned, **pointer**, or double	AE

Table 15-4: Converting TACKY Operands to Assembly

TACKY operand		Assembly operand
Var(identifier)	**Scalar value**	Pseudo(identifier)
	Aggregate value	PseudoMem(identifier, 0)

Table 15-5: Converting Types to Assembly

Source type		Assembly type	Alignment
Array(element, size)	Variables that are 16 bytes or larger	ByteArray(*<size of element>* * size, 16)	16
	Everything else	ByteArray(*<size of element>* * size, *<alignment of element>*)	Same alignment as element

Next, we'll replace PseudoMem operands with concrete addresses.

Replacing PseudoMem Operands

We can't call this pass "pseudoregister replacement" anymore, because we're replacing aggregate values too. Just like we'll allocate 4 bytes of stack space for a Longword and 8 bytes for a Quadword, we'll allocate *size* bytes for an object with type ByteArray(*size, alignment*). As usual, we'll round down the array's address to the appropriate alignment.

Once an array has been assigned a memory address, we'll replace any PseudoMem operands that refer to it. A PseudoMem operand includes an offset from the start of the array, and the array's concrete address includes an offset from the address in RBP. We'll add these two offsets to construct a new concrete memory address. For example, suppose we encounter the following instruction:

```
Mov(Longword, Imm(3), PseudoMem("arr", 4))
```

Let's say that we previously assigned arr the stack address -12(%rbp). We compute −12 + 4 to determine that our new, concrete operand is -8(%rbp). We then rewrite the instruction accordingly:

```
Mov(Longword, Imm(3), Memory(BP, -8))
```

To access an array with static storage duration, we use the existing Data operand. If arr is a static array, we convert

```
PseudoMem("arr", 0)
```

to:

```
Data("arr")
```

If we encountered PseudoMem("arr", *n*) for any nonzero *n*, we'd be in trouble, because the Data operand doesn't include an offset. Luckily, this situation won't come up. At the moment, we use PseudoMem operands with nonzero offsets only to initialize arrays with automatic storage duration, not to access arrays with static storage duration.

RIP-relative addressing *does* support constant offsets—for example, foo+4(%rip) represents the address 4 bytes past the symbol foo—but we can't represent these offsets in the assembly AST yet. We'll add them in Chapter 18 to support operations on structures.

Fixing Up Instructions

We didn't introduce any new instructions, so we don't need any new instruction fix-up rules. This pass must recognize that the new Indexed operand specifies a memory address and therefore can't be used where a register or immediate value is required. Otherwise, we don't need to change anything.

TEST THE ASSEMBLY GENERATION STAGE

To test that your compiler can generate assembly programs without throwing an error, run:

```
$ ./test_compiler /path/to/your_compiler --chapter 15 --stage codegen
```

Code Emission

We'll make four small additions to this stage. First, we'll emit the new Indexed operand. Second, we'll emit the static ZeroInit initializer as a .zero assembly directive. For example, we'll emit ZeroInit(32) as:

```
.zero 32
```

Third, if a variable's only initializer is ZeroInit, we'll write it to the BSS section instead of the data section.

And finally, when we define a static variable, we'll emit each item in the associated initializer list. The file scope declaration

```
int arr[4] = {1, 2, 3};
```

will ultimately be translated to the assembly in Listing 15-37.

```
    .globl arr
    .data
    .align 16
arr:
    .long 1
    .long 2
    .long 3
    .zero 4
```

Listing 15-37: Initializing a static array in assembly

Note that we initialize the last element of this array to zero because it wasn't initialized explicitly.

Tables 15-6 through 15-8 summarize these additions to the code emission stage, with new constructs and changes to the way we emit existing constructs bolded.

Table 15-6: Formatting Top-Level Assembly Constructs

Assembly top-level construct		Output
StaticVariable(name, global, alignment, **init_list**)	Integer initialized to zero, **or** **any variable initialized only with** ZeroInit	*\<global-directive>* .bss *\<alignment-directive>* *\<name>*: ***\<init_list>***
	All other variables	*\<global-directive>* .data *\<alignment-directive>* *\<name>*: *\<init_list>*

Table 15-7: Formatting Static Initializers

Static initializer	Output
ZeroInit(n)	**.zero** *\<n>*

Table 15-8: Formatting Assembly Operands

Assembly operand	Output
Indexed(reg1, reg2, int)	(*\<reg1>*, *\<reg2>*, *\<int>*)

After making these changes, you can test out your compiler.

TEST THE WHOLE COMPILER

To test out the whole compiler, run:

```
$ ./test_compiler /path/to/your_compiler --chapter 15
```

Summary

You've just implemented your first aggregate type! In this chapter, you learned how to parse array declarators and compound initializers. In the type checker, you made implicit conversions from arrays to pointers explicit and analyzed the types of pointer arithmetic expressions. During TACKY generation, you relied on those conversions and that type information to handle operations on pointers cleanly, regardless of whether they point to arrays or scalar values. And on the backend, you added new, more flexible ways to address values in memory.

In the next chapter, you'll implement three more integer types: char, signed char, and unsigned char. You'll also implement string literals, which can be either array initializers or char arrays that decay to pointers, depending on context. Because you've already implemented integer types, pointers, and arrays, a lot of the groundwork for the work you'll do there is already in place.

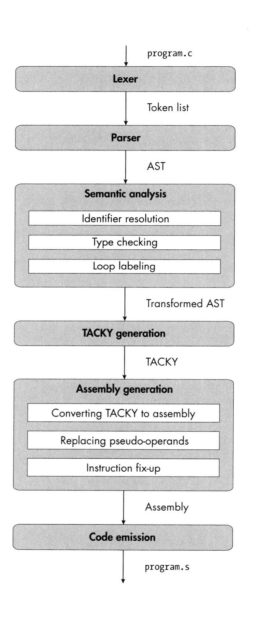

16

CHARACTERS AND STRINGS

In this chapter, you'll implement three new integer types: char, signed char, and unsigned char. These are the *character types*, which have a size of 1 byte. Because your compiler already supports signed and unsigned integers in multiple sizes, you can add these new types with minimal effort. You'll also add support for string literals and character constants. String literals play a weird role in C: sometimes they behave like compound initializers, and at other times they represent constant char arrays. To support the latter case, you'll store constant strings alongside variables in the symbol table, and you'll introduce static constants as a top-level construct in TACKY.

At the end of the chapter, we'll compile "Hello, World!" In Chapter 9, we compiled a version of this program that printed one character at a time. This time, we'll compile a more reasonable version that prints out an entire string. Before we get started, I'll give you a bit of background information: I'll first touch on a few notable differences between the character types and the other integers, then describe how strings work in C and assembly.

Character Traits

The most surprising thing about the character types is that there are three of them. There's no distinction between int and signed int or between long and signed long, but the specifiers char and signed char refer to two distinct types. Whether "plain" char is signed or unsigned is implementation-defined. We'll follow the System V ABI, which specifies that char is signed.

Even though char and signed char will behave identically in our implementation, the fact that they're different types has real consequences. For instance, Listing 16-1 is illegal because it declares the same global variable as both a char and a signed char.

```
char c;
signed char c;
```

Listing 16-1: Conflicting file scope variable declarations with different character types

Declaring a global variable as both an int and a signed int, on the other hand, is perfectly legal, since both declarations specify the same type.

The character types also follow slightly different type conversion rules than the other integer types. When a character is used in a unary +, -, or ~ operation; a bitwise binary operation; or the usual arithmetic conversions, it's first converted to an int. These conversions are called the *integer promotions*. (If int can't fit every value of a particular character type, the character is converted to unsigned int instead. In our implementation, int can hold every value of every character type, so this is a moot point. Of course, we can also ignore the typing rules for operations we haven't implemented, like unary + and the bitwise binary operations; I'm mentioning them here only for the sake of completeness.)

There's one more noteworthy difference between characters and other integers: in C17, there are no scalar constants of character type. Tokens like 'a' all have type int, despite being called "character constants." There are constants with *wide character types* like char16_t, char32_t, and wchar_t, which are intended to represent multibyte characters, but we won't implement them.

NOTE *C23 introduces u8 character constants with type* unsigned char. *These represent 1-byte UTF-8 characters.*

String Literals

Throughout this chapter, I'll distinguish between string literals and strings. A *string literal* is an expression that appears in the source code, like "abc". A *string* is an object that lives in memory—specifically, a null-terminated char array. Some strings can't be modified at runtime; I'll call these *constant strings*, although this isn't a standard term.

You can use a string literal in two distinct ways. First, it can initialize an array of any character type:

```
signed char array[4] = "abc";
```

We'll include a terminating null byte if there's space and omit it if there isn't. This coincides with our usual rules for array initialization: if the initializer is shorter than the target object, we pad out the remainder with zeros. Therefore, the previous declaration is equivalent to:

```
signed char array[4] = {'a', 'b', 'c', 0};
```

In Listing 16-2, on the other hand, we leave out the null byte in array1 because the array isn't large enough to include it. Therefore, array1 and array2 have identical contents.

```
char array1[3] = "abc";
char array2[3] = {'a', 'b', 'c'};
```

Listing 16-2: Using a string literal as an array initializer without the null byte

When a string literal appears anywhere other than as an array initializer, it designates a constant string. In this context, string literals act a lot like other expressions of array type. They decay to pointers like other array expressions, so you can subscript them or assign them to char * objects. The following declaration initializes the variable str_ptr with the address of the first character in the constant string "abc":

```
char *str_ptr = "abc";
```

String literals are also lvalues, so they support the & operator. Here, we use this operator to take the address of the constant string "abc", then assign it to array_ptr:

```
char (*array_ptr)[4] = &"abc";
```

The only difference from the previous example is that the string literal doesn't undergo array decay. We end up with a pointer to the whole string, with type char (*)[4], instead of a pointer to its first element, with type char *. In both examples, we treat "abc" like any other expression of array type.

Unlike other arrays, constant strings are, well, constant. Attempting to modify them, as in Listing 16-3, produces undefined behavior.

```
char *ptr = "abc";
ptr[0] = 'x';
```

Listing 16-3: Illegally modifying a constant string

Although this code compiles, it will probably throw a runtime error, because most C implementations—including ours—store constant strings in read-only memory. (The const qualifier, which we won't implement, informs the compiler that an object cannot be modified. If Listing 16-3 were part of a real C program, it would be a good idea to add a const qualifier to ptr.)

Let's look at one more example, shown in Listing 16-4, to clarify the difference between string literals that designate constant strings and string literals that initialize arrays.

```
char arr[3] = "abc";
arr[0] = 'x';
```

Listing 16-4: Legally modifying an array initialized from a string literal

Unlike Listing 16-3, this code is perfectly legal. In Listing 16-3, ptr points to the start of the constant string "abc". In Listing 16-4, on the other hand, we use each character of the string literal "abc" to initialize one element of arr, which is an ordinary, non-constant char array.

Both cases are easier to understand once we see how they translate to assembly.

Working with Strings in Assembly

We'll use two different assembly directives to initialize strings in assembly. The .ascii and .asciz directives both tell the assembler to write an ASCII string to the object file, much like .quad tells it to write a quadword. The difference is that .asciz will include a terminating null byte and .ascii won't. The three declarations

```
static char null_terminated[4] = "abc";
static char not_null_terminated[3] = "abc";
static char extra_padding[5] = "abc";
```

correspond to the assembly in Listing 16-5.

```
        .data
null_terminated:
        .asciz "abc"
not_null_terminated:
        .ascii "abc"
extra_padding:
        .asciz "abc"
        .zero 1
```

Listing 16-5: Initializing three static char arrays from string literals in assembly

Because null_terminated is long enough to accommodate a null byte, we initialize it with the .asciz directive. We use .ascii to initialize not_null _terminated so we don't go past the bounds of the array. Since extra_padding needs two zero bytes to reach the correct length, we write a null-terminated string, then write an extra zero byte with the .zero directive. Note that none of these variables needs an .align directive. The character types are all 1-byte aligned, so arrays of characters are too. (Array variables containing 16 or more characters are the exception; they're 16-byte aligned, like all array variables that are 16 bytes or larger.)

The .ascii and .asciz directives initialize objects with static storage duration. Next, let's consider Listing 16-6, which initializes a non-static array.

```
int main(void) {
    char letters[6] = "abcde";
    return 0;
}
```

Listing 16-6: Using a string literal to initialize a non-static array

Listing 16-7 illustrates one way to initialize letters in assembly, by copying "abcde" onto the stack one byte at a time.

```
movb    $97,  -8(%rbp)
movb    $98,  -7(%rbp)
movb    $99,  -6(%rbp)
movb    $100, -5(%rbp)
movb    $101, -4(%rbp)
movb    $0,   -3(%rbp)
```

Listing 16-7: Initializing a non-static char array in assembly

The characters 'a', 'b', 'c', 'd', and 'e' have ASCII values 97, 98, 99, 100, and 101, respectively. Assuming letters starts at stack address -8(%rbp), the instructions in Listing 16-7 copy each character to the appropriate location in the array. The b suffix in each movb instruction indicates that it operates on a single byte.

Listing 16-8 demonstrates a more efficient approach. We initialize the first 4 bytes of this string with a single movl instruction, then use movb instructions to initialize the remaining 2 bytes.

```
movl    $1684234849, -8(%rbp)
movb    $101, -4(%rbp)
movb    $0,   -3(%rbp)
```

Listing 16-8: A more efficient way to initialize a non-static char array in assembly

We get 1684234849 when we interpret the first 4 bytes of our string as an integer. (I'll discuss how we get this integer in more detail later in the chapter.) This listing has the same effect as Listing 16-7, but it saves us a few instructions.

Next, let's look at constant strings. We write these to read-only sections of the object file, just like floating-point constants. On Linux, we store constant strings in `.rodata`; on macOS, we store them in the `.cstring` section. Consider the code fragment in Listing 16-9, which returns a pointer to the start of a constant string.

```
return "A profound statement.";
```

Listing 16-9: Returning a pointer to the start of a string

We'll generate a unique label for this string, then define it in the appropriate section. Listing 16-10 gives the resulting assembly.

```
    .section .rodata
.Lstring.0:
    .asciz "A profound statement."
```

Listing 16-10: Defining a constant string in assembly

Constant strings are always null-terminated, since they don't need to fit into any particular array dimensions. Once we've defined a constant string, we can access it with RIP-relative addressing, like any other static object. In this particular example, we want to return the string's address, so we'll load it into RAX with this instruction:

```
leaq    .Lstring.0(%rip), %rax
```

Finally, let's see how to initialize a static pointer with a string literal, like in Listing 16-11.

```
static char *ptr = "A profound statement.";
```

Listing 16-11: Initializing a static char * from a string literal

We'll define the string the same way as in Listing 16-10. However, we can't load it into ptr with an `lea` instruction. Because ptr is static, it must be initialized before the program starts. Luckily, the `.quad` directive accepts labels as well as constants. Listing 16-12 illustrates how to initialize ptr with this directive.

```
    .data
    .align 8
ptr:
    .quad .Lstring.0
```

Listing 16-12: Initializing a static variable with the address of a static constant

The directive `.quad .Lstring.0` tells the assembler and linker to write the address of `.Lstring.0`.

As a side note, it's possible to initialize any static pointer this way, not just pointers to strings. While our implementation doesn't accept expressions like &x as static initializers, a more complete compiler might translate

```
static int x = 10;
static int *ptr = &x;
```

into:

```
        .data
        .align 4
x:
        .long 10
        .align 8
ptr:
        .quad x
```

At this point, you know enough about how to use strings in C and assembly to get started. The first step is to extend the lexer to recognize string literals and character constants.

The Lexer

You'll add three new tokens in this chapter:

char A keyword, used to specify character types

Character constants Individual characters, like 'a' and '\n'

String literals Sequences of characters, like "Hello, World!"

A character constant consists of one character (like a) or escape sequence (like \n) wrapped in single quotes. Section 6.4.4.4 of the C standard defines a set of escape sequences to represent special characters. Table 16-1 lists these escape sequences and their ASCII codes.

Table 16-1: Escape Sequences for Special Characters

Escape sequence	Description	ASCII code
\'	Single quote	39
\"	Double quote	34
\?	Question mark	63
\\	Backslash	92
\a	Audible alert	7
\b	Backspace	8
\f	Form feed	12
\n	New line	10
\r	Carriage return	13
\t	Horizontal tab	9
\v	Vertical tab	11

The new line, single quote ('), and backslash (\) characters can't appear on their own as character constants and must be escaped. Any other character can be used directly as a character constant as long as it's in the *source character set*, the complete set of characters that can appear in a source file.

The source character set is implementation-defined, but it has to include at least the *basic source character set*, which is specified in section 5.2.1 of the C standard. In our implementation, the source character set includes all the printable ASCII characters, plus the required control characters: the new line, horizontal tab, vertical tab, and form feed. You don't need to explicitly reject characters outside of this set; you can simply assume that they never show up in source files.

Some of the characters in Table 16-1, like the audible alert (\a) and backspace (\b), aren't in our source character set, so they can be represented only by escape characters. Other characters, including the double quote ("), question mark (?), form feed, and horizontal and vertical tabs, are in the source character set; they can be escaped in character constants, but they don't have to be. For example, the character constants '?' and '\?' are equivalent; they both represent the question mark character. The new line, single quote, and backslash are all in the source character set but still need to be escaped.

We can recognize character constants with the truly egregious regular expression in Listing 16-13.

```
'([^'\\\n]|\\['"?\\abfnrtv])'
```

Listing 16-13: The regular expression to recognize a character constant

Let's break this down. The first alternative in the parenthesized expression, the character class [^'\\\n], matches any single character except for a single quote, backslash, or new line. We have to escape the backslash, because it's a control character in PCRE regexes as well as in C string literals. Similarly, we use the escape sequence \n in this regex to match a literal new line character. The second alternative, \\['"?\\abfnrtv], matches an escape sequence. The first \\ matches a single backslash, and the character class that follows includes every character that can follow the backslash in an escape sequence. The whole thing must start and end with single quotes.

A string literal consists of a possibly empty sequence of characters and escape sequences, wrapped in double quotes. A single quote can appear on its own in a string literal, but a double quote must be escaped. Listing 16-14 shows the regular expression to recognize a string literal.

```
"([^"\\\n]|\\['"\\?abfnrtv])*"
```

Listing 16-14: The regular expression to recognize a string literal

Here, [^"\\\n] matches any single character except a double quote, backslash, or new line. Like in Listing 16-13, the second alternative matches every escape sequence. We apply the * quantifier to the whole parenthesized expression because it can repeat zero or more times, and we delimit it all with double quotes.

After lexing a string literal or character token, you need to unescape it. In other words, you need to convert every escape sequence in that token to the corresponding ASCII character. You can do that either now or in the parser.

The standard defines a few other types of string literals and character constants that we won't implement. In particular, we won't support hexadecimal escape sequences like \xff, octal escape sequences like \012, or multicharacter constants like 'ab'. We also won't support any of the types or constants used for non-ASCII encodings, like wide character types, wide string literals, or UTF-8 string literals.

TEST THE LEXER

To test out the lexer, run:

```
$ ./test_compiler /path/to/your_compiler --chapter 16 --stage lex
```

Your lexer should reject every test case in *tests/chapter_16/invalid_lex*. These tests include invalid escape sequences, unescaped special characters, and unterminated character constants and string literals. The lexer should successfully process all the other test cases for this chapter.

The Parser

We'll extend the AST definition in three ways. First, we'll add char, signed char, and unsigned char types. Second, we'll add a new kind of expression to represent string literals. Third, we'll extend the const AST node to represent constants with character types:

```
const = ConstInt(int) | ConstLong(int) | ConstUInt(int) | ConstULong(int)
      | ConstDouble(double) | ConstChar(int) | ConstUChar(int)
```

These new constant constructors are a little unusual because they don't correspond to constant literals that actually appear in C programs. Character constants like 'a' have type int, so the parser will convert them to ConstInt nodes; it won't use the new ConstChar and ConstUChar constructors at all. But we'll need these constructors later, when we pad out partially initialized character arrays during type checking and when we initialize character arrays in TACKY.

Listing 16-15 gives the complete AST definition, with this chapter's changes bolded.

```
program = Program(declaration*)
declaration = FunDecl(function_declaration) | VarDecl(variable_declaration)
variable_declaration = (identifier name, initializer? init,
                        type var_type, storage_class?)
function_declaration = (identifier name, identifier* params, block? body,
                        type fun_type, storage_class?)
initializer = SingleInit(exp) | CompoundInit(initializer*)
type = Char | SChar | UChar | Int | Long | UInt | ULong | Double
     | FunType(type* params, type ret)
     | Pointer(type referenced)
     | Array(type element, int size)
storage_class = Static | Extern
block_item = S(statement) | D(declaration)
block = Block(block_item*)
for_init = InitDecl(variable_declaration) | InitExp(exp?)
statement = Return(exp)
          | Expression(exp)
          | If(exp condition, statement then, statement? else)
          | Compound(block)
          | Break
          | Continue
          | While(exp condition, statement body)
          | DoWhile(statement body, exp condition)
          | For(for_init init, exp? condition, exp? post, statement body)
          | Null
exp = Constant(const)
    | String(string)
    | Var(identifier)
    | Cast(type target_type, exp)
    | Unary(unary_operator, exp)
    | Binary(binary_operator, exp, exp)
    | Assignment(exp, exp)
    | Conditional(exp condition, exp, exp)
    | FunctionCall(identifier, exp* args)
    | Dereference(exp)
    | AddrOf(exp)
    | Subscript(exp, exp)
unary_operator = Complement | Negate | Not
binary_operator = Add | Subtract | Multiply | Divide | Remainder | And | Or
                | Equal | NotEqual | LessThan | LessOrEqual
                | GreaterThan | GreaterOrEqual
const = ConstInt(int) | ConstLong(int) | ConstUInt(int) | ConstULong(int)
      | ConstDouble(double) | ConstChar(int) | ConstUChar(int)
```

Listing 16-15: The abstract syntax tree with character types, character constants, and string literals

It's tempting to extend const, rather than exp, to include string literals, but string literals are distinct enough from other kinds of constants that it's easiest to define them separately. For example, the type checker will need to handle them differently than other constants when it processes initializers.

Parsing Type Specifiers

We'll need to extend parse_type, which converts a list of type specifiers into a type AST node, to handle character types. I won't provide the pseudocode for this, because the logic is pretty simple. If char appears in a declaration by itself, it specifies the plain char type. If it appears with the unsigned keyword, it specifies the unsigned char type. If it appears with the signed keyword, it specifies the signed char type. As usual, the order of type specifiers doesn't matter. It's illegal for char to appear in a declaration with any other type specifier.

Parsing Character Constants

The parser should convert each character constant token to a ConstInt with the appropriate ASCII value. It should convert the token 'a' to ConstInt(97), '\n' to ConstInt(10), and so on.

Parsing String Literals

The parser should unescape string literals if the lexer hasn't done that already. Each character in the string literal, including characters represented by escape sequences in the original source code, must be represented as a single byte internally. Otherwise, we'll calculate inaccurate string lengths in the type checker and initialize arrays with incorrect values at runtime.

Adjacent string literal tokens should be concatenated into a single String AST node. For example, the parser should convert the statement

```
return "foo" "bar";
```

to the AST node Return(String("foobar")).

Putting It All Together

Listing 16-16 defines the complete grammar, with this chapter's changes bolded.

```
<program> ::= { <declaration> }
<declaration> ::= <variable-declaration> | <function-declaration>
<variable-declaration> ::= { <specifier> }+ <declarator> [ "=" <initializer> ] ";"
<function-declaration> ::= { <specifier> }+ <declarator> ( <block> | ";")
<declarator> ::= "*" <declarator> | <direct-declarator>
<direct-declarator> ::= <simple-declarator> [ <declarator-suffix> ]
<declarator-suffix> ::= <param-list> | { "[" <const> "]" }+
<param-list> ::= "(" "void" ")" | "(" <param> { "," <param> } ")"
<param> ::= { <type-specifier> }+ <declarator>
<simple-declarator> ::= <identifier> | "(" <declarator> ")"
<type-specifier> ::= "int" | "long" | "unsigned" | "signed" | "double" | ❶ "char"
<specifier> ::= <type-specifier> | "static" | "extern"
<block> ::= "{" { <block-item> } "}"
<block-item> ::= <statement> | <declaration>
```

```
<initializer> ::= <exp> | "{" <initializer> { "," <initializer> } [ "," ] "}"
<for-init> ::= <variable-declaration> | [ <exp> ] ";"
<statement> ::= "return" <exp> ";"
              | <exp> ";"
              | "if" "(" <exp> ")" <statement> [ "else" <statement> ]
              | <block>
              | "break" ";"
              | "continue" ";"
              | "while" "(" <exp> ")" <statement>
              | "do" <statement> "while" "(" <exp> ")" ";"
              | "for" "(" <for-init> [ <exp> ] ";" [ <exp> ] ")" <statement>
              | ";"
<exp> ::= <unary-exp> | <exp> <binop> <exp> | <exp> "?" <exp> ":" <exp>
<unary-exp> ::= <unop> <unary-exp>
              | "(" { <type-specifier> }+ [ <abstract-declarator> ] ")" <unary-exp>
              | <postfix-exp>
<postfix-exp> ::= <primary-exp> { "[" <exp> "]" }
<primary-exp> ::= <const> | <identifier> | "(" <exp> ")" | ❷ { <string> }+
                | <identifier> "(" [ <argument-list> ] ")"
<argument-list> ::= <exp> { "," <exp> }
<abstract-declarator> ::= "*" [ <abstract-declarator> ]
                        | <direct-abstract-declarator>
<direct-abstract-declarator> ::= "(" <abstract-declarator> ")" { "[" <const> "]" }
                               | { "[" <const> "]" }+
<unop> ::= "-" | "~" | "!" | "*" | "&"
<binop> ::= "-" | "+" | "*" | "/" | "%" | "&&" | "||"
          | "==" | "!=" | "<" | "<=" | ">" | ">=" | "="
<const> ::= <int> | <long> | <uint> | <ulong> | <double> | ❸ <char>
<identifier> ::= ? An identifier token ?
<string> ::= ? A string token ? ❹
<int> ::= ? An int token ?
<char> ::= ? A char token ? ❺
<long> ::= ? An int or long token ?
<uint> ::= ? An unsigned int token ?
<ulong> ::= ? An unsigned int or unsigned long token ?
<double> ::= ? A floating-point constant token ?
```

Listing 16-16: The grammar with character types, character constants, and string literals

The bolded additions to the grammar correspond to the three changes to the parser we just discussed. The grammar now includes a "char" type specifier ❶ and <string> ❹ and <char> tokens ❺. We recognize a sequence of one or more string literals as a primary expression ❷ and a character token as a constant ❸.

TEST THE PARSER

To test your parser, run:

```
$ ./test_compiler /path/to/your_compiler --chapter 16 --stage parse
```

The Type Checker

For the most part, the type checker can treat characters like the other integer types. They follow the same typing rules and support the same operations. The integer promotions are the one exception to this pattern, so we'll implement them in this section. We'll also introduce static initializers for the character types.

String literals are more challenging to type check, particularly when they appear in initializers. We'll need to track whether each string should be used directly or converted to a pointer and which strings should be terminated with null bytes. We'll add a few new constructs to the symbol table to represent each of these cases.

Characters

We'll promote character types to int as part of the usual arithmetic conversions. Listing 16-17 shows how to perform this promotion in get_common_type.

```
get_common_type(type1, type2):
    if type1 is a character type:
        type1 = Int
    if type2 is a character type:
        type2 = Int
    --snip--
```

Listing 16-17: Applying the integer promotions during the usual arithmetic conversions

After promoting the types of both operands, we'll find their common type as usual. We'll also promote the operands of the unary - and ~ operations. Listing 16-18 demonstrates how to promote a negated operand.

```
typecheck_exp(e, symbols):
    match e with
    | --snip--
    | Unary(Negate, inner) ->
        typed_inner = typecheck_and_convert(inner, symbols)
        inner_t = get_type(typed_inner)
        if inner_t is a pointer type:
            fail("Can't negate a pointer")
      ❶ if inner_t is a character type:
            typed_inner = convert_to(typed_inner, Int)
        unary_exp = Unary(Negate, typed_inner)
      ❷ return set_type(unary_exp, get_type(typed_inner))
```

Listing 16-18: Applying the integer promotions to a negation expression

First, we make sure the operand isn't a pointer (we introduced this validation in Chapter 14). Then, we apply the integer promotions. We check whether the operand is one of the character types ❶; if it is, we convert it to Int and then negate the promoted value. The result of the expression has the same type as its promoted operand ❷. We'll handle ~ the same way, so I won't provide the pseudocode for that here.

We'll always recognize characters as integer types during type checking. For example, we'll accept characters as operands in ~ and % expressions and as indices in pointer arithmetic. Because all integer types are also arithmetic types, we'll permit implicit conversions between the character types and any other arithmetic type in convert_by_assignment.

We'll add two static initializers for the character types. Listing 16-19 gives the updated definition of static_init.

```
static_init = IntInit(int) | LongInit(int) | UIntInit(int) | ULongInit(int)
            | CharInit(int) | UCharInit(int)
            | DoubleInit(double) | ZeroInit(int bytes)
```

Listing 16-19: Adding the static initializers for character types

Since signed char and plain char are both signed types, we'll use CharInit to initialize both of them. We'll convert each initializer to the type it initializes according to the type conversion rules we covered in Chapters 11 and 12. For example, if an unsigned char is initialized with a value greater than 255, we'll reduce its value modulo 256.

Finally, we'll make one small, straightforward update to the way we type check compound initializers for non-static arrays. (We'll handle string literals that initialize arrays as a separate case in the next section.) In the previous chapter, we dealt with partly initialized arrays by padding out the remaining elements with zeros. I suggested writing a zero_initializer helper function to generate these zeroed-out initializers. Now we can extend that function to emit ConstChar and ConstUChar to zero out elements of character type.

String Literals in Expressions

When we encounter a string literal in an expression, rather than in an array initializer, we'll annotate it as a char array of the appropriate size. Listing 16-20 shows how to handle string literals in typecheck_exp.

```
typecheck_exp(e, symbols):
    match e with
    | --snip--
    | String(s) -> return set_type(e, Array(Char, length(s) + 1))
```

Listing 16-20: Type checking a string literal

Note that the array size accounts for a terminating null byte. The type checker already handles implicit conversions from arrays to pointers in typecheck_and_convert. Now typecheck_and_convert will convert string literals to pointers too, since they also have array type.

Next, we'll update the type checker to recognize String expressions as lvalues, along with variables, subscript operators, and dereference expressions. This allows programs to take their address with the & operator.

That takes care of string literals in ordinary expressions; now we'll type check string literals in initializers.

String Literals Initializing Non-static Variables

Usually, we type check SingleInit constructs with typecheck_and_convert, which converts values of array type to pointers. This approach correctly handles string literals that initialize pointers. But when a string literal is used to initialize an array, we'll type check it differently. Listing 16-21 shows how to handle this case.

```
typecheck_init(target_type, init, symbols):
    match target_type, init with
    | Array(elem_t, size), SingleInit(String(s)) ->
    ❶ if elem_t is not a character type:
          fail("Can't initialize a non-character type with a string literal")
    ❷ if length(s) > size:
          fail("Too many characters in string literal")
    ❸ return set_type(init, target_type)
    | --snip--
```

Listing 16-21: Type checking a string literal that initializes an array

First, we make sure the target type is an array of characters, since string literals can't initialize arrays of any other type ❶. Then, we validate that the string isn't too long to initialize the array ❷. Finally, we annotate the initializer with the target type ❸. We'll use this annotation later to figure out how many null bytes to append to the string.

String Literals Initializing Static Variables

Our final task is to process string literals that initialize static variables. We'll need to represent two new kinds of initial values in the symbol table: ASCII strings (which correspond to the .ascii and .asciz directives) and the addresses of static objects (which correspond to directives like .quad .Lstring.0). We'll update static_init once again to include both kinds of initializers. Listing 16-22 gives the new definition with these two additions bolded.

```
static_init = IntInit(int) | LongInit(int)
            | UIntInit(int) | ULongInit(int)
            | CharInit(int) | UCharInit(int)
            | DoubleInit(double) | ZeroInit(int bytes)
            | StringInit(string, bool null_terminated)
            | PointerInit(string name)
```

Listing 16-22: Adding the static initializers for strings and pointers

StringInit defines an ASCII string initializer. We'll use it to initialize both constant strings and character arrays. The null_terminated argument specifies whether to include a null byte at the end; we'll use this argument to choose between the .ascii and .asciz directives during code emission. PointerInit initializes a pointer with the address of another static object.

We'll also start tracking constant strings in the symbol table. Listing 16-23 gives the updated definition of identifier_attrs, which includes constants.

```
identifier_attrs = FunAttr(bool defined, bool global)
                 | StaticAttr(initial_value init, bool global)
                 | ConstantAttr(static_init init)
                 | LocalAttr
```

Listing 16-23: Tracking constants in the symbol table

Unlike a variable, which may be uninitialized, tentatively initialized, or initialized with a list of values, a constant is initialized with a single value. It also doesn't need a global flag, since we'll never define a global constant.

Now that we've extended static_init and identifier_attrs, let's discuss how to process string initializers for both character arrays and char pointers.

Initializing a Static Array with a String Literal

If a string literal initializes a static array, we first validate the array's type: we make sure that the array elements have character type and that the array is long enough to contain the string. (This is the same validation we performed for non-static arrays back in Listing 16-21.) We then convert the string literal to a StringInit initializer, setting the null_terminated flag if the array has enough space for the terminating null byte. We add ZeroInit to the initializer list if we need to pad it out with additional null bytes. For example, we'll convert the declaration

```
static char letters[10] = "abc";
```

to the symbol table entry in Listing 16-24.

```
name="letters"
type=Array(Char, 10)
attrs=StaticAttr(init=Initial([StringInit("abc", True), ZeroInit(6)]),
                global=False)
```

Listing 16-24: The symbol table entry for an array initialized from a string literal

This entry initializes letters with the null-terminated string "abc", followed by 6 bytes of zeros.

Initializing a Static Pointer with a String Literal

If a string literal initializes a static variable of type char *, we create two entries in the symbol table. The first defines the string itself, and the second defines the variable that points to that string. Let's look at an example:

```
static char *message = "Hello!";
```

First, we generate an identifier for the constant string "Hello!"; let's say this identifier is "string.0". Then, we add the entry shown in Listing 16-25 to the symbol table.

```
name="string.0"
type=Array(Char, 7)
attrs=ConstantAttr(StringInit("Hello!", True))
```

Listing 16-25: Defining a constant string in the symbol table

This identifier must be globally unique and must be a syntactically valid label in assembly. In other words, it should follow the same constraints as the identifiers we generate for floating-point constants. Because Listing 16-25 defines a constant string, we use the new ConstantAttr construct, and we'll initialize it with the null-terminated string "Hello!".

Then, when we add message itself to the symbol table, we initialize it with a pointer to the symbol we just added. Listing 16-26 shows the symbol table entry for message.

```
name="message"
type=Pointer(Char)
attrs=StaticAttr(init=Initial([PointerInit("string.0")]), global=False)
```

Listing 16-26: Defining a static pointer to a string in the symbol table

If a string literal initializes a pointer to a type other than char, we throw an error. (Note that typecheck_init already catches this error in the non-static case.) Even using a string literal to initialize a signed char * or unsigned char * is illegal. This is in keeping with the ordinary rules for type conversions: string literals have type char *, and we can't implicitly convert from one pointer type to another. By contrast, a string literal can initialize an *array* of any character type because it's legal to implicitly convert each individual character from one character type to another.

At this point, we have symbol table entries for all the strings that appear in static initializers. During TACKY generation, we'll add all the other constant strings in the program to the symbol table too.

TEST THE TYPE CHECKER

To test the type checker, run:

```
$ ./test_compiler /path/to/your_compiler --chapter 16 --stage validate
```

Type checking should fail for all the test cases in *tests/chapter_16/invalid _types*. These tests include string literals that initialize arrays of non-character type, assignments to string literals, and implicit conversions between pointers to different character types. Your type checker should successfully process all the test cases in *tests/chapter_16/valid*.

TACKY Generation

When we convert a program to TACKY, we can treat characters exactly like all the other integers. In particular, we'll implement casts to and from character types with the existing type conversion instructions. For example, we'll implement casts from double to unsigned char with the DoubleToUInt instruction, and we'll implement casts from char to int with SignExtend. Processing string literals, however, requires a bit more work.

String Literals as Array Initializers

In the type checker, we dealt with string literals that initialized static arrays. Now we'll do the same for arrays with automatic storage duration.

As we saw earlier in the chapter, there are two options here. The simpler option is to initialize these arrays one character at a time. The more efficient option is to initialize entire 4- or 8-byte chunks at once. Either way, we'll copy the string into the array with a sequence of CopyToOffset instructions.

Let's walk through both options. We'll use the initializer from Listing 16-6, reproduced here, as a running example:

```
int main(void) {
    char letters[6] = "abcde";
    return 0;
}
```

When we first looked at this example, we learned that the ASCII values of 'a', 'b', 'c', 'd', and 'e' are 97, 98, 99, 100, and 101. Using the simple one-byte-at-a-time approach, we'll initialize letters with the TACKY instructions in Listing 16-27.

```
CopyToOffset(Constant(ConstChar(97)),  "letters", 0)
CopyToOffset(Constant(ConstChar(98)),  "letters", 1)
CopyToOffset(Constant(ConstChar(99)),  "letters", 2)
CopyToOffset(Constant(ConstChar(100)), "letters", 3)
CopyToOffset(Constant(ConstChar(101)), "letters", 4)
CopyToOffset(Constant(ConstChar(0)),   "letters", 5)
```

Listing 16-27: Initializing a non-static array in TACKY, one byte at a time

Using the more efficient approach, we'll initialize letters with a single 4-byte integer, followed by 2 individual bytes:

```
CopyToOffset(Constant(ConstInt(1684234849)), "letters", 0)
CopyToOffset(Constant(ConstChar(101)),       "letters", 4)
CopyToOffset(Constant(ConstChar(0)),         "letters", 5)
```

To come up with the integer 1684234849, we take the 4 bytes 97, 98, 99, and 100 and interpret them as a single little-endian integer. In hexadecimal, these bytes are 0x61, 0x62, 0x63, and 0x64. The first byte in little-endian integers is least significant, so interpreting this byte sequence as an integer gives us 0x64636261, or 1684234849 in decimal. Whatever language you're implementing your compiler in, it likely has utility functions to manipulate byte buffers and interpret them as integers, so you won't need to implement this fiddly logic yourself.

To initialize eight characters at once, we'll use a ConstLong instead of a ConstInt. We need to be careful not to overrun the bounds of the array we're initializing; in this example, it would be incorrect to initialize letters with two 4-byte integers, because it would clobber neighboring values.

It's up to you which of these approaches to use; they're both equally correct. In either case, make sure to initialize the correct number of null bytes at the end of the string. In the type checker, you annotated every initializer, including string literals, with type information. Now you'll use that type information to figure out how many null bytes to include. If a string literal is longer than the array it initializes, copy in only as many characters as the array can hold. In other words, leave off the null byte. If the string literal is too short, copy zeros into the rest of the array.

String Literals in Expressions

When we encounter a string literal outside of an array initializer, we'll add it to the symbol table as a constant string. Then, we'll use its identifier as a TACKY Var. Let's revisit Listing 16-9, which returns a pointer to the first character in a string:

```
return "A profound statement.";
```

The parser and type checker transform this into the following AST node:

```
Return(AddrOf(String("A profound statement.")))
```

To convert this AST node to TACKY, we first define "A profound statement." in the symbol table:

```
name="string.1"
type=Array(Char, 22)
attrs=ConstantAttr(StringInit("A profound statement.", True))
```

This entry is no different from the constant strings we defined in the type checker. It has a globally unique, automatically generated label. It's a char array that's just large enough to contain the whole string, including the terminating null byte. It's initialized with the new ConstantAttr construct because we'll ultimately store it in read-only memory.

Now we can refer to the identifier we just defined—string.1, in this example—to load the string's address:

```
GetAddress(Var("string.1"), Var("tmp2"))
Return(Var("tmp2"))
```

In short, we use string.1 like any other symbol of array type.

Top-Level Constants in TACKY

We need to account for all these new constant strings when we convert entries in the symbol table to top-level TACKY definitions. The assembly AST already has a top-level constant construct. Now we'll add the corresponding construct to TACKY:

```
top_level = --snip-- | StaticConstant(identifier, type t, static_init init)
```

When we're generating top-level TACKY definitions from the symbol table, we'll generate a StaticConstant for every constant in the symbol table, just like we generate a StaticVariable for each static variable. Make sure to convert function definitions to TACKY before traversing the symbol table; otherwise, you'll miss the constant strings that get added to the symbol table during this pass.

Listing 16-28 summarizes the TACKY IR, with this chapter's addition bolded.

```
program = Program(top_level*)
top_level = Function(identifier, bool global, identifier* params, instruction* body)
          | StaticVariable(identifier, bool global, type t, static_init* init_list)
          | StaticConstant(identifier, type t, static_init init)
instruction = Return(val)
            | SignExtend(val src, val dst)
            | Truncate(val src, val dst)
            | ZeroExtend(val src, val dst)
            | DoubleToInt(val src, val dst)
            | DoubleToUInt(val src, val dst)
            | IntToDouble(val src, val dst)
            | UIntToDouble(val src, val dst)
            | Unary(unary_operator, val src, val dst)
            | Binary(binary_operator, val src1, val src2, val dst)
            | Copy(val src, val dst)
            | GetAddress(val src, val dst)
            | Load(val src_ptr, val dst)
            | Store(val src, val dst_ptr)
            | AddPtr(val ptr, val index, int scale, val dst)
            | CopyToOffset(val src, identifier dst, int offset)
            | Jump(identifier target)
            | JumpIfZero(val condition, identifier target)
            | JumpIfNotZero(val condition, identifier target)
            | Label(identifier)
            | FunCall(identifier fun_name, val* args, val dst)
val = Constant(const) | Var(identifier)
unary_operator = Complement | Negate | Not
binary_operator = Add | Subtract | Multiply | Divide | Remainder | Equal | NotEqual
                | LessThan | LessOrEqual | GreaterThan | GreaterOrEqual
```

Listing 16-28: Adding static constants to the TACKY IR

At this point, your TACKY generation pass should be good to go: it can handle individual characters, string literals that are implicitly converted to pointers, and string literals that initialize arrays.

TEST THE TACKY GENERATION STAGE

To test out TACKY generation, run:

```
$ ./test_compiler /path/to/your_compiler --chapter 16 --stage tacky
```

Assembly Generation

We won't do anything too fancy in this stage. First, we'll convert operations on individual characters to assembly. This will require a few changes to the assembly AST. Then, we'll handle TACKY StaticConstant constructs and add constant strings to the backend symbol table.

Operations on Characters

Most instructions support 1-byte operands as well as longwords and quadwords. A b suffix, like in the instructions movb and andb, indicates that an instruction operates on a single byte. We'll introduce a new Byte assembly type to represent this new operand size:

```
assembly_type = Byte | --snip--
```

We'll convert the char, signed char, and unsigned char types to Byte. The general-purpose registers have 1-byte aliases too; for example, %al is the 1-byte alias for RAX. Luckily, our code emission pass already supports these aliases.

Aside from adding the Byte type, we'll need to convert to and from character types correctly. You can zero extend a 1-byte value to a wider type with the movz instruction. This instruction takes a two-letter suffix, indicating the types of the source and destination. The movzbl instruction extends a byte to a longword, and movzbq extends a byte to a quadword. (You can also use movzwl or movzwq to extend a 2-byte word to a larger type, but we don't use 2-byte operands.) We'll represent movz with the existing MovZeroExtend instruction in the assembly AST, but we'll add the types of both operands:

```
MovZeroExtend(assembly_type src_type, assembly_type dst_type, operand src, operand dst)
```

If src_type is Byte, we'll ultimately emit a movz instruction with the correct suffix. If src_type is Longword, we'll rewrite this to an ordinary mov instruction during the fix-up pass, just like in earlier chapters.

To sign extend a byte to a larger type, we'll use the existing Movsx instruction. This instruction also takes a suffix to specify the types of both the source and the destination: movsbl extends a byte to a longword, movsbq extends a byte to a quadword, and movslq extends a longword into a quadword. We'll add type information to this instruction in the assembly AST too:

```
Movsx(assembly_type src_type, assembly_type dst_type, operand src, operand dst)
```

You can truncate a larger integer to a single byte with a movb instruction, just like you can truncate a quadword to a longword with movl. Note that when you copy a value to a register with the movb instruction, the register's upper bytes aren't zeroed out. This isn't a problem; whether we're operating on a single byte or a longword, we use only the part of the register that holds the value itself, and we ignore the register's upper bytes.

CLANG GOES ROGUE

There is one case where the contents of a register's upper bytes might matter: when you're calling a function that was compiled with Clang. If a function argument is narrower than 4 bytes, Clang always has the caller sign extend or zero extend it to 4 bytes. Then, in the callee, it assumes the argument has been extended to 4 bytes already.

This assumption violates the System V ABI, which doesn't require callers to extend narrow function arguments. Take the following C code:

```
int accept_int(int i);

int accept_char(char c) {
    return accept_int(c);
}
```

When a function calls accept_char, it passes the parameter c in the least significant byte of EDI, which has the alias %dil. Then, when accept_char calls accept_int, it passes the 4-byte representation of c's value in EDI. If we're strictly following the ABI, we assume that the 3 highest bytes of EDI are garbage at the start of accept_char, so we explicitly sign extend c before passing it to accept_int:

```
movsbl  %dil, %edi
call    accept_int
```

But Clang doesn't strictly follow the ABI: when optimizations are enabled, it leaves out the movsbl instruction. This means that if accept_char's caller didn't

---

already sign extend c, we might get the wrong result! This isn't just a hypothetical concern: ICC, Intel's legacy C compiler, doesn't extend narrow arguments, so it's not ABI-compatible with Clang. (Intel's newer C compiler, which is built on Clang and LLVM, doesn't have this problem.)

GCC takes the most conservative approach: it has callers extend narrow arguments but doesn't assume they've been extended in the callee. It therefore interoperates correctly with both ICC and Clang.

In Clang's defense, the ABI isn't very explicit on this point. Ideally, the maintainers of the System V ABI would either specifically permit what Clang is doing or specifically forbid it.

So where does that leave us? We'll follow ICC and not bother to extend narrow arguments. But if you want to make your compiler more robust, you can take GCC's approach: when you generate assembly code to call a function, zero extend any unsigned char arguments and sign extend any char or signed char arguments.

I learned about this ugly corner case from Peter Cordes's excellent answer on Stack Overflow (https://stackoverflow.com/a/36760539). His answer was written in 2016; as of spring 2024, neither the ABI nor Clang's behavior has changed.

Finally, let's consider how to convert between double and the character types. There's no assembly instruction to convert double directly to a 1-byte integer or vice versa. Instead, we'll convert to or from int as an intermediate step. To convert a double to any character type, we'll first convert it to an int and then truncate it, as Listing 16-29 demonstrates.

```
Cvttsd2si(Longword, src, Reg(AX))
Mov(Byte, Reg(AX), dst)
```

Listing 16-29: Converting a double to a character type

Listing 16-30 gives the assembly to convert an unsigned char to a double. We'll zero extend it to an int, then convert the result to a double.

```
MovZeroExtend(Byte, Longword, src, Reg(AX))
Cvtsi2sd(Longword, Reg(AX), dst)
```

Listing 16-30: Converting an unsigned char to a double

And to convert either signed character type to a double, we'll sign extend it to an int first, as Listing 16-31 demonstrates.

```
Movsx(Byte, Longword, src, Reg(AX))
Cvtsi2sd(Longword, Reg(AX), dst)
```

Listing 16-31: Converting a char or signed char to a double

Next, we'll deal with our second task: converting top-level constants from TACKY to assembly.

Top-Level Constants

Processing a TACKY StaticConstant is extremely simple: we just convert it to an assembly StaticConstant. You'll also need to convert each constant string in the symbol table to an equivalent entry in the backend symbol table, like you do for variables. When you add a constant string to the backend symbol table, set its is_static attribute to True. If your backend symbol table includes an is_constant attribute, set this to True as well. (Remember that is_constant was an optional addition in Chapter 13; it tells us when to use local labels during code emission.)

The Complete Conversion from TACKY to Assembly

Listing 16-32 shows this chapter's additions to the assembly AST.

```
program = Program(top_level*)
assembly_type = Byte | Longword | Quadword | Double | ByteArray(int size, int alignment)
top_level = Function(identifier name, bool global, instruction* instructions)
          | StaticVariable(identifier name, bool global, int alignment, static_init* init_list)
          | StaticConstant(identifier name, int alignment, static_init init)
instruction = Mov(assembly_type, operand src, operand dst)
            | Movsx(assembly_type src_type, assembly_type dst_type, operand src, operand dst)
            | MovZeroExtend(assembly_type src_type, assembly_type dst_type, operand src,
                           operand dst)
            | Lea(operand src, operand dst)
            | Cvttsd2si(assembly_type dst_type, operand src, operand dst)
            | Cvtsi2sd(assembly_type src_type, operand src, operand dst)
            | Unary(unary_operator, assembly_type, operand)
            | Binary(binary_operator, assembly_type, operand, operand)
            | Cmp(assembly_type, operand, operand)
            | Idiv(assembly_type, operand)
            | Div(assembly_type, operand)
            | Cdq(assembly_type)
            | Jmp(identifier)
            | JmpCC(cond_code, identifier)
            | SetCC(cond_code, operand)
            | Label(identifier)
            | Push(operand)
            | Call(identifier)
            | Ret
unary_operator = Neg | Not | Shr
binary_operator = Add | Sub | Mult | DivDouble | And | Or | Xor
operand = Imm(int) | Reg(reg) | Pseudo(identifier) | Memory(reg, int) | Data(identifier)
        | PseudoMem(identifier, int) | Indexed(reg base, reg index, int scale)
cond_code = E | NE | G | GE | L | LE | A | AE | B | BE
reg = AX | CX | DX | DI | SI | R8 | R9 | R10 | R11 | SP | BP
    | XMM0 | XMM1 | XMM2 | XMM3 | XMM4 | XMM5 | XMM6 | XMM7 | XMM14 | XMM15
```

Listing 16-32: The assembly AST with byte operands

Tables 16-2 through 16-5 summarize the latest updates to the conversion from TACKY to assembly, with new constructs and changes to the conversions for existing constructs bolded.

Table 16-2: Converting Top-Level TACKY Constructs to Assembly

TACKY top-level construct	Assembly top-level construct
StaticConstant(name, t, init)	StaticConstant(name, *\<alignment of t\>*, init)

Table 16-3: Converting TACKY Instructions to Assembly

TACKY instruction		Assembly instructions
ZeroExtend(src, dst)		MovZeroExtend(**\<src type\>**, **\<dst type\>**, src, dst)
SignExtend(src, dst)		Movsx(**\<src type\>**, **\<dst type\>**, src, dst)
Truncate(src, dst)		Mov(**\<dst type\>**, src, dst)
IntToDouble(src, dst)	**char or signed char**	**Movsx(Byte, Longword, src, Reg(\<R\>))** **Cvtsi2sd(Longword, Reg(\<R\>), dst)**
	int or long	Cvtsi2sd(*\<src type\>*, src, dst)
DoubleToInt(src, dst)	**char or signed char**	**Cvttsd2si(Longword, src, Reg(\<R\>))** **Mov(Byte, Reg(\<R\>), dst)**
	int or long	Cvttsd2si(*\<dst type\>*, src, dst)
UIntToDouble(src, dst)	**unsigned char**	**MovZeroExtend(Byte, Longword, src, Reg(\<R\>))** **Cvtsi2sd(Longword, Reg(\<R\>), dst)**
	unsigned int	MovZeroExtend(**Longword, Quadword**, src, Reg(\<R\>)) Cvtsi2sd(Quadword, Reg(\<R\>), dst)
	unsigned long	Cmp(Quadword, Imm(0), src) JmpCC(L, *\<label1\>*) Cvtsi2sd(Quadword, src, dst) Jmp(*\<label2\>*) Label(*\<label1\>*) Mov(Quadword, src, Reg(\<R1\>)) Mov(Quadword, Reg(\<R1\>), Reg(\<R2\>)) Unary(Shr, Quadword, Reg(\<R2\>)) Binary(And, Quadword, Imm(1), Reg(\<R1\>)) Binary(Or, Quadword, Reg(\<R1\>), Reg(\<R2\>)) Cvtsi2sd(Quadword, Reg(\<R2\>), dst) Binary(Add, Double, dst, dst) Label(*\<label2\>*)

(continued)

Table 16-3: Converting TACKY Instructions to Assembly *(continued)*

TACKY instruction		Assembly instructions
DoubleToUInt(src, dst)	unsigned char	Cvttsd2si(Longword, src, Reg(<R>)) Mov(Byte, Reg(<R>), dst)
	unsigned int	Cvttsd2si(Quadword, src, Reg(<R>)) Mov(Longword, Reg(<R>), dst)
	unsigned long	Cmp(Double, Data(<upper-bound>), src) JmpCC(AE, <label1>) Cvttsd2si(Quadword, src, dst) Jmp(<label2>) Label(<label1>) Mov(Double, src, Reg(<X>)) Binary(Sub, Double, Data(<upper-bound>), Reg(<X>)) Cvttsd2si(Quadword, Reg(<X>), dst) Mov(Quadword, Imm(9223372036854775808), Reg(<R>)) Binary(Add, Quadword, Reg(<R>), dst) Label(<label2>) And add a top-level constant: StaticConstant(<upper-bound>, 8, DoubleInit(9223372036854775808.0))

Table 16-4: Converting TACKY Operands to Assembly

TACKY operand	Assembly operand
Constant(ConstChar(int))	Imm(int)
Constant(ConstUChar(int))	Imm(int)

Table 16-5: Converting Types to Assembly

Source type	Assembly type	Alignment
Char	Byte	1
SChar	Byte	1
UChar	Byte	1

Next, let's move on to pseudo-operand replacement and instruction fix-up. The updates to both of these passes are pretty straightforward.

Pseudo-Operand Replacement

We'll allocate 1 byte on the stack for each Byte object. We don't need to worry about rounding these down to the right alignment, because they're all 1-byte aligned.

This pass shouldn't require any dedicated logic to deal with constant strings. We've already recorded that they have static storage duration in the backend symbol table. Now we'll access them with Data operands like any other static object.

Instruction Fix-Up

The destination of a movz instruction must be a register, and its source must not be an immediate value. If the size of the source operand of a MovZeroExtend instruction is 1 byte and its source or destination is invalid, we rewrite it according to the usual pattern. For instance, we rewrite

```
movzbl  $10, -4(%rbp)
```

as:

```
movb    $10, %r10b
movzbl  %r10b, %r11d
movl    %r11d, -4(%rbp)
```

If its source operand is a longword, we replace it with one or more mov instructions, like in earlier chapters.

If the source of a movb instruction is an immediate value that can't fit in a single byte, we'll reduce it modulo 256. For example, we'll rewrite

```
movb    $258, %al
```

as:

```
movb    $2, %al
```

This is the same pattern we introduced in Chapter 11 to handle movl instructions whose source operands are 8-byte immediate values.

TEST THE ASSEMBLY GENERATION STAGE

To test that your compiler can generate assembly programs without throwing an error, run:

```
$ ./test_compiler /path/to/your_compiler --chapter 16 --stage codegen
```

Code Emission

The code emission stage needs to support string constants, pointer initializers, and a handful of other changes. We'll emit each StringInit as either an .ascii or an .asciz directive, depending on whether it should include a null byte. Double quotes, backslashes, and new lines in ASCII strings must be escaped. To escape these characters, you can use either the \", \\, and \n escape sequences or three-digit octal escape sequences that specify their

ASCII values. For example, the ASCII code for the backslash character is 92, or 134 in octal, so you could represent it with the escape sequence \134. You can escape other special characters too, but you don't need to. Some escape sequences, like \a, are valid in C but not assembly, so octal escape sequences are the safest way to escape arbitrary characters.

We'll emit each PointerInit as a .quad directive, followed by the label we want to point to. We'll convert CharInit and UCharInit to the .byte directive, which works exactly like .long and .quad. When you emit a 1-byte-aligned object, you can either include the .align directive or omit it. Every object is at least 1-byte aligned by definition, so specifying a 1-byte alignment has no effect.

On Linux, string constants will live in the .rodata section along with floating-point constants. On macOS, they'll live in the .cstring section. If you use local labels (which begin with a .L or L prefix) for floating-point constants, you should use them for string constants too. The logic to add this prefix to Data operands won't change; we'll still look up each Data operand in the backend symbol table and add this prefix if its is_constant attribute is true.

The movz and movsx instructions should include suffixes to indicate both the source and destination types. Other instructions should include a b suffix when they operate on bytes. Tables 16-6 through 16-9 summarize the latest updates to the code emission pass; new constructs and changes to the way we emit existing constructs are bolded.

Table 16-6: Formatting Top-Level Assembly Constructs

Assembly top-level construct	Output	
StaticConstant(name, alignment, init)	Linux	.section .rodata *\<alignment-directive\>* *\<name\>*: *\<init\>*
	macOS (8-byte-aligned numeric constants)	.literal8 .balign 8 *\<name\>*: *\<init\>*

	macOS (16-byte-aligned numeric constants)	.literal16
		.balign 16
		\<name\>:
		    \<init\>
		    .quad 0

	macOS (string constants)	**.cstring** ***\<name\>*:** ***\<init\>***

Table 16-7: Formatting Static Initializers

Static initializer	Output
CharInit(0)	.zero 1
CharInit(i)	.byte <i>
UCharInit(0)	.zero 1
UCharInit(i)	.byte <i>
StringInit(s, True)	.asciz "<s>"
StringInit(s, False)	.ascii "<s>"
PointerInit(label)	.quad <label>

Table 16-8: Formatting Assembly Instructions

Assembly instruction	Output	
Movsx(src_t, dst_t, src, dst)	movs<src_t><dst_t>	<src>, <dst>
MovZeroExtend(src_t, dst_t, src, dst)	movz<src_t><dst_t>	<src>, <dst>

Table 16-9: Instruction Suffixes for Assembly Types

Assembly type	Instruction suffix
Byte	b

Your compiler now supports strings and characters! You still need to run this chapter's tests to make sure you've implemented these features correctly, but first, we'll try out a couple of examples.

Hello Again, World!

Back in Chapter 9, we printed "Hello, World!" one character at a time. Now we can write a more traditional "Hello, World!" program using the puts standard library function, which has the following signature:

```
int puts(const char *s);
```

Since we don't support const, we'll declare puts without it. Listing 16-33 shows our new "Hello, World!" program.

```
int puts(char *c);
int main(void) {
    puts("Hello, World!");
    return 0;
}
```

Listing 16-33: Printing out a string with puts

This code is not entirely legal, since the declaration of puts isn't compatible with the definition in the standard library. However, the program should work correctly in spite of this minor bit of rule breaking. Compile it, then run it to print a message to stdout:

```
$ ./hello_world
Hello, World!
```

If you want to get really wild, you can even compile Listing 16-34, which reads from stdin.

```
int getchar(void);
int puts(char *c);
char *strncat(char *s1, char *s2, unsigned long n);
char *strcat(char *s1, char *s2);
unsigned long strlen(char *s);

❶ static char name[30];
❷ static char message[40] = "Hello, ";

int main(void) {
    puts("Please enter your name: ");

    int idx = 0;
    while (idx < 29) {
        int c = getchar();

        // treat EOF, null byte, or line break as end of input
        if (c <= 0 || c == '\n') {
            break;
        }

        name[idx] = c;
        idx = idx + 1;
    }

  ❸ name[idx] = 0; // add terminating null byte to name

    // append name to message, leaving space for null byte
    // and exclamation point
    strncat(message, name, 40 - strlen(message) - 2);

    // append exclamation point
    strcat(message, "!");
    puts(message);
    return 0;
}
```

Listing 16-34: Reading from stdin

Much like Listing 16-33 declares puts without the const qualifier, this program declares several library functions without their usual qualifiers, including const and restrict. We use getchar to read from stdin one character at a time, since our compiler can't easily handle most other ways to read from stdin using C standard library functions.

Listing 16-34 declares two static arrays: name and message. Because name is static but has no explicit initializer, it will be initialized with all zeros ❶. The beginning of message is initialized with the string "Hello, ", and the remainder is filled with null bytes ❷. This program calls puts to emit a prompt, then calls getchar in a loop to read the user's response into the name array, one character at a time. We exit the loop when getchar returns a negative number (which indicates end-of-file or an error), a null byte, or a new line character, or after we've read in 29 characters, whichever comes first. (We check whether the result is negative, instead of comparing it to the EOF macro like a normal C program would, because we can't include <stdio.h>, where EOF is defined.) Reading in at most 29 characters leaves room for a terminating null byte, which we add to name after exiting the loop ❸.

The call to strncat appends the user's name to message, and the subsequent call to strcat appends an exclamation point. Finally, the second call to puts writes the whole message to stdout. Your compiler should be able to handle this listing; go ahead and give it a try! I'll use the program to say hello to my dog, Arlo. (I promised him I'd mention him in this book at least once.)

```
$ ./hello_name
Please enter your name:
Arlo
Hello, Arlo!
```

If this program works correctly, you're ready to run the full test suite.

TEST THE WHOLE COMPILER

To test out the whole compiler, run:

```
$ ./test_compiler /path/to/your_compiler --chapter 16
```

The test programs in *tests/chapter_16/valid/char_constants* exercise your compiler's support for character constant tokens. The programs in *tests/chapter_16/valid/chars* test its support for values of scalar character type, and the programs in *tests/chapter_16/valid/strings_as_initializers* and *tests/chapter_16/valid/strings_as_lvalues* test its support for string literals. As usual, the tests in *tests/chapter_16/valid/libraries* validate that your compiler handles strings and characters according to the System V ABI.

Summary

Your compiler can now process programs that work with text. In this chapter, you learned how to lex string literals and character constants, and you extended the type checker to distinguish between constant strings and string literals that initialize arrays. You also introduced new ways to define constants in the symbol table and the TACKY IR. In the next chapter, you'll introduce two features that make it easier to dynamically allocate memory: the sizeof operator and the void type.

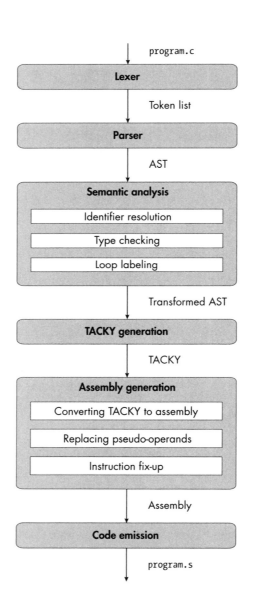

17

SUPPORTING DYNAMIC MEMORY ALLOCATION

Over the course of Part II, you've compiled programs that call an increasingly wide range of standard library functions. At the end of Part I, your compiler supported only functions with parameters and return values of type int, like putchar. Now you can compile programs that call floating-point math functions like fmax and string processing functions like puts. In this chapter, you'll implement the remaining features you need to call a particularly important part of the standard library: the memory management functions. These include malloc, calloc, and aligned _alloc, which allocate memory dynamically; free, which deallocates dynamically allocated memory; and realloc, which deallocates one block of memory and reallocates another with the same contents.

To compile programs that declare and call these functions, you'll need to implement the void type. Up until now, we've used the void keyword only to specify an empty parameter list; now we'll treat it as a proper type specifier. In C, void * represents the address of a chunk of memory with no particular type; the standard library functions that allocate memory all return this type. The void type on its own is also useful. For instance, you can use it to declare functions that don't return a value, like free. In addition to void, we'll implement the sizeof operator, which gets the size of a type or object. C programs often use sizeof to figure out how many bytes of memory to allocate.

This chapter's not-so-secret agenda is to get you ready to implement structure types in Chapter 18. Real-life C programs frequently store structures in dynamically allocated memory, and so do many of that chapter's tests. The changes we make to the type checker will also come in handy in Chapter 18 because some of the typing rules that apply to void will apply to structure types too.

The void Type

The C standard (section 6.2.5, paragraph 19) gives the following rather mysterious definition of void: "The void type comprises an empty set of values; it is an incomplete object type that cannot be completed." We'll talk more about what "incomplete object type" means in a moment. For now, the main idea is that void is a type with no values. You can't do a whole lot with this type, but it does have a few uses.

You can give a function a void return type if it doesn't return anything. To leave a function with a void return type, you can use a return statement with no expression, like in Listing 17-1.

```
void return_nothing(void) {
    return;
}
```

Listing 17-1: A function with a void return type

As Listing 17-2 demonstrates, you can also leave out the return statement entirely. In that case, the function will return once you reach the end of the function body.

```
void perform_side_effect(void) {
    extern int some_variable;
    some_variable = 100;
}
```

Listing 17-2: A void function with no return statement

A *void expression* is an expression whose type is void; it has no value, but you can evaluate it for its side effects. There are three ways to produce a void expression. First, you can call a void function. Second, you can evaluate a conditional expression whose branches are both void:

```
flag ? perform_side_effect() : return_nothing();
```

Third, you can cast a value to void:

```
(void) (1 + 1);
```

Here, the cast to void has no effect on program execution; its only purpose is to tell the compiler, and human readers, that the value of the expression should be discarded. This is a common way to silence compiler warnings about unused values.

If you're particularly zealous about following C's typing rules, you might also cast to void in code like that in Listing 17-3 to get the types of two conditional branches to agree.

```
int i = 0;
flag ? perform_side_effect() : (void) (i = 3);
```

Listing 17-3: A conditional expression with type void

If we left out the cast to void in this conditional expression, one branch would have type void and the other would have type int. This would be illegal, although most compilers won't complain about it unless you use the -pedantic flag to enable extra warnings. Our compiler will reject conditional expressions with one void branch, because it's pedantic all the time.

There are four places where you can use a void expression. First, it can appear as a clause in a conditional expression, as in Listing 17-3. Second, you can use it as a stand-alone expression:

```
perform_side_effect();
```

Third, it can appear as the first or third clause of a for loop header, like in Listing 17-4.

```
for (perform_side_effect(); i < 10; perform_side_effect())
    --snip--
```

Listing 17-4: Using void expressions in a for loop header

And fourth, you can cast a void expression to void:

```
(void) perform_side_effect();
```

That last one isn't particularly useful, but it is legal.

As you already know, you can also use the void keyword to specify an empty parameter list in a function declaration. This is a special case, since it doesn't actually specify an expression, object, or return value with type void. Even once we extend the compiler to fully support the void type, we'll handle this particular case exactly the same way as before.

Memory Management with void *

Now let's look at how the memory management functions use void * to represent allocated memory. The malloc function has the following signature:

```
void *malloc(size_t size);
```

The size argument specifies the number of bytes to allocate. Its type, size_t, is an implementation-defined unsigned integer type. Under the System V x64 ABI, size_t is an alias for unsigned long. Because we don't support type aliases, our test programs and examples use this declaration instead:

```
void *malloc(unsigned long size);
```

The malloc function allocates a chunk of memory and returns its address. Since malloc doesn't know what type of object will be stored in this chunk of memory, it would be misleading to return a pointer to int, char, or any of the other types we've seen so far. Instead, it returns void *. You can't read or write memory through a void * pointer, though. So, before you can access the memory that you allocated with malloc, you need to specify what type of object it should contain by converting its address from void * to a different pointer type.

You can convert other pointer types to and from void * without an explicit cast. For example, you might use malloc to allocate an array of 100 int elements:

```
int *many_ints = malloc(100 * sizeof (int));
```

When you assign the result of malloc to many_ints, it's implicitly converted from void * to int *. Then, you can subscript many_ints like any other pointer into an int array:

```
many_ints[10] = 10;
```

The free function accepts a void * argument that designates the chunk of memory to deallocate:

```
void free(void *ptr);
```

This pointer must be the same value that was returned earlier by `malloc` or one of the other memory allocation functions. Here's how you'd use `free` to deallocate the memory that `many_ints` points to:

```
free(many_ints);
```

This function call implicitly converts the value of `many_ints` from `int *` back to `void *`, resulting in the same pointer that `malloc` returned in the first place.

The `calloc` and `aligned_alloc` functions provide slightly different ways to allocate memory; like `malloc`, they return pointers to the allocated space with type `void *`. The `realloc` function accepts a size and a `void *` pointer to previously allocated storage that should now be freed, and it returns a `void *` pointer to a newly allocated block of storage with the new size and the original contents. For our purposes, the details of these functions aren't important; the key idea is that they all use `void *` pointers to identify the blocks of memory they allocate and deallocate.

These blocks of memory are objects that we can read and write, much like variables, but their lifetimes are managed differently. As we know, variables have either automatic storage duration (their lifetime lasts through the execution of a single block) or static storage duration (their lifetime lasts for the whole program). A block of allocated memory has *allocated storage duration*: its lifetime starts when it's allocated and ends when it's deallocated.

The compiler has to keep track of all the variables with static or automatic storage duration, record details about their size and lifetime in the symbol table, and reserve space for them in the data section or on the stack. But the compiler doesn't need to know anything about objects with allocated storage duration, because the programmer and the memory management library are responsible for keeping track of them.

Complete and Incomplete Types

An object type is *complete* if we know its size and *incomplete* if we don't. The `void` type is the first incomplete type we've seen. We don't know its size because it doesn't *have* a size. In the next chapter, we'll encounter incomplete structure types, whose size and members aren't visible to the compiler. Incomplete structure types can be completed later in the program if the compiler learns more about them. The `void` type, on the other hand, can't be completed.

The C standard states that "an incomplete type can only be used when the size of an object of that type is not needed" (section 6.7.2.3, footnote 132). For example, you can't define a variable with an incomplete type, because you don't know how much space to allocate for it. And you can't assign to an object with an incomplete type or use its value, since you would need to know how many bytes to read or write. With a few exceptions, other incomplete types are subject to the same restrictions as `void`, and the type checker will handle them the same way.

All pointers are complete types, even if the types they point to are incomplete; we know that the size of a pointer is always 8 bytes. That's

why you can declare variables and parameters of type void *, return void *
values from functions, convert them to other pointer types, and so on. As
you'll see in the next chapter, you can use pointers to incomplete structure
types in the same way.

The sizeof Operator

The sizeof operator accepts either an expression or the name of a type.
When it takes a type name, it returns the size of that type in bytes. When it
takes an expression, it returns the size of the expression's type. Listing 17-5
illustrates both cases.

```
sizeof (long);
sizeof 10.0;
```

Listing 17-5: The two uses of sizeof

Both of these sizeof expressions evaluate to 8 because the long and
double types are both 8 bytes. Note that type names in sizeof expressions
must be parenthesized, but expressions don't need to be.

When you use an array in a sizeof expression, it doesn't decay to a
pointer. Consider the sizeof expression in Listing 17-6.

```
int array[3];
return sizeof array;
```

Listing 17-6: Getting the size of an array

This code returns 12, which is the size of a three-int array, rather than 8,
the size of a pointer.

You can always determine an expression's type—and therefore its size—
without evaluating it. In fact, the C standard requires that we *don't* evaluate
the operand of a sizeof expression. Instead, we infer the operand's type and
evaluate sizeof at compile time. This implies that a sizeof expression won't
produce side effects. For example, the statement

```
return sizeof puts("Shouting into the void");
```

won't call puts. It will just return 4 because the puts function's return type
is int.

You can also apply sizeof to expressions that would typically produce
runtime errors, as Listing 17-7 demonstrates.

```
double *null_ptr = 0;
return sizeof *null_ptr;
```

Listing 17-7: Getting the size of an expression without evaluating it

Normally, dereferencing null_ptr would lead to undefined behavior.
But this example is well defined, because it will never evaluate *null_ptr.

Instead, it will return 8, because the compiler can determine that the type of *null_ptr is double.

Variable-length arrays are the one exception to this rule. The size of a variable-length array isn't known at compile time, so it has to be evaluated at runtime. Because we don't support variable-length arrays, we can ignore this case.

Now that we know how C programs use void, void *, and sizeof, let's work on the compiler. As usual, we'll start by updating the lexer.

The Lexer

You'll add one new keyword in this chapter:

sizeof

You don't need to add the void keyword; the lexer already recognizes it.

TEST THE LEXER

To test the lexer, run:

```
$ ./test_compiler /path/to/your_compiler --chapter 17 --stage lex
```

It should process all of this chapter's tests without error.

The Parser

Listing 17-8 shows this chapter's changes to the AST.

```
program = Program(declaration*)
declaration = FunDecl(function_declaration) | VarDecl(variable_declaration)
variable_declaration = (identifier name, initializer? init,
                        type var_type, storage_class?)
function_declaration = (identifier name, identifier* params, block? body,
                        type fun_type, storage_class?)
initializer = SingleInit(exp) | CompoundInit(initializer*)
type = Char | SChar | UChar | Int | Long | UInt | ULong | Double | Void
     | FunType(type* params, type ret)
     | Pointer(type referenced)
     | Array(type element, int size)
storage_class = Static | Extern
block_item = S(statement) | D(declaration)
block = Block(block_item*)
for_init = InitDecl(variable_declaration) | InitExp(exp?)
statement = Return(exp?)
          | Expression(exp)
```

```
               | If(exp condition, statement then, statement? else)
               | Compound(block)
               | Break
               | Continue
               | While(exp condition, statement body)
               | DoWhile(statement body, exp condition)
               | For(for_init init, exp? condition, exp? post, statement body)
               | Null
exp = Constant(const)
    | String(string)
    | Var(identifier)
    | Cast(type target_type, exp)
    | Unary(unary_operator, exp)
    | Binary(binary_operator, exp, exp)
    | Assignment(exp, exp)
    | Conditional(exp condition, exp, exp)
    | FunctionCall(identifier, exp* args)
    | Dereference(exp)
    | AddrOf(exp)
    | Subscript(exp, exp)
    | SizeOf(exp)
    | SizeOfT(type)
unary_operator = Complement | Negate | Not
binary_operator = Add | Subtract | Multiply | Divide | Remainder | And | Or
                | Equal | NotEqual | LessThan | LessOrEqual
                | GreaterThan | GreaterOrEqual
const = ConstInt(int) | ConstLong(int) | ConstUInt(int) | ConstULong(int)
      | ConstDouble(double) | ConstChar(int) | ConstUChar(int)
```

Listing 17-8: The abstract syntax tree with void, sizeof, *and* return *statements with no return value*

We've made four small changes here. First, we added a void type. Second, the expression in the Return statement is now optional so that it can represent return statements with and without return values. Finally, there are two new expressions to represent the two ways you can use the sizeof operator.

Next, we'll make the corresponding changes to the grammar. The one wrinkle here is that we can't apply sizeof to a cast expression unless that expression is parenthesized. For example, this is a syntax error:

```
sizeof (int) a;
```

Wrapping the cast expression in parentheses fixes the error:

```
sizeof ((int) a);
```

This restriction makes it easier for the parser to distinguish between sizeof operations on type names and on expressions. To capture this restriction in the grammar, we need to break out cast expressions into a separate symbol from other unary expressions.

Let's start by refactoring type names into a symbol that we can use in both cast and sizeof expressions:

```
<type-name> ::= { <type-specifier> }+ [ <abstract-declarator> ]
```

Next, we'll define the new `<cast-exp>` symbol, which includes one rule for cast expressions and another for all the other unary expressions:

```
<cast-exp> ::= "(" <type-name> ")" <cast-exp>
             | <unary-exp>
```

We'll then update `<unary-exp>` to include every unary expression except for casts:

```
<unary-exp> ::= <unop> ❶ <cast-exp>
              | "sizeof" ❷ <unary-exp>
              | "sizeof" "(" <type-name> ")"
              | <postfix-exp>
```

The rule for unary operations like -, ~, !, and & allows cast expressions as operands ❶, while the rule for sizeof doesn't ❷.

Finally, we'll use the new `<cast-exp>` symbol, instead of the more restrictive `<unary-exp>`, to represent a single term in a binary or ternary expression:

```
<exp> ::= <cast-exp> | <exp> <binop> <exp> | <exp> "?" <exp> ":" <exp>
```

Listing 17-9 gives the complete grammar for this chapter.

```
<program> ::= { <declaration> }
<declaration> ::= <variable-declaration> | <function-declaration>
<variable-declaration> ::= { <specifier> }+ <declarator> [ "=" <initializer> ] ";"
<function-declaration> ::= { <specifier> }+ <declarator> ( <block> | ";")
<declarator> ::= "*" <declarator> | <direct-declarator>
<direct-declarator> ::= <simple-declarator> [ <declarator-suffix> ]
<declarator-suffix> ::= <param-list> | { "[" <const> "]" }+
<param-list> ::= "(" "void" ")" | "(" <param> { "," <param> } ")"
<param> ::= { <type-specifier> }+ <declarator>
<simple-declarator> ::= <identifier> | "(" <declarator> ")"
<type-specifier> ::= "int" | "long" | "unsigned" | "signed" | "double" | "char" | "void"
<specifier> ::= <type-specifier> | "static" | "extern"
<block> ::= "{" { <block-item> } "}"
<block-item> ::= <statement> | <declaration>
<initializer> ::= <exp> | "{" <initializer> { "," <initializer> } [ "," ] "}"
<for-init> ::= <variable-declaration> | [ <exp> ] ";"
<statement> ::= "return" [ <exp> ] ";"
              | <exp> ";"
              | "if" "(" <exp> ")" <statement> [ "else" <statement> ]
              | <block>
              | "break" ";"
              | "continue" ";"
              | "while" "(" <exp> ")" <statement>
              | "do" <statement> "while" "(" <exp> ")" ";"
```

```
                | "for" "(" <for-init> [ <exp> ] ";" [ <exp> ] ")" <statement>
                | ";"
<exp> ::= <cast-exp> | <exp> <binop> <exp> | <exp> "?" <exp> ":" <exp>
<cast-exp> ::= "(" <type-name> ")" <cast-exp>
                | <unary-exp>
<unary-exp> ::= <unop> <cast-exp>
                | "sizeof" <unary-exp>
                | "sizeof" "(" <type-name> ")"
                | <postfix-exp>
<type-name> ::= { <type-specifier> }+ [ <abstract-declarator> ]
<postfix-exp> ::= <primary-exp> { "[" <exp> "]" }
<primary-exp> ::= <const> | <identifier> | "(" <exp> ")" | { <string> }+
                | <identifier> "(" [ <argument-list> ] ")"
<argument-list> ::= <exp> { "," <exp> }
<abstract-declarator> ::= "*" [ <abstract-declarator> ]
                        | <direct-abstract-declarator>
<direct-abstract-declarator> ::= "(" <abstract-declarator> ")" { "[" <const> "]" }
                        | { "[" <const> "]" }+
<unop> ::= "-" | "~" | "!" | "*" | "&"
<binop> ::= "-" | "+" | "*" | "/" | "%" | "&&" | "||"
          | "==" | "!=" | "<" | "<=" | ">" | ">=" | "="
<const> ::= <int> | <long> | <uint> | <ulong> | <double> | <char>
<identifier> ::= ? An identifier token ?
<string> ::= ? A string token ?
<int> ::= ? An int token ?
<char> ::= ? A char token ?
<long> ::= ? An int or long token ?
<uint> ::= ? An unsigned int token ?
<ulong> ::= ? An unsigned int or unsigned long token ?
<double> ::= ? A floating-point constant token ?
```

Listing 17-9: The grammar with void, sizeof, *and optional return values*

The parse_type helper function, which converts a list of type specifiers into a type AST node, should reject any declarations where the void specifier appears alongside other type specifiers, like long or unsigned. Otherwise, the parser should treat void like any other type. The void type can be modified by pointer, array, and function declarators; pointers to void and functions returning void are both perfectly legal, while other ways of using void are syntactically valid but semantically illegal. For example, it's a semantic error to declare an array of void elements, define a void variable, or declare a function with void parameters. The parser won't catch these semantic errors, but the type checker will.

You may need to change your parsing logic for <param-list>, even though the grammar rule itself hasn't changed. If the opening (is followed by a void keyword, you'll need to look ahead one more token. If the next token is), the parameter list is empty. Otherwise, the list is not empty, and the void keyword is the start of a parameter declaration.

Note that when a void keyword indicates an empty parameter list, we do *not* translate it to a Void type in the AST. For example, given the function declaration

```
int main(void);
```

the resulting AST node will have this type:

```
FunType(params=[], ret=Int)
```

The params list is empty, just like in prior chapters; it doesn't contain Void.

The Type Checker

Now let's figure out how to type check void, void *, and sizeof. We'll begin with implicit conversions between void * and the other pointer types. These are permitted in a few cases, even though most implicit conversions between pointer types are not. Next, we'll detect all of the new and exciting type errors that void can trigger. We'll handle the sizeof operator last.

Conversions to and from void *

Implicit conversions between void * and the other pointer types are legal in three cases. First, you can compare a value of type void * with another pointer type using == or !=:

```
int *a;
void *b;
--snip--
return a == b;
```

Second, in a conditional expression of the form *<cond>* ? *<clause1>* : *<clause2>*, one clause can have type void * and the other clause can have another pointer type:

```
int *a;
void *b;
--snip--
return flag ? a : b;
```

In both of these cases, the non-void pointer is converted to void *.

Third, you can implicitly convert to and from void * during assignment. You can assign a value with any pointer type to an object of type void *:

```
int *a = 0;
void *b = a;
```

And along the same lines, you can assign a value with type void * to an object with another pointer type.

This last case doesn't just include simple assignment; it covers all the conversions "as if by assignment" that we talked about in Chapter 14. For example, it's legal to pass void * arguments to a function that expects parameters of some other pointer type:

```
int use_int_pointer(int *a);
void *ptr = 0;
use_int_pointer(ptr);
```

Not coincidentally, these are the same three cases where you can implicitly convert a null pointer constant to some other pointer type. To support implicit conversions to and from void *, we'll extend two helper functions we defined back in Chapter 14: get_common_pointer_type and convert_by_assignment.

Let's revisit Listing 14-14, which defined get_common_pointer_type. It's reproduced here as Listing 17-10, with this chapter's changes bolded.

```
get_common_pointer_type(e1, e2):
    e1_t = get_type(e1)
    e2_t = get_type(e2)
    if e1_t == e2_t:
        return e1_t
    else if is_null_pointer_constant(e1):
        return e2_t
    else if is_null_pointer_constant(e2):
        return e1_t
    else if e1_t == Pointer(Void) and e2_t is a pointer type:
        return Pointer(Void)
    else if e2_t == Pointer(Void) and e1_t is a pointer type:
        return Pointer(Void)
    else:
        fail("Expressions have incompatible types")
```

Listing 17-10: Getting the common type of two expressions, where at least one has pointer type

The bolded code permits implicit conversions between void * and other pointer types but not between void * and arithmetic types, array types, or void. Next, we'll take another look at Listing 14-16, reproduced here as Listing 17-11, with changes bolded.

```
convert_by_assignment(e, target_type):
    if get_type(e) == target_type:
        return e
    if get_type(e) is arithmetic and target_type is arithmetic:
        return convert_to(e, target_type)
    if is_null_pointer_constant(e) and target_type is a pointer type:
        return convert_to(e, target_type)
    if target_type == Pointer(Void) and get_type(e) is a pointer type:
        return convert_to(e, target_type)
    if target_type is a pointer type and get_type(e) == Pointer(Void):
        return convert_to(e, target_type)
    else:
        fail("Cannot convert type for assignment")
```

Listing 17-11: Converting an expression to a target type as if by assignment

The bolded additions permit us to convert void * to other pointer types, and vice versa, during assignment. Note that nothing in this listing would prevent us from assigning a void expression to a void target type. However, we'll introduce other restrictions on void elsewhere in the type checker that will ensure that we never call convert_by_assignment with a target type of void. For instance, we'll never try to convert a function argument to void, because we'll reject function declarations with void parameters.

Functions with void Return Types

Next, we'll type check return statements with and without expressions. Which return statement you should use depends on the function's return type. A function with a void return type must not return an expression. A function with any other return type must include an expression when it returns. Therefore, these two function definitions are legal:

```
int return_int(void) {
    return 1;
}

void return_void(void) {
    return;
}
```

And these are both illegal:

```
int return_int(void) {
    return;
}

void return_void(void) {
    return 1;
}
```

You can't even return a void expression from a function with a void return type, which makes the following example illegal too:

```
void return_void(void) {
    return (void) 1;
}
```

Both GCC and Clang accept this program, but they'll warn if you include the -pedantic flag. You can handle this edge case however you like; the test suite doesn't cover it.

I'll skip the pseudocode for this section, since it's a pretty straightforward extension to our existing logic to type check return statements.

Scalar and Non-scalar Types

Several C constructs require scalar expressions, including the operands of the &&, ||, and ! expressions; the first operand of a conditional expression; and the controlling conditions in loops and if statements. The common thread is that all of these language constructs compare the value of the expression to zero. Comparing a pointer or arithmetic value to zero makes sense; comparing a non-scalar value to zero does not.

In earlier chapters, there was no way to write a program that violated these type constraints. Arrays were our only non-scalar type, and they decay to pointers wherever scalar expressions are required. But once we throw void into the mix, we need to enforce these constraints explicitly. (Although void isn't an aggregate type, it isn't scalar, either. A scalar expression has a single value, but a void expression has *no* value.) Listing 17-12 defines a tiny helper function to tell us whether a type is scalar.

```
is_scalar(t):
    match t with
    | Void -> return False
    | Array(elem_t, size) -> return False
    | FunType(param_ts, ret_t) -> return False
    | _ -> return True
```

Listing 17-12: Checking whether a type is scalar

We can use this helper function to validate controlling conditions and logical operands. For example, Listing 17-13 illustrates how to validate the operand of a logical ! expression.

```
typecheck_exp(e, symbols):
    match e with
    | --snip--
    | Unary(Not, inner) ->
        typed_inner = typecheck_and_convert(inner, symbols)
        if not is_scalar(get_type(typed_inner)):
            fail("Logical operators only apply to scalar expressions")
        --snip--
```

Listing 17-13: Validating that a logical operand is scalar

Cast expressions are a bit different. Except for casts between double and pointers, which we already prohibit, you can cast a scalar expression to any scalar type. You can also cast any type to void. Listing 17-14 shows how to type check cast expressions.

```
| Cast(t, inner) ->
    typed_inner = typecheck_and_convert(inner, symbols)
    --snip--
❶ if t == Void:
      return set_type(Cast(t, typed_inner), Void)
❷ if not is_scalar(t):
      fail("Can only cast to scalar type or void")
❸ if not is_scalar(get_type(typed_inner)):
      fail("Cannot cast non-scalar expression to scalar type")
  else:
      return set_type(Cast(t, typed_inner), t)
```

Listing 17-14: Type checking cast expressions

First, we explicitly reject casts between double and pointers. That check is snipped out of Listing 17-14, since it's the same as in previous chapters. Then, we check whether the target type is void ❶. If it is, we record that the type of the whole expression is void. Otherwise, we validate that both the target type ❷ and the inner expression ❸ are scalar. This rejects casts from void to any non-void type. It also forbids casts to array and function types, which we already know are illegal.

The type checking logic in Listings 17-13 and 17-14 will also apply to structures, which we'll implement in the next chapter. Structures are aggregate types, but they don't decay to pointers like arrays do. We'll therefore need to validate that programs don't use structures where scalar types are required.

Restrictions on Incomplete Types

A program will run into type errors if it uses an incomplete type where a complete type is required. For now, we'll require complete types in three cases. First, you can't add, subtract, or subscript pointers to incomplete types, since you can't determine the sizes of the array elements they point to. Second, you can't apply sizeof to an incomplete type, since its size is unknown. Third, whenever you specify an array type, its element type must be complete.

NOTE *As a language extension, Clang and GCC permit pointer arithmetic with void pointers and sizeof operations on void. These expressions are implemented as if the size of void were 1.*

Listing 17-15 defines a couple of helper functions to support this validation.

```
is_complete(t):
    return t != Void

is_pointer_to_complete(t):
    match t with
    | Pointer(t) -> return is_complete(t)
    | _ -> return False
```

Listing 17-15: Checking for incomplete types and pointers to incomplete types

We'll use is_complete whenever we need to check for a complete type. We'll use is_pointer_to_complete when we need to check for a pointer to a complete type—specifically, when we type check pointer addition, subtraction, and subscripting. For example, Listing 17-16 demonstrates how to type check pointer addition. It reproduces Listing 15-21, with this chapter's changes bolded and some unchanged code omitted.

```
    | Binary(Add, e1, e2) ->
        typed_e1 = typecheck_and_convert(e1, symbols)
        typed_e2 = typecheck_and_convert(e2, symbols)
        t1 = get_type(typed_e1)
        t2 = get_type(typed_e2)
        if t1 and t2 are arithmetic:
            --snip--
        else if is_pointer_to_complete(t1) and t2 is an integer type:
            --snip--
        else if is_pointer_to_complete(t2) and t1 is an integer type:
            --snip--
        else:
            fail("Invalid operands for addition")
```

Listing 17-16: Type checking pointer addition, with extra validation that the pointer's referenced type is complete

In the next chapter, we'll extend is_complete to distinguish between complete and incomplete structure types too.

We won't worry about sizeof just yet; we'll type check it a little later, in "sizeof Expressions" on page 477. That means we just have to handle our third case, by making sure that every array element type is complete. This applies to arrays nested in larger types too. The following declaration, for example, is invalid:

```
void (*ptr_to_void_array)[3];
```

Even though every pointer is a complete type, it's illegal to declare a pointer to an array of void elements. In Listing 17-17, we define one more helper function to catch these invalid type specifiers.

```
validate_type_specifier(t):
    match t with
    | Array(elem_t, size) ->
    ❶ if not is_complete(elem_t):
        fail("Illegal array of incomplete type")
```

```
        validate_type_specifier(elem_t)
    | Pointer(referenced_t) -> ❷ validate_type_specifier(referenced_t)
    | FunType(param_ts, ret_t) ->
        for param_t in param_ts:
            validate_type_specifier(param_t)
        validate_type_specifier(ret_t)
❸ | _ -> return
```

Listing 17-17: Validating type specifiers

When we see an array type, we'll make sure that its element type is complete ❶ and then validate that element type recursively. This ensures that we'll reject nested arrays of void elements, arrays of pointers to arrays of void elements, and so on. To handle another derived type, we'll recursively validate any types it refers to ❷. Non-derived types, including void itself, are all valid ❸. We'll call validate_type_specifier to validate type specifiers everywhere they appear: in variable declarations, function declarations, sizeof expressions, and cast expressions.

We'll introduce more restrictions on incomplete types in the next chapter. For example, it's illegal to use incomplete types besides void in the branches of conditional expressions. It's also illegal to assign to an lvalue with an incomplete type, but we can ignore this rule for now because there are no void lvalues, thanks to the rules we'll implement next.

Extra Restrictions on void

On top of the restrictions on all incomplete types that we just implemented, we'll enforce two extra restrictions on void in particular: you can't declare void variables or parameters, and you can't dereference pointers to void. (Both of these uses of void are legal gray areas; see the box "When void Is Valid: An Excessively Detailed Discussion" for the gory details.)

These restrictions on void don't apply to other incomplete types. In the next chapter, you'll see that you can declare—but not define—a variable with an incomplete structure type. You can then define the variable at a different point in the program, once the type is completed. Similarly, you can declare a function that uses an incomplete structure type as a parameter or return type, as long as you complete the type before you call or define that function. Finally, it's legal to dereference a pointer to an incomplete structure type, although this isn't terribly useful; the only thing you're allowed to do with the result of the dereference is take its address, which just gives back the pointer you started with.

WHEN VOID IS VALID: AN EXCESSIVELY

DETAILED DISCUSSION

Very few C programmers need to declare void variables or dereference void * expressions. Nonetheless, it's worth digging into exactly what the C standard

(continued)

---

has to say about these niche cases and how a few widely used compilers handle them. This corner of the language turns out to be particularly confusing and ill defined, which makes it a fun illustration of just how difficult language standards are to write and implement.

For starters, the C standard allows you to declare an extern void variable, but it doesn't allow you to use that variable. Assigning to it or using its value is, unsurprisingly, undefined behavior. This is true for variables with other incomplete types as well. The one thing you *can* do with most variables with incomplete types is take their address:

```
extern struct s my_incomplete_var;
struct s *ptr = &my_incomplete_var;
```

As Stephen Kell, this book's technical reviewer, pointed out to me, you might want to take the address of void variables too. For example, if you're writing a program that examines the layout of memory, such as a debugger, you might need to refer to arbitrary memory locations without a specific type. Most Unix-like systems define special symbols for exactly this purpose: etext, edata, and end, whose addresses mark the ends of the text, data, and BSS segments, respectively. Programs that need to access these symbols normally declare them as char or some other arbitrary type, like this:

```
extern char etext;
void *text_segment = &etext;
```

It would arguably make more sense to declare them as void variables, since they don't really designate objects with values. But if you did that, it would be illegal to take their address, because void variables aren't lvalues. Section 6.3.2.1, paragraph 1, of the C standard states that "an *lvalue* is an expression (with an object type other than void) that potentially designates an object." And section 6.5.3.2, paragraph 1, lays out the constraints on the & operator: "The operand of the unary & operator shall be either a function designator, the result of a [] or unary * operator, or an lvalue that designates an object [that satisfies a couple of other constraints]."

Because a void variable isn't any of these things, we can't take its address, which means we can't do anything with it. In practice, both Clang and GCC let you declare and take the address of void variables, although they'll warn you that your code doesn't strictly conform to the standard. The Microsoft Visual Studio compiler (MSVC) is much less permissive; it won't let you declare void variables at all.

You can declare function parameters with incomplete types, and there's no indication in the standard that void parameters would be an exception, so this appears to be legal:

```
void my_sketchy_function(void a, void b);
```

But GCC warns about functions with void parameters, while Clang and MSVC reject them outright. There are at least two good reasons to reject these parameters: there's no conceivable use for them, and they potentially conflict with the special case of a single void parameter that specifies an empty parameter list. The fact that the standard doesn't just prohibit void parameters aside from that special case seems like an oversight.

Finally, let's try to figure out what happens when you dereference a void * value and discard the result:

```
void *void_ptr = malloc(4);
(void) *void_ptr;
```

GCC warns about this, and as of version 16.0.0, Clang does as well. MSVC, still the most cantankerous of the bunch, considers it an error. The standard itself is no help at all. Section 6.5.3.2 says that the operand of the pointer dereference operator must be a pointer, but it doesn't place any restrictions on what type it can point to. It goes on to say: "If the operand . . . points to an object, the result is an lvalue designating the object. If the operand has type 'pointer to *type*', the result has type '*type*'. If an invalid value has been assigned to the pointer, the behavior of the unary * operator is undefined."

You can't really argue that a pointer to void is an "invalid value." As we've seen, well-formed programs use pointers to void all the time. The next question is whether a pointer to void can point to an object; if so, it sounds like dereferencing it should give us an lvalue. Other parts of the standard suggest that it can indeed point to an object. For example, the first paragraph of section 7.22.3, which introduces malloc and the other memory management functions, states that "the lifetime of an allocated object extends from the allocation until the deallocation. Each such allocation shall yield a pointer to an object disjoint from any other object."

This all suggests that void_ptr is a valid pointer to an object, so *void_ptr should return an lvalue with type void—except that void expressions can't be lvalues. It's a paradox! According to Aaron Ballman (who's on the C standards committee), this means that dereferencing a pointer to void and discarding the result is undefined behavior by omission (*https://github.com/llvm/llvm-project/ issues/53631#issuecomment-1253653888*). It would be nice for the C standard to actually spell this out, but I guess the standards committee has higher priorities.

We're fudging one corner case here. Strictly speaking, it's legal to take the address of *any* dereferenced pointer, whether it's a pointer to a complete type, an incomplete structure type, or void. As we saw back in Chapter 14, taking the address of a dereferenced pointer is a special case; the two operations cancel each other out and the result is well defined, even if the dereference expression by itself would be undefined. That means this code fragment is legal:

```
void *void_ptr = malloc(4);
void *another_ptr = &*void_ptr;
```

Our compiler will reject all dereference operations on void * operands, even in this edge case. But we're not alone here: GCC issues a warning about this code fragment and MSVC rejects it entirely. (Of course, you can handle this edge case correctly if you want; our test suite doesn't cover it.)

Conditional Expressions with void Operands

We'll explicitly allow void operands in conditional expressions, as Listing 17-18 illustrates.

```
typecheck_exp(e, symbols):
    match e with
    | --snip--
    | Conditional(condition, e1, e2) ->
        typed_cond = typecheck_and_convert(condition, symbols)
        typed_e1 = typecheck_and_convert(e1, symbols)
        typed_e2 = typecheck_and_convert(e2, symbols)
    ❶ if not is_scalar(get_type(typed_cond)):
            fail("Condition in conditional operator must be scalar")
        t1 = get_type(typed_e1)
        t2 = get_type(typed_e2)
        if t1 == Void and t2 == Void:
          ❷ result_type = Void
        else if t1 and t2 are arithmetic types:
            result_type = get_common_type(t1, t2)
        else if t1 or t2 is a pointer type:
            result_type = get_common_pointer_type(typed_e1, typed_e2)
        else:
            fail("Cannot convert branches of conditional to a common type")
        --snip--
```

Listing 17-18: Type checking a conditional expression

To type check a conditional expression, we first validate that its controlling condition is scalar ❶. Then, we consider the types of both clauses. If they're both void, the result is void too ❷. Otherwise, we find the result type as before: by applying the usual arithmetic conversions if both operands are arithmetic or finding their common pointer type if either is a pointer. If none of these cases applies—for example, because one operand is void and the other is a pointer or arithmetic value—we throw an error.

Existing Validation for Arithmetic Expressions and Comparisons

Next, we'll make sure that our existing logic to type check arithmetic operations and comparisons works even with void in the mix. Earlier, we could assume that every expression had either arithmetic or pointer type. Now we can't rely on that assumption. For example, let's revisit Listing 14-15, which demonstrated how to type check Equal expressions. Listing 17-19 reproduces that code with the extra validation logic that we need to add.

```
typecheck_exp(e, symbols):
    match e with
    | --snip--
    | Binary(Equal, e1, e2) ->
        typed_e1 = typecheck_and_convert(e1, symbols)
        typed_e2 = typecheck_and_convert(e2, symbols)
        t1 = get_type(typed_e1)
        t2 = get_type(typed_e2)
        if t1 or t2 is a pointer type:
            common_type = get_common_pointer_type(typed_e1, typed_e2)
        else if t1 and t2 are arithmetic types:
            common_type = get_common_type(t1, t2)
        else:
            fail("Invalid operands to equality expression")
        --snip--
```

Listing 17-19: Type checking an Equal expression, with extra validation

NOTE *If you compare this code to Listing 14-15, you'll notice that we've replaced the recursive calls to* typecheck_exp *with* typecheck_and_convert. *We made that change back in Chapter 15, so it's not bolded here.*

In Chapter 14, if neither t1 nor t2 was a pointer type, we knew they were both arithmetic types, so we could go ahead and perform the usual arithmetic conversions. Now we'll explicitly check that they're either pointer or arithmetic types; if they're anything else, we'll fail.

More broadly, we should type check each expression's operands by accepting valid types instead of rejecting invalid ones. For example, we should validate that the operands to Multiply and Divide *are* arithmetic values, instead of making sure they *aren't* pointers. Take a moment to look over your type checking logic for all the relational and arithmetic operations, tightening up any validation that's too permissive.

sizeof Expressions

A sizeof expression has type size_t; in our implementation, that's just unsigned long. To type check sizeof, we first validate its operand and then record unsigned long as the result type, as Listing 17-20 demonstrates.

```
typecheck_exp(e, symbols):
    match e with
    | --snip--
    | SizeOfT(t) ->
      ❶ validate_type_specifier(t)
      ❷ if not is_complete(t):
            fail("Can't get the size of an incomplete type")
        return set_type(e, ULong)
    | SizeOf(inner) ->
```

```
❸ typed_inner = typecheck_exp(inner, symbols)
❹ if not is_complete(get_type(typed_inner)):
        fail("Can't get the size of an incomplete type")
  return set_type(SizeOf(typed_inner), ULong)
```

Listing 17-20: Type checking sizeof

If sizeof operates on a type, we enforce two rules about incomplete types that we discussed in "Restrictions on Incomplete Types" on page 471: you can never specify an array with an incomplete element type ❶, and you can't apply sizeof to an incomplete type ❷. (You can't apply sizeof to a function type either, but we already catch that error in the parser.)

If the operand is an expression, we first infer that expression's type ❸. To avoid converting arrays to pointers, we use typecheck_exp instead of typecheck_and_convert. Once we've determined the expression's type, we make sure that type is complete ❹.

TEST THE TYPE CHECKER

To test out the type checker, run:

```
$ ./test_compiler /path/to/your_compiler --chapter 17 --stage validate
```

The invalid test cases for this stage are broken up into several subdirectories. The tests in *tests/chapter_17/invalid_types/pointer_conversions* cover invalid conversions to and from void *. The tests in *tests/chapter_17/invalid_types/scalar_expressions* use non-scalar expressions where scalar expressions are required, and the tests in *tests/chapter_17/invalid_types/incomplete_types* use incomplete types where complete types are required. The tests in *tests/chapter_17/invalid_types/void* cover other invalid uses of void (like returning a value from a function with a void return type or comparing two void expressions). Finally, *tests/chapter_17/valid* contains valid programs, which your type checker should process successfully.

TACKY Generation

Next, we'll convert sizeof and void expressions to TACKY. We'll need to update the Return and FunCall instructions to account for functions with a void return type. We'll also process casts and conditional expressions of type void slightly differently from their non-void counterparts; in particular, we won't create any void temporary variables. We'll evaluate sizeof expressions during this pass as well, replacing them with integer constants. We won't need to change anything to support pointers to void.

Functions with void Return Types

We'll make two changes to the TACKY IR so that we can call and return from functions with a void return type. First, we'll make the destination of the FunCall instruction optional:

```
FunCall(identifier fun_name, val* args, val? dst)
```

For calls to void functions, we'll leave dst empty. For calls to any other function, dst will be the temporary variable that holds the return value, like it is now. We'll make a similar change to the Return instruction:

```
Return(val?)
```

Then, we'll translate each return statement with no expression to a TACKY Return instruction without a value.

A void function might not use an explicit return statement; in this case, it returns once control reaches the end of the function. We already handle this case correctly by adding a Return instruction to the end of every TACKY function.

Casts to void

Listing 17-21 shows how to handle a cast to void: just process the inner expression without emitting any other instructions.

```
emit_tacky(e, instructions, symbols):
    match e with
    | --snip--
    | Cast(Void, inner) ->
        emit_tacky_and_convert(inner, instructions, symbols)
        return PlainOperand(Var("DUMMY"))
```

Listing 17-21: Converting a cast to void to TACKY

You can return whatever operand you want here; the caller won't use it.

Conditional Expressions with void Operands

Listing 17-22 demonstrates how we currently convert conditional expressions to TACKY.

```
    | Conditional(condition, e1, e2) ->
        --snip--
        cond = emit_tacky_and_convert(condition, instructions, symbols)
        instructions.append(JumpIfZero(cond, e2_label))
        dst = make_tacky_variable(get_type(e), symbols)
        v1 = emit_tacky_and_convert(e1, instructions, symbols)
        instructions.append_all(
        ❶ [ Copy(v1, dst),
            Jump(end),
            Label(e2_label) ])
```

```
        v2 = emit_tacky_and_convert(e2, instructions, symbols)
        instructions.append_all(
      ❷ [ Copy(v2, dst),
            Label(end) ])
        return PlainOperand(dst)
```

Listing 17-22: Converting a non-void conditional expression to TACKY

If e1 and e2 are void expressions, the Copy instructions ❶❷ are problematic. We shouldn't create a dst temporary variable with type void, and we definitely shouldn't copy anything into it. To handle void expressions in conditionals, we'll stick with the basic approach from Listing 17-22, but without generating dst or emitting either Copy instruction. Listing 17-23 shows the updated pseudocode to handle void conditional expressions.

```
| Conditional(condition, e1, e2) ->
    --snip--
    cond = emit_tacky_and_convert(condition, instructions, symbols)
    instructions.append(JumpIfZero(cond, e2_label))
    if get_type(e) == Void:
        emit_tacky_and_convert(e1, instructions, symbols)
        instructions.append_all(
        [ Jump(end),
          Label(e2_label) ])
        emit_tacky_and_convert(e2, instructions, symbols)
        instructions.append(Label(end))
      ❶ return PlainOperand(Var("DUMMY"))
    else:
        --snip--
```

Listing 17-23: Converting a conditional expression with a void result to TACKY

Since we don't create the temporary variable dst, we need to return some other operand to the caller. We can return a dummy value ❶ because we know the caller won't use it. To handle non-void expressions, we'll generate the same instructions as before, so I've omitted the pseudocode for that case.

sizeof Expressions

We'll evaluate sizeof expressions during TACKY generation and represent the results as unsigned long constants, as Listing 17-24 illustrates.

```
| SizeOf(inner) ->
    t = get_type(inner)
    result = size(t)
    return PlainOperand(Constant(ConstULong(result)))
| SizeOfT(t) ->
    result = size(t)
    return PlainOperand(Constant(ConstULong(result)))
```

Listing 17-24: Evaluating sizeof during TACKY generation

Since we don't convert the operand of sizeof to TACKY, it won't be evaluated at runtime.

The Latest and Greatest TACKY IR

Listing 17-25 defines the current TACKY IR, with this chapter's two changes bolded.

```
program = Program(top_level*)
top_level = Function(identifier, bool global, identifier* params, instruction* body)
          | StaticVariable(identifier, bool global, type t, static_init* init_list)
          | StaticConstant(identifier, type t, static_init init)
instruction = Return(val?)
            | SignExtend(val src, val dst)
            | Truncate(val src, val dst)
            | ZeroExtend(val src, val dst)
            | DoubleToInt(val src, val dst)
            | DoubleToUInt(val src, val dst)
            | IntToDouble(val src, val dst)
            | UIntToDouble(val src, val dst)
            | Unary(unary_operator, val src, val dst)
            | Binary(binary_operator, val src1, val src2, val dst)
            | Copy(val src, val dst)
            | GetAddress(val src, val dst)
            | Load(val src_ptr, val dst)
            | Store(val src, val dst_ptr)
            | AddPtr(val ptr, val index, int scale, val dst)
            | CopyToOffset(val src, identifier dst, int offset)
            | Jump(identifier target)
            | JumpIfZero(val condition, identifier target)
            | JumpIfNotZero(val condition, identifier target)
            | Label(identifier)
            | FunCall(identifier fun_name, val* args, val? dst)
val = Constant(const) | Var(identifier)
unary_operator = Complement | Negate | Not
binary_operator = Add | Subtract | Multiply | Divide | Remainder | Equal | NotEqual
                | LessThan | LessOrEqual | GreaterThan | GreaterOrEqual
```

Listing 17-25: Adding support for functions with void return types to the TACKY IR

Most of the changes in this section—to support void casts, void conditional expressions, and sizeof—didn't impact the TACKY IR. We'll process the two instructions that did change in the next section.

TEST THE TACKY GENERATION STAGE

To test out TACKY generation, run:

```
$ ./test_compiler /path/to/your_compiler --chapter 17 --stage tacky
```

Assembly Generation

To finish off the chapter, we'll generate assembly for Return instructions with no value and FunCall instructions with no destination. We can handle both instructions with minor changes to the assembly generation pass.

Normally, an instruction of the form Return(val) is converted to the following assembly:

```
Mov(<val type>, val, <dst register>)
Ret
```

If the return value is absent, we'll skip the Mov instruction and just generate the Ret instruction. Along the same lines, Listing 17-26 summarizes how we usually convert a FunCall instruction to assembly.

```
<fix stack alignment>
<move arguments to general-purpose registers>
<move arguments to XMM registers>
<push arguments onto the stack>
Call(fun_name)
<deallocate arguments/padding>
❶ Mov(<dst type>, <dst register>, dst)
```

Listing 17-26: Converting FunCall to assembly when the function returns a value

If dst is absent, we won't generate the final Mov instruction ❶, but everything else will remain the same. Table 17-1 summarizes the latest updates to the conversion from TACKY to assembly, with these two small changes bolded.

Table 17-1: Converting TACKY Instructions to Assembly

TACKY instruction		Assembly instructions
Return(val)	Integer	Mov(<val type>, val, Reg(AX)) Ret
	double	Mov(Double, val, Reg(XMM0)) Ret
	void	**Ret**
FunCall(fun_name, args, dst)	dst is present	<fix stack alignment> <move arguments to general-purpose registers> <move arguments to XMM registers> <push arguments onto the stack> Call(fun_name) <deallocate arguments/padding> Mov(<dst type>, <dst register>, dst)
	dst is absent	**<fix stack alignment>** **<move arguments to general-purpose registers>** **<move arguments to XMM registers>** **<push arguments onto the stack>** **Call(fun_name)** **<deallocate arguments/padding>**

Because the assembly AST didn't change, we won't touch the rest of the backend.

TEST THE WHOLE COMPILER

To test out the whole compiler, run:

```
$ ./test_compiler /path/to/your_compiler --chapter 17
```

The test programs in *tests/chapter_17/valid/void_pointer* perform various operations on void * values, including assignments, comparisons, type conversions, and calls to all the memory management functions we discussed at the beginning of the chapter. The tests in *tests/chapter_17/valid/void* exercise your compiler's support for void expressions, including function calls, casts, and conditional expressions. The tests in *tests/chapter_17/valid/sizeof* validate that your compiler can handle both forms of sizeof, that the operand to sizeof isn't evaluated at runtime, and that your compiler correctly calculates the size of a wide range of types. Finally, the tests in *tests/chapter_17/valid/libraries* validate that when you compile code that uses void and pointers to void, it will interoperate correctly with code compiled by your system's C compiler.

Summary

In this chapter, you implemented the void type and the sizeof operator. You learned about the difference between complete and incomplete types and the ways that C programs can use void expressions. Then, you extended the type checker to detect invalid uses of incomplete and non-scalar types, modified the TACKY generation stage to evaluate sizeof operators without evaluating their operands, and tweaked the backend to support functions that don't return a value. Next, we'll finish up Part II by adding structure types. Structures are the very last language feature you'll implement in the book, and perhaps the most challenging. Luckily, you're well prepared to take on this challenge, thanks to the skills you learned and the groundwork you laid in previous chapters.

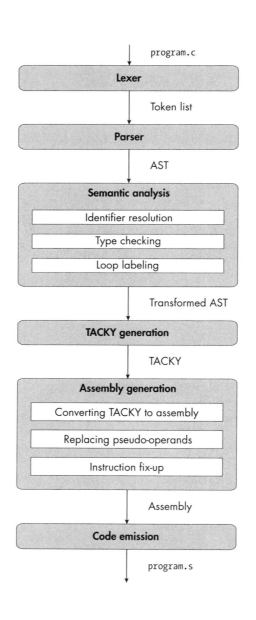

18

STRUCTURES

In this chapter, you'll add one final language feature: structures. You'll also implement the . and -> operators to access structure members. In a fitting end to Part II, you'll draw on many of the skills, concepts, and techniques you learned in earlier chapters. In the identifier resolution stage, you'll resolve structure tags along with function and variable identifiers. In the type checker, you'll record structure definitions in a type table, much like you already record function and variable declarations in the symbol table. During TACKY generation, you'll build on the strategy you used in Chapter 14 to handle operations on dereferenced pointers and other objects. And on the backend, you'll implement the part of the System V calling convention that specifies how to pass structures as function parameters and return values. Since unions are a close cousin to structures, you might want to implement those too. We won't cover them in detail, but you can add them as an extra credit feature.

Declaring Structure Types

You have to declare a structure type before you can use it. There are two kinds of structure type declarations. The first, shown in Listing 18-1, specifies the structure's members.

```
struct complete_struct {
    long member1;
    double member2;
};
```

Listing 18-1: A complete structure type declaration

This listing declares a complete structure type with two members: a long and a double. The identifier complete_struct is this type's *tag*, which we can use to specify the type later in the program. A complete structure type must have at least one member, so it's illegal to declare a structure type with an empty member list:

```
struct empty {};
```

The second kind of structure type declaration, shown in Listing 18-2, specifies a structure's tag but not its members.

```
struct incomplete_struct;
```

Listing 18-2: An incomplete structure type declaration

Listing 18-2 declares an incomplete structure type. As you learned in the previous chapter, you can use incomplete types only in certain limited circumstances. For example, you can't define a variable of type struct incomplete_struct, but you can define a pointer to a struct incomplete_struct. (That's because we know how much memory a pointer requires, but not how much memory this structure requires.) We'll say that a structure declaration with no member list *declares* a type, while a structure declaration with a member list both *declares* and *defines* a type. This differs from the terminology you'll see in the C standard and elsewhere; in particular, when people talk about "type definitions," they usually mean aliases introduced with the typedef keyword.

Structure tags are visible only in the scope in which they're declared, just like function and variable names. If a structure tag is declared at file scope, it's visible from the point where it's declared until the end of the file. If it's declared at block scope, it's visible until the end of the block. If two structure type declarations with the same tag appear in the same scope, they always declare the same type; if they appear in different scopes, they declare distinct types. (Type declarations don't have linkage, so you can't apply the static or extern keywords to them.) You can declare the same structure type multiple times, but you can't define it more than once.

A structure type is complete once its definition is in scope, as Listing 18-3 illustrates.

```
❶ struct s;

   struct s *ptr = 0;

   struct s {
       int a;
       int b;
   }; ❷

❸ struct s x = {0,0};
```

Listing 18-3: Declaring an incomplete type and then completing it

Between ❶ and ❷, struct s is an incomplete type. It wouldn't be legal to define a variable with type struct s between these two points in the program, but it's legal to define ptr, which is a pointer to struct s. After the end of the type declaration that specifies its member list ❷, struct s is a complete type, so it's legal to define a variable with that type ❸.

When the same structure tag is declared in two different scopes, one can shadow the other, as Listing 18-4 illustrates.

```
   #include <stdio.h>

❶ struct s {
       int a;
   };

   int main(void) {
       printf("Outer struct size: %lu\n", ❷ sizeof (struct s));

     ❸ struct s {
           long l;
       };

       printf("Inner struct size: %lu\n", ❹ sizeof (struct s));
       return 0;
   }
```

Listing 18-4: One structure type shadowing another

First, we define a struct s type at file scope ❶. Its size is 4 bytes because it contains a single int. The first sizeof expression in main refers to this type ❷. Then, we define another struct s type at block scope ❸, shadowing the first type. This type contains a single long, so its size is 8 bytes. The two definitions of struct s don't conflict, because they appear in different scopes. In the second sizeof expression ❹, the specifier struct s refers to the 8-byte structure type defined in the inner scope. Running this program gives the following output:

```
$ ./listing_18_4
Outer struct size: 4
Inner struct size: 8
```

Even when a structure's tag is shadowed, its members are still visible. Consider Listing 18-5.

```
int main(void) {

❶ struct shadow {
      int x;
  };
  struct shadow outer;
  outer.x = 2;
  {
    ❷ struct shadow {
          int y;
      };
      struct shadow inner;
      inner.y = 3;
    ❸ return outer.x + inner.y;
  }
}
```

Listing 18-5: Using a variable with a shadowed structure type

In this listing, we first declare a structure type, struct shadow ❶. Then, we define a variable, outer, with that type. In the inner scope, we declare another structure type with the same tag ❷, which shadows the outer declaration. We then declare a variable with this new type, inner. In the return statement, we can still access the members of both variables ❸. Even in the inner scope, the compiler knows about the original struct shadow type, and it still knows that outer belongs to that type; we just can't specify that type with the shadow tag.

To keep all our structure types straight, we'll treat structure tags a lot like variable names: in the identifier resolution pass, we'll replace each user-defined tag with a unique identifier.

Structure Member Declarations

The members of a structure can have any complete type, including primitive types like int and derived types like arrays, pointers, or other structures. It's illegal to declare a structure member with an incomplete type, however, because that makes it impossible to determine the size of the whole structure. This implies, as section 6.7.2.1, paragraph 3, of the C standard puts it, that "a structure shall not contain an instance of itself." That is, a `struct s` can't contain a member of type `struct s`. On the other hand, a structure can contain a pointer to itself because pointer types are always complete. The canonical example, shown in Listing 18-6, is a node in a linked list, which holds a value and a pointer to the next list entry.

```
struct linked_list_node ❶ {
    int val;
    struct linked_list_node *next;
}; ❷
```

Listing 18-6: A structure type definition that contains a pointer to itself

After ❶, `struct linked_list_node` is visible as an incomplete type, so we can declare the member `next` as a pointer to this type. After ❷, the type is complete.

It's also illegal to declare functions as structure members. A structure can hold function pointers—which are complete types, just like any other pointer—but we don't support function pointers, so that doesn't matter to us.

Tag and Member Namespaces

Structure tags are in a different namespace from functions and variables. This means the same identifier can be used as both a tag and a function or variable name, and neither identifier will shadow or conflict with the other. It's perfectly legal, for example, to declare the type `struct s` and a variable `s` in the same scope. It's possible to maintain these separate namespaces because the `struct` keyword tells the compiler that a particular identifier is a structure tag.

Similarly, each structure member list is its own namespace. A structure member can share a name with any function, variable, or structure type, including the structure type that contains it, like in the following example:

```
struct s {
    int s;
};
```

It's also legal for members in different structures to have the same name:

```
struct s1 {
    int x;
};

struct s2 {
    int x;
};
```

When the identifier x appears in an expression, like var->x, the compiler can figure out from context whether it refers to the member in s1, the member in s2, or a function or variable. Unsurprisingly, it's illegal for two members of the same structure to share a name.

Structure Type Declarations We Aren't Implementing

C syntax doesn't distinguish between structure type specifiers and type declarations, so you can simultaneously declare a new structure type and use that structure type in some larger construct. In Listing 18-7, for example, a single declaration defines a new structure type, struct s, and a variable x of type struct s.

```
struct s {
    int member;
} x;
```

Listing 18-7: Defining and specifying a structure type in the same declaration

To simplify parsing and semantic analysis, we'll require every declaration to declare exactly one function, variable, or type. We won't support declarations like Listing 18-7 that declare a new type and some other entity at the same time. This goes for incomplete types as well. The C standard lets you implicitly declare an incomplete structure type, just by specifying it:

```
struct s *f(void);
```

Even if struct s hasn't yet been declared, this declaration is legal: it simultaneously declares struct s as an incomplete type and declares a function that returns a pointer to struct s. However, our implementation won't permit this. Instead, we'll require a separate declaration of struct s first:

```
struct s;
struct s *f(void);
```

Requiring types to be declared before they're used also implies that you can't nest one structure declaration inside another, like in Listing 18-8.

```
struct outer {
    struct inner {
        int a;
        long l;
    } i;
    double d;
};
```

Listing 18-8: Declaring an inner structure type and declaring member i with that type in the same declaration

We'll impose a few other restrictions too. We'll reject structure declarations without tags and structure members without names, even though the C standard permits them. We also won't support *bit-field members*, which make it possible to address individual bits within a structure.

Operating on Structures

You can access the members of a structure with the . operator:

```
struct s var;
--snip--
long l = var.member1;
```

If you have a pointer to a structure, you can access the structure's members with the -> operator. Continuing with the same example:

```
struct s *ptr = &var;
long l2 = ptr->member1;
```

You can apply the . and -> operators only to complete structure types. You can't access the members of an incomplete structure type, since those members haven't been defined yet.

Structures are aggregate types, like arrays. But structures don't decay to pointers like arrays do, so you can use them in several ways that you can't use arrays. For example, you can pass them as function arguments and return values. You can also assign to them, like in Listing 18-9.

```
struct s foo;
struct s bar;
--snip--
foo = bar;
```

Listing 18-9: Assigning to a structure

You can assign to individual members of a structure too, as long as they're lvalues. A structure member specified with the -> operator is always an lvalue:

```
ptr->member2 = 2.0;
```

Recall that all dereferenced pointers are lvalues. The -> operator produces a dereferenced pointer, much like the * and [] operators do, so the same rules apply.

If a structure is an lvalue, any members you access with the . operator are lvalues too. If a structure isn't an lvalue, neither are its members. Therefore, this assignment expression is legal:

```
var.member2 = 2.0;
```

But, because the result of a function call isn't an lvalue, this is illegal:

```
return_struct().member2 = 2.0;
```

Structures can appear in a few other expressions, pretty much where you'd expect. They can appear in the branches of conditional expressions, as long as both branches have the same structure type. You can get their size with sizeof and cast them to void, but you can't otherwise cast to or from structure types. And if a structure or structure member is an lvalue, you can take its address.

There are two ways to initialize a structure. You can initialize it with an expression of the same structure type:

```
struct s return_struct(void);
struct s var = return_struct();
```

Or, you can use a compound initializer to initialize each member individually, like in Listing 18-10.

```
struct example {
    int member1;
    double member2;
    char array[3];
};

struct example var = {1, 2.0, ❶ {'a', 'b', 'c'}};
```

Listing 18-10: Initializing a structure with a compound initializer

A compound initializer initializes a structure's members in order. The initializer in Listing 18-10 initializes member1 with the value 1 and member2 with 2.0. The inner compound initializer initializes the three array elements in array_member ❶. Note that compound initializers for arrays and structures have identical syntax. (The syntax for *designated initializers*, which initialize specific subobjects in an aggregate object, is different for array elements and structure members, but we won't implement designated initializers.) By nesting compound initializers, you can initialize arrays of structures, structures that contain other structures, and so on.

Structure Layout in Memory

At this point, we have a pretty good sense of how structure types work in source code. Now let's look at how they're laid out in memory at runtime. This is specified partly by the C standard and partly by the System V ABI. It's important to lay out structures exactly as the ABI specifies so that the code we compile can interoperate with other code that uses structures.

A structure's members appear in the same order in memory as in the original structure declaration. The first member must have the same address as the structure as a whole; you can always convert a pointer to a structure into a pointer to its first member, and vice versa. Each subsequent member will be stored at the earliest free address with the correct alignment. Let's use the struct example type from Listing 18-10 as an example. Listing 18-11 reproduces the definition of struct example.

```
struct example {
    int member1;
    double member2;
    char array[3];
};
```

Listing 18-11: A structure type with several members with different alignments

The first member must start at the very beginning of the structure. Because member1 is an int, it occupies the structure's first 4 bytes. Bytes in a structure are typically zero-indexed, so we'll say that member1 occupies bytes 0 through 3. The next unused space is therefore at byte 4. But member2 is a double, which is 8-byte aligned; its starting address must be a multiple of 8. Therefore, member2 will be stored in bytes 8 through 15. We say that member2 has an offset of 8 bytes from the start of the structure. Between member1 and member2, in bytes 4 through 7, we have 4 bytes of padding.

The last member, array, takes up 3 bytes and has an alignment of 1 byte. Since we don't need any padding to align it correctly, we'll store it right after member2, in bytes 16 through 18.

We'll also need padding at the end of the structure, after array. According to the System V ABI, the size of a type must be a multiple of its alignment. The ABI also states that a structure takes on the same alignment as its most strictly aligned member. The most strictly aligned member of struct example is the double, member2. Therefore, the whole structure must be 8-byte aligned, and its size must be a multiple of 8. The three members of struct example and the padding between them occupy 19 bytes. We'll add 5 bytes of padding to the end of the structure, bringing its total size to 24 bytes. Figure 18-1 illustrates the layout of the whole structure.

Member	member1	<padding>	member2	array [0]	[1]	[2]	<padding>
Bytes	0–3	4–7	8–15	16	17	18	19–23

Figure 18-1: The structure layout in memory

The padding between members guarantees that each member will end up at a correctly aligned memory address. If the starting address of the entire structure is a multiple of 8 and the offset of member2 from the start is also a multiple of 8, we know that member2's runtime memory address will be a multiple of 8 too. The padding at the end of the structure guarantees that each element in an array of structures will have the correct alignment; if the initial element in an array of struct example objects is 8-byte aligned and its total size is 24 bytes, each subsequent element will be 8-byte aligned as well.

Now that you understand how to work with structures in C and how they're laid out in memory, let's get to work on implementing them.

The Lexer

You'll add three new tokens in this chapter:

struct   A keyword indicating a structure type specifier

.   A period, the structure member access operator

->   An arrow, the operator to access a structure member through a pointer

Keep in mind that a period can be either a structure member access operator or part of a floating-point constant. We'll recognize a period as a . token only if it's followed by a non-digit character. If a period is followed by a digit, either it's the start of a floating-point constant or it's invalid. For example, if the lexer sees the input .100u, it should try to parse this as a constant. It will then raise an error, since this doesn't match the regular expression for any kind of constant. It should *not* lex this as a . token followed by the constant 100u.

TEST THE LEXER

To test out the lexer, run:

```
$ ./test_compiler /path/to/your_compiler --chapter 18 --stage lex
```

The lexer should reject the test programs in *tests/chapter_18/invalid_lex*; these include . characters that are followed by digits but aren't part of valid floating-point constants. The lexer should accept all the other test programs in this chapter.

The Parser

We'll add several new constructs to the AST in this chapter: structure declarations, structure type specifiers, and the two new structure operators. Listing 18-12 gives the AST definition for structure declarations.

```
struct_declaration = (identifier tag, member_declaration* members)
member_declaration = (identifier member_name, type member_type)
```

Listing 18-12: Representing structure declarations in the AST

A struct_declaration consists of a tag and a list of members. To represent an incomplete structure type declaration, we'll leave the member list empty.

(Remember that a complete structure type must have at least one member.) We'll represent each member with a `member_declaration`, which includes a member name and a type.

Next, we'll extend the `declaration` AST node to support structure type declarations as well as function and variable declarations:

```
declaration = --snip-- | StructDecl(struct_declaration)
```

We'll also extend the `type` AST node to include structure type specifiers like `struct s`:

```
type = --snip-- | Structure(identifier tag)
```

Finally, we'll add two new expressions: the `.` and `->` operators, sometimes called the *structure member operator* and *structure pointer operator*, respectively. We'll use the more concise names `Dot` and `Arrow`:

```
exp = --snip--
    | Dot(exp structure, identifier member)
    | Arrow(exp pointer, identifier member)
```

Each of these operators takes an expression as its first operand and the name of a structure member as its second operand. Listing 18-13 defines the complete AST, with this chapter's changes bolded.

```
program = Program(declaration*)
declaration = FunDecl(function_declaration) | VarDecl(variable_declaration)
            | StructDecl(struct_declaration)
variable_declaration = (identifier name, initializer? init,
                           type var_type, storage_class?)
function_declaration = (identifier name, identifier* params, block? body,
                           type fun_type, storage_class?)
struct_declaration = (identifier tag, member_declaration* members)
member_declaration = (identifier member_name, type member_type)
initializer = SingleInit(exp) | CompoundInit(initializer*)
type = Char | SChar | UChar | Int | Long | UInt | ULong | Double | Void
     | FunType(type* params, type ret)
     | Pointer(type referenced)
     | Array(type element, int size)
     | Structure(identifier tag)
storage_class = Static | Extern
block_item = S(statement) | D(declaration)
block = Block(block_item*)
for_init = InitDecl(variable_declaration) | InitExp(exp?)
statement = Return(exp?)
          | Expression(exp)
          | If(exp condition, statement then, statement? else)
          | Compound(block)
          | Break
          | Continue
          | While(exp condition, statement body)
          | DoWhile(statement body, exp condition)
```

```
                        | For(for_init init, exp? condition, exp? post, statement body)
                        | Null
            exp = Constant(const)
                | String(string)
                | Var(identifier)
                | Cast(type target_type, exp)
                | Unary(unary_operator, exp)
                | Binary(binary_operator, exp, exp)
                | Assignment(exp, exp)
                | Conditional(exp condition, exp, exp)
                | FunctionCall(identifier, exp* args)
                | Dereference(exp)
                | AddrOf(exp)
                | Subscript(exp, exp)
                | SizeOf(exp)
                | SizeOfT(type)
                | Dot(exp structure, identifier member)
                | Arrow(exp pointer, identifier member)
            unary_operator = Complement | Negate | Not
            binary_operator = Add | Subtract | Multiply | Divide | Remainder | And | Or
                            | Equal | NotEqual | LessThan | LessOrEqual
                            | GreaterThan | GreaterOrEqual
            const = ConstInt(int) | ConstLong(int) | ConstUInt(int) | ConstULong(int)
                  | ConstDouble(double) | ConstChar(int) | ConstUChar(int)
```

Listing 18-13: The abstract syntax tree with structure types and the . and -> operators

Listing 18-14 shows the corresponding changes to the grammar.

```
<program> ::= { <declaration> }
<declaration> ::= <variable-declaration> | <function-declaration> | <struct-declaration>
<variable-declaration> ::= { <specifier> }+ <declarator> [ "=" <initializer> ] ";"
<function-declaration> ::= { <specifier> }+ <declarator> ( <block> | ";")
<struct-declaration> ::= "struct" <identifier> ❶ [ "{" { <member-declaration> }+ "}" ] ";"
<member-declaration> ::= { <type-specifier> }+ <declarator> ";"
<declarator> ::= "*" <declarator> | <direct-declarator>
<direct-declarator> ::= <simple-declarator> [ <declarator-suffix> ]
<declarator-suffix> ::= <param-list> | { "[" <const> "]" }+
<param-list> ::= "(" "void" ")" | "(" <param> { "," <param> } ")"
<param> ::= { <type-specifier> }+ <declarator>
<simple-declarator> ::= <identifier> | "(" <declarator> ")"
<type-specifier> ::= "int" | "long" | "unsigned" | "signed" | "double" | "char" | "void"
                   | "struct" <identifier>
<specifier> ::= <type-specifier> | "static" | "extern"
<block> ::= "{" { <block-item> } "}"
<block-item> ::= <statement> | <declaration>
<initializer> ::= <exp> | "{" <initializer> { "," <initializer> } [ "," ] "}"
<for-init> ::= <variable-declaration> | [ <exp> ] ";"
<statement> ::= "return" [ <exp> ] ";"
              | <exp> ";"
              | "if" "(" <exp> ")" <statement> [ "else" <statement> ]
              | <block>
              | "break" ";"
              | "continue" ";"
              | "while" "(" <exp> ")" <statement>
```

```
                 | "do" <statement> "while" "(" <exp> ")" ";"
                 | "for" "(" <for-init> [ <exp> ] ";" [ <exp> ] ")" <statement>
                 | ";"
<exp> ::= <cast-exp> | <exp> <binop> <exp> | <exp> "?" <exp> ":" <exp>
<cast-exp> ::= "(" <type-name> ")" <cast-exp>
                 | <unary-exp>
<unary-exp> ::= <unop> <cast-exp>
                 | "sizeof" <unary-exp>
                 | "sizeof" "(" <type-name> ")"
                 | <postfix-exp>
<type-name> ::= { <type-specifier> }+ [ <abstract-declarator> ]
<postfix-exp> ::= <primary-exp> { <postfix-op> }
<postfix-op> ::= "[" <exp> "]"
                 | "." <identifier>
                 | "->" <identifier>
<primary-exp> ::= <const> | <identifier> | "(" <exp> ")" | { <string> }+
                 | <identifier> "(" [ <argument-list> ] ")"
<argument-list> ::= <exp> { "," <exp> }
<abstract-declarator> ::= "*" [ <abstract-declarator> ]
                          | <direct-abstract-declarator>
<direct-abstract-declarator> ::= "(" <abstract-declarator> ")" { "[" <const> "]" }
                                 | { "[" <const> "]" }+
<unop> ::= "-" | "~" | "!" | "*" | "&"
<binop> ::= "-" | "+" | "*" | "/" | "%" | "&&" | "||"
            | "==" | "!=" | "<" | "<=" | ">" | ">=" | "="
<const> ::= <int> | <long> | <uint> | <ulong> | <double> | <char>
<identifier> ::= ? An identifier token ?
<string> ::= ? A string token ?
<int> ::= ? An int token ?
<char> ::= ? A char token ?
<long> ::= ? An int or long token ?
<uint> ::= ? An unsigned int token ?
<ulong> ::= ? An unsigned int or unsigned long token ?
<double> ::= ? A floating-point constant token ?
```

Listing 18-14: The grammar with structure types and the . and -> operators

A <struct-declaration> may include a brace-enclosed list of structure members ❶. This member list is optional, but if the braces are present they must contain at least one member.

A structure member declaration has the same form as a variable declaration; it includes a list of type specifiers and a declarator and ends with a semicolon. Unlike a variable declaration, however, a structure member can't have an initializer or a storage class. We'll impose one syntactic requirement that isn't reflected in the grammar: the parser should reject function declarators in structure member declarations, even though the <member -declaration> grammar rule allows them. For example, the parser should reject this declaration:

```
struct contains_function {
    int foo(void);
};
```

A structure type specifier consists of two tokens: the struct keyword and an identifier token, which specifies the structure tag. This specifier can't be combined with other type specifiers, but it can be modified by a pointer, array, or function declarator.

The new . and -> operators are postfix operators, like the subscript operator we added in Chapter 15. All three postfix operators have higher precedence than any prefix operator. The new <postfix-op> symbol includes all three operators, which ensures that they're all parsed with the correct precedence.

TEST THE PARSER

To test your parser, run:

```
$ ./test_compiler /path/to/your_compiler --chapter 18 --stage parse
```

Semantic Analysis

We haven't made any substantive changes to the identifier resolution pass in a while. Now we'll have it resolve structure tags along with function and variable names. This pass will assign every structure type a unique ID, replacing its original user-defined tag. It will also throw an error if a program tries to specify a structure type before declaring it.

In the type checker, we'll introduce a new table to track structure definitions. We'll refer to these definitions when we type check initializers, member access operators, and other operations on structures. We'll also use them to generate TACKY and assembly in later stages.

Resolving Structure Tags

Let's walk through how to handle structure tags during identifier resolution. We'll rename these tags in basically the same way that we rename local variables. We'll maintain a map from user-defined tags to unique identifiers. When we find a declaration of a new structure type, we'll generate a new identifier and add it to the map. And when we encounter a structure type specifier, we'll replace it with the corresponding unique identifier from the map. Because structure tags exist in a separate namespace from functions and variables, we'll track them in a separate map.

Defining the Structure Tag Map

In our existing identifier map, we track three pieces of information about each user-defined function or variable name: the unique identifier we'll replace it with, whether it has linkage, and whether it was defined in the current scope. In the structure tag map, we'll track each tag's unique identifier and whether it was defined in the current scope, but we won't track linkage, because that concept doesn't apply to types. Go ahead and define this data structure. Then, we'll look at how to resolve tags in type specifiers and declarations.

Resolving Type Specifiers

Listing 18-15 illustrates how to resolve a type specifier.

```
resolve_type(type_specifier, structure_map):
    match type_specifier with
    | Structure(tag) ->
        if tag is in structure_map:
            unique_tag = structure_map.get(tag).new_tag
          ❶ return Structure(unique_tag)
        else:
          ❷ fail("Specified an undeclared structure type")
    | Pointer(referenced_t) ->
        resolved_t = resolve_type(referenced_t, structure_map)
        return Pointer(resolved_t)
    | Array(elem_t, size) ->
        --snip--
    | FunType(param_ts, ret_t) ->
        --snip--
    | t -> return t
```

Listing 18-15: Replacing structure tags in a type specifier

The resolve_type function accepts a type specifier and returns a copy of that specifier in which any structure tags have been replaced with unique IDs. When resolve_type encounters a structure type, it replaces the tag with the corresponding identifier from structure_map ❶. If the tag isn't in structure _map, the structure hasn't been declared yet, so it throws an error ❷. To resolve a derived type, like Pointer, we resolve its constituent types recursively. I've omitted the pseudocode for Array and FunType, which we'll handle the same way as Pointer. We return any other type unchanged. We'll process every type specifier in the AST with resolve_type, including specifiers in function and variable declarations, cast and sizeof expressions, and structure member declarations.

Resolving Structure Type Declarations

Next, let's look at the pseudocode in Listing 18-16, which illustrates how to resolve a structure type declaration.

```
resolve_structure_declaration(decl, structure_map):
    prev_entry = structure_map.get(decl.tag) ❶
    if (prev_entry is null) or (not prev_entry.from_current_scope):
        unique_tag = make_temporary()
        structure_map.add(decl.tag, MapEntry(new_tag=unique_tag, from_current_scope=True)) ❷
    else:
        unique_tag = prev_entry.new_tag ❸
    processed_members = []
```

```
for member in decl.members:
    processed_type = resolve_type(member.member_type, structure_map) ❹
    processed_member = (member_name=member.member_name, member_type=processed_type)
    processed_members.append(processed_member)
resolved_decl = (tag=unique_tag, members=processed_members)
return resolved_decl ❺
```

Listing 18-16: Adding structure type declarations to the structure tag map

First, we look up the declaration's tag in the structure tag map ❶. If this tag hasn't been declared yet, or if it was declared in an outer scope, this declaration introduces a new type. We therefore generate a new identifier and add it to the structure tag map ❷. If the structure's tag was already declared in the current scope, the current declaration just redeclares the same type. In this case, we don't generate a new unique ID; instead, we use the one that's already in the map ❸.

At this point, the structure tag map is up to date. Now we transform the structure type declaration itself. If this declaration specifies the structure's members, we resolve its member types by calling resolve_type on each of them ❹. We replace the declaration's user-defined tag with unique_tag, the ID that we generated or looked up earlier in the function. Finally, we return the transformed declaration ❺.

Note that we add the new tag to structure_map before processing any structure members. This lets us accept self-referential structures, like the linked list node from Listing 18-6:

```
struct linked_list_node {
    int val;
    struct linked_list_node *next;
};
```

Also note that we don't generate unique names for structure members. Variables and functions need unique identifiers because they're all stored in a single symbol table, and structure tags need to be unique because they're all stored in a single type table, but structure members won't all be stored in one table. Instead, we'll maintain a separate member list for each structure type, so members in different structures with the same name won't conflict with each other.

We'll make two more updates to the identifier resolution pass. First, at the start of each new scope, we'll make a copy of the structure tag map with each entry's from_current_scope attribute set to False, just like we do for the identifier map. The second change is purely mechanical: we'll extend resolve_exp to process the new Dot and Arrow expressions the same way it processes all the other kinds of expressions. I'll skip the pseudocode for these changes, since they're both straightforward.

Type Checking Structures

Much like the type checker records information about every function and variable in the symbol table, it will also record information about every complete structure type in the *type table*. Let's start by defining the type table; then, we'll look at how to convert structure type declarations to type table entries. Finally, we'll use the information in the type table to type check declarations, expressions, and initializers.

Defining the Type Table

The type table maps the structure tags we generated in the previous stage to struct_entry constructs. Listing 18-17 defines struct_entry.

```
struct_entry = StructEntry(int alignment, int size, member_entry* members)
member_entry = MemberEntry(identifier member_name, type member_type, int offset)
```

Listing 18-17: An entry in the type table

A struct_entry describes a structure type's alignment, size, and members. We describe each member with a member_entry construct, which specifies the member's name, its type, and its offset in bytes from the start of the structure. A struct_entry should support two different ways of accessing members: looking up specific members by name and getting the whole list of members in order. You might want to represent members as an ordered dictionary if your implementation language supports it.

Like the symbol table, the type table should be a global variable or singleton that you can easily access from any stage of the compiler. (We'll pass it explicitly in this section's pseudocode for the sake of clarity.)

Next, we'll see how to add structure definitions to the type table as we traverse the AST.

Populating the Type Table

When the type checker encounters a definition of a complete structure type, it should validate the definition, then convert it into a struct_entry and add it to the type table. The type checker can ignore any structure type declaration without a member list; a declaration with no member list either declares an incomplete type or redeclares a type that was already defined.

To validate a structure type definition, we'll start by checking whether this structure is in the type table already. If it is, that means there's another definition of the same tag in the same scope, so we'll throw an error. Then, we'll make sure that no members of the structure share the same name, that no member has an incomplete type, and that no member type specifies an array with an incomplete element type. (Remember that arrays of incomplete type are illegal everywhere, not just in structure definitions.) You might also want to validate that no structure members have function type, but it isn't strictly necessary since we already validated that during parsing.

After validating that a structure type satisfies all these requirements, we'll calculate each member's offset and the whole structure's size and alignment. Earlier in the chapter, we saw how to perform these calculations and walked through an example. Now let's look at Listing 18-18, which demonstrates the whole process in pseudocode.

```
typecheck_struct_declaration(struct_decl, type_table):
❶ if struct_decl.members is empty:
      return
❷ validate_struct_definition(struct_decl, type_table)

   // define a member_entry for each member
❸ member_entries = []
   struct_size = 0
   struct_alignment = 1
   for member in struct_decl.members:
       member_alignment = alignment(member.member_type, type_table)
     ❹ member_offset = round_up(struct_size, member_alignment)
     ❺ m = MemberEntry(member.member_name, member.member_type,
                        member_offset)
       member_entries.append(m)
       struct_alignment = max(struct_alignment, member_alignment)
       struct_size = member_offset + size(member.member_type, type_table)

   // define a struct_entry for the whole structure
❻ struct_size = round_up(struct_size, struct_alignment)
   struct_def = StructEntry(struct_alignment, struct_size, member_entries)
❼ type_table.add(struct_decl.tag, struct_def)
```

Listing 18-18: Calculating a structure definition

We start by checking whether this declaration includes a member list ❶. If it doesn't, we return immediately, without making any changes to the type table. If it does have a member list, we validate that it meets the requirements described earlier in this section ❷. I won't give you the pseudocode for validate_struct_definition, since it isn't too complicated.

Then, we get to the interesting part: figuring out each member's layout in memory. Here, we'll define a member_entry for each structure member ❸. As we go, we'll maintain a running total of the structure's size in bytes, struct_size. We'll also track the strictest member alignment we've seen so far as struct_alignment.

To calculate a structure member's offset, we take the next available offset, which is given by struct_size, and round it up to that member's alignment ❹. (We'll walk through how to look up each type's size and alignment in a moment.) We construct its member_entry ❺, then update struct_alignment and struct_size.

Once we've processed every member, we calculate the structure's total size by rounding struct_size up to the nearest multiple of its alignment ❻. This rounded-up size will account for any padding at the end of the structure. Finally, we add the whole struct_entry to the type table ❼.

Handling Structures in Helper Functions

We've centralized a lot of type checking logic into a handful of helper functions, including is_scalar and is_complete. You've probably also written a few helper functions to look up each type's size, alignment, and other properties, although I haven't provided pseudocode for those yet. Now we'll extend these helpers to handle structure types too.

We defined is_scalar back in Listing 17-12. Listing 18-19 gives the updated definition, with this chapter's addition bolded.

```
is_scalar(t):
    match t with
    | Void -> return False
    | Array(elem_t, size) -> return False
    | FunType(param_ts, ret_t) -> return False
    | Structure(tag) -> return False
    | _ -> return True
```

Listing 18-19: Checking whether a type is scalar

Structure types aren't scalar, so this is pretty simple. I'm guessing you've written similar helper functions to test whether a type is arithmetic, whether it's an integer type, and so on. These will require similarly straightforward updates, which we won't get into here.

Updating is_complete is slightly more involved; we'll need to consult the type table. Listing 18-20 gives the new definition of this function.

```
is_complete(t, type_table):
    match t with
    | Void -> return False
    | Structure(tag) ->
        if tag is in type_table:
            return True
        else:
            return False
    | _ -> return True
```

Listing 18-20: Checking whether a type is complete

If a structure type is in the type table, it's complete; if not, it's incomplete. As we saw earlier, a structure type may be incomplete at one point in the program but complete later on. During type checking, the type table tells us whether the structure type is complete at the current point in the AST. Consider the code fragment in Listing 18-21.

```
❶ struct s;
❷ struct t {
      struct s member;
  };
❸ struct s {
      int a;
      int b;
  };
```

Listing 18-21: Declaring a variable with an incomplete structure type

Because the first declaration of struct s ❶ doesn't specify any members, we won't add it to the type table. Then, when we validate the definition of struct t ❷, we'll look up struct s in the type table. (Strictly speaking, we'll look up the unique identifier that replaced s during the identifier resolution stage.) When we don't find it, we'll correctly conclude that struct s is incomplete and throw an error. If the declaration of struct t appeared after the definition of struct s ❸, we'd add struct s to the type table before processing struct t, so we wouldn't throw an error.

We also need helper functions to find a type's size and alignment. Listing 18-22 shows the pseudocode for the alignment function.

```
alignment(t, type_table):
    match t with
    | Structure(tag) ->
        struct_def = type_table.get(tag)
        return struct_def.alignment
    | Array(elem_t, size) ->
        return alignment(elem_t, type_table)
    | --snip--
```

Listing 18-22: Calculating a type's alignment

To find a structure's alignment, we'll look it up in the type table. To find an array's alignment, we'll recursively calculate the alignment of its element type. We'll hardcode the alignments of other types, which are dictated by the ABI. I won't provide pseudocode for size, which will look similar to alignment.

NOTE *We learned earlier that if a variable of array type is 16 bytes or larger, it must be 16-byte aligned. Listing 18-22 doesn't reflect this requirement because it calculates the alignment of types, not variables. You'll probably want to write a different helper function to calculate the alignment of variables, if you haven't already.*

The other helper functions we defined in earlier chapters should handle structures correctly without any changes. Consider convert_by_assignment, which we use to type check assignment expressions and other places where we convert a value to a specific type "as if by assignment." Listing 18-23 reproduces the latest version of this code from Listing 17-11.

```
convert_by_assignment(e, target_type):
    if get_type(e) == target_type:
        return e
    if get_type(e) is arithmetic and target_type is arithmetic:
        return convert_to(e, target_type)
    if is_null_pointer_constant(e) and target_type is a pointer type:
        return convert_to(e, target_type)
    if target_type == Pointer(Void) and get_type(e) is a pointer type:
        return convert_to(e, target_type)
    if target_type is a pointer type and get_type(e) == Pointer(Void):
        return convert_to(e, target_type)
    else:
        fail("Cannot convert type for assignment")
```

Listing 18-23: Converting an expression to a target type

If we pass `convert_by_assignment` an expression that already has the correct structure type, it will return the expression unchanged. In any other case with a source or target structure type, it will fail. That's the correct behavior, since there's no way to convert to or from a structure type.

Handling Incomplete Structure Types

We need to enforce several restrictions on incomplete structure types. First, we'll validate the use of these types in declarations; then, we'll validate their use in expressions.

It's legal to declare, but not define, a function with parameters or a return value of incomplete structure type. (Remember that a function definition is a function declaration with a body.) If `struct s` is an incomplete type, the type checker should accept this declaration:

```
void take_a_struct(struct s incomplete);
```

But it should reject this definition:

```
void take_a_struct(struct s incomplete) {
    return;
}
```

Similarly, we'll accept declarations of variables with incomplete structure type but reject any definitions of these variables, including tentative definitions. (This is more restrictive than the C standard, which permits tentative definitions of variables with incomplete types in certain limited circumstances.) Concretely, we'll accept a variable declaration with an incomplete structure type only if it has the `extern` storage class and no initializer.

That takes care of declarations; now let's consider expressions. There's exactly one way to use a variable with incomplete type in an expression. You can take its address, as the following example demonstrates:

```
extern struct s my_incomplete_struct;
struct s *ptr = &my_incomplete_struct;
```

You can then use `ptr` like any other pointer to an incomplete type.

Similarly, it's legal (if not especially useful) to dereference a pointer to an incomplete structure and then take its address, resulting in the pointer you started with:

```
struct s *another_ptr = &*ptr;
```

Any other use of an expression with an incomplete structure type is invalid. You can't even cast it to `void` or use it as an expression statement, so the type checker should reject both of the following statements:

```
(void) my_incomplete_struct;
*ptr;
```

We'll extend typecheck_and_convert to catch these invalid expressions. Listing 18-24 gives the updated definition of this function, with changes from the original definition in Listing 15-19 bolded.

```
typecheck_and_convert(e, symbols, type_table):
    typed_e = typecheck_exp(e, symbols, type_table)
    match get_type(typed_e) with
    | Array(elem_t, size) ->
        --snip--
    | Structure(tag) ->
        if tag is not in type_table:
            fail("Invalid use of incomplete structure type")
        return typed_e
    | _ -> return typed_e
```

Listing 18-24: Rejecting incomplete structure types in typecheck_and_convert

Remember that typecheck_and_convert processes every expression in the AST except for static initializers (which must be constants) and the operands of the SizeOf and AddrOf expressions (which don't undergo array decay). This makes typecheck_and_convert the most convenient place to put the new validation, even though it has nothing to do with the function's original purpose, which is to implicitly convert arrays to pointers. With this new validation in place, we'll handle incomplete types correctly in every kind of expression: we'll permit incomplete structure types in AddrOf expressions, our existing validation will reject all incomplete types (including void) in SizeOf expressions, and typecheck_and_convert will reject incomplete structure types everywhere else. Note that typecheck_and_convert still accepts void expressions, which are legal in several places where expressions with incomplete structure types are not.

We've already implemented all the other validation we need for incomplete types. For example, we already require the pointer operands in pointer arithmetic expressions to point to complete types, and we already require the element types in array type specifiers to be complete.

Type Checking the Member Access Operators

Next, let's type check the . and -> operators. In both cases, we'll validate the expression, figure out the member type, and record that as the type of the whole expression. Listing 18-25 demonstrates how to type check a . operator.

```
typecheck_exp(e, symbols, type_table):
    match e with
    | --snip--
    | Dot(structure, member) ->
        typed_structure = typecheck_and_convert(structure, symbols, type_table)
      ❶ match get_type(typed_structure) with
        | Structure(tag) ->
          ❷ struct_def = type_table.get(tag)
```

```
    ❸ member_def = <find member in struct_def.members>
      if member_def is not found:
          fail("Structure has no member with this name")
      member_exp = Dot(typed_structure, member)
    ❹ return set_type(member_exp, member_def.member_type)
    | _ -> fail("Tried to get member of non-structure")
 | Arrow(pointer, member) ->
      --snip--
```

Listing 18-25: Type checking the . operator

We start by type checking the first operand, structure, with a call to typecheck_and_convert (which throws an error if structure has an incomplete type). Then, we validate that structure really is a structure ❶. If it is, we look up its type in the type table ❷, then look up member in the resulting type table entry ❸. Finally, we annotate the expression with the member type ❹. If structure isn't a structure or doesn't have a member with this name, we throw an error.

I won't provide pseudocode for type checking the -> operator, since it's nearly identical; the only difference is that we validate that the first operand is a pointer to a structure, rather than a structure itself.

Validating Lvalues

An -> expression is always an lvalue. To determine whether a . expression is an lvalue, the type checker must recursively check whether its first operand is an lvalue. For example, the type checker should reject the expression f().member = 3. Because f() isn't an lvalue, f().member isn't either.

This means we might encounter arrays that aren't lvalues! It's a type error to explicitly take the address of such an array, like in Listing 18-26.

```
struct s {
    int arr[3];
};

struct s f(void);

int main(void) {
    int *pointer_to_array[3] = &(f().arr);
    --snip--
}
```

Listing 18-26: Illegally taking the address of a non-lvalue

However, these arrays still decay to pointers, so their addresses are still loaded implicitly. The program in Listing 18-27, for example, is entirely legal.

```
struct s {
    int arr[3];
};

struct s f(void);
```

```
int main(void) {
    return f().arr[0];
}
```

Listing 18-27: Implicitly converting a non-lvalue array to a pointer

When we type check this program, we'll insert AddrOf to take the address of f().arr, just like when we type check any other expression of array type.

THE CURIOUS CASE OF TEMPORARY LIFETIMES

There's something wonky happening here. The expression f().arr isn't an lvalue, but in order to have an address that we can load, it has to designate an object. Section 6.2.4, paragraph 8, of the C standard resolves this dilemma: "A non-lvalue expression with structure or union type, where the structure or union contains a member with array type . . . refers to an object with automatic storage duration and *temporary lifetime*. . . . Its lifetime ends when the evaluation of the containing full expression ends. Any attempt to modify an object with temporary lifetime results in undefined behavior."

An object with temporary lifetime is similar to the temporary variables we create during TACKY generation. The compiler allocates it to hold the result of an expression, and it's never used again after that expression is evaluated. The key difference is that it's possible to get a pointer to an object with temporary lifetime in the source program. This makes it easy to inadvertently use that object after the end of its lifetime. Consider this example, which you might expect to be equivalent to the return statement in Listing 18-27:

```
int *arr_pointer = f().arr;
return arr_pointer[0];
```

The lifetime of the structure returned by f() ends once we finish evaluating the expression f().arr. This means that arr_ptr points to an object whose lifetime has ended, so subscripting it is undefined behavior.

Type Checking Structures in Conditional Expressions

The type checker should accept conditional expressions where both branches have the same structure type. It should reject conditional expressions where only one branch has a structure type or where the branches have two different structure types. To determine whether two structure types are identical, compare their tags, not their contents.

Type Checking Structure Initializers

Finally, we'll deal with structure initializers. As you learned earlier in this chapter, you can initialize a structure either with a single expression of that structure type or with a compound initializer. The first case shouldn't require any changes to the type checker.

To handle compound initializers, we'll type check each item in the initializer list against the corresponding member type, as Listing 18-28 demonstrates.

```
typecheck_init(target_type, init, symbols, type_table):
    match target_type, init with
    | Structure(tag), CompoundInit(init_list) ->
        struct_def = type_table.get(tag) ❶
        if length(init_list) > length(struct_def.members): ❷
            fail("Too many elements in structure initializer")
        i = 0
        typechecked_list = []
        for init_elem in init_list: ❸
            t = struct_def.members[i].member_type
            typechecked_elem = typecheck_init(t, init_elem, symbols, type_table)
            typechecked_list.append(typechecked_elem)
            i += 1
        while i < length(struct_def.members): ❹
            t = struct_def.members[i].member_type
            typechecked_list.append(zero_initializer(t))
            i += 1
        return set_type(CompoundInit(typechecked_list), target_type)
    | --snip--
```

Listing 18-28: Type checking compound initializers for structures

We'll start by looking up the structure in the type table ❶. We should have already validated that target_type is complete before calling typecheck _init, so at this point it's safe to assume that the structure has been defined. Next, we'll make sure the initializer list isn't too long ❷. Just like when we process array initializers, we'll reject an initializer list with too many elements but accept one with too few elements to initialize the whole object.

After performing this check, we'll iterate through the initializer list ❸. To type check each initializer, we'll look up the corresponding member type in the structure's member list, then call typecheck_init recursively to make sure the initializer is compatible with that type. Finally, we'll pad out any uninitialized structure members with zeros ❹.

Once you've updated typecheck_init, you'll need to extend zero_initializer to handle structure types. To initialize a structure to zero, zero_initializer should call itself recursively for each member type and return the results in a compound initializer.

Initializing Static Structures

If a structure has static storage duration, we'll store its initial value as a static_init list in the symbol table, just like we do for arrays. The key difference is that we'll initialize any padding in the structure too. Let's return to the example from Listing 18-10:

```
struct example {
    int member1;
    double member2;
    char array[3];
};

struct example var = {1, 2.0, {'a', 'b', 'c'}};
```

We figured out that this structure included 4 bytes of padding between member1 and member2 and 5 bytes of padding after array. If var is a static variable, we'll use the construct in Listing 18-29 to represent its initial value.

```
Initial([IntInit(1),
    ❶ ZeroInit(4),
        DoubleInit(2.0),
        CharInit(97),
        CharInit(98),
        CharInit(99),
    ❷ ZeroInit(5)])
```

Listing 18-29: Representing the initializer from Listing 18-10 as a static_init list

We initialize padding with the ZeroInit construct ❶❷ because the C standard requires the padding in static structures to be initialized to zero. Listing 18-30 demonstrates how to generate static initializer lists like the one in Listing 18-29.

```
create_static_init_list(init_type, initializer, type_table):
    match init_type, initializer with
    | Structure(tag), CompoundInit(init_list) ->
    ❶ struct_def = type_table.get(tag)
        if length(init_list) > length(struct_def.members):
            fail("Too many elements in structure initializer")
        current_offset = 0
        static_inits = []
        i = 0
        for init_elem in init_list:
            member = struct_def.members[i]
            if member.offset != current_offset:
            ❷ static_inits.append(ZeroInit(member.offset - current_offset))
        ❸ more_static_inits = create_static_init_list(member.member_type,
                                                      init_elem,
                                                      type_table)
            static_inits.append_all(more_static_inits)
            current_offset = member.offset + size(member.member_type,
                                                  type_table)
            i += 1
        if struct_def.size != current_offset:
        ❹ static_inits.append(ZeroInit(struct_def.size - current_offset))
        return static_inits
```

```
| Structure(tag), SingleInit(e) ->
    ❺ fail("Cannot initialize static structure with scalar expression")
| --snip--
```

Listing 18-30: Generating a static initializer for a structure

To process a compound initializer for a static structure, we first look up the structure in the type table ❶. We make sure the initializer list isn't too long, just like we did for non-static initializers in typecheck_init. Then, we iterate over the initializer list, looking up the corresponding member definition for each element in the structure's member list. As we go, we update the current_offset variable to track how many bytes we've initialized so far.

Each time we process the initializer for a structure member, we first check whether we've initialized enough bytes to bring us up to the expected offset. If we haven't, we add the necessary padding with a ZeroInit initializer ❷. We then create the initializer list for the structure member itself with a recursive call to create_static_init_list ❸. Next, we update current _offset based on the offset and size of the member we just initialized.

Once we've initialized every structure member, we add another ZeroInit, if necessary, to pad out the structure to the correct size ❹. This last ZeroInit zeroes out any structure members that weren't explicitly initialized as well as any trailing padding after the last member.

Because there are no constants of structure type, initializing a static structure with a SingleInit expression is a type error ❺.

TEST THE SEMANTIC ANALYSIS STAGE

To test out the changes to identifier resolution and type checking, run:

```
$ ./test_compiler /path/to/your_compiler --chapter 18 --stage validate
```

You'll find the invalid test cases for this stage in *tests/chapter_18/invalid _struct_tags* and *tests/chapter_18/invalid_types*. The programs in *tests/chapter _18/invalid_struct_tags* refer to undeclared structure tags, so your compiler should reject them during identifier resolution. (Since the C standard doesn't require you to declare structure tags before using them, a fully conforming compiler will reject these programs for different reasons, usually because they refer to incomplete types when complete types are required.)

The programs in *tests/chapter_18/invalid_types* cover all sorts of type errors, like conflicting definitions of the same structure, structure declarations with incomplete member types, and member access operations that refer to nonexistent members. Several of these programs are designed to test out

(continued)

identifier resolution, even though they cause type errors. Here's an example of this sort of test case:

```
struct s;
struct s *ptr1 = 0;
int main(void) {
    struct s;
    struct s *ptr2 = 0;
    return ptr1 == ptr2;
}
```

Your compiler should reject this program during type checking because it compares pointers to two distinct types. But in order for the type checker to recognize that ptr1 and ptr2 point to distinct types, the identifier resolution pass needs to generate different IDs for the two declarations of struct s.

TACKY Generation

In this section, we'll introduce one last TACKY instruction:

```
CopyFromOffset(identifier src, int offset, val dst)
```

This instruction mirrors the CopyToOffset instruction we added back in Chapter 15. The src identifier in CopyFromOffset is the name of an aggregate variable, offset is the byte offset of a subobject within that variable, and dst is the variable we'll copy that subobject to. Listing 18-31 defines the complete TACKY IR, including the new CopyFromOffset instruction.

```
program = Program(top_level*)
top_level = Function(identifier, bool global, identifier* params, instruction* body)
          | StaticVariable(identifier, bool global, type t, static_init* init_list)
          | StaticConstant(identifier, type t, static_init init)
instruction = Return(val?)
            | SignExtend(val src, val dst)
            | Truncate(val src, val dst)
            | ZeroExtend(val src, val dst)
            | DoubleToInt(val src, val dst)
            | DoubleToUInt(val src, val dst)
            | IntToDouble(val src, val dst)
            | UIntToDouble(val src, val dst)
            | Unary(unary_operator, val src, val dst)
            | Binary(binary_operator, val src1, val src2, val dst)
            | Copy(val src, val dst)
            | GetAddress(val src, val dst)
            | Load(val src_ptr, val dst)
            | Store(val src, val dst_ptr)
            | AddPtr(val ptr, val index, int scale, val dst)
```

```
| CopyToOffset(val src, identifier dst, int offset)
| CopyFromOffset(identifier src, int offset, val dst)
| Jump(identifier target)
| JumpIfZero(val condition, identifier target)
| JumpIfNotZero(val condition, identifier target)
| Label(identifier)
| FunCall(identifier fun_name, val* args, val? dst)
val = Constant(const) | Var(identifier)
unary_operator = Complement | Negate | Not
binary_operator = Add | Subtract | Multiply | Divide | Remainder | Equal | NotEqual
                | LessThan | LessOrEqual | GreaterThan | GreaterOrEqual
```

Listing 18-31: Adding CopyFromOffset *to the TACKY IR*

Not only can you access subobjects in a structure with the CopyToOffset and CopyFromOffset instructions, but you can also copy entire structures from one location to another using Copy, Load, and Store or pass them between functions with Return and FunCall, just like scalar variables. We'll represent variables of structure type as ordinary TACKY Vars.

Next, we'll convert the member access operators to TACKY. Then, we'll process compound structure initializers. We won't change how we process most constructs that can use structures, like function calls, return statements, and conditional expressions. We also won't need to do anything with the new top-level StructDecl construct; we'll discard structure declarations at this stage, just like we discard function declarations without bodies and variable declarations without initializers.

Implementing the Member Access Operators

In earlier chapters, you learned that you can use an object in one of three ways: you can lvalue convert it, assign to it, or take its address. Now there's a fourth option: if the object is a structure, you can access one of its members. And because that structure member is itself an object, you can lvalue convert it, assign to it, take its address, or access one of *its* members. Let's look at the TACKY we should generate in each of these cases. Then, building on the approach we used to handle dereferenced pointers in Chapter 14, we'll introduce a new kind of exp_result to designate structure members.

Accessing Structure Members in TACKY

To implement any sort of operation on a structure member, we'll start by looking up the member's offset in the type table. First, let's consider cases where the structure itself is a TACKY variable, rather than a dereferenced pointer or a subobject in some larger structure. To lvalue convert a structure member, we'll use the CopyFromOffset instruction. We'll translate <struct>.<member> to:

```
<instructions for struct>
s = <result of struct>
result = CopyFromOffset(s, <member offset>)
```

We'll assign to structure members with CopyToOffset, converting `<struct>.<member>` = `<right>` to:

```
<instructions for struct>
dst = <result of struct>
<instructions for right>
src = <result of right>
CopyToOffset(src, dst, <member offset>)
```

To get a structure member's address, we'll first load the address of the object that contains it, then add the member's offset. We'll convert `&<struct>.<member>` to:

```
<instructions for struct>
s = <result of struct>
result = GetAddress(s)
result = AddPtr(ptr=result, index=<member offset>, scale=1)
```

To process a sequence of nested member accesses, we'll add all their offsets together and then issue an instruction depending on how the final member in the sequence is used. Consider the structure declarations in Listing 18-32.

```
struct inner {
    char c;
    int i;
};

struct outer {
    int member1;
    struct inner member2;
};
```

Listing 18-32: Declaring a structure that contains a nested structure

If `my_struct` is a struct `outer` and we need to lvalue convert `my_struct.member2.i`, we'll emit:

```
result = CopyFromOffset("my_struct", 8)
```

Because `member2` has an offset of 4 bytes in struct `outer` and `i` has an offset of 4 bytes in struct `inner`, the object designated by `my_struct.member2.i` has a total offset of 8 bytes from the start of `my_struct`.

Finally, let's consider how to access structure members through dereferenced pointers. The most idiomatic way to do this is with an arrow operator, of the form `<exp>-><member>`. This is equivalent to the expression `(*<exp>).<member>`. Either way, you'll add the member offset to the pointer and then dereference the result. As with any dereferenced pointer, whether you issue a Load or Store instruction or simply use the pointer's value will depend on how it's used. Suppose inner_struct_pointer has type struct inner *. We'll convert the expression

```
inner_struct_pointer->i = 1
```

to:

```
ptr = AddPtr(ptr=inner_struct_pointer, index=4, scale=1)
Store(1, ptr)
```

We can implement the equivalent expression

```
(*inner_struct_pointer).i = 1
```

with exactly the same instructions. Now that we know what instructions we'd like to generate, we'll update the TACKY generation pass accordingly.

Designating Structure Members with SubObject

Let's extend the exp_result construct to designate a member of an aggregate object. Listing 18-33 gives the updated definition of exp_result.

```
exp_result = PlainOperand(val)
           | DereferencedPointer(val)
           | SubObject(identifier base, int offset)
```

Listing 18-33: Extending exp_result to represent subobjects

The base argument to SubObject is an aggregate object, not a pointer. The second argument, offset, is a byte offset into that object. The object that SubObject designates might be scalar, or it might be an aggregate itself. In Listing 18-34, we use this construct to represent the result of a Dot operator.

```
emit_tacky(e, instructions, symbols, type_table):
    match e with
    | --snip--
    | Dot(structure, member) ->
        struct_def = <look up structure's type in the type table>
        member_offset = <look up member offset in struct_def>
        inner_object = emit_tacky(structure, instructions, symbols, type_table)
        match inner_object with
        | PlainOperand(Var(v)) -> return SubObject(v, member_offset) ❶
        | SubObject(base, offset) -> return SubObject(base, offset + member_offset) ❷
        | DereferencedPointer(ptr) -> ❸
            dst_ptr = make_tacky_variable(Pointer(get_type(e)), symbols)
            instr = AddPtr(ptr=ptr, index=Constant(ConstLong(member_offset)),
                        scale=1, dst=dst_ptr)
            instructions.append(instr)
            return DereferencedPointer(dst_ptr)
```

Listing 18-34: Converting the Dot operator to TACKY

First, we look up member's offset in the structure. Then, we process this expression's first operand without lvalue converting it. The resulting object is either a plain TACKY variable, a subobject of a TACKY variable, or a dereferenced pointer. (We know the result isn't a constant because TACKY doesn't have constants of structure type.)

If inner_object is just a variable, we return a SubObject designating the object at member_offset within that variable ❶. If inner_object is itself a sub-object in some larger variable, we add its offset to member_offset ❷. This takes care of nested member operators, like the expression my_struct .member2.i that we considered earlier in this section.

Finally, if the inner structure is a dereferenced pointer, we access the structure member with pointer arithmetic ❸. Since DereferencedPointer(ptr) designates the whole structure, ptr must point to the start of the structure. We add member_offset to ptr to get a pointer to the specified structure member. Then, we dereference this pointer to designate the structure member itself.

Processing SubObject

Next, we'll process SubObject constructs in lvalue conversions, assignment expressions, and AddrOf expressions. To lvalue convert a SubObject, we copy it into a new variable with the CopyFromOffset instruction, as Listing 18-35 demonstrates.

```
emit_tacky_and_convert(e, instructions, symbols, type_table):
    result = emit_tacky(e, instructions, symbols, type_table)
    match result with
    | SubObject(base, offset) ->
        dst = make_tacky_variable(get_type(e), symbols)
        instructions.append(CopyFromOffset(base, offset, dst))
        return dst
    | --snip--
```

Listing 18-35: Lvalue converting a SubObject

Conversely, when a SubObject appears on the left-hand side of an assignment expression, we write to it with a CopyToOffset instruction, as Listing 18-36 demonstrates.

```
emit_tacky(e, instructions, symbols, type_table):
    match e with
    | --snip--
    | Assignment(left, right) ->
        lval = emit_tacky(left, instructions, symbols, type_table)
        rval = emit_tacky_and_convert(right, instructions, symbols,
                                      type_table)
        match lval with
        | SubObject(base, offset) ->
            instructions.append(CopyToOffset(rval, base, offset))
            return PlainOperand(rval)
        | --snip--
```

Listing 18-36: Assigning to a SubObject

Finally, Listing 18-37 shows how to calculate the address of a SubObject. We load the address of the base object, then add the offset.

```
| AddrOf(inner) ->
    v = emit_tacky(inner, instructions, symbols, type_table)
    match v with
    | SubObject(base, offset) ->
        dst = make_tacky_variable(get_type(e), symbols)
        instructions.append(GetAddress(Var(base), dst))
        instructions.append(AddPtr(ptr=dst,
                                  index=Constant(ConstLong(offset)),
                        ❶ scale=1,
                                  dst=dst))
        return PlainOperand(dst)
    | --snip--
```

Listing 18-37: Taking the address of a SubObject

We reuse the same temporary variable, dst, to point to both the base of the structure and its member. We could also generate two different temporary variables, but we don't need to. Because the offset in a SubObject construct is in bytes, the scale of this AddPtr instruction is 1 ❶.

Implementing the Arrow Operator

Now that we've implemented Dot, we can easily implement Arrow too. To calculate ptr->member, we'll first evaluate and lvalue convert ptr. Then, we'll use AddPtr to add the offset of member. This will give us a pointer to the designated structure member. Finally, we'll dereference this pointer with a DereferencedPointer construct. I'll omit the pseudocode for this; you've already seen how to convert (*ptr).member to TACKY, and converting ptr->member to TACKY is very similar.

We don't need any extra logic to handle the result of an Arrow expression. This expression will always produce a DereferencedPointer construct, which we already know how to handle.

Omitting Useless AddPtr Instructions

The first member in a structure always has an offset of zero. As an optional optimization, you can skip the AddPtr instruction when calculating this member's address. This affects Listings 18-34 and 18-37, as well as the implementation of Arrow, which I didn't give the pseudocode for. In all three cases, you don't need to generate an AddPtr instruction if member_offset is 0.

Converting Compound Initializers to TACKY

To finish up this section, we'll convert compound structure initializers to TACKY. The basic approach is the same as in previous chapters: we'll evaluate each expression in the initializer list in turn, copying the result of each one to the correct offset in the destination with a CopyToOffset instruction. But now we'll need to check the type table to find the correct offset for each expression. We'll also need to calculate the offsets of subobjects deep within nested structures, arrays of structures, structures that contain arrays, and so on.

Listing 18-38 demonstrates how to track these offsets and emit CopyToOffset instructions as we traverse a compound initializer for a structure or array.

```
compound_initializer_to_tacky(var_name, offset, init, instructions, symbols, type_table):
    match init, get_type(init) with
    | SingleInit(String(s)), Array(elem_t, size) ->
        --snip--
    | SingleInit(e), t ->
        v = emit_tacky_and_convert(e, instructions, symbols, type_table)
        instructions.append(CopyToOffset(v, var_name, offset)) ❶
    | CompoundInit(init_list), Structure(tag) ->
        members = type_table.get(tag).members
        for mem_init, member in zip(init_list, members):
            mem_offset = offset + member.offset ❷
            compound_initializer_to_tacky(var_name, mem_offset, mem_init, instructions,
                                          symbols, type_table)
    | CompoundInit(init_list), Array(elem_t, size) ->
        --snip--
```

Listing 18-38: Converting a compound initializer to TACKY

The parameters of compound_initializer_to_tacky include var_name (the name of the array or structure variable being initialized), offset (the byte offset of the current subobject within that variable), and init (the initializer itself). In the top-level call to initialize an entire variable, the offset argument will be 0.

In the base case, we initialize a subobject with the value of a single expression. This expression may be a string literal that initializes an array; I've omitted the pseudocode for this case, which we covered back in Chapter 16. Otherwise, we evaluate the expression and copy the result into place with a CopyToOffset instruction ❶. Even if the result has structure type, we can copy it to its destination with a single instruction.

When we encounter a compound initializer for a structure, we look up the structure's member list in the type table. We calculate the offset of each item in the initializer list by adding the corresponding member offset to the starting offset argument ❷. Then, we process the item recursively. I won't talk through the case of a compound initializer for an array, since you already know how to handle that.

Our implementation deviates slightly from the C standard here. Under certain circumstances, the standard requires padding to be initialized to zero; Listing 18-38 doesn't initialize structure padding, and none of our tests check the value of padding in non-static structures.

ALL ABOUT PADDING

The C standard tries to ensure that padding is initialized in a consistent, predictable way. Unfortunately, it doesn't really succeed, so it's easy to accidentally leave padding uninitialized. This is a potential security risk because uninitialized padding might leak sensitive data that was previously stored at that spot in memory. The 2012 blog post "C11 Defects: Initialization of Padding" by Jens Gustedt provides a good overview of this confusing corner of the standard (*https://gustedt.wordpress.com/2012/10/24/c11-defects-initialization-of-padding/*).

Luckily, the situation gets somewhat better in C23. This revision introduces an empty initializer of the form {} that initializes a whole union or aggregate object to zero, including any padding. This doesn't completely address the inconsistencies that Gustedt highlighted, but it makes life easier for every C programmer who just needs to zero out a structure. For a delightful introduction to this feature (and a bunch of other changes in C23), see JeanHeyd Meneide's blog post "Ever Closer—C23 Draws Nearer" (*https://thephd.dev/ever-closer-c23-improvements*).

At this point, you know how to convert both member access operators and compound structure initializers to TACKY. Once you've implemented these conversions, you can test out this compiler pass.

TEST THE TACKY GENERATION STAGE

To test out TACKY generation, run:

```
$ ./test_compiler /path/to/your_compiler --chapter 18 --stage tacky
```

Structures in the System V Calling Convention

The trickiest part of assembly generation in this chapter is dealing with function calls. As always, we need to pass parameters and return values according to the System V x64 calling convention. The rules for passing and returning structures are particularly gnarly, so we'll take a look at them before we make any changes to the backend.

Classifying Structures

In the System V x64 ABI, every parameter and return value has a *class*, which dictates how it's transferred during function calls. We've already encountered two of the classes defined in the ABI, although I didn't use the term *class* to describe them. Values with integer, character, and pointer types all belong to the INTEGER class; they're transferred in general-purpose registers. Values with type double all belong to the SSE class; they're transferred in XMM registers.

In this chapter we'll encounter a third class, MEMORY, for large values that must be transferred in memory. We've passed function arguments in memory before, but passing return values in memory is a new concept; we'll see exactly how that works in a moment.

The ABI presents a somewhat complicated algorithm for classifying structures and unions. We can use a simplified version of this algorithm because there are a bunch of types that we don't handle, like float and unions. We'll walk through the simplified rules for classifying structures in this section. For the complete algorithm, see the documentation listed in "Additional Resources" on page 553.

Splitting a Structure into Eightbytes

We'll assign a separate class to each 8-byte chunk of a structure. The ABI calls these chunks *eightbytes*. If the structure's size isn't exactly divisible by 8, the last eightbyte may be shorter than 8 bytes (which makes the term a little misleading). Consider Listing 18-39, which declares a 12-byte structure.

```
struct twelve_bytes {
    int i;
    char arr[8];
};
```

Listing 18-39: A structure with two eightbytes

The first eightbyte of this structure contains i and the first four elements of arr. The second eightbyte is 4 bytes long and contains the last four elements of arr. Figure 18-2 shows this structure's layout in memory.

Member	i				arr							
					[0]	[1]	[2]	[3]	[4]	[5]	[6]	[7]
Byte number	0	1	2	3	4	5	6	7	8	9	10	11

First eightbyte · Second eightbyte

Figure 18-2: The layout of struct twelve_bytes in memory

Figure 18-2 illustrates that a nested array like arr can span multiple eightbytes. A nested structure can too. Consider the structure declaration in Listing 18-40.

```
struct inner {
    int i;
    char ch2;
};

struct nested_ints {
    char ch1;
```

```
    struct inner nested;
};
```

Listing 18-40: A structure type containing a nested structure that spans two eightbytes

Figure 18-3 shows how a struct nested_ints will be laid out in memory.

Member	ch1	<padding>			nested							
					i				ch2	<padding>		
Byte number	0	1	2	3	4	5	6	7	8	9	10	11

First eightbyte   Second eightbyte

Figure 18-3: The layout of struct nested_ints in memory

The first eightbyte of this structure holds two scalar values: ch1 and the nested member nested.i. The second eightbyte holds nested.ch2. When we classify a structure, we care about what scalar values each eightbyte contains, but we don't care how those values are grouped into nested structures or arrays. As far as our classification algorithm is concerned, struct nested _ints is equivalent to the struct flattened_ints type defined in Listing 18-41.

```
struct flattened_ints {
    char c;
    int i;
    char a;
};
```

Listing 18-41: A structure with the same layout as struct nested_ints in memory

This structure looks identical to struct nested_ints in memory: its first eightbyte holds a char and an int, and its second eightbyte holds another char.

Classifying Eightbytes

If a structure is larger than 16 bytes—in other words, if it consists of three or more eightbytes—we'll assign every eightbyte to the MEMORY class. For example, struct large consists of four eightbytes, which are all classified as MEMORY:

```
struct large {
    int i;
    double d;
    char arr[10];
};
```

If a structure is 16 bytes or smaller, we'll assign each eightbyte to either the INTEGER or the SSE class, according to its contents. An eightbyte belongs to the SSE class if it contains a double and the INTEGER class if it contains anything else. For example, both eightbytes of struct twelve_bytes, from Listing 18-39, belong to the INTEGER class. We'll assign both eightbytes of struct nested_ints from Listing 18-40 and both eightbytes of struct flattened_ints from Listing 18-41 to the INTEGER class too, since none of them hold a double.

Listing 18-42 defines a few more structure types. Let's classify each of them.

```
struct two_ints {
    int i;
    int i2;
};

struct nested_double {
    double array[1];
};

struct two_eightbytes {
    double d;
    char c;
};
```

Listing 18-42: More structure types

A struct two_ints consists of a single eightbyte, which belongs to the INTEGER class. A struct nested_double consists of a single eightbyte in the SSE class. A struct two_eightbytes consists of two eightbytes: the first is in the SSE class because it contains a double, and the second is in the INTEGER class because it contains a char.

Passing Parameters of Structure Type

Once we've classified a structure, we can figure out how to pass it as a parameter. If a structure consists of one or two eightbytes, we'll pass each eightbyte of the structure in the next available register for its class. If a structure consists of a single eightbyte in the INTEGER class, we'll pass it in the next general-purpose parameter passing register. If it consists of a single eightbyte in the SSE class, we'll pass it in the next available parameter passing XMM register. If it consists of one INTEGER eightbyte and one SSE eightbyte, we'll pass the first eightbyte in a general-purpose register and the next eightbyte in an XMM register, and so forth. If there aren't enough registers available to pass the entire structure, we'll push the whole thing onto the stack.

Let's look at a few examples. First, in Listing 18-43, we reproduce the struct two_eightbytes type that we defined in Listing 18-42 and declare a function that takes a parameter with that type.

```
struct two_eightbytes {
    double d;
    char c;
};

void pass_struct(struct two_eightbytes param);
```

Listing 18-43: A function declaration with a struct two_eightbytes *parameter*

Suppose x is a variable of type struct two_eightbytes, which is stored on the stack at address -16(%rbp). We might convert the function call pass _struct(x) to the assembly in Listing 18-44.

```
movsd   -16(%rbp), %xmm0
movq    -8(%rbp), %rdi
call    pass_struct
```

Listing 18-44: Passing a structure parameter in two registers

Because the first eightbyte of this structure belongs to the SSE class, we pass it in the first parameter passing XMM register, XMM0. The second eightbyte of the structure belongs to the INTEGER class, so we pass it in the first general-purpose parameter passing register, RDI.

Next, let's look at Listing 18-45. This listing declares a function with a structure parameter that we'll need to push onto the stack.

```
struct two_longs {
    long a;
    long b;
};

void a_bunch_of_arguments(int i0, int i1, int i2, int i3, int i4,
                          struct two_longs param, int i5);
```

Listing 18-45: A function declaration with a structure parameter that must be passed in memory

When we call a_bunch_of_arguments, we'll pass parameters i0 through i4 in registers EDI, ESI, EDX, ECX, and R8D. This doesn't leave enough registers open to pass the param parameter; both eightbytes belong to the INTEGER class, but only one general-purpose parameter passing register, R9, is available. Therefore, we'll push the whole structure onto the stack. Then, since R9D is still open, we'll use it to transfer i5. If arg is a struct two_longs with static storage duration, we could convert the function call

```
a_bunch_of_arguments(0, 1, 2, 3, 4, arg, 5);
```

to the assembly in Listing 18-46.

```
movl    $0, %edi
movl    $1, %esi
movl    $2, %edx
```

```
        movl    $3, %ecx
        movl    $4, %r8d
        movl    $5, %r9d
    ❶ pushq   arg+8(%rip)
        pushq   arg(%rip)
        call    a_bunch_of_arguments
```

Listing 18-46: Passing a structure on the stack

Because arg lives in the data section, we access it with RIP-relative addressing. We're using a bit of new assembly syntax here: arg+8(%rip) indicates the address 8 bytes after the label arg. Our first push instruction will therefore push the second eightbyte of the structure, which contains member b, onto the stack ❶. This preserves the structure's layout in memory, as Figure 18-4 demonstrates.

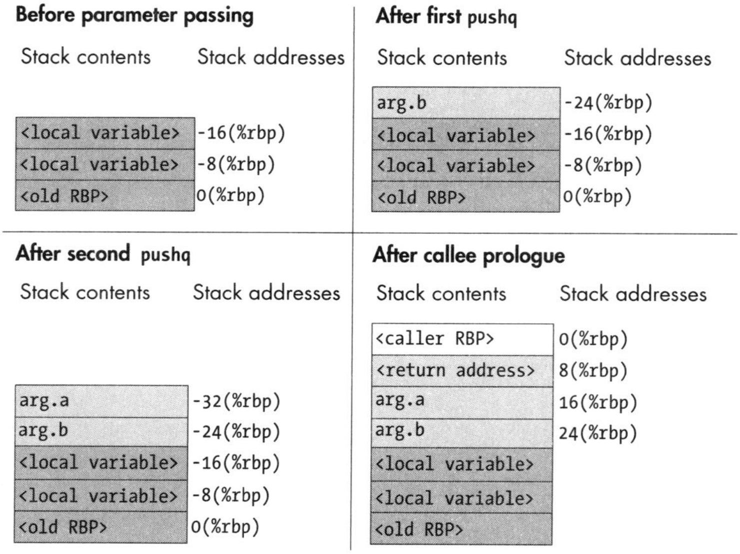

Figure 18-4: Pushing a structure onto the stack

The two pushq instructions in Listing 18-46 push a copy of arg onto the stack with the correct layout. After the callee sets up its stack frame, it can access arg at 16(%rbp), which is where we always expect to find a function's first stack parameter.

If a structure belongs to the MEMORY class, we'll always push it onto the stack. Consider the structure type declaration and function declaration in Listing 18-47.

```
struct pass_in_memory {
    double w;
    double x;
    int y;
```

```
    long z;
};

void accept_struct(struct pass_in_memory arg);
```

Listing 18-47: A function declaration with a structure parameter that belongs to the MEMORY class

Listing 18-48 demonstrates how to pass a structure stored at -32(%rbp) as an argument to accept_struct.

```
pushq   -8(%rbp)
pushq   -16(%rbp)
pushq   -24(%rbp)
pushq   -32 (%rbp)
call    accept_struct
```

Listing 18-48: Passing a structure that belongs to the MEMORY class on the stack

In this case, like in Listing 18-46, we maintain the structure's layout in memory by pushing it onto the stack from back to front.

Returning Structures

If a structure fits into a single register, returning it is straightforward. We'll return structures that belong to the INTEGER class in RAX and structures that belong to the SSE class in XMM0. If a structure is between 8 and 16 bytes, we'll return it in two registers. To accommodate these structures, we'll designate two more registers to transfer return values: RDX and XMM1. We'll transfer each eightbyte of a structure in the next available return register of the appropriate class. For example, if the first part of a structure belongs to the SSE class and the second part belongs to the INTEGER class, we'll transfer the first part in XMM0 and the second part in RAX. If both parts belong to the SSE class, we'll transfer the structure in XMM0 and XMM1; if both parts belong to the INTEGER class, we'll transfer it in RAX and RDX.

Things get even hairier if a structure is in the MEMORY class. In that case, the caller allocates space for the return value and passes the address of that space to the callee in the RDI register, as if it were the first integer parameter. This means the actual first integer parameter must be passed in RSI, the second in RDX, and so on. To return a value, the callee copies it into the space pointed to by RDI and copies the pointer itself into RAX. Let's look at the example in Listing 18-49.

```
struct large_struct {
    long array[3];
};

struct large_struct return_a_struct(long i) {
    struct large_struct callee_result = { {0, 1, i } };
    return callee_result;
}
```

```
int main(void) {
❶ struct large_struct caller_result = return_a_struct(10);
    --snip--
}
```

Listing 18-49: Calling function that returns a structure in memory

Because struct large_struct is 24 bytes, we'll return the result of the
return_a_struct function in memory. In main, we call return_a_struct and
assign the result to caller_result ❶. Assuming main has reserved stack space
for caller_result at -24(%rbp), Listing 18-50 shows how to implement this
function call.

```
leaq    -24(%rbp), %rdi
movq    $10, %rsi
call    return_a_struct
```

Listing 18-50: Calling return_a_struct in assembly

First, we pass the address of caller_result, which will hold the result of
return_a_struct, in RDI. We then pass the argument 10 in the next available parameter passing register, RSI. Finally, we issue a call instruction.
Figure 18-5 illustrates the program's state just before the call instruction.

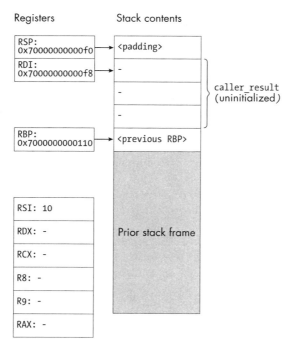

*Figure 18-5: The state of the stack and registers before
calling return_a_struct*

RSP and RBP point to the top and bottom of the current stack frame, as usual. RDI points to caller_result, which hasn't been initialized yet. RSI holds the first argument to return_a_struct, 10.

Note that Listing 18-50 doesn't allocate additional stack space to hold the result of return_a_struct; it just loads the address of the caller_result variable. That's typically fine, with one caveat: according to the ABI, the memory that will hold the return value "must not overlap any data visible to the callee through other names than this argument." For example, if you needed to implement the function call var = foo(1, 2, &var), it would violate the ABI to pass the address of var in RDI as the storage for the return value *and* in RCX as an ordinary argument. Instead, you'd need to allocate additional stack space to hold the result of foo and copy the result to var after the function returned. We don't need to worry about this case, since we generate a new variable to hold the result of each function call during TACKY generation.

Now let's look at Listing 18-51, which implements return_a_struct in assembly.

```
return_a_struct:
    pushq   %rbp
    movq    %rsp, %rbp
    subq    $32, %rsp
    movq    $0, -24(%rbp)
    movq    $1, -16(%rbp)
    movq    %rsi, -8(%rbp)
  ❶ movq    -24(%rbp), %r10
    movq    %r10, (%rdi)
    movq    -16(%rbp), %r10
    movq    %r10, 8(%rdi)
    movq    -8(%rbp), %r10
    movq    %r10, 16(%rdi)
  ❷ movq    %rdi, %rax
    --snip--
```

Listing 18-51: Returning a structure in memory

At the start of the function, we set up the stack frame, allocate stack space for the local callee_result variable at -24(%rbp), and then initialize it. The assembly code to return result starts at ❶. First, we copy result into the memory location that RDI points to, 8 bytes at a time; we'll copy the first 8 bytes to (%rdi), the next 8 bytes to 8(%rdi), and the last 8 bytes to 16(%rdi). Then, we copy the pointer to the return value from RDI into RAX ❷. Finally, we execute the function epilogue, which is omitted from this listing. Figure 18-6 illustrates the state of the program just before the function epilogue.

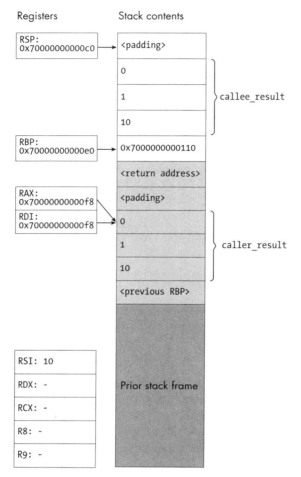

Figure 18-6: The state of the stack and registers just before returning from return_a_struct

The caller_result variable in the caller's stack frame now holds the function's return value, and RAX holds the address of caller_result. In this example, the RDI register holds that address too, but this isn't required by the ABI.

We've covered everything we need to know about the calling convention for structures. Now we're ready to work on the assembly generation pass!

Assembly Generation

This pass will change in a couple of ways. First, we'll need to generate assembly to copy entire structures from one location to another. The Copy, Load, Store, and CopyToOffset instructions can all transfer both scalar and aggregate values. So can the new CopyFromOffset instruction, which we'll need to implement. Second, we'll implement the System V calling convention that we just learned about.

We'll start by making a few small changes to the assembly AST.

Extending the Assembly AST

In Listing 18-46, we used the operand arg+8(%rip) to access data at a constant offset from a RIP-relative label. We'll often need these sorts of operands to access members of structures with static storage duration. The assembly AST can already specify constant offsets from most memory addresses, but not from RIP-relative addresses. We'll remove this limitation by adding an offset to the Data operand:

```
operand = --snip-- | Data(identifier, int)
```

We'll also introduce two new assembly instructions. First, we'll add the left-shift instruction, shl. This instruction takes an immediate value as its source operand and a memory address or register as its destination. It shifts its destination left by the number of bits specified by its source. For example, the instruction

```
shlq    $8, %rax
```

shifts the value in RAX 1 byte to the left, setting its lowest byte to 0. If the value in RAX were 0x8 before this instruction, it would be 0x800 afterward. The shl instruction will help us copy irregularly sized structures into registers in order to pass them as arguments and return values. Because we can't directly access every individual byte within a register, we'll use shl to shift each byte into place.

Second, we'll add the two-operand form of the logical right-shift instruction, shr. (We added the one-operand form, which shifts its operand 1 bit to the right, back in Chapter 13.) Similar to shl, it shifts its destination right by the number of bits its source specifies. It will serve a similar purpose to shl, helping us transfer irregularly sized structures *out* of registers and into memory.

NOTE *The shl instruction also has a one-operand form, which we won't use; it's the counterpart to the one-operand form of shr that we're already familiar with. Both instructions have yet another form we won't use, which uses the CL register as the source operand.*

We'll extend binary_operator to represent shl and shr:

```
binary_operator = --snip-- | Shl | ShrTwoOp
```

The new binary shr instruction gets the rather clunky name ShrTwoOp to distinguish it from the existing unary Shr instruction in the assembly AST.

Listing 18-52 defines the updated assembly AST, with these changes bolded.

```
program = Program(top_level*)
assembly_type = Byte | Longword | Quadword | Double | ByteArray(int size, int alignment)
top_level = Function(identifier name, bool global, instruction* instructions)
            | StaticVariable(identifier name, bool global, int alignment, static_init* init_list)
            | StaticConstant(identifier name, int alignment, static_init init)
instruction = Mov(assembly_type, operand src, operand dst)
            | Movsx(assembly_type src_type, assembly_type dst_type, operand src, operand dst)
            | MovZeroExtend(assembly_type src_type, assembly_type dst_type,
                            operand src, operand dst)
            | Lea(operand src, operand dst)
            | Cvttsd2si(assembly_type dst_type, operand src, operand dst)
            | Cvtsi2sd(assembly_type src_type, operand src, operand dst)
            | Unary(unary_operator, assembly_type, operand)
            | Binary(binary_operator, assembly_type, operand, operand)
            | Cmp(assembly_type, operand, operand)
            | Idiv(assembly_type, operand)
            | Div(assembly_type, operand)
            | Cdq(assembly_type)
            | Jmp(identifier)
            | JmpCC(cond_code, identifier)
            | SetCC(cond_code, operand)
            | Label(identifier)
            | Push(operand)
            | Call(identifier)
            | Ret
unary_operator = Neg | Not | Shr
binary_operator = Add | Sub | Mult | DivDouble | And | Or | Xor | Shl | ShrTwoOp
operand = Imm(int) | Reg(reg) | Pseudo(identifier) | Memory(reg, int) | Data(identifier, int)
        | PseudoMem(identifier, int) | Indexed(reg base, reg index, int scale)
cond_code = E | NE | G | GE | L | LE | A | AE | B | BE
reg = AX | CX | DX | DI | SI | R8 | R9 | R10 | R11 | SP | BP
    | XMM0 | XMM1 | XMM2 | XMM3 | XMM4 | XMM5 | XMM6 | XMM7 | XMM14 | XMM15
```

Listing 18-52: The assembly AST with offsets on static operands and bit shift instructions

Converting types and TACKY operands to assembly is pretty simple. Structure types, like array types, are converted to the ByteArray assembly type. To convert a structure type to assembly, you'll need to look up its size and alignment in the type table. We'll convert TACKY variables of structure type to PseudoMem assembly operands, just like we do with arrays. We'll always store arrays and structures in memory rather than registers, even once we implement register allocation in Part III.

Some of the TACKY variables you encounter may have incomplete structure types. (Remember that it's legal to declare an extern variable with an incomplete type and take its address, but it's illegal to define it or use it in any other way.) Convert these variables to PseudoMem operands, like other variables of structure type. You can give these variables a dummy assembly type when you add them to the backend symbol table; that dummy type will never be used.

Next, let's handle the Copy, Load, Store, CopyToOffset, and CopyFromOffset instructions. Then, we'll deal with function calls.

Copying Structures

To copy a structure to a new location, you don't need to consider its members' types or offsets; you just need to copy the right number of bytes. To minimize the number of mov instructions required, copy 8 bytes at a time until there are fewer than 8 bytes left to move. Then, copy 4 bytes at a time. Finally, when there are fewer than 4 bytes left to move, copy 1 byte at a time. (There's also a 2-byte mov instruction in x64 assembly, but our assembly AST doesn't support it.) For example, if a and b are 20-byte structures, you should translate

```
Copy(Var("a"), Var("b"))
```

to the assembly in Listing 18-53.

```
Mov(Quadword, PseudoMem("a", 0), PseudoMem("b", 0))
Mov(Quadword, PseudoMem("a", 8), PseudoMem("b", 8))
Mov(Longword, PseudoMem("a", 16), PseudoMem("b", 16))
```

Listing 18-53: Implementing Copy for non-scalar values

The first Mov instruction copies the first 8 bytes of a to b; the second instruction copies the next 8 bytes of a to the corresponding offset in b, and the final instruction copies the remaining 4 bytes. These Mov instructions are invalid, since their source and destination operands are both in memory, but they'll be rewritten in the instruction fix-up pass.

You can use the same approach to translate the Load and Store instructions. For example, if y is a 6-byte structure, you'll translate

```
Load(Var("ptr"), Var("y"))
```

to Listing 18-54.

```
Mov(Quadword, Pseudo("ptr"), Reg(AX))
Mov(Longword, Memory(AX, 0), PseudoMem("y", 0))
Mov(Byte, Memory(AX, 4), PseudoMem("y", 4))
Mov(Byte, Memory(AX, 5), PseudoMem("y", 5))
```

Listing 18-54: Implementing Load for non-scalar values

The first instruction copies the pointer into the RAX register. Each subsequent Mov instruction copies a chunk of data stored at some offset from the address in RAX to the corresponding offset in y.

You can also implement CopyToOffset for non-scalar values with a sequence of Mov instructions; the only difference is that you'll add the specified offset to each instruction's destination. To give another example with the 6-byte structure y, you'll translate

```
CopyToOffset(src=Var("y"), dst="z", offset=8)
```

to Listing 18-55.

```
Mov(Longword, PseudoMem("y", 0), PseudoMem("z", 8))
Mov(Byte, PseudoMem("y", 4), PseudoMem("z", 12))
Mov(Byte, PseudoMem("y", 5), PseudoMem("z", 13))
```

Listing 18-55: Implementing CopyToOffset for non-scalar values

Finally, you'll need to implement the new CopyFromOffset instruction. Like the other TACKY instructions that copy data, it accepts both scalar and non-scalar operands. I won't talk through this instruction in detail; you should handle it basically the same way as CopyToOffset.

I recommend writing a helper function, which I'll call copy_bytes, that generates assembly instructions to copy an arbitrary number of bytes from one Memory or PseudoMem operand to another. You can use this helper function to implement all five of the TACKY copying instructions. It will come in handy again when you need to pass structures in memory as arguments and return values.

Once you've implemented CopyFromOffset and extended the other copy instructions to support non-scalar values, you're ready to move on to function calls.

Using Structures in Function Calls

Since the rules for passing and returning structures are complex, let's talk about our overall strategy before diving into the pseudocode. First, we'll write a function to classify each eightbyte of a structure type. Then, we'll extend the classify_parameters helper function, which we introduced back in Chapter 13 to help with parameter passing on both the caller and callee sides. Remember that this function returns three lists: operands passed in general-purpose registers, operands passed in XMM registers, and operands passed on the stack. Once we update this function, these lists may include both scalar values and eightbytes of structure values.

Next, we'll introduce another helper function, classify_return_value, to split up return values in a similar way. It will return a list of operands returned in general-purpose registers, a list of operands returned in XMM registers, and a Boolean flag that indicates whether the return value is passed in memory. This flag will be True only when both lists are empty.

When classify_return_value processes a scalar value, it will return one empty list, one list with a single element, and a False flag. When it processes a structure, it might produce a more interesting result. Its main purpose is to massage both scalar and structure return values into the same shape, so we can process them in a uniform way.

Once these helpers are in place, we'll update how we convert the FunCall TACKY instruction to assembly. For the most part, we can pass parameters the same way as in earlier chapters. We'll copy each operand we get from classify_parameters into the appropriate register or push it onto the stack, without worrying about whether it's a scalar value or part of a structure. Only a few details will change. First, we'll account for the fact that RDI may not be available if it holds the address of the space reserved for the return value. We'll also need to pass irregularly sized eightbytes that can't be transferred with a single mov instruction. We'll write a new helper function to move these eightbytes into registers.

Retrieving the function's return value will require larger changes. We'll use classify_return_value to learn where we can find each part of the return value, then copy each part from the appropriate register or memory address to its final destination. This will require yet another helper function to copy irregularly sized eightbytes *out* of registers.

Finally, we'll tackle things on the callee side. Here, like on the caller side, the way we process parameters will change only slightly, but the way we handle return values will change quite a bit. We'll use classify_return_value again to figure out where to put each part of the return value.

Classifying Structure Types

We'll start with a helper function to classify structure types. We'll use the class construct defined in Listing 18-56 to represent the three classes we discussed earlier.

```
class = MEMORY | SSE | INTEGER
```

Listing 18-56: The class *construct*

The classification function will return a list of class elements, one for each eightbyte of the structure being classified. To classify a structure, we'll first consider its size and then look at the types of its members. Listing 18-57 gives the pseudocode for this process.

```
classify_structure(StructEntry(alignment, size, members)):
    if size > 16:
        result = []
        while size > 0:
            result.append(MEMORY)
            size -= 8
        return result
 ❶ scalar_types = <flatten out list of member types>
 ❷ if size > 8:
        if first and last type in scalar_types are Double:
            return [SSE, SSE]
        if first type in scalar_types is Double:
            return [SSE, INTEGER]
        if last type in scalar_types is Double:
            return [INTEGER, SSE]
        return [INTEGER, INTEGER]
    else if first type in scalar_types is Double:
      ❸ return [SSE]
    else:
      ❹ return [INTEGER]
```

Listing 18-57: Classifying structure types

The classify_structure function takes a structure definition from the type table. If the structure is larger than 16 bytes, it must be passed in memory, so we return a list of enough MEMORY elements to cover the whole structure. For example, if the structure's size is 17 bytes, `classify _structure` should return [MEMORY, MEMORY, MEMORY].

Otherwise, the structure's classification depends on its member types. We construct a list of every scalar type the structure contains, including the types of nested values ❶. Suppose a structure contains two members: an int * and a char[3]. The resulting scalar_types list will be [Pointer(Int), Char, Char, Char].

If a structure is between 8 and 16 bytes, we return a list of two classes ❷. Because a double has a size and alignment of 8 bytes, any double that appears in a structure of this size must completely occupy either the first or second eightbyte. Taking advantage of this fact, we examine only the first and last elements of scalar_type. If the first element is Double, the first eightbyte must be in the SSE class; otherwise, it must be in the INTEGER class. Likewise, the second eightbyte is in the SSE class only if the last element of scalar_type is Double.

Finally, we classify structures that are 8 bytes or smaller. A structure of this size belongs to the SSE class if the first (and only) scalar type it contains is Double ❸. Otherwise, it belongs to the INTEGER class ❹.

If you want, you can improve on the code in Listing 18-57 by caching the results. You'll need to maintain a mapping from structure tags to their classifications. The first time you classify a particular structure type, add the result to this mapping. Then, if you need to classify that structure type again, you can just retrieve the result instead of recomputing it.

Classifying Parameters

Next, we'll extend the classify_parameters function. This function partitions a list of parameters or arguments in three, based on whether each one is passed in a general-purpose register, in an XMM register, or on the stack. Now, when it processes a value of structure type, it will split up the value into eightbytes and add each one to the correct list. Listing 18-58 reproduces the definition of classify_parameters from Listing 13-29, with changes bolded.

```
classify_parameters(values, return_in_memory):
    int_reg_args = []
    double_reg_args = []
    stack_args = []

    if return_in_memory:
        int_regs_available = 5
    else:
        int_regs_available = 6

    for v in values:
        operand = convert_val(v)
        t = assembly_type_of(v)
        typed_operand = (t, operand)

        if t == Double:
```

```
            --snip--
        else if t is scalar:
            if length(int_reg_args) < int_regs_available:
                int_reg_args.append(typed_operand)
            else:
                stack_args.append(typed_operand)

        else:
            // v is a structure
            // partition it into eightbytes by class
            classes = classify_structure(<struct definition for v>) ❶
            use_stack = True
            struct_size = t.size
            if classes[0] != MEMORY: ❷

                // make tentative assignments to registers
                tentative_ints = []
                tentative_doubles = []
                offset = 0
                for class in classes:
                    operand = PseudoMem(<name of v>, offset) ❸
                    if class == SSE:
                        tentative_doubles.append(operand)
                    else:
                        eightbyte_type = get_eightbyte_type(offset, struct_size) ❹
                        tentative_ints.append((eightbyte_type, operand))
                    offset += 8

                // finalize them if there are enough free registers
                if ((length(tentative_doubles) + length(double_reg_args)) <= 8 and
                    (length(tentative_ints) + length(int_reg_args)) <= int_regs_available): ❺
                    double_reg_args.append_all(tentative_doubles)
                    int_reg_args.append_all(tentative_ints)
                    use_stack = False

            if use_stack:
                // add each eightbyte of the structure to stack_args
                offset = 0
                for class in classes:
                    operand = PseudoMem(<name of v>, offset)
                    eightbyte_type = get_eightbyte_type(offset, struct_size)
                    stack_args.append((eightbyte_type, operand)) ❻
                    offset += 8

    return (int_reg_args, double_reg_args, stack_args)
```

Listing 18-58: Extending classify_parameters *to support structures*

The first change to this function is the new Boolean return_in_memory
parameter. As the name suggests, this indicates whether the function's
return value is passed in memory. If it is, that memory address will be
passed in the RDI register, leaving one fewer general-purpose register
available for other parameters. We'll set int_regs_available accordingly.

Then, when we process parameters of integer or pointer type, we'll use int _regs_available, instead of the constant 6, as the number of usable general-purpose registers. (We'll process parameters of double type exactly the same way we did in Chapter 13, so I've snipped out that bit of the listing.)

Now we've reached the interesting part: processing parameters of structure type. We'll start with a call to classify_structure ❶. Then, we'll check whether the first eightbyte of the structure is in the MEMORY class ❷. If it is, the rest of the structure must be too. If not, we'll try to assign each eightbyte to a register. We'll convert each eightbyte to a PseudoMem operand ❸, then add it to one of two lists, tentative_doubles or tentative_ints, based on its class. We know that v is a variable, rather than a constant, because there are no aggregate constants in TACKY; the name of that variable will be the base of the PseudoMem operand.

When we add an eightbyte to tentative_ints, we need to figure out what assembly type to associate it with. Most eightbytes are exactly 8 bytes long, so we associate them with the Quadword type. But the final eightbyte in a structure might be shorter. We'll find each eightbyte's assembly type using the get_eightbyte_type helper function ❹, which we'll walk through in a moment. This function takes two arguments: the eightbyte's offset and the total size of the structure. It will use these to figure out the eightbyte's size, which dictates its assembly type.

Once we've partitioned the whole structure into two tentative lists, we check that we have enough free registers to accommodate both of them ❺. If we do, we append both lists to their non-tentative equivalents. If we don't have enough registers available, or if the structure belongs to the MEMORY class, we add each eightbyte to stack_args instead ❻. We use get_eightbyte _type to determine the type of each eightbyte we pass on the stack.

Now let's walk through get_eightbyte_type, defined in Listing 18-59.

```
get_eightbyte_type(offset, struct_size):
  ❶ bytes_from_end = struct_size - offset
    if bytes_from_end >= 8:
        return Quadword
    if bytes_from_end == 4:
        return Longword
    if bytes_from_end == 1:
        return Byte
  ❷ return ByteArray(bytes_from_end, 8)
```

Listing 18-59: Associating an eightbyte with an assembly_type

The goal here is to figure out what operand size to use when moving this eightbyte into a register or onto the stack. First, we calculate the number of bytes between the start of this eightbyte and the end of the whole structure ❶. If there are more than 8 bytes left in the structure, this isn't the last eightbyte, so we use the Quadword type. If this eightbyte is exactly 8 bytes, 4 bytes, or 1 byte long, we use the Quadword, Longword, or Byte type, respectively.

Otherwise, the eightbyte's size is irregular; it's not a valid operand size for assembly instructions. In this case, we use the ByteArray type to record the eightbyte's exact size in bytes ❷. (The alignment in this ByteArray is a dummy value; we won't need it later.) We can't safely transfer an irregularly sized eightbyte with a single Mov instruction. As you learned in Chapter 9, reading past the end of a value in memory—by pushing a 4-byte value with an 8-byte pushq instruction, for example—could trigger a memory access violation. By the same logic, it's not safe to transfer a 5-, 6-, or 7-byte operand with an 8-byte movq instruction or a 3-byte operand with a 4-byte movl instruction. We'll look at how to transfer irregularly sized eightbytes in a moment.

Note that get_eightbyte_type doesn't consider the eightbyte's class; it will return Quadword for any full-length eightbyte, even if it belongs to the SSE class. This is correct because we use get_eightbyte_type only to find the types of values we're going to transfer in general-purpose registers or on the stack. When we push 8 bytes of a structure onto the stack, we don't care whether those bytes contain a floating-point value or an integer.

Classifying Return Values

Next, we'll write a similar helper function to classify return values. This function is simpler than classify_parameters. We have one value to deal with, instead of a whole list, so we don't need to worry about running out of registers. We also don't need to split up the value into eightbytes if it will be returned in memory, like we did in classify_parameters. Listing 18-60 shows the pseudocode for the classify_return_value helper function.

```
classify_return_value(retval):

    t = assembly_type_of(retval)

    if t == Double:
        operand = convert_val(retval)
    ❶ return ([], [operand], False)
    else if t is scalar:
        typed_operand = (t, convert_val(retval))
    ❷ return ([typed_operand], [], False)
    else:
        classes = classify_structure(<struct definition for retval>)
        struct_size = t.size
        if classes[0] == MEMORY:
            // the whole structure is returned in memory,
            // not in registers
          ❸ return ([], [], True)
        else:
            // the structure is returned in registers;
            // partition it into eightbytes by class
            int_retvals = []
            double_retvals = []
            offset = 0
```

```
                    for class in classes:
                        operand = PseudoMem(<name of retval>, offset)
                    ❹ match class with
                        | SSE ->
                            double_retvals.append(operand)
                        | INTEGER ->
                            eightbyte_type = get_eightbyte_type(offset, struct_size)
                            int_retvals.append((eightbyte_type, operand))
                        | MEMORY -> fail("Internal error")
                        offset += 8
                return (int_retvals, double_retvals, False)
```

Listing 18-60: Classifying return values

If the return value is a double, the first of our two lists, which contains operands returned in general-purpose registers, will be empty. The second list, which holds operands returned in XMM registers, will contain the return value. The flag signaling that the value is returned in memory will be False ❶. If the return value is some other scalar type, we'll add it to the list of operands returned in general-purpose registers, along with its type. The list of operands in XMM registers will be empty, and the flag will still be False ❷.

Otherwise, the return value must be a structure. We'll look up its classes with classify_structure, then check whether it belongs to the MEMORY class. If it does, we'll return two empty lists, which indicate that nothing will be returned in registers, and a True flag, which indicates that the return value will be passed in memory ❸.

If the structure isn't in the MEMORY class, it will be returned in registers. We'll convert each eightbyte to a PseudoMem operand and add it to either double_retvals or int_retvals, according to its class ❹. Here, as in classify _parameters, we'll use get_eightbyte_type to find the assembly type of each operand in int_retvals. Finally, we'll return both lists, along with a False flag.

Implementing FunCall

Next, let's update how we implement function calls in assembly. Listing 18-61 reproduces the definition of convert_function_call from Listing 13-31, with changes bolded and some unchanged code omitted.

```
convert_function_call(FunCall(fun_name, args, dst)):
    int_registers = [ DI, SI, DX, CX, R8, R9 ]
    double_registers = [ XMM0, XMM1, XMM2, XMM3, XMM4, XMM5, XMM6, XMM7 ]

    return_in_memory = False
    int_dests = []
    double_dests = []
    reg_index = 0

    // classify return value
    if dst is not null:
        int_dests, double_dests, return_in_memory = classify_return_value(dst) ❶
```

```
if return_in_memory:
    dst_operand = convert_val(dst)
    emit(Lea(dst_operand, Reg(DI))) ❷
    reg_index = 1

// classify arguments
int_args, double_args, stack_args = classify_parameters(args, return_in_memory)

--snip--

// pass args in registers
for (assembly_type, assembly_arg) in int_args:
    r = int_registers[reg_index]
    if assembly_type is ByteArray(size, alignment):
        copy_bytes_to_reg(assembly_arg, r, size) ❸
    else:
        emit(Mov(assembly_type, assembly_arg, Reg(r)))
    reg_index += 1

--snip--

// pass args on stack
for (assembly_type, assembly_arg) in reverse(stack_args):
    if assembly_type is ByteArray(size, alignment):
        emit(Binary(Sub, Quadword, Imm(8), Reg(SP))) ❹
        copy_bytes(from=assembly_arg, to=Memory(SP, 0), count=size)
    else if (assembly_arg is a Reg or Imm operand
            or assembly_type == Quadword
            or assembly_type == Double):
        emit(Push(assembly_arg))
    else:
        emit(Mov(assembly_type, assembly_arg, Reg(AX)))
        emit(Push(Reg(AX)))

--snip--

// retrieve return value
if (dst is not null) and (not return_in_memory):
    int_return_registers = [ AX, DX ]
    double_return_registers = [ XMM0, XMM1 ]

    // retrieve values returned in general-purpose registers
    reg_index = 0
    for (t, op) in int_dests:
        r = int_return_registers[reg_index]
        if t is ByteArray(size, alignment):
            copy_bytes_from_reg(r, op, size) ❺
        else:
            emit(Mov(t, Reg(r), op)) ❻
        reg_index += 1

    // retrieve values returned in XMM registers
    reg_index = 0
```

```
for op in double_dests:
    r = double_return_registers[reg_index]
    emit(Mov(Double, Reg(r), op)) ❼
    reg_index += 1
```

Listing 18-61: Supporting structures in function calls

We start by calling classify_return_value (unless the function call doesn't have a return value because its return type is void) ❶. If we find that the return value will be passed in memory, we convert dst into an assembly operand, then emit an instruction to load its address into RDI ❷. We also increment reg_index so that we'll pass the first integer argument in RSI instead of RDI.

Next, we call classify_parameters, passing it the new return_in_memory flag. Then, we adjust the stack pointer (I've omitted this step because it's the same as in earlier chapters).

We then pass arguments in the general-purpose registers. If an argument has the ByteArray type, its size isn't exactly 1, 4, or 8 bytes, so transferring it into the register will take multiple instructions. We emit those instructions with the copy_bytes_to_reg helper function ❸, which we'll look at in a moment. If an argument has any other type, we transfer it with a single Mov instruction, as in earlier chapters. The way we pass arguments in XMM registers won't change, so I've snipped out that step.

The next step is passing arguments on the stack. The way we pass operands with type Byte, Longword, Quadword, or Double won't change. To pass an irregular operand with a ByteArray type, we first need to subtract 8 bytes from RSP to allocate the stack slot for that operand ❹. (Remember that the ABI reserves an entire 8-byte stack slot for each eightbyte of a structure parameter, even if the actual eightbyte is smaller than that.) To copy the operand into that stack slot, we use the copy_bytes helper function we've already written. Suppose x is a global variable and its size is 3 bytes. We'll issue these instructions to pass it as an argument on the stack:

```
subq    $8, %rsp
movb    x(%rip), (%rsp)
movb    x+1(%rip), 1(%rsp)
movb    x+2(%rip), 2(%rsp)
```

These movb instructions are invalid, since both operands are in memory; we'll rewrite them in the instruction fix-up pass.

Next, we issue the call instruction and restore the stack pointer to its original location. I've snipped out these steps because they're unchanged from earlier chapters.

Finally, we copy the return value to the destination. If the return value is transferred in memory, we don't do anything; the callee already copied it for us. Otherwise, we iterate over the two lists of destination operands returned by classify_return_value—first int_dests, then double_dests—and retrieve each operand from the corresponding register. To retrieve an irregularly sized eightbyte from a general-purpose register, we use the copy_bytes_from_reg helper function ❺, which we'll define in a moment. This

540   Chapter 18

is the counterpart to `copy_bytes_to_reg`, which we used to pass parameters. We emit a single Mov instruction to retrieve a Byte, Longword, or Quadword value from a general-purpose register ❻ or to retrieve a Double value from an XMM register ❼.

The code to copy the return value to dst works whether dst is a structure or a scalar object. If it's a structure, each item in int_dests and double _dests is an eightbyte of dst, which we'll populate from the corresponding return register. If dst is scalar, either int_dests or double_dests will have exactly one element, and the other list will be empty. In that case, this code will emit a single Mov instruction to transfer the return value from RAX or XMM0 to its destination.

Transferring Irregular Structures in Registers

We still need to implement `copy_bytes_to_reg` and `copy_bytes_from_reg`, which copy irregularly sized eightbytes to and from general-purpose registers. This is trickier than copying between two locations in memory, like we do in `copy_bytes`, because we can't directly access every individual byte in a general-purpose register. We can access a general-purpose register's lowest byte with the appropriate 1-byte alias, like AL or DIL, but we can't access its other bytes individually. (Each register's second-lowest byte also has its own alias—for instance, AH is the second-lowest byte of RAX—but our assembly AST doesn't support these aliases. Even if it did, we still couldn't access the other 6 bytes.)

We'll use our new bit-shifting instructions to work around this limitation. Let's revisit the 3-byte global variable x from our last example. If we need to copy x into RDI, we'll issue the following instructions:

```
movb    x+2(%rip), %dil
shlq    $8, %rdi
movb    x+1(%rip), %dil
shlq    $8, %rdi
movb    x(%rip), %dil
```

We start by copying the *last* byte of x into the lowest byte of RDI, whose alias is DIL. Then, we issue a shl instruction to shift RDI 1 byte to the left. This moves the byte we just copied into the second-lowest byte of RDI and zeroes out DIL. Next, we copy the middle byte of x into DIL and issue another shl instruction. At this point, the last 2 bytes of x are in the correct place in the register, so we just move the first byte of x into DIL, and we're done. Figure 18-7 shows the contents of RDI (in hexadecimal) after each instruction, if x contains the bytes 0x1, 0x2, and 0x3, and RDI's initial value is 0.

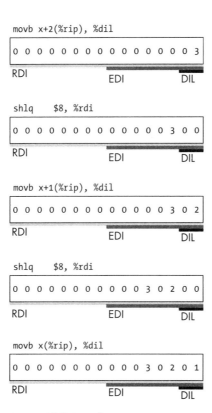

Figure 18-7: Transferring a structure into
a register a byte at a time

Don't let the byte ordering here throw you off: because our system is little-endian, the least significant (rightmost) byte in RDI corresponds to the lowest memory address when we copy the value from RDI into memory, or vice versa. This means—somewhat counterintuitively—that shifting a value to the *left* moves each byte to a location that corresponds to a *higher* memory address. If, after copying this structure into RDI, we issue the instruction

```
movl    %edi, -4(%rbp)
```

then the contents of memory will look like Figure 18-8.

Contents	0x01	0x02	0x03	0x00
Address	-4(%rbp)	-3(%rbp)	-2(%rbp)	-1(%rbp)

Figure 18-8: The contents of memory after copying a structure
from a register

Now the structure is laid out in memory in the correct order. (This movl instruction also writes 1 byte of memory past the end of the structure, which is fine if you aren't using that byte for anything else. We'll transfer irregularly sized structures in and out of registers 1 byte at a time, but code in other translation units that we interact with may transfer them in 4- and 8-byte chunks when it's safe to do so.)

That's the basic idea of copy_bytes_to_reg; now let's implement it. Listing 18-62 gives the pseudocode.

```
copy_bytes_to_reg(src_op, dst_reg, byte_count):
    offset = byte_count - 1
    while offset >= 0:
        src_byte = add_offset(src_op, offset)
        emit(Mov(Byte, src_byte, Reg(dst_reg)))
        if offset > 0:
            emit(Binary(Shl, Quadword, Imm(8), Reg(dst_reg)))
        offset -= 1
```

Listing 18-62: Generating instructions to copy bytes from memory into a register

This function copies byte_count bytes from src_op into dst_reg. Because src_op is part of a structure, we can assume it's a memory operand that accepts an offset, like PseudoMem or Memory. We iterate over the bytes of src_op in reverse order: we start at its final byte, with offset byte_count - 1, and end at byte zero. We use a simple helper function, add_offset, to construct the assembly operand for each byte. I won't give you the pseudocode for this function, since it just adds the specified offset to src_op. For example, if src_op is PseudoMem("x", 2), add_offset(src_op, 3) should return PseudoMem("x", 5).

Once we have the assembly operand for the current byte, we emit a Mov instruction to copy that byte into the destination register. Next, on all but the last loop iteration, we emit a Shl instruction to shift the whole register left by 8 bits. We then decrement the offset and move on to the next byte.

To copy bytes out of a register, we do the whole thing in reverse. Here's how we would copy 3 bytes from RDI onto the stack at -4(%rbp):

```
movb    %dil, -4(%rbp)
shrq    $8, %rdi
movb    %dil, -3(%rbp)
shrq    $8, %rdi
movb    %dil, -2(%rbp)
```

First, we copy the lowest byte of RDI into memory. Then, we shift RDI 1 byte to the right, so DIL now contains the second-lowest byte of the structure. We repeat this process until we've transferred every byte. Listing 18-63 gives the pseudocode to generate these instructions.

```
copy_bytes_from_reg(src_reg, dst_op, byte_count):
    offset = 0
    while offset < byte_count:
        dst_byte = add_offset(dst_op, offset)
        emit(Mov(Byte, Reg(src_reg), dst_byte))
        if offset < byte_count - 1:
            emit(Binary(ShrTwoOp, Quadword, Imm(8), Reg(src_reg)))
        offset += 1
```

Listing 18-63: Generating instructions to copy bytes from a register into memory

As in Listing 18-62, we can assume that dst_op is a memory operand with an offset. We iterate through the bytes of dst_op in order, starting with byte zero. On each iteration, we copy the lowest byte of src_reg into the current byte of dst_op. Then, on all but the last iteration, we shift src_reg 8 bits to the right.

With these two helper functions, we've finished our implementation of function calls. Next, we'll handle the callee side.

Setting Up Function Parameters

At the start of a function, we copy every parameter into that function's stack frame. Now we'll copy parameters of structure type too. The main wrinkle is that RDI might hold a pointer to the return value's destination, instead of an ordinary parameter. Let's revisit set_up_parameters, from Listing 13-30, and see what's changed. Listing 18-64 gives the new definition of set_up _parameters, with this chapter's changes bolded.

```
set_up_parameters(parameters, return_in_memory):

    // classify them
    int_reg_params, double_reg_params, stack_params = classify_parameters(parameters,
                                                                          return_in_memory)

    // copy parameters from general-purpose registers
    int_regs = [ DI, SI, DX, CX, R8, R9 ]
    reg_index = 0

    if return_in_memory:
        emit(Mov(Quadword, Reg(DI), Memory(BP, -8)))
        reg_index = 1

    for (param_type, param) in int_reg_params:
        r = int_regs[reg_index]
        if param_type is ByteArray(size, alignment):
            copy_bytes_from_reg(r, param, size)
        else:
            emit(Mov(param_type, Reg(r), param))
        reg_index += 1

    --snip--

    // copy parameters from the stack
    offset = 16
    for (param_type, param) in stack_params:
        if param_type is ByteArray(size, alignment):
            copy_bytes(from=Memory(BP, offset), to=param, count=size)
        else:
            emit(Mov(param_type, Memory(BP, offset), param))
        offset += 8
```

Listing 18-64: Copying function parameters to the stack

We've added a return_in_memory flag, which we'll pass through to classify _parameters. This flag also dictates how we'll handle the value in RDI. If RDI points to the return value's destination, we'll copy it to the first open slot on the stack, -8(%rbp); we'll retrieve it from this slot when we need to return a value. (In the next section, we'll update the pseudo-operand replacement pass so it doesn't clobber this pointer by assigning a local variable to the same spot.) In this case, we'll also increment reg_index, just like we did when we passed arguments in Listing 18-61, so that we'll look for ordinary parameters starting in RSI instead of RDI.

To copy irregularly sized operands out of registers, we'll use the copy_bytes_from_reg helper function from Listing 18-63. To copy irregularly sized operands that were passed on the stack, we'll use the copy_bytes helper function. If an operand has type Byte, Longword, Quadword, or Double, we'll copy it into place with a single Mov instruction, regardless of whether it represents a scalar value or a chunk of a structure.

Implementing Return

Listing 18-65 illustrates how to convert the Return instruction to assembly.

```
convert_return_instruction(Return(retval)):
    if retval is null:
        emit(Ret)
        return

    int_retvals, double_retvals, return_in_memory = classify_return_value(retval)

    if return_in_memory:
        emit(Mov(Quadword, Memory(BP, -8), Reg(AX))) ❶
        return_storage = Memory(AX, 0)
        ret_operand = convert_val(retval)
        t = assembly_type_of(retval)
        copy_bytes(from=ret_operand, to=return_storage, count=t.size) ❷
    else:
        int_return_registers = [ AX, DX ]
        double_return_registers = [ XMM0, XMM1 ]

        reg_index = 0
        for (t, op) in int_retvals: ❸
            r = int_return_registers[reg_index]
            if t is ByteArray(size, alignment):
                copy_bytes_to_reg(op, r, size)
            else:
                emit(Mov(t, op, Reg(r)))
            reg_index += 1

        reg_index = 0
        for op in double_retvals: ❹
            r = double_return_registers[reg_index]
            emit(Mov(Double, op, Reg(r)))
            reg_index += 1

    emit(Ret)
```

Listing 18-65: Implementing the Return instruction

Assuming the function returns a value, rather than void, we start by classifying that value. Then, we check whether we need to return it in memory or in registers. To return it in memory, we first retrieve the pointer to the destination from -8(%rbp). We copy that pointer into RAX, as the System V calling convention requires ❶. Then, we copy the return value into the block of memory that RAX points to. We perform this copy using the copy_bytes helper function ❷.

If the return value is passed in one or more registers, we iterate through the operands in int_retvals, copying each one into the corresponding general-purpose register ❸. We then iterate through double_retvals, copying these values into XMM0 and XMM1 ❹. Once we've copied every part of the return value to the correct location, we emit a Ret instruction.

Tracking Which Functions Pass Return Values in Memory

Finally, we'll extend the backend symbol table to track which functions return values in memory. Listing 18-66 shows how to update our definition of a backend symbol table entry.

```
asm_symtab_entry = ObjEntry(assembly_type, bool is_static, bool is_constant)
                 | FunEntry(bool defined, bool return_on_stack)
```

Listing 18-66: The updated definition of an entry in the backend symbol table

As you'd expect, we'll set return_on_stack to True if a function passes its return value on the stack and False if it passes its return value in registers or returns void. The pseudo-operand replacement pass will use this flag to figure out if the quadword starting at -8(%rbp) is available or if it holds the pointer to the memory where the return value will be passed. If a function has an incomplete return type other than void (which can happen if it's declared but never defined or called), the return_on_stack flag will never be used, so we can just set it to False.

Putting It All Together

We've now covered all the pieces of assembly generation! Tables 18-1 through 18-4 summarize the latest updates to the conversion from TACKY to assembly; as usual, new constructs and changes to the conversions for existing constructs are bolded. Appendix B includes the complete conversion from TACKY to assembly for this chapter, since this is the final chapter in Part II.

Table 18-1: Converting Top-Level TACKY Constructs to Assembly

TACKY top-level construct	Assembly top-level construct	

Function(name,
     global,
     params,
     instructions)
	Return value
	in registers
	or no return
	value
		Function(name, global,
		[*\<copy Reg(DI) into first int param/eightbyte\>*,
		   \<copy Reg(SI) into second int param/eightbyte\>,
		   \<copy next four int params/eightbytes from registers\>,
		   Mov(Double,
		       Reg(XMM0),
		       \<first double param/eightbyte\>),
		   Mov(Double,
		       Reg(XMM1),
		       \<second double param/eightbyte\>),
		   \<copy next six double params/eightbytes from registers\>,
		   \<copy Memory(BP, 16) into first stack param/eightbyte\>,
		   \<copy Memory(BP, 24) into second stack param/eightbyte\>,
		   \<copy remaining params/eightbytes from stack\>] +
		instructions)

	Return value
	on stack
		Function(name, global,
		[Mov(Quadword,
		       Reg(DI),
		       Memory(BP, -8)),
		   \<copy Reg(SI) into first int param/eightbyte\>,
		   \<copy Reg(DX) into second int param/eightbyte\>,
		   \<copy next three int params/eightbytes from registers\>,
		   Mov(Double,
		       Reg(XMM0),
		       \<first double param/eightbyte\>),
		   Mov(Double,
		       Reg(XMM1),
		       \<second double param/eightbyte\>),
		   \<copy next six double params/eightbytes from registers\>,
		   \<copy Memory(BP, 16) into first stack param/eightbyte\>,
		   \<copy Memory(BP, 24) into second stack param/eightbyte\>,
		   \<copy remaining params/eightbytes from stack\>] +
		instructions)

Table 18-2: Converting TACKY Instructions to Assembly

TACKY instruction	Assembly instructions	

Return(val)	Return on
	stack
		Mov(Quadword, Memory(BP, -8), Reg(AX))
		Mov(Quadword,
		    \<first eightbyte of return value\>,
		    Memory(AX, 0))
		Mov(Quadword,
		    \<second eightbyte of return value\>,
		    Memory(AX, 8))
		\<copy rest of return value\>
		Ret

	Return in registers	*\<move integer parts of return value into RAX, RDX\>* *\<move double parts of return value into XMM0, XMM1\>* Ret
	No return value	Ret

(continued)

Table 18-2: Converting TACKY Instructions to Assembly *(continued)*

TACKY instruction		Assembly instructions
Unary(Negate, src, dst) (double negation)		Mov(Double, src, dst) Binary(Xor, Double, Data(*<negative-zero>*, 0), dst) And add a top-level constant: StaticConstant(*<negative-zero>*, 16, DoubleInit(-0.0))
Copy(src, dst)	Scalar	Mov(*<src type>*, src, dst)
	Structure	Mov(*<first chunk type>*, PseudoMem(src, 0), PseudoMem(dst, 0)) Mov(*<next chunk type>*, PseudoMem(src, *<first chunk size>*), PseudoMem(dst, *<first chunk size>*)) *<copy remaining chunks>*
Load(ptr, dst)	Scalar	Mov(Quadword, ptr, Reg(*<R>*)) Mov(*<dst type>*, Memory(*<R>*, 0), dst)
	Structure	Mov(Quadword, ptr, Reg(*<R>*)) Mov(*<first chunk type>*, Memory(*<R>*, 0), PseudoMem(dst, 0)) Mov(*<next chunk type>*, Memory(*<R>*, *<first chunk size>*), PseudoMem(dst, *<first chunk size>*)) *<copy remaining chunks>*
Store(src, ptr)	Scalar	Mov(Quadword, ptr, Reg(*<R>*)) Mov(*<src type>*, src, Memory(*<R>*, 0))
	Structure	Mov(Quadword, ptr, Reg(*<R>*)) Mov(*<first chunk type>*, PseudoMem(src, 0), Memory(*<R>*, 0)) Mov(*<next chunk type>*, PseudoMem(src, *<first chunk size>*), Memory(*<R>*, *<first chunk size>*)) *<copy remaining chunks>*
CopyToOffset(src, dst, offset)	src is scalar	Mov(*<src type>*, src, PseudoMem(dst, offset))
	src **is a structure**	Mov(*<first chunk type>*, PseudoMem(src, 0), PseudoMem(dst, offset)) Mov(*<next chunk type>*, PseudoMem(src, *<first chunk size>*), PseudoMem(dst, offset + *<first chunk size>*)) *<copy remaining chunks>*
CopyFromOffset(src, offset, dst)	dst is scalar	Mov(*<dst type>*, PseudoMem(src, offset), dst)
	dst **is a structure**	Mov(*<first chunk type>*, PseudoMem(src, offset), PseudoMem(dst, 0)) Mov(*<next chunk type>*, PseudoMem(src, offset + *<first chunk size>*), PseudoMem(dst, *<first chunk size>*)) *<copy remaining chunks>*

TACKY instruction		Assembly instructions
FunCall(fun_name, args, dst)	dst **will be returned in memory**	Lea(dst, Reg(DI)) *\<fix stack alignment\>* *\<move arguments to general-purpose registers, **starting with RSI**\>* *\<move arguments to XMM registers\>* *\<push arguments onto the stack\>* Call(fun_name) *\<deallocate arguments/padding\>*
	dst **will be returned in registers**	*\<fix stack alignment\>* *\<move arguments to general-purpose registers\>* *\<move arguments to XMM registers\>* *\<push arguments onto the stack\>* Call(fun_name) *\<deallocate arguments/padding\>* ***\<move integer parts of return value from RAX, RDX into dst\>*** ***\<move double parts of return value from XMM0, XMM1 into dst\>***
	dst is absent	*\<fix stack alignment\>* *\<move arguments to general-purpose registers\>* *\<move arguments to XMM registers\>* *\<push arguments onto the stack\>* Call(fun_name) *\<deallocate arguments/padding\>*
DoubleToUInt(src, dst)	unsigned char	Cvttsd2si(Longword, src, Reg(*\<R\>*)) Mov(Byte, Reg(*\<R\>*), dst)
	unsigned int	Cvttsd2si(Quadword, src, Reg(*\<R\>*)) Mov(Longword, Reg(*\<R\>*), dst)
	unsigned long	Cmp(Double, Data(*\<upper-bound\>*, **0**), src) JmpCC(AE, *\<label1\>*) Cvttsd2si(Quadword, src, dst) Jmp(*\<label2\>*) Label(*\<label1\>*) Mov(Double, src, Reg(*\<X\>*)) Binary(Sub, Double, Data(*\<upper-bound\>*, **0**), Reg(*\<X\>*)) Cvttsd2si(Quadword, Reg(*\<X\>*), dst) Mov(Quadword, Imm(9223372036854775808), Reg(*\<R\>*)) Binary(Add, Quadword, Reg(*\<R\>*), dst) Label(*\<label2\>*) And add a top-level constant: StaticConstant(*\<upper-bound\>*, 8, DoubleInit(9223372036854775808.0))

Table 18-3: Converting TACKY Operands to Assembly

TACKY operand	Assembly operand
Constant(ConstDouble(double))	Data(*\<ident\>*, **0**) And add a top-level constant: StaticConstant(*\<ident\>*, 8, DoubleInit(double))

Table 18-4: Converting Types to Assembly

Source type	Assembly type	Alignment
Structure(tag)	ByteArray(*<size from type table>*, *<alignment from type table>*)	**Alignment from type table**

Note that we now include offsets on every Data operand we generate. The only Data operands at this point represent floating-point constants; these include the constants we use in the conversions for floating-point Negate and DoubleToUInt in Table 18-2 and ordinary floating-point TACKY constants in Table 18-3. These operands all have an offset of zero.

Replacing Pseudo-operands

We'll make two small changes to this pass. First, we'll supply offsets for Data operands. For example, if v is a static variable, we'll convert

```
PseudoMem("v", 0)
```

to

```
Data("v", 0)
```

and

```
PseudoMem("v", 10)
```

to:

```
Data("v", 10)
```

Second, we need to avoid clobbering the return value pointer in -8(%rbp). Before we start allocating stack space, we'll check the backend symbol table to see whether the function's return value will be passed in memory. If it will, we'll reserve the quadword starting at -8(%rbp) for the return value pointer and allocate space for pseudoregisters only at addresses lower than -8(%rbp). For example, if the first pseudoregister we encounter is a Longword, we'll map it to -12(%rbp).

The instruction fix-up pass won't change in this chapter. The shl and shr instructions we emit during code generation are already valid and don't need to be fixed up, since the destination operand is always a register and the source operand is always the immediate value 8.

Code Emission

The code emission pass requires two small changes. First, we'll include the offsets on Data operands. For example, we'll emit Data("x", 4) as:

```
x+4(%rip)
```

If the offset is zero, you can either include it or omit it.

Second, we'll emit the new Shl and ShrTwoOp assembly instructions as shl and shr, respectively. These take the usual operand size suffixes.

Tables 18-5 and 18-6 show these changes to the code emission pass. Appendix B includes the complete code emission pass for this chapter, since this is the final chapter of Part II.

Table 18-5: Instruction Names for Assembly Operators

Assembly operator	Instruction name
Shl	shl
ShrTwoOp	shr

Table 18-6: Formatting Assembly Operands

Assembly operand	Output
Data(identifier, *int*)	*<identifier>*+*<int>*(%rip)

And with that, you're done with the chapter; your compiler now supports structures!

I recommend debugging the valid test cases for this chapter in several stages. Start with the tests in *tests/chapter_18/valid/no_structure_parameters*. These test programs don't include any parameters or return values of structure type, but they exercise all the other functionality you added in this chapter. They declare structures, assign to them, and access structure members using the . and -> operators. These tests also pass and return pointers to structures.

The last tests you should debug in the *no_structure_parameters* directory are the multifile tests in *tests/chapter_18/valid/no_structure_parameters/libraries*. These tests pass pointers to structures between functions in different compilation units; they also define structures and arrays of structures as global variables. They test that each structure's size, alignment, and layout in memory match the System V ABI, but they don't test the changes to the calling convention.

The tests in *tests/chapter_18/valid/parameters* include parameters, but not return values, of structure type. This directory also includes multifile tests (in *tests/chapter_18/valid/parameters/libraries*), to make sure your compiler passes parameters according to the System V ABI. The tests in *tests/chapter_18/valid/params_and_returns*, including the multifile tests in *tests/chapter_18/valid/params_and_returns/libraries*, include functions with both parameters and return values of structure type.

Extra Credit: Unions

Structure and union types have a lot in common. Their type declarations share the same syntax and declare tags in the same namespace. They follow the same typing rules and support the same operations, including the -> and . operators. The difference is that the members of a structure are laid out sequentially in memory, whereas the members of a union all start at the same address, such that writing to one overwrites the others. From the compiler's perspective, a union is basically a structure where every member's offset is zero. This makes it relatively straightforward to extend the work you did in this chapter to support unions too. Still, this is a bigger challenge than previous extra credit features. It's an opportunity to add a new language feature on your own.

If you implement union types, there are a few points you should keep in mind. First, remember that we restricted where structures can be declared to make compilation easier. The test cases for unions also follow the same restrictions; that means you don't need to support anonymous union declarations or union declarations that are part of declarations of some other type or variable.

In the type checker, you'll add union definitions to the type table. Structure and union tags share a namespace, so defining a structure and a union type with the same tag in the same scope is an error. You'll need to track each union's size and alignment (you can look up how to calculate these in the System V ABI). You'll also need to type check compound initializers for unions. A union initializer should have a single element, which initializes the union's first member. (C provides syntax to specify which union member to initialize, but you don't have to implement it.)

On the backend, the System V calling convention treats unions similarly to structures; a union will be passed in memory, in two registers, or in one register, depending on its size and the types of its members. For all the gory details, see the links in "Additional Resources." Good luck!

You can use the --union flag to test your compiler's support for union types:

```
$ ./test_compiler /path/to/your_compiler --chapter 18 --union
```

Or, you can use the --extra-credit flag to test every extra credit feature.

Summary

You've finished Part II! In this chapter, you learned how to analyze structure type declarations, manipulate aggregate objects in TACKY, and transfer structures according to the System V calling convention. Your compiler now supports every language feature this book covers, including most of the statements, expressions, and types in the C language. You can officially tell people that you've written a C compiler.

If you want, you can stop here. Or, you can move on to Part III, where you'll implement several compiler optimizations to generate more efficient assembly code. In Chapter 19, you'll optimize TACKY programs by eliminating useless instructions and evaluating constant expressions at compile time. In Chapter 20, you'll write a register allocator, which maps pseudoregisters to hardware registers instead of locations on the stack. These optimizations aren't specific to C or x64 assembly; you'll find them in compilers with lots of different source and target languages.

Additional Resources

If you want to learn about the complete System V x64 calling convention, including all the rules for passing structures and unions, you have a couple of options:

- The official System V x86-64 ABI is available at *https://gitlab.com/x86 -psABIs/x86-64-ABI*. (I've linked to this a couple of times already.) Section 3.2.3 discusses parameter passing.

- Agner Fog has written a helpful manual describing the calling conventions of different C++ compilers (*https://www.agner.org/optimize/calling _conventions.pdf*). Tables 6 and 7, in Section 7.1, cover how structures are passed and returned. The document covers C++, so parts of it aren't relevant, but the description of how to pass plain structures and unions applies to C as well as C++.

I found Fog's summary of calling conventions easier to follow than the official ABI. If you decide to implement unions for extra credit, you'll probably need to refer to both documents.

PART III

OPTIMIZATIONS

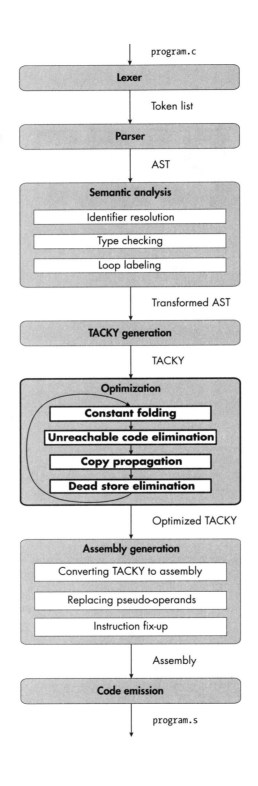

19

OPTIMIZING TACKY PROGRAMS

In the first two parts of this book, you wrote a compiler that supported much of the C language. You made sure that the executable programs you produced were correct—in other words, that their behavior conformed to the C standard—but you didn't worry about their performance. You didn't try to make them run faster, take up less storage space, or consume less memory. In Part III, you'll focus on *optimizing* these programs—that is, making them smaller and faster without changing their behavior.

Some compiler optimizations are *machine-independent*. This means they aren't affected by the details of the target architecture, like the number of available registers or constraints on specific assembly instructions. A compiler typically performs these optimizations on an intermediate representation like TACKY before converting it to assembly. *Machine-dependent* optimizations, on the other hand, need to take the target architecture into account, so these are usually performed later, after the program has been converted to assembly. This chapter covers four widely used machine-independent optimizations: constant folding, unreachable code elimination, copy propagation, and dead store elimination. You'll add a new optimization stage, bolded in the diagram at the start of the chapter, to apply these four optimizations to TACKY programs. The next chapter covers register allocation, a machine-dependent optimization.

You don't need to complete Part II before you start on Part III. For each optimization, we'll start with an implementation that doesn't account for the language features from Part II. Then, if necessary, we'll extend it to support those features; you'll skip this step if you didn't do Part II. We'll need this extra step for every optimization except unreachable code elimination, which isn't affected by the features from Part II.

These two chapters include just a few of the optimizations you'd find in a production compiler, but the basic concepts we'll cover apply to lots of other optimizations too. Before we get started, let's consider a question that's fundamental to every compiler optimization: How do we know our optimized code is correct?

Safety and Observable Behavior

First and foremost, compiler optimizations must be *safe*, meaning they cannot change the program's semantics. (It doesn't matter how speedy your program is if it doesn't behave correctly!) In particular, an optimization must not change the program's *observable behavior*, which is the behavior visible to its execution environment. Returning an exit status, printing a message to stdout, and writing to a file are all examples of observable behavior. Most of the actions that a program takes—like calculating values, updating local variables, and transferring control from one statement to another—are not visible to the execution environment, so they affect the program's observable behavior only indirectly. This gives us lots of flexibility to transform the program. We can reorder, replace, and even delete code as long as the observable behavior doesn't change.

Let's look at how GCC optimizes a simple C program. Listing 19-1 initializes three variables with the values 1, 2, and 3, then adds them up and returns the result.

```
int main(void) {
    int x = 1;
    int y = 2;
    int z = 3;
    return x + y + z;
}
```

Listing 19-1: A C program that adds three variables

This program will have the same observable behavior every time it runs: it will terminate with an exit status of 6. You can run the following command to compile the program without optimizations:

```
$ gcc -S -fno-asynchronous-unwind-tables -fcf-protection=none listing_19_1.c
```

This will produce the assembly in Listing 19-2, or something similar.

```
        .text
        .globl main
main:
        pushq   %rbp
        movq    %rsp, %rbp
        movl    $1, -4(%rbp)
        movl    $2, -8(%rbp)
        movl    $3, -12(%rbp)
        movl    -4(%rbp), %edx
        movl    -8(%rbp), %eax
        addl    %eax, %edx
        movl    -12(%rbp), %eax
        addl    %edx, %eax
        popq    %rbp
        ret
```

Listing 19-2: The unoptimized assembly for Listing 19-1

This assembly program faithfully implements Listing 19-1's source code: it initializes three locations on the stack with the values 1, 2, and 3; adds them up; and then returns the result in EAX. Now let's compile the same source code with the -O switch to enable optimizations:

```
$ gcc -S -O -fno-asynchronous-unwind-tables -fcf-protection=none listing_19_1.c
```

This will generate the assembly in Listing 19-3.

```
        .text
        .globl main
main:
        movl    $6, %eax
        ret
```

Listing 19-3: The optimized assembly for Listing 19-1

Instead of initializing three variables and then adding them up, this assembly program just returns the constant 6. Listings 19-2 and 19-3 look quite different, but they both produce the right observable behavior.

Four TACKY Optimizations

This section introduces the optimizations we'll implement in this chapter: constant folding, unreachable code elimination, copy propagation, and dead store elimination. These optimizations aim to speed up our code and reduce the amount of space it takes up. Individually, some of them further one or both of these goals, while others aren't particularly helpful on their own. The real payoff comes from the way they work together, because running any one of them creates new opportunities to apply the other three. We'll look at these four optimizations in turn, then discuss how each one makes the others more effective.

Before we jump in, be aware that I'll use minimal notation in most of this chapter's TACKY listings. I'll write copies as x = y instead of Copy(Var("x"), Var("y")), as I've occasionally done in earlier chapters, and I'll take similar shortcuts with other instructions. For example, I'll write binary operations as x = a + b instead of Binary(Add, Var("a"), Var("b"), Var("x")) and labels as Target: instead of Label(Target). This notation lets us focus on the high-level logic of our TACKY programs, not the details of each TACKY instruction.

Constant Folding

The *constant folding* pass evaluates constant expressions at compile time. For example, constant folding will replace the Binary TACKY instruction

```
a = 6 / 2
```

with a Copy instruction:

```
a = 3
```

Constant folding can also turn conditional jumps into unconditional jumps or eliminate them entirely. It will transform

```
JumpIfZero(0, Target)
```

into

```
Jump(Target)
```

because the program will always make this jump. It will also delete the instruction

```
JumpIfZero(1, Target)
```

because the program will never make this jump. (Deleting useless jumps is often considered a type of dead code elimination rather than constant folding, but we're transforming conditional jumps in this pass anyway, so we might as well delete the useless ones too.)

Constant folding helps with both speed and code size. A single arithmetic operation or comparison might require several assembly instructions. Some of those instructions, like idiv, are quite slow. Constant folding ultimately replaces that assembly code with a single mov instruction.

Unreachable Code Elimination

Unreachable code elimination removes instructions that we know will never run. Consider the fragment of TACKY in Listing 19-4.

```
x = 5
Jump(Target)
x = my_function()
```

```
Target:
Return(x)
```

Listing 19-4: A fragment of TACKY with an unreachable instruction

Since we'll always jump over the call to my_function, we can get rid of it:

```
x = 5
Jump(Target)
Target:
Return(x)
```

Now the Jump instruction is useless, since it jumps to the instruction that we'd execute next anyway. We'll remove this instruction too:

```
x = 5
Target:
Return(x)
```

Finally, we can also eliminate the Target label, assuming no other instruction jumps to it:

```
x = 5
Return(x)
```

Strictly speaking, the Jump and Label instructions we just removed aren't unreachable code; a running program will reach both of them, though they won't have any effect. But removing unreachable code often makes jumps and labels useless, so this pass is a logical place to remove them.

Eliminating unreachable code clearly reduces code size. It's also pretty clear that removing useless jumps saves time; even a useless instruction takes some amount of time to execute. It turns out that removing truly unreachable instructions, like the FunCall in Listing 19-4, can speed up the program too, by reducing memory pressure and freeing up space in the processor's instruction cache.

Removing unused labels, on the other hand, won't impact speed or code size, since labels don't become machine instructions in the final executable. We'll remove these labels anyway because it makes our TACKY programs a bit easier to read and debug and requires very little extra work.

This pass is especially handy for cleaning up the extra Return instruction we add to the end of every TACKY function. Recall that we add this instruction as a backstop in case the source code is missing a return statement. When we convert a program to TACKY, we can't tell whether this extra Return is necessary, so we end up adding it to functions that don't need it. The unreachable code elimination pass removes all the Return instructions that we added unnecessarily, while retaining any that we actually need. This is one example of a broader principle: generating inefficient code and optimizing it later is often easier than generating efficient code to begin with.

Copy Propagation

When a program includes the Copy instruction dst = src, the *copy propagation* pass tries to replace dst with src in later instructions. Take the following snippet of TACKY:

```
x = 3
Return(x)
```

We can replace x with its current value, 3, in the Return instruction:

```
x = 3
Return(3)
```

Replacing a variable with a constant is a special case of copy propagation called *constant propagation*. In other cases, we'll replace one variable with another. For instance, we can rewrite

```
x = y
Return(x)
```

as:

```
x = y
Return(y)
```

Sometimes, figuring out whether it's safe to perform copy propagation can be tricky. Take the following example:

```
x = 4
JumpIfZero(flag, Target)
x = 3
Target:
Return(x)
```

Depending on which path we take, x's value will be either 3 or 4 when we reach the Return instruction. Since we don't know which path we'll take to that instruction, we can't safely replace x with either value. To handle cases like this one, we'll need to analyze every possible path to the instruction we'd like to rewrite. We'll use a technique called *data-flow analysis* to look at all the paths through a function and find the places where we can perform copy propagation safely. Data-flow analysis isn't just useful for copy propagation; it's used in lots of different compiler optimizations, including dead store elimination, which we'll discuss next.

Some of the copies we analyze will involve variables with static storage duration, which can be accessed by multiple functions (or just multiple invocations of the same function, in the case of local static variables). We won't always be able to tell exactly when these variables are updated, so our data-flow analysis will need to treat them a bit differently than variables with automatic storage duration. If you completed Part II, you'll need to account for similar uncertainty around variables whose address is taken with the & operator, since they can be updated through pointers.

Copy propagation isn't useful by itself, but it makes our other optimizations more effective. When we propagate constants, we create new opportunities for constant folding. And we'll sometimes replace every use of a Copy instruction's destination with its source, which makes the Copy itself useless. We'll remove these useless instructions in our last optimization pass: dead store elimination.

Dead Store Elimination

When an instruction updates a variable's value but we never use that new value, the instruction is called a *dead store*. (The term *store* here refers to any instruction that stores a value in a variable, not the TACKY Store instruction we introduced in Part II.) Because dead stores don't impact a program's observable behavior, it's safe to remove them. Let's look at a simple example:

```
x = 10
Return(y)
```

Assuming x has automatic storage duration, the instruction x = 10 is a dead store. We don't use x between this instruction and the end of the function, which is also the end of x's lifetime.

Here's another kind of dead store:

```
x = a + b
x = 2
Return(x)
```

In this example, we'll never use the result of a + b, because we'll overwrite it first; this means x = a + b is a dead store. The dead store elimination pass will identify such useless instructions and remove them. The challenge is proving that an instruction really is a dead store; to do this, we'll need to analyze every path through the function and make sure that the value it assigns to its destination is never used. Once again, we'll use data-flow analysis to figure out when we can apply this optimization safely.

Like copy propagation, dead store elimination gets more complicated when you factor in objects that can be accessed by multiple functions or through pointers. For instance, if x is a global variable, the instruction x = 10 in our first example is *not* a dead store; x might be used after the function returns. Our data-flow analysis will have to take this possibility into account.

WHEN OPTIMIZATIONS ATTACK!

Dead store elimination is safe in the sense that it won't change a program's observable behavior. But in another, more intuitive sense, it's unsafe: it can

---

make a program less secure. A conscientious, security-minded programmer will overwrite sensitive data as soon as they're done processing it. The longer a secret lives in memory, the greater the risk that an attacker will be able to read it, perhaps by exploiting another vulnerability in the program or even dumping the entire system's memory. Unfortunately, operations that clear sensitive data are often dead stores. Dead store elimination tends to, well, eliminate them. Consider this code fragment that tries to zero out an encryption key:

```c
char *encryption_key = malloc(encryption_key_size);
// initialize encryption_key and use it to encrypt some things
--snip--
memset(encryption_key, 0, encryption_key_size);
free(encryption_key);
return 0;
```

Normally, calling memset would zero out the buffer that encryption_key points to, preventing the data in that buffer from being leaked later on. But the compiler might optimize away the call to memset because it's technically a dead store; it just updates a buffer that we'll never use again. Our implementation of dead store elimination wouldn't remove memset from this example, because it never optimizes away function calls, but GCC and Clang actually do eliminate memset in code like this. You can compile a toy example to see for yourself.

C programs can avoid this problem by clearing memory with a dedicated library function that the compiler knows not to optimize away. There are several platform-specific functions that serve this purpose, like SecureZeroMemory on Windows and explicit_bzero on many Linux distributions. The memset_s function to write to memory securely was added to the C standard library back in the C11 revision of the standard, but it's part of an optional annex that was never widely implemented. C23 introduces a similar function that isn't optional, memset_explicit, so C programmers *finally* have a standard, portable way to clear sensitive data from memory.

Functions like memset_explicit solve the immediate problem with dead stores. But they don't address the more fundamental issue: the concept of observable behavior doesn't cover every kind of behavior that programmers care about. The C standard guarantees that your code will behave the way you intended it to when everything goes right—when your code has no undefined behavior, the libraries it relies on have no undefined behavior, and nobody tampers with the underlying system—but it provides no guarantees about what happens when things go wrong. Without those guarantees, it's difficult, and sometimes impossible, to write secure code. (If you'd like to learn more about the security impact of compiler optimizations, see "Additional Resources" on page 610 for links to a couple of relevant papers.)

We won't worry about the security impact of the optimizations we implement here. If you're using the compiler you wrote for this book to compile security-critical software, dead store elimination is the least of your problems.

With Our Powers Combined . . .

Now let's look at how the four optimizations we'll implement in this chapter work together. We'll use the TACKY program in Listing 19-5 as a running example.

```
my_function(flag):
    x = 4
    y = 4 - x
    JumpIfZero(y, Target)
    x = 3
    Target:
    JumpIfNotZero(flag, End)
    z = 10
    End:
    z = x + 5
    Return(z)
```

Listing 19-5: An unoptimized TACKY program

Using all four optimizations, we can reduce this function to a single Return instruction. I'll display the results of each round of optimization, highlighting any changed instructions. Because each optimization can create more opportunities to apply the other three, we'll need to run most of them several times to fully optimize this function. For now, we'll decide which optimization to run at each step in an ad hoc way, by looking at the code and seeing which one will be most useful. We'll use a more systematic approach when we actually implement our optimization pipeline.

Let's start with a copy propagation pass, substituting 4 for x in y = 4 - x:

```
my_function(flag):
    x = 4
    y = 4 - 4
    JumpIfZero(y, Target)
    x = 3
    Target:
    JumpIfNotZero(flag, End)
    z = 10
    End:
    z = x + 5
    Return(z)
```

We can't replace the second use of x, in z = x + 5, because x has more than one possible value at that point: it might be 3 or 4, depending on whether we take the conditional jump. Next, we'll apply constant folding to evaluate y = 4 - 4:

```
my_function(flag):
    x = 4
    y = 0
    JumpIfZero(y, Target)
    x = 3
```

```
    Target:
    JumpIfNotZero(flag, End)
    z = 10
    End:
    z = x + 5
    Return(z)
```

By replacing a binary operation with a Copy instruction, we've created another opportunity for copy propagation. We can replace y with its value, 0, in the JumpIfZero instruction:

```
my_function(flag):
    x = 4
    y = 0
    JumpIfZero(0, Target)
    x = 3
    Target:
    JumpIfNotZero(flag, End)
    z = 10
    End:
    z = x + 5
    Return(z)
```

Now that JumpIfZero depends on a constant condition, we can run constant folding again to turn it into an unconditional Jump:

```
my_function(flag):
    x = 4
    y = 0
    Jump(Target)
    x = 3
    Target:
    JumpIfNotZero(flag, End)
    z = 10
    End:
    z = x + 5
    Return(z)
```

This change makes x = 3 unreachable, so we'll run unreachable code elimination to delete it. This pass will also remove the Jump instruction and Target label, which have no effect once we've removed x = 3:

```
my_function(flag):
    x = 4
    y = 0
    JumpIfNotZero(flag, End)
    z = 10
    End:
    z = x + 5
    Return(z)
```

We couldn't rewrite z = x + 5 earlier, because x had two different values on the different paths to that instruction. We just solved that problem by eliminating the path through x = 3. Now we can run copy propagation again:

```
my_function(flag):
    x = 4
    y = 0
    JumpIfNotZero(flag, End)
    z = 10
    End:
    z = 4 + 5
    Return(z)
```

Then we'll run another round of constant folding:

```
my_function(flag):
    x = 4
    y = 0
    JumpIfNotZero(flag, End)
    z = 10
    End:
    z = 9
    Return(z)
```

And we'll run copy propagation one last time:

```
my_function(flag):
    x = 4
    y = 0
    JumpIfNotZero(flag, End)
    z = 10
    End:
    z = 9
    Return(9)
```

We've managed to calculate this function's return value at compile time, eliminating every use of x, y, and z in the process. Now we'll run dead store elimination to clean up the instructions that assign to these three variables:

```
my_function(flag):
    JumpIfNotZero(flag, End)
    End:
    Return(9)
```

Finally, we'll run unreachable code elimination to remove the JumpIfNot Zero instruction and the End label. These are both redundant, since we just eliminated the one instruction that JumpIfNotZero jumps over. This last round of optimization will reduce our function to a single instruction:

```
my_function(flag):
    Return(9)
```

This example highlighted some of the ways our optimizations work together. Copy propagation may replace variables with constants, creating new opportunities for constant folding; constant folding rewrites arithmetic operations as Copy instructions, creating new opportunities for copy propagation. Constant folding can replace conditional jumps with unconditional ones, making some instructions unreachable; eliminating unreachable code simplifies the program's control flow, which promotes copy propagation. Copy propagation may make Copy instructions redundant, which lets us remove them during dead store elimination. And dead store elimination can potentially remove every instruction between a jump and the label it jumps to, which makes the jump, and possibly the label, candidates for unreachable code elimination.

Now we know what each optimization does and how they all work together. Next, we'll add a few new command line options that will allow us to test them out.

Testing the Optimization Passes

This chapter's tests work differently than the tests in earlier chapters. We need to verify that our optimizations don't change the program's observable behavior but do simplify constant expressions and remove useless code. Our current strategy—compiling C programs, running them, and making sure they behave correctly—satisfies the first requirement but not the second. Just running a program can't tell you whether the optimization phase *did* anything. To address the second point, the test script will inspect your compiler's assembly output for each test program. To address the first point, it will also run each test program and verify its behavior, like in earlier chapters.

To support this chapter's tests, you'll need to add a few command line options to your compiler:

-S Directs your compiler to emit an assembly file, but not assemble or link it. Running *./YOUR_COMPILER* -S */path/to/program.c* should write an assembly file to */path/to/program.s*. (I suggested adding this option to help with debugging back in Chapter 1; you'll need to add it now if you haven't already.)

--fold-constants Enables constant folding.

--propagate-copies Enables copy propagation.

--eliminate-unreachable-code Enables unreachable code elimination.

`--eliminate-dead-stores`   Enables dead store elimination.

`--optimize`   Enables all four optimizations.

The options to enable optimizations should be passed to the optimization stage, which we'll implement next. It should be possible to enable more than one individual optimization; for example, `./YOUR_COMPILER --fold-constants --propagate-copies` should enable both constant folding and copy propagation, but not the other two optimizations.

If your compiler doesn't generate assembly exactly the way I've laid out in this book, the test script should still be able to validate your assembly output for this chapter's tests, but there are a couple of caveats to keep in mind. First, the test script understands only AT&T assembly syntax, which is the syntax we've been using throughout the book. Second, the script doesn't recognize every single assembly instruction; it only knows about the instructions we've used in this book and a handful of others that are particularly common in real-world assembly code. If you emit instructions that the test script doesn't understand, some tests may fail.

Next, we'll wire up the new optimization stage, which will control when we call each individual optimization.

Wiring Up the Optimization Stage

The optimization stage will run right after we convert the program to TACKY. This stage will optimize each TACKY function independently, without any knowledge of the other functions defined in the program. For example, it won't try to evaluate function calls during the constant folding pass or remove them during dead store elimination. (We can't remove function calls during dead store elimination because we don't know whether they have side effects. We *can* remove them during unreachable code elimination, though—if a function call will never execute, it doesn't matter what side effects the function has.) Optimizations like these, which transform one function at a time, are called *intraprocedural optimizations*. Most production compilers also perform *interprocedural optimizations*, which transform whole translation units instead of individual functions.

Each individual optimization will take the body of a TACKY function as input and return a semantically equivalent function body as output. In the constant folding pass, we'll represent the function body as a list of TACKY instructions, like we normally do. But in the other three optimization passes, we'll represent each function as a *control-flow graph*. This is an intermediate representation that explicitly models the different execution paths through a piece of code. We'll talk more about how to construct control-flow graphs and why they're useful later in the chapter.

The optimization stage will process each function by running through all of the enabled optimizations over and over. It will stop once it reaches a *fixed point*, where running them again doesn't change the function further. Listing 19-6 illustrates this optimization pipeline.

```
optimize(function_body, enabled_optimizations):
    if function_body is empty:
        return function_body

    while True:
        if enabled_optimizations contains "CONSTANT_FOLDING":
          ❶ post_constant_folding = constant_folding(function_body)
        else:
            post_constant_folding = function_body

      ❷ cfg = make_control_flow_graph(post_constant_folding)

        if enabled_optimizations contains "UNREACHABLE_CODE_ELIM":
            cfg = unreachable_code_elimination(cfg)

        if enabled_optimizations contains "COPY_PROP":
            cfg = copy_propagation(cfg)

        if enabled_optimizations contains "DEAD_STORE_ELIM":
            cfg = dead_store_elimination(cfg)

      ❸ optimized_function_body = cfg_to_instructions(cfg)

      ❹ if (optimized_function_body == function_body
            or optimized_function_body is empty):
            return optimized_function_body

        function_body = optimized_function_body
```

Listing 19-6: The TACKY optimization pipeline

In this listing, function_body is the list of instructions in the body of a
TACKY function and enabled_optimizations is a list of strings representing
the optimizations that we enabled on the command line. (This would be
a pretty kludgy way to store command line options in a real program; feel
free to represent these options differently in your own code.) If function_body
is empty, we'll just return it, since there's nothing to optimize. Otherwise,
we'll perform constant folding if it's enabled ❶.

Next, we'll convert the function body from a list of instructions into a
control-flow graph ❷. We'll apply all the other enabled optimizations to
this representation. Then, we'll convert the optimized control-flow graph
back to a list of instructions ❸, which we'll compare to the original list ❹. If
it's different, and if we haven't optimized away the entire function, we'll go
through the loop again to take advantage of any new optimization opportunities. If it's the same, we can't optimize it any further, so we're done.

HOW DO WE KNOW LISTING 19-6 WILL TERMINATE?

At first glance, it looks like the optimize function in Listing 19-6 might get caught in an infinite loop. The TACKY function we're optimizing could keep changing on every iteration, without ever converging on a final result. But if we think about these optimizations more carefully, we can convince ourselves that the optimization pipeline must terminate.

First, both dead store elimination and unreachable code elimination remove instructions, and none of our optimizations ever add new instructions. These two optimizations can't keep changing a function forever, because we'll eventually run out of instructions. To be more precise, if our TACKY function initially has n instructions, we'll see at most n loop iterations where either of these optimizations changes anything.

Similarly, constant folding replaces several kinds of TACKY instructions (including Unary, Binary, type conversions, and conditional jumps) with other kinds of TACKY instructions (specifically Copy and the unconditional Jump instruction). None of our other optimizations will introduce the kinds of instructions that constant folding replaces. The constant folding pass can change a function only so many times before we've eliminated every instruction it could potentially rewrite.

That leaves copy propagation. We've already put an upper bound on how many times each of the other optimizations can change a function, so optimize will terminate unless copy propagation by itself can get stuck in an infinite loop, changing the function every time we apply it. To see why this is impossible, let's think about how many times copy propagation could rewrite a single instruction, i. We'll assume this instruction has one operand, but it's easy to extend this logic to instructions with multiple operands. If there are no Copy instructions on the shortest path to i, we know that i will never be rewritten. (Keep in mind that we can propagate a Copy instruction only if it appears on *every* path to i.) Now imagine there's exactly one Copy on the path to i. In that case, we'll be able to rewrite i at most once. We might propagate the value from that Copy instruction to i, but we won't be able to rewrite it again after that. Now let's generalize this: if there are n Copy instructions on the shortest path to i, we'll rewrite i at most n times. Whenever we rewrite i, we replace its operand with another operand that was defined earlier on the shortest path to i (or with a constant). If we rewrite i multiple times, each rewrite must propagate a Copy instruction from earlier in the program than the one before, until there are no copies left to propagate.

It's helpful to look at an example:

```
w = foo()
x = w
y = x
Return(y)
```

Initially, this code snippet returns y, which is defined by y = x. After one round of copy propagation, we'll rewrite the final instruction as Return(x). Of course, x is defined before y, in the instruction x = w. The next round of copy propagation will replace x with w, which is defined even earlier, in the instruction w = foo(). The key point here is that we'll never replace one operand with another that's defined later on the path to the instruction that we're rewriting, so we can replace each operand only a finite number of times. Therefore, the optimize function has to terminate.

Using the optimization pipeline in Listing 19-6, we'll never miss an optimization opportunity. Whenever one optimization changes the program, we'll rerun the other three to take advantage of those changes. This is feasible because we're implementing only four optimizations, and all of our test programs are small enough to optimize pretty quickly. Production compilers, which implement dozens of optimizations and compile much larger programs, don't take this approach; if they did, compilation would take way too long. Instead, they apply a fixed sequence of optimizations just once, running each individual optimization in the place where it's likely to have the biggest impact. As a result, they can end up missing optimization opportunities. (Finding the best order to run optimizations for any given program is an open research question called the *phase ordering problem*.)

Go ahead and add the optimization pipeline to your compiler. For now, define each individual optimization as a stub that takes a list of instructions and returns them unchanged. You can stub out the conversions to and from control-flow graphs the same way. Write this plumbing code now so that you can test the individual optimization passes as you implement them.

Once everything is wired up, you can start on your first optimization: constant folding!

Constant Folding

Constant folding is the simplest optimization in this chapter. This pass iterates through all the instructions in a TACKY function and evaluates any instructions with constant source operands. First, we'll talk briefly about how to add constant folding to the version of the compiler you implemented in Part I. Then, we'll discuss how to handle the types and TACKY instructions you added in Part II. If you haven't worked through Part II yet, feel free to skip the latter discussion.

Constant Folding for Part I TACKY Programs

The constant folding pass should evaluate four of the TACKY instructions from Part I: Unary, Binary, JumpIfZero, and JumpIfNotZero. When you find a Unary instruction with a constant source operand, or a Binary instruction with two constant source operands, replace it with a Copy. For example, you should replace

```
Binary(binary_operator=Add, src1=Constant(1), src2=Constant(2), dst=Var("b"))
```

with:

```
Copy(src=Constant(3), dst=Var("b"))
```

Your constant folding pass could run into two kinds of invalid expressions: division by zero and operations that result in integer overflow. These are both undefined behaviors, so it doesn't matter how you evaluate them. However, your compiler can't just fail if it encounters one of these invalid expressions, because the program's behavior is undefined only if it actually reaches the invalid expression at runtime. For example, if a program includes division by zero in a branch that's never taken, you should still be able to compile it.

You should also evaluate JumpIfZero and JumpIfNotZero instructions with constant conditions. If the condition is met, replace the instruction with an unconditional Jump. If the condition isn't met, remove the instruction from the program. That's all there is to it! If you completed only Part I, you can skip to the test suite once you've implemented constant folding for these four instructions. If you completed Part II, there are a few more instructions you'll need to handle.

Supporting Part II TACKY Programs

When we added the new arithmetic types in Part II, we also added type conversion instructions: Truncate, SignExtend, ZeroExtend, DoubleToInt, DoubleToUInt, IntToDouble, and UIntToDouble. The constant folding pass should evaluate all of these instructions when their source operands are constants.

The Copy instruction can perform type conversions too; we use it to convert between signed and unsigned integers of the same size. When a Copy instruction copies an unsigned constant to a signed variable, or vice versa, this pass should convert the constant to the correct type. For example, if a is a signed char, you should replace

```
Copy(src=Constant(ConstUChar(255)), dst=Var("a"))
```

with:

```
Copy(src=Constant(ConstChar(-1)), dst=Var("a"))
```

Be careful to perform every type conversion with exactly the same semantics that the program would use at runtime. For example, when you convert a double to an integer type, truncate its value toward zero; when you convert an integer to a double, round to the nearest representable value. The good news is that you already know how to perform all of these type conversions at compile time, since you had to convert static initializers to the correct type throughout Part II. Ideally, you'll be able to reuse the code you've already written to perform these type conversions.

You'll also need to adhere to C semantics when you evaluate unsigned arithmetic operations. In particular, you should ensure that unsigned arithmetic wraps around, like it would at runtime. How you accomplish this will depend entirely on what language you're writing your compiler in. Some languages support wraparound unsigned arithmetic as part of their standard library. In Rust, for example, methods like `wrapping_add` and `wrapping_sub` provide the same semantics as unsigned arithmetic in C. In other languages, you might use a third-party library for unsigned arithmetic. For example, Python doesn't provide unsigned integer types, but the NumPy library does. If you don't want to use an external library, or you can't find a suitable one, it isn't terribly difficult to implement wraparound unsigned arithmetic yourself.

Finally, when you evaluate floating-point operations, you'll need to use round-to-nearest, ties-to-even rounding and handle negative zero and infinity correctly. If you added support for NaN for extra credit in Chapter 13, you'll need to evaluate operations on NaN correctly too. This shouldn't require any special effort on your part—the vast majority of programming languages use IEEE 754 semantics—but there's a small chance that your implementation language handles negative zero, NaN, or infinity differently than C. Start with a simple implementation of constant folding that doesn't try to address these edge cases; you can rely on the test suite to catch any problems. If you run into any cases that your implementation language doesn't evaluate correctly, you have two options: either find a third-party library to handle them for you or evaluate them yourself as a special case.

TEST THE CONSTANT FOLDING PASS

If you completed Part I but not Part II, use the following command to test your constant folding implementation:

```
$ ./test_compiler /path/to/your_compiler --chapter 19 --fold-constants
--int-only
```

This will run the tests in *tests/chapter_19/constant_folding/int_only*, which use only language features from Part I. It will also compile all the test programs from Part I with constant folding enabled. It won't inspect the assembly output for these earlier test programs, but it will run them to confirm that they still behave correctly.

If you completed Parts I and II, run the same command without the `--int-only` option:

```
$ ./test_compiler /path/to/your_compiler --chapter 19 --fold-constants
```

(continued)

Control-Flow Graphs

For the rest of the chapter, we'll represent TACKY functions as control-flow graphs. A graph representation is a good fit for our remaining optimizations, which have to account for the different paths we might take through a function. The nodes in the control-flow graph represent sequences of straight-line code called *basic blocks*, except for two special nodes that represent the function's entry and exit points. Each node has outgoing edges to the nodes that could execute immediately after it.

As an example, let's look at the control-flow graph for Listing 19-7.

```
processing_loop():
    LoopStart:
    input = get_input()
    JumpIfNotZero(input, ProcessIt)
    Return(-1)
    ProcessIt:
    done = process_input(input)
    JumpIfNotZero(done, LoopStart)
    Return(0)
```

Listing 19-7: A TACKY function with multiple execution paths

This function executes a loop that repeatedly retrieves a value by calling get_input, then processes that value by calling process_input. If get_input ever returns 0, this function immediately returns -1. If process_input ever returns 0, the function immediately returns 0. Figure 19-1 shows the corresponding control-flow graph.

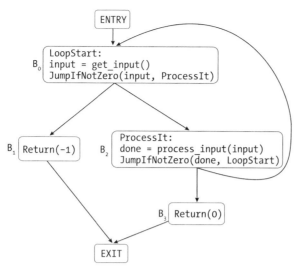

Figure 19-1: The control-flow graph for Listing 19-7

There's a single outgoing edge from the special ENTRY node to block B_0, since we'll always execute B_0 at the start of the function. (ENTRY will have exactly one outgoing edge in every control-flow graph, since C functions have only one entry point.) After we execute B_0, there are two possibilities: we can execute the next block in the program, B_1, or we can jump to block B_2. Therefore, B_0 has outgoing edges to both of those blocks. By the same logic, B_2 has outgoing edges to both B_0 and B_3. A Return instruction exits the function, so B_1 and B_3 each have a single outgoing edge to EXIT.

Defining the Control-Flow Graph

Now that you know what a control-flow graph looks like, let's look at how to construct one. First, we'll define the graph data structure. Listing 19-8 sketches out one possible representation.

```
node_id = ENTRY | EXIT | BlockId(int num)
node = BasicBlock(node_id id, instruction* instructions,
                  node_id* predecessors, node_id* successors)
     | EntryNode(node_id* successors)
     | ExitNode(node_id* predecessors)
graph = Graph(node* nodes)
```

Listing 19-8: One way to represent the control-flow graph

Every node in the graph has a unique node_id, which identifies it as ENTRY, EXIT, or a numbered basic block. We'll assign numeric IDs to basic blocks according to their order in the original TACKY function. Each basic block holds a list of TACKY instructions, a list of *successors* (the blocks that could execute right after it), and another list of *predecessors* (the blocks that could execute right before it). The entry and exit nodes don't hold any instructions. ENTRY, as the very first point in the function, has successors but no predecessors. EXIT, on the other hand, has predecessors but no successors.

You'll need a way to associate both basic blocks and individual instructions with extra information so that you can track the results of data-flow analysis in the copy propagation and dead store elimination passes. The definition in Listing 19-8 doesn't include a way to track this information. You could either attach it directly to the graph or store it in a separate data structure. The pseudocode throughout this chapter will use annotate _instruction and get_instruction_annotation to save and look up information about individual instructions. It will use annotate_block and get_block _annotation to save and look up information about basic blocks by block ID.

NOTE *Your graph data structure might look quite different from Listing 19-8. For instance, you might want to represent the graph as a map from node_id to node, instead of a list of nodes, or track the entry and exit nodes separately from the nodes that represent basic blocks. You can define your control-flow graph in whatever way makes sense to you and suits your implementation language, as long as it includes all the information you'll need.*

Creating Basic Blocks

Next, let's see how to partition the body of a TACKY function into basic blocks. You can't have any jumps into or out of the middle of a basic block. The only way to execute a basic block is to start at its first instruction and continue all the way to the end. This implies that Label can appear only as the first instruction in a block, and a Return or jump instruction can appear only as the last instruction. Listing 19-9 demonstrates how to split a list of instructions into basic blocks along these boundaries.

```
partition_into_basic_blocks(instructions):
    finished_blocks = []
    current_block = []
    for instruction in instructions:
      ❶ if instruction is Label:
            if current_block is not empty:
                finished_blocks.append(current_block)
            current_block = [instruction]

      ❷ else if instruction is Jump, JumpIfZero, JumpIfNotZero, or Return:
            current_block.append(instruction)
            finished_blocks.append(current_block)
            current_block = []

        else:
          ❸ current_block.append(instruction)

    if current_block is not empty:
        finished_blocks.append(current_block)

    return finished_blocks
```

Listing 19-9: Partitioning a list of instructions into basic blocks

When we encounter a `Label` instruction, we start a new basic block beginning with that `Label` ❶. When we encounter a `Return` instruction or a conditional or unconditional jump, we add it to the current block, then start a new empty block ❷. When we encounter any other instruction, we add it to the current block without starting a new block ❸.

Listing 19-9 just partitions a function body into a list of lists of instructions. The next step (which I won't provide pseudocode for) is to convert these lists of instructions into `BasicBlock` nodes with increasing block IDs. We'll then add these nodes to the graph, along with the entry and exit nodes.

Adding Edges to the Control-Flow Graph

After adding every node to the graph, we'll add edges from each node to its successors, as Listing 19-10 demonstrates.

```
add_all_edges(❶ graph):

  ❷ add_edge(ENTRY, BlockId(0))

    for node in graph.nodes:
        if node is EntryNode or ExitNode:
            continue

        if node.id == max_block_id(graph.nodes):
            next_id = EXIT
        else:
          ❸ next_id = BlockId(node.id.num + 1)

        instr = get_last(node.instructions)
        match instr with
        | Return(maybe_val) -> add_edge(node.id, EXIT)
        | Jump(target) ->
            target_id = get_block_by_label(target)
            add_edge(node.id, target_id)
        | JumpIfZero(condition, target) ->
            target_id = get_block_by_label(target)
          ❹ add_edge(node.id, target_id)
          ❺ add_edge(node.id, next_id)
        | JumpIfNotZero(condition, target) ->
            // same as JumpIfZero
            --snip--
        | _ -> add_edge(node.id, next_id)
```

Listing 19-10: Adding edges to the control-flow graph

The graph argument to `add_all_edges` ❶ is our unfinished control-flow graph, which has nodes but no edges. We'll begin by adding an edge from ENTRY to the first basic block ❷. (We can assume that the function contains at least one basic block, since we don't optimize empty functions.) Throughout this listing, we'll use the `add_edge` function, which takes two node IDs, to add edges to the graph. Keep in mind that whenever we add an edge from node1 to node2, we must update both the successors of node1 and the predecessors of node2. I've omitted the pseudocode for add_edge, since it will depend on how you've defined your control-flow graph.

Next, we'll add outgoing edges from the nodes that correspond to basic blocks. To process one of these nodes, we'll first determine which other node will follow it by default if we don't jump or return at the end of the block. If we're processing the very last block, the next node will be EXIT. Otherwise, it will just be whatever basic block comes next in the original TACKY function ❸.

We'll figure out what edges to add by inspecting the last instruction in the current basic block. If it's a Return instruction, we'll add one outgoing edge to EXIT. If it's an unconditional Jump, we'll add an edge to the block that begins with the corresponding Label. We use the get_block_by_label helper function, which I won't show the pseudocode for, to look up which block begins with a particular label. I recommend building a map from labels to block IDs ahead of time so that this function can just perform a map lookup.

If a block ends with a conditional jump, we'll add two outgoing edges. The first edge, which represents taking the jump, will go to the block that starts with the corresponding Label ❹. The other edge, which represents not taking the jump ❺, will go to the default next node, identified by next_id. If a block ends with any other instruction, we'll add a single outgoing edge to the default next node.

Converting a Control-Flow Graph to a List of Instructions

At this point, you should have working code to convert a TACKY function into a control-flow graph. You'll also need code to go in the other direction and convert a control-flow graph back to a list of instructions. This operation is much simpler: just sort all the basic blocks by ID, then concatenate all their instructions.

Making Your Control-Flow Graph Code Reusable

In the next chapter, we'll build control-flow graphs of assembly programs. We'll use the same algorithm to construct these graphs, but we'll look for different individual control-flow instructions. For instance, jmp, ret, and conditional jump instructions like jne and je all signal the end of a basic block in assembly.

Once you have working code to construct control-flow graphs, you might want to refactor it so you can use it for assembly programs too. This is completely optional, but it will save you some effort in the next chapter.

First, you'll need to generalize the graph data type so that a block can contain either TACKY or assembly instructions. Next, you'll need to generalize the logic to analyze specific instructions in Listings 19-9 and 19-10. For instance, you could define a one-off data type to represent both assembly and TACKY instructions, which captures just the information you need to build the control-flow graph:

```
generic_instruction = Return
                    | Jump
                    | ConditionalJump(identifier label)
                    | Label(identifier)
                    | Other
```

Instead of inspecting individual TACKY instructions to determine where a basic block ends or what its successors are, you can convert each instruction to a generic_instruction and inspect that. Then, when you need to build control-flow graphs for assembly programs, you'll use a different helper function to convert an assembly instruction to a generic_instruction but leave everything else the same.

That wraps up our discussion of control-flow graphs. We're now ready to move on to our second optimization pass: unreachable code elimination.

Unreachable Code Elimination

We'll split up this pass into three steps, first removing basic blocks that will never execute, then useless jumps, and finally useless labels. The last two steps might leave us with empty blocks that don't contain any instructions. Optionally, we can clean up after this optimization by removing these empty blocks from the control-flow graph.

Eliminating Unreachable Blocks

To find every block that might possibly execute, we'll traverse the control-flow graph starting at ENTRY. We'll visit ENTRY's successor, then all of that node's successors, and so on, until we run out of nodes to explore. If this traversal never reaches a particular basic block, we'll know that block is safe to remove. Let's try out this approach on the example from Listing 19-4, which we looked at when we first introduced unreachable code elimination:

```
x = 5
Jump(Target)
x = my_function()
Target:
Return(x)
```

We determined earlier that x = my_function() is unreachable. Assuming this listing is the entire body of a TACKY function, it will have the control-flow graph shown in Figure 19-2.

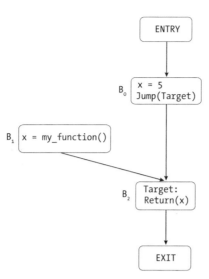

Figure 19-2: The control-flow graph for
Listing 19-4

Note that there's no path from ENTRY to B_1. If we traverse this graph
starting at ENTRY, we'll visit B_0, B_2, and EXIT. Along the way, we'll keep track of
which nodes we've visited so far. Once we're done, we'll see that we never
visited B_1, so we'll remove it. I won't provide the pseudocode for exploring
the graph, since it's just an ordinary breadth- or depth-first graph traversal.

When you remove a node from the graph, remember to remove its
outgoing edges too. For example, when we remove B_1 from the graph in
Figure 19-2, we should also remove it from B_2's list of predecessors.

Removing Useless Jumps

Next, we'll remove any useless jump instructions. Remember that by default,
if a block doesn't end with a jump or Return instruction, control falls through
to the next block from the original program order. We can delete a jump
instruction if it targets this default next block.

We'll look at each basic block that ends with a conditional or unconditional jump and figure out which block would follow it by default if the
jump weren't taken. If this default next block is its only successor, the jump
instruction is redundant. Listing 19-11 demonstrates this approach.

```
remove_redundant_jumps(graph):
  ❶ sorted_blocks = sort_basic_blocks(graph)
    i = 0
  ❷ while i < length(sorted_blocks) - 1:
        block = sorted_blocks[i]
        if block.instructions ends with Jump, JumpIfZero, or JumpIfNotZero:
            keep_jump = False
            default_succ = sorted_blocks[i + 1]
```

```
        for succ_id in block.successors:
            if succ_id != default_succ.id:
                keep_jump = True
                break
        if not keep_jump:
        ❸ remove_last(block.instructions)
    i += 1
```

Listing 19-11: Removing redundant jumps

First, we'll sort the basic blocks by their position in the original TACKY function ❶; this is one reason we numbered the blocks when we first constructed the graph. Next, we'll iterate over this sorted list of basic blocks (except the last one, since a jump at the very end of the function is never redundant) ❷. If a block ends with a jump, we'll search for a successor other than the next block in the list. If we find one, we'll keep the jump instruction. Otherwise, we'll remove it ❸.

Note that the next block in the list won't necessarily have the next consecutive numerical ID, since we may have deleted blocks earlier. Block 2, for example, might be followed by block 4. That's why we can't just increment a block's ID number to find its default successor.

Removing Useless Labels

Removing useless labels is similar to removing useless jumps. After sorting basic blocks by numeric ID, we can delete the Label instruction at the start of a block if we'll enter it only by falling through from the previous block, rather than jumping to it explicitly. More concretely, we can delete the Label at the start of sorted_blocks[i] if its only predecessor is sorted_blocks[i - 1]. We can also delete the Label at the start of sorted_blocks[0] if its only predecessor is ENTRY. This transformation is safe because we just deleted redundant jump instructions; we know that sorted_blocks[i - 1] won't end with an explicit jump to sorted_blocks[i]. I won't provide pseudocode for this step, since it would look basically the same as Listing 19-11.

Removing Empty Blocks

Eliminating unreachable jumps and labels might result in blocks with no instructions. If you want, you can remove them; this will shrink the graph and might speed up later optimization passes a bit. When you remove a block, make sure to update the edges in the control-flow graph accordingly. For example, if the graph has edges from B_0 to B_1 and B_1 to B_2, and you delete B_1, you'll need to add an edge from B_0 to B_2.

A Little Bit About Data-Flow Analysis

This section will give a quick overview of data-flow analysis, which we'll rely on in the next two optimization passes. You'll learn what it is, when it's useful, and what features all data-flow analyses have in common. This isn't intended to be a complete explanation of data-flow analysis; my goal here is just to introduce a few key ideas and describe how they fit together, to make the specific analyses in later sections easier to follow.

Data-flow analysis answers questions about how values are defined and used throughout a function. Different data-flow analyses answer different questions. In the copy propagation pass, for example, we'll implement *reaching copies analysis*. This answers the question: Given some instruction i in a TACKY function, and two operands u and v that appear in that function, can we guarantee that u and v are equal at the point just before i executes?

We can divide all data-flow analyses into two broad categories: forward and backward analyses. In a *forward analysis*, information travels forward through the control-flow graph. Reaching copies analysis is a forward analysis. When we see a Copy instruction x = y, that tells us that x and y might have the same value later in the same basic block or in one of that block's successors. In a *backward analysis*, the reverse is true. In the dead store elimination pass, we'll implement a backward analysis called *liveness analysis*. This analysis tells us whether a variable's current value will ever be used. If we see an instruction that uses x, that tells us that x may be live earlier in the same basic block or in one of that block's predecessors.

Each data-flow analysis has its own transfer function and meet operator. The *transfer function* calculates the analysis results within a single basic block. This function analyzes how individual instructions impact the results, but it doesn't need to deal with multiple execution paths. The *meet operator* combines information from multiple paths to calculate how each basic block is impacted by its neighbors. We'll use an *iterative algorithm* to drive the entire analysis. This algorithm calls the transfer function and meet operator on each basic block and keeps track of which blocks still need to be analyzed. It's iterative because we may need to visit some blocks multiple times as we propagate information along different execution paths. This algorithm will traverse the control-flow graph, analyzing each basic block it visits, until it reaches a fixed point where the analysis results no longer change. At that point, we'll know that every possible execution path is accounted for. The iterative algorithm isn't the only way to solve data-flow analysis problems, but it's the only one we'll discuss in this book.

While different analyses use different transfer functions and meet operators, they all use essentially the same iterative algorithm. Forward and backward analyses use different versions of this algorithm because they propagate data in opposite directions. We'll implement both versions in the next two sections.

Copy Propagation

If the instruction x = y appears in a function, we can sometimes replace x with y later in that function. Let's call the instruction where we'd like to perform this substitution *i*. The substitution is safe when two conditions are met. First, x = y must appear on every path from the program's entry point to *i*. Consider the control-flow graph in Figure 19-3, which doesn't meet this condition.

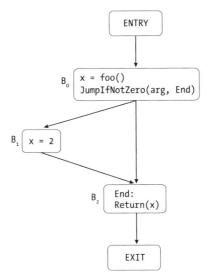

Figure 19-3: A control-flow graph for a function where we cannot perform copy propagation

In this control-flow graph, there are two paths from the start of the function to Return(x). Because only one of these paths passes through x = 2, it isn't safe to substitute 2 for x in this Return instruction. In Figure 19-4, on the other hand, every path to Return(x) passes through x = 2.

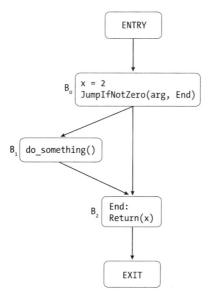

Figure 19-4: A control-flow graph for a function where we can perform copy propagation

No matter which path we take through Figure 19-4, we'll execute x = 2 before we reach the Return instruction, so we can safely rewrite that instruction as Return(2).

Figure 19-5 shows another, slightly trickier example.

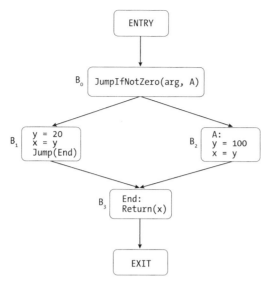

Figure 19-5: Another control-flow graph where copy propagation is safe

Once again, there are two different paths to Return(x). Both paths pass through x = y, but they pass through different instances of this instruction that appear in different blocks. In B_1, y's value is 20; in B_2, it's 100. But in either case, x and y will have the same value when we reach the Return instruction. That means it's still safe to rewrite Return(x) as Return(y).

Before we rewrite instruction i, there's a second condition that each path to i must satisfy: between the instruction x = y and i, neither x nor y can be updated again. Consider this fragment of TACKY:

```
x = 10
x = foo()
Return(x)
```

We can't replace x with 10 in Return(x), because x's value is no longer 10 at that point. Updating the variable that appeared on the right-hand side of a Copy instruction causes the same problem:

```
x = y
y = 0
Return(x)
```

Right before y = 0, we know that x and y have the same value. But after that instruction, their values will be different, so we can't rewrite Return(x). When a Copy instruction's source or destination is updated, we say the copy is *killed*. Once a copy is killed, we can't propagate it to later points in the program.

It's possible for x = y to appear multiple times on some path to *i*. It's unsafe to propagate it only if it's killed after the *last* time it appears. In the following example, it's safe to rewrite Return(x) as Return(2):

```
x = 2
x = foo()
x = 2
Return(x)
```

If there are multiple paths to *i*, the Copy instruction we're interested in must not be killed on any of them. Take a look at Figure 19-6, where x = y is killed on one path but not another.

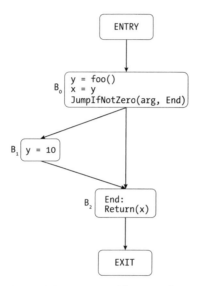

Figure 19-6: A control-flow graph where a reaching copy is killed along one path

If we jump over B₁, x and y will have the same value when we reach the Return instruction in B₂. But if we take the path through B₁, their values will be different. Because we don't know ahead of time which path the program will take, we can't rewrite Return(x).

Let's consider one final edge case. Suppose that x = y is followed by y = x, with no intervening kills:

```
x = y
--snip--
y = x
z = x + y
```

Normally, updating y would kill the earlier Copy instruction. But after y = x, x and y still have the same value. There are multiple correct ways to handle this case. One option is to say that y = x kills x = y, so only y = x reaches z = x + y. In that case, we'd rewrite the final instruction as z = x + x. This might let us remove y = x later, during dead store elimination, depending on where else y is used. Another option is to simply ignore y = x during our analysis, on the grounds that it has no effect; it just assigns y the same value it already had. Then, when we're rewriting instructions, we can go ahead and eliminate y = x and rewrite the last instruction as z = y + y. A third option is to propagate *both* copies in the final instruction, substituting x for y and y for x. This substitution is safe but not particularly helpful, since it won't help us get rid of either Copy instruction. We'll go with the second option and eliminate the redundant Copy.

If a Copy instruction appears on every path to instruction i, and it isn't killed on any of those paths, we say that it *reaches* instruction i. At the start of the copy propagation pass, we'll perform reaching copies analysis to determine which copies reach each instruction in the TACKY function. Then, we'll use the results of this analysis to identify instructions that we can rewrite safely.

We'll implement this whole optimization for the subset of TACKY we defined in Part I, then extend it to handle the new language features from Part II.

Reaching Copies Analysis

To implement reaching copies analysis, we'll define each of the elements of data-flow analysis that we discussed earlier: the transfer function, meet operator, and iterative algorithm. The transfer function and meet operator we'll discuss in this section are specific to reaching copies analysis, while the iterative algorithm applies to every forward data-flow analysis.

The Transfer Function

The transfer function takes all the Copy instructions that reach the beginning of a basic block and calculates which copies reach each individual instruction within the block. It also calculates which copies reach the end of the block, just after the final instruction. The rules here are pretty simple. First, if i is a Copy instruction, it reaches the instruction that comes right after it. Second, if some Copy instruction reaches i, it also reaches the instruction right after i, unless i kills it. Let's work through an example. Suppose a basic block contains the instructions in Listing 19-12.

```
x = a
y = 10
x = y * 3
Return(x)
```

Listing 19-12: A basic block

Let's assume that one Copy instruction, a = y, reaches the start of this basic block. This Copy will reach the first instruction, x = a. Once we encounter x = a, we add it to the current set of reaching copies, so both a = y and x = a reach the next instruction, y = 10. Because this next instruction updates y, it kills a = y. We therefore remove a = y from the set of reaching copies, but we add y = 10. Finally, x = y * 3 kills x = a. We don't add x = y * 3 as a reaching copy because it's not a Copy instruction. The final Return instruction doesn't add or remove any reaching copies. Table 19-1 lists which copies reach each instruction in this basic block.

Table 19-1: Copies Reaching Each Instruction in Listing 19-12

Instruction	Reaching copies
x = a	{ a = y }
y = 10	{ a = y, x = a }
x = y * 3	{ x = a, y = 10 }
Return(x)	{ y = 10 }
End of block	{ y = 10 }

Things get a little trickier when we consider variables with static storage duration. As Listing 19-13 demonstrates, these variables can be updated in other functions.

```
int static_var = 0;

int update_var(void) {
    static_var = 4;
    return 0;
}

int main(void) {
    static_var = 5;
❶ update_var();
    return static_var;
}
```

Listing 19-13: A C program where multiple functions access the same variable with static storage duration

Our reaching copies analysis should recognize that the call to update_var in main kills static_var = 5 ❶. Otherwise, it will incorrectly rewrite main to return the constant 5. At first glance, it might look like this problem applies only to file scope variables, but as Listing 19-14 illustrates, it impacts static local variables too.

```
int indirect_update(void);

int f(int new_total) {
    static int total = 0;
    total = new_total;
    if (total > 100)
        return 0;
    total = 10;
❶ indirect_update();
    return total;
}
```

```
int indirect_update(void) {
    f(101);
    return 0;
}
```

Listing 19-14: A C program where a function call indirectly updates a static local variable

When we analyze f, we'll need to know that the call to indirect_update at ❶ can update total. Otherwise, we'll incorrectly rewrite f to return 10.

There are a couple of ways to solve this problem. One option is to figure out which function calls will update which static variables. This would make reaching copies analysis an interprocedural analysis, which gathers information about multiple functions. This approach gets complicated very quickly. Our other option is to assume that every function call updates every static variable. We'll go with this option because it's much simpler. Whenever we encounter a function call, we'll kill any copies to or from static variables. This approach is *conservative*; it guarantees that we'll never perform an unsafe optimization, but it may lead us to kill some reaching copies unnecessarily and miss some safe optimizations. In contrast, using interprocedural analysis would be a more *aggressive* approach because it would miss fewer optimizations. More aggressive optimization techniques aren't always better; they often come at the cost of increased complexity and longer compilation times.

Listing 19-15 gives the pseudocode for the transfer function.

```
transfer(block, initial_reaching_copies):
    current_reaching_copies = initial_reaching_copies

    for instruction in block.instructions:
      ❶ annotate_instruction(instruction, current_reaching_copies)
        match instruction with
        | Copy(src, dst) ->
          ❷ if Copy(dst, src) is in current_reaching_copies:
                continue

          ❸ for copy in current_reaching_copies:
                if copy.src == dst or copy.dst == dst:
                    current_reaching_copies.remove(copy)

          ❹ current_reaching_copies.add(instruction)
        | FunCall(fun_name, args, dst) ->
            for copy in current_reaching_copies:
              ❺ if (copy.src is static
                    or copy.dst is static
                    or copy.src == dst
                    or copy.dst == dst):
                    current_reaching_copies.remove(copy)
        | Unary(operator, src, dst) ->
          ❻ for copy in current_reaching_copies:
                if copy.src == dst or copy.dst == dst:
                    current_reaching_copies.remove(copy)
        | Binary(operator, src1, src2, dst) ->
            // same as Unary
```

```
        --snip--
    |  _  -> continue

❼ annotate_block(block.id, current_reaching_copies)
```

Listing 19-15: The transfer function for reaching copies analysis

To process an instruction, we'll first record the set of copies that reach the point just before that instruction executes ❶. (We'll refer to this information later when we actually rewrite the instruction.) Then, we'll inspect the instruction itself to calculate which copies reach the point just after it. In the special case where x = y reaches y = x, we won't add or remove any reaching copies ❷. As we saw earlier, y = x will have no effect, since x and y already have the same value. Otherwise, we'll handle the Copy instruction x = y by killing any copies to or from x ❸, then adding x = y to the set of reaching copies ❹.

When we encounter a FunCall instruction, we'll kill any copies to or from variables with static storage duration along with any copies to or from dst, the variable that will hold the result of the function call ❺. The two other instructions from Part I that update variables are Unary and Binary. To handle either of these, we'll kill any copies to or from its destination ❻. The remaining TACKY instructions from Part I, like Jump, Return, and Label, don't add or kill any reaching copies. After processing every instruction, we'll record which copies reach the very end of the block ❼.

The Meet Operator

Next, we'll implement the meet operator, which propagates information about reaching copies from one block to another. This operator calculates the set of initial reaching copies that we'll pass to the transfer function. Recall that a copy reaches some point in the program only if it appears, and isn't killed, on *every* path to that point. Therefore, a copy reaches the beginning of a block only if it reaches the end of all of that block's predecessors. In other words, we'll just take the set intersection of the results from every predecessor. Listing 19-16 gives the pseudocode for the meet operator.

```
meet(block, all_copies):

❶ incoming_copies = all_copies
   for pred_id in block.predecessors:
       match pred_id with
❷    | ENTRY -> return {}
     | BlockId(id) ->
❸        pred_out_copies = get_block_annotation(pred_id)
          incoming_copies = intersection(incoming_copies, pred_out_copies)
     | EXIT -> fail("Malformed control-flow graph")

   return incoming_copies
```

Listing 19-16: The meet operator for reaching copies analysis

The meet operator takes two arguments. The first is the block whose incoming copies we want to calculate. The second, all_copies, is the set of all `Copy` instructions that appear in the function. We initialize the set of incoming copies to this value ❶, because it's the *identity element* for set intersection. That is, given any set of reaching copies, S, the intersection of S with `all_copies` is just S.

Next, we iterate over the block's predecessors, which might include other basic blocks, the `ENTRY` node, or both. No copies reach the very start of a function, so if we find `ENTRY` in the list of predecessors we just return the empty set ❷. (The intersection of the empty set and anything else is still the empty set, so there's no need to look at the block's other predecessors.) Otherwise, we look up the set of copies that reach the end of each predecessor ❸, which we recorded at the end of Listing 19-15, and take the intersection of `incoming_copies` with each of these sets.

We have one edge case to consider. If unreachable code elimination is disabled, the block we're analyzing might not have any predecessors. Calling `meet` on a block with no predecessors will return `all_copies`, so we assume that every possible `Copy` instruction reaches the start of the block. We don't care how this ultimately impacts the block itself, which will never execute anyway. We *do* care how this impacts the block's successors, which might be reachable. For instance, if a reachable block `A` and unreachable block `B` both jump to block `C`, then block `C` is reachable.

Luckily, our analysis is still safe. The intersection of the real results from `A` and the junk results from `B` will always be a subset of the copies that actually reach `C` from `A`; this is a conservative approximation of the results we'd get if we enabled unreachable code elimination and deleted `B` entirely.

The Iterative Algorithm

We can analyze a basic block with the meet operator and transfer function once we know the results from the blocks that preceded it. Now we'll tie everything together and analyze the entire function. There's just one problem: control-flow graphs can have loops! We can't analyze a block until we've analyzed all of its predecessors, which requires us to analyze all of their predecessors, and so on. Once we hit a loop, it seems like we're stuck; we can't analyze any of the blocks in the loop, because each block directly or indirectly precedes itself.

To get unstuck, we need some way to analyze a block even if we don't have complete results from all of its predecessors. The solution is to maintain a provisional result for every block; if we need to analyze a block before some of its predecessors, we can use those predecessors' provisional results. At first, before we've explored any paths to a block, its provisional result includes every `Copy` instruction in the function. Then, with each new path to the block (or rather, the end of the block) that we explore, we eliminate any copies that don't appear, or are killed, along that path. This means a block's provisional result always tells us which reaching copies appear (and aren't killed) on *every* path to the end of that block that we've explored so far. Once we've explored every possible path, we'll have the block's final result.

That's the basic idea; now let's put it into practice. First, we'll annotate each basic block with the set of all `Copy` instructions in the function. As we learned earlier, this set is the identity element for our meet operator. Initializing every block with the identity element ensures that blocks we haven't yet analyzed don't change the result of the meet operator. Let's try out this approach on the control-flow graph in Figure 19-7.

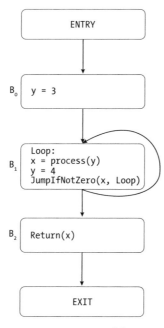

Figure 19-7: A control-flow graph with a loop

This control-flow graph contains two Copy instructions: y = 3 and y = 4. We'll initially annotate each block with the set containing both copies. Then, we'll analyze the blocks in order. We can calculate the final results for B_0 in just one pass because its only predecessor is ENTRY. Figure 19-8 illustrates the annotations on each block after we've processed B_0.

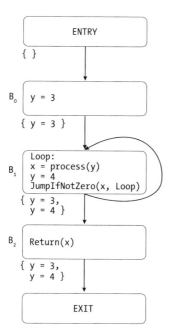

Figure 19-8: The provisional results of reaching copies analysis for Figure 19-7, after processing B_0

At this point, the annotation on B_0 is correct: only y = 3 reaches the end of that block. The other two blocks are still annotated with every copy. Next, we'll apply the meet operator to see which copies reach the start of B_1. This block has two predecessors: B_0 and itself. We'll therefore take the intersection of { y = 3 } and { y = 3, y = 4 }, which is { y = 3 }. This is the same result we'd get if B_0 were B_1's only predecessor. That's exactly the behavior we want: because we haven't analyzed B_1 yet, it shouldn't contribute to the result of the meet operator. Once we apply the transfer function to B_1, we'll recognize that only y = 4 reaches the end of the block. We'll then have all the information we need to process B_2 too. Figure 19-9 shows the annotations on each block after we've analyzed B_1 and B_2.

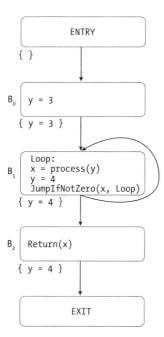

Figure 19-9: The provisional
results of reaching copies
analysis after analyzing
each basic block once

Each block now has the correct set of reaching copies. But we don't yet
have the right answer for each individual instruction in B_1. (Figures 19-8
and 19-9 don't show the annotations on individual instructions.) When we
last analyzed B_1, we assumed that y = 3 reached the start of the block, which
would imply that it also reaches x = process(y). Now that we have more accurate information, we need to analyze B_1 again. This time, the meet operator
will take the intersection of { y = 3 } and { y = 4 }, which is the empty set.
We'll pass this result to the transfer function to recalculate the results for
individual instructions in B_1. This time around, we'll correctly conclude that
no Copy instructions reach x = process(y) (or any point in the block before
y = 4, for that matter).

Now that we've seen the iterative algorithm in action, let's implement it.
Listing 19-17 gives the pseudocode for this algorithm.

```
find_reaching_copies(graph):

    all_copies = find_all_copy_instructions(graph)
    worklist = []

    for node in graph.nodes:
        if node is EntryNode or ExitNode:
            continue
      ❶ worklist.append(node)
        annotate_block(node.id, all_copies)
```

```
while worklist is not empty:
  ❷ block = take_first(worklist)
     old_annotation = get_block_annotation(block.id)
     incoming_copies = meet(block, all_copies)
     transfer(block, incoming_copies)
  ❸ if old_annotation != get_block_annotation(block.id):
       for successor_id in block.successors:
           match successor_id with
           | EXIT -> continue
           | ENTRY -> fail("Malformed control-flow graph")
           | BlockId(id) ->
               successor = get_block_by_id(successor_id)
               if successor is not in worklist:
                   worklist.append(successor)
```

Listing 19-17: The iterative algorithm for reaching copies analysis

We'll maintain a worklist of basic blocks we need to process, including blocks that we need to revisit after updating one of their predecessors. In the initial setup for this algorithm, we'll add each basic block to the worklist ❶, since we need to analyze every block at least once. We'll also initialize each block with the set of all Copy instructions that appear in the function.

Next, we enter our main processing loop, where we'll remove a block from the front of the worklist ❷, then analyze it using the meet operator and transfer function. If this analysis changes the block's outgoing reaching copies, we'll add all of its successors to the worklist so we can reanalyze them using those new results ❸. If a successor is already in the worklist, we don't need to add it again. We'll repeat this process until the worklist is empty.

GETTING MORE BANG FOR YOUR BLOCK

It's possible to improve on the code in Listing 19-17: when you initialize the worklist, you could add blocks in *reverse postorder*. To sort the nodes of a graph in postorder, you perform a depth-first search, adding each node to the sorted list after you return from traversing its successors. To sort them in reverse postorder, you take the list of nodes sorted in postorder and reverse it. In a reverse postorder traversal, you generally don't visit a block until you've visited all of its predecessors. (If you're traversing a graph with a loop, of course, you'll hit a few exceptions to this general rule.) This helps you gather as much information as possible about a block's predecessors before you try to analyze it, which minimizes how many times you need to revisit each block. If you don't add blocks to the worklist in this order, the algorithm will still be correct; it will just take longer. "Additional Resources" on page 610 lists a couple of references with more details about how to sort a graph in postorder or reverse postorder.

Listing 19-17 works for any forward data-flow analysis. Only the transfer function, the meet operator, and the identity element used to initialize each basic block will vary.

Rewriting TACKY Instructions

After running reaching copies analysis, we'll look for opportunities to rewrite, or even remove, each instruction in the TACKY function. To rewrite an instruction, we'll check whether the copies that reach it define any of its operands. If they do, we'll replace those operands with their values. If we encounter a Copy instruction of the form x = y and its reaching copies include x = y or y = x, we'll remove it instead of trying to rewrite it; the instruction has no effect if x and y already have the same value. Listing 19-18 demonstrates how to process each instruction.

```
replace_operand(op, reaching_copies):
    if op is a constant:
        return op

    for copy in reaching_copies:
        if copy.dst == op:
            return copy.src
    return op

rewrite_instruction(instr):
  ❶ reaching_copies = get_instruction_annotation(instr)
    match instr with
    | Copy(src, dst) ->
        for copy in reaching_copies:
          ❷ if (copy == instr) or (copy.src == dst and copy.dst == src):
                return null
      ❸ new_src = replace_operand(src, reaching_copies)
        return Copy(new_src, dst)
    | Unary(operator, src, dst) ->
        new_src = replace_operand(src, reaching_copies)
        return Unary(operator, new_src, dst)
    | Binary(operator, src1, src2, dst) ->
        new_src1 = replace_operand(src1, reaching_copies)
        new_src2 = replace_operand(src2, reaching_copies)
        return Binary(operator, new_src1, new_src2, dst)
    | --snip--
```

Listing 19-18: Rewriting an instruction based on the results of reaching copies analysis

Given the set of copies that reach the current instruction, replace_operand replaces a single TACKY operand with its value. If the operand is a constant or we can't find a reaching copy that assigns to it, we just return the original value.

In rewrite_instruction, we start by looking up the set of copies that reach the current instruction, instr ❶. If instr is a Copy instruction, we'll search this set, which we call reaching_copies, for a copy from its source to its destination or vice versa ❷. If we find one, instr's operands already have the same value, so we can delete it. (Listing 19-18 returns `null` to indicate that we should delete the instruction; your code might indicate this differently.) Otherwise, we try to replace the instruction's source operand using `replace_operand` ❸. We'll attempt to replace the source operands of other TACKY instructions in the same way. Listing 19-18 demonstrates how to rewrite the source operands in `Unary` and `Binary`; I've omitted the remaining TACKY instructions from Part I because the logic is the same.

At this point, you have a complete copy propagation pass that performs reaching copies analysis and uses the results to optimize a TACKY function. If you skipped Part II, you can move on to this section's test suite. But if you completed Part II, you still have some work to do.

Supporting Part II TACKY Programs

To make copy propagation work with the TACKY code we generate in Part II, we need to solve a couple of problems. The first problem is that we sometimes use `Copy` instructions to perform type conversions. We don't want to propagate copies between signed and unsigned types, because we sometimes generate different assembly code for operations on signed and unsigned values. If we replace a signed value with an unsigned one in a comparison, for example, we'll end up generating the wrong condition code for that comparison. Our reaching copies analysis will treat any `Copy` between signed and unsigned operands like a type conversion instruction instead of a normal copy operation. We won't add it as a reaching copy in the transfer function, and we won't include it in the set of initial reaching copies at the start of the iterative algorithm.

NOTE *Another solution would be to introduce separate signed and unsigned TACKY operators for comparisons, remainder operations, and division, so we wouldn't have to check the types of operands to distinguish between these cases during code generation. The LLVM IR uses this approach.*

The second problem is that variables can be updated through pointers. These updates are difficult to analyze. If we see the instruction `Store(v, ptr)`, we don't know which object `ptr` points to, so we don't know which copies to kill. This is similar to the issue we ran into with static variables, which could be updated in other functions. To solve this problem, we'll find all the variables that could be accessed through pointers (these are called *aliased variables*). We'll assume that every `Store` instruction updates every one of these variables. We'll assume that function calls update these variables too, since we can declare a variable in one function and then update it through a pointer in a different function. Let's use this approach to analyze Listing 19-19.

```
function_with_pointers():
    x = 1
    y = 2
    z = 3
    ptr1 = GetAddress(x)
```

```
Store(10, ptr1)
ptr2 = GetAddress(y)
z = x + y
Return(z)
```

Listing 19-19: A TACKY function that updates variables through pointers

First, we'll identify the aliased variables in function_with_pointers. Both x and y are aliased because they're both used in GetAddress instructions. (Let's assume that none of the variables in this listing are static, so we don't have to worry about whether other functions take their address.) Next, we'll run reaching copies analysis. Since this whole function body is one basic block, we can just apply the transfer function to the entire thing. We'll add x = 1, y = 2, and z = 3 to the set of reaching copies, as usual. Then, when we reach the Store instruction, we'll kill the copies to our two aliased variables, x and y. Table 19-2 describes which copies will reach each instruction in this function.

Table 19-2: Copies Reaching Each Instruction in Listing 19-19

Instruction	Reaching copies
x = 1	{ }
y = 2	{ x = 1 }
z = 3	{ x = 1, y = 2 }
ptr1 = GetAddress(x)	{ x = 1, y = 2, z = 3 }
Store(10, ptr1)	{ x = 1, y = 2, z = 3 }
ptr2 = GetAddress(y)	{ z = 3 }
z = x + y	{ z = 3 }
Return(z)	{ }
End of block	{ }

We correctly recognize that the Store instruction might overwrite x, which means that we can't replace x with 1 in z = x + y. We also assume that the Store instruction might overwrite y because our analysis isn't smart enough to realize that ptr1 couldn't possibly point to y. Therefore, we won't replace y with 2 in z = x + y, even though it would be safe to do so. Once again, we're making a conservative assumption; we'll miss some safe optimizations, but we'll never apply any that are unsafe.

Implementing Address-Taken Analysis

The approach we just used to identify aliased variables is called *address-taken analysis*. To perform this analysis, we'll inspect each instruction in a TACKY function and identify every variable that either has static storage duration or has its address taken by a GetAddress instruction. (We'll assume that all static variables are aliased, because their addresses might be taken in other functions.) We'll rerun this analysis on every iteration through the optimization pipeline because the results can change if we optimize away any

GetAddress instructions. Listing 19-20 demonstrates how it fits into the overall optimization pipeline we defined in Listing 19-6.

```
optimize(function_body, enabled_optimizations):
    --snip--
    while True:
        aliased_vars = address_taken_analysis(function_body)
        --snip--
        if enabled_optimizations contains "COPY_PROP":
            cfg = copy_propagation(cfg, aliased_vars)
        if enabled_optimizations contains "DEAD_STORE_ELIM":
            cfg = dead_store_elimination(cfg, aliased_vars)
        --snip--
```

Listing 19-20: Adding address-taken analysis to the TACKY optimization pipeline

Address-taken analysis is just one kind of *alias analysis*, also known as *pointer analysis*, which tries to determine whether two pointers or variables can refer to the same object. Most pointer analysis algorithms are more powerful than address-taken analysis. For example, they could figure out that ptr1 will never point to y in Listing 19-19.

Updating the Transfer Function

Next, we'll extend the transfer function to support the new types and instructions we added in Part II.

Listing 19-21 illustrates our new and improved transfer function. It reproduces Listing 19-15, with the changes to support additional types bolded.

```
transfer(block, initial_reaching_copies, aliased_vars):
    current_reaching_copies = initial_reaching_copies

    for instruction in block.instructions:
        annotate_instruction(instruction, current_reaching_copies)
        match instruction with
        | Copy(src, dst) ->
            --snip--
            if (get_type(src) == get_type(dst)) or (signedness(src) == signedness(dst)):
                current_reaching_copies.add(instruction)
        | FunCall(fun_name, args, dst) ->
            for copy in current_reaching_copies:
                if (copy.src is in aliased_vars
                    or copy.dst is in aliased_vars
                    or (dst is not null and (copy.src == dst or copy.dst == dst))):
                    current_reaching_copies.remove(copy)
        | Store(src, dst_ptr) ->
            for copy in current_reaching_copies:
                if (copy.src is in aliased_vars) or (copy.dst is in aliased_vars):
                    current_reaching_copies.remove(copy)
        | Unary(operator, src, dst) or any other instruction with dst field ->
            --snip--
```

```
    |  _ -> continue

annotate_block(block.id, current_reaching_copies)
```

Listing 19-21: The transfer function for reaching copies analysis, with support for features from Part II

We've already touched on most of the changes in this listing. Before we add a Copy instruction to current_reaching_copies, we'll make sure that its source and destination have the same type, or at least types with the same signedness. The signedness helper function should count char as a signed type and all pointer types as unsigned types, so we can propagate copies between char and signed char, between different pointer types, and between pointers and unsigned long. (The concept of signedness doesn't apply to double or non-scalar types. That's fine, because we don't use Copy instructions to convert to or from these types. If a Copy uses a double or non-scalar operand, both operands will have the same type, so we won't need to check their signedness.)

When we encounter a function call or Store instruction, we'll kill any copies to or from aliased variables. We'll also account for the fact that a function call may not have a destination operand. Note that we don't kill the Store instruction's dst_ptr operand. Store doesn't change the value of the destination pointer itself, just the value of the object it points to. Finally, when we encounter any of the other instructions we added in Part II— including type conversions, CopyToOffset, and CopyFromOffset—we'll kill any copies to or from its destination. We won't track copies to or from individual subobjects within structures or arrays, so CopyToOffset and CopyFromOffset will kill reaching copies without generating any new ones.

Updating rewrite_instruction

We'll rewrite most of the new TACKY instructions from Part II in the same way as the instructions from Part I, replacing any source operands that are defined by reaching copies. The one exception is GetAddress, which we'll never rewrite. It wouldn't make sense to apply copy propagation to GetAddress, because it uses its source operand's address rather than its value.

TEST THE COPY PROPAGATION PASS

If you completed only Part I, run the following command to test your implementation of copy propagation:

```
$ ./test_compiler /path/to/your_compiler --chapter 19 --propagate-copies
--int-only
```

If you completed Parts I and II, run:

```
$ ./test_compiler /path/to/your_compiler --chapter 19 --propagate-copies
```

Dead Store Elimination

Our last optimization is dead store elimination. We'll use liveness analysis, a backward data-flow analysis, to calculate which variables are live at every point in the function we're optimizing. Then, we'll use the results of this analysis to identify dead stores and eliminate them.

A variable is *live* at a particular point if its value at that point might be read later in the program. Otherwise, it's *dead*. To be more precise, a variable x is live at any given point p when two conditions are met. First, there must be at least one path from p to some later instruction that uses x. We say that x is *generated* by any instruction that uses it. Second, x must not be updated on the path from p to that later instruction. We say that x is *killed* by any instruction that updates it, just like a reaching copy is killed when either of its operands is updated. (You'll see the terms *generate* and *kill* in discussions of most data-flow analyses, not just the two in this chapter.) Consider the control-flow graph in Figure 19-10.

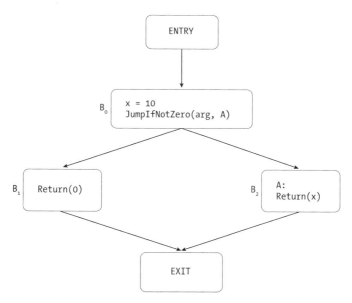

Figure 19-10: A control-flow graph in which x is live just after it's defined

There are two paths from x = 10 to EXIT. On the path through B_1, x is never used. On the path through B_2, x is used in a Return instruction. We know that x is live at the point after x = 10 because it's generated on one of these paths. By the same logic, x is also live at the end of B_0, at the beginning of B_2, and just before the Return instruction in B_2. On the other hand, x is dead at the end of B_2 and at every point in B_1, since there are no paths from those points to an instruction that uses x. Note that x is also dead at the very beginning of B_0, since we don't use its (uninitialized) value before we assign it a new value in x = 10.

Now let's look at the control-flow graph in Figure 19-11.

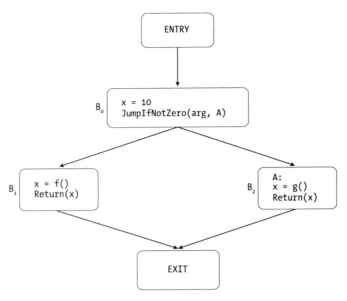

Figure 19-11: A control-flow graph with a dead store to x

Again, we have two paths from x = 10 to EXIT. Both paths pass through Return instructions that use x, but on both paths x is killed between x = 10 and the Return instruction that generates it. This means that x is dead right after x = 10. It's alive at just two points in this control-flow graph: right after x = f() in B_1 and right after x = g() in B_2.

An instruction is a dead store if it assigns to a dead variable and has no other side effects. Therefore, x = 10 is a dead store in Figure 19-11 but not in Figure 19-10. Note that we care whether the variable is dead just *after* the instruction, not before it. In the code fragment

```
x = x + 1
Return(0)
```

x is live just before x = x + 1 but dead after it. The fact that x is dead just after we update it means that this instruction is a dead store, so we can eliminate it.

Liveness Analysis

Like every data-flow analysis, liveness analysis requires a transfer function, a meet operator, and an iterative algorithm. Because this is a backward-flow problem, the transfer function will start at the end of a basic block and work its way to the beginning, instead of working from start to finish like we did in reaching copies analysis. Similarly, the meet operator will gather information from a block's successors, not its predecessors. We'll also use a slightly different iterative algorithm to send data backward through the control-flow graph. Let's take a closer look at each of these pieces.

The Transfer Function

The transfer function takes the set of variables that are live at the end of a basic block and figures out which variables are live just before each instruction. As we saw in Figures 19-10 and 19-11, an instruction generates any variables that it reads and kills any variables that it updates. For example, to calculate the live variables before the instruction x = y * z, we would take the set of variables that are live right after the instruction, add y and z, and remove x. If an instruction reads and writes the same variable, it generates the variable instead of killing it. For example, x = x + 1 generates x.

Let's apply the transfer function to the basic block in Listing 19-22.

```
x = 4
x = x + 1
y = 3 * x
Return(y)
```

Listing 19-22: A basic block

The transfer function will start at the bottom of this basic block and work its way up. Let's assume that there are no live variables at the end of the block, after the Return instruction. (This assumption might not hold if the function deals with static variables, but we'll worry about that later.) When we process the Return instruction, we'll add y to the set of live variables. Then, y = 3 * x will kill y and generate x. The next instruction, x = x + 1, generates x. This has no effect because x is already live. Finally, x = 4 will kill x, leaving no live variables at the start of the basic block. Table 19-3 summarizes which variables are live just after each instruction in Listing 19-22.

Table 19-3: The Live Variables After Each Instruction in Listing 19-22

Instruction	Live variables
Beginning of block	{ }
x = 4	{ x }
x = x + 1	{ x }
y = 3 * x	{ y }
Return(y)	{ }

Static variables complicate things, much like they did during reaching copies analysis. We don't know how other functions will interact with any static variables that we encounter; they could read them, update them, or both. We'll assume that every function reads every static variable. This assumption is conservative, since it prevents us from eliminating earlier writes to those variables. Listing 19-23 gives the pseudocode for the transfer function.

```
transfer(block, end_live_variables, all_static_variables):
  ❶ current_live_variables = end_live_variables
```

```
❷ for instruction in reverse(block.instructions):
    ❸ annotate_instruction(instruction, current_live_variables)

       match instruction with
       | Binary(operator, src1, src2, dst) ->
           current_live_variables.remove(dst)
           if src1 is a variable:
               current_live_variables.add(src1)
           if src2 is a variable:
               current_live_variables.add(src2)
       | JumpIfZero(condition, target) ->
           if condition is a variable:
               current_live_variables.add(condition)
       | --snip--
       | FunCall(fun_name, args, dst) ->
           current_live_variables.remove(dst)
           for arg in args:
               if arg is a variable:
                   current_live_variables.add(arg)
         ❹ current_live_variables.add_all(all_static_variables)

❺ annotate_block(block.id, current_live_variables)
```

Listing 19-23: The transfer function for liveness analysis

We'll start with the set of variables that are live at the end of the block ❶, then process the list of instructions in reverse ❷. We annotate each instruction with the set of variables that are live just after it executes ❸; we'll use this annotation later to figure out whether the instruction is a dead store. Then, we calculate which variables are live just before the instruction. We'll kill its destination if it has one, then add every variable that it reads. Listing 19-23 includes the pseudocode to handle the Binary instruction, which updates one operand and reads two others, and the JumpIfZero instruction, which reads an operand but doesn't update anything. It omits the pseudocode to handle most of the other instructions, since they follow the same pattern. FunCall is the one special case; we'll kill its destination and add its arguments, as usual, but we'll add every static variable too ❹. Finally, we'll annotate the whole block with the variables that are live before the first instruction ❺. The meet operator will use this information later.

There are a couple of ways to calculate all_static_variables. One option is to scan this TACKY function and look for static variables before you start the dead store elimination pass. Another option is to scan the whole symbol table for static variables, without worrying about which variables show up in which functions. There's no harm in adding superfluous static variables here, since they won't change which instructions we eventually eliminate.

The Meet Operator

The meet operator calculates which variables are live at the end of a basic block. To find the live variables at the end of some block B, we'll look at all of its successors. If a variable is live at the start of at least one successor, it must also be live at the end of B, because there's at least one path from the end of B through that successor to an instruction that generates that variable. Basically, we'll take the set union of all the live variables at the start of all the block's successors.

We'll assume that every static variable is live at the EXIT node. Other functions, or other invocations of the current function, might read those variables. Variables with automatic storage duration are all dead at EXIT, since they're not accessible after we leave the function. The pseudocode in Listing 19-24 defines the meet operator.

```
meet(block, all_static_variables):
    live_vars = {}
    for succ_id in block.successors:
        match succ_id with
        | EXIT -> live_vars.add_all(all_static_variables)
        | ENTRY -> fail("Malformed control-flow graph")
        | BlockId(id) ->
            succ_live_vars = get_block_annotation(succ_id)
            live_vars.add_all(succ_live_vars)

    return live_vars
```

Listing 19-24: The meet operator for liveness analysis

In reaching copies analysis, we were looking for copies that appeared on *every* path to a point, so we used set intersection as our meet operator. In liveness analysis, we want to know if a variable is used on *any* path from a point, so we use set union instead. This is unrelated to the fact that one analysis is forward and the other is backward. Some forward analyses use set union because they care whether at least one path to a point has some property. Some backward analyses use set intersection because they care whether every path from a point has some property. Other, more complex analyses don't use set union or intersection, and instead use different meet operators entirely.

The Iterative Algorithm

Finally, we'll implement the iterative algorithm for liveness analysis. This differs from the iterative algorithm in Listing 19-17 in a couple of ways. First, when the annotation on a block changes, we'll add its predecessors, rather than its successors, to the worklist. Second, we'll use a different initial block annotation. Recall that each block's initial annotation should be the identity element for the meet operator. Since our meet operator is set union, the initial annotation is the empty set. As we analyze more paths from a block to later points in the program, we'll add more live variables to this set.

I won't provide the pseudocode for the backward iterative algorithm, since it's so similar to the forward algorithm we've already defined. But I will give you a couple of tips about how to implement it. First, you may want to initialize the worklist in postorder. (Recall that you sort the nodes of a graph in postorder by performing a depth-first traversal and visiting each node after you've visited its successors.) This makes the backward algorithm terminate faster, just like initializing the worklist in reverse postorder helps the forward algorithm terminate faster. This ordering means that whenever possible, you'll visit each block only after you've visited all of its successors.

My second tip is to make your backward iterative algorithm reusable. In the next chapter, we'll implement liveness analysis again, this time for assembly programs. The details of the meet operator and transfer function will change, but the iterative algorithm won't. Try to structure your code so that you'll be able to reuse the same iterative algorithm with a different meet operator and transfer function; then, you'll be able to use it to analyze assembly programs in the next chapter.

Removing Dead Stores

After we run liveness analysis, we'll find any dead stores in the TACKY function and remove them. An instruction is a dead store if its destination is dead as soon as we execute it, like in the following example:

```
x = 1
x = 2
```

Liveness analysis will tell us that x is dead right after x = 1, making that instruction safe to delete. We'll never delete function calls, even when they update dead variables, because they may have other side effects. We also won't delete instructions without destinations, like Jump and Label. Listing 19-25 demonstrates how to identify a dead store.

```
is_dead_store(instr):
    if instr is FunCall:
        return False

    if instr has a dst field:
        live_variables = get_instruction_annotation(instr)
        if instr.dst is not in live_variables:
            return True

    return False
```

Listing 19-25: Identifying a dead store

If you completed only Part I, you've learned everything you need to know about dead store elimination! You can skip straight to the test suite. Otherwise, read on to learn how to handle the types and instructions we added in Part II.

Supporting Part II TACKY Programs

To update the transfer function, we'll need to think through which live variables each new instruction might generate or kill. The type conversion instructions, like `Truncate` and `SignExtend`, are straightforward. Each one generates its source operand and kills its destination, much like the `Copy` and `Unary` instructions we already handle. `AddPtr` also follows the usual pattern: it generates both source operands and kills its destination.

The operations on pointers and aggregate types are trickier. Pointers cause essentially the same problem they did in reaching copies analysis: when we read or write through a pointer, we can't tell which underlying object is being accessed. When in doubt, we should err on the conservative side and assume that a variable is live. Therefore, reading through a pointer should generate every aliased variable, but writing through a pointer shouldn't kill any of them. We'll take a similar approach to aggregate variables: reading part of an aggregate variable will generate it, but updating part of it won't kill it. I won't provide updated pseudocode for the transfer function; now that we've covered the key points, I'll let you work through the remaining details on your own. The meet operator won't change; in particular, static variables are still live at `EXIT`, but other aliased variables aren't, because their lifetimes end when the function returns.

Finally, let's update the last step in this optimization, where we use the results of liveness analysis to find dead stores and eliminate them. We'll never eliminate a `Store` instruction, since we don't know whether its destination is dead. Even if every single variable in the current function is dead, a `Store` might still have a visible side effect. For instance, it could update an object defined in a different function, like in the following example:

```
update_through_pointer(param):
    Store(10, param)
    Return(0)
```

After the `Store` instruction, there are no live variables in `update_through_pointer`. But that instruction clearly isn't a dead store; it updates an object that our analysis didn't track but that will likely be read later in the program.

The usual logic for spotting dead stores applies to all the other instructions from Part II, including `Load`, `GetAddress`, `CopyToOffset`, and `CopyFromOffset`.

TEST THE WHOLE OPTIMIZATION PIPELINE

Now that you've implemented the whole optimization pipeline, you can test it out. You might want to start by testing just the dead store elimination pass. If you completed only Part I, you can do that with the following command:

```
$ ./test_compiler /path/to/your_compiler --chapter 19
--eliminate-dead-stores
--int-only
```

(continued)

If you completed Parts I and II, run:

```
$ ./test_compiler /path/to/your_compiler --chapter 19
--eliminate-dead-stores
```

The --eliminate-dead-stores option will run the dead store elimination–specific tests in *tests/chapter_19/dead_store_elimination*. It will also run the tests from earlier chapters with all four optimizations enabled.

To test the whole optimization pipeline, run

```
$ ./test_compiler /path/to/your_compiler --chapter 19 --int-only
```

or:

```
$ ./test_compiler /path/to/your_compiler --chapter 19
```

This command will run all the tests of individual optimizations and all the tests from previous chapters with all four optimizations enabled (as usual, the --int-only option excludes any tests that rely on language features from Part II). It will also run the tests in *tests/chapter_19/whole_pipeline*, which focus on how the different optimizations work together. These tests validate that each optimization takes advantage of any optimization opportunities that the others create.

Summary

In this chapter, you implemented four important compiler optimizations: constant folding, unreachable code elimination, copy propagation, and dead store elimination. You learned how these optimizations work together to transform the TACKY representation of a program, resulting in smaller, faster, simpler assembly code than your compiler produced before. You also learned how to construct a control-flow graph and perform data-flow analysis. These techniques are fundamental to many different optimizations, not just the ones we covered in this chapter. If you ever want to implement more TACKY optimizations on your own, you'll be well prepared.

In the next chapter, you'll write a register allocator. You'll use a graph coloring algorithm to map pseudoregisters to hardware registers, and you'll learn how to spill a register when graph coloring fails and you run out of registers. You'll also use a technique called register coalescing to clean up many of the unnecessary mov instructions in your assembly code. By the end of the chapter, your assembly programs still won't look quite like what a production compiler would generate, but they'll be a lot closer.

Additional Resources

This section lists the resources I referred to while writing this chapter, organized by topic.

Security implications of compiler optimizations

- "Dead Store Elimination (Still) Considered Harmful" by Zhaomo Yang et al. surveys the different ways programmers try to avoid unwanted dead store elimination and the limits of each approach (*https://www .usenix.org/system/files/conference/usenixsecurity17/sec17-yang.pdf*).

- "The Correctness-Security Gap in Compiler Optimization" by Vijay D'Silva, Mathias Payer, and Dawn Song looks at the security impact of a few different compiler optimizations and formalizes some of the security properties that optimizations should preserve (*https://ieeexplore.ieee .org/stamp/stamp.jsp?tp=&arnumber=7163211*).

Data-flow analysis

- Chapter 9 of *Compilers: Principles, Techniques, and Tools*, 2nd edition, by Alfred V. Aho et al. (Addison-Wesley, 2006) defines data-flow analysis more rigorously than I did here. It also proves that the iterative algorithm is correct and terminates in a reasonable amount of time and discusses the use of reverse postorder traversal (which it calls *depth-first ordering*) in this algorithm.

- Paul Hilfinger's lecture slides from CS164 at UC Berkeley give an example-heavy overview of the same material (*https://inst.eecs.berkeley.edu/ ~cs164/sp11/lectures/lecture37-2x2.pdf*). I found the explanation of liveness analysis in these slides particularly helpful.

- Eli Bendersky's blog post "Directed Graph Traversal, Orderings and Applications to Data-Flow Analysis" describes how to sort graphs in postorder and reverse postorder to speed up data-flow analysis (*https:// eli.thegreenplace.net/2015/directed-graph-traversal-orderings-and-applications -to-data-flow-analysis*).

Copy propagation

- Every discussion of reaching copies analysis seems to formulate it slightly differently. The version in this chapter draws on Jeffrey Ullman's lecture notes on *Compilers: Principles, Techniques, and Tools* (*http://infolab.stanford .edu/~ullman/dragon/slides3.pdf* and *http://infolab.stanford.edu/~ullman/ dragon/slides4.pdf*).

- I've borrowed the idea of deleting redundant copies from LLVM's low-level copy propagation pass (*https://llvm.org/doxygen/MachineCopyPropagation _8cpp_source.html*).

Alias analysis

- You can find a quick overview of alias analysis algorithms in Phillip Gibbons's lecture slides from his Carnegie Mellon course on compiler optimizations (*https://www.cs.cmu.edu/afs/cs/academic/class/15745-s16/www/ lectures/L16-Pointer-Analysis.pdf*).

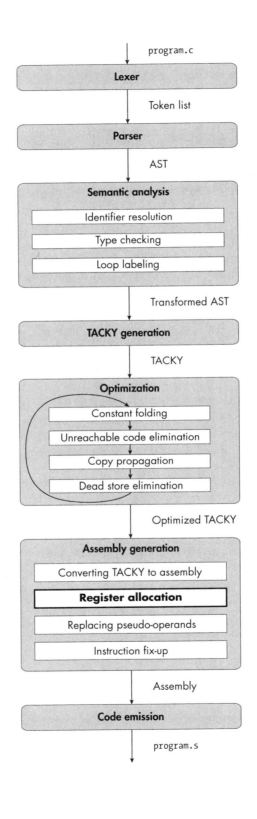

program.c

Lexer

Token list

Parser

AST

Semantic analysis

Identifier resolution

Type checking

Loop labeling

Transformed AST

TACKY generation

TACKY

Optimization

Constant folding

Unreachable code elimination

Copy propagation

Dead store elimination

Optimized TACKY

Assembly generation

Converting TACKY to assembly

Register allocation

Replacing pseudo-operands

Instruction fix-up

Assembly

Code emission

program.s

20

REGISTER ALLOCATION

Up until now, you've allocated space for every pseudoregister on the stack. This strategy is simple but painfully inefficient. Because instructions can't always operate on values in memory directly, you sometimes need to generate extra instructions to copy values between these stack locations and registers. Even worse, the assembly code you generate has to access memory constantly, even though registers are faster. Now you'll solve those problems. You'll finish up your compiler by adding a *register allocation* pass, bolded in the diagram at the start of the chapter, to assign pseudoregisters to hard registers instead of locations in memory. You'll use graph coloring, a classic register allocation technique, to come up with this assignment.

Once the initial version of the register allocator is up and running, you'll give it one more job: to clean up some of the unnecessary mov instructions produced during assembly generation. The final version of your allocator will perform *register coalescing* before assigning pseudoregisters to hard registers. The register coalescing step will look for mov instructions whose source and destination can be merged, or coalesced, into a single operand, which allows you to delete the instruction.

Register allocation has a little bit of everything: high-level theory, low-level details, brand-new concepts, and familiar techniques from earlier chapters. And the payoff is very satisfying: at the end of the chapter, you'll be generating dramatically more efficient code. I think it's a good note to end the book on.

To get started, let's look at an example that illustrates why register allocation is such a powerful optimization.

Register Allocation in Action

Consider the tiny C function in Listing 20-1.

```
int f(int x, int y) {
    return 10 - (3 * y + x);
}
```

Listing 20-1: A tiny C function

First, our compiler will turn this into the tiny TACKY function in Listing 20-2.

```
f(x, y):
    tmp0 = 3 * y
    tmp1 = tmp0 + x
    tmp2 = 10 - tmp1
    Return(tmp2)
```

Listing 20-2: The TACKY code for Listing 20-1

This listing gives the definition of f after the optimization stage. (In particular, we've optimized out the extra Return(0) that we add to the end of each TACKY function as a backstop for missing return statements.)

Next, we'll convert Listing 20-2 to the assembly code in Listing 20-3.

```
f:
  ❶ movl    %edi, %x
    movl    %esi, %y
  ❷ movl    $3, %tmp0
    imull   %y, %tmp0
    movl    %tmp0, %tmp1
```

```
        addl    %x, %tmp1
        movl    $10, %tmp2
        subl    %tmp1, %tmp2
 ❸ movl    %tmp2, %eax
        ret
```

Listing 20-3: The assembly code for Listing 20-2

We set up the function's parameters ❶, then we calculate tmp0, tmp1, and tmp2 ❷. Finally, we return tmp2 ❸. The operands %x, %y, %tmp0, %tmp1, and %tmp2 in this listing refer to the corresponding pseudoregisters; I'll use this notation throughout the chapter.

Now we'll walk through three approaches to replacing these pseudoregisters with real operands. First, we'll replace them with stack addresses, which is what our compiler does right now. On our next attempt, we'll replace them with hard registers, without performing register coalescing first; this is what the initial version of our register allocator will do. The third time around, we'll perform register coalescing before replacing the pseudoregisters with hard registers. That's how our finished allocator will handle this program. (A quick note on terminology: throughout this chapter, I'll use the word *register* to refer to pseudoregisters and hard registers collectively.)

Take One: Put Everything on the Stack

In its current form, our compiler will replace each pseudoregister with a stack slot according to Table 20-1.

Table 20-1: Replacing Pseudoregisters with Stack Addresses

Pseudoregister	Real location
x	-4(%rbp)
y	-8(%rbp)
tmp0	-12(%rbp)
tmp1	-16(%rbp)
tmp2	-20(%rbp)

This will give us the assembly code in Listing 20-4.

```
f:
        movl    %edi, -4(%rbp)
        movl    %esi, -8(%rbp)
        movl    $3, -12(%rbp)
 ❶ imull   -8(%rbp), -12(%rbp)
 ❷ movl    -12(%rbp), -16(%rbp)
 ❸ addl    -4(%rbp), -16(%rbp)
        movl    $10, -20(%rbp)
 ❹ subl    -16(%rbp), -20(%rbp)
        movl    -20(%rbp), %eax
        ret
```

Listing 20-4: Listing 20-3 after replacing pseudoregisters with stack addresses

Once we replace every pseudoregister with a memory address, instructions ❶, ❷, ❸, and ❹ are invalid, so the instruction fix-up pass will need to repair them. It will insert an extra instruction before ❶ to load its destination into a hard register, and it will add another to store the result back to -12(%rbp) afterward. It will also insert instructions to load the source operands of ❷, ❸, and ❹ into hard registers. In the context of register allocation, we say a pseudoregister is *spilled* to memory if we store its contents on the stack instead of in a hard register. The extra instructions we insert to move spilled values between registers and memory are called *spill code*.

We'll ultimately end up with the assembly code in Listing 20-5. I've bolded the spill code to make it easier to spot. (I've also snipped out the instructions to set up and tear down the stack frame, which aren't relevant here. These are snipped out of assembly programs later in the chapter too.)

```
f:
    --snip--
    movl    %edi, -4(%rbp)
    movl    %esi, -8(%rbp)
    movl    $3, -12(%rbp)
    movl    -12(%rbp), %r11d
    imull   -8(%rbp), %r11d
    movl    %r11d, -12(%rbp)
    movl    -12(%rbp), %r10d
    movl    %r10d, -16(%rbp)
    movl    -4(%rbp), %r10d
    addl    %r10d, -16(%rbp)
    movl    $10, -20(%rbp)
    movl    -16(%rbp), %r10d
    subl    %r10d, -20(%rbp)
    movl    -20(%rbp), %eax
    --snip--
    ret
```

Listing 20-5: Listing 20-4 with spill code

This code is incredibly inefficient. Almost every instruction accesses memory, and we waste a huge amount of time copying data from one place to another. To take one particularly egregious example, we store the result of 3 * y in -12(%rbp), then immediately copy it into -16(%rbp)—which takes two mov instructions—and never use -12(%rbp) again.

Take Two: Register Allocation

Let's try a more reasonable strategy. This time, we'll replace each pseudoregister with a hard register instead of a stack address, as shown in Table 20-2.

Table 20-2: Replacing Pseudoregisters with Hard Registers

Pseudoregister	Real location
x	%edx
y	%ecx
tmp0	%r8d
tmp1	%r9d
tmp2	%edi

We'll replace x, y, tmp0, and tmp1 with registers that don't appear at all in the original assembly program. We'll replace tmp2 with EDI, which *is* used in the original program. This is fine, since we use tmp2 only once we're done using EDI for anything else. Later in the chapter, we'll see how to reason more systematically about which mappings from pseudoregisters to hard registers are safe and which ones might cause conflicts.

There's no spill code this time, so I won't include separate listings from before and after the instruction fix-up pass. Instead, we'll skip right to the final assembly code, shown in Listing 20-6.

```
f:
    --snip--
    movl    %edi, %edx
    movl    %esi, %ecx
    movl    $3, %r8d
    imull   %ecx, %r8d
    movl    %r8d, %r9d
    addl    %edx, %r9d
    movl    $10, %edi
    subl    %r9d, %edi
    movl    %edi, %eax
    --snip--
    ret
```

Listing 20-6: The final assembly code for Listing 20-3 after register allocation

This is a major improvement; we don't access memory, and we have fewer instructions overall. If we wanted to, we could even omit the instructions to set up and tear down the stack frame, since we never use the stack. But we're still moving data around more than we need to. For instance, we copy our function parameters from EDI and ESI to new locations, instead of leaving them where they are. We also copy tmp0 (now in %r8d) to tmp1 (now in %r9d), when we could just as easily use tmp0 for two calculations in a row. This isn't the register allocator's fault; it's just that we generated inefficient TACKY and assembly code in earlier passes. But if we're thoughtful about how we allocate registers, we can clean up after those earlier passes. That's why our register allocator will include one more step: register coalescing.

Take Three: Register Allocation with Coalescing

Our last approach has two steps. First, we'll coalesce registers: we'll look at each mov instruction in the function and decide whether its operands can be merged together. Then, we'll replace any remaining pseudoregisters with hard registers, like we did in our previous attempt.

Let's take another look at the original assembly program from Listing 20-3. This program includes four mov instructions whose source and destination are both registers, which are bolded here:

```
f:
    movl    %edi, %x
    movl    %esi, %y
    movl    $3, %tmp0
    imull   %y, %tmp0
    movl    %tmp0, %tmp1
    addl    %x, %tmp1
    movl    $10, %tmp2
    subl    %tmp1, %tmp2
    movl    %tmp2, %eax
    ret
```

Sometimes, copying values from one register to another is genuinely necessary. For example, we might need to copy x out of EDI if we were going to pass another function argument in EDI later. But in this case, it's safe to merge x into EDI, since we don't need EDI for anything else after that first mov instruction. The same logic applies to each of the other three mov instructions. We won't need to store different values in the source and destination operands at the same time, so it's safe to merge them together. We'll merge x into EDI, y into ESI, tmp1 into tmp0, and tmp2 into EAX.

Table 20-3 summarizes which pairs of registers we'll coalesce and shows which member of each pair will remain in the program.

Table 20-3: Coalescing Registers

Coalesced pair	Remaining register
%edi, %x	%edi
%esi, %y	%esi
%tmp0, %tmp1	%tmp0
%tmp2, %eax	%eax

We'll also delete all four mov instructions, since they no longer serve any purpose. Listing 20-7 gives the resulting assembly code, with the updated operands bolded.

```
f:
    movl    $3, %tmp0
    imull   %esi, %tmp0
    addl    %edi, %tmp0
    movl    $10, %eax
```

```
     subl     %tmp0, %eax
     ret
```

Listing 20-7: Listing 20-3 after register coalescing

This looks a lot more reasonable! We leave x and y in EDI and ESI, where they were passed to begin with, instead of copying them to new locations. When we calculate the return value, we store the result in EAX right away, instead of copying it into EAX after we've calculated it. And we no longer use two separate temporary registers to calculate the intermediate and final results in 3 * y + x; we stick with tmp0 the whole time.

We're not quite done; we still need to replace tmp0 with a hard register. Any register besides ESI, EDI, or EAX will do—let's go with ECX. Listing 20-8 shows the assembly code we'll ultimately wind up with.

```
f:
     --snip--
     movl     $3, %ecx
     imull    %esi, %ecx
     addl     %edi, %ecx
     movl     $10, %eax
     subl     %ecx, %eax
     --snip--
     ret
```

Listing 20-8: The final assembly code for Listing 20-3 after register allocation with coalescing

Register allocation without coalescing improved our code in two ways: it reduced the number of memory accesses and the amount of spill code in our program. With register coalescing, we improve our code even further by removing the many unnecessary mov instructions generated by earlier passes.

Now that we have a sense of what we want to accomplish, let's look at how register allocation fits into the whole compiler pipeline.

Updating the Compiler Pipeline

Register allocators work best when there are lots of hard registers available, so the very first thing we'll do is add every remaining hard register to the assembly AST, including the callee-saved registers that we've avoided so far. We'll also make one small change to the conversion from TACKY to assembly: during this pass, we'll store extra information in the backend symbol table about which hard registers each function uses to pass parameters and return values.

Next, we'll implement the register allocator itself. The register allocator will run just after we convert the program from TACKY to assembly, before any of the other backend compiler passes. Much like the optimizations we implemented in Chapter 19, this pass will process each assembly function independently.

Even after register allocation, there may still be some pseudoregisters left in the program. This could happen for a couple of reasons. First, if a function uses lots of pseudoregisters at once, there might not be enough hard registers to accommodate all of them. When that happens, we'll have to spill some pseudoregisters to memory. Our register allocator won't replace spilled pseudoregisters; it will just leave them in the program for the next pass to deal with. Second, some pseudoregisters represent variables with static storage duration. These must live in memory instead of registers. If you completed Part II, you'll encounter a few other objects that must live in memory, including aliased variables, structures, and arrays. The register allocator won't touch these either.

To deal with all these stragglers, we'll run our old pseudo-operand replacement pass immediately after the register allocator. We won't make any changes to this pass. It will handle any pseudo-operands it finds exactly the same way it did before; it will just find a lot fewer of them.

Next, we'll update the instruction fix-up pass to take care of saving and restoring callee-saved registers. All our existing rewrite rules—including the rules to generate spill code—will stay the same. Since we still replace some pseudoregisters with locations in memory, we'll still have to generate spill code some of the time.

Finally, we'll extend the code emission stage to support the new hard registers we introduce in this chapter. You might want to stub out the new register allocation stage at this point. Then, we'll update the assembly AST one last time.

Extending the Assembly AST

So far, the assembly AST has included only the registers that we used for a particular purpose, such as passing parameters or rewriting instructions. It doesn't include any of the callee-saved registers: RBX, R12, R13, R14, and R15. Now we'll add these five registers so the register allocator can use them. We'll also add the pop instruction, which we'll use to restore callee-saved registers at the end of a function. If you completed Part II, you should also add the remaining XMM registers, XMM8 through XMM13. These registers are not callee-saved.

Listing 20-9 shows the complete assembly AST that includes everything we covered in Parts I, II, and III, with this chapter's additions bolded.

```
program = Program(top_level*)
assembly_type = Byte | Longword | Quadword | Double | ByteArray(int size, int alignment)
top_level = Function(identifier name, bool global, instruction* instructions)
          | StaticVariable(identifier name, bool global, int alignment, static_init* init_list)
          | StaticConstant(identifier name, int alignment, static_init init)
instruction = Mov(assembly_type, operand src, operand dst)
            | Movsx(assembly_type src_type, assembly_type dst_type, operand src, operand dst)
            | MovZeroExtend(assembly_type src_type, assembly_type dst_type,
                            operand src, operand dst)
            | Lea(operand src, operand dst)
```

```
        | Cvttsd2si(assembly_type dst_type, operand src, operand dst)
        | Cvtsi2sd(assembly_type src_type, operand src, operand dst)
        | Unary(unary_operator, assembly_type, operand)
        | Binary(binary_operator, assembly_type, operand, operand)
        | Cmp(assembly_type, operand, operand)
        | Idiv(assembly_type, operand)
        | Div(assembly_type, operand)
        | Cdq(assembly_type)
        | Jmp(identifier)
        | JmpCC(cond_code, identifier)
        | SetCC(cond_code, operand)
        | Label(identifier)
        | Push(operand)
        | Pop(reg)
        | Call(identifier)
        | Ret
unary_operator = Neg | Not | Shr
binary_operator = Add | Sub | Mult | DivDouble | And | Or | Xor | Shl | ShrTwoOp
operand = Imm(int) | Reg(reg) | Pseudo(identifier) | Memory(reg, int) | Data(identifier, int)
        | PseudoMem(identifier, int) | Indexed(reg base, reg index, int scale)
cond_code = E | NE | G | GE | L | LE | A | AE | B | BE
reg = AX | BX | CX | DX | DI | SI | R8 | R9 | R10 | R11 | R12 | R13 | R14 | R15 | SP | BP
    | XMM0 | XMM1 | XMM2 | XMM3 | XMM4 | XMM5 | XMM6 | XMM7
    | XMM8 | XMM9 | XMM10 | XMM11 | XMM12 | XMM13 | XMM14 | XMM15
```

Listing 20-9: The complete assembly AST with the pop instruction and additional registers

Note that pop accepts only registers, not other operands. Now that we've updated the AST, let's move on to the conversion from TACKY to assembly.

Converting TACKY to Assembly

We'll make just one change to this pass. We aren't changing what assembly we generate; we're just recording extra information in the backend symbol table. Specifically, we'll record which registers are used to pass each function's parameters. As you'll see in the next section, the register allocator needs this information to figure out which hard registers and pseudoregisters conflict.

Suppose we have the following function declaration:

```
int foo(int i, int j);
```

We'll record that foo's parameters are passed in the first two parameter passing registers, RDI and RSI. We'll track this information even if foo is defined in a different translation unit, because we'll need it to allocate registers in functions that call foo.

If you completed Part II, you should also track which registers are used to pass each function's return value. Given the function declaration

```
double foo(int i, double d);
```

we'll record that foo's parameters are passed in RDI and XMM0 and that its return value is also passed in XMM0. To figure out which registers a function uses to pass parameters and return values, we'll use the same logic we implemented in the classify_parameters and classify_return_value helper functions in Chapter 18. Note that we might run into function declarations with incomplete return types or parameter types. It doesn't matter what information we record about these functions, since it would be illegal to either define or call them in the current translation unit; we just need to handle them without crashing. It's easiest to simply record that they don't pass any values in registers.

Next, we'll build the register allocator itself.

Register Allocation by Graph Coloring

Our compiler will model register allocation as a *graph coloring* problem. Coloring a graph means assigning every node a label (traditionally called a "color") so that each node has a different color from all its neighbors. A graph is *k-colorable* if you can color it with *k* or fewer colors. Figure 20-1 illustrates a 3-colored graph.

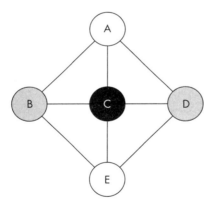

Figure 20-1: A 3-colored graph

Graph coloring is an important area of research in its own right; mathematicians have been investigating how to color graphs since the 19th century! It's relevant to register allocation because it captures two fundamental constraints on how we can assign pseudoregisters to hard registers: we have a limited number of hard registers to work with, and some registers will *interfere* with each other, meaning they can't occupy the same physical location. If two pseudoregisters interfere, we need to assign them to two different hard registers. A pseudoregister might also interfere with a hard register, which means we can't assign it to that hard register.

Graph coloring lets us express both kinds of interference and handle them in a uniform way. To turn register allocation into a graph coloring problem, we'll first build a *register interference graph* with nodes representing pseudoregisters and hard registers and with edges between any registers that interfere. Then, we'll color the graph, using one color per hard register. Finally, we'll assign each pseudoregister to a hard register according to its color. Because each register gets a different color from all of its neighbors, we'll never assign two pseudoregisters that interfere to the same hard register or assign a pseudoregister to a hard register that it interferes with.

Let's try out this technique on the assembly function in Listing 20-10.

```
divide_and_subtract:
 ❶ movl     %edi, %a
 ❷ movl     %esi, %b
   movl     %a, %eax
 ❸ cdq
   idivl    %b
 ❹ movl     %eax, %tmp
   subl     %b, %tmp
   movl     %tmp, %eax
   ret
```

Listing 20-10: A small assembly function

This function takes two parameters, which it copies into the pseudoregisters a and b. It calculates a / b - b and stores the result in tmp. Finally, it returns the value of tmp in EAX. We need to figure out which registers in this function interfere so we can build the interference graph. To start off, it's easy to see that a and b interfere. If we map them to the same hard register, we'll clobber a when we define b ❷. This is a problem because a is still live at this point. You learned in Chapter 19 that a variable is live if its current value might be used later in the program, and otherwise it's dead. This definition applies to registers too. When a register is live, we need to preserve its value, so we can't store a different value in the same location. When it's dead, we're free to overwrite its value with something else. This gives us an easy rule for detecting interference: two registers interfere if we update one while the other is live.

This rule also tells us that b interferes with tmp, since b is live when we define tmp ❹. But a and tmp don't interfere; a is already dead by the time we define tmp, so it's fine to map them to the same hard register.

Now let's think through which hard registers interfere with pseudoregisters. ESI interferes with a because ESI is live when we define a ❶. If we mapped a to ESI, we'd clobber the function's second parameter before we had a chance to copy it to b. EAX interferes with b because b is live when we copy a to EAX to prepare for division. The last source of interference is less obvious. Remember that the cdq instruction sign extends the value from EAX into EDX ❸. Because cdq implicitly updates EDX while b is live, it makes EDX interfere with b; if we mapped b to EDX, this instruction would clobber it. (Similarly, the idiv instruction updates EAX and EDX implicitly, so it would make both of these registers interfere with b if they didn't already.)

Finally, the hard registers all interfere with each other. This is sort of tautological; they can't occupy the same physical location because they represent different physical locations to begin with. Still, we need to capture this in the interference graph to make sure that each hard register gets its own color.

Now that we've figured out which registers interfere, we'll construct the graph. To keep this graph relatively small and readable, we'll pretend that the only hard registers are EDI, ESI, EAX, and EDX. Our real register interference graphs will include every hard register we can assign pseudoregisters to, even if the assembly program doesn't use them. However, they'll exclude RSP, RBP, and the scratch registers that we use during instruction fix-up.

Figure 20-2 illustrates the interference graph for the function in Listing 20-10.

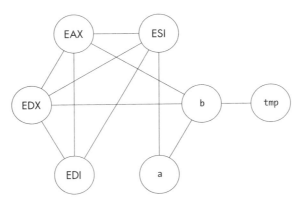

Figure 20-2: The register interference graph for divide_and_subtract

This graph encodes all the interferences we just identified: a interferes with ESI and b; b interferes with tmp, EAX, and EDX as well as a; and all four hard registers interfere with each other.

Now we'll try to *k*-color this graph, where *k* is the number of hard registers in the graph. In this small example, *k* is 4. There are several possible 4-colorings of Figure 20-2. Figure 20-3 shows a few of them.

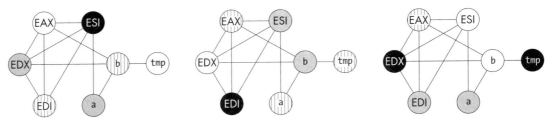

Figure 20-3: Three valid 4-colorings of the register interference graph for divide_and_subtract

Any one of these colorings—or any other 4-coloring we can come up with—will give us a valid register assignment. Each register will receive a different color from any of its neighbors. And because the k hard registers all interfere with each other, we'll assign each color to exactly one hard register, which creates a 1:1 mapping from colors to hard registers.

After we color the graph, we'll replace each pseudoregister with the hard register that received the same color. If we use the first coloring from Figure 20-3, we'll replace a with EDX, b with EDI, and tmp with EAX, which gives us the assembly code in Listing 20-11.

```
divide_and_subtract:
    movl    %edi, %edx
    movl    %esi, %edi
    movl    %edx, %eax
    cdq
    idivl   %edi
    movl    %eax, %eax
    subl    %edi, %eax
    movl    %eax, %eax
    ret
```

Listing 20-11: Replacing registers in divide_and_subtract based on the first coloring in Figure 20-3

If you like, you can work through this listing and confirm that it produces the same result as the original code for divide_and_subtract in Listing 20-10. You can also try this out with the other colorings in Figure 20-3.

Note that coloring the graph produces two different mappings: one from all registers to colors and one from colors to hard registers. Conceptually, each color represents a hard register, but we don't know *which* hard register until after we've colored the graph. If instead we used the names of the hard registers themselves as colors, or associated each hard register with a color ahead of time, then we would have to *precolor* each hard register with the corresponding color before we tried to color the rest of the graph. Precoloring adds more constraints to the graph coloring problem, which makes it harder to find a valid coloring. Some graph coloring implementations require precolored nodes; luckily, ours isn't one of them.

USING LIVE RANGES INSTEAD OF PSEUDOREGISTERS

Our register allocator will map pseudoregisters to hard registers. Most register allocators, however, solve a slightly different problem: they map *live ranges* to hard registers. A live range is a region of the program in which a particular pseudoregister is live. A single pseudoregister may have multiple live ranges (that is, it may be live in several unconnected regions of a program). These live

(continued)

---

ranges can safely be assigned to different hard registers. Here's a simple, if unrealistic, example:

```
two_live_ranges:
  ❶ movl    $1, %x
     addl    %x, var(%rip)
  ❷ movl    $2, %x
     movl    %x, %eax
     ret
```

In this example, x has two live ranges. The first starts when we define x ❶ and ends after we add it to the static variable var in the next instruction. The second starts when we redefine x ❷ and ends after we use it in the instruction right after that. Let's rewrite the program to refer to these live ranges explicitly:

```
two_live_ranges:
     movl    $1, %x.1
     addl    %x.1, var(%rip)
     movl    $2, %x.2
     movl    %x.2, %eax
     ret
```

Now it's clear that we don't need to assign x.1 and x.2 to the same hard register. A typical register allocator starts by identifying the distinct live ranges for each pseudoregister and giving each one its own name, like we just did for two_live_ranges. It then uses these live ranges, rather than pseudoregisters, as nodes in the interference graph. This puts fewer constraints on where the allocator can place each live range, which makes it easier to find a valid register assignment.

We're building a simplified register allocator that doesn't identify live ranges, so we'll just use pseudoregisters from the original assembly code as nodes in the interference graph. (Confusingly, identifying live ranges isn't quite the same as *liveness analysis*, which we discussed in Chapter 19. Our allocator will perform liveness analysis to learn when each register is live, but identifying live ranges is a more involved process in which liveness analysis is just the first step.)

If you want to build a more sophisticated register allocator that works with live ranges instead of pseudoregisters, you'll find a few useful references listed in "Additional Resources" on page 669.

Detecting Interference

Earlier, I said that two registers interfered if we updated one while the other was live. We used this rule to figure out which registers interfered in divide _and_subtract; it helped us identify both interference between pseudoregisters and interference between pseudoregisters and hard registers. But there are a couple of important points about this rule that we still need to cover.

The first point is that two registers interfere only if one is live *immediately after* we update the other. Here's a short example:

```
movl    4(%rdi), %x
movl    %x, %eax
ret
```

In this code snippet, RDI holds some memory address—presumably the address of a structure or array. The first instruction in this snippet takes the value stored in memory at RDI + 4 and copies it into x. Before this instruction, RDI is live; afterward, it's dead. RDI and x don't interfere. If we map x to RDI, the first mov instruction will overwrite the address in RDI. But that's okay, because we won't use that address again.

The second point is that two registers interfere only if they have different values. Concretely, this means the instruction mov src, dst won't make src and dst interfere, even if src is still live afterward. In Listing 20-12, for example, x and y don't interfere.

```
movl    $1, %y
movl    %y, %x
addl    %x, %ecx
addl    %y, %eax
```

Listing 20-12: A snippet of assembly where the source operand of a mov instruction is still live after that instruction

If we assign x and y to the same hard register, the second mov instruction won't clobber x with a new value. Instead, it will have no effect at all. When we perform register coalescing, we'll even go out of our way to put x and y in the same register so that we can delete this instruction entirely.

Two registers connected by a mov instruction could still interfere for other reasons, as Listing 20-13 demonstrates.

```
movl    $1, %y
movl    %y, %x
addl    $1, %y
addl    %x, %y
```

Listing 20-13: A snippet of assembly where a later instruction makes the operands of a mov instruction interfere

In this snippet, the second mov instruction doesn't make x and y interfere, but the subsequent add instruction does, because it updates y while x is live. In this case, putting x and y in the same register would be unsafe.

Spilling Registers

We can't always *k*-color the interference graph. Consider the assembly function in Listing 20-14, which calculates 10 / arg1 + arg1 / arg2.

```
uncolorable:
    movl    %edi, %arg1
    movl    %esi, %arg2
    movl    $10, %eax
    cdq
    idivl   %arg1
    movl    %eax, %tmp
    movl    %arg1, %eax
    cdq
    idivl   %arg2
    addl    %tmp, %eax
    ret
```

Listing 20-14: Calculating 10 / arg1 + arg1 / arg2

For the purpose of this example, we'll pretend that we have four hardware registers: ESI, EDI, EDX, and EAX. Figure 20-4 shows the interference graph for the listing. I won't walk you through how to construct the graph, but you can verify it on your own if you like.

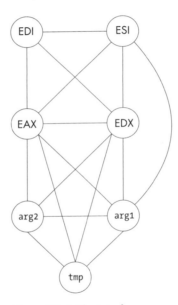

Figure 20-4: The interference graph for Listing 20-14

It's impossible to 4-color this graph. Note that EAX, EDX, arg1, arg2, and tmp all interfere with each other. That means each of them must receive a different color than the other four, which would require five distinct colors. We'll solve this problem by spilling a register—in other words, removing it from the graph instead of coloring it. Spilling any one of arg1, arg2, or tmp will make the graph colorable. If we spill tmp, for example, we can use the coloring shown in Figure 20-5.

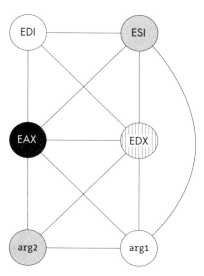

Figure 20-5: Coloring the interference
graph after spilling tmp

Now we can replace the two pseudoregisters that we colored, but not
tmp. Listing 20-15 gives the resulting assembly code, with changes from
Listing 20-14 bolded.

```
uncolorable:
    movl    %edi, %edi
    movl    %esi, %esi
    movl    $10, %eax
    cdq
    idivl   %edi
    movl    %eax, %tmp
    movl    %edi, %eax
    cdq
    idivl   %esi
    addl    %tmp, %eax
    ret
```

Listing 20-15: The uncolorable function after register allocation

Note that we've made the first two instructions in this listing redundant. We could optimize the code further by deleting them, but we won't
worry about this optimization for now.

After the register allocator has assigned arg1 and arg2 to hard registers,
the pseudo-operand replacement pass will put tmp on the stack. Listing 20-16
gives the final assembly code for this function, with the changes from
Listing 20-15 bolded.

```
uncolorable:
    --snip--
    movl    %edi, %edi
```

```
movl    %esi, %esi
movl    $10, %eax
cdq
idivl   %edi
movl    %eax, -4(%rbp)
movl    %edi, %eax
cdq
idivl   %esi
addl    -4(%rbp), %eax
--snip--
ret
```

Listing 20-16: The final assembly code for uncolorable

Spilling one pseudoregister made it possible to replace all the others with hard registers. But *which* registers we decide to spill matters a lot! As a general rule, the more frequently a pseudoregister is accessed, the more it will hurt performance to spill that pseudoregister. Our allocator will calculate a *spill cost* for each register in the interference graph. This is an estimate of how much spilling that register will hurt performance. Then, when we color the graph, we'll use that information to minimize the overall performance impact of spills.

The Basic Register Allocator

Now that we have some idea of how our register allocator will work, let's implement it! Listing 20-17 describes how to allocate registers for a single function.

```
allocate_registers(instructions):
    interference_graph = build_graph(instructions)
    add_spill_costs(interference_graph, instructions)
    color_graph(interference_graph)
    register_map = create_register_map(interference_graph)
    transformed_instructions = replace_pseudoregs(instructions, register_map)
    return transformed_instructions
```

Listing 20-17: The top-level register allocation algorithm

We start by building the interference graph. Then, we calculate a spill cost for each register based on how frequently it's used and annotate the graph with that information. Next, we color the graph, annotating each node with its color. If we can't color every node, we'll use the spill costs we calculated in the previous step to decide what to spill. To spill a node, we'll just leave it uncolored.

The last step is replacing all the pseudoregisters we colored. In create_register_map, we construct a map from colored pseudoregisters to hard registers with the same color. Finally, we rewrite the body of the function, replacing each pseudoregister with the corresponding hard register from the map.

Go ahead and stub out `allocate_registers`. Then, we'll walk through how to implement each of these steps.

Handling Multiple Types During Register Allocation

If you completed Part II, then you'll need to run the whole algorithm in Listing 20-17 twice: once to allocate general-purpose registers and once to allocate XMM registers. On each run, you'll include only registers of the appropriate type in the interference graph. The new features we added in Part II will change a few other details about how we build the interference graph too. We'll take a closer look at these changes when we implement `build_graph`.

The individual steps after building the interference graph—including calculating spill costs, coloring the graph, and replacing pseudoregisters—look exactly the same whether we're dealing with floating-point or general-purpose registers. The other features we added in Part II won't impact these steps either.

Defining the Interference Graph

To get started, we'll define the data structure for the interference graph. Listing 20-18 presents one possible representation.

```
node = Node(operand id, operand* neighbors, double spill_cost, int? color, bool pruned)
graph = Graph(node* nodes)
```

Listing 20-18: The definition of the register interference graph

Each node in the graph corresponds to a `Pseudo` or `Register` operand from the assembly AST. We'll track each node's neighbors, spill cost, and color. We'll represent colors with the integers 1 through k, where k is the number of available hard registers. The `color` field is optional because we may not be able to color every node. We'll use the `pruned` flag when we color the graph; you can ignore it until then. When you create a new node, you should initialize `spill_cost` to 0.0, `color` to null, and `pruned` to False.

This definition of `node` is a bit more permissive than it needs to be; the `operand` type includes constants and memory locations, which we'll never add to the interference graph. Alternatively, you could replace `operand` with a dedicated `node_id` type that can represent only registers. I'm using a more permissive definition so that we don't have to constantly convert back and forth between `operand` and `node_id` throughout the allocator.

Building the Interference Graph

We're finally ready to build the interference graph! First, we'll walk through an implementation of `build_graph` that supports the assembly AST from Part I. Then, we'll discuss how to modify it to support the assembly AST from Part II.

Since building this graph is a fairly involved process, we'll break it down into several steps. Listing 20-19 illustrates these steps in pseudocode.

```
build_graph(instructions):
  ❶ interference_graph = base_graph
  ❷ add_pseudoregisters(interference_graph, instructions)
    cfg = make_control_flow_graph(instructions)
  ❸ analyze_liveness(cfg)
  ❹ add_edges(cfg, interference_graph)
    return interference_graph
```

Listing 20-19: Building the interference graph

We'll start with a graph that includes every hard register ❶. (As far as I know, there's no standard term for this graph, so I'll call it the *base graph*.) Next, we'll insert a node for each pseudoregister that appears in the function ❷. Finally, we'll figure out which registers interfere with each other. Since this depends on which registers are live at each point, we'll need to run liveness analysis on our assembly code. Just like in Chapter 19, this analysis will take a control-flow graph (which is different from the interference graph!) and annotate it with liveness information ❸. Finally, we'll use that information to figure out which edges to add to the interference graph ❹. Let's take a closer look at each of these steps.

The Base Graph

The base graph, shown in Figure 20-6, includes 12 registers: RAX, RBX, RCX, RDX, RDI, RSI, R8, R9, R12, R13, R14, and R15.

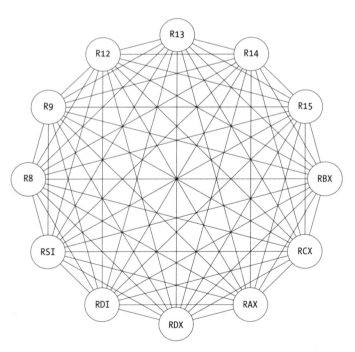

Figure 20-6: The base register interference graph

We won't include RSP or RBP in the graph because we're already using them to manage the stack frame, and we won't include R10 or R11 because we'll need them in the instruction fix-up pass. Since the hard registers all interfere with each other, the base graph includes an edge between each pair of nodes. In graph theory jargon, this makes the base graph a *complete graph*.

NOTE *Because the example programs in this chapter deal with 4-byte pseudoregisters, most of the diagrams of interference graphs use 4-byte aliases for hard registers. I've used 8-byte aliases in Figure 20-6, since it represents the base graph you'll use for all programs rather than the interference graph for any specific program. The interference graphs we actually construct will represent hard registers using* reg *assembly AST nodes, which don't specify a size.*

Adding Pseudoregisters to the Graph

This bit is straightforward: we just loop over every operand in every instruction and decide whether to add it to the graph. Every pseudoregister that appears in the assembly function should go in the graph, unless it has static storage duration. I'll skip the pseudocode for add_pseudoregisters because there's not a lot to it.

Liveness Analysis

We already know how liveness analysis works, since we implemented it back in Chapter 19. Now we'll need a new implementation that analyzes assembly instead of TACKY and tracks registers instead of variables. Luckily, the basic logic is the same. We can even reuse some of our existing code.

First, we'll construct a control-flow graph. This works just like building a control-flow graph from a TACKY function; only the specific instructions at the boundaries between basic blocks are different. Instead of looking for TACKY control-flow instructions like Label, Return, Jump, JumpIfZero, and JumpIfNotZero, we'll look for their assembly equivalents: the assembly Label instruction, Ret, Jmp, and JmpCC. You've already written code to convert TACKY into a control-flow graph; ideally, you'll be able to refactor it to handle assembly too.

Next, we'll look at the three components of liveness analysis itself: the iterative algorithm, the meet operator, and the transfer function. The iterative algorithm is exactly the same as in Chapter 19, so you should be able to use the implementation of this algorithm that you already wrote.

We'll use set union as our meet operator, just like we did before. However, we'll handle the EXIT node in the control-flow graph differently. Our original meet operator assumed that static variables were live when a function exited. Now we don't care about static variables, because they're not in the interference graph. Instead, we have to worry about hard registers: specifically EAX, which holds the function's return value. Listing 20-20 defines our new meet operator, with the one change from the original meet operator defined in Listing 19-24 in bold.

```
meet(block):
    live_registers = {}
    for succ_id in block.successors:
        match succ_id with
        | EXIT -> live_registers.add(Reg(AX))
        | ENTRY -> fail("Malformed control-flow graph")
        | BlockId(id) ->
            succ_live_registers = get_block_annotation(succ_id)
            live_registers.add_all(succ_live_registers)

    return live_registers
```

Listing 20-20: The meet operator for liveness analysis of assembly code

We're ignoring the fact that the callee-saved registers are *also* live at EXIT. We can get away with this because the instruction fix-up pass will spill these registers if we end up using them; that is, it will save their values onto the stack at the start of the function and restore them before we return. Assuming that these registers are dead at EXIT makes it possible to actually use them. If we added them to the set of live registers here, we'd conclude that they were live throughout the whole function and interfered with every single pseudoregister.

The transfer function is the one part of liveness analysis that differs significantly from the previous chapter. The basic idea is the same: we add registers to the live set when they're used and remove them when they're updated. But the specifics are different because we're working with a different set of instructions than we were before.

First, let's write a helper function, find_used_and_updated, that tells us which operands each instruction uses and updates. Both the transfer function and the add_edges function that we'll implement next will use this helper function. Listing 20-21 gives the pseudocode for find_used_and_updated.

```
find_used_and_updated(instruction):
    match instruction with
    | Mov(src, dst) -> ❶
        used = [src]
        updated = [dst]
    | Binary(op, src, dst) -> ❷
        used = [src, dst]
        updated = [dst]
    | Unary(op, dst) ->
        used = [dst]
        updated = [dst]
    | Cmp(v1, v2) ->
        used = [v1, v2]
        updated = []
    | SetCC(cond, dst) ->
        used = []
        updated = [dst]
    | Push(v) ->
        used = [v]
```

```
      updated = []
| Idiv(divisor) ->
    used = [ divisor, Reg(AX), Reg(DX) ]
    updated = [ Reg(AX), Reg(DX) ]
| Cdq ->
    used = [ Reg(AX) ]
    updated = [ Reg(DX) ]
| Call(f) ->
    used = <look up parameter passing registers in the backend symbol table> ❸
    updated = [ Reg(DI), Reg(SI), Reg(DX), Reg(CX), Reg(R8), Reg(R9), Reg(AX) ]
| _ ->
    used = []
    updated = []
return (used, updated)
```

Listing 20-21: Identifying the operands used and updated by each instruction

Keep in mind that this listing covers only the assembly instructions from Part I. Mov is the most straightforward case: it uses its source and updates its destination ❶. A binary instruction like add src, dst uses its source and destination and updates its destination ❷. It's also easy to see which operands the Unary, Cmp, SetCC, and Push instructions read and update.

Some instructions use registers that they don't mention explicitly. Idiv divides the value stored in the EAX and EDX registers by its source operand, so it uses all three values. It stores its results in EAX and EDX, so it updates those two registers. Cdq sign extends EAX into EDX, which means it uses EAX and updates EDX.

Call uses the registers that hold the callee's parameters; we can look these up in the backend symbol table, where we recorded them during the assembly generation pass ❸. It updates all the caller-saved registers—whether we're passing the callee's parameters in them or not—since these may be clobbered by the callee. This makes all the caller-saved registers interfere with any pseudoregisters that are live when we call this function, so our graph coloring algorithm will assign these pseudoregisters to callee-saved registers instead.

If an instruction both uses and updates the same register—like a Binary instruction both uses and updates its destination, for example—it's important to include that register in both the used and updated lists. In the transfer function, we'll only care that the register is used, since that will make it live. But when we use this helper function again in add_edges, we'll only care that the register is updated, since that will make it interfere with any other registers that are live at the same time.

Now we can write the transfer function, which is defined in Listing 20-22.

```
transfer(block, end_live_registers):
    current_live_registers = end_live_registers

    for instruction in reverse(block.instructions):
        ❶ annotate_instruction(instruction, current_live_registers)
        ❷ used, updated = find_used_and_updated(instruction)
```

```
        for v in updated:
            if v is a register:
                current_live_registers.remove(v)

        for v in used:
            if v is a register:
                current_live_registers.add(v)

❸ annotate_block(block.id, current_live_registers)
```

Listing 20-22: The transfer function for liveness analysis in assembly

Since this is a backward analysis, we analyze the assembly instructions in reverse order. To process an instruction, we first record which registers are live immediately after it ❶. Then, we calculate which registers are live just before it. We call the helper function we just wrote to figure out what operands it uses and updates ❷. We then remove any registers it updates from the set of current live registers, and we add any registers it uses. (If an instruction uses and updates the same register, we'll remove that register from the set of live registers and then immediately add it again.) Once we've processed every instruction, we record which registers are live at the start of the block ❸.

We won't track constants and memory operands, but our set of live registers might still include some operands that we don't care about (specifically, pseudoregisters with static storage duration). There's no harm in including them in our liveness results; we'll just ignore them when we use those results in the next step.

Adding Edges

With liveness information in hand, we can finally figure out which edges to add to the graph. Listing 20-23 gives the pseudocode for this step.

```
add_edges(liveness_cfg, interference_graph):
    for node in liveness_cfg.nodes:
        if node is EntryNode or ExitNode:
            continue

        for instr in node.instructions:
            used, updated = find_used_and_updated(instr)

        ❶ live_registers = get_instruction_annotation(instr)

            for l in live_registers:
            ❷ if (instr is Mov) and (l == instr.src):
                    continue

                for u in updated:
                ❸ if (l and u are in interference_graph) and (l != u):
                        add_edge(interference_graph, l, u)
```

Listing 20-23: Adding edges to the interference graph

We learned earlier that two registers interfere if one is updated while the other is live. Now we'll look at each instruction and figure out which interferences it creates. To process a single instruction, we'll first call find_used_and_updated to look up what operands it updates. (We'll ignore the first list this function returns, used, because don't care what operands the instruction uses.) Next, we'll look up which registers are live immediately after the instruction ❶.

We then add an edge between each register in live_registers and each register in updated. The Mov instruction is a special case. If the current instruction is a Mov, we'll skip over its source as we iterate over the set of live registers so that we don't add an edge between its source and destination ❷.

Before we add an edge between two nodes, we'll make sure that both nodes are already in the interference graph. We'll also make sure that they're different, since we don't want to add an edge from a node to itself ❸.

Handling Other Types While Constructing the Graph

Now we'll deal with all the features we added in Part II. Since we allocate XMM and general-purpose registers separately, we'll build two interference graphs. We'll start with a separate base graph for each register class. The base graph for XMM registers should have 14 nodes; it will include XMM0 through XMM13, but not the scratch registers XMM14 and XMM15. In add_pseudoregisters, we'll check that a pseudoregister has the correct type before adding it to the graph. When we allocate XMM registers, we'll add only pseudoregisters of Double type to the graph. When we allocate general-purpose registers, we'll exclude Double pseudoregisters and include all the other scalar types: Longword, Quadword, and Byte.

Floating-point registers aside, there are a few other details we need to change. We'll exclude aliased pseudoregisters from the graph, since they shouldn't be assigned to registers. You can reuse the previous chapter's address-taken analysis here; just rerun the analysis immediately before converting the program from TACKY to assembly. If a variable was aliased in the TACKY program, it will still be aliased in assembly.

Liveness analysis should reflect the new calling conventions we implemented in Part II. The meet function can't assume that EAX is live when the function exits; it should check the backend symbol table to learn which registers the function uses to pass its return value. These registers will all be live at EXIT.

We'll also update the find_used_and_updated helper function. First, this function needs to handle the Memory and Indexed operands correctly. These operands designate locations in memory, but they use registers in their address calculations. When we use one of these operands, we *read* any registers it refers to, even if we *write* to the memory location it designates. For example, the instruction movl $1, 4(%rax) uses RAX instead of updating it, and the instruction leaq (%rax, %rcx, 4), %rdi uses both RAX and RCX but updates RDI. Second, find_used_and_updated must recognize that all the XMM registers are caller-saved and therefore updated by Call instructions. Finally, this function will need to handle all the new assembly instructions we added in Part II, but there's nothing particularly tricky about them.

Calculating Spill Costs

After constructing the graph, we annotate each register with a spill cost. If we can't color every node in the graph, these costs will help us decide which node (or nodes) to spill. We'll try to color the graph in a way that minimizes the total cost of all spilled nodes.

Since we can't spill hard registers, we assign each of them an infinite spill cost. To estimate the spill cost of each pseudoregister, we just count up the number of times it appears in our assembly code. For example, if we encounter the instruction movl $1, %x, we increase x's spill cost by one. If we see the instruction addl %x, %x, we increase x's spill cost by two. The rationale here is that the more often a pseudoregister is used, the more memory accesses and new instructions we'll introduce if we spill it.

Frankly, this is a lousy way to calculate spill cost. It ignores the basic fact that some instructions are executed more frequently than others. Clearly, using a pseudoregister inside a loop that executes a million times should increase its spill cost a lot more than using it in an instruction that runs just once. It's hard to predict exactly how many times a particular instruction will execute, but one approach is to use loop nesting depth as a rough proxy for execution frequency. When compilers that take this approach calculate spill costs, they give more weight to instructions in more deeply nested loops.

Unfortunately, we have no idea where the loops in our program are. Discovering loops would require us to implement a whole new type of analysis, and this chapter is long enough. I've included a couple of references about identifying loops in "Additional Resources" on page 669 in case you want to implement this analysis on your own.

Coloring the Interference Graph

It's time to color the graph! Our goal is to minimize the total spill cost of the nodes we leave uncolored (ideally by coloring every node so that the total spill cost is zero). But exact graph coloring algorithms, which find the best possible coloring, are too slow to use in practice. Instead, we'll use an approximate algorithm. This algorithm may not find the best coloring, but it can usually find a pretty good one.

Our graph coloring algorithm is based on a simple observation: you can always color a node with fewer than k neighbors, because there's always at least one color that none of its neighbors uses. This observation is called the *degree* < k *rule*. (The number of neighbors a node has is called its *degree*; we say that a node has *significant degree* if it has k or more neighbors.) The degree < k rule gives us a way to break down the problem. First, we'll temporarily remove any node with fewer than k neighbors. This is called *pruning* the graph. Then, we'll color the rest of the graph somehow (we won't worry about how to do this just yet). Finally, we'll put back the nodes that we pruned, one at a time. When we put back a node, we'll assign it some color that doesn't conflict with any neighbors that we've already colored. There will always be at least one available color, since each node has fewer than k neighbors.

Let's try to 3-color the graph shown in Figure 20-7 using this approach and see how far we get.

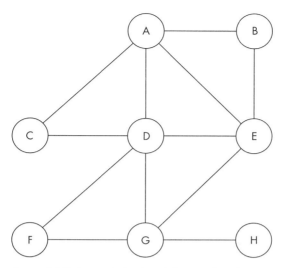

Figure 20-7: A graph that hasn't been colored yet

This graph has four nodes with fewer than three neighbors: *B*, *C*, *F*, and *H*. We'll prune these nodes from the graph and then figure out how to color the smaller graph. We'll also define a stack to keep track of the pruned nodes that we'll eventually need to put back in the graph. Figure 20-8 shows the pruned graph and the stack.

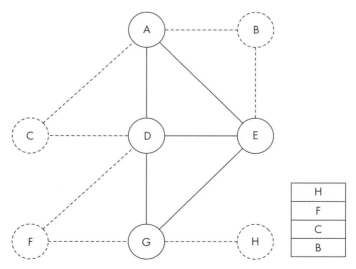

Figure 20-8: The graph from Figure 20-7 with low-degree nodes removed

In this pruned graph, *A* and *G* both have fewer than three neighbors. That means we can apply the same trick to prune the graph again! We'll push *A* and *G* onto the top of the stack; later on, we'll pop them off and color them before we color *B*, *C*, *F*, and *H*. When we pop *A* and *G* off the stack and put them back in the graph, they'll have the same degree they do now, so we know we'll be able to find a color for each of them.

Figure 20-9 shows how the graph and stack look after we prune *A* and *G*.

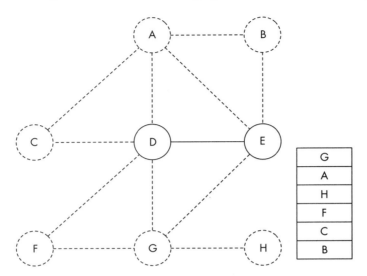

Figure 20-9: The graph from Figure 20-7 after two rounds of pruning

Our two remaining nodes each have fewer than three neighbors, so we could just color them. But we'll take a slightly different approach to accomplish the same thing: we'll prune them from the graph, then put them back. After we prune them, the graph is empty. Figure 20-10 shows how things look after we've pruned every node.

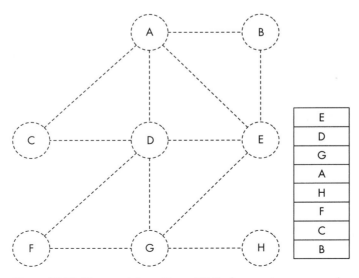

Figure 20-10: The graph from Figure 20-7 after pruning every node

Our original plan was to prune the graph, color the remaining nodes, then put back the nodes we had pruned. Now that we're done pruning, we don't have to do anything for the second step: there are no nodes left to color! We won't get this lucky with every graph; sometimes we'll end up with nodes we can't prune. We'll talk about how to handle that situation in a moment. For now, let's finish coloring this graph.

As the last step in our plan, we'll take each of the nodes we pruned earlier, assign it a color, and put it back in the graph. We'll start with the last node we removed, which is at the top of the stack, then repeat this process until the stack is empty. The sequence of diagrams in Figure 20-11 illustrates how we'll rebuild the graph in this example.

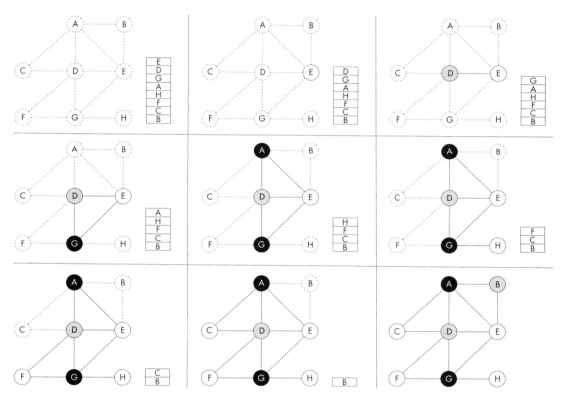

Figure 20-11: Adding nodes back to the graph and assigning colors

When we add E back to the graph, it has no neighbors, so we can assign it any color. Let's color it white. Then, when we add D, its only neighbor is E, so we can assign it either black or gray. When we add G, we find that it has a white neighbor and a gray neighbor, so we must color it black. We continue until the stack is empty and every node in the graph has been assigned a color.

Dealing with Spills

For many interference graphs, we can prune every node using the approach we took in the previous section. We can color those graphs without any spills. But there are other graphs where we'll get stuck: we'll hit a point where every node has k or more neighbors. Suppose we want to 3-color the graph shown in Figure 20-12.

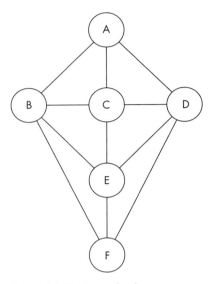

Figure 20-12: A graph where every
node has three or more neighbors

If we try to prune this graph, we'll immediately get stuck: every node has at least three neighbors! To get unstuck, we'll choose a node to prune anyway. We'll put this node on the stack, then continue with the algorithm as usual. This node is a *spill candidate* because we might not be able to color it when we put it back in the graph. If we're lucky, its neighbors won't use up every color, so we'll be able to color it. If we're unlucky, its neighbors will use all k colors, so we'll have to spill it.

We want to choose a spill candidate with a low spill cost. But we also want to choose a spill candidate with lots of neighbors that haven't been pruned yet, because pruning our spill candidate lowers its neighbors' degrees and helps us avoid spilling them later on. To balance these two priorities, we'll choose the node with the smallest value of *spill cost / degree*, where degree is the number of neighbors that haven't been pruned yet.

Note that we'll never choose a hard register as a spill candidate, because *spill cost / degree* for each of these registers is always infinity. If there are any pseudoregisters left in the graph, we'll always choose one of them as a spill candidate instead of choosing a hard register. If there are no pseudoregisters left, the total number of registers must be k or fewer, so we'll be able to prune every register.

Some graphs have no valid *k*-colorings, which makes spilling unavoidable. For other graphs, a valid coloring exists, but whether we find it is a matter of chance; it depends on the exact order in which we remove nodes from the graph and how we happen to color them when we put them back.

To illustrate the element of chance in this approach, we'll make a couple of attempts to color the graph in Figure 20-12. This graph is 3-colorable, but only one of our attempts will find a spill-free coloring. In both cases, we'll choose *C* as our spill candidate, then prune *A* and *B*, leaving *D*, *E*, and *F*. And in both cases, we'll use the same strategy to color nodes as we add them back into the graph: we'll choose the first available color from the list *[white, gray, black]*. The only difference will be the order in which we prune the three nodes. In the first case, we'll prune *D*, then *E*, then *F*. Figure 20-13 shows what will happen when we try to add the nodes back in.

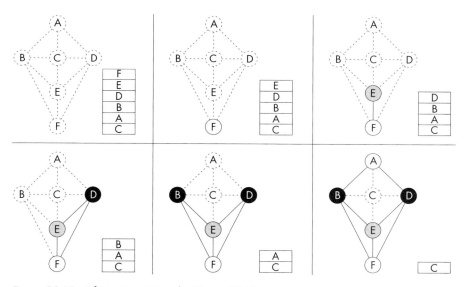

Figure 20-13: A first attempt to color Figure 20-12

When we reach *C*, we'll see that its neighbors are already using all three colors, so we'll be forced to spill it.

Now let's repeat this process; on this attempt, we'll prune *F*, then *E*, then *D*. Figure 20-14 shows what will happen when we put the nodes back in the graph this time around.

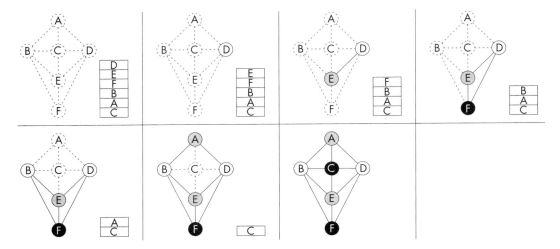

Figure 20-14: A more successful attempt to color Figure 20-12

This time, we assigned *A* and *E* the same color, which allowed us to assign *C* a color instead of spilling it. In a small example like this one, it's easy to see that assigning these nodes the same color is the better choice. But there's no general rule that lets us avoid unnecessary spills like the one in Figure 20-13; that's what makes this algorithm approximate. We *could* avoid unnecessary spills if we used an exact algorithm instead, but as I mentioned earlier, exact algorithms are too expensive to be practical.

Implementing the Graph Coloring Algorithm

Now that we've worked through a few examples using this algorithm, let's look at the pseudocode, which is shown in Listing 20-24.

```
color_graph(g):
    remaining = <unpruned nodes in g>
  ❶ if remaining is empty:
        return

    // choose next node to prune
    chosen_node = null

    for node in remaining:
        degree = length(<unpruned neighbors of node>)
        if degree < k:
          ❷ chosen_node = node
            break

    if chosen_node is null:
        // choose a spill candidate
        best_spill_metric = infinity
        for node in remaining:
            degree = length(<unpruned neighbors of node>)
            spill_metric = node.spill_cost / degree
```

```
            if spill_metric < best_spill_metric:
        ❸ chosen_node = node
                best_spill_metric = spill_metric

    chosen_node.pruned = True

    // color the rest of the graph
❹ color_graph(g)

    // color this node
    colors = [ 1, 2, ..., k ]
    for neighbor_id in chosen_node.neighbors:
        neighbor = get_node_by_id(g, neighbor_id)
        if neighbor.color is not null:
            colors.remove(neighbor.color)

❺ if colors is not empty:
        if chosen_node is a callee-saved hard register:
            chosen_node.color = max(colors)
        else:
            chosen_node.color = min(colors)
        chosen_node.pruned = False

    return
```

Listing 20-24: The graph coloring algorithm

We'll color the graph recursively. At each step, we'll prune a node, then make a recursive call to color the rest of the graph, then put the node back and assign it a color. In the base case, we've already pruned every node, so we have nothing left to do ❶.

In the recursive case, we'll start by choosing a node to prune, which this listing calls chosen_node. We'll pick the first node we find with fewer than k unpruned neighbors ❷. (If you're allocating general-purpose registers, k is 12; if you're allocating XMM registers, it's 14.) If that search comes up empty, we'll pick the node with the minimum value of *spill cost / degree* ❸. To prune a node, we'll just set its pruned attribute to True. Then, we'll call color_graph recursively to color the remaining nodes in the graph ❹.

After we return from this recursive call, we'll try to assign chosen_node a color. We'll take the list of integers 1 through k, which represent every possible color, and remove any color that we've already assigned to one of chosen _node's neighbors. Some of chosen_node's neighbors may not have a color, either because we spilled them or because we pruned them before chosen _node and will therefore color them later. We can simply ignore these nodes.

If there are any colors left in the list, we'll assign one of them to chosen _node ❺. If there's more than one color available, the algorithm isn't fussy about which one we choose. Although the color we choose here might impact how many nodes we ultimately spill, the effect is unpredictable; there's no color selection strategy that minimizes spills across the board. So, we'll choose a color with a different goal in mind: assigning pseudoregisters to caller-saved rather than callee-saved hard registers. (We'd like to use as few callee-saved registers as possible, to avoid the cost of saving and restoring them.) When chosen_node represents a callee-saved hard register, we'll assign it the available color with the highest number. Otherwise, we assign it the lowest-numbered available color. Using this strategy, the coloring algorithm will tend to assign higher-numbered colors to callee-saved registers and lower-numbered colors to caller-saved registers and pseudoregisters. A pseudoregister will end up with a higher-numbered color only when there are no lower-numbered colors available (for example, because it conflicts with every caller-saved register). Once we've picked a color, we set the pruned attribute back to False. This isn't strictly necessary, because we won't use this attribute again, but it marks that we've put the node back in the graph.

If there are no colors left in the list, we'll have to spill chosen_node. Concretely, this just means we won't assign it a color. We also won't update its pruned attribute, since we aren't putting this node back in the graph. Note that we don't explicitly push nodes onto a stack or pop them off afterward. Our recursive algorithm naturally colors nodes in the correct order, starting with the last node we pruned.

Building the Register Map and Rewriting the Function Body

Once we've colored the graph, the rest of the register allocator is pretty simple. We'll build a map from pseudoregisters to hard registers, which we'll use to replace the pseudoregisters in our assembly code. As we build this map, we'll also keep track of which callee-saved registers we've allocated so that we can save and restore them in the instruction fix-up pass. Listing 20-25 demonstrates how to construct the map.

```
create_register_map(colored_graph):

    // build map from colors to hard registers
    color_map = <empty map>
    for node in colored_graph.nodes:
        match node.id with
        | Reg(r) ->
            color_map.add(node.color, r)
        | Pseudo(p) -> continue

    // build map from pseudoregisters to hard registers
    register_map = <empty map>
    callee_saved_regs = {}
    for node in colored_graph.nodes:
        match node.id with
        | Pseudo(p) ->
            if node.color is not null:
              ❶ hardreg = color_map.get(node.color)
                register_map.add(p, hardreg)
                if hardreg is callee saved:
                  ❷ callee_saved_regs.add(hardreg)
        | Reg(r) -> continue
```

❸ record_callee_saved_regs(*<current function name>*, callee_saved_regs)

```
    return register_map
```

Listing 20-25: Building a map from pseudoregisters to hard registers

First, we'll iterate through the hard registers in the graph, building up a map from colors to hard registers. Remember that we'll have a 1:1 mapping between colors and hard registers because each of the *k* hard registers must be assigned a different one of the *k* possible colors. Next, we'll iterate through all the pseudoregisters. If a pseudoregister was assigned a color, we'll map it to the hard register with the same color, which we can find in color_map ❶. If a pseudoregister wasn't assigned a color, we won't add it to the map.

As we build up register_map, we also track the set of callee-saved registers this function will use. Whenever we add a mapping from a pseudoregister to a callee-saved hard register, we'll add the hard register to this set ❷. We'll record each function's callee_saved_regs set so that we can pass that information on to the instruction fix-up phase ❸. (This listing doesn't specify *where* to record that information; you can add it to the function definition itself, the backend symbol table, or some other data structure, depending on what's most convenient.) We can skip this step when we allocate XMM registers, because none of the XMM registers are callee-saved.

Finally, we'll rewrite the assembly code. We'll replace each pseudoregister in each instruction with the corresponding hard register from the register map. If a pseudoregister is missing from the map, we won't replace it. While we're at it, we'll remove any mov instruction whose source and destination ended up in the same hard register. For instance, if we've mapped both tmp1 and tmp2 to EAX, we can rewrite

```
my_fun:
    movl    %edi, %tmp1
    addl    $5, %tmp1
❶ movl    %tmp1, %tmp2
❷ movl    %tmp2, %eax
    ret
```

as:

```
my_fun:
    movl    %edi, %eax
    addl    $5, %eax
    ret
```

Both ❶ and ❷ would be rewritten as movl %eax, %eax, which doesn't do anything, so we can drop them both from the final assembly program.

This bit of cleanup where we delete unnecessary mov instructions is related to register coalescing, which we'll implement later in this chapter. But there are some important differences. The register coalescing step will deliberately merge together registers connected by a mov, like tmp1 and tmp2, then delete the mov instructions between them. This whole process will happen before we color the rest of the graph. What we're doing here is much simpler; we're not trying to merge registers, but if we happen to assign both operands of a mov instruction the same color, we'll take advantage of it.

Even once we implement register coalescing, this post-coloring cleanup will still be useful. As we'll see, the register coalescing pass isn't perfect; sometimes it will miss a pair of registers that it would have been helpful to coalesce. If we get lucky and assign that pair of registers the same color, this final step will still be able to delete mov instructions between them.

At this point, we have a working register allocator! We just need to update the instruction fix-up and code emission passes before we test it out.

Instruction Fix-Up with Callee-Saved Registers

If a function uses any callee-saved registers, we need to save their values at the start of the function and restore them at the end. We'll save them by pushing them onto the stack on top of the rest of the current stack frame. For example, if a function needs 16 bytes of stack space for local variables and uses R12 and R13, we'll insert the following three instructions at the very beginning of the function body:

```
Binary(Sub, Quadword, Imm(16), Reg(SP))
Push(Reg(R12))
Push(Reg(R13))
```

The initial Sub instruction allocates the current stack frame, just like in earlier chapters. The new Push instructions come immediately after it. (If you skipped Part II, the first instruction will be AllocateStack rather than Sub.)

Before we return, we'll restore the values of these registers by popping them off the stack. That is, we'll rewrite each Ret instruction in this function as:

```
Pop(R13)
Pop(R12)
Ret
```

We can push callee-saved registers onto the stack in any order, but we'll always need to pop them back off in the reverse order so that each register ends up with its original value. Since we add the rest of the function epilogue during code emission, we'll end up deallocating the stack frame just after restoring the callee-saved registers:

```
popq    %r13
popq    %r12
movq    %rbp, %rsp
popq    %rbp
ret
```

We also need to ensure that the entire stack frame, including the values of any callee-saved registers that we save to the stack, is 16-byte aligned.

Suppose the pseudo-operand replacement pass has allocated 20 bytes of stack space to store local variables in a particular function. We'd normally subtract 32 bytes from RSP to maintain the proper stack alignment. But if the function uses a single callee-saved register, we should initially subtract 24 bytes instead:

```
Binary(Sub, Quadword, Imm(24), Reg(SP))
Push(Reg(BX))
```

If we subtract 24 bytes from RSP explicitly and subtract another 8 bytes by pushing RBX, we still end up subtracting a total of 32 bytes, so the stack will be properly aligned. Listing 20-26 demonstrates one way to perform this tricky calculation.

```
calculate_stack_adjustment(bytes_for_locals, callee_saved_count):
    callee_saved_bytes = 8 * callee_saved_count
    total_stack_bytes = callee_saved_bytes + bytes_for_locals
❶ adjusted_stack_bytes = round_up(total_stack_bytes, 16)
❷ stack_adjustment = adjusted_stack_bytes - callee_saved_bytes
    return stack_adjustment
```

Listing 20-26: The stack space calculation that accounts for callee-saved registers

In this listing, bytes_for_locals is the number of bytes of stack space we allocated during pseudo-operand replacement, and callee_saved_count is the number of callee-saved registers the function uses. We start by calculating how many bytes the callee-saved values will occupy. Then, we add this to bytes_for_locals and round up to the nearest multiple of 16 to get the total size of the stack frame ❶. Working backward from this value, we subtract the number of bytes the callee-saved values will occupy to find the number of bytes we need to explicitly subtract from RSP ❷.

Code Emission

Finally, we'll update the code emission pass to handle the pop instruction and all the new registers we added in this chapter. Like push, pop will always use the 8-byte names for registers. Tables 20-4 and 20-5 describe how to print out these constructs. (I haven't bolded new and changed constructs like I did in most code emission tables in earlier chapters, because all of these constructs are new.) For a summary of the complete code emission pass at the end of this chapter, see Appendix B, which includes two sets of code emission tables for Part III: one with the features from Part II and one without them.

Table 20-4: Formatting Assembly Instructions

Assembly instruction	Output
Pop(reg)	popq <reg>

Table 20-5: Formatting Assembly Operands

Assembly operand		Output
Reg(BX)	8-byte	%rbx
	4-byte	%ebx
	1-byte	%bl
Reg(R12)	8-byte	%r12
	4-byte	%r12d
	1-byte	%r12b
Reg(R13)	8-byte	%r13
	4-byte	%r13d
	1-byte	%r13b
Reg(R14)	8-byte	%r14
	4-byte	%r14d
	1-byte	%r14b
Reg(R15)	8-byte	%r15
	4-byte	%r15d
	1-byte	%r15b
Reg(XMM8)		%xmm8
Reg(XMM9)		%xmm9
Reg(XMM10)		%xmm10
Reg(XMM11)		%xmm11
Reg(XMM12)		%xmm12
Reg(XMM13)		%xmm13

Now you're ready to try out your register allocator on some real programs!

TEST THE BASIC REGISTER ALLOCATOR

If you completed only Part I, test out your register allocator with the following command:

```
$ ./test_compiler /path/to/your_compiler --chapter 20 --no-coalescing
--int-only
```

This will run all the test programs in *tests/chapter_20/int_only*, all the tests from Part I, and all the Part I–specific tests from Chapter 19. It will also inspect the assembly output for the test programs in *tests/chapter_20/int_only/no _coalescing* to make sure that your compiler doesn't spill registers unnecessarily.

If you completed Parts I and II, run the same command without the `--int -only` option:

```
$ ./test_compiler /path/to/your_compiler --chapter 20 --no-coalescing
```

There are a couple of things you should know about this chapter's tests. First, many of them are designed to produce specific interference graphs or use every hard register. If your compiler generates different assembly code or includes extra optimizations beyond what this book covers, these tests may not cover the edge cases they're intended to target, so you should write your own unit tests too.

Second, if your code to recognize interference is buggy, the test suite might not catch those bugs until you implement register coalescing. Several tests include pairs of registers that could be coalesced, except that they interfere in some specific way. Once you've implemented coalescing, your allocator must recognize that they interfere to avoid coalescing them. Without coalescing, the test suite can't reliably detect this sort of bug; even if your allocator doesn't know that two registers interfere, it might still get lucky and assign them different colors. To thoroughly test your register allocator before you move on to coalescing, you might want to write your own unit tests for the code that builds the interference graph.

Third, the test commands in this chapter always compile test programs with the optimizations from Chapter 19 enabled. This doesn't have any particular implications; it's just something to be aware of while you're debugging your tests.

Register Coalescing

Our register allocator already works correctly. But as we saw in the example at the start of the chapter, it will produce even more efficient code if we include a coalescing step. That early example also gave us a general sense of how this process works: we look at each mov instruction that copies a value from one register to another and decide whether to coalesce its source and destination. Once we've made these decisions, we rewrite the assembly code, replacing the registers we coalesced and deleting any mov instructions that we no longer need.

To decide which registers to coalesce, we'll consult the interference graph. We'll coalesce a pair of registers when two conditions are met. The first condition is obvious: the registers can't interfere with each other. The example from Listing 20-13, reproduced here, illustrates why this condition is necessary:

```
movl    $1, %y
movl    %y, %x
addl    $1, %y
addl    %x, %y
```

Since we update y while x is live, these two registers interfere. If we coalesced them, the first add instruction would clobber x, and we'd end up calculating $2 + 2$ instead of $1 + 2$.

The second condition is subtler: we'll coalesce a pair of registers only if that won't force us to spill more registers. To understand why coalescing can lead to spills, let's look at Listing 20-27.

```
f:
    movl    %edi, %arg
    movl    %arg, %tmp
    addl    $1, %tmp
    imull   %arg, %tmp
    movl    $10, %eax
    subl    %tmp, %eax
    ret
```

Listing 20-27: An assembly function where coalescing would cause a spill

This assembly function calculates 10 - (arg + 1) * arg. For this example, we'll pretend that EDI and EAX are the only available hard registers, so k is 2. Figure 20-15 shows this listing's interference graph, which is clearly 2-colorable.

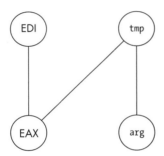

Figure 20-15: The interference graph for Listing 20-27

The first mov instruction in Listing 20-27 looks like a possible candidate for coalescing. (The second instruction isn't, since arg and tmp interfere.) But if we try to coalesce arg into EDI, we'll run into trouble. We'll end up with the assembly code in Listing 20-28.

```
f:
    movl    %edi, %tmp
    addl    $1, %tmp
    imull   %edi, %tmp
    movl    $10, %eax
    subl    %tmp, %eax
    ret
```

Listing 20-28: Listing 20-27 after coalescing arg into EDI

Figure 20-16 shows the interference graph for this coalesced code.

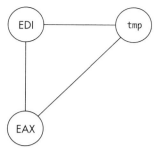

Figure 20-16: The interference graph for Listing 20-28

Now we can't 2-color the graph anymore. Since tmp interferes with both hard registers, we'll have to spill it. Instead of improving performance, we've made it worse! The cost of spilling tmp to memory outweighs the benefit of removing a single mov instruction. To avoid this situation, we'll use a strategy called *conservative coalescing*: we'll coalesce two registers only when we can tell in advance that it won't make the interference graph harder to color. But before we dig into conservative coalescing, we need to learn how to keep the graph up to date.

Updating the Interference Graph

Whenever we decide to coalesce a pair of registers, we need to update the interference graph. Otherwise, we'll make later coalescing decisions based on bad information. There are two ways to perform this update. The first is to rewrite the assembly code immediately and rebuild the graph from scratch. The problem with this approach is that building the interference graph is slow. We might coalesce dozens or even hundreds of mov instructions in a single function, but we can't afford to rebuild the interference graph hundreds of times.

A much quicker approach is to merge the two nodes together in the existing interference graph, without referring back to the assembly code. In Figure 20-17, we use this approach to coalesce the pseudoregister tmp2 into EAX.

Original interference graph

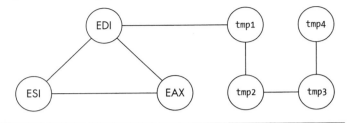

After coalescing tmp2 into EAX

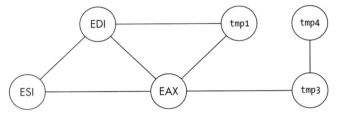

Figure 20-17: Updating the interference graph to reflect coalescing decisions

We'll assume that any register that originally interfered with tmp2 now interferes with EAX. To make the interference graph reflect this change, we just add an edge from each of tmp2's neighbors to EAX and then remove tmp2.

But this way of updating the graph has a problem too: it's not always accurate! It might include some extra edges between registers that don't really interfere. Listing 20-29 gives a slightly contrived example.

```
f:
    movl    %edi, %tmp1
    movl    %edi, %tmp2
    addl    %tmp1, %tmp2
    movl    %tmp2, %eax
    ret
```

Listing 20-29: A function that copies its first argument into two different pseudoregisters

Note that tmp1 and tmp2 interfere: the second mov instruction updates tmp2 while tmp1 is still live. Let's try to coalesce tmp1 into EDI and use our speedy, simple method to update the graph accordingly. Figure 20-18 shows how the graph will change.

Original interference graph

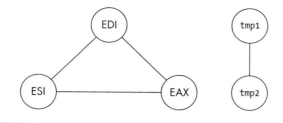

After coalescing tmp1 into EDI

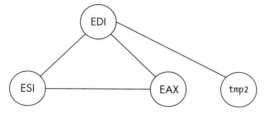

Figure 20-18: Updating the interference graph for Listing 20-29

But when we actually replace tmp1 with EDI, we'll find that the interference with tmp2 goes away! Listing 20-30 shows the updated assembly code.

```
f:
    movl    %edi, %tmp2
    addl    %edi, %tmp2
    movl    %tmp2, %eax
    ret
```

Listing 20-30: Listing 20-29 after coalescing tmp1 into EDI

We learned earlier that the instruction mov src, dst will never make src and dst interfere. Initially, the instruction movl %edi, %tmp2 caused an interference between tmp1 and tmp2. Now that we've merged tmp1 into EDI, it doesn't cause an interference anymore.

Even though it isn't completely accurate, our quick update method is still useful. It produces a conservative approximation of the true interference graph; it has all the nodes and edges that should be in the graph, but it might have a few extra edges too. If this graph tells us that two registers are safe to coalesce, we can be sure they really are. But if we rely solely on this method, we'll leave some coalescing opportunities on the table. If, for instance, we only look at the graph in Figure 20-18, we won't realize that we can coalesce tmp2 into EDI. Worse, if we attempted to color this graph, we might end up spilling registers unnecessarily.

So, we'll use *both* approaches to update the graph. Each time we decide to coalesce a pair of registers, we'll perform a quick update by merging their nodes together. Then, after we've looked at every mov instruction and rewritten the assembly code, we'll rebuild the graph from scratch. We'll repeat this build-coalesce loop until we can't find any more registers to coalesce. Combining a speedy, approximate inner loop with a slow, precise outer loop gives us the best of both worlds. We'll catch every coalescing opportunity and send an accurate interference graph on to the coloring stage, but we won't waste time rebuilding the graph after every single coalescing decision.

Conservative Coalescing

Now that we understand how coalescing changes the graph, we can reason about when it might lead to spills. The basic issue is that when we coalesce two nodes, the merged node will have a higher degree than either of them, which could make it more difficult to prune. It's also likely to have a higher spill cost than either of the original nodes, since it's used more frequently.

We'll use two conservative coalescing tests to ensure that a merged node doesn't cause problems when we color the graph. The *Briggs test* guarantees that we won't spill the merged node. The *George test* guarantees that we won't spill any other nodes unless they were already potential spill candidates in the original graph. We'll only coalesce two pseudoregisters if they pass the Briggs test. We'll coalesce a pseudoregister into a hard register if the two registers pass either test; we can be more permissive in this case because we already know that the hard register won't spill. Both tests are named after the people who invented them; you can find links to the papers that first proposed them in "Additional Resources" on page 669.

It's worth clarifying exactly what the conservative coalescing tests guarantee, because it's a little unintuitive. If you could completely prune the original graph without ever having to choose a spill candidate, these tests guarantee that the same will be true for the coalesced graph. In this case, we can say for sure that coalescing won't cause any spills.

But if you couldn't totally prune the original graph, it's harder to predict the impact of coalescing, because a lot of what happens after you pick a spill candidate comes down to chance. We saw an example of this earlier in the chapter, when we tried to color the graph in Figure 20-12; pruning nodes in a different order made the difference between being able to color a spill candidate and actually spilling it. Coalescing registers can have similar ripple effects. If we're unlucky, these effects might lead to a spill that we otherwise would have avoided.

In other words, if coloring the original graph required us to choose a spill candidate, coloring the coalesced graph might too—and at that point, it's impossible to say with any certainty what's going to happen. In this case, the conservative coalescing tests still give us two valuable guarantees. First, the coalesced node itself won't spill. Second, at the point where we get stuck and have to choose our first spill candidate, every node's degree will be the same or lower than it would have been when we got stuck if we hadn't performed coalescing. This means that, on balance, we're likely to successfully prune more nodes and spill fewer than we would have without coalescing.

Now we'll take a closer look at the Briggs and George tests. We'll define both of them and walk through some examples that demonstrate why they work.

The Briggs Test

Remember that a node has significant degree if it has k or more neighbors. The Briggs test allows us to merge two nodes if the merged node will have fewer than k neighbors with significant degree. When we color the graph, we'll be able to prune every neighbor with insignificant degree. The merged node itself will then have insignificant degree—it will have fewer than k neighbors left—so we'll be able to prune that node too.

Let's look at an example. Consider the interference graph in Figure 20-19.

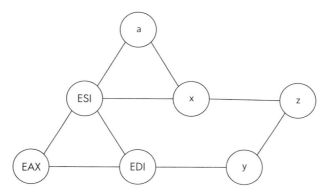

Figure 20-19: An interference graph before coalescing

Our coloring algorithm can prune this entire graph without any difficulty. Now let's apply the Briggs test to see if we can coalesce x into y. Figure 20-20 shows how the graph will look once we merge these two nodes together.

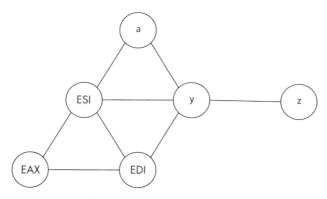

Figure 20-20: The graph in Figure 20-19 after merging x into y

After coalescing, y will have four neighbors: a, z, ESI, and EDI. Only two of these nodes, ESI and EDI, have significant degree. Since k is 3, this example passes the Briggs test. And in fact, we'll be able to prune y after we've pruned a and z, then finish pruning the rest of the graph like we did before.

Next, let's look at a case that fails the Briggs test. The graph in Figure 20-21 is almost identical to the one in Figure 20-19, except for an extra edge from a to EDI.

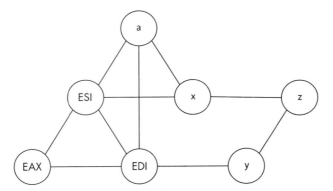

Figure 20-21: A variation on the graph in Figure 20-19 where x and y can no longer be coalesced

Even with this extra edge, our coloring algorithm can still prune the whole graph. But Figure 20-22 shows what happens when we coalesce x into y this time around.

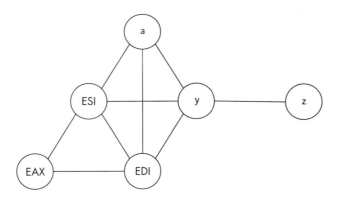

Figure 20-22: The graph in Figure 20-21 after merging x into y

Now y has three neighbors with significant degree: ESI, EDI, and a. This example fails the Briggs test, and y really is impossible to prune. After we prune z and EAX we'll get stuck, and we'll be forced to choose y or a as a spill candidate.

As these examples show us, the Briggs test stops us from transforming a colorable graph into an uncolorable one. It also gives us another guarantee: we'll never coalesce two nodes if the resulting node might spill. Take a look at Figure 20-23.

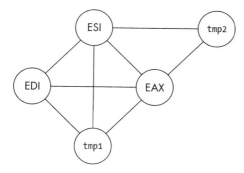

Figure 20-23: An interference graph where we can't coalesce tmp1 and tmp2

Suppose we want to coalesce `tmp2` into `tmp1`. This clearly won't make the graph harder to color; it will have the same effect on the interference graph as removing `tmp2` entirely. But coalescing these nodes is a bad idea for another reason. We won't be able to color `tmp1` whether we coalesce it with `tmp2` or not, so coalescing will just make things worse by increasing `tmp1`'s spill cost.

This example fails the Briggs test, since `tmp1` will have three neighbors with significant degree after coalescing (just like it did before coalescing). If we might not be able to color it, the Briggs test won't let us coalesce it.

Finally, let's tweak this example to illustrate one of the limits of the Briggs test. Imagine that we want to coalesce `tmp2` into EDI instead of `tmp1`. Like in our previous example, this won't make the graph harder to color. And this also fails the Briggs test, because EDI will have three neighbors with significant degree. But there's one important difference: as a hard register, EDI can't spill. This means that there's no downside to coalescing `tmp2` into EDI; it won't force us to spill EDI, and it won't make other nodes harder to color either. In cases like this, we'll use the George test to find coalescing opportunities that the Briggs test misses.

The George Test

When we coalesce a pseudoregister with a hard register, we know the coalesced register can't spill. Instead, we're worried about a slightly different outcome: if the hard register becomes more difficult to prune, its neighbors could become harder to prune too. Ultimately, this change could force us to spill nodes that we were able to color before. In cases that involve a hard register, we'll use both the Briggs test and the George test to identify as many coalescing opportunities as possible. The Briggs test proves that we can prune the merged node, so it won't interfere with attempts to color other nodes. The George test proves that we won't make the merged node's neighbors harder to prune (and therefore won't make those nodes or the rest of the graph more difficult to color), even if we can't prune the merged node itself. We can coalesce a pair of nodes that passes either of these tests.

The George test says that you can coalesce a pseudoregister *p* into a hard register *h* if each of *p*'s neighbors meets either of two conditions:

1. It has fewer than *k* neighbors.
2. It already interferes with *h*.

If a neighbor meets the first condition, we'll definitely be able to prune it when we color the graph. If it meets the second condition, it will have exactly the same neighbors as before (except for *p*) after coalescing, so we won't have made it any harder to prune; if anything, we might have made it easier.

Coalescing *h* and *p* won't make any of *h*'s neighbors harder to prune, either. The only way it could do that would be by preventing us from pruning *h* itself, but any new neighbors that *h* acquires through coalescing will have insignificant degree, so they won't affect our ability to prune it.

Let's take another look at the graph from Figure 20-23 to see why this works:

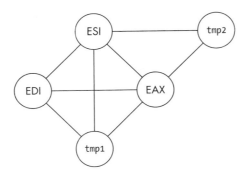

Earlier, we decided that coalescing tmp2 into EDI was safe, because EDI couldn't spill and this change wouldn't make any of the other nodes harder to color. But we also saw that this case failed the Briggs test, since EDI would then have three neighbors with significant degree. Now we'll try the George test instead. This test will pass, since both neighbors of tmp2 already interfere with EDI. Our allocator will coalesce tmp2 into EDI, since it coalesces moves that pass either of our two tests.

For our last example, let's revisit the graph from Figure 20-15:

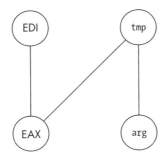

The last time we looked at this graph, we were considering whether to coalesce arg into EDI. Now we know that we shouldn't coalesce them, because this case doesn't pass either of our two tests. It fails the Briggs test because the coalesced node would have two neighbors with significant degree, tmp and EAX. It also fails the George test; arg's one neighbor, tmp, has significant degree and doesn't interfere with EDI. The George test tells us that tmp *might* become harder to color if we made this change; we'd be making it interfere with an additional register, and we don't know what impact that would have. In this small example, we can tell by looking at the graph that tmp actually would be harder to color if we coalesced arg into EDI, since it would interfere with both hard registers.

There's one ugly detail about the George test that I want to mention. Remember that we're using a quick, approximate method to update the graph after each coalescing decision. This approximate method might leave edges in the graph between registers that do not, in fact, interfere. As a result, when applying the George test to registers p and h, we might think that some neighbor n of p also interferes with h when it actually doesn't. We might then incorrectly conclude that p and h pass the George test and coalesce them.

That sounds pretty bad, but it only slightly weakens the guarantee that the George test provides. Earlier, I claimed that the George test guarantees that we won't make the merged node's neighbors harder to prune. It actually guarantees that we won't make them harder to prune than they were *before we started the current round of coalescing*—that is, the last time we rebuilt the interference graph from scratch.

This weaker guarantee still holds because our approximate graph will include an edge between n and h only if n did interfere with h when we built the interference graph, but some earlier coalescing decision removed that interference. Essentially, if an earlier coalescing decision made n or h easier to prune by removing the edge between them, we might accidentally make them more difficult to prune again by putting that edge back. However, we'll never make things worse than they were before the current round of coalescing. (It's also worth keeping in mind that the purpose of the Briggs and George tests is to improve performance, *not* to guarantee correctness; even a "bad" coalescing decision that fails both tests won't change the program's observable behavior.)

THE LIMITS OF THE BRIGGS AND GEORGE TESTS

The Briggs and George tests share a basic limitation: they both guess whether a node can be pruned by examining only the node and its neighbors, without considering its neighbors' neighbors, and their neighbors, and so on. That's not always enough information to recognize that we'll eventually be able to prune

(continued)

a node. The following interference graph illustrates the problem: it fails the Briggs test even though coalescing would be safe.

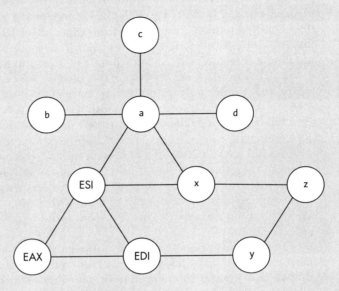

This graph is identical to the one in Figure 20-19, which we looked at when we discussed the Briggs test earlier, except that we've given a some extra neighbors. These extra neighbors don't impact our ability to color the graph, since we can prune all of them right away. Now let's try to coalesce x into y.

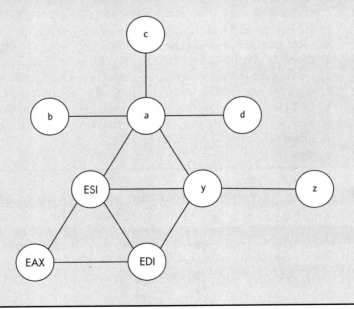

It's easy to see that this graph is still colorable. However, it fails the Briggs test because y now has three neighbors with significant degree: ESI, EDI, and a. If the test went one step further, we would see that ESI, EDI, and a themselves all have fewer than three neighbors with significant degree, so we'll be able to prune all of them—but it doesn't. Instead, it stops after considering y's immediate neighbors. The George test has exactly the same issue: it gets tripped up by nodes that have lots of neighbors to start with but that would have fewer than k neighbors after a few rounds of pruning.

The same paper that introduced the George test proposed an algorithm called *iterated register coalescing* to overcome this limitation. The gist of this technique is that you can alternate between pruning the graph and coalescing. After a round of pruning, the Briggs and George tests can often identify coalescing opportunities that they couldn't find before. For example, we could prune the nodes with insignificant degree from the first interference graph in this box and then apply the Briggs test to coalesce x and y. Iterated register coalescing is still a conservative approach, so it won't find every single coalescing opportunity, but it will catch many opportunities that our simpler strategy misses.

We've looked at both conservative coalescing tests, what guarantees they provide, and why they work. Now we just have to implement them.

Implementing Register Coalescing

Our first task is to add the build-coalesce loop to the top-level register allocation algorithm. Listing 20-31 gives the updated algorithm, with this addition bolded.

```
allocate_registers(instructions):
    while True:
        interference_graph = build_graph(instructions)
        coalesced_regs = coalesce(interference_graph, instructions)
        if nothing_was_coalesced(coalesced_regs):
            break
        instructions = rewrite_coalesced(instructions, coalesced_regs)
    add_spill_costs(interference_graph, instructions)
    color_graph(interference_graph)
    register_map = create_register_map(interference_graph)
    transformed_instructions = replace_pseudoregs(instructions, register_map)
    return transformed_instructions
```

Listing 20-31: Adding register coalescing to the top-level register allocation algorithm

Within this loop, we build the interference graph, then look for registers to coalesce. If we find any, we rewrite the assembly code and start the whole process again. Otherwise, we exit the loop and run the rest of the allocator as usual.

We record which registers we've coalesced together in coalesced_regs, which is a *disjoint-set* data structure. Let's write a simple implementation of this data structure; then we'll define the coalesce and rewrite_coalesced functions.

Disjoint Sets

As the name suggests, a disjoint-set data structure represents multiple disjoint sets of values. Each set is identified by one representative member. Disjoint sets support two operations: union merges two sets, and find looks up the representative member of a set. In our case, the values in each set are Reg and Pseudo operands. Initially, each register is in a set by itself. As we coalesce registers, we'll use the union operation to merge these sets together. When we rewrite the assembly code, we'll use find to replace each register with the representative member of its set.

There are a few different ways to implement disjoint sets. We'll use a simple implementation that's easy to understand. Listing 20-32 defines our implementation.

```
init_disjoint_sets():
  ❶ return <empty map>

union(x, y, reg_map):
  ❷ reg_map.add(x, y)

find(r, reg_map):
  ❸ if r is in reg_map:
        result = reg_map.get(r)
      ❹ return find(result, reg_map)
    return r

nothing_was_coalesced(reg_map):
  ❺ if reg_map is empty:
        return True
    return False
```

Listing 20-32: A basic implementation of disjoint sets

We use a map to track which sets have been merged together. At first, this map is empty ❶. To merge two sets whose representative members are x and y, the union operation inserts a mapping from x to y ❷. This makes y the representative member of the new set. When we coalesce a pseudoregister into a hard register, it's important to make the hard register the set's representative member; we don't want to replace hard registers with pseudoregisters when we rewrite the code later on.

To look up the representative member of the set that contains the register r, the find operation first checks whether r maps to some other register ❸. If it doesn't, r itself is the representative member of its set, so we return it. Otherwise, looking it up in the map will give us result, which is the register we merged r into previously. We then call find recursively ❹, which leads us up the chain of mappings from r to its representative member. For example, if we've merged a into b and then merged b into c, we'll follow the mappings from a to b to c to determine that c is the representative member for a.

The last operation we define in this listing is `nothing_was_coalesced`, which just checks whether the map is empty ❺.

The coalesce Function

The coalesce function will look at each `mov` instruction in the assembly code, deciding which registers to coalesce and keeping track of those decisions in the disjoint-set structure we just defined. Let's walk through Listing 20-33, which gives the pseudocode for this function.

```
coalesce(graph, instructions):
    coalesced_regs = init_disjoint_sets()

    for i in instructions:
        match i with
        | Mov(src, dst) ->
          ❶ src = find(src, coalesced_regs)
            dst = find(dst, coalesced_regs)

          ❷ if (src is in graph
                and dst is in graph
                and src != dst
              ❸ and (not are_neighbors(graph, src, dst))
              ❹ and conservative_coalesceable(graph, src, dst)):

                if src is a hard register:
                    to_keep = src
                    to_merge = dst
                else:
                    to_keep = dst
                    to_merge = src

              ❺ union(to_merge, to_keep, coalesced_regs)
                update_graph(graph, to_merge, to_keep)

        | _ -> continue

    return coalesced_regs
```

Listing 20-33: Deciding which registers to coalesce

We start by initializing a new disjoint-set structure, `coalesced_regs`, to track which registers we've coalesced. Then, we iterate through the instruction list. When we hit a `Mov` instruction, we use `find` to look up its current source and destination ❶, since we might have coalesced `src` and `dst` into other registers already. Note that these operands might be constants or memory addresses instead of registers. This is fine; if there's no mapping for x in `coalesced_regs`, `find(x, coalesced_regs)` just returns x, regardless of whether x is a register or some other kind of operand.

Next, we decide whether to coalesce the instruction's source and destination ❷. First, we check whether they're both in the interference graph. (This stops us from trying to coalesce constants or memory operands.)

We then make sure they're two different registers, since there's no reason to coalesce a register with itself. If these checks pass, we test the two conditions we learned about earlier: src and dst must not interfere ❸, and coalescing them must not make the graph harder to color ❹. We check the second of these conditions with the conservative_coalesceable function, which we'll come back to in a moment.

If src and dst meet all these conditions, we'll coalesce them! Now we have to figure out which one to keep in the assembly code and which one to replace. If either operand is a hard register, we'll keep that one and replace the other one. If they're both pseudoregisters, we'll arbitrarily choose to keep dst. We call union to actually coalesce these registers ❺, then we update the interference graph. Listing 20-34 defines the function that performs this update.

```
update_graph(graph, x, y):

    node_to_remove = get_node_by_id(graph, x)
    for neighbor in node_to_remove.neighbors:
        add_edge(graph, y, neighbor)
        remove_edge(graph, x, neighbor)

    remove_node_by_id(graph, x)
```

Listing 20-34: Updating the interference graph

This function takes each of x's neighbors, removes its edge to x, and adds an edge to y instead. Then, it removes x from the graph.

The conservative_coalesceable Function

Now that the rest of coalesce is in place, let's take a look at Listing 20-35, which defines the conservative coalescing tests.

```
conservative_coalesceable(graph, src, dst):
  ❶ if briggs_test(graph, src, dst):
        return True
  ❷ if src is a hard register:
        return george_test(graph, src, dst)
    if dst is a hard register:
        return george_test(graph, dst, src)
    return False

briggs_test(graph, x, y):
    significant_neighbors = 0

    x_node = get_node_by_id(graph, x)
    y_node = get_node_by_id(graph, y)

    combined_neighbors = set(x_node.neighbors)
    combined_neighbors.add_all(y_node.neighbors)
    for n in combined_neighbors:
        neighbor_node = get_node_by_id(graph, n)
```

```
   ❸ degree = length(neighbor_node.neighbors)
        if are_neighbors(graph, n, x) and are_neighbors(graph, n, y):
          ❹ degree -= 1
        if degree >= k:
            significant_neighbors += 1

  ❺ return (significant_neighbors < k)

george_test(graph, hardreg, pseudoreg):
    pseudo_node = get_node_by_id(graph, pseudoreg)
    for n in pseudo_node.neighbors:
      ❻ if are_neighbors(graph, n, hardreg):
            continue

        neighbor_node = get_node_by_id(graph, n)
      ❼ if length(neighbor_node.neighbors) < k:
            continue

        return False
    return True
```

Listing 20-35: The conservative coalescing tests

In `conservative_coalesceable`, we try the Briggs test first ❶. Then, if the Briggs test fails and either src or dst is a hard register, we try the George test ❷. When we use the George test, we'll make sure to pass the hard register as its first argument and the pseudoregister as its second, since it doesn't treat these registers interchangeably.

To apply the Briggs test, we first construct `combined_neighbors`, which is the set of nodes that interfere with either x or y. We then iterate through this set, looking up each neighbor's degree ❸. If a node interferes with both of them, coalescing x and y would decrease its degree by one, so we adjust degree accordingly ❹. We'll return True if fewer than *k* of the nodes in `combined_neighbors` have significant degree ❺.

To apply the George test, we iterate through the pseudoregister's neighbors, making sure each one either interferes with the hard register ❻ or has insignificant degree ❼. If we find a neighbor that doesn't satisfy either condition, we'll return False. If every neighbor meets both conditions, we'll return True.

The rewrite_coalesced Function

We'll wrap up by rewriting the assembly code. Listing 20-36 gives the pseudocode for this step.

```
rewrite_coalesced(instructions, coalesced_regs):
    new_instructions = []
    for i in instructions:
        match i with
        | Mov(src, dst) ->
            src = find(src, coalesced_regs)
            dst = find(dst, coalesced_regs)
```

```
❶ if src != dst:
        new_instructions.append(Mov(src, dst))
  | Binary(op, src, dst) ->
      src = find(src, coalesced_regs)
      dst = find(dst, coalesced_regs)
      new_instructions.append(Binary(op, src, dst))
  | --snip--

return new_instructions
```

Listing 20-36: Rewriting instructions after deciding which registers to coalesce

We use the `find` operation to replace each operand in each instruction. (Here, like in `coalesce`, we rely on `find` to handle non-registers correctly.) If a `Mov` instruction's updated source and destination are the same, we'll omit the instruction from the rewritten code ❶. As a side benefit, this will also remove any `Mov` instructions that were redundant before we coalesced registers.

And with that, you've finished your register allocator! We don't need to change any other passes, so you can go ahead and test it out.

TEST THE WHOLE COMPILER

If you completed only Part I, run:

```
$ ./test_compiler /path/to/your_compiler --chapter 20 --int-only
```

If you also completed Part II, run:

```
$ ./test_compiler /path/to/your_compiler --chapter 20
```

These commands run the same test programs as the earlier commands with the --no-coalescing option, and they perform the same validation, except that they also validate the assembly output for the programs in *tests/chapter_20/int_only/with_coalescing* and (for the second command) *tests/chapter_20/all_types/with_coalescing* to make sure you're coalescing registers properly.

Summary

In this chapter, you built a register allocator. You used everything you'd already learned about liveness analysis to build an interference graph, and then you implemented a classic graph coloring algorithm to color it. You introduced callee-saved registers and learned how to save and restore them. Then, you used register coalescing to clean up the mess that earlier stages of the compiler left behind. You've written your last optimization and completed the project!

Over the course of this book, you've built an impressive piece of software: an optimizing compiler for a substantial chunk of the C language. You've covered a lot of ground, from the intricacies of the C standard to the gory details of the System V calling convention to the fundamentals of data-flow analysis. But if you want to push your compiler even further, you have plenty of options. I'll close out this part of the book with a few ideas for what to work on next.

Additional Resources

The register allocator you built in this chapter uses a simplified version of the classic *Chaitin-Briggs algorithm.* This section tells you where to find the original papers about this algorithm, a couple of textbook chapters that present them in a more approachable way, and some other useful references on more specific topics.

Key papers

- "Register Allocation via Coloring," a 1981 paper by Gregory Chaitin et al., described the original graph coloring register allocator (*https:// doi.org/10.1016/0096-0551(81)90048-5*). It introduced most of the fundamental concepts in this chapter, including how to build and color an interference graph.

- Chaitin published an updated description of the same allocator, "Register Allocation & Spilling via Graph Coloring," in 1982 (*https://doi.org/10.1145/ 872726.806984*).

- "Improvements to Graph Coloring Register Allocation," a 1994 paper by Preston Briggs, Keith Cooper, and Linda Torczon, describes an improved version of Chaitin's design (*https://doi.org/10.1145/177492 .177575*). The name *Chaitin-Briggs* refers to this improved algorithm. This paper presented the technique of putting spill candidates on the stack and trying to color them later instead of spilling them immediately. (Briggs et al. call this technique *optimistic coloring.*) It also introduced the Briggs test and the general concept of conservative coalescing; Chaitin's original design coalesced aggressively, even when it made the graph harder to color. This paper described some techniques that we didn't cover in this chapter, like rematerialization, as well.

Textbook chapters

- Chapter 16 of Steven Muchnick's *Advanced Compiler Design and Implementation* (Morgan Kaufmann, 1997) presents a register allocator that uses an algorithm similar to Chaitin-Briggs. The most notable difference is that it doesn't use conservative coalescing; like Chaitin's original allocator, it coalesces aggressively. I found Muchnick's explanations of how to include hard registers in the interference graph, how to detect interference, and the overall structure of the allocator especially useful.

- Chapter 13 of Keith Cooper and Linda Torczon's *Engineering a Compiler,* 2nd edition (Morgan Kaufmann, 2011), provides an excellent overview of a wide range of approaches to register allocation, including the Chaitin-Briggs algorithm and several others that we didn't discuss here. I've drawn on their definition of interference and their discussion of how to update the interference graph while coalescing; they provide a particularly helpful explanation of why both fast, imprecise updates and slow, complete updates are needed. (You can also consult the third edition of this book, published in 2022.)

NOTE *These are both good resources if you want to implement the parts of Chaitin-Briggs that we skipped. The chapter by Muchnick is particularly useful if you want to integrate spill code generation into your register allocator. Both books discuss how to use live ranges (which Muchnick calls* webs) *instead of pseudoregisters as the nodes in your interference graph, and both provide better spill cost metrics than the one we used.*

Conservative coalescing

- The George test comes from "Iterated Register Coalescing," by Lal George and Andrew Appel (*https://doi.org/10.1145/229542.229546*). The main point of the paper is that you can coalesce more registers if you alternate between coalescing and pruning; the George test is presented as a minor implementation detail.

- For an informal discussion of the George and Briggs tests with lots of examples, see the slides from Phillip Gibbons's course on compiler optimizations at Carnegie Mellon (*https://www.cs.cmu.edu/afs/cs/academic/class/15745-s19/www/lectures/L23-Register-Coalescing.pdf*).

- "Comparing Conservative Coalescing Criteria" by Max Hailperin rigorously defines what the Briggs and George tests actually prove, which is something that the authors of the original papers never bothered to do (*https://doi.org/10.1145/1065887.1065894*). My discussion of what these tests guarantee at the start of "Conservative Coalescing" on page 656 relies heavily on Hailperin's paper. Note that some of his claims don't apply to our graph coloring implementation because he uses precoloring and we don't.

Identifying loops

To calculate more accurate spill costs, you need to detect the loops in your program. These resources talk about how to identify loops:

- Chapter 9, section 6, of *Compilers: Principles, Techniques, and Tools*, 2nd edition, by Alfred Aho et al. (Addison-Wesley, 2006).

- Phillip Gibbons's lecture slides on induction variable optimizations, from his Carnegie Mellon compiler optimizations course (*https://www.cs.cmu.edu/afs/cs/academic/class/15745-s19/www/lectures/L8-Induction-Variables.pdf*). This is a great starting point, but the slides aren't detailed enough to use as a stand-alone guide to loop analysis. You might want to use them alongside the previous reference or another textbook.

NEXT STEPS

The world of programming languages is wide, and there's a lot more for you to explore. Extending your compiler on your own is a great way to keep learning about the topics you're most interested in.

I'll leave you with a few ideas to get you started.

Add Some Missing Features

The most obvious next step is to implement the major parts of C that this book didn't cover. If you already have a list of features you're particularly excited to add, start with those. Then, if you want to keep going, pick a real-world C program—think something small, not the Linux kernel—and build out your compiler until it can compile that program successfully. You can choose another program and repeat this process until you're satisfied with how much of the language you've implemented. Make sure to add new language features one at a time, testing each one thoroughly before moving on to the next one.

Handle Undefined Behavior Safely

We've seen that C compilers can deal with undefined behavior however they like. But just because you *can* do something doesn't mean you *should*. There are huge benefits to dealing with undefined behavior in a clean, predictable way: it makes C programs more secure, easier to debug, and less terrifying in general. For example, you could guarantee that signed integer overflow always wraps around (this is what the -fwrapv compiler option does). Or you could have the program raise an error and exit when it encounters undefined behavior; Clang and GCC both have a feature called UndefinedBehaviorSanitizer that supports this sort of error handling (*https://clang.llvm.org/docs/UndefinedBehaviorSanitizer.html*).

Think about a few examples of undefined behavior that we discussed in this book. How do you think your compiler should handle them? How would that impact any optimizations you've implemented? Some types of undefined behavior are tricky to detect, but others aren't too difficult to deal with; choose one that seems manageable and see if you can handle it cleanly.

Write More TACKY Optimizations

Chapter 19 covered just a few of the IR optimizations you'd find in a production compiler. If you like, you can implement more on your own. Do some research on common compiler optimizations and pick the ones that sound most interesting. If you go this route, you may want to convert your TACKY code into *static single assignment (SSA) form*, where every variable is defined exactly once. SSA form is widely used in real-world compilers, including Clang and GCC, because it makes many optimizations easier to implement.

Support Another Target Architecture

Most production compilers have several different backends to support different target architectures.

You can use the same strategy, converting TACKY into different assembly code depending on which system you're targeting. If you use a Windows or ARM system and needed a virtualization or emulation layer to complete this project, a new backend would let you compile code that runs natively on your machine.

If you add support for Windows, you'll be able to reuse most of your existing code generation pass. Only the ABI will be different. Adding an ARM backend is a more ambitious project; you'll need to learn a completely new instruction set.

Contribute to an Open Source Programming Language Project

Improving your own compiler is a great way to learn, but consider branching out and working on other projects too. Many widely used compilers are open source and welcome new contributors. The same goes for a whole range of related projects, like interpreters, linters, and static analysis tools. Pick one that you like, and find out how to get involved. This is a great way to put your new skills to work and maybe even make your favorite programming language a little faster, safer, more usable, or easier to learn.

That's a Wrap!

I hope this book has laid the foundation for you to keep building compilers and programming languages. I also hope it's changed your perspective on the programming languages you use day to day. You'll now be better able to appreciate the care, effort, and ingenuity that went into creating those languages, and when things go wrong, you won't be afraid to dig into the language internals to figure out what's really happening. Compilers will stop seeming like magic and start to look like something much more interesting: ordinary software.

A

DEBUGGING ASSEMBLY CODE WITH GDB OR LLDB

At some point, your compiler is going to generate assembly code that doesn't behave correctly, and you'll need to figure out why. When that happens, a command line debugger is indispensable for understanding what's going wrong. A debugger lets you pause a running program, step through it one instruction at a time, and examine the program state at different points. You can use either GDB (the GNU debugger) or LLDB (the debugger from the LLVM Project) to debug the assembly code your compiler generates. I recommend using GDB if you're on Linux and LLDB if you're on macOS (I think GDB has a slightly nicer UI for working with assembly, but getting it to run on macOS can be a challenge).

This appendix is a brief guide to debugging assembly programs with GDB or LLDB. It introduces the basics that you'll need to know if you've never used a debugger before. It also covers the most important commands and options that you'll need to use to work with assembly code in particular, which may be new to you even if you're comfortable using these tools to debug source code. I've included separate walk-throughs for the two debuggers; even though they have very similar functionality, the details of many commands are different. Follow the walk-through for whichever debugger you're using.

Before you get started, you should be familiar with the basics of assembly code covered in Chapters 1 and 2. A few aspects of assembly from later chapters will also come up, but you can gloss over those if you haven't gotten to them yet.

The Program

We'll use the assembly program in Listing A-1 as a running example.

```
        .data
        .align 4
❶ integer:
        .long 100
        .align 8
❷ dbl:
        .double 3.5
        .text
        .globl main
❸ main:
        pushq   %rbp
        movq    %rsp, %rbp
        subq    $16, %rsp
        # call a function
❹ callq   f
❺ # put some stuff in registers
        movl    $0x87654321, %eax
        movsd   dbl(%rip), %xmm0
        # put some stuff on the stack
        movl    $0xdeadbeef, -4(%rbp)
        movl    $0, -8(%rbp)
        movl    $-1, -12(%rbp)
        movl    $0xfeedface, -16(%rbp)
❻ # initialize loop counter
        movl    $25, %ecx
.L_loop_start:
        # decrement counter
        subl    $1, %ecx
        cmpl    $0, %ecx
        # jump back to start of loop
        jne     .L_loop_start
        # return 0
        movl    $0, %eax
```

```
        movq    %rbp, %rsp
        popq    %rbp
        ret
        .text
        .globl  f
f:
        movl    $1, %eax
        ret
        .section .note.GNU-stack,"",@progbits
```

Listing A-1: A pointless assembly program

This program doesn't do anything useful; it just gives us the opportunity to try out the most important features of the debuggers. It includes a couple of static variables for us to inspect: integer ❶ and dbl ❷. In main ❸, it first calls a very small function, f, so we can practice stepping into and out of function calls ❹, then moves some data into registers and onto the stack so we can practice examining the state of the program ❺. It ends with a loop that decrements ECX on every iteration, stopping once it reaches 0 ❻. We'll use this loop to practice setting conditional breakpoints.

Download this program from *https://norasandler.com/book/#appendix-a*, then save it as *hello_debugger.s.* There are two different versions of this file for Linux and macOS, so make sure to pick the right one for your operating system.

Once you've saved the file, assemble and link it and confirm that it runs:

```
$ gcc hello_debugger.s -o hello_debugger
$ ./hello_debugger
```

On macOS, include the -g option when you assemble and link the file:

```
$ gcc -g hello_debugger.s -o hello_debugger
```

The -g option generates extra debug information. Make sure to include it when assembling and linking your own compiler's assembly output for debugging too.

Now you can start the walk-through. If you're using GDB, follow the walk-through in the next section. If you're using LLDB, skip to "Debugging with LLDB" on page 687.

Debugging with GDB

Run this command to start up GDB:

```
$ gdb hello_debugger
--snip--
(gdb)
```

This sets hello_debugger as the executable to debug but doesn't actually execute it. Before we start running this executable, let's configure the UI to make working with assembly code easier.

Configuring the GDB UI

During a GDB session, you can open up different text windows that display different information about the running program. For our purposes, the most important of these is the *assembly window*, which displays the assembly code as we step through it. The *register window* is also useful; by default, it shows the current contents of every general-purpose register.

The layout command controls which windows are visible. Let's open up the assembly and register windows:

```
(gdb) layout asm
(gdb) layout reg
```

You should now see three windows in your terminal: the register window, the assembly window, and the command window with the (gdb) prompt. It should look similar to Figure A-1.

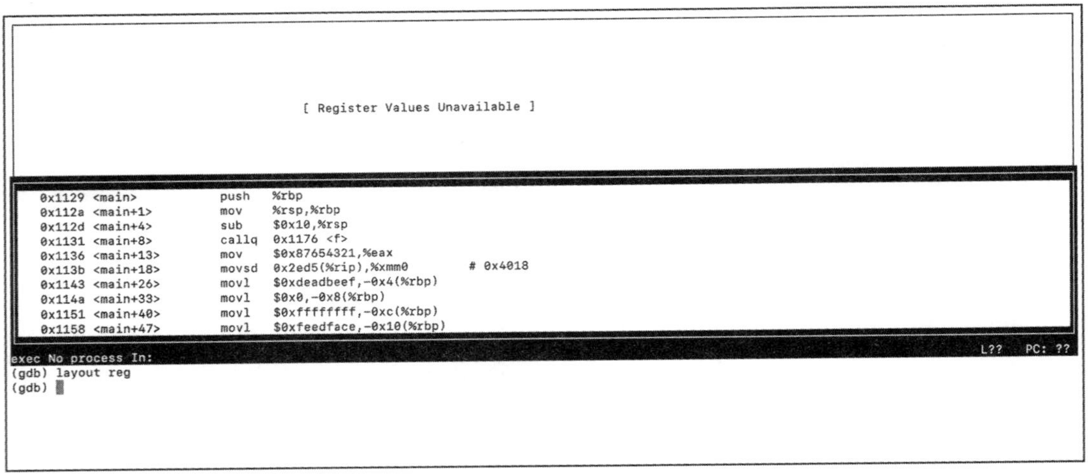

```
                              [ Register Values Unavailable ]




  0x1129 <main>          push   %rbp
  0x112a <main+1>        mov    %rsp,%rbp
  0x112d <main+4>        sub    $0x10,%rsp
  0x1131 <main+8>        callq  0x1176 <f>
  0x1136 <main+13>       mov    $0x87654321,%eax
  0x113b <main+18>       movsd  0x2ed5(%rip),%xmm0        # 0x4018
  0x1143 <main+26>       movl   $0xdeadbeef,-0x4(%rbp)
  0x114a <main+33>       movl   $0x0,-0x8(%rbp)
  0x1151 <main+40>       movl   $0xffffffff,-0xc(%rbp)
  0x1158 <main+47>       movl   $0xfeedface,-0x10(%rbp)
exec No process In:                                                       L??   PC: ??
(gdb) layout reg
(gdb) █
```

Figure A-1: A GDB session with the assembly and register windows open

The register window won't display any information until you start the program.

You can scroll in whichever window is currently in focus. Use the focus command to change the in-focus window:

```
(gdb) focus cmd
(gdb) focus asm
(gdb) focus regs
```

Starting and Stopping the Program

Next, we'll set a *breakpoint*—a location where the debugger will pause the program—and run the program up to that breakpoint. If we start the program without setting a breakpoint first, it will run all the way through without stopping, which isn't very useful.

The command break `<function name>` sets a breakpoint at the start of a function. Let's set a breakpoint at the entrance to main:

```
(gdb) break main
Breakpoint 1 at 0x112d
```

Now let's start the program:

```
(gdb) run
Starting program: /home/ubuntu/hello_debugger
```

❶ Breakpoint 1, 0x000055555555512d in main ()

The output of this command tells us that the program has hit the breakpoint we just set ❶. Notice that the current instruction is highlighted in the assembly window and the current values of the general-purpose registers are displayed in the register window, as shown in Figure A-2.

```
┌─Register group: general──────────────────────────────────────────────────────────────────────────┐
│rax          0x555555555129      93824992235817              rbx      0x555555555180      93824992235904
│rcx          0x555555555180      93824992235904              rdx      0x7fffffffe3b8      140737488348088
│rsi          0x7fffffffe3a8      140737488348072             rdi      0x1                 1
│rbp          0x7fffffffe2b0      0x7fffffffe2b0              rsp      0x7fffffffe2b0      0x7fffffffe2b0
│r8           0x0                 0                           r9       0x7ffff7fe0d50      140737354009936
│r10          0x0                 0                           r11      0x0                 0
│r12          0x555555555040      93824992235584              r13      0x7fffffffe3a0      140737488348064
│r14          0x0                 0                           r15      0x0                 0
│rip          0x55555555512d      0x55555555512d <main+4>     eflags   0x246               [ PF ZF IF ]
│cs           0x33                51                          ss       0x2b                43
└────────────────────────────────────────────────────────────────────────────────────────────────────┘
   0x555555555129 <main>       push    %rbp
   0x55555555512a <main+1>     mov     %rsp,%rbp
B+>0x55555555512d <main+4>     sub     $0x10,%rsp
   0x555555555131 <main+8>     callq   0x555555555176 <f>
   0x555555555136 <main+13>    mov     $0x87654321,%eax
   0x55555555513b <main+18>    movsd   0x2ed5(%rip),%xmm0        # 0x555555558018
   0x555555555143 <main+26>    movl    $0xdeadbeef,-0x4(%rbp)
   0x55555555514a <main+33>    movl    $0x0,-0x8(%rbp)
   0x555555555151 <main+40>    movl    $0xffffffff,-0xc(%rbp)
   0x555555555158 <main+47>    movl    $0xfeedface,-0x10(%rbp)
native process 93349 In: main                                        L??    PC: 0x55555555512d
(gdb) break main
Breakpoint 1 at 0x112d
(gdb) run
Starting program: /home/ubuntu/hello_debugger

Breakpoint 1, 0x000055555555512d in main ()
(gdb) ▋
```

Figure A-2: A GDB session when the program is stopped at a breakpoint

Once a program is paused, there are a few commands you can use to move it forward:

continue resumes the program and runs until we hit another breakpoint or exit.

finish resumes the program and pauses again when we return from the current function.

stepi executes the next instruction, then pauses. It steps into call instructions, pausing at the first instruction in the callee. The command stepi <n> will execute *n* instructions.

nexti executes the next instruction, then pauses. It steps over call instructions, pausing at the next instruction after call in the current function. The command nexti <n> will execute *n* instructions.

Most GDB instructions can be abbreviated to one or two letters: you can type c instead of continue, b instead of break, si instead of stepi, and so on. Table A-1 on page 687 gives full and shortened versions of all the commands we discuss.

WARNING   *While the nexti and stepi commands step through assembly instructions, the next and step commands step through lines in the original source file. Since we don't have any information about the original source file, entering one of these commands will run the program until the end of the current function. These commands are abbreviated to n and s, respectively, so it's easy to run them by accident when you meant to use nexti or stepi.*

Let's try out our new commands. First, we'll execute two instructions, which should take us into the call to f:

```
(gdb) stepi 2
0x0000555555555176 in ❶ f ()
```

We can see from the command output ❶ and from the highlighted instruction in the assembly window that we're stopped in f instead of main. Next, we'll return from f:

```
(gdb) finish
Run till exit from #0  0x0000555555555176 in f ()
0x0000555555555136 in main ()
```

We're now back in main, at the instruction right after callq. Let's continue:

```
(gdb) continue
Continuing.
[Inferior 1 (process 82326) exited normally]
```

Since we didn't hit any more breakpoints, the program ran until it exited. To keep debugging it, we'll have to restart it:

```
(gdb) run
Starting program: /home/ubuntu/hello_debugger

Breakpoint 1, 0x000055555555512d in main ()
```

Now we're paused at the start of main again. We'll step forward two instructions one more time, but this time we'll use nexti to step over f instead of stepping into it:

```
(gdb) nexti 2
0x0000555555555136 in main ()
```

This puts us back at the instruction right after callq.

Setting Breakpoints by Address

In addition to setting breakpoints on functions, you can break on specific machine instructions. Let's set a breakpoint on the instruction movl 0xdeadbeef, -4(%rbp). First, we'll find this instruction in the assembly window. It should look something like this:

❶ 0x555555555143 ❷ <main+26>   movl   0xdeadbeef, -4(%rbp)

The instruction's address in memory is at the beginning of the line ❶, followed by the byte offset of that address from the start of the function ❷. The exact address may be different on your machine, but the offset should be the same. To set this breakpoint, you can type either

```
(gdb) break *main+26
```

or

```
(gdb) break *MEMORY_ADDRESS
```

where MEMORY_ADDRESS is the address you found in the assembly window. The * symbol tells GDB that we're specifying an exact address rather than a function name.

Managing Breakpoints

Let's list all the breakpoints we've set:

```
(gdb) info break
Num     Type           Disp Enb Address            What
1       breakpoint     keep y   0x000055555555512d <main+4>
        breakpoint already hit 1 time
2       breakpoint     keep y   0x0000555555555143 <main+26>
```

Every breakpoint has a unique number, which you can refer to if you need to delete, disable, or modify it. Let's delete breakpoint 1:

```
(gdb) delete 1
```

Next, we'll look at a couple of different ways to examine the program's state.

Printing Expressions

You can print out expressions with the command print/*<format>* *<expr>*, where:

> *<format>* is a one-letter format specifier. You can use most of the same format specifiers you'd use in printf: x to display a value as a hexadecimal integer, d to display it as a signed integer, and so on.

> *<expr>* is an arbitrary expression. This expression can refer to registers, memory addresses, and symbols in the running program. It can also include C operations like arithmetic, pointer dereferencing, and cast expressions.

Let's try some examples. Right now, the program should be paused at the instruction movl 0x87654321, %eax. We'll step through this instruction, then print out the value of EAX in a few different formats:

```
(gdb) stepi
--snip--
(gdb) print $eax
$1 = ❶ -2023406815
(gdb) print/x $eax
$2 = ❷ 0x87654321
(gdb) print/u $eax
$3 = ❸ 2271560481
```

By default, GDB formats the values in general-purpose registers as signed integers ❶. Here, we also display the value in EAX in hexadecimal ❷ and as an unsigned integer ❸. The symbols $1, $2, and so on are *convenience variables*, which GDB automatically generates to store the result of each expression.

You can find the full list of format specifiers in the documentation for the x command, which we'll talk more about in a moment:

```
(gdb) help x
--snip--
Format letters are o(octal), x(hex), d(decimal), u(unsigned decimal),
  t(binary), f(float), a(address), i(instruction), c(char), s(string)
  and z(hex, zero padded on the left).
--snip--
```

Chapter 13 introduces the XMM registers, which hold floating-point values. The next instruction in our program, movsd dbl(%rip), %xmm0, copies the value 3.5 from the static dbl variable into XMM0.

Let's step through this instruction, then inspect XMM0:

```
(gdb) stepi
--snip--
(gdb) print $xmm0
$4 = {v4_float = {0, 2.1875, 0, 0}, v2_double = {3.5, 0}, v16_int8 = {0, 0, 0, 0,
0, 0, 12, 64, 0, 0, 0, 0, 0, 0, 0, 0}, v8_int16 = {0, 0, 0, 16396, 0, 0, 0, 0},
```

```
v4_int32 = {0, 1074528256, 0, 0}, v2_int64 = {4615063718147915776, 0}, uint128 =
4615063718147915776}
```

GDB is showing us lots of different views of the same data: `v4_float` displays this register's contents as an array of four 32-bit floats, `v2_double` displays it as an array of 64-bit doubles, and so on. Since we'll use XMM registers only to store individual doubles, you can always examine them with a command like this:

```
(gdb) print $xmm0.v2_double[0]
$5 = 3.5
```

This prints out the value in the register's lower 64 bits, interpreted as a double.

In addition to registers, we can print out the values of objects in the symbol table. Let's inspect the two static variables in this program, `integer` and `dbl`:

```
(gdb) print (long) integer
$6 = 100
(gdb) print (double) dbl
$7 = 3.5
```

Since GDB doesn't have any information about these objects' types, we have to cast them to the correct type explicitly.

Let's look at a few examples of more complex expressions. Aside from the fact that they refer directly to hardware registers, these expressions all use ordinary C syntax.

We can perform basic arithmetic:

```
(gdb) print/x $eax + 0x10
$8 = 0x87654331
```

We can call functions that are defined in the current program or the standard library. Here, we call `f`, which returns `1`:

```
(gdb) print (int) f()
$9 = 1
```

We can also dereference pointers. Let's execute the next instruction, `movl 0xdeadbeef, -4(%rbp)`, then inspect the value at `-4(%rbp)`:

```
(gdb) stepi
--snip--
(gdb) print/x *(int *)($rbp - 4)
$10 = 0xdeadbeef
```

First, we calculate the memory address we want to inspect, `$rbp - 4`. Then, we cast this address to the correct pointer type, `(int *)`. Finally, we dereference it with the dereference operator, *. This produces an integer, which we print out in hexadecimal with the /x specifier.

Next, we'll look at a more flexible way to inspect values in memory.

Examining Memory

We can examine memory with the command x/<n><format><unit> <expr>, where:

<n> is the number of units of memory to display (given the unit size specified by <unit>).

<format> specifies how to format each unit. These are the same format specifiers we used in the print command.

<unit> is a one-letter specifier for the size of a unit: b for a byte, h for a 2-byte halfword, w for a 4-byte word, or g for an 8-byte "giant" word.

<expr> is an arbitrary expression that evaluates to some valid memory address. These are the same kinds of expressions we can use in the print command.

Let's use the x command to inspect the integer at -4(%rbp):

```
(gdb) x/1xw ($rbp - 4)
❶ 0x7fffffffe2ac: ❷ 0xdeadbeef
```

This command tells GDB to print out one 4-byte word in hexadecimal. The output includes both the memory address ❶ and the value at that address ❷.

The next three instructions in Listing A-1 store three more integers on the stack:

```
movl    $0, -8(%rbp)
movl    $-1, -12(%rbp)
movl    $0xfeedface, -16(%rbp)
```

We'll use the commands in Listing A-2 to step through these instructions, then print out the whole stack frame.

```
(gdb) stepi 3
(gdb) x/6xw $rsp
0x7fffffffe2a0: ❶ 0xfeedface     0xffffffff    0x00000000    ❷ 0xdeadbeef
0x7fffffffe2b0: ❸ 0x00000000     0x00000000
```

Listing A-2: Stepping forward three instructions, then printing out the current stack frame

The command x/6xw $rsp tells GDB to print out six 4-byte words, starting at the address in RSP. We print out six words because the stack frame for this particular function is 24 bytes. At the start of main, we saved the old value of RBP onto the stack. That's 8 bytes. Then, we allocated another 16 bytes with the command subq $16, %rsp. Keep in mind that RSP always holds the address of the top of the stack, which is the *lowest* stack address.

This command displays the four integers we saved to the stack, with 0xfeedface at the top ❶ and 0xdeadbeef at the bottom ❷, followed by the old value of RBP ❸. On some systems, this value will be 0 because we're in the outermost stack frame; on others, it will be a valid memory address.

The saved value of RBP is at the bottom of the current stack frame. Right after it, on top of the *caller's* stack frame, we'll find the caller's return address—that is, the address we'll jump to when we return from main. (We covered this in detail when we implemented function calls in Chapter 9.) Let's inspect this return address:

```
(gdb) x/4ag $rsp
0x7fffffffe2a0: 0xfffffffffeedface      0xdeadbeef00000000
0x7fffffffe2b0: 0x0      ❶ 0x7ffff7dee083 <__libc_start_main+243>
```

This command will print out four 8-byte "giant" words, starting with the value at the address in RSP. The a specifier tells GDB to format these values as memory addresses; this means it will print each address in hexadecimal and, if possible, print out its offset from the nearest symbol in the program. Because function and static variable names are defined in the symbol table, GDB can display the relative offsets of assembly instructions and static data. It won't display relative offsets of stack addresses, heap addresses, or invalid addresses, because they would be completely meaningless.

The first line of output includes the four integers we saved onto the stack, now displayed as two 8-byte values instead of four 4-byte values. The null pointer 0x0 on the next line is the saved value of RBP. None of these three 8-byte values are valid addresses, so GDB can't display their offsets from symbols. The next value on the stack is the return address ❶. GDB tells us that this is the address of an instruction in _libc_start_main, the standard library function responsible for calling main and cleaning up after it exits.

The a specifier makes it easy to spot return addresses and pointers to static variables. This is particularly useful if your program's stack frame is corrupted; finding each stack frame's return address can help you get your bearings.

Setting Conditional Breakpoints

To wrap up this walk-through, we'll look at how to set *conditional breakpoints*. The program will pause at a conditional breakpoint only if the associated condition is true. This condition can be an arbitrary expression; GDB will consider it false if it evaluates to 0 and true otherwise.

Let's set a breakpoint on the jne instruction at the end of the last loop iteration in hello_debugger. First, we need to find this instruction in the assembly window. It should be 65 bytes after the start of the function:

```
0x55555555516a <main+65>      jne      0x555555555164 <main+59>
```

We'll set a conditional breakpoint to pause on this instruction if ECX is 0:

```
(gdb) break *main+65 if $ecx == 0
```

Since this loop repeats until ECX is 0, the condition $ecx == 0 will be true only on the last iteration. Let's continue until this breakpoint, then verify that the condition is true:

```
(gdb) c
Continuing.

Breakpoint 3, 0x000055555555516a in main ()
(gdb) print $ecx
$11 = 0
```

So far, so good. If you get a different value for ECX, check whether you set the breakpoint correctly:

```
(gdb) info break
--snip--
3        breakpoint     keep y    0x000055555555516a ❶ <main+65>
         stop only if ❷ $ecx == 0
```

Make sure that your breakpoint is at the location main+65 ❶ and that it includes the condition $ecx == 0 ❷. If your breakpoint looks different, you might have mistyped something; delete it and try again.

We should be on the last loop iteration, so let's step forward one instruction and make sure that the jump isn't taken:

```
(gdb) stepi
```

Usually, jne will jump back to the start of the loop, but on the last iteration it moves forward to the next instruction.

Getting Help

To learn about commands and options that we didn't cover here, see the GDB documentation at *https://sourceware.org/gdb/current/onlinedocs/gdb/index.html*. As you saw earlier, you can also type help at the prompt to learn more about any GDB command. For example, to see the documentation for the run command, type:

```
(gdb) help run
Start debugged program.
You may specify arguments to give it.
--snip--
```

Table A-1 summarizes the commands and options we covered, including full and abbreviated forms for each command (except x, which can't be abbreviated any further). Both forms take the same arguments.

Table A-1: A Summary of GDB Commands

Command	Description
run r	Start the program.
continue c	Resume the program.
finish fin	Resume the program and continue until the current function exits.
stepi [<n>] si	Execute one instruction (or n instructions), stepping into function calls.
nexti [<n>] ni	Execute one instruction (or n instructions), stepping over function calls.
break <loc> [if <cond>] b	Set a breakpoint at <loc> (conditional on <cond>, if provided).
info break i b	List all breakpoints. (Other info subcommands display other information.)
delete [<id>] d	Delete all breakpoints (or the breakpoint specified by <id>).
print/<format> <expr> p	Evaluate <expr> and display the result according to format specifier <format>.
x/<n><format><unit> <addr>	Print out memory starting at <addr> in n chunks of size <unit>, formatted according to <format>.
layout <window> la	Open <window>.
focus <window> fs	Change focus to <window>.
help <cmd> h	Display help text about <cmd>.

Now you're ready to start debugging with GDB!

Debugging with LLDB

Run this command to start up LLDB:

```
$ lldb hello_debugger
(lldb) target create "hello_debugger"
Current executable set to 'hello_debugger' (x86_64).
(lldb)
```

This will set hello_debugger as the executable to debug but won't execute it yet. If prompted, enter your username and password to give LLDB permission to control hello_debugger.

Starting and Stopping the Program

Next, we'll set a *breakpoint*—a location where the debugger will pause the program—and run the program up to that breakpoint. If we start the program without setting a breakpoint first, it will run all the way through without stopping, which isn't very useful.

Let's set a breakpoint at the entrance to main:

```
(lldb) break set -n main
Breakpoint 1: where = hello_debugger`main, address = 0x0000000100003f65
```

Note that main may be at a different memory address on your machine. The break set command creates a new breakpoint; the -n option specifies the name of the function where we want to break. We'll look at other ways to set breakpoints in a moment.

Now let's run the program:

```
(lldb) run
Process 6750 launched: '/Users/me/hello_debugger' (x86_64)
Process 6750 stopped
* thread #1, queue = 'com.apple.main-thread', ❶ stop reason = breakpoint 1.1
    frame #0: 0x0000000100003f65 hello_debugger`main
❷ hello_debugger`main:
❸ ->  0x100003f65 <+0>: pushq   %rbp
      0x100003f66 <+1>: movq    %rsp, %rbp
      0x100003f69 <+4>: subq    $0x10, %rsp
      0x100003f6d <+8>: callq   0x100003fb2              ; f
Target 0: (hello_debugger) stopped.
(lldb)
```

The stop reason ❶ tells us that the program has hit the breakpoint we just set. LLDB also helpfully tells us that we're stopped in the main function in hello_debugger ❷ and prints out the next few assembly instructions ❸.

Once a program is paused, there are a few commands we can use to keep executing it:

continue resumes the program and runs until we hit another breakpoint or exit.

finish resumes the program and pauses again when we return from the current function.

stepi executes the next instruction, then pauses. It steps into call instructions, pausing at the first instruction in the callee. The command stepi -c <*n*> steps through *n* instructions.

nexti executes the next instruction, then pauses. It steps over call instructions, pausing at the next instruction after call in the current function. The command nexti -c <*n*> steps through *n* instructions.

Most LLDB commands have several aliases. For example, `continue` is a shortcut for `process continue`, and it can be shortened even further to the one-letter command c. See Table A-2 on page 697 for full and abbreviated versions of all the commands we cover.

Let's try out these new commands. First, we'll execute four instructions, which should take us into the call to f:

```
(lldb) stepi -c 4
--snip--
❶ hello_debugger`f:
-> 0x100003fb2 <+0>: movl    $0x1, %eax
--snip--
```

We can see from the command output that we're stopped in f instead of main ❶. Now we'll return from f:

```
(lldb) finish
--snip--
hello_debugger`main:
-> 0x100003f72 <+13>: movl    $0x87654321, %eax          ; imm = 0x87654321
--snip--
```

This puts us back in main, at the instruction right after `callq`. Let's continue:

```
(lldb) continue
Process 6750 resuming
Process 6750 exited with status = 0 (0x00000000)
```

Since we didn't hit any more breakpoints, the program ran until it exited. To keep debugging it, we have to restart it:

```
(lldb) run
```

Now we're paused at the start of main again. Once again, we'll move forward four instructions, but this time we'll use `nexti` to step over f instead of stepping into it:

```
(lldb) nexti -c 4
--snip--
hello_debugger`main:
-> 0x100003f72 <+13>: movl    $0x87654321, %eax          ; imm = 0x87654321
--snip--
```

This puts us back at the instruction right after `callq`.

Setting Breakpoints by Address

In addition to setting breakpoints on functions, you can break on specific machine instructions. Let's set a breakpoint on the instruction `movl 0xdeadbeef, -4(%rbp)`. First, we need to find this instruction's address.

Luckily, LLDB has already given us this information. The output from the last command should look something like this:

```
hello_debugger`main:
->  0x100003f72 <+13>: movl    $0x87654321, %eax          ; imm = 0x87654321
    0x100003f77 <+18>: movsd   0x181(%rip), %xmm0         ; dbl, xmm0 = mem[0],zero
  ❶ 0x100003f7f ❷ <+26>: movl    $0xdeadbeef, -0x4(%rbp)    ; imm = 0xDEADBEEF
    0x100003f86 <+33>: movl    $0x0, -0x8(%rbp)
```

This shows the next few instructions, including the one we want to break on. We can see that instruction's memory address ❶ and the byte offset of that address from the start of the function ❷. The exact address may be different on your machine, but the offset should be the same. To set this breakpoint, type

```
(lldb) break set -a MEMORY_ADDRESS
```

where *MEMORY_ADDRESS* is the instruction's address on your machine. The -a option indicates that we're specifying an address rather than a function name. We can also use more complex expressions to specify instruction addresses. Here's another way to set a breakpoint on the same instruction:

```
(lldb) break set -a '(void()) main + 26'
```

First, we cast main to a function type so that LLDB can use it in address calculations. (It doesn't matter which function type we cast it to.) Then, we add a 26-byte offset to get the address of the movl instruction we want to break on. Since this address expression includes spaces and special characters, we have to wrap the whole thing in quotes.

In a minute, we'll see how to disassemble the whole function and see every instruction's address. First, let's look at a couple of other useful commands for managing breakpoints.

Managing Breakpoints

Let's list all the breakpoints we've set:

```
(lldb) break list
Current breakpoints:
1: name = 'main', locations = 1, resolved = 1, hit count = 1
  1.1: where = hello_debugger`main, address = 0x0000000100003f65, resolved, hit count = 1

2: address = hello_debugger[0x0000000100003f7f], locations = 1, resolved = 1, hit count = 0
  2.1: where = hello_debugger`main + 26, address = 0x0000000100003f7f, resolved, hit count = 0

3: address = hello_debugger[0x0000000100003f7f], locations = 1, resolved = 1, hit count = 0
  3.1: where = hello_debugger`main + 26, address = 0x0000000100003f7f, resolved, hit count = 0
```

Every breakpoint has a unique number, which you can refer to if you need to delete, disable, or modify it. In the last section, we set breakpoints 2 and 3 at the same location, main+26. Let's delete one of them:

```
(lldb) break delete 3
```

Next, we'll look at how to display all the assembly instructions in a function, along with their addresses.

Displaying Assembly Code

The command disassemble -n <*function name*> tells LLDB to print out all the assembly instructions in a function. Let's try this out on main:

```
(lldb) disassemble -n main
hello_debugger`main:
    0x100003f65 <+0>:   pushq   %rbp
    0x100003f66 <+1>:   movq    %rsp, %rbp
    0x100003f69 <+4>:   subq    $0x10, %rsp
    0x100003f6d <+8>:   callq   0x100003fb2               ; f
->  0x100003f72 <+13>:  movl    $0x87654321, %eax         ; imm = 0x87654321
    0x100003f77 <+18>:  movsd   0x181(%rip), %xmm0        ; dbl, xmm0 = mem[0],zero
    0x100003f7f <+26>:  movl    $0xdeadbeef, -0x4(%rbp)   ; imm = 0xDEADBEEF
    0x100003f86 <+33>:  movl    $0x0, -0x8(%rbp)
    0x100003f8d <+40>:  movl    $0xffffffff, -0xc(%rbp)   ; imm = 0xFFFFFFFF
    0x100003f94 <+47>:  movl    $0xfeedface, -0x10(%rbp)  ; imm = 0xFEEDFACE
    0x100003f9b <+54>:  movl    $0x19, %ecx
    0x100003fa0 <+59>:  subl    $0x1, %ecx
    0x100003fa3 <+62>:  cmpl    $0x0, %ecx
    0x100003fa6 <+65>:  jne     0x100003fa0              ; <+59>
    0x100003fa8 <+67>:  movl    $0x0, %eax
    0x100003fad <+72>:  movq    %rbp, %rsp
    0x100003fb0 <+75>:  popq    %rbp
    0x100003fb1 <+76>:  retq
(lldb)
```

The -> symbol points to the current instruction. We can also print out a fixed number of instructions, starting at a specific address. Let's disassemble five instructions, starting with the third instruction in main. In the disassembled code shown here, this instruction's address is 0x100003f69; it might have a different address on your machine. The -s option specifies the address where LLDB should start disassembling, and -c specifies how many instructions to display, so we'll disassemble these five instructions with the following command:

```
(lldb) disassemble -s 0x100003f69 -c 5
hello_debug`main:
    0x100003f69 <+4>:   subq    $0x10, %rsp
    0x100003f6d <+8>:   callq   0x100003fb2               ; f
->  0x100003f72 <+13>:  movl    $0x87654321, %eax         ; imm = 0x87654321
    0x100003f77 <+18>:  movsd   0x181(%rip), %xmm0        ; dbl, xmm0 = mem[0],zero
    0x100003f7f <+26>:  movl    $0xdeadbeef, -0x4(%rbp)   ; imm = 0xDEADBEEF
```

Finally, we can use the `--pc` option to start disassembling at the current instruction:

```
(lldb) disassemble --pc -c 3
->  0x100003f72 <+13>: movl   $0x87654321, %eax        ; imm = 0x87654321
    0x100003f77 <+18>: movsd  0x181(%rip), %xmm0       ; dbl, xmm0 = mem[0],zero
    0x100003f7f <+26>: movl   $0xdeadbeef, -0x4(%rbp)  ; imm = 0xDEADBEEF
```

This command displays three instructions, starting with the current instruction. We can use the -c option when we specify a starting address with -s or --pc but not when we disassemble a whole function with -n.

Printing Expressions

You can evaluate expressions with the command exp -f *<format>* -- *<expr>*, where:

<format> is a format specifier that tells LLDB how to display the result of the expression.

<expr> is an arbitrary expression. This expression can refer to registers, memory addresses, and symbols in the running program. It can also include C operations like arithmetic, pointer dereferencing, and cast expressions.

Let's try some examples. Right now, the program should be paused at the instruction movl 0x87654321, %eax. We'll step through this instruction, then print out the value of EAX in a few different formats:

```
(lldb) stepi
--snip--
hello_debugger`main:
->  0x100003f77 <+18>: movsd  0x181(%rip), %xmm0       ; dbl, xmm0 = mem[0],zero
--snip--
(lldb) exp -- $eax
(unsigned int) $0 = ❶ 2271560481
(lldb) exp -f x -- $eax
(unsigned int) $1 = ❷ 0x87654321
(lldb) exp -f d -- $eax
(unsigned int) $2 = ❸ -2023406815
```

By default, LLDB formats the values in general-purpose registers as unsigned integers ❶. Here, we also display the value of EAX in hexadecimal ❷ and as a signed integer ❸. (For a full list of formats, use the help format command.) The symbols $0, $1, and so on are *convenience variables*, which LLDB automatically generates to store the result of each expression.

Chapter 13 introduces the XMM registers, which hold floating-point values. The next instruction in our program, movsd dbl(%rip), %xmm0, copies the value 3.5 from the static dbl variable into XMM0. Let's step through this instruction, then inspect XMM0. We'll use the float64[] format, which displays the register's contents as an array of two doubles:

```
(lldb) stepi
--snip--
hello_debugger`main:
-> 0x100003f7f <+26>: movl   $0xdeadbeef, -0x4(%rbp)   ; imm = 0
--snip--
(lldb) exp -f float64[] -- $xmm0
(unsigned char __attribute__((ext_vector_type(16)))) $3 = (❶ 3.5, 0)
```

The first array element corresponds to the register's lower 64 bits ❶, which we updated with the movsd instruction. The second element corresponds to the register's upper 64 bits, which we can ignore.

In addition to registers, we can print out the values of objects in the symbol table. Let's inspect the two static variables in this program, integer and dbl:

```
(lldb) exp -f d -- integer
(void *) $4 = 100
(lldb) exp -f f -- dbl
(void *) $5 = 3.5
```

Now let's look at a few examples of more complex expressions. We can perform basic arithmetic:

```
(lldb) exp -f x -- $eax + 0x10
(unsigned int) $6 = 0x87654331
```

We can call functions from the current program or the standard library. Here we call f, which returns 1:

```
(lldb) exp -- (int) f()
(int) $7 = 1
```

We can also dereference pointers. Let's execute the next instruction, movl 0xdeadbeef, -4(%rbp), then inspect the value at -4(%rbp):

```
(lldb) stepi
--snip--
hello_debugger`main:
-> 0x100003f86 <+33>: movl   $0x0, -0x8(%rbp)
--snip--
(lldb) exp -f x -- *(int *)($rbp - 4)
(int) $8 = 0xdeadbeef
```

First, we calculate the memory address we want to inspect, $rbp - 4. Then, we cast this address to the correct pointer type, (int *). Finally, we dereference it with the dereference operator, *. This produces an integer, which we print out in hexadecimal with the option -f x.

Next, we'll look at a more flexible way to inspect values in memory.

Examining Memory

We can examine memory with the `memory read` command. Like `exp`, it takes an arbitrary expression, which must evaluate to a valid memory address. This gives us another way to inspect the integer at `-4(%rbp)`:

```
(lldb) memory read -f x -s 4 -c 1 '$rbp - 4'
0x3040bb93c: 0xdeadbeef
```

The `-f x` option says to print the output in hexadecimal; `-s 4` says to interpret the contents of memory as a sequence of 4-byte values; and `-c 1` says to print just one of those values. In other words, this command prints out the single 4-byte integer at `$rbp - 4`, formatted as hexadecimal. We have to wrap the expression `$rbp - 4` in quotes because it contains spaces.

The next three instructions in Listing A-1 store three more integers on the stack:

```
movl    $0, -8(%rbp)
movl    $-1, -12(%rbp)
movl    $0xfeedface, -16(%rbp)
```

Let's step through these instructions, then print out the whole stack frame. We'll tell LLDB to print out six 4-byte words, starting at the address in RSP. We'll use the option `-l 1` to print out each word on a separate line:

```
(lldb) stepi -c 3
--snip--
hello_debugger`main:
->  0x100003f9b <+54>: movl    $0x19, %ecx
--snip--
(lldb) memory read -f x -s 4 -c 6 -l 1 $rsp
0x3040bb930: ❶ 0xfeedface
0x3040bb934: 0xffffffff
0x3040bb938: 0x00000000
0x3040bb93c: 0xdeadbeef
0x3040bb940: ❷ 0x040bba50
0x3040bb944: 0x00000003
```

We print out six words because the stack is 24 bytes in this particular function. At the start of `main`, we saved the old value of RBP onto the stack. That's 8 bytes. Then, we allocated another 16 bytes with the command `subq $16, %rsp`. Keep in mind that RSP always holds the address of the top of the stack, which is the *lowest* stack address.

This command shows us the four integers we saved to the stack, with `0xfeedface` at the top ❶ and the old value of RBP at the bottom ❷. Since the value at ❷ is really an 8-byte address, we can read it more easily if we group the stack into 8-byte values:

```
(lldb) memory read -f x -s 8 -c 3 -l 1 $rsp
0x3040bb930: 0xfffffffffeedface
```

```
0x3040bb938: 0xdeadbeef00000000
0x3040bb940: ❶ 0x00000003040bba50
```

Now it's clear that the bottom 8 bytes on the stack hold a single memory address ❶.

Just below the saved value of RBP, on top of the caller's stack frame, we'd expect to find the caller's return address—that is, the address we'll jump to when we return from main. (We cover this in detail when we implement function calls in Chapter 9.) Let's inspect this address:

```
(lldb) memory read -f A -s 8 -c 4 -l 1 $rsp
0x3040bb930: 0xffffffffffeedface
0x3040bb938: 0xdeadbeef00000000
0x3040bb940: 0x00000003040bba50
0x3040bb948: ❶ 0x0000000200012310 dyld`start + 2432
```

This command is almost identical to the previous one, except that we use the option -c 4 to print out four values instead of three and the option -f A to format each value as a memory address. The A format specifier tells LLDB to print each address in hexadecimal and, if possible, print out its offset from the nearest symbol in the program. Because function and static variable names are defined in the symbol table, LLDB can display the relative offsets of assembly instructions and static data. It won't display relative offsets of stack addresses, heap addresses, or invalid addresses, because they would be completely meaningless.

The first three lines of output are the same as before. The first two values aren't valid memory addresses and the third is a stack address, so LLDB can't display their offsets from symbols. The next value on the stack is the return address ❶. The label dyld`start tells us this is the address of an instruction in the start function in the dyld shared library. (The start function is responsible for calling main and cleaning up after it exits; dyld is the dynamic linker.)

The -f A option makes it easy to spot return addresses and pointers to static variables. This is particularly useful if your program's stack frame is corrupted; finding each stack frame's return address can help you get your bearings.

Setting Conditional Breakpoints

To wrap up this walk-through, we'll look at how to set *conditional breakpoints*. The program will pause at a conditional breakpoint only if the associated condition is true. This condition can be an arbitrary expression; LLDB will consider it false if it evaluates to 0 and true otherwise.

Let's set a breakpoint on the jne instruction at the end of the last loop iteration in hello_debugger. First, we'll find this instruction's address in the disassembled main function:

```
(lldb) disassemble -n main
hello_debugger`main:
```

```
--snip--
❶ 0x100003fa6 <+65>:   jne     0x100003fa0                    ; <+59>
--snip--
```

Here, the address of jne is 0x100003fa6 ❶. Now we'll set a conditional breakpoint to pause on the jne instruction if ECX is 0. We can use the -c option to specify a condition:

```
(lldb) break set -a MEMORY_ADDRESS -c '$ecx == 0'
```

Since this loop repeats until ECX is 0, the condition $ecx == 0 will be true only on the last iteration. Let's continue until the breakpoint, then verify that this condition is true:

```
(lldb) continue
--snip--
hello_debugger`main:
-> 0x100003fa6 <+65>:   jne     0x100003fa0                    ; <+59>
--snip--
(lldb) exp -- $ecx
(unsigned int) $9 = 0
```

If you get a different value for ECX, check whether you set the breakpoint correctly:

```
(lldb) break list
--snip--
4: address = hello_debugger[0x0000000100003fa6], locations = 1, resolved = 1, hit count = 0
Condition: $ecx == 0 ❶

  4.1: where = ❷ hello_debugger`main + 65, address = 0x0000000100003fa6, resolved, hit count
= 0
```

Make sure that your breakpoint includes the condition $ecx == 0 ❶ and that it's at the location hello_debugger`main + 65 ❷. If your breakpoint looks different, you might have mistyped something; delete it and try again.

We should be on the last loop iteration, so let's step forward one instruction and make sure that the jump isn't taken:

```
(lldb) stepi
--snip--
hello_debugger`main:
-> 0x100003fa8 <+67>:   movl    $0x0, %eax
--snip--
```

Usually, jne will jump back to the start of the loop, but on the last iteration it moves forward to the next instruction.

Getting Help

To learn more about the commands and options we didn't cover here, see the LLDB documentation at *https://lldb.llvm.org/index.html*. You can also type help at the prompt to learn more about any LLDB command. For example, to see the documentation for the run command, type:

```
(lldb) help run
    Launch the executable in the debugger
--snip--
```

Table A-2 summarizes the commands and options we covered. The version of each command that we used in the walk-through is listed first, followed by a shorter abbreviation (except for exp, which isn't normally shortened further), then the full form when it differs from the one we used. All versions of each command take the same arguments.

Table A-2: A Summary of LLDB Commands

Command	Description
run r process launch --	Start the program.
continue c process continue	Resume the program.
finish fin thread step-out	Resume the program and continue until the current function exits.
stepi [-c <n>] si thread step-inst	Execute one instruction (or *n* instructions), stepping into function calls.
nexti [-c <n>] ni thread step-inst-over	Execute one instruction (or *n* instructions), stepping over function calls.
break set [-n <fun> | -a <addr>] [-c <cond>] br s breakpoint set	Set a breakpoint at start of function <fun> or at address <addr> (conditional on <cond>, if provided).
break list br l breakpoint list	List all breakpoints.

(continued)

Table A-2: A Summary of LLDB Commands *(continued)*

Command	Description

`break delete [ <id> ]`
`br del`
`breakpoint delete`
	Delete all breakpoints (or the breakpoint specified by *<id>*).

`exp -f <format> -- <expr>` `expression`	Evaluate *<expr>* and display the result in format *<format>*.

`memory read -f <format> -s <size>`
`-c <count> -l <num-per-line>`
`<addr>`
`me read`
	Print out memory in *<count>* chunks of *<size>* bytes, starting at address *<addr>*. Display *<num -per-line>* chunks on each line in format *<format>*.

`disassemble [ -n <fun> | -s`
`<addr> -c <count> | --pc -c`
`<count> ]`
`di`
	Disassemble all instructions in function *<fun>*, or *<count>* instructions starting at address *<addr>*, or *<count>* instructions starting at the current instruction.

`help <cmd>` `h`	Display help text about *<cmd>*.

Now you're ready to start debugging with LLDB!

B

ASSEMBLY GENERATION AND CODE EMISSION TABLES

In each chapter where we updated the conversion from TACKY to assembly or the code emission pass, I included tables summarizing those passes. From Chapter 4 on, these tables showed only the changes made in that chapter, not the entire pass. This appendix presents the complete tables summarizing these passes at the end of Part I, Part II, and Part III.

Part I

The first set of tables in this section illustrates how your compiler should convert every TACKY construct to assembly at the end of Part I. The second set of tables illustrates how your compiler should emit every assembly construct at the end of Part I.

Converting TACKY to Assembly

Tables B-1 through B-5 show the complete conversion from TACKY to assembly at the end of Part I.

Table B-1: Converting Top-Level TACKY Constructs to Assembly

TACKY top-level construct	Assembly top-level construct
Program(top_level_defs)	Program(top_level_defs)

Function(name, global, params, instructions)	Function(name, global,
	    [Mov(Reg(DI), param1),
	      Mov(Reg(SI), param2),
	      <copy next four parameters from registers>,
	      Mov(Stack(16), param7),
	      Mov(Stack(24), param8),
	      <copy remaining parameters from stack>] +
	    instructions)

StaticVariable(name, global, init)	StaticVariable(name, global, init)

Table B-2: Converting TACKY Instructions to Assembly

TACKY instruction	Assembly instructions
Return(val)	Mov(val, Reg(AX)) Ret
Unary(Not, src, dst)	Cmp(Imm(0), src) Mov(Imm(0), dst) SetCC(E, dst)
Unary(unary_operator, src, dst)	Mov(src, dst) Unary(unary_operator, dst)
Binary(Divide, src1, src2, dst)	Mov(src1, Reg(AX)) Cdq Idiv(src2) Mov(Reg(AX), dst)
Binary(Remainder, src1, src2, dst)	Mov(src1, Reg(AX)) Cdq Idiv(src2) Mov(Reg(DX), dst)
Binary(arithmetic_operator, src1, src2, dst)	Mov(src1, dst) Binary(arithmetic_operator, src2, dst)
Binary(relational_operator, src1, src2, dst)	Cmp(src2, src1) Mov(Imm(0), dst) SetCC(relational_operator, dst)
Jump(target)	Jmp(target)
JumpIfZero(condition, target)	Cmp(Imm(0), condition) JmpCC(E, target)
JumpIfNotZero(condition, target)	Cmp(Imm(0), condition) JmpCC(NE, target)
Copy(src, dst)	Mov(src, dst)

TACKY instruction	Assembly instructions
Label(identifier)	Label(identifier)
FunCall(fun_name, args, dst)	*<fix stack alignment>* *<set up arguments>* Call(fun_name) *<deallocate arguments/padding>* Mov(Reg(AX), dst)

Table B-3: Converting TACKY Arithmetic Operators to Assembly

TACKY operator	Assembly operator
Complement	Not
Negate	Neg
Add	Add
Subtract	Sub
Multiply	Mult

Table B-4: Converting TACKY Comparisons to Assembly

TACKY comparison	Assembly condition code
Equal	E
NotEqual	NE
LessThan	L
LessOrEqual	LE
GreaterThan	G
GreaterOrEqual	GE

Table B-5: Converting TACKY Operands to Assembly

TACKY operand	Assembly operand
Constant(int)	Imm(int)
Var(identifier)	Pseudo(identifier)

Code Emission

Tables B-6 through B-10 show the complete code emission pass at the end of Part I.

Table B-6: Formatting Top-Level Assembly Constructs

Assembly top-level construct		Output
Program(top_levels)		Print out each top-level construct. On Linux, add at end of file: `.section .note.GNU-stack,"",@progbits`

Function(name, global, instructions)		`<global-directive>`
		`.text`
		`<name>:`
		`    pushq    %rbp`
		`    movq     %rsp, %rbp`
		`    <instructions>`

StaticVariable(name, global, init)	Initialized to zero	`<global-directive>`
		`.bss`
		`<alignment-directive>`
		`<name>:`
		`    .zero 4`

	Initialized to nonzero value	`<global-directive>`
		`.data`
		`<alignment-directive>`
		`<name>:`
		`    .long <init>`

Global directive		If global is true: `.globl <identifier>` Otherwise, omit this directive.
Alignment directive	Linux only	`.align 4`
	macOS or Linux	`.balign 4`

Table B-7: Formatting Assembly Instructions

Assembly instruction	Output
Mov(src, dst)	`movl    <src>, <dst>`

Ret	`movq    %rbp, %rsp`
	`popq    %rbp`
	`ret`

Unary(unary_operator, operand)	`<unary_operator>    <operand>`
Binary(binary_operator, src, dst)	`<binary_operator>    <src>, <dst>`
Idiv(operand)	`idivl    <operand>`
Cdq	`cdq`
AllocateStack(int)	`subq    $<int>, %rsp`
DeallocateStack(int)	`addq    $<int>, %rsp`
Push(operand)	`pushq    <operand>`

Call(label)	`call    <label>`
	or
	`call    <label>@PLT`

Cmp(operand, operand)	`cmpl    <operand>, <operand>`
Jmp(label)	`jmp    .L<label>`
JmpCC(cond_code, label)	`j<cond_code>    .L<label>`
SetCC(cond_code, operand)	`set<cond_code>    <operand>`
Label(label)	`.L<label>:`

Table B-8: Instruction Names for Assembly Operators

Assembly operator	Instruction name
Neg	negl
Not	notl
Add	addl
Sub	subl
Mult	imull

Table B-9: Instruction Suffixes for Condition Codes

Condition code	Instruction suffix
E	e
NE	ne
L	l
LE	le
G	g
GE	ge

Table B-10: Formatting Assembly Operands

Assembly operand		Output
Reg(AX)	8-byte	%rax
	4-byte	%eax
	1-byte	%al
Reg(DX)	8-byte	%rdx
	4-byte	%edx
	1-byte	%dl
Reg(CX)	8-byte	%rcx
	4-byte	%ecx
	1-byte	%cl
Reg(DI)	8-byte	%rdi
	4-byte	%edi
	1-byte	%dil
Reg(SI)	8-byte	%rsi
	4-byte	%esi
	1-byte	%sil
Reg(R8)	8-byte	%r8
	4-byte	%r8d
	1-byte	%r8b

(continued)

Table B-10: Formatting Assembly Operands *(continued)*

Assembly operand		Output
Reg(R9)	8-byte	%r9
	4-byte	%r9d
	1-byte	%r9b
Reg(R10)	8-byte	%r10
	4-byte	%r10d
	1-byte	%r10b
Reg(R11)	8-byte	%r11
	4-byte	%r11d
	1-byte	%r11b
Stack(int)		*<int>*(%rbp)
Imm(int)		$*<int>*
Data(identifier)		*<identifier>*(%rip)

Part II

The first set of tables in this section illustrates how your compiler should convert every TACKY construct to assembly at the end of Part II. The second set of tables illustrates how your compiler should emit every assembly construct at the end of Part II.

Converting TACKY to Assembly

Tables B-11 through B-16 show the complete conversion from TACKY to assembly at the end of Part II.

Table B-11: Converting Top-Level TACKY Constructs to Assembly

TACKY top-level construct		Assembly top-level construct
Program(top_level_defs)		Program(top_level_defs + *<all StaticConstant constructs for floating-point constants>*)
Function(name, global, params, instructions)	Return value in registers or no return value	Function(name, global, [*<copy Reg(DI) into first int param/eightbyte>*, *<copy Reg(SI) into second int param/eightbyte>*, *<copy next four int params/eightbytes from registers>*, Mov(Double, Reg(XMM0), *<first double param/eightbyte>*),

TACKY top-level construct		Assembly top-level construct
		Mov(Double, Reg(XMM1), <second double param/eightbyte>), <copy next six double params/eightbytes from registers>, <copy Memory(BP, 16) into first stack param/eightbyte>, <copy Memory(BP, 24) into second stack param/eightbyte>, <copy remaining params/eightbytes from stack>] + instructions)

	Return value
	on stack
		Function(name, global,
		[Mov(Quadword,
		    Reg(DI),
		    Memory(BP, -8)),
		<copy Reg(SI) into first int param/eightbyte>,
		<copy Reg(DX) into second int param/eightbyte>,
		<copy next three int params/eightbytes from registers>,
		Mov(Double,
		    Reg(XMM0),
		    <first double param/eightbyte>),
		Mov(Double,
		    Reg(XMM1),
		    <second double param/eightbyte>),
		<copy next six double params/eightbytes from registers>,
		<copy Memory(BP, 16) into first stack param/eightbyte>,
		<copy Memory(BP, 24) into second stack param/eightbyte>,
		<copy remaining params/eightbytes from stack>] +
		instructions)

StaticVariable(name, global, t,
        init_list)
		StaticVariable(name, global, <alignment of t>,
		        init_list)

StaticConstant(name, t, init)		StaticConstant(name, <alignment of t>, init)

Table B-12: Converting TACKY Instructions to Assembly

TACKY instruction	Assembly instructions	

Return(val)	Return on
	stack
		Mov(Quadword, Memory(BP, -8), Reg(AX))
		Mov(Quadword,
		    <first eightbyte of return value>,
		    Memory(AX, 0))
		Mov(Quadword,
		    <second eightbyte of return value>,
		    Memory(AX, 8))
		<copy rest of return value>
		Ret

	Return in registers	<move integer parts of return value into RAX, RDX> <move double parts of return value into XMM0, XMM1> Ret
	No return value	Ret

(continued)

TACKY instruction	Assembly instructions	
Unary(Not, src, dst)	Integer	Cmp(*<src type>*, Imm(0), src) Mov(*<dst type>*, Imm(0), dst) SetCC(E, dst)
	double	Binary(Xor, Double, Reg(*<X>*), Reg(*<X>*)) Cmp(Double, src, Reg(*<X>*)) Mov(*<dst type>*, Imm(0), dst) SetCC(E, dst)
Unary(Negate, src, dst) (double negation)		Mov(Double, src, dst) Binary(Xor, Double, Data(*<negative-zero>*, 0), dst) And add a top-level constant: StaticConstant(*<negative-zero>*, 16, DoubleInit(-0.0))
Unary(unary_operator, src, dst)		Mov(*<src type>*, src, dst) Unary(unary_operator, *<src type>*, dst)
Binary(Divide, src1, src2, dst) (integer division)	Signed	Mov(*<src1 type>*, src1, Reg(AX)) Cdq(*<src1 type>*) Idiv(*<src1 type>*, src2) Mov(*<src1 type>*, Reg(AX), dst)
	Unsigned	Mov(*<src1 type>*, src1, Reg(AX)) Mov(*<src1 type>*, Imm(0), Reg(DX)) Div(*<src1 type>*, src2) Mov(*<src1 type>*, Reg(AX), dst)
Binary(Remainder, src1, src2, dst)	Signed	Mov(*<src1 type>*, src1, Reg(AX)) Cdq(*<src1 type>*) Idiv(*<src1 type>*, src2) Mov(*<src1 type>*, Reg(DX), dst)
	Unsigned	Mov(*<src1 type>*, src1, Reg(AX)) Mov(*<src1 type>*, Imm(0), Reg(DX)) Div(*<src1 type>*, src2) Mov(*<src1 type>*, Reg(DX), dst)
Binary(arithmetic_operator, src1, src2, dst)		Mov(*<src1 type>*, src1, dst) Binary(arithmetic_operator, *<src1 type>*, src2, dst)
Binary(relational_operator, src1, src2, dst)		Cmp(*<src1 type>*, src2, src1) Mov(*<dst type>*, Imm(0), dst) SetCC(relational_operator, dst)
Jump(target)		Jmp(target)
JumpIfZero(condition, target)	Integer	Cmp(*<condition type>*, Imm(0), condition) JmpCC(E, target)
	double	Binary(Xor, Double, Reg(*<X>*), Reg(*<X>*)) Cmp(Double, condition, Reg(*<X>*)) JmpCC(E, target)
JumpIfNotZero(condition, target)	Integer	Cmp(*<condition type>*, Imm(0), condition) JmpCC(NE, target)
	double	Binary(Xor, Double, Reg(*<X>*), Reg(*<X>*)) Cmp(Double, condition, Reg(*<X>*)) JmpCC(NE, target)

TACKY instruction	Assembly instructions	
Copy(src, dst)	Scalar	Mov(*<src type>*, src, dst)
	Structure	Mov(*<first chunk type>*, PseudoMem(src, 0), PseudoMem(dst, 0)) Mov(*<next chunk type>*, PseudoMem(src, *<first chunk size>*), PseudoMem(dst, *<first chunk size>*)) *<copy remaining chunks>*
Load(ptr, dst)	Scalar	Mov(Quadword, ptr, Reg(*<R>*)) Mov(*<dst type>*, Memory(*<R>*, 0), dst)
	Structure	Mov(Quadword, ptr, Reg(*<R>*)) Mov(*<first chunk type>*, Memory(*<R>*, 0), PseudoMem(dst, 0)) Mov(*<next chunk type>*, Memory(*<R>*, *<first chunk size>*), PseudoMem(dst, *<first chunk size>*)) *<copy remaining chunks>*
Store(src, ptr)	Scalar	Mov(Quadword, ptr, Reg(*<R>*)) Mov(*<src type>*, src, Memory(*<R>*, 0))
	Structure	Mov(Quadword, ptr, Reg(*<R>*)) Mov(*<first chunk type>*, PseudoMem(src, 0), Memory(*<R>*, 0)) Mov(*<next chunk type>*, PseudoMem(src, *<first chunk size>*), Memory(*<R>*, *<first chunk size>*)) *<copy remaining chunks>*
GetAddress(src, dst)		Lea(src, dst)
AddPtr(ptr, index, scale, dst)	Constant index	Mov(Quadword, ptr, Reg(*<R>*)) Lea(Memory(*<R>*, index * scale), dst)
	Variable index and scale of 1, 2, 4, or 8	Mov(Quadword, ptr, Reg(*<R1>*)) Mov(Quadword, index, Reg(*<R2>*)) Lea(Indexed(*<R1>*, *<R2>*, scale), dst)
	Variable index and other scale	Mov(Quadword, ptr, Reg(*<R1>*)) Mov(Quadword, index, Reg(*<R2>*)) Binary(Mult, Quadword, Imm(scale), Reg(*<R2>*)) Lea(Indexed(*<R1>*, *<R2>*, 1), dst)
CopyToOffset(src, dst, offset)	src is scalar	Mov(*<src type>*, src, PseudoMem(dst, offset))
	src is a structure	Mov(*<first chunk type>*, PseudoMem(src, 0), PseudoMem(dst, offset)) Mov(*<next chunk type>*, PseudoMem(src, *<first chunk size>*), PseudoMem(dst, offset + *<first chunk size>*)) *<copy remaining chunks>*

(continued)

TACKY instruction	Assembly instructions	
CopyFromOffset(src, offset, dst)	dst is scalar	Mov(*<dst type>*, PseudoMem(src, offset), dst)

	dst is a structure	Mov(*<first chunk type>*,
		    PseudoMem(src, offset),
		    PseudoMem(dst, 0))
		Mov(*<next chunk type>*,
		    PseudoMem(src, offset + *<first chunk size>*),
		    PseudoMem(dst, *<first chunk size>*))
		<copy remaining chunks>

Label(identifier)		Label(identifier)
FunCall(fun_name, args, dst)	dst will be returned in memory	Lea(dst, Reg(DI)) *<fix stack alignment>* *<move arguments to general-purpose registers, starting with RSI>* *<move arguments to XMM registers>* *<push arguments onto the stack>* Call(fun_name) *<deallocate arguments/padding>*
	dst will be returned in registers	*<fix stack alignment>* *<move arguments to general-purpose registers>* *<move arguments to XMM registers>* *<push arguments onto the stack>* Call(fun_name) *<deallocate arguments/padding>* *<move integer parts of return value from RAX, RDX into dst>* *<move double parts of return value from XMM0, XMM1 into dst>*
	dst is absent	*<fix stack alignment>* *<move arguments to general-purpose registers>* *<move arguments to XMM registers>* *<push arguments onto the stack>* Call(fun_name) *<deallocate arguments/padding>*
ZeroExtend(src, dst)		MovZeroExtend(*<src type>*, *<dst type>*, src, dst)
SignExtend(src, dst)		Movsx(*<src type>*, *<dst type>*, src, dst)
Truncate(src, dst)		Mov(*<dst type>*, src, dst)
IntToDouble(src, dst)	char or signed char	Movsx(Byte, Longword, src, Reg(*<R>*)) Cvtsi2sd(Longword, Reg(*<R>*), dst)
	int or long	Cvtsi2sd(*<src type>*, src, dst)
DoubleToInt(src, dst)	char or signed char	Cvttsd2si(Longword, src, Reg(*<R>*)) Mov(Byte, Reg(*<R>*), dst)
	int or long	Cvttsd2si(*<dst type>*, src, dst)
UIntToDouble(src, dst)	unsigned char	MovZeroExtend(Byte, Longword, src, Reg(*<R>*)) Cvtsi2sd(Longword, Reg(*<R>*), dst)
	unsigned int	MovZeroExtend(Longword, Quadword, src, Reg(*<R>*)) Cvtsi2sd(Quadword, Reg(*<R>*), dst)

TACKY instruction	Assembly instructions	
	unsigned long	Cmp(Quadword, Imm(0), src) JmpCC(L, <*label1*>) Cvtsi2sd(Quadword, src, dst) Jmp(<*label2*>) Label(<*label1*>) Mov(Quadword, src, Reg(<*R1*>)) Mov(Quadword, Reg(<*R1*>), Reg(<*R2*>)) Unary(Shr, Quadword, Reg(<*R2*>)) Binary(And, Quadword, Imm(1), Reg(<*R1*>)) Binary(Or, Quadword, Reg(<*R1*>), Reg(<*R2*>)) Cvtsi2sd(Quadword, Reg(<*R2*>), dst) Binary(Add, Double, dst, dst) Label(<*label2*>)
DoubleToUInt(src, dst)	unsigned char	Cvttsd2si(Longword, src, Reg(<*R*>)) Mov(Byte, Reg(<*R*>), dst)
	unsigned int	Cvttsd2si(Quadword, src, Reg(<*R*>)) Mov(Longword, Reg(<*R*>), dst)
	unsigned long	Cmp(Double, Data(<*upper-bound*>, 0), src) JmpCC(AE, <*label1*>) Cvttsd2si(Quadword, src, dst) Jmp(<*label2*>) Label(<*label1*>) Mov(Double, src, Reg(<*X*>)) Binary(Sub, Double, Data(<*upper-bound*>, 0), Reg(<*X*>)) Cvttsd2si(Quadword, Reg(<*X*>), dst) Mov(Quadword, Imm(9223372036854775808), Reg(<*R*>)) Binary(Add, Quadword, Reg(<*R*>), dst) Label(<*label2*>) And add a top-level constant: StaticConstant(<*upper-bound*>, 8, DoubleInit(9223372036854775808.0))

Table B-13: Converting TACKY Arithmetic Operators to Assembly

TACKY operator	Assembly operator
Complement	Not
Negate (integer negation)	Neg
Add	Add
Subtract	Sub
Multiply	Mult
Divide (double division)	DivDouble

Table B-14: Converting TACKY Comparisons to Assembly

TACKY comparison		Assembly condition code
Equal		E
NotEqual		NE
LessThan	Signed	L
	Unsigned, pointer, or double	B
LessOrEqual	Signed	LE
	Unsigned, pointer, or double	BE
GreaterThan	Signed	G
	Unsigned, pointer, or double	A
GreaterOrEqual	Signed	GE
	Unsigned, pointer, or double	AE

Table B-15: Converting TACKY Operands to Assembly

TACKY operand		Assembly operand
Constant(ConstChar(int))		Imm(int)
Constant(ConstInt(int))		Imm(int)
Constant(ConstLong(int))		Imm(int)
Constant(ConstUChar(int))		Imm(int)
Constant(ConstUInt(int))		Imm(int)
Constant(ConstULong(int))		Imm(int)
Constant(ConstDouble(double))		Data(*<ident>*, 0) And add a top-level constant: StaticConstant(*<ident>*, 8, DoubleInit(double))
Var(identifier)	Scalar value	Pseudo(identifier)
	Aggregate value	PseudoMem(identifier, 0)

Table B-16: Converting Types to Assembly

Source type	Assembly type	Alignment
Char	Byte	1
SChar	Byte	1
UChar	Byte	1
Int	Longword	4
UInt	Longword	4
Long	Quadword	8
ULong	Quadword	8
Double	Double	8

Source type		Assembly type	Alignment
Pointer(referenced_t)		Quadword	8
Array(element, size)	Variables that are 16 bytes or larger	ByteArray(*<size of element>* * size, 16)	16
	Everything else	ByteArray(*<size of element>* * size, *<alignment of element>*)	Same alignment as element
Structure(tag)		ByteArray(*<size from type table>*, *<alignment from type table>*)	Alignment from type table

Code Emission

Tables B-17 through B-23 show the complete code emission pass at the end of Part II.

Table B-17: Formatting Top-Level Assembly Constructs

Assembly top-level construct		Output
Program(top_levels)		Print out each top-level construct. On Linux, add at end of file: .section .note.GNU-stack,"",@progbits

Function(name, global, instructions)		*<global-directive>*
		    .text
		<name>:
		    pushq %rbp
		    movq %rsp, %rbp
		<instructions>

StaticVariable(name, global, alignment, init_list)	Integer initialized to zero, or any variable initialized only with ZeroInit	*<global-directive>*
		    .bss
		<alignment-directive>
		<name>:
		    <init_list>

	All other variables	*<global-directive>*
		    .data
		<alignment-directive>
		<name>:
		    <init_list>

StaticConstant(name, alignment, init)	Linux	.section .rodata *<alignment-directive>* *<name>*: *<init>*

	macOS (8-byte-aligned numeric constants)	.literal8
		    .balign 8
		<name>:
		    <init>

	macOS (16-byte-aligned numeric constants)	.literal16
		    .balign 16
		<name>:
		    <init>
		    .quad 0

(continued)

Table B-17: Formatting Top-Level Assembly Constructs *(continued)*

Assembly top-level construct		Output

	macOS (string constants)	`.cstring`
		`<name>:`
		`    <init>`

Global directive		If global is true: `.globl <identifier>` Otherwise, omit this directive.
Alignment directive	Linux only	`.align <alignment>`
	macOS or Linux	`.balign <alignment>`

Table B-18: Formatting Static Initializers

Static initializer	Output
`CharInit(0)`	`.zero 1`
`CharInit(i)`	`.byte <i>`
`IntInit(0)`	`.zero 4`
`IntInit(i)`	`.long <i>`
`LongInit(0)`	`.zero 8`
`LongInit(i)`	`.quad <i>`
`UCharInit(0)`	`.zero 1`
`UCharInit(i)`	`.byte <i>`
`UIntInit(0)`	`.zero 4`
`UIntInit(i)`	`.long <i>`
`ULongInit(0)`	`.zero 8`
`ULongInit(i)`	`.quad <i>`
`ZeroInit(n)`	`.zero <n>`

`DoubleInit(d)`	`.double <d>`
	or
	`.quad <d-interpreted-as-long>`

`StringInit(s, True)`	`.asciz "<s>"`
`StringInit(s, False)`	`.ascii "<s>"`
`PointerInit(label)`	`.quad <label>`

Table B-19: Formatting Assembly Instructions

Assembly instruction	Output
`Mov(t, src, dst)`	`mov<t>    <src>, <dst>`
`Movsx(src_t, dst_t, src, dst)`	`movs<src_t><dst_t>    <src>, <dst>`
`MovZeroExtend(src_t, dst_t, src, dst)`	`movz<src_t><dst_t>    <src>, <dst>`
`Lea`	`leaq    <src>, <dst>`

Assembly instruction	Output
Cvtsi2sd(t, src, dst)	cvtsi2sd*<t>* *<src>*, *<dst>*
Cvttsd2si(t, src, dst)	cvttsd2si*<t>* *<src>*, *<dst>*
Ret	movq %rbp, %rsp popq %rbp ret
Unary(unary_operator, t, operand)	*<unary_operator><t>* *<operand>*
Binary(Xor, Double, src, dst)	xorpd *<src>*, *<dst>*
Binary(Mult, Double, src, dst)	mulsd *<src>*, *<dst>*
Binary(binary_operator, t, src, dst)	*<binary_operator><t>* *<src>*, *<dst>*
Idiv(t, operand)	idiv*<t>* *<operand>*
Div(t, operand)	div*<t>* *<operand>*
Cdq(Longword)	cdq
Cdq(Quadword)	cqo
Push(operand)	pushq *<operand>*
Call(label)	call *<label>* or call *<label>*@PLT
Cmp(Double, operand, operand)	comisd *<operand>*, *<operand>*
Cmp(t, operand, operand)	cmp*<t>* *<operand>*, *<operand>*
Jmp(label)	jmp .L*<label>*
JmpCC(cond_code, label)	j*<cond_code>* .L*<label>*
SetCC(cond_code, operand)	set*<cond_code>* *<operand>*
Label(label)	.L*<label>*:

Table B-20: Instruction Names for Assembly Operators

Assembly operator	Instruction name
Neg	neg
Not	not
Shr	shr
Add	add
Sub	sub
Mult (integer multiplication only)	imul
DivDouble	div
And	and
Or	or
Shl	shl
ShrTwoOp	shr

Table B-21: Instruction Suffixes for Assembly Types

Assembly type	Instruction suffix
Byte	b
Longword	l
Quadword	q
Double	sd

Table B-22: Instruction Suffixes for Condition Codes

Condition code	Instruction suffix
E	e
NE	ne
L	l
LE	le
G	g
GE	ge
A	a
AE	ae
B	b
BE	be

Table B-23: Formatting Assembly Operands

Assembly operand		Output
Reg(AX)	8-byte	%rax
	4-byte	%eax
	1-byte	%al
Reg(DX)	8-byte	%rdx
	4-byte	%edx
	1-byte	%dl
Reg(CX)	8-byte	%rcx
	4-byte	%ecx
	1-byte	%cl
Reg(DI)	8-byte	%rdi
	4-byte	%edi
	1-byte	%dil
Reg(SI)	8-byte	%rsi
	4-byte	%esi
	1-byte	%sil

Assembly operand		Output
Reg(R8)	8-byte	%r8
	4-byte	%r8d
	1-byte	%r8b
Reg(R9)	8-byte	%r9
	4-byte	%r9d
	1-byte	%r9b
Reg(R10)	8-byte	%r10
	4-byte	%r10d
	1-byte	%r10b
Reg(R11)	8-byte	%r11
	4-byte	%r11d
	1-byte	%r11b
Reg(SP)		%rsp
Reg(BP)		%rbp
Reg(XMM0)		%xmm0
Reg(XMM1)		%xmm1
Reg(XMM2)		%xmm2
Reg(XMM3)		%xmm3
Reg(XMM4)		%xmm4
Reg(XMM5)		%xmm5
Reg(XMM6)		%xmm6
Reg(XMM7)		%xmm7
Reg(XMM14)		%xmm14
Reg(XMM15)		%xmm15
Memory(reg, int)		*<int>*(*<reg>*)
Indexed(reg1, reg2, int)		(*<reg1>*, *<reg2>*, *<int>*)
Imm(int)		$*<int>*
Data(identifier, int)		*<identifier>* +*<int>*(%rip)

Part III

In Part III, we don't change the conversion from TACKY to assembly, but we do add some new registers to the assembly AST and update the code emission pass accordingly. How the code emission pass looks at the end of this section depends on whether you completed Part II first or skipped straight from Part I to Part III.

Tables B-24 through B-28 show the complete code emission pass at the end of Part III if you skipped over Part II.

Table B-24: Formatting Top-Level Assembly Constructs

Assembly top-level construct		Output
Program(top_levels)		Print out each top-level construct. On Linux, add at end of file: `.section .note.GNU-stack,"",@progbits`

Function(name, global, instructions)		`<global-directive>`
		`.text`
		`<name>:`
		`    pushq    %rbp`
		`    movq     %rsp, %rbp`
		`    <instructions>`

StaticVariable(name, global, init)	Initialized to zero	`<global-directive>`
		`.bss`
		`<alignment-directive>`
		`<name>:`
		`    .zero 4`

	Initialized to nonzero value	`<global-directive>`
		`.data`
		`<alignment-directive>`
		`<name>:`
		`    .long <init>`

Global directive		If global is true: `.globl <identifier>` Otherwise, omit this directive.
Alignment directive	Linux only	`.align 4`
	macOS or Linux	`.balign 4`

Table B-25: Formatting Assembly Instructions

Assembly instruction	Output	
Mov(src, dst)	`movl`	`<src>, <dst>`

Ret	`movq` `%rbp, %rsp`
	`popq` `%rbp`
	`ret`	

Unary(unary_operator, operand)	`<unary_operator>`	`<operand>`
Binary(binary_operator, src, dst)	`<binary_operator>`	`<src>, <dst>`
Idiv(operand)	`idivl`	`<operand>`
Cdq	`cdq`	
AllocateStack(int)	`subq`	`$<int>, %rsp`
DeallocateStack(int)	`addq`	`$<int>, %rsp`
Push(operand)	`pushq`	`<operand>`
Pop(reg)	`popq`	`<reg>`

Assembly instruction	Output	
Call(label)	call	<label>
	or	
	call	<label>@PLT
Cmp(operand, operand)	cmpl	<operand>, <operand>
Jmp(label)	jmp	.L<label>
JmpCC(cond_code, label)	j<cond_code>	.L<label>
SetCC(cond_code, operand)	set<cond_code>	<operand>
Label(label)	.L<label>:	

Table B-26: Instruction Names for Assembly Operators

Assembly operator	Instruction name
Neg	negl
Not	notl
Add	addl
Sub	subl
Mult	imull

Table B-27: Instruction Suffixes for Condition Codes

Condition code	Instruction suffix
E	e
NE	ne
L	l
LE	le
G	g
GE	ge

Table B-28: Formatting Assembly Operands

Assembly operand		Output
Reg(AX)	8-byte	%rax
	4-byte	%eax
	1-byte	%al
Reg(DX)	8-byte	%rdx
	4-byte	%edx
	1-byte	%dl

(continued)

Table B-28: Formatting Assembly Operands *(continued)*

Assembly operand		Output
Reg(CX)	8-byte	`%rcx`
	4-byte	`%ecx`
	1-byte	`%cl`
Reg(BX)	8-byte	`%rbx`
	4-byte	`%ebx`
	1-byte	`%bl`
Reg(DI)	8-byte	`%rdi`
	4-byte	`%edi`
	1-byte	`%dil`
Reg(SI)	8-byte	`%rsi`
	4-byte	`%esi`
	1-byte	`%sil`
Reg(R8)	8-byte	`%r8`
	4-byte	`%r8d`
	1-byte	`%r8b`
Reg(R9)	8-byte	`%r9`
	4-byte	`%r9d`
	1-byte	`%r9b`
Reg(R10)	8-byte	`%r10`
	4-byte	`%r10d`
	1-byte	`%r10b`
Reg(R11)	8-byte	`%r11`
	4-byte	`%r11d`
	1-byte	`%r11b`
Reg(R12)	8-byte	`%r12`
	4-byte	`%r12d`
	1-byte	`%r12b`
Reg(R13)	8-byte	`%r13`
	4-byte	`%r13d`
	1-byte	`%r13b`
Reg(R14)	8-byte	`%r14`
	4-byte	`%r14d`
	1-byte	`%r14b`
Reg(R15)	8-byte	`%r15`
	4-byte	`%r15d`
	1-byte	`%r15b`
Stack(int)		`<int>(%rbp)`
Imm(int)		`$<int>`
Data(identifier)		`<identifier>(%rip)`

Tables B-29 through B-35 show the complete code emission pass after completing Parts I, II, and III.

Table B-29: Formatting Top-Level Assembly Constructs

Assembly top-level construct		Output
`Program(top_levels)`		Print out each top-level construct. On Linux, add at end of file: `.section .note.GNU-stack,"",@progbits`

`Function(name, global, instructions)`		`<global-directive>`
		`.text`
		`<name>:`
		`    pushq    %rbp`
		`    movq     %rsp, %rbp`
		`    <instructions>`

`StaticVariable(name, global, alignment, init_list)`	Integer initialized to zero, or any variable initialized only with ZeroInit	`<global-directive>`
		`.bss`
		`<alignment-directive>`
		`<name>:`
		`    <init_list>`

	All other variables	`<global-directive>`
		`.data`
		`<alignment-directive>`
		`<name>:`
		`    <init_list>`

`StaticConstant(name, alignment, init)`	Linux	`.section .rodata`
		`<alignment-directive>`
		`<name>:`
		`    <init>`

	macOS (8-byte-aligned numeric constants)	`.literal8`
		`.balign 8`
		`<name>:`
		`    <init>`

	macOS (16-byte-aligned numeric constants)	`.literal16`
		`.balign 16`
		`<name>:`
		`    <init>`
		`.quad 0`

	macOS (string constants)	`.cstring`
		`<name>:`
		`    <init>`

Global directive		If global is true: `.globl <identifier>` Otherwise, omit this directive.
Alignment directive	Linux only	`.align <alignment>`
	macOS or Linux	`.balign <alignment>`

Table B-30: Formatting Static Initializers

Static initializer	Output
CharInit(0)	.zero 1
CharInit(i)	.byte <i>
IntInit(0)	.zero 4
IntInit(i)	.long <i>
LongInit(0)	.zero 8
LongInit(i)	.quad <i>
UCharInit(0)	.zero 1
UCharInit(i)	.byte <i>
UIntInit(0)	.zero 4
UIntInit(i)	.long <i>
ULongInit(0)	.zero 8
ULongInit(i)	.quad <i>
ZeroInit(n)	.zero <n>
DoubleInit(d)	.double <d> or .quad <d-interpreted-as-long>
StringInit(s, True)	.asciz "<s>"
StringInit(s, False)	.ascii "<s>"
PointerInit(label)	.quad <label>

Table B-31: Formatting Assembly Instructions

Assembly instruction	Output
Mov(t, src, dst)	mov<t> <src>, <dst>
Movsx(src_t, dst_t, src, dst)	movs<src_t><dst_t> <src>, <dst>
MovZeroExtend(src_t, dst_t, src, dst)	movz<src_t><dst_t> <src>, <dst>
Lea	leaq <src>, <dst>
Cvtsi2sd(t, src, dst)	cvtsi2sd<t> <src>, <dst>
Cvttsd2si(t, src, dst)	cvttsd2si<t> <src>, <dst>
Ret	movq %rbp, %rsp popq %rbp ret
Unary(unary_operator, t, operand)	<unary_operator><t> <operand>
Binary(Xor, Double, src, dst)	xorpd <src>, <dst>
Binary(Mult, Double, src, dst)	mulsd <src>, <dst>
Binary(binary_operator, t, src, dst)	<binary_operator><t> <src>, <dst>
Idiv(t, operand)	idiv<t> <operand>

Assembly instruction	Output	
Div(t, operand)	div\<t\>	*\<operand\>*
Cdq(Longword)	cdq	
Cdq(Quadword)	cqo	
Push(operand)	pushq	*\<operand\>*
Pop(reg)	popq	*\<reg\>*
Call(label)	call	*\<label\>*
	or	
	call	*\<label\>*@PLT
Cmp(Double, operand, operand)	comisd	*\<operand\>*, *\<operand\>*
Cmp(t, operand, operand)	cmp\<t\>	*\<operand\>*, *\<operand\>*
Jmp(label)	jmp	.L*\<label\>*
JmpCC(cond_code, label)	j*\<cond_code\>*	.L*\<label\>*
SetCC(cond_code, operand)	set*\<cond_code\>*	*\<operand\>*
Label(label)	.L*\<label\>*:	

Table B-32: Instruction Names for Assembly Operators

Assembly operator	Instruction name
Neg	neg
Not	not
Shr	shr
Add	add
Sub	sub
Mult (integer multiplication only)	imul
DivDouble	div
And	and
Or	or
Shl	shl
ShrTwoOp	shr

Table B-33: Instruction Suffixes for Assembly Types

Assembly type	Instruction suffix
Byte	b
Longword	l
Quadword	q
Double	sd

Table B-34: Instruction Suffixes for Condition Codes

Condition code	Instruction suffix
E	e
NE	ne
L	l
LE	le
G	g
GE	ge
A	a
AE	ae
B	b
BE	be

Table B-35: Formatting Assembly Operands

Assembly operand		Output
Reg(AX)	8-byte	%rax
	4-byte	%eax
	1-byte	%al
Reg(DX)	8-byte	%rdx
	4-byte	%edx
	1-byte	%dl
Reg(CX)	8-byte	%rcx
	4-byte	%ecx
	1-byte	%cl
Reg(BX)	8-byte	%rbx
	4-byte	%ebx
	1-byte	%bl
Reg(DI)	8-byte	%rdi
	4-byte	%edi
	1-byte	%dil
Reg(SI)	8-byte	%rsi
	4-byte	%esi
	1-byte	%sil
Reg(R8)	8-byte	%r8
	4-byte	%r8d
	1-byte	%r8b

Assembly operand		Output
Reg(R9)	8-byte	%r9
	4-byte	%r9d
	1-byte	%r9b
Reg(R10)	8-byte	%r10
	4-byte	%r10d
	1-byte	%r10b
Reg(R11)	8-byte	%r11
	4-byte	%r11d
	1-byte	%r11b
Reg(R12)	8-byte	%r12
	4-byte	%r12d
	1-byte	%r12b
Reg(R13)	8-byte	%r13
	4-byte	%r13d
	1-byte	%r13b
Reg(R14)	8-byte	%r14
	4-byte	%r14d
	1-byte	%r14b
Reg(R15)	8-byte	%r15
	4-byte	%r15d
	1-byte	%r15b
Reg(SP)		%rsp
Reg(BP)		%rbp
Reg(XMM0)		%xmm0
Reg(XMM1)		%xmm1
Reg(XMM2)		%xmm2
Reg(XMM3)		%xmm3
Reg(XMM4)		%xmm4
Reg(XMM5)		%xmm5
Reg(XMM6)		%xmm6
Reg(XMM7)		%xmm7
Reg(XMM8)		%xmm8
Reg(XMM9)		%xmm9
Reg(XMM10)		%xmm10
Reg(XMM11)		%xmm11

(continued)

Table B-35: Formatting Assembly Operands *(continued)*

Assembly operand	Output
Reg(XMM12)	%xmm12
Reg(XMM13)	%xmm13
Reg(XMM14)	%xmm14
Reg(XMM15)	%xmm15
Memory(reg, int)	*<int>*(*<reg>*)
Indexed(reg1, reg2, int)	(*<reg1>*, *<reg2>*, *<int>*)
Imm(int)	$*<int>*
Data(identifier, 0)	*<identifier>*(%rip)
Data(identifier, int)	*<identifier>*+*<int>*(%rip)

REFERENCES

Aho, Alfred V., Monica S. Lam, Ravi Sethi, and Jeffrey D. Ullman. "Machine-Independent Optimizations." Chapter 9 in *Compilers: Principles, Techniques, & Tools*, 2nd ed. Boston: Addison-Wesley, 2006.

Ballman, Aaron. Comment on Issue 53631: "C Compiler: Missing Diagnostics 'Dereferencing "void *" Pointer.'" LLVM issue tracker. GitHub, September 21, 2022. *https://github.com/llvm/llvm-project/issues/53631#issuecomment-1253653888*.

Bendersky, Eli. "The Context Sensitivity of C's Grammar, Revisited." *Eli Bendersky's Website*, May 2, 2011. *https://eli.thegreenplace.net/2011/05/02/the-context-sensitivity-of-cs-grammar-revisited*.

Bendersky, Eli. "Directed Graph Traversal, Orderings and Applications to Data-Flow Analysis." *Eli Bendersky's Website*, October 16, 2015. *https://eli.thegreenplace.net/2015/directed-graph-traversal-orderings-and-applications-to-data-flow-analysis*.

Bendersky, Eli. "Parsing Expressions by Precedence Climbing." *Eli Bendersky's Website*, August 2, 2012. *https://eli.thegreenplace.net/2012/08/02/parsing-expressions-by-precedence-climbing*.

Bendersky, Eli. "Position Independent Code (PIC) in Shared Libraries." *Eli Bendersky's Website*, November 3, 2011. *https://eli.thegreenplace.net/2011/11/03/position-independent-code-pic-in-shared-libraries*.

Bendersky, Eli. "Position Independent Code (PIC) in Shared Libraries on x64." *Eli Bendersky's Website*, November 11, 2011. *https://eli.thegreenplace.net/2011/11/11/position-independent-code-pic-in-shared-libraries-on-x64.*

Bendersky, Eli. "Some Problems of Recursive Descent Parsers." *Eli Bendersky's Website*, March 14, 2009. *https://eli.thegreenplace.net/2009/03/14/some-problems-of-recursive-descent-parsers.*

Borgwardt, Michael. The Floating-Point Guide. Accessed January 12, 2023. *https://floating-point-gui.de.*

Briggs, Preston, Keith D. Cooper, and Linda Torczon. "Improvements to Graph Coloring Register Allocation." *ACM Transactions on Programming Languages and Systems* 16, no. 3 (May 1994): 428–455. *https://doi.org/10.1145/177492.177575.*

Chaitin, G. J. "Register Allocation & Spilling via Graph Coloring." *ACM SIGPLAN Notices* 17, no. 6 (June 1982): 98–101. *https://doi.org/10.1145/872726.806984.*

Chaitin, Gregory J., Marc A. Auslander, Ashok K. Chandra, John Cocke, Martin E. Hopkins, and Peter W. Markstein. "Register Allocation via Coloring." *Computer Languages* 6, no. 1 (January 1981): 47–57. *https://doi.org/10.1016/0096-0551(81)90048-5.*

Chu, Andy. "Pratt Parsing and Precedence Climbing Are the Same Algorithm." *Oils Blog*, November 1, 2016. *https://www.oilshell.org/blog/2016/11/01.html.*

Chu, Andy. "Precedence Climbing Is Widely Used." *Oils Blog*, March 30, 2017. *https://www.oilshell.org/blog/2017/03/30.html.*

Ciechanowski, Bartosz. Float Exposed. Accessed March 29, 2023. *https://float.exposed.*

Cooper, Keith D., and Linda Torczon. "Register Allocation." Chapter 13 in *Engineering a Compiler*, 2nd ed. Boston: Morgan Kaufmann, 2011.

Cordes, Peter. Answer to "Is a Sign or Zero Extension Required When Adding a 32bit Offset to a Pointer for the x86-64 ABI?" Stack Overflow, April 21, 2016, updated April 30, 2019. *https://stackoverflow.com/a/36760539.*

cppreference.com. "C23." Updated September 25, 2023. *https://en.cppreference.com/w/c/23.*

cppreference.com. "Order of Evaluation." Updated September 20, 2023. *https://en.cppreference.com/w/c/language/eval_order.*

Cuoq, Pascal. Answer to "Unsigned 64-Bit to Double Conversion: Why This Algorithm from g++." Stack Overflow, November 7, 2014, updated October 23, 2018. *https://stackoverflow.com/a/26799227.*

David542 and Peter Cordes. "Integer Overflow in gas." Forum discussion. Stack Overflow, October 10, 2020. *https://stackoverflow.com/q/64289590.*

Dawson, Bruce. "Sometimes Floating Point Math Is Perfect." *Random ASCII*, June 19, 2017. *https://randomascii.wordpress.com/2017/06/19/sometimes-floating -point-math-is-perfect/.*

Drysdale, David. "Beginner's Guide to Linkers." Updated 2009. *https://www .lurklurk.org/linkers/linkers.html.*

D'Silva, Vijay, Mathias Payer, and Dawn Song. "The Correctness-Security Gap in Compiler Optimization." In *Proceedings of the 2015 IEEE Security and Privacy Workshops*, 73–87. San Jose, CA, 2015. *https://doi.org/10.1109/ SPW.2015.33.*

Finley, Thomas. "Two's Complement." Department of Computer Science, Cornell University, April 2000. *https://www.cs.cornell.edu/~tomf/notes/cps104/ twoscomp.html.*

Fog, Agner. "Calling Conventions for Different C++ Compilers and Operating Systems." Updated February 1, 2023. *https://www.agner.org/optimize/calling _conventions.pdf.*

Friedl, Steve. "Reading C Type Declarations." December 27, 2003. *http:// unixwiz.net/techtips/reading-cdecl.html.*

GCC Wiki. "Semantics of Floating Point Math in GCC." Updated April 13, 2021. *https://gcc.gnu.org/wiki/FloatingPointMath.*

George, Lal, and Andrew W. Appel. "Iterated Register Coalescing." *ACM Transactions on Programming Languages and Systems* 18, no. 3 (May 1996): 300–324. *https://doi.org/10.1145/229542.229546.*

Ghuloum, Abdulaziz. "An Incremental Approach to Compiler Construction." In *Proceedings of the 2006 Scheme and Functional Programming Workshop*, 27–37. Portland, OR, 2006. *http://scheme2006.cs.uchicago.edu/11-ghuloum.pdf.*

Gibbons, Phillip B. "Lecture 8: Induction Variable Optimizations." Lecture slides for 15-745 Optimizing Compilers for Modern Architectures, Carnegie Mellon University, Spring 2019. *https://www.cs.cmu.edu/afs/cs/ academic/class/15745-s19/www/lectures/L8-Induction-Variables.pdf.*

Gibbons, Phillip B. "Lecture 16: Pointer Analysis." Lecture slides for 15-745 Optimizing Compilers for Modern Architectures, Carnegie Mellon University, Spring 2016. *https://www.cs.cmu.edu/afs/cs/academic/class/15745 -s16/www/lectures/L16-Pointer-Analysis.pdf.*

Gibbons, Phillip B. "Lecture 23: Register Allocation: Coalescing." Lecture slides for 15-745 Optimizing Compilers for Modern Architectures, Carnegie Mellon University, Spring 2019. *https://www.cs.cmu.edu/afs/cs/ academic/class/15745-s19/www/lectures/L23-Register-Coalescing.pdf.*

Godbolt, Matt. Compiler Explorer. Updated September 27, 2023. *https:// godbolt.org.*

Goldberg, David. "What Every Computer Scientist Should Know about Floating-Point Arithmetic." *ACM Computing Surveys* 23, no. 1 (March 1991): 5–48. *https://doi.org/10.1145/103162.103163*. Edited reprint included as Appendix D of *Numerical Computation Guide*. Palo Alto: Sun Microsystems, 2000. *https://docs.oracle.com/cd/E19957-01/806-3568/ncg_goldberg.html*.

Gustedt, Jens. "C11 Defects: Initialization of Padding." *Jens Gustedt's Blog*, October 24, 2012. *https://gustedt.wordpress.com/2012/10/24/c11-defects -initialization-of-padding/*.

Gustedt, Jens. "Checked Integer Arithmetic in the Prospect of C23." *Jens Gustedt's Blog*, December 18, 2022. *https://gustedt.wordpress.com/2022/12/18/ checked-integer-arithmetic-in-the-prospect-of-c23/*.

Hailperin, Max. "Comparing Conservative Coalescing Criteria." *ACM Transactions on Programming Languages and Systems* 27, no. 3 (May 2005): 571–582. *https://doi.org/10.1145/1065887.1065894*.

Hilfinger, Paul. "Lecture 37: Global Optimization." Lecture slides for CS 164: Programming Languages and Compilers, University of California, Berkeley, Spring 2011. *https://inst.eecs.berkeley.edu/~cs164/sp11/lectures/ lecture37-2x2.pdf*.

Hyde, Randall. "Procedures." Chap. 5 in *The Art of 64-Bit Assembly*, Vol. 1. San Francisco: No Starch Press, 2021.

IEEE. *IEEE Standard for Floating-Point Arithmetic*. IEEE Std. 754-2019. New York: IEEE, 2019. *https://doi.org/10.1109/IEEESTD.2019.8766229*.

Intel Corporation. *Intel® 64 and IA-32 Architectures Software Developer's Manual*. Vol. 2, *Instruction Set Reference, A-Z*. Updated September 2023. *https:// www.intel.com/content/www/us/en/developer/articles/technical/intel-sdm.html*. Unofficial copy also available online at *https://www.felixcloutier.com/x86/*.

ISO/IEC. *Information Technology—Programming Languages—C*. 4th ed. ISO/ IEC 9899:2018. Geneva, Switzerland: ISO, 2018.

ISO/IEC. *Information Technology—Programming Languages—C*. N3096 (work-ing draft), April 1, 2023. *https://open-std.org/JTC1/SC22/WG14/www/docs/ n3096.pdf*.

Jones, Joel. "Abstract Syntax Tree Implementation Idioms." In *Proceedings of the 10th Conference on Pattern Languages of Programs (PLoP2003)*, 2003. *https://hillside.net/plop/plop2003/Papers/Jones-ImplementingASTs.pdf*.

Levien, Raph. "With Undefined Behavior, Anything Is Possible." *Raph Levien's Blog*, August 17, 2018. *https://raphlinus.github.io/programming/rust/ 2018/08/17/undefined-behavior.html*.

LLVM. "LLVM: lib/CodeGen/MachineCopyPropagation.Cpp Source File." Source code. Accessed December 24, 2021. *https://llvm.org/doxygen/ MachineCopyPropagation_8cpp_source.html*.

LLVM Project. "Controlling Floating Point Behavior." Clang Compiler User's Manual. Accessed April 11, 2023. *https://clang.llvm.org/docs/ UsersManual.html#controlling-floating-point-behavior.*

LLVM Project. LLDB documentation. Updated October 4, 2023. *https://lldb .llvm.org.*

Lu, H.J., Michael Matz, Milind Girkar, Jan Hubička, Andreas Jaeger, and Mark Mitchell, eds. *System V Application Binary Interface AMD64 Architecture Processor Supplement (With LP64 and ILP32 Programming Models).* Updated September 26, 2023. *https://gitlab.com/x86-psABIs/x86-64-ABI.*

MaskRay. "Copy Relocations, Canonical PLT Entries and Protected Visibility." *MaskRay,* January 9, 2021. *https://maskray.me/blog/2021-01-09 -copy-relocations-canonical-plt-entries-and-protected.*

Meneide, JeanHeyd. "Ever Closer—C23 Draws Nearer." *The Pasture,* February 28, 2022. *https://thephd.dev/ever-closer-c23-improvements.*

Muchnick, Steven S. "Register Allocation." Chapter 16 in *Advanced Compiler Design and Implementation.* San Francisco: Morgan Kaufmann, 1997.

Myers, Joseph. Comment on Bug 90472: "'extern int i;' Declaration Inside Function Isn't Allowed to Shadow 'static int i;' at File Scope." GCC Bugzilla, May 16, 2019. *https://gcc.gnu.org/bugzilla/show_bug.cgi?id =90472#c3.*

Nisan, Noam, and Shimon Schocken. "Boolean Arithmetic." Chapter 2 in *The Elements of Computing Systems: Building a Modern Computer from First Principles,* 1st ed. Cambridge: MIT Press, 2008. *https://www.nand2tetris.org/ _files/ugd/44046b_f0eaab042ba042dcb58f3e08b46bb4d7.pdf.*

Regan, Rick. "Decimal to Floating-Point Converter." *Exploring Binary.* Accessed June 2, 2023. *https://www.exploringbinary.com/floating-point -converter/.*

Regan, Rick. "GCC Avoids Double Rounding Errors with Round-to-Odd." *Exploring Binary,* January 15, 2014. *https://www.exploringbinary.com/gcc -avoids-double-rounding-errors-with-round-to-odd/.*

Regan, Rick. "Hexadecimal Floating-Point Constants." *Exploring Binary,* October 4, 2010. *https://www.exploringbinary.com/hexadecimal-floating-point -constants/.*

Regan, Rick. "Number of Digits Required for Round-Trip Conversions." *Exploring Binary,* April 9, 2015. *https://www.exploringbinary.com/number-of -digits-required-for-round-trip-conversions/.*

Regan, Rick. "The Spacing of Binary Floating-Point Numbers." *Exploring Binary,* March 15, 2015. *https://www.exploringbinary.com/the-spacing-of-binary -floating-point-numbers/.*

Regehr, John. "A Guide to Undefined Behavior in C and C++, Part 1." *Embedded in Academia,* July 9, 2010. *https://blog.regehr.org/archives/213.*

Ritchie, Dennis M. "The Development of the C Language." In *The Second ACM SIGPLAN Conference on History of Programming Languages*, 201–8. Cambridge: ACM, 1993. *https://doi.org/10.1145/154766.155580*. Reproduced on the author's home page, Bell Labs, 2003. *https://www.bell-labs.com/usr/dmr/www/chist.html*.

Stallman, Richard M., and the GCC Developer Community. "Integers." *Using the GNU Compiler Collection (GCC)*. Accessed January 12, 2023. *https://gcc.gnu.org/onlinedocs/gcc/Integers-implementation.html*.

Stallman, Richard, Roland Pesch, Stan Shebs, et al. *Debugging with GDB: The GNU Source-Level Debugger*. Accessed January 29, 2024. *https://sourceware.org/gdb/current/onlinedocs/gdb/index.html*.

Taylor, Ian Lance. "Linkers." Series of blog posts. *Airs – Ian Lance Taylor*, September 2007. First post available at *https://www.airs.com/blog/archives/38*, table of contents available at *https://lwn.net/Articles/276782/*.

Ullman, Jeffrey D. "Code Optimization I." Lecture notes. Stanford University InfoLab, Stanford University. Accessed October 6, 2023. *http://infolab.stanford.edu/~ullman/dragon/slides3.pdf*.

Ullman, Jeffrey D. "Code Optimization II." Lecture notes. Stanford University InfoLab, Stanford University. Accessed October 6, 2023. *http://infolab.stanford.edu/~ullman/dragon/slides4.pdf*.

Wang, Daniel C., Andrew W. Appel, Jeff L. Korn, and Christopher S. Serra. "The Zephyr Abstract Syntax Description Language." In *Proceeedings of the Conference on Domain Specific Languages (DSL '97)*. Santa Barbara, CA, 1997. *https://www.cs.princeton.edu/~appel/papers/asdl97.pdf*.

Wikipedia. "Double-Precision Floating-Point Format." Last modified March 26, 2024. *https://en.wikipedia.org/wiki/Double-precision_floating-point_format*.

Yang, Edward Z. "The AST Typing Problem." *Ezyang's Blog*, May 28, 2013. *http://blog.ezyang.com/2013/05/the-ast-typing-problem/*.

Yang, Zhaomo, Brian Johannesmeyer, Anders Trier Olesen, Sorin Lerner, and Kirill Levchenko. "Dead Store Elimination (Still) Considered Harmful." In *Proceedings of the 26th USENIX Security Symposium*, 1025–1040. Vancouver, BC, 2017. *https://www.usenix.org/system/files/conference/usenixsecurity17/sec17-yang.pdf*.

INDEX

build_graph function, 631–632
.byte directive, 450

C

caller-saved and callee-saved registers, 185,
    648–649
    callee-saved registers in assembly AST,
        620–621
    in graph coloring algorithm, 645–646
    saving and restoring, 187, 193–194,
        196–197, 648–649
    tracking callee-saved register usage,
        646–647
calling convention, 161, 184. *See also* System
    V x64 calling convention
call instruction, 186, 189–190
    emitting, 201–202
    generating, 198–199
calloc function, 461
case statements, 159
Cast expression, 248
    implicit type conversions represented
        by, 255
cast expressions. *See also* type conversions
    parsing, 247–249, 464–466
    pointer types as operands, 351–352
    TACKY for, 259–260, 281–283, 309–
        310, 375, 440, 479
    type checking, 254, 369, 402, 471, 505
    to void, 459, 471, 479
cdq instruction, 61–63, 262
    emitting, 66, 269
Chaitin, Gregory, 669
Chaitin-Briggs algorithm, 669–670
character constants, 424
    lexing, 429–431
    parsing, 433
    type of, 424
    UTF-8, 424
character types, 423–424
    assembly type, 443
    char, 423–424
    integer promotions, 424, 435
    signed char, 423–424
    specifiers, parsing, 433
    static initializers for, 436
    type conversions
        assembly for, 443–445
        TACKY for, 440
    unsigned char, 423–424
    wide, 424
char keyword, 429
char type, 423–424
    signedness, 424
    static initializer for, 436–438
Chu, Andy, 68
Ciechanowski, Bartosz, 345

Clang, xxxiv–xxxv, 4–5
    floating-point support, 296–297,
        317–318, 344
    installing, xxxiv
    invoking with gcc command, xxxv, 4
    language extensions, 395, 401, 471
    System V ABI violation, 444–445
    void, treatment of, 474–475
classify_parameters function, 329–330,
    534–536
classify_return_value function, 532–533,
    537–538
classify_structure function, 533–534
cmp instruction, 79–80, 85–86, 262
    emitting, 90, 270
    fixing up, 88, 268
coalesce function, 665–666
    in build-coalesce loop, 663
code emission, 4, 19–20. *See also entries for*
    individual instructions and
    language constructs
    floating-point constants, 338–339
    function names, 201
    function prologue and epilogue,
        43–44
    instruction size suffixes, 269–271,
        340–341, 443
    local labels, 89, 339, 450
    non-executable stack note, 19
    @PLT suffix, 201–202
    reference tables
        Part I, 702–704
        Part II, 711–715
        Part III, 716–724
    register aliases, 88, 90, 203
    string literals, 449–450
color_graph function, 644–646
comisd instruction, 317, 324, 328
    emitting, 341
    fixing up, 337
common real type, 254–255, 279–280,
    308, 435
comparisons, 78–83. *See also* pointer
    comparisons; relational
    operators
    floating-point, 317, 328
    unsigned, 283–286
compiler, xxvii
    stages, 3–4
compiler driver, xxviii, 7–8
    command line options, 8
        -c, 169–170
        --codegen, 8, 43
        --eliminate-dead-stores, 570
        --eliminate-unreachable-code, 569
        --fold-constants, 569
        -l, 301

pointers to void as operands,
473–475
TACKY for, 371–374
type checking, 364–365
DereferencedPointer construct, 372–374,
408, 410, 515–517
derived types, 354
disjoint-set data structures, 663–664
div instruction, 286, 287–288
fixing up, 290
division (/) operator, 47–48
assembly for, 60–63
floating-point, 315, 327
unsigned, 286, 288
parsing, 50–55
TACKY for, 58
type checking, 254–255, 369
division assignment (/=) operator, 113
divsd instruction, 315
DivDouble, 324–325
fixing up, 337
do statements, 144, 148–151, 152–155, 156
Dot operator, 495. *See also* structure member
operator
.double directive, 312, 338–339
double extended precision floating-point
format, 299
double-precision floating-point format,
297–299
double rounding error, 306
additional resources, 344
type conversion with, 320–323
DoubleToInt instruction, 309–310
assembly for, 317–318
DoubleToUInt instruction, 309–310
assembly for, 318–320
double type, 295–301. *See also* floating-point
constants; floating-point
operations
alignment, 336
assembly type, 324
conversions. *See* conversions to and
from double *under* integer
types; double *under* type
conversions
in function calls, 312–315,
329–333
representation, 297–299
precision, 301
rounding, 299–301
size, 336
specifier, 302, 305, 306–307
static initializers for, 308–309, 340
type checking, 308–309
Drysdale, David, 21
D'Silva, Vijay, 611
dynamic linkers, 202

E

EAX register, 5–6, 40–41, 60–62, 185,
193, 525
EBNF. *See* Extended Backus-Naur Form
notation
EDX register, 60–64, 185, 525
effective type, 352
Elements of Computing Systems, The (Nisan
and Schocken), 45
ELF (Executable and Linkable Format), 201
else clause, 118–121, 126–127
dangling else ambiguity, 120–121
Engineering a Compiler, 2nd edition
(Cooper and Torczon),
669–670
equal to (==) operator, 71–74
assembly for, 85–87
floating-point, 317, 328
pointer comparisons, 352
TACKY for, 75–76, 77
type checking, 254–255, 366–367,
476–477
escape sequences, 429–431
in assembly, 449–450
Executable and Linkable Format (ELF), 201
executable stacks, 19
additional resources, 22
expect function, 16
expressions, 14
converting to TACKY, 38
full, 374
lvalue vs. non-lvalue, 348
parsing, 34. *See also* precedence
climbing
resolving variables in, 107
type checking, 251–256
result types, 251
void, 459–460
expression statements, 95, 98, 110
Extended Backus-Naur Form (EBNF)
notation, 15
optional sequences, 101
repeated sequences, 100
at least once, 225
external linkage, 167–168, 209–211
external variables, 208
resolving, 227–229
extern specifier, 207, 208, 210–212, 213,
214–217
on declarations with incomplete types,
474, 505
in identifier resolution, 228–229
parsing, 225–226
in the type checker, 230–233
extra credit features, xxxii–xxxiii
bitwise operators, 67
case statements, 159

parsing, 50–55
TACKY for, 58
type checking, 254–255, 369
multiplication assignment (*=) operator, 113
Myers, Joseph, 218

N

NaNs (not-a-number), 299, 342–343
    comparing, 299, 317, 342
    extra credit, 342
    quiet, 299
    signaling, 299
negation (-) operator, 26
    assembly for, 26–27, 40–41
        floating-point, 315–316, 327–328
    parsing, 33–34
    TACKY for, 36–38
    token for, 31–32
    type checking, 254, 369, 435
negative infinity, 298
negative zero, 298, 317, 326, 340
neg instruction, 26–27, 40–41, 44
    emitting, 44, 270
nested function definitions, 163
Nisan, Noam, 45
non-scalar types, 470–471
non-terminal symbols, 15
NOT (!) operator, 71–74
    assembly for, 86, 328
    TACKY for, 75–76, 77
    type checking, 254, 369, 470
not equal to (!=) operator, 71–74
    assembly for, 85–87
        floating-point, 317, 328
    pointer comparisons, 352
    TACKY for, 75–76, 77
    type checking, 254–255, 366–367
not instruction, 26–27, 40–41
    emitting, 44, 270
null pointers, 351–352
    comparisons, 352
    constants, 351, 366–368, 401
    as static initializers, 369
null statements, 98, 110

O

object code, xxviii
object files, xxviii, 5
    generating, 169–170
    sections of, 5
        BSS, 222, 340, 418
        data, 221–222
        read-only data, 311–312, 339
        text, 5
objects, 348
    lifetime of, 212–213, 461, 508

observable behavior, 558–560
OF. *See* overflow flag
optimistic coloring, 669
optimization pipeline, 570–573, 600–601
optimizations. *See also* machine-independent
             optimizations *and entries for*
             individual optimizations
    constant folding, 561, 573–576
    copy propagation, 563–564, 585–602
    dead store elimination, 564–565,
        603–609
    interprocedural, 570
    intraprocedural, 570
    machine-dependent, 558
    safety of, 558
    security impact, 564–565
    unreachable code elimination,
        561–562, 581–584
optimize function, 570–573, 601
    termination, 572–573
OR (||) operator, 71–77
    short-circuiting, 72
    TACKY for, 75–77, 259
    type checking, 255, 470
or instruction, 323–325, 337, 341
overflow, 78–82
overflow flag (OF), 78–80, 83
    not applicable, 284–285, 317

P

packed operands, 310, 316
parameter-passing registers, 185, 312
parameters, 162–163, 165, 177, 195–197
parity flag (PF), 342
parse_exp function, 16, 34, 51–57,
    101–102, 124
parser generators, 11
parsers, 4, 10–17. *See also* recursive descent
        parsing
    handwritten, 11
    precedence climbing, 51–57
    predictive, 16
parse_type function, 249–250, 277, 307,
    433, 466
pattern matching, xxxiii–xxxiv
Payer, Mathias, 611
PF (parity flag), 342
phase ordering problem, 573
PlainOperand construct, 372–374
PLT (procedure linkage table), 201–202
pointer analysis, 601
pointer arithmetic, 387–390
    addition, 387–390
    assembly for, 414–415
    relationship to subscript operator,
        387–389
    subtraction, 388–390

shift left (shl) instruction, 529–530,
  541–543, 551
shift right (shr) instruction, 320–321,
  323–325, 529
  two-operand form, 529, 543, 551
short-circuiting operators, 72, 76–77
signed char type, 423–424
signed integers, 243
  overflow, 78–82
  representation, 26, 61, 244
  type conversions, 244–246, 274–275
signed keyword, 275
SignExtend instruction, 259–260, 263,
  282–283
sign extension, 61, 244–245, 275
  in assembly, 263, 444
  in TACKY, 259–260, 282–283
sign flag (SF), 78–80, 83
significant degree, 638
single-precision format, 299
sizeof operator, 458, 462–466, 471,
  477–478, 480–481
Song, Dawn, 611
source character set, 430
source file, xxviii, 7–8, 208
special characters, 429, 450
special sequences (EBNF), 15
spilling, 616, 627–630, 642–644, 646
  candidates for, 642
  spill code, 616, 620
  spill cost, 630–631, 638, 642, 644–645
SSA (static single assignment) form, 672
SSE. *See* Streaming SIMD Extension
  instructions
SSE class, 519
stack, 19, 27–31
  alignment, 185, 197–198, 648–649
  executable, 19
    additional resources, 22
  frames, 29–31
    allocating, 42, 197–199, 200–201
  pointer, 27
stack frames, 29–31
Stack operand, 40, 42, 44
  replaced with Memory operand, 375
StaticConstant construct (assembly), 324,
  326, 336, 446
  emitting, 340
StaticConstant construct (TACKY), 442, 446
static initializers, 213–214. *See also* ZeroInit
  construct
  in assembly, 221–222, 238–239
  for characters, 436
  compound, 404–405
    in assembly, 418–419
    for structures, 509–511
  for double type, 308–309, 340

for long integers, 246, 257–258, 270
for pointers, 369–370, 428–429, 437,
  438–439
  null pointers as, 369
strings as, 437–439
in the symbol table, 257
type checking, 257–258
for unsigned integers, 280–281
static single assignment (SSA) form, 672
static specifier, 208, 209–211, 213, 216–217,
  230–233
static storage duration, 213–214. *See also*
  static variables
  replacing pseudoregisters with, 237
StaticVariable construct (assembly),
  235–236, 263–264, 413
  emitting, 238–239
StaticVariable construct (TACKY),
  234–235, 258–259, 406
static variables, 213–214
  assembly for, 221–222, 235–239, 246
  initializing, 213–214. *See also* static
    initializers
  in TACKY, 234–235
  type checking, 229–230, 231–233
status flags, 78–80
  carry, 284–285, 317
  overflow, 78–80, 83
  parity, 342
  sign, 78–80, 83
  zero, 78–80, 83
Sterbenz lemma, 319
storage-class specifiers, 207–208, 223
  effects, 209–217
  parsing, 225–226
storage duration, 207, 212–213
  allocated, 213, 461
  in assembly, 221–222
  automatic, 212–213, 217
  vs. scope, 213
  static, 213–214, 237
  in the symbol table, 229–230
  thread, 213
Store instruction, 370–374
  and liveness analysis, 609
  and reaching copies analysis, 599–600,
    601–602
Streaming SIMD Extension (SSE)
  instructions, 310–312
  arithmetic, 315–316
  comparisons, 317
  type conversions, 317, 320
strict aliasing rules, 352
string literals, 425–426
  as array initializers, 425, 426
    TACKY for, 440–441
  type checking, 437–438

rounding behavior, 300–301
undefined, 308, 371
implementation-defined, 245, 352
implicit, 254–255, 279, 351, 467–469
as if by assignment, 368, 468–469,
504–505
Cast expression representing, 255
usual arithmetic conversions,
254–255, 279–280, 308, 435
integer, 244–245, 274–275
pointer, 351–352, 460
in TACKY, 259–260, 281–283, 309–310
Copy, 259–260
to and from double, 309–310
SignExtend, 259–260
Truncate, 259–260
ZeroExtend, 281–283
typedef declarations, 108–109
type errors, 174. *See also* type checking
type names, 361–363, 462, 465–466
types, 178–179. *See also* character types;
integer types; void type
aggregate, 384
arithmetic, 347, 476–477
array, 384–392
derived, 354
on exp nodes, 252–253
floating-point, 295–299
function, 178–179, 247–248
incomplete, 461–462
non-scalar, 470–471
pointer, 347, 349–353
scalar, 384, 470–471
type specifiers
char, 429
character, 433
double, 302, 306–307
int, 8
integer, 249–250, 277–278
long, 247
signed, 275
structures, 498
unsigned, 275
void, 8
type table, 500–502, 503–504, 506–507,
509–511, 515, 517–518

U

UIntToDouble instruction, 309–310
assembly for, 320–324
Ullman, Jeffrey, 611
unary expressions, 25–27, 31–38
AST definition, 33
parsing, 33–34
formal grammar, 33, 397, 465
TACKY for, 36–38
type checking, 254

unary operators. *See* unary expressions *and*
names of individual operators
unconditional jump instructions. *See* jump
instructions (assembly);
jump instructions (TACKY)
undeclared variables, 104, 107, 134
undefined behavior, 80–82
additional resources, 91
conflicting linkage, 218–219
handling safely, 672
integer overflow, 80–82
missing return statement, 111–112
modifying objects, 425–426, 508
out-of-range type conversions, 308, 317
pointer arithmetic, 388, 390
pointer dereferences, 351–352
tentative definitions, 219–220
variable accesses, 96, 106–107
UndefinedBehaviorSanitizer, 672
union types, 552–553
universal character names, 10
unreachable code elimination, 561–562,
581–584
combining with other
optimizations, 569
unsequenced evaluations, 58–59, 82
unsigned char type, 424
unsigned integers, 273–289
in assembly, 283–289
assembly type, 287
unsigned comparisons, 283–285,
287–288
unsigned division, 286, 288
constants, 275–278
regular expression for, 304
static initializers for, 280–281
type conversions, 274–275, 279–280,
282–283
unsigned int type, 273–281
unsigned long type, 273–281
wraparound, 79, 285–286, 575
unsigned keyword, 275
usual arithmetic conversions, 254–255,
279–280, 308, 435

V

values, 348
variable declarations, 94–95, 208–220
of array type, 384–385
AST definition, 98, 171
linkage, 209–212
parsing, 100–101, 224–227
resolving identifiers in, 105–106,
138–139, 227–229
scopes, 131–134, 208–209
block scope, 208
file scope, 208

variable declarations *(continued)*
  storage duration, 212–214
  type checking, 179–180, 231–233,
    257–258
variable resolution, 104–108, 136–139,
    227–229
  conditional expressions, 125–126
  if statements, 125–126
  loops, 151–152
  multiple scopes, 136–139
  renamed identifier resolution, 174
variables, 93–97, 208–222. *See also*
    static variables
  aliased, 599–602, 609, 637
  automatic, 208
  external, 208, 227–229
  live, 603
  local, 93–95
  resolving, 104–107, 227–229
  scopes, 131–134, 208–209
  in TACKY, 36–38, 110
    temporary, 36–38, 260–261
  type checking, 181, 253
  variable resolution, 107
variadic functions, 191
void expressions, 459
void keyword, 8–9
  as parameter list, 162, 459, 466–467
void type, 458–460
  casts to, 459, 471, 479
  conditional expressions with, 459, 476,
    479–480
  in C standard, 458, 474–475
  functions returning, 458, 469–470,
    479, 482
  pointers to, 460–461, 475
    conversions to and from, 467–469
  restrictions on, 473–476
  when valid, 473–475
volatile objects, 560

W

Wang, Daniel, 22
while statements, 144, 148–150, 151–155, 157
whitespace, 9–10
wide character types, 424
Windows Subsystem for Linux (WSL), xxxiv
w suffix, 28

X

x64 instruction set, xxvii. *See also* assembly
    code *and names of individual*
    instructions
  AT&T vs. Intel syntax, 6, 244, 570
  documentation, xxxvi
  Streaming SIMD Extension
    instructions, 310–312
x64 processor, xxxiv
  little-endian, 86
  memory address size, 28
x86-64. *See* x64 instruction set; x64
    processor
Xcode, xxxiv–xxxv
XMM registers, 311–312, 325
  allocating, 631
    building register interference
      graph, 637
  in function calls, 312–315, 329–333,
    519, 532–541, 545–546
  zeroing, 316
XOR (^) operator, 67
XOR assignment (^=) operator, 113
xorpd instruction, 316, 324–325, 328
  emitting, 341
  fixing up, 337

Y

Yang, Edward, 253
Yang, Zhaomo, 611

Z

Zephyr Abstract Syntax Description
    Language. *See* ASDL
.zero directive, 222
ZeroExtend instruction, 281–283, 288
zero extension, 274, 281–282, 286–288,
    443–444
zero flag (ZF), 78–80, 83
  comisd, set by, 317
  in unsigned comparisons, 284–285
ZeroInit construct, 405
  emitting, 418–419
  initializing padding, 510–511
  initializing scalar variables, 405
  initializing tentatively defined
    arrays, 411

RESOURCES

Visit *https://nostarch.com/writing-c-compiler* for errata and more information.

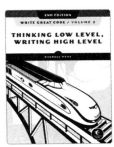

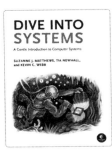

Never before has the world relied so heavily on the Internet to stay connected and informed. That makes the Electronic Frontier Foundation's mission—to ensure that technology supports freedom, justice, and innovation for all people—more urgent than ever.

For over 30 years, EFF has fought for tech users through activism, in the courts, and by developing software to overcome obstacles to your privacy, security, and free expression. This dedication empowers all of us through darkness. With your help we can navigate toward a brighter digital future.